☐ Contributors ☐

Dean J. Barron
Boris I. Bittker
Edmond Cahn
Mortimer M. Caplin
Marvin K. Collie
Hugh F. Culverhouse
Norris Darrell
Erwin N. Griswold
Thomas J. Graves
Crane C. Hauser
Jerome R. Hellerstein
H. Brian Holland

Paul F. Icerman
Mark H. Johnson
John M. Maguire
Thomas P. Marinis, Jr.
Merle H. Miller
Seymour S. Mintz
Francis C. Oatway
Randolph E. Paul
Bruno Schachner
T. T. Shaw
Thomas N. Tarleau
F. S. A. Wheatcroft

Milton Young

"PROFESSIONAL RESPONSIBILITY
☐ IN FEDERAL TAX PRACTICE"☐

☐ Edited by Boris I. Bittker ☐

☐ FEDERAL TAX PRESS, INC. ☐   BRANFORD, CONN. ☐

KF6320
.A75B5

Sources and Acknowledgments

Chapter 1: 63 Harv. L. Rev. 377 (1950), © 1950 by The Harvard Law Review Association and reprinted by permission.
Chapter 2: 8 Tax L. Rev. 1 (1952), © 1953 by New York University School of Law and reprinted by permission.
Chapter 3: 10 N.Y.U. Inst. Fed. Tax. 1067 (1952), © 1952 by New York University and reprinted by permission.
Chapter 4: 25 Rocky Mt. L. Rev. 412 (1953), © 1953 by Rocky Mountain Law Review and reprinted by permission of University of Colorado Law Review.
Chapter 5: Trumbull, Materials on the Lawyer's Professional Responsibility 291 (1957), © 1953 by American Law Student Association and reprinted by permission of American Bar Association (Law Student Division).
Chapter 6: 13 Tax L. Rev. 27 (1957), © 1958 by New York University School of Law and reprinted by permission.
Chapter 7: 7 The Practical Lawyer No. 3, 23 (1961), © 1961 by American Law Institute and reprinted by permission.
Chapter 8: 114 J. Acc'y No. 6, 33 (1962), © 1962 by American Institute of Certified Public Accountants, and 40 Taxes 1040 (1962), © 1962 by Commerce Clearing House, Inc. and reprinted by permission.
Chapter 9: 15 So. Calif. Tax Inst. 25 (1963), © 1963 by Matthew Bender Co., Inc. and reprinted by permission.
Chapter 10: 15 So. Calif. Tax Inst. 39 (1963), © 1963 by Matthew Bender Co., Inc. and reprinted by permission.
Chapter 11: 21 N.Y.U. Inst. Fed. Tax. 23 (1963), © 1963 by New York University and reprinted by permission.
Chapter 12: Bittker, Professional Responsibility and Federal Tax Practice (1965), © 1965 by New York University and reprinted by permission of Federal Tax Press, Inc.
Chapter 13: 20 Tax L. Rev. 237 (1965), © 1965 by New York University School of Law and reprinted by permission.
Chapter 14: 22 Tax Lawyer 455 (1969), © 1969 by American Bar Association and reprinted by permission.
Chapter 15: 111 J. Acc'y No. 2, 259 (1961), © 1961 by American Institute of Certified Public Accountants and reprinted by permission.
Appendix: AICPA Statements © 1964, 1965, 1966, and 1969 by American Institute of Certified Public Accountants and reprinted by permission.

© 1970 by Federal Tax Press, Inc.
Library of Congress Catalog Card No. 73-96147
Printed in the United States of America

Preface

The busier a man is, the more ready he is to take on additional assignments. Among lawyers and accountants, those who concentrate on federal taxation are surely among the busiest; but they are also conspicuous among their colleagues for the amount of time they devote to extra-curricular writing and lecturing. Many of them, indeed, are teachers without classrooms, who ceaselessly and doggedly crisscross the country to lecture at tax institutes and other professional meetings.

This voluntary teacher corps has produced not only a torrent of explanation, analysis, and criticism of the tax law, but also a large body of introspection about the relationship of the tax lawyer and accountant to the client, to the government, and to each other. Although lawyers and accountants who specialize in other areas (e.g., anti-trust, public utility, and banking law) must encounter similar problems, they have not speculated so extensively, at least not in public, about their roles and responsibilities. Whatever its cause, this preoccupation of tax experts with questions of professional responsibility seems to me to warrant a compendium of their contributions. The choices were not always easy, but I believe that this collection fairly reflects the range of ideas and suggestions.

While the texts are reprinted here in their original form, without cuts or revisions, I have added a series of editor's notes to explain a few obscure or short-hand references, and to supply the current statutory references for provisions of the Internal Revenue Code that have been amended in a significant way. These notes, which commence at page 477, are signaled by asterisks in the margin of the text. The Documentary Appendix contains a number of judicial opinions, official announcements, and statements of professional associations to which references are made in the text, and these are also indicated by asterisks in the margin.

I am very much indebted to the authors and publishers who have consented to the reprinting of these essays, and to Miss Suzanne Meyer, Yale Law School class of 1970, who proofread parts of the book and prepared the index.

B.I.B.

Contents

1. The Responsibilities of the Tax Adviser
   Randolph E. Paul   1
2. Ethical Problems of Tax Practitioners
   Edmond Cahn, Chairman   13
3. Morality in Tax Planning
   Merle H. Miller   47
4. The Lawyer as a Tax Adviser
   Randolph E. Paul   64
5. Responsibilities of the Lawyer in Tax Practice
   Norris Darrell   87
6. Conscience and Propriety in Lawyer's Tax Practice
   John M. Maguire   109
7. The Tax Practitioner's Duty to his Client and his Government
   Norris Darrell   131
8. Responsibility of the Tax Adviser
   Thomas J. Graves   149
9. Does the Tax Practitioner Owe a Dual Responsibility to his Client and to the Government? — The Theory
   Mark H. Johnson   161
10. Does the Tax Practitioner Owe a Dual Responsibility to his Client and to the Government? — The Practice
    Milton Young   175
11. What is Good Tax Practice: A Panel Discussion
    H. Brian Holland, Chairman   187
12. Professional Responsibility in Federal Tax Practice
    Boris I. Bittker   233
13. Motivation and Responsibility in Tax Practice: The Need for Definition
    Francis C. Oatway   293
14. Ethical Considerations on Discovery of Error in Tax Returns
    Marvin K. Collie and *Thomas P. Marinis, Jr.*   315
15. Ethical Restraints on Tax Practice in Great Britain
    F. S. A. Wheatcroft   327

Documentary Appendix

Treasury Circular 230 (1959 version)   343
Treasury Interpretation of Circular 230   357
Treasury Circular 230 (1966 version)   359
Rev. Proc. 68-20 (Practice by Unenrolled Preparers of Tax Returns)   369

National Conference of Lawyers and Certified Public Accountants (1944 and 1951 Statements)	373
ABA Committee on Professional Ethics, Opinion 314	377
AICPA Committee on Federal Taxation, Statements on Responsibilities in Tax Practice	382
Lowell Bar Ass'n v. Loeb	395
Application of N. Y. Country Lawyers Ass'n (In re Bercu)	400
Gardner v. Conway	411
Agran v. Shapiro	419
Oregon State Bar v. John H. Miller & Co.	432
Blumenberg v. Neubecker	435
Rassieur v. Charles	439
Anderson v. Knox	443
Lindner v. Barlow, Davis & Wood	454
Bancroft v. Indemnity Ins. Co. of No. America	461
Miles v. Livingstone	468
United States v. Bowman	472
U. S. Code, Title 5 (Appendix), § 1012	475

Editor's Notes and Index

Editor's Notes	477
Index	483

Contributors

Dean J. Barron, Bradley University, J.D., American University, member of the Virginia and Pennsylvania bars; C.P.A., Illinois; Director, Office of International Operations, Internal Revenue Service, 1960; Director, Audit Division, National Office, Internal Revenue Service, 1960-1962; Regional Commissioner, Internal Revenue Service, Mid-Atlantic Region, 1962 to date.

Boris I. Bittker, B.A., Cornell University, 1938, LL.B., Yale University, 1941; member of Connecticut and New York bars; Southmayd Professor of Law, Yale University; author of Federal Income, Estate and Gift Taxation (3d ed., 1964) and Federal Income Taxation of Corporations and Shareholders (2d ed., 1966, with J. S. Eustice).

Edmond Cahn (1906-64), A.B., Tulane University, 1925, J.D., 1927; practiced law, New York City, 1927-50; professor of law, New York University, 1948-64; editor-in-chief, Tax Law Review, 1945-53; author of The Sense of Injustice, The Moral Decision, and other books and articles.

Mortimer M. Caplin, B.S., 1937, LL.B. University of Virginia, 1940, J.S.D., New York University, 1953; member of Virginia, New York, and D. C. bars; professor of law, University of Virginia (1950-61); Commissioner of Internal Revenue (1961-64); member, Caplin & Drysdale, Washington, D. C.

Marvin K. Collie, B.A., LL.B., University of Texas, 1941; member of Texas bar; member, Vinson, Elkins, Searls & Connally, Houston.

Hugh F. Culverhouse, B.S., University of Alabama, 1941; LL.B., University of Alabama, 1947; member of Florida and Alabama bars; Assistant Attorney General, State of Alabama (1947-1949); Special Attorney, Office of Chief Counsel, Internal Revenue Service (1949-1954); Assistant Regional Counsel, Internal Revenue Service, Atlanta Region, (1954-1956); member of Advisory Group to Commissioner of Internal Revenue (1961-1962); member, Culverhouse, Tomlinson, Taylor & DeCarion.

Norris Darrell, LL.B., University of Minnesota, 1923; member of Minnesota and New York bars; President, American Law Institute; member, Sullivan & Cromwell, New York City.

Thomas J. Graves, B.S., University of Notre Dame, 1938; C.P.A., California and other states; Chairman, 1962-65, Committee on Federal Taxation, American Institute of Certified Public Accountants; member, Haskins & Sells, San Francisco.

Erwin N. Griswold, A.B., A.M., Oberlin College, 1925, LL.B., Harvard University, 1928, S.J.D., 1929; member of Ohio and Massachusetts bars; attorney, Department of Justice (1929-34); faculty, Harvard Law School (1934-46), dean (1946-67); author of Cases on Federal Taxation (5th ed., 1960), The Fifth Amendment Today, and other books and articles on legal matters; Solicitor General of United States (1967-date).

Crane C. Hauser, A.B., Franklin and Marshall College, 1946, J.D., Northwestern University, 1950; C.P.A., Illinois, 1953; member of Illinois bar; Chief Counsel, Internal Revenue Service (1961-63); member, Planning Committees, New York University Institute on Federal Taxation and University of Chicago Federal Tax Conference; member, Winston, Strawn, Smith & Patterson, Chicago.

Jerome R. Hellerstein, B.A., University of Denver, 1927, M.A., University of Iowa, 1928, LL.B., Harvard University, 1928; member of New York bar; Professor, New York University Law School; author of Cases and Materials on State and Local Taxation (2d ed., 1961); member, Hellerstein, Rosier, & Rembar, New York City.

H. Brian Holland, Ph.B., Yale University, 1925, LL.B., Harvard University, 1928; member Pennsylvania and Massachusetts bars; Assistant Attorney General, Tax Division, Department of Justice (1953-56); member, Ropes & Gray, Boston.

Paul F. Icerman, A.B., M.B.A., University of Michigan, 1933; C.P.A.; formerly adjunct professor of accounting, University of Michigan; member, Icerman, Johnson & Hoffman, Ann Arbor, Michigan.

Mark H. Johnson, B.S.S., College of the City of New York, 1932, J.D., New York University, 1935; co-author of Rabkin and Johnson, Federal Income, Gift and Estate Taxation and co-author of Rabkin and Johnson Current Legal Forms; counsel, Roberts & Holland, New York City.

John M. Maguire, A.B., Colorado College, 1908, LL.B., Harvard University, 1911, LL.D., Colorado College, 1949; member of Massachusetts bar; Royall professor of law, emeritus, Harvard University; author of Evidence: Common Sense and Common Law, The Lance of Justice, and other books and articles on taxation and evidence.

Thomas P. Marinis, Jr., B.A., Yale University, 1965, LL.B., University of Texas, 1968; member of Texas bar; associate, Vinson, Elkins, Searls & Connally, Houston.

Merle H. Miller, A.B., Butler University, 1927, LL.B., Harvard University, 1930; member of Indiana bar; member, Ice, Miller, Donadio, & Ryan, Indianapolis.

Seymour S. Mintz, A.B., George Washington University, 1933, LL.B., 1936; member of District of Columbia bar; professor, George Washington University Law School (1952-55); member, Hogan & Hartson, Washington, D. C.

Francis C. Oatway, B.S.B.A., Boston College, 1960; C.P.A., Massachusetts and New York; contributing editor, Federal Income Taxation of Banks and Financial Institutions; member, American Institute of Certified Public Accountants and New York State Society of Certified Public Accountants; Principal, Haskins & Sells, New York City.

Randolph E. Paul, (1890-1956), A.B., Amherst College, 1911, LL.B., New York Law School, 1913; General Counsel of Treasury; Sterling lecturer, Yale University School of Law; visiting associate professor, Harvard Law School; author of Law of Federal Income Taxation (with Jacob Mertens), Studies in Federal Taxation (3 series), and other books and articles on taxation.

Bruno Schachner, J.D., Columbia University, 1933; Assistant United States Attorney, Southern District of New York (1938-1951); Associate Professor of Law, New York Law School (1948-1950); Special Counsel to Subcommittee on Internal Revenue Administration, House Ways and Means Committee (1951-1952); law practice, New York City.

T. T. Shaw, C.P.A., member, American Institute of Certified Public Accountants; former editor, Tax Clinic — Journal of Accountancy; former member of Advisory Committee, New York University Institute on Federal Taxation; member, Arthur Young & Company, New York.

Thomas N. Tarleau, LL.B., Columbia University (1929); member of New York bar; Tax Legislative Counsel, Treasury Department (1936-42); President, The Tax Institute (1947); Chairman, Tax Section of American Bar Association (1952-54); member, Willkie Farr & Gallagher, New York City.

G. S. A. Wheatcroft, M.A., Oxford; Solicitor of Supreme Court (1929-1951), Master of Supreme Court (Chancery Division) (1951-59); Professor of English Law, emeritus, London University; author of Estate and Gift Taxation (1965), Capital Gains Tax (1968) and other books on taxation; Editor, British Tax Review (1956 to date).

Milton Young, LL.B., Fordham University, 1931; member of New York bar; member of Advisory Group to Commissioner of Internal Revenue (1964); member of faculty, New York University School of Law (1949-1952), member of Advisory Committee, New York University Institute on Federal Taxation (1950-1963), lecturer, Practising Law Institute; firm, Young, Kaplan & Edelstein, New York City.

PROFESSIONAL RESPONSIBILITY
☐ IN FEDERAL TAX PRACTICE ☐

1. The Responsibilities of the Tax Adviser
Randolph E. Paul

"Hast any philosophy in thee, shepherd?"
Touchstone in *As You Like It*, Act III, Scene 2.

IT IS probably as difficult to enumerate the responsibilities of a tax adviser as it is to advise taxpayers. Even long experience may fail a tax adviser who has never put himself to the acid test of reducing to writing the philosophy that consciously or subconsciously guides him. The tax adviser is in the position of a pianist who is suddenly asked to write the notes that express the music he has played all his life by ear. Indeed, he is being asked to write more than the notes — he is being called upon to express the melody which the notes collectively create.[1]

But difficulty is an old story to tax advisers. They have one of the hardest jobs in the world. Their subject is intensely fluid. Too often the rule of today is gone tomorrow. Sources are legion. We start with the words of a statute, but, in the vivid language of Judge Learned Hand, these words "dance before [our] eyes in a meaningless procession: cross-reference to cross-reference, exception upon exception — couched in abstract terms that offer no handle to seize hold of" — leaving in our minds "only a confused sense of some vitally important, but successfully concealed pur-

---

[1] *Cf.* Helvering v. Gregory, 69 F.2d 809, 811 (2d Cir. 1934), *aff'd*, 293 U.S. 465 (1935).

port," which it is our duty to extract, but which is within our power to extract, if at all, "only after the most inordinate expenditure of time." [2] One is between the devil and the deep blue sea. If there is not this abundance of verbiage, there may not be enough verbiage to suggest the questions — much less provide answers to them.[3]

But though tax law begins with the statute, it has no ending there.[4] Voluminous regulations and rulings do their honest best to interpret and apply the statute. And the language of this supplementary gloss on the statute is not always an outstanding improvement on the statute itself. Court decisions follow years later — sometimes too late [5] — at the thankless task of "interstitial" judicial legislation; [6] many will probably say that the word "interstitial" is an understatement.[7] Magazines, law reviews, periodicals of all sorts, constantly pour out their wearisome quota of suggestion and criticism and dogma.[8] There is no last word, and there are few clear words. The mills of tax law in their perpetual motion grind exceedingly fast and exceedingly fine. The end product is a recalcitrant, ambiguous body of turbulent law with no fields of black and white, where exactness would be only delusive, where logic makes frequent concession to practical values, and where considerations of policy tip many nicely balanced scales.[9]

Tax experts make a habit of pretending that they are intimately familiar with all this material. They do try their best to keep current with the help of tax institutes and by the expenditure of almost unbelievable time, if not industry. In a competitive area they must impress clients, particularly clients who long passionately for the vanished certainties supposedly had in days of long ago. But few tax experts would boast that their grasp of the whole vast subject is more than skin-deep.

---

[2] Learned Hand, *Thomas Walter Swan*, 57 YALE L.J. 167, 169 (1947).

[3] See Frankfurter, *Some Reflections on the Reading of Statutes*, 47 COL. L. REV. 527, 528–29 (1947); 1 PAUL, FEDERAL ESTATE AND GIFT TAXATION 487 (1942); PAUL, STUDIES IN FEDERAL TAXATION 164 (3d ser. 1940).

[4] See Frankfurter, *supra* note 3, at 535.

[5] Griswold, *The Need for a Court of Tax Appeals*, 57 HARV. L. REV. 1153, 1154 (1944).

[6] See Southern Pac. R.R. v. Jensen, 244 U.S. 205, 221 (1917).

[7] *Cf.* Eisenstein, *A Case of Deferred Compensation*, 4 TAX L. REV. 391, 397 (1949).

[8] For a brief inventory of the growing mass of tax material, see STANLEY AND KILCULLEN, THE FEDERAL INCOME TAX vii (1948).

[9] *Cf.* Woolford Realty Co. v. Rose, 286 U.S. 319, 330 (1932).

The difficulties of the tax adviser have even more remote origins. It is no trade secret that the emotions of tax clients sometimes make them "keen for lawsuits and the reckless fray." [10] This is not strange, "For where your treasure is, there will your heart be also." And in tax matters the heart is hardly a satisfactory substitute for the head. If he would save a client from his worst enemy — the client himself — the tax adviser must supply the deficiency. He must wash all his conclusions with the cynical acid of distrust. He must be a completely detached skeptic, discounting everything he reads. It may be emotional claptrap, a misplaced general maxim, wish-fathered thoughts, or verbal agility rationalizing subconscious predilections. The tax adviser must watch for inarticulate law. His thinking must be precise, but he must think, as the Chinese express it, "with his profound intestines." In short, he must have the gift of controlled intuition. He must read between every line on every page, catching elusive overtones, freely translating words which are, at best, inexact tools for the expression of the subtleties that abound in taxation.

It is even more disconcerting to remember that the function of a tax adviser is systematized prediction.[11] He must constantly make accurate appraisals of changes in the climate of judicial, legislative, and administrative opinion.[12] His clients are not interested in history, but rather in what will happen to them in their cases. The tax adviser must, therefore, know the trend of tax law; a large part of his job is guessing the shape of things to come. And woe unto the adviser who guesses wrong. Clients are not fond of alibis; the tax adviser's failure will be measurable in dollars and cents, the client's dollars and cents — and the tax adviser's, as well.

It is not even enough that the tax adviser know the present and future of tax law. Tax law covers many waterfronts; to mix metaphors, it is a melting pot of many other branches of the law. The tax adviser who draws a trust instrument is a bold man [13] if he

---

[10] HORACE, ODES, Book III, XIV.

[11] HOLMES, THE COMMON LAW 126 (1881); HOLMES, COLLECTED LEGAL PAPERS 167, 173 (1921); CARDOZO, THE GROWTH OF THE LAW 31 (1924).

[12] Two recent appraisals of past and prospective change in an important area of tax law illustrate the difficulties and hazards confronting the appraiser. See Darrell, *Recent Developments in Nontaxable Reorganizations and Stock Dividends*, 61 HARV. L. REV. 958 (1948); DeWind, *Preferred Stock "Bail-Outs" and the Income Tax*, 62 HARV. L. REV. 1126 (1949).

[13] There is only one bolder and more helpless man — he who draws a trust instrument without knowing something about tax law.

moves forward without knowing the applicable law of perpetuities and the relevant rules governing powers of appointment; he had better have a bowing acquaintance with the subject of conflict of laws.[14] The same is true in the field of trusts and estates,[15] corporate reorganizations,[16] partnerships,[17] domestic relations,[18] real estate,[19] evidence;[20] the list can be stretched to cover almost the whole area of law — even patents and copyrights.[21] The knowledge of a tax adviser can extend even further into the morasses of accounting.[22] At times a little knowledge of economics may not be too dangerous a thing.[23]

Yet there is a sense in which too many qualifications in other areas of the law may be a handicap to the tax lawyer. This may happen if a lawyer's knowledge of other branches of the law adds up to a vested intellectual interest. Too much knowledge can then become a perilous possession; the lawyer may be overanxious to apply in tax territory principles which will not be welcome there.[24]

---

[14] See, *e.g.*, Barclay v. United States, 175 F.2d 48 (3d Cir. 1949); Leser v. Burnet, 46 F.2d 756 (4th Cir. 1931). For the application of conflict of laws concepts to power of appointment problems, see 1 PAUL, FEDERAL ESTATE AND GIFT TAXATION § 9.23 (1942).

[15] See, *e.g.*, Estate of Spiegel v. Commissioner, 335 U.S. 701 (1949); Helvering v. Stuart, 317 U.S. 154 (1942); McAllister v. Commissioner, 157 F.2d 235 (2d Cir. 1946), *cert. denied*, 330 U.S. 826 (1947); Brewster v. Gage, 280 U.S. 327 (1930); Commissioner v. Dravo, 119 F.2d 97 (3d Cir. 1941).

[16] See, *e.g.*, Helvering v. Cement Investors, Inc., 316 U.S. 527 (1942); Helvering v. Alabama Asphaltic Limestone Co., 315 U.S. 179 (1942).

[17] See, *e.g.*, Heiner v. Mellon, 304 U.S. 271 (1938); Commissioner v. Smith, 173 F.2d 470 (5th Cir.), *cert. denied*, 70 Sup. Ct. 61 (1949); Commissioner v. Lehman, 165 F.2d 383 (2d Cir.), *cert. denied*, 334 U.S. 819 (1948); Williams v. McGowan, 152 F.2d 570 (2d Cir. 1945).

[18] See, *e.g.*, Cox v. Commissioner, 176 F.2d 226 (3d Cir. 1949); Murray v. Commissioner, 174 F.2d 816 (2d Cir. 1949); INT. REV. CODE §§ 22(k), 23(u).

[19] See, *e.g.*, Crane v. Commissioner, 331 U.S. 1 (1947); Magruder v. Supplee, 316 U.S. 394 (1942); Helvering v. Hammel, 311 U.S. 504 (1941); Helvering v. Lazarus & Co., 308 U.S. 252 (1939).

[20] See, *e.g.*, Baldwin v. Commissioner, 125 F.2d 812 (9th Cir. 1942).

[21] See, *e.g.*, Commissioner v. Wodehouse, 337 U.S. 369 (1949); Fulda, *Copyright Assignments and the Capital Gains Tax*, 58 YALE L.J. 245 (1949).

[22] See, *e.g.*, INT. REV. CODE §§ 41, 45, 102; Chicago Stockyards Co. v. Helvering, 318 U.S. 693 (1943); Helvering v. National Grocery Co., 304 U.S. 282 (1938); May, *Accounting and the Accountant in the Administration of Income Taxation*, 47 COL. L. REV. 377 (1947).

[23] The economists' approach is particularly important in the area of the excess profits tax covered by INT. REV. CODE §§ 721, 722. See, *e.g.*, George Kemp Real Estate Co. v. Commissioner, 12 T.C. 943 (1949); Pantasote Leather Co. v. Commissioner, 12 T.C. 635 (1949).

[24] See, *e.g.*, Commissioner v. Culbertson, 337 U.S. 733 (1949); Commissioner v. Tower, 327 U.S. 280 (1946); Commissioner v. Court Holding Co., 324 U.S.

He will then be ignoring an important distinction between tax law and many other branches of the law.

That distinction is hard to state, yet I believe it to be real and significant. For several decades there has been a movement in all law away from emphasis upon what for lack of better terms we can call form and technicality, and toward a search for underlying substance and basic realities.[25] This movement has perhaps been more rapid in tax law; it may be that there has never been much of the older attitude in a body of law which started its existence only a little more than a quarter of a century ago.[26] At least the absolutes of the common law, as some of us older lawyers tried to learn them in law school, had only a limited opportunity to entrench themselves in tax law, where so many of the important issues are lively questions of degree.[27] By that token tax law may be more interesting, depending upon one's outlook on life, but those who are too eager for certainties get many dusty answers.[28]

It would be pleasant to say that the tax adviser's responsibilities stopped at this far point on a dim horizon. Unfortunately they do not. There is another important respect in which tax law differs from other law. Its disputes are not between private litigants, as in an action on a contract or in tort. The controversies of tax law are between *taxpayers and their government*. This puts the public

---

331 (1945); Helvering v. Clifford, 309 U.S. 33 (1940); see also 1 PAUL, FEDERAL ESTATE AND GIFT TAXATION §§ 1.11, 1.12 (1942); PAUL, SELECTED STUDIES IN FEDERAL TAXATION 19 (2d ser. 1938).

[25] See Eisenstein, *supra* note 7, at 393, 397.

[26] Many ancient legal concepts which established themselves in earlier tax decisions, see, *e.g.*, Becker v. St. Louis Union Trust Co., 296 U.S. 48 (1935); May v. Heiner, 281 U.S. 238 (1930), have been rooted out by supervening court decisions. Helvering v. Hallock, 309 U.S. 106, 122 (1940); Commissioner v. Estate of Church, 335 U.S. 632 (1949).

[27] See, *e.g.*, Harrison v. Schaffner, 312 U.S. 579, 581 (1941); Irwin v. Gavit, 268 U.S. 161, 168 (1925).

[28] Advice to a particular client in a specific case too often turns upon answers to riddles such as: What is the scope of the "business purpose" doctrine? See, *e.g.*, Lewis v. Commissioner, 176 F.2d 646, 649 (1st Cir. 1949); Bazley v. Commissioner, 155 F.2d 237, 243 (3d Cir. 1946), *aff'd*, 331 U.S. 737 (1947). In what circumstances will the Commissioner and the courts disregard corporate entities? *Compare* Moline Properties, Inc. v. Commissioner, 319 U.S. 436 (1943), *with* National Carbide Corp. v. Commissioner, 336 U.S. 422 (1949). What family partnerships will be recognized for tax purposes? See Commissioner v. Culbertson, *supra* note 24. What corporate distributions will be taxed as dividends under the provisions of INT. REV. CODE § 115(g)? *Compare* Darrell, *supra* note 12, *with* DeWind, *supra* note 12. What are unreasonable accumulations of corporate earnings under the provisions of INT. REV. CODE § 102? See World Publishing Co. v. United States, 169 F.2d 186, 187–88 (10th Cir. 1948), *cert. denied*, 335 U.S. 911 (1949).

interest into the equation and enormously complicates the responsibilities of the tax adviser. He cannot safely act like an adviser in a completely private dispute because he must allow for the breaks a sovereign government may receive and also for his own special duty in the circumstances.[29]

For the purpose of further discussion, I should like for the sake of convenient arrangement to make an assumption which has troubled me in another context.[30] The assumption is that there is in tax law a distinction between fact and law questions.[31] On the basis of this assumption, I will first discuss the tax adviser's special responsibilities in connection with the *facts* of a tax case. I will then pass on to a brief discussion of his responsibilities in connection with the *law* of a tax case.

I have said that the tax adviser must be a prophet; I now say without fear of exaggeration that he must also be a historian, gathering as best he can the elusive facts of his case.[32] Too often facts are the shyest birds in tax law.[33] They are not objective entities; in tax law as elsewhere they are frequently fugitive imponderables. The most painstaking industry of the tax lawyer and the most willing co-operation of clients are sometimes insufficient to assemble in accurate array the complicated facts that raise tax questions in these troublesome days.

But tax clients, like other clients, are not invariably co-operative. On the contrary, their ingenuity and uncanny cunning at concealing and suppressing facts pass my poor powers of description. They are experts at forgetting what needs to be remembered and at remembering what needs to be forgotten. I have known clients to tell a long story full of irrelevant detail, and then suddenly, without the slightest warning, introduce the critical fact of

---

[29] For example, the taxpayer is generally saddled with the burden of proof in a civil tax case; the Commissioner's determinations enjoy a presumption of correctness. See also New Colonial Ice Co. v. Helvering, 292 U.S. 426 (1934); Porto Rico Coal Co. v. Commissioner, 126 F.2d 212 (2d Cir. 1942). *But cf.* Griswold, Note, *An Argument against the Doctrine that Deductions Should Be Narrowly Construed as a Matter of Legislative Grace*, 56 HARV. L. REV. 1142 (1943).

[30] See Paul, *Dobson v. Commissioner: The Strange Ways of Law and Fact*, 57 HARV. L. REV. 753 (1944); *cf.* FRANK, COURTS ON TRIAL 321 (1949).

[31] See FRANK, COURTS ON TRIAL c. III (1949).

[32] *Cf.* CUTLER, SUCCESSFUL TRIAL TACTICS 4 (1949).

[33] Proof of the absence of tax avoidance motives, so crucial to many tax cases, often requires inquiry into remote corners of motive and intent to establish, for example, what a reasonably prudent man would do in a similar situation if there were no taxes to consider or avoid.

the case with a deprecatory "by the way." A tax lawyer should always shiver when he hears the phrase: "To be frank with you . . . ." The tax adviser will sometimes have to dynamite the facts of his case out of unwilling witnesses on his own side — witnesses who are nervous, witnesses who are confused about their own interest, witnesses who try to be too smart for their own good, and witnesses who subconsciously do not want to understand what has happened despite the fact that they must if they are to testify coherently.

One effective way to induce a full fact statement is to submit to the client in writing exactly what he has told his lawyer orally. He will hardly be able to resist the temptation to demonstrate the mistakes his lawyer has made. The process may be humiliating to the lawyer, but it is often effective. And a little mortification is a small price for the discovery of essential facts.

It is true that in some instances taxpayers are unaware of the safety inherent in the confidential relationship which exists between tax clients and their attorneys. Of course, it would be a breach of a sacred duty for tax attorneys to disclose anything which is confidentially revealed to them by their clients. Nor can they be compelled to testify as to the contents of any confidential disclosure. In this respect they have a status superior to that of accountants, who may not plead privilege.

The tax adviser has a responsibility to himself. Clients sometimes come to a lawyer to cover their own tracks. They want to follow a given course of action; they want the lawyer to share blame if results are disappointing. Some will pressure their advisers; others adopt the more subtle technique of misstatement. The lawyer's reputation depends upon the record. Oral opinions are easily forgotten. Written opinions do well to begin: "You state that . . ." and to proceed: "On the above facts, my opinion is . . . ."

An emphasis upon the importance of facts sometimes saves the tax adviser from the consequences of horseback opinions. A good many clients want the answer in a hurry — a desire which is wholly unreasonable in view of their tardiness in seeking legal advice at all. And there are clients who think that tax opinions are simple matters which may be recited like sums at school. It is not easy to resist the temptation to snatch at the prestige which is too often associated with facile responses; it is very easy to yield to the temptation to give an immediate opinion with the hope that one will find it to be right when the client has left the office. It is a perilous practice.

Poincaré once said that "a collection of facts is no more a science than a heap of stones is a house." The remark is certainly true of the facts of a tax case. Once they are found, facts must be sorted, arranged, classified, identified with their connotation, interpreted. Interpretation is the hardest part of the process. Into what ultimate pattern do the primary facts fit? Does one first adopt a theory and arrange the facts around that theory, or does one first find the facts and then select a theory which fits what is found? This question is one of fundamental technique. Every tax adviser might profitably ask himself the question in privacy, and answer it with absolute candor — in the same privacy.

One peculiar responsibility of tax advisers derives from the fact that tax controversies are between the client and the Government, rather than between two private litigants. Our established procedures make the Government more dependent upon the taxpayer than is the private litigant upon the other side in an ordinary controversy.[34] The advice of Holmes in another context is applicable: "Men must turn square corners when they deal with the Government." [35]

This responsibility of tax advisers begins long before the making of a return. Long-distance tax planning is a first order of personal business. The tax aspects of business transactions are becoming so important that the tax adviser must participate in negotiations. Tax attorneys must advise with respect to placing the evidence of transactions squarely upon the taxpayer's books. In connection with tax advice as to impending transactions the tax adviser's responsibility is not to shape the transaction so that there may be a maximum tax liability; but insofar as the objective is tax minimization, documents should fairly reflect the transaction. We should advise open covenants even if they may not be openly arrived at. At the point of filing returns there need not be disclosure of every detail, but there should be disclosure of every essential fact. Reasonable disclosure not only is honest, but also has the virtue of being the best policy. In all subsequent dealings with the Bureau of Internal Revenue and in litigation, the tax adviser will gain little by suppression of the facts.

---

[34] This is particularly true when subjective factors like motive and purpose determine results.

[35] Rock Island, A. & L.R.R. v. United States, 254 U.S. 141, 143 (1920).

Turning to the law side of the case, the tax adviser needs to beware of competitive pressures. There are always the heathen to beguile him to their temples, and the sirens with their songs. It is necessary to resist the temptation to slant opinions in the direction of a client's desires. An honest doubt can easily find expression in an opinion which evaluates calculated risks. Delays sometimes have dangerous ends, and misgivings are better stated frankly at the beginning than acknowledged ungracefully at the end, even though prompt revelation may send a client to another attorney who wears his heart nearer to his sleeve. In tax law the day of reckoning is often on earth and not in heaven.

I have sometimes been asked the question whether in making arguments as an advocate, the tax attorney should consult his personal views on tax policy. Should he argue for an interpretation of the statute which he does not believe to be correct or which he thinks may, if accepted, be harmful precedent from the public standpoint?

The question deserves a candid answer. One may say in parenthesis that it is rarely possible to be dogmatic about the public interest in tax law. Almost every tax question cuts in at least two directions. It is frequently more important that there be an answer than that the answer arrived at be a perfect one. But sometimes issues are fairly black and white, and the equities clearly favor the taxpayer in many cases where the law is muddy — or even hostile to his position. When that happens I never hesitate myself to make any argument that I think will advance the client's financial interest even though I may feel that acceptance of the argument in an opinion which is not carefully narrowed to the facts may create a precedent unfriendly to the best interests of the revenue. By the same token, I would not refuse to protect for a taxpayer a right secured to him by a statutory loophole, which as a legislator I would promptly close. But it is the function of Congress to pass tax laws; and it is the duty of the Treasury and the courts to administer and interpret tax laws. In representing a client I am not the keeper of the Congressional conscience. It is my duty to present fairly, but forcibly, the arguments that will benefit that client. I may be in grave doubt at times in my selection of what will help the client. Considerations of policy may influence my choice of arguments, but I should be careful not to let my private notions of policy intrude into work for a client in his tax case. I am free at a different time, on my own time, to present to appropriate Congressional committees or to the Treasury my personal views on social and economic and fiscal policy.

Conversely, I do not think that it is a tax adviser's duty to suggest arguments to government counsel. Most experienced practitioners will agree, I am sure, that suggesting arguments to government counsel is a prime example of carrying coals to Newcastle.

The responsibilities of the tax adviser, *qua* tax adviser, may be said to end at the point of faithful attendance to his client's interest. But this is not, in my opinion, the end of the tax adviser's responsibility. He is a *citizen* as well as a *tax adviser*. He is more than the ordinary citizen; he is a specially qualified person in one of the most important areas of the public interest. His experience equips him with a peculiar knowledge of what is wrong with tax law and makes especially valuable his objective opinion about what should be done — and sometimes what should not be done — to remedy defects. Special qualifications bring special responsibilities which may not be passively discharged.

I have said that the tax adviser should not mix into his work for his client his own personal notions of tax policy. I repeat this statement. But I hasten to add that the tax adviser should use for his government, as well as for his clients, the special knowledge his education and experience have bestowed upon him. He should use this knowledge actively, affirmatively, and even aggressively. He is not disqualified because he has represented taxpayers. On the contrary, he is for that reason all the more qualified to aid the public interest.

What precisely should the tax adviser do in the performance of this supplementary duty? A number of things — speaking, writing, appearing before committees — could be listed. We all know that it is not lack of knowledge of what to do that accounts for the inertia of tax advisers in this territory. Rather it is doubt whether tax advisers should or dare do such things.

Many tax advisers will protest that they devote a large portion of their time to all kinds of efforts looking toward the improvement of tax law. They write articles — sometimes of great length and learning — telling us that the Treasury is unfair, and that the courts too jealously protect the revenue. They zealously point out some of the inequities of the statute. Many even go so far as to repeat — sometimes with the citation of a case decided in 1873 [36] — the rusty platitude that taxpayers have a right to avoid

---

[36] United States v. Isham, 17 Wall. 496, 506 (U.S. 1873).

taxes if they confine themselves to means that are legal to that end. Without further description I am sure that almost everyone will recognize the type of literature to which I am referring. Sometimes it is smug and pious; often it is vehement; generally it is sincere. Yet it has, always, the same hollow ring.

I will go so far as to say that the writers of this literature perform a helpful function in the development of tax law. They police overzealous legislators and administrators. Many of the defects to which they call attention should be remedied. Time and time again the role of the Bureau of Internal Revenue has been that of a responsible rule-making agency seriously engaged in the trying task of implementing Congressional tax policy. But too often its role has been that of a mere litigant. The legislative process is frequently too unwieldy to react sensitively and quickly to each tax dilemma. The courts are often necessarily impotent at the job of interpreting tax statutes because they must be passive rather than dynamic, and can deal with generic problems only as they are presented in the context of specific litigation.[37]

But in the contributions of these protesting friends one type of suggestion is made conspicuous by its absence. Their writings consistently fail to espouse amendments of the statute which will operate in favor of the government. Their silence about flagrant loopholes is unrelieved. The steps they advocate do not add up to a tax law that raises the necessary revenue and at the same time distributes the required tax burden in a way which treats alike those who are similarly situated.

In short, these tax advisers are representing taxpayers, if not a particular taxpayer in a particular case. They are taxpayer-minded, as some others are government-minded.

I know that many tax advisers would like nothing better than to spend part of their time working for a better tax system, but leave the job to others because they honestly think that they cannot afford that luxury. They have accepted the doctrine that they will attract and hold tax business only if they remain completely conventional, voicing opinions that will be popular with taxpayers. They believe that silence is golden when measures objectively looking to the improvement of our tax system are being canvassed. They have become mental prisoners of the views and interests of clients.

---

[37] Eisenstein, *Some Iconoclastic Reflections on Tax Administration*, 58 HARV. L. REV. 477 (1945).

I wish I could confidently say that there is no rational foundation for this attitude. The most I can say is that I do not think surrender needs to be unconditional. I know several tax advisers who manage the double job of ably representing their clients in particular cases and faithfully working for the tax system taxpayers deserve. At the bread and butter level there is no evidence that these tax advisers lack clients. At another level, I venture the opinion that they lead a more comfortable life than do many of their colleagues. Of one thing I am very sure — that both taxpayers and their government need many more of these tax advisers.

2. Ethical Problems of Tax Practitioners
Edmond Cahn, Chairman

EDMOND CAHN: WE COME now to the main business of this evening, and we were cautioned last year by Dean Niles [1] not to allow the subject to be treated lightly or facetiously. It is one that I think no one present is disposed to treat that way. I think that we all feel deeply concerned and, to some extent, unhappy over the subject which we are met to discuss.

The problem of a departure from ethical standards has always been with us. It is not new in our generation.

A current example of it (outside the field of taxation) which makes excellent reading is Chief Justice Arthur Vanderbilt's opinion in *Driscoll v. Burlington-Bristol Bridge Co.*[2] It is interesting to compare that case, which reads like a detective story in which the miscreants are brought to justice in the final chapter, with something that I am going to read to you from a decision some seventy-five years old, a unanimous opinion of the United States Supreme Court, *Trist v. Child*,[3] delivered in the October Term 1874 by Mr. Justice Swayne. He says:

> The foundation of a republic is the virtue of its citizens. They are at once sovereigns and subjects. As the foundation is undermined, the structure is weakened. When it is destroyed, the fabric must fall. Such is the voice of universal history. The theory of our government is, that all public stations are trusts, and that those clothed with them are to be animated in the discharge of their duties solely by considerations of right, justice, and the public good. They are never to descend to a lower plane. But there is a correlative duty resting upon the citizen. In his intercourse with those in authority, whether executive or legislative, touching the performance of their functions, he is bound to exhibit truth, frankness, and integrity. Any departure from the line of rectitude in such cases, is not only bad in morals, but involves a public wrong. No people can have any higher public interest, except the preservation of their liberties, than integrity in the administration of their government in all its departments.

That part read as though it were written yesterday.

But, in order to show this picture in full contrast and to underline the virulence of the present situation, let me read this further statement:

> If any of the great corporations of the country were to hire adventurers who make market of themselves in this way, to procure the passage of a general

---
[1] *See* 7 TAX L. REV. at 17 (1951).
[2] 8 N.J. 433 (1952).
[3] 88 U.S. 441 (1874).

law with a view to the promotion of their private interests, the moral sense of every right-minded man would instinctively denounce the employer and employed as steeped in corruption, and the employment as infamous.

If the instances were numerous, open and tolerated, they would be regarded as measuring the decay of the public morals and the degeneracy of the times. No prophetic spirit would be needed to foretell the consequences near at hand.

As you know, this subject matter is one of peculiar interest to me, because I approach it in two capacities: as a student of the philosophy of law and as editor of the TAX LAW REVIEW. I have tried to understand what the causes are in our times that have worked for this degeneracy of morals in government and on the part of citizens dealing with government.

As a philosopher it was my first reaction that possibly the skepticism of the past two generations had undermined moral fabric; but then I remembered that it was the greatest skeptic of them all who had said these famous words: "Men must turn square corners when they deal with the Government." [4]

I think, rather, that the basic cause of this pestilence is the conformism that characterizes our society: the obsessive need to be like everyone else, to have the same possessions as everyone else, to follow the same pattern in the pursuit of material goods. I believe we have lost much of the individuality in action and in expression in our society, and also the sense of moral responsibility that came from that individuality in the past.

One of the things that is conspicuously changed in our society is the absence of cranks. We don't have enough cranks. This conformism involves keeping up with the Joneses in terms of possessions and keeping down with the Joneses in terms of morals. From the standpoint of the bar, it involves those things particularly with relation to the mercantile community. In respect of morals there are lawyers who have become what the communists have always said the lawyers were in a capitalist society: with characteristic politeness, they have called us "jackals of the bourgeoisie." Lawyers may become worthy of the compliment if all they desire is to participate in the same standards as their mercantile neighbors, live the same lives, obtain for their wives the same type of coats, and ride around in the same automobiles.

In short, with respect to a capacity to distinguish in ethical matters, we may be fast losing our status as a profession and becoming nothing more than skilled merchant-clerks.

---

[4] Here we have a good illustration of the risks one incurs in using a quotation in the course of extemporaneous remarks. I quoted Holmes accurately but out of context: he was referring only to strict compliance with formal statutory conditions attached to the Government's consent to be sued. *Rock Island R.R. v. United States,* 254 U.S. 141, 143 (1920). I feel confident, however, that Holmes would approve my wider application of his aphorism.

There are heavy guilts on both the law schools and the bar in this connection. I believe that within limits, even in a society as corrupt, as avaricious, as unscrupulous as our society seems to have become, there are real things that can be accomplished to overcome this trend and to bring about a bar which will have a sense of moral responsibility and will hold itself up as a sort of civic nobility, which is, as I see it, our duty and our role.

From the standpoint of the law schools, I think everything that we can do must be done during the impressionable period of the beginning of the study of law. I believe further that that must not be done merely by precept or by preaching "thou shalt nots" to young men.

I think the same thing applies with respect to the bar. The second impressionable period in a young lawyer's life is when he gets out of law school and first enters a law office and has association with an older man. The opportunity arises then to teach him things that are rather more important in the long run than the latest provision of the Civil Practice Act or the Federal Rules or the Internal Revenue Code, things in a code which is considerably older and which he will ultimately need more.

Nothing is more impressive to him than the example of the man who is where he expects to be a few years hence, or at least hopes to be. Here again, I think, it is not a matter of precept but of the living example of the older man.

Let me give an illustration of that.

About thirty years ago my father came home one night and was in an obviously happy mood. When he was happy, he showed it in a stereotyped fashion: He had a rich, resonant voice and he knew only one song, and it was to the effect that he "stood on the bridge at midnight when the clock was striking the hour." He could accompany himself on the Steinway to this song, but only in chords, and he would sit there and throw his head back, the way you feel when you are in the shower, and let out his exuberance, and then, after he had sung this song, he would go mix himself the very best of Sazerac cocktails.

Observing this, I asked him whether he had won a particularly good case that day. He rubbed his hands together and said, "I won the biggest case a lawyer can win. I threw a rich client out of my office for asking me to do something wrong."

You can imagine what that meant to a sixteen-year-old boy who hoped to become a lawyer, and I looked forward to the day when I could have that same thrill. Unfortunately, for years after I began to practice law, no rich client ever asked me to do anything wrong. Then, after the lapse of some time, they started, once in a while, asking me to do something wrong, but the first nine or so of them conformed obediently when I told them they couldn't do that and indicated the proper thing to do. I had to wait for the tenth rich man who wanted to do something wrong before I succeeded in throwing him out of the office and having the belated celebration.

But I want to say that in the meantime there must have been half a dozen not-so-rich men who had to be thrown out for the same reason.

It is interesting when you read the great figures in the literature of our profession that they virtually never mention the subject of professional dishonesty. You don't find that sort of thing in their writings, and the reason for it is not so much that they are trying to hide it from their public, nor is it so much that no one ever attempted improperly to influence, say, Learned Hand's opinions; it is rather that the profession has held for them so many non-pecuniary satisfactions, satisfactions having to do with public service, culture, the advancement of justice, scholarship, and law reform and bar-association activities, that they have kept their eyes on those concerns, and so the pecuniary side has become secondary and has been pretty much taken for granted in their thinking as legitimate but not central.

I believe that that is a way and the only way that we in the schools and the law offices can guide young men as their mentors into becoming the kind of lawyers we have had in the past: Not by telling them, "You must not do this." "Why must I not?" If you have nothing else to offer but the type of picture that prevails in a merchant's establishment, your only answer will be, "Because you will be caught." That then becomes not a matter of honesty but of prudence and self-preservation. But if you have the kind of vision of the profession in which it is possible for a man to obtain these other satisfactions I have talked about, I believe it is very easy to make him see that what you ask him not to do is something that is incompatible with these other ends—not incompatible with his safety, but incompatible with his act of self-dedication in becoming a lawyer, and the causes he is supposed to serve.

In short—and I think it is high time I became short—I submit that these days the very possibility of the honest lawyer is directly dependent on the possibility of a lawyer who is making more than a living out of the profession, but is building in it a life.

With these introductory comments, I think we can move on to our form papers.

Ethical Problems in Office Counselling
Jerome R. Hellerstein

The word "ethics," which is derived from the Greek, has a broader significance than the related Greek term "ethos," meaning "customs."

The term ethics embraces not only the mores of the community, but more than that, its morals. Legal ethics, therefore, refer not merely to customary standards of conduct of the legal community, but also to the principles by which that conduct ought to be governed. This distinction between mores and morals, between what is and what ought to be, is basic to a dynamic philosophy of ethics.[1] For morals influence mores, just as mores influence morals.

Nor is ethics to be equated with the law. The standards of conduct imposed by law may or may not be in conformity with our ethical standards. The law to a large measure falls short of the moral standards by which we evaluate our conduct. And certainly, that is true of the legal community in the practice of its profession, for we are dedicated to a code of ethics which transcends the code of law.[2] Hence I start with the premise that *by legal ethics we mean not merely the customary conduct of the bar, or the requirements of law, but a code of conduct setting higher moral standards.*

To suggest the contours of an acceptable system of ethics by which to guide the conduct of a tax practitioner in the area of office counselling, I should like to set out several types of ethical problems which recur day by day in tax practice.

1. Fraudulent, illegal acts participated in by the tax lawyer. A client comes into your office on January 10, 1952 and informs you that he would like to sell his boat to a friend. Inquiry reveals that he will have a taxable gain and that had the boat been sold in 1951, the client could have offset the gain against a capital loss carry-over from 1946. The client says, "That's easy. Just date the documents of sale December 28, 1951, and I'll report the gain in my 1951 return."

What should you do? This is an illegal and a fraudulent act, which if carried out would constitute tax evasion. Generally speaking, the members of the tax bar would, I think, refuse to pre-date or mis-date documents and would lend no assistance to such fraudulent conduct.

The principle of ethics which I deduce from this illustration—a principle to which I think there would be universal assent in theory and widespread acceptance in practice—is this: *It is unethical for a tax lawyer to draw legal documents or otherwise give advice, as a result of which, by*

---

[1] Dean Pound has drawn a similar distinction between the term "morality," as referring to a body of accepted conduct, and the term "morals," as referring to a system of ideal precepts as to conduct. *Law and Morals, Jurisprudence and Ethics,* 23 N. Car. L. Rev. 185 (1945).

[2] James, in The Professional Ideals of the Lawyer 4 (1925), quotes Henry Wade Rogers as saying:

"A lawyer is unworthy of membership in the profession who would regulate his conduct solely according to what the law permits rather than what morality and honor require."

18 [6]   ETHICAL PROBLEMS

deliberate misrepresentation of facts or circumstances, tax evasion will result.

    Let us now vary the case. Your client asks you to review its position under section 102. After examining the facts, you are worried about the case, but find the client unwilling to pay a substantial dividend. You recommend the consideration of plans for expansion and a review of inventory needs, of working capital and future contingencies. The corporate officers are unwilling to undertake or to commit the corporation to any serious expansion. By carefully chosen questions, you find that the officers are not unwilling to have a report prepared directing that steps looking toward expansion be taken, or to have a corporate record made that the inventory and working capital are too low for its current, and especially for anticipated needs—though far in excess of any such needs in the corporation's history. Passing the question as to whether it is good tax advice to draw such a resolution or to have such a report made to the Board of Directors, is it ethical for you to recommend such a course or to draw the resolution or to assist in preparing the report? I am assuming a factual situation which will not always but will often be the case, that is, put in its best light, you will be exaggerating and overstating the facts in an effort to suggest serious consideration of expansion which is not intended, and to give an appearance of cash needs which you and your client know do not exist. Does this case differ in essence from pre-dating the bill of sale for the boat? I think not, except perhaps in the obviousness of the distortion of facts and in our use of self-deception in order to persuade ourselves that we are not misstating the facts or seeking to mislead the Treasury.

    There are numerous illustrations of the same type of problem, which arise day in and day out to plague the tax practitioner. In trying to avoid the *Court Holding Company* case and fall within *Cumberland Public Service,* should you recite in the contract of sale that the seller desired to sell only stock and the purchaser refused to buy stock but demanded a sale of assets, when you know that the deal was strictly a simple sale of assets until the clients came to you and were apprised of the tax problem? Or take the problem of allocating a lump-sum purchase price of a business to machinery, inventory, and good-will in a case where you know and the parties know that good-will is a substantial factor of value. Are you justified in recommending an allocation of a nominal amount to good-will and a correspondingly larger amount to machinery in order to increase the purchaser's depreciation base and in drawing the contract so as to recite such an allocation? Or take the all-important area of particular concern to the accountants but on which the lawyers are increasingly encroaching—the matter of how transactions should be recorded in the taxpayer's books of account. Are we justified in advising the client to bury in an expense account an item which is indisputably a capital expenditure and if properly recorded would have to be amortized over a long period, whereas the client desires an ordinary expense deduction?

In principle, I can find no justification for regarding the section 102 case, the *Court Holding Company* problem, the allocation problem, and the misleading accounting—on the facts which I have stated—as anything less than a fraud on the fisc, a violation of law, and an attempt by the taxpayer and his counsel to evade taxes. My guess is that this type of tax fraud is widely encouraged and indulged in by tax practitioners who would be horrified at the thought of pre-dating corporate minutes or a contract of sale.

2. *Advice as to unwarranted deductions.* The second type of ethical problem presented to the tax practitioner which I should like to consider may be illustrated by the following example. Your client Brown, an officer of a small, closely-held corporation, informs you that his neighbor Jones, similarly occupied, told him that for years he has had his personal car, which is never used for the business, purchased, owned, serviced, and insured by his corporation, and that the Bureau has never questioned the item. "If Jones can do it, why can't I?" asks Brown. Jones, like Brown, is known as a fine, upstanding citizen, who makes generous contributions to deductible charities. I take it that most members of the tax bar would not hesitate to tell Brown that such a practice would be a tax fraud and urge him to have nothing to do with it. The reason for this result is this: *It is unethical for a tax lawyer to advise his client to take admittedly unauthorized deductions or to exclude income which is incontrovertibly taxable.*

Let us vary the illustration. Brown tells you that Jones gets a $5,000-a-year flat allowance from his corporation for unreimbursed entertainment and business expenses, which he does not report as income. "Why can't I do that?" asks Brown. On examination you find that a $500 allowance would be a generous provision for all Brown's unreimbursed business expenses. Should you admonish Brown in the same way as you would in the case of the car, that this would be fraudulent and an evasion of the law? I am fearful that many of our brethren would advise Brown that, while as a matter of law he is required to prove the actual expenditures, as a practical matter, it is a good tax-saving scheme; that maybe $5,000 is too high, perhaps it ought to be $4,000; that even if his return should be examined, he has a pretty fair chance of settling for perhaps half the amount in question. Yet, is there any difference between the expense allowance case, on the facts which I have stated, and the automobile case, other than the difference in the likelihood of being caught at the fraud, the greater difficulty of proof? Ethical standards cannot properly be made to yield to the difficulties of proof of misdeed.

In dealing with the type of problem under discussion, we delude ourselves into believing that the facts justify the results desired by the clients. To still our consciences, we suddenly lose our great skill in developing the facts. This, I fear, is one of the weakest points in our moral armor. In this connection, a statement in the Canons of Ethics deserves quotation.

No client, corporate or individual, however powerful, nor any cause, civil or political, however important, is entitled to receive nor should any lawyer render any service or advice involving disloyalty to the law, whose ministers we are. . . .[3]

3. Resolving questions of law in the taxpayer's favor. The third and last category of problems which I should like to discuss is perhaps the most troublesome one of all. To illustrate, your client is the settlor of a trust which you are fearful may be taxable to him under the Clifford doctrine and regulations, but the question is in doubt. Or a corporation has taken a deduction for interest payments on notes held pro rata by its stockholders which, under the so-called thin incorporation doctrine, is highly questionable. In these cases you are reasonably clear that if the facts are brought to the Bureau's attention, the Bureau will decide the issue adversely to the client, but you are not clear as to what the results will be in the courts. In these circumstances, do our ethics call for a full and fair disclosure? Should you recommend that the client in his return set forth the facts as to the Clifford issue or that the corporation call attention in its return to the circumstances as to thin incorporation, in such a manner that the issue will not be overlooked by the Bureau? The answer in practice is, I think, in most cases, perfectly clear. Such disclosure is not required and we go along hoping, with some anxiety but with no feeling of guilt, that the Revenue Agent will miss the item. In short, it is the ethic of the profession that: *The tax practitioner does not regard it as his duty to recommend full and fair disclosure of the facts as to items questionable in law.*

Let us generalize from these illustrations. We regard it as unethical to draw obviously and easily detected false documents which aid in tax evasion, but we are ready to play fast and loose with the facts in our documents where we can put a semblance of truth on the false impressions we seek to create. We regard it as unethical to advise taking an obviously unwarranted deduction or to fail to include obviously taxable income, but where there is basis for a deduction, we have no compunction about encouraging and advising an unwarranted expansion in amount. We regard

---
[3] Canon 32, Canons of Professional Ethics.

it as entirely proper to advise clients not to call attention to items of exclusion of income or to deductions which, as a matter of law, we have advised the client are highly doubtful.

These, then, if I have correctly appraised the picture, are our mores and morals. Is this an acceptable ethic? I think the heart of our problem is in the ethical judgment we make as to the relations between the taxpayer and his government. If you think of the citizen's relationship to his government as comparable as that of a plaintiff or a defendant to his adversary in a litigation, perhaps you can justify the absence of an ethical standard of full and fair disclosure, but even on that basis not the looseness with which we draw misleading contracts and resolutions, and advise as to swollen deductions or misleading accounting. But is that a proper standard by which to conduct the citizen's relations to his government in the taxing area? Does not the citizen owe his government and his neighbors the duty of paying his share of taxes as required by law? As ministers of the law, can we countenance or be accessory to an escape by taxpayers of their duty to their government?

By and large I suspect that the tax bar will merely echo the ethics of the business man and the taxpayer. If it's "smart" to evade payment of one's fair share of the tax load, if one is a "sucker" when he files a fair return making full disclosure, then I think that the tax bar, regarding itself as the handmaiden of the taxpayer, will largely use its skill and knowledge to make such practices successful.

We have, therefore, a large task at hand if we are to conform the mores of the tax bar to acceptable moral standards. We must set out to do no less than to conform the tax mores of the general community to acceptable moral standards. Our task is to use our skill and experience and the great confidence which our clients repose in us—our advice, our writing, and our teaching—to improve the tax morality of the community. We are professional men not mere hired hands. We have a tradition at the bar which has commanded respect and honor. We can have great impact on our clients and on the community generally. We must bring that influence to bear in order to develop in the community generally ethical standards which require full and fair disclosure by the taxpayer, which abhor fraud, whether obvious or cloaked in elegantly drawn documents or befuddled by the stretching of judgments or the magnifying of doubts.[4] This, I think, we owe to our Government and to ourselves.

---

[4] "The only alternative to moral schizophrenia or chaos is the intellectual effort at the integration of human ideals which men have dubbed, reverently or contemptuously, moral philosophy or ethics or the science of values." M. R. COHEN AND F. S. COHEN, READINGS IN JURISPRUDENCE AND LEGAL PHILOSOPHY 595 (1951). *See generally* the chapter in this work on "Law and Ethics."

THOMAS N. TARLEAU: I hope you will give me a moment or two, before I go into my paper, to comment on the talk that you gave us, Mr. Chairman, because it interested me and moved me profoundly.

The scandals which we are all familiar with and which undoubtedly color the thinking of all of us today have moved me as profoundly as anything that has happened in my lifetime. Nevertheless, I felt somewhat taken aback by your feeling, which I may have misinterpreted, that we are living in a degenerate age, that we are behind our forefathers, that the practice of the tax law has gone down in ethical and moral standards compared to what it was a generation ago.

My own belief is that that is not so. My own belief is that immorality and corruption in government can be illustrated in every age and in every generation from Francis Bacon to Martin Manton. I don't believe that we are in a degenerate age. I believe we are in a more self-conscious age than those of our predecessors. That doesn't relieve us from the responsibilities of living up to our ethical standards, but I only go through this vale of tears once, and I would hate to feel that I am dwelling with a group of persons who are in a society of practitioners that measure up less to their sense of duty and fitness than those of my father and grandfather.

I profoundly feel that that is not so. I think that the current wave of dismay, justified as it is and needing cure as it does, should not blind us to our position in the long history of the practice of law. I think we have made advances. I think the setbacks that befall us every once in a while cause us greater concern each time that they happen.

I don't believe, therefore, that we should look upon ourselves as lower than our fathers, even though we are considerably lower than the angels.

Ethical Problems in Dealing with Treasury Representatives
THOMAS N. TARLEAU

The ethical problems facing the tax practitioner in dealing with Treasury representatives are, of course, largely the same as those of any lawyer dealing with an adversary. The necessity for the avoidance of any false statement, misrepresentation, or trickery is as obvious here as in all other fields of legal practice. The conflict between the lawyer's zeal as an advocate and his ethical responsibilities as a member of the bar is always present. But there is another factor which cannot be overlooked. In dealing with the Treasury the lawyer is not only an advocate in an adversary proceeding but he is dealing with the Department of whose Bar he is an enrolled member. When the Treasury, through its Bureau representatives, asks for data and information pertaining to a case of a particular taxpayer, the Government is entitled to such information if it is pertinent to the issue, and the lawyer assumes the responsibility for the accuracy of the information furnished. In arguing the legal merits from the information that is available, the lawyer can, of course, put the most favorable face on the facts. He is not bound to support interpretations of the facts which might help the Government, but is duty-bound not to conceal facts which are material to the issue which is being considered. In the ordinary case a lawyer is generally free to furnish his adversary facts or refuse to furnish them, depending upon the tactics of the case. This, of course, is one of the striking differences between the ordinary situation and the tax situation.

The effect of the lawyer-client relationship on this problem creates certain difficulties. For example, let us suppose that an individual claims on his return a deduction for depreciation with respect to certain property. Let us assume further that the Revenue Agent in his 30-day letter denies the deduction on the ground that the property was not held in the taxpayer's trade or business but was inherited non-business property. The taxpayer's lawyer, in his protest and in his hearings in the Agent's office, is able to show that the inherited property was converted to a business use shortly after its inheritance ten years before the taxable year and that the property was rented or held out for rent for a considerable period. The taxpayer is also able to show the value on the date on which it was converted to a business use. The Treasury representative seems to be convinced and asks for some supporting information. In the course of the preparation of the supporting information, the lawyer learns for the first time that although the real estate is still held by the taxpayer the building upon which the depreciation is claimed was actually no longer in existence during the taxable year but had been torn down. Must the taxpayer's lawyer disclose to the Agent that the depreciation should be disallowed because of other facts of which the Agent was not cognizant? This is an extreme case and, therefore, the answer is comparatively easy. I doubt whether anyone would disagree that unless the client permits disclosure of the full facts, the lawyer must withdraw from the case.

The desire to present only the favorable facts and not the unfavorable ones, the desire to comply only with the minimum necessary to satisfy the Agent and not to furnish the complete story is an everyday problem. The temptation to disclose only those facts which support the taxpayer may be great. Yet, because of the tax practitioner's dual responsibility, he is obliged to reveal every fundamental fact which is pertinent to the issue under consideration. Admittedly, situations are bound to arise which call for close decisions on whether particular facts are material facts which must be disclosed or whether they are merely evidentiary in nature. It is not possible to provide a copybook rule for resolving such decisions. Nevertheless, the general principle is clear that the lawyer practicing before the

Treasury Department has an obligation to engage in open-handed dealing with the representatives of the Department, and to avoid anything suggesting concealment or trickery.

Because of the very nature of a tax proceeding, the danger of deception is always present. Normally, all of the facts involved in the case are known only to the taxpayer and his representatives. The Revenue Agent conducts an examination in the nature of an inquest. Ordinarily, however, he receives no more than the data or facts made available to him by the taxpayer, his accountant or his lawyer. This control of the facts which are being disclosed to an adversary makes deception a very simple matter. Correspondingly, the lawyer's duty to avoid overreaching, either by the taxpayer or himself, is that much greater.

Let us assume that in the course of an audit of an individual's tax return the examining agent requests the details of a deduction for travelling expenses incurred by the taxpayer in connection with his business. In the taxable year in question the taxpayer has travelled extensively throughout Europe for the purpose of purchasing merchandise to be resold in his business. The taxpayer's lawyer is able to supply the agent with cancelled checks for steamship and railroad fares, hotel charges, etc. These items of expense all appeared reasonable in amount considering the taxpayer's station and the length of the business trip. This evidence ordinarily would be sufficient to sustain the deduction.

However, the lawyer's examination of the facts also uncovers the fact that the taxpayer's wife, who had no connection whatsoever with the business, had accompanied him on this trip. Innocently or otherwise, the taxpayer had assumed that he had had no choice but to have his wife make this extended trip with him and, therefore, that the cost was a necessary business expense. Without commenting upon this client's questionable tax logic, is this not a situation which requires the lawyer to disclose to the agent that part of the travelling expenses was incurred for the taxpayer's wife and that her business purpose on this trip was, to say the least, highly remote?

This rather obvious example has a thousand counterparts in the daily experience of tax practitioners. Most often, it is simple from an ethical standpoint to judge when facts should be furnished to the Bureau and when to fail to do so would be tantamount to concealment. Occasionally the decision may be difficult. Certainly there are many instances where some circumstances having no direct bearing on the tax issue involved, if made available to the Bureau, could be used by it to the detriment of the taxpayer's case. Of course, the obligation to avoid concealment or subterfuge does not go so far as to require counsel to furnish the Government with ammunition to defeat a taxpayer's valid claims.

A striking difference between the general practice of law and tax practice is that the tax lawyer has the same adversary in every matter. His opponent is always the Government and his dealings are mainly with its agents and lawyers. While this may not be a very small group, the lawyer finds himself meeting and dealing with the same Government people with some regularity. If the lawyer is of good repute he soon finds that these Government representatives are ready to rely upon his integrity. This may manifest itself in a variety of ways: the acceptance of a statement of facts without verification, the adoption of data submitted by counsel without an independent audit, etc.

Although this situation makes the practice of tax law a pleasant one, it also saddles the lawyer with a great responsibility. Because he knows that his word, his version of the facts, or the data he submits may be accepted without further verification, he is under a duty to make certain of the accuracy of the material he presents to these Government representatives. In effect, he is regarded as having vouched for the correctness of the material he submits unless he expressly disavows responsibility for it. Obviously, while the latter course may frequently be the safest, it is also one which can arouse suspicion and thereby prove detrimental to the client's interests.

Such a relationship between counsel and the Government's agents also makes it possible for the client, either innocently or deliberately, to trade upon his lawyer's good reputation. Loose or careless representations may be made to the lawyer, knowing that they will be passed on to the Bureau as undisputed facts. If the lawyer does not take steps to satisfy himself as to the accuracy of his information, not only is he being imposed upon but he will in turn be imposing upon others. It hardly seems necessary to mention that it does not take many innocent misrepresentations to damage a lawyer's reputation. Word quickly gets about in Government circles that some lawyer is "unreliable" and from that point he will be dealt with cautiously. Apart from purely ethical considerations, therefore, it is obvious that a lawyer's fidelity in dealing with his Government adversary insures and protects his own most available asset—his good reputation.

Our discussion to this point has been concerned with the ethical problems facing a lawyer in his dealings with Government representatives. I would note, in passing, that the problems involved in this connection, so far as the client is concerned, are largely the same as those arising in general practice. As a matter of fact, Treasury Circular 230 provides that the tax lawyer is required to observe the canons of ethics as adopted by the American Bar Association.

Where the lawyer is dealing with a Treasury representative in connection with questions arising on a return which the lawyer has prepared for the client, does the privilege extend to the information furnished the lawyer for inclusion in the return? For example, where misinformation has been given to the lawyer as to the amount of a client's gross income and the error is later discovered by the lawyer, I doubt that the information is privileged.

Because of the brief time available to me I will not be able to discuss the many unique ethical questions which may arise in fraud cases. However, in view of the extensive newspaper publicity on the subject, I feel I should make brief mention of the corrupt Treasury agent or the one who seeks to be corrupted. What is the duty of the lawyer who meets with a brazen demand for a bribe? Were it not for the client's position in these situations there would be little room for question. However, it is generally the case that the client is reluctant to become involved in a criminal or disciplinary proceeding and would prefer to have his lawyer ignore and forget the suggested bribe. It is my sincere conviction that the lawyer's duty to his client is not involved in this situation. Assuming that the lawyer is dealing with an out-and-out attempt to secure a bribe and not a mere suspicion that the Agent would be interested in one, I believe the lawyer is under a duty to reveal the fact to the Agent's superiors, notwithstanding the feelings of the client. I know of no surer way of eradicating the corruption recently revealed.

I do not wish to leave you with the impression that encounters with fraudulent Agents are a frequent experience for the tax lawyer. Contrary to the impression one would get from the current newspaper stories, I would say that it is a rare occurrence. I am thankful that in my own experience of 25 years in the tax field it is one that I have not encountered.

EDMOND CAHN: May I say that I did not mean to indicate that our age was either more or less degenerate than its predecessors. I meant only to indicate that the degeneracy we witness takes on a special form in our age. I am referring to the kind of analysis that you find in David Riesman's book called *The Lonely Crowd*. In that book he makes a very sound distinction between past generations of Americans, who he says were inner-directed, and our generation, who are generally outer-directed.

The man of the past, if he was crooked, did not characteristically claim that he was only doing what everybody else was doing, nor did he resort to the kind of defense which, if my memory serves, Mr. Steuer used on behalf of Mitchell: "Why pick on Mitchell? Everybody is doing it." It is this abnegation of personal moral responsibility in deference to the mores of the society which I believe is distinctive in our period.

BRUNO SCHACHNER: Before starting in on my paper, I think I ought not let the opportunity pass, now that I have the floor, to say a word or two about whether our generation is worse or better than previous generations have been.

Of course, I have little personal experience with previous generations, but I have some idea that the problem is strictly akin to the problem which you have, taken from my own field of criminal law, in larceny, where if you have an inflationary period and your limit of grand larceny stays constant at $500, you are going to have a great deal more grand larceny.

I think we have a great deal less morality in dealing with taxes, because we exact from the community a moral standard up to which the community is not prepared to live. It is perfectly ludicrous to have laws prohibiting sexual intercourse among married people. When you don't even enforce them among unmarried people, you are never going to enforce them among married people.

I feel that various laws, of which the tax law is just one example, make demands on the moral standards of the community to which the community is just not prepared to conform. In the olden days—and I still have some slight personal experience with it—we had prohibition. Well, people wanted to drink. Other people thought it was unethical to drink. People stayed unethical, but, in addition, they became criminals.

We have a very similar problem with us now. What the solution of this problem is, I am not prepared to say here and now, but it does seem to me that this is a fact that should bear on a consideration of these problems, which I am sure all those who spoke before will readily agree with me on.

Ethical Problems in Tax Prosecutions

BRUNO SCHACHNER

The limitation of my own subject-matter to criminal proceedings may seem capriciously narrow, but criminal litigation is usually less familiar to the tax practitioner, and it is governed by special rules. It is unique in its aims and its methods, and the position of defendant's counsel reflects that uniqueness.

Basically, in civil litigation we expect counsel not to suppress evidence of advantage to the other side and in criminal litigation we exact the same duty from the prosecutor on pain of having the verdict voided. Must counsel for the defense turn over evidence of guilt to the prosecution, or is he at least permitted to do so with propriety? Further, should he refuse to defend one accused of crime whom he believes to be guilty?

The last issue was posed dramatically in an English murder case, in which counsel had accepted the brief for the defense because he believed in the innocence of the accused, incidentally a belief that is often dangerous and always unprofessional in criminal cases. On the second day of the trial the defendant suddenly turned to his counsel and confessed his guilt to him, yet he refused to plead guilty and insisted that the counsel proceed with the defense. Of course, the attorney-client privilege forbade the disclosure of the confession, but counsel was reluctant to argue the innocence of one whom he now knew to be guilty. In this dilemma he turned to one of the judges who was not involved in the case, and who advised him that he was bound to continue the defense and to do his utmost to secure the acquittal of his client. The defendant was convicted in due course, but not without the solace of a stirring address in his behalf. For contrast with the English notion of an advocate's duty in a civil case a fictional incident comes to mind. In Galsworthy's *Loyalties,* counsel was retained for the plaintiff in a defamation action, under the representation that the client was innocent of a theft with which he had been charged. Suddenly, counsel is confronted in his chambers with a new witness who possesses irrefutable proof that the client had committed the theft. Without hesitation he abandons the client and transmits the proof of guilt to the public prosecutor, and the propriety of this action is taken for granted in the play.

Perhaps the two examples given do not embody American notions of what is proper. They serve, however, to illustrate a fundamental difference between the duties of an attorney in a criminal, as contrasted with a civil, case—which in turn reflects an underlying difference in policy.

The stress in civil cases is primarily on a speedy and just determination of the controversy, and society has little interest in affording every cantankerous person his day in court. Lawyers should not engage in frivolous litigation, and they live up to the highest standards of the profession if they refuse to do so. In criminal cases the stress is much more on the lawyer's duty to hold himself available to defend seemingly hopeless causes and even disreputable persons, lest the innocent accused find himself without a champion. In theory, at least, we have come a long way from the common law, which refused counsel to the defendant because, as he was mockingly assured, he was presumed to be innocent. Now we are unwilling to have anyone convicted unless every effort has been made to have him represented by counsel.

However, have we in fact as well as in theory abandoned the medieval common law? The question is likely to be tested in tax prosecutions in the near future.

The Bureau of Internal Revenue has recently concentrated on fraud investigations of persons who are popularly suspected of being "racketeers." This concentration will undoubtedly, in the fullness of time, result in prosecutions. Will persons suspected of being racketeers and accused of tax evasion be able to retain reputable law firms to undertake their defense? I think they will in the end, but only at considerable and unjustifiable cost to the reputation of their counsel. We may put to one side the leaders of the bar, whose reputations would survive any attack, and the dregs of the profession, whose reputations could not be materially lowered, but the middle ranks of the profession face a serious problem. The general public will be prone to identify them with their clients, with consequent damage to their reputation and pocketbook. If they are ambitious for public office, the defense of a racketeer may constitute a serious handicap.

In cases involving crimes verging on treason, a solution has been worked out in practice. Reputable lawyers refused to accept employment for pay, but accepted appointments by the courts. Since the accused was usually not financially able to afford competent counsel, he would in any event have had to accept court-appointed counsel. In some cases there were rumors that reputable lawyers would not undertake to defend, although money was available, but equally reliable rumor had it that the real difficulty was the unwillingness of counsel to cater to the client's caprice in the conduct of the case.

In tax cases the accused is rarely without funds and to assign counsel to him is unfair to him because it deprives him of free choice of counsel, and unfair to the lawyer because it deprives him of just compensation for professional services. It is to be hoped, therefore, that lawyers will hold themselves freely available even to disreputable clients. Bar associations might suitably support them in that determination.

The term "lawyer" rather than "tax practitioner" is used, for representation by accountants is fraught with special dangers in criminal situations. Treasury agents may be eager to deal with accountants on such matters, and Bureau officials and even Department of Justice officials may be willing to receive them, but let them be wary, because a criminal tax case is primarily a criminal case involving taxes and not a tax case involving criminal law. Above all, the client's confidences are not protected if they are entrusted to an accountant and he should guard himself against receiving them, lest he have to disgorge them under oath. The foregoing, of course, does not mean that accountants are not frequently and properly employed to aid lawyers in the investigation of facts and in the preparation of accounting data which help them to present the case. It is desirable, however, that the accountant restrict his activities to the books and not obtain dangerous admissions from the client, for it is by no means sure that such admissions are protected even if the accountant is the lawyer's employee *pro tem*.

Perhaps the development of our customs in this respect has been unfortunate, and it would be preferable if the accountant were to come to occupy the position of the British solicitor in tax cases, and the lawyer were to content himself with the position of the barrister. But no sign of such a development is discernible. A special problem in criminal cases is also raised by the practice of representing more than one defendant or prospective defendant. In civil cases the chances of conflict between taxpayers in the same case are remote. In tax fraud cases, however, it may well be, for example, that the person who profited mostly by the fraud had to obtain the cooperation of his clerical employees who are now in danger of becoming co-defendants. Frequently the employer is quite willing to have his representative act also for employees. The employees, however, may find it to their advantage, under these circumstances, to confess and to testify against the employer. Needless to say, it is not always improper to represent more than one person in the same criminal case, just as it may not always be proper to represent more than one in a civil case; but much more careful exploration of possible sources of conflict should be made in criminal cases.

In the actual conduct of a criminal case, it is generally not considered improper to refuse concession of even the most obvious fact, while a similar refusal to stipulate might be intolerable chicanery on the civil side. Naturally, the defendant (and that includes his representative) has no duty to aid in bringing about his own conviction. But while he may remain passive, he may, of course, do nothing to destroy or fabricate evidence, and if his representative finds that the client is engaged in such activities he must, of course, relinquish the representation.

The duty not to tamper with evidence, however, does not by the remotest stretch of the imagination include a duty not to learn the strength and possible weaknesses of the Government's case. It is widely and mistakenly believed that witnesses who are likely to be subpoenaed by the Government are not to be interviewed by the defense. On the contrary, if prospective witnesses are willing to be interviewed, preparation for trial would not be complete without ascertaining all that they will tell. It is well, however, to be cautious in such interviews, for witnesses in criminal cases are notoriously treacherous, and the line between an attorney's expressions of doubt and subornation of perjury can easily be misplaced by the bias of a witness.

It is difficult to discuss ethics in the tax field, and particularly in the criminal tax field, without hypocrisy. Such discussions are apt to sound like discussions by missionary societies of table manners among cannibals, in which strong views are expressed on the use of forks but no mention is made of the fact that the main course is usually *ragout de missionary*. By now it is no secret either to the general public or to tax practitioners that a good deal of "missionary" had been consumed and that questions of outright dishonesty are more pressing than questions of ethics. For the near future, however, there is genuine hope that we will have tax administration that is reasonably honest and resistant to political pressure. The professionally trained tax practitioner, apart from his interest as a citizen, has a special and vital interest that this be and remain so. As long as cases can readily be "fixed" there is no need to resort to the employment of persons proficient at winning them on the merits. In the years just past the value of a Treasury card was debatable, since persons who called themselves "investigators," "public relations men," or "insurance agents," or even nothing at all, were able to bring comfort to a surprising number of taxpayers—at a price.

Yet, it is still possible that a tax practitioner may encounter a demand for a bribe, either directly or through his client. The approach is likely to be devious and naturally the practitioner will not want to encourage it to the point at which it becomes unequivocal. If, however, it is unequivocally made to the practitioner directly, he has a duty to inform the Inspection Service of the Bureau of Internal Revenue, irrespective of the client's wishes. If he learns about it through his client it is at least colorably covered by the attorney-client privilege, and the client's consent to complain must be obtained. Certainly, if the client gives any indication of future compliance with the demand, the representation should end.

A complaint to the Inspection Service is protection against extortion. This agency may, however, ask the taxpayer to feign compliance so that corroborating evidence of crucial conversations can be obtained. Sometimes this may entail the use of special apparatus to overhear conversations. It may be legitimate to cooperate in this manner, but many persons might feel that they would thereby debase themselves. *Lee v. United States,* 343 U.S. 747 (1952) shows that even the Supreme Court is divided on this problem. No easy answer of what is proper occurs to me. There is, of course, the natural reluctance to inform and to engage in double-dealing even on the side of the angels, but it seems counterbalanced by the interest in rooting out bribery and extortion. In the final analysis, this—like many other ethical problems—involves balancing one's own immediate discomfort against ultimate good to the community.

Ethical Problems in Lobbying for Legislation
Merle H. Miller

There is a natural reticence concerning ethical problems in connection with any field of endeavor, for it is difficult to speak without seeming to impose your standards upon someone else. And also there is the fear that in proclaiming the laxity of your standards, others with higher standards may feel inclined to relax. Fortunately, this particular subject is covered in the Canons of Professional Ethics adopted by the American Bar Association in 1908, so that we may first direct our inquiry to determining whether the standards found desirable by the committee headed by William Howard Taft meet today's problems.

* Canon 26, relating to "Professional Advocacy Other Than Before Courts," provides:

> A lawyer openly, and in his true character may render professional services before legislative or other bodies, regarding proposed legislation and in advocacy of claims before departments of government, upon the same principles of ethics which justify his appearance before the Courts; but it is unprofessional for a lawyer so engaged to conceal his attorneyship, or to employ secret personal solicitations, or to use means other than those addressed to the reason and understanding, to influence action.

Being governed by the same principles of ethics which justify his appearance before the courts, a lawyer is limited in his advocacy to that in which he himself believes. Canon 30 states that the appearance of a lawyer in court should be deemed equivalent to an assertion on his honor that in his opinion his client's case is one proper for judicial determination. In urging a case before a court a lawyer can ask for a result in which he himself does not believe, but which result is required by the applicable law. One who believes the defense of the Statute of Limitations to be unethical may nevertheless plead it as a defense to which his client is entitled.

However, in requesting new legislation there normally is no other law to rely upon to justify advocating a result in which one does not believe. Consistency, fairness, and public good are suitable grounds for urging legislation, and if the lawyer himself does not believe that the legislation for which he is asked to lobby is justified on the grounds which he urges, then the Canon of Ethics would preclude his professional activity for that legislation. Canon 31 takes away the excuse that he is only following his client's instructions.

The limitation on the advocacy of causes in which one does not believe is, however, largely theoretical as a practical matter. It is usually impossible to examine a problem at the behest of a client without soon becoming so enmeshed with its solution as to be disqualified to judge its merits in relation to the public good. So the more practical inquiry relates to the *methods* a lawyer may employ. It is in this area that the lawyer will find the greatest difficulty in following the principles applicable to his appearance before a court.

The canon specifically calls for the revelation of his attorneyship. This would probably be automatic in appearing before the Ways and Means Committee or the Senate Finance Committee. However, much remedial legislation originates in organizations such as the American Bar Association and the state and local bar associations. Any lawyer presenting a request to such an organization for a recommendation to Congress would seem to be required by the spirit of these principles to reveal his attorneyship. Then if that association does recommend the requested legislation to Congress, the attorney who, on behalf of his client, urges upon Congressmen the passage of that legislation, should reveal his attorneyship, since otherwise he will be appearing to act solely for the good of the public, whereas he is actually employed by a client to procure that specific legislation.

Some of the principles applicable to presenting cases to a court do not seem applicable in the promoting of legislation in Congress. One does not discuss the case with a judge in the absence of the other party, yet it is doubtful that such a limitation would be placed upon calls on Congressmen. The limitation, however, is not so much on the physical act of calling, or writing, as upon what is said by the lawyer. Lawyers are precluded from "using means other than those addressed to the reason and understanding, to influence action." Presumably he may call upon his Congressman, but his discussion is limited to an appeal to reason, which presumably relates to the merits of the legislation and not to the chances of reelection of a Congressman if a request is not granted.

When we consider the many forces that are brought to bear to influence members of Congress to vote one way or the other, one wonders how an attorney may follow Canon 26 and still earn his pay in representing a client. However, on the types of legislation for which an *attorney* is needed, as contrasted with a pressure-worker, the measured appeal to reason may well be more effective if only because of its contrast to other methods to which Congressmen are subjected. But whether effective or not, the cultivation of legislators, the incurring of political and other obligations, even the use of friendships, are not for the lawyer as he seeks to obtain legislation for the benefit of those whom he represents.

Strangely, the greatest ethical problem confronts those who do not lobby for legislation. At least that is true if the field of ethics which we are discussing includes affirmative obligations as well as negative prohibitions. What then about the duty of the tax bar to lobby *against* special legislation? Although Government representatives usually oppose special legislation which grants favors to a selected number, the Government is usually carrying such a burden in getting through the necessary legislation to raise its revenues that it cannot always take an adamant stand against every piece of special legislation. In fact, the principle that the Government's interest is in raising the revenue often leads the special legislation to become even more selective as its proponents narrow the field so as to cost as little as possible in revenue and yet give the desired benefit to the specific taxpayers' representatives. Thus the legislation becomes more inequitable and yet more acceptable to a Government which must, of necessity, continue to worry about the source of its revenue. Thus we find some most peculiar specifications in our tax laws giving benefits not only to a class but to selected persons within the class, without apparent cause or logic.

But while Washington is swarming with those seeking to change a particular section of the law, there is no one to speak out on behalf of the rest of the taxpayers who stand the cost of the special concessions so granted. This cost to all taxpayers over a period of time is considerable, but at no one time is it sufficient to warrant them to rise up and send agents to Congress to speak out against special benefits to others.

Over a lifetime each tax practitioner has a greater interest in a fair and symmetrical body of tax laws than any group has in special legislation in any single year. Every word added to the Code for the benefit of some particular taxpayer may well prove a trap and a very costly one for some other unsuspecting taxpayers. Yet tax practitioners are sitting idly by, while year by year the lobbyists are making of our body of tax laws a more cumbersome instrument with which to ply our trade.

The one voice to be heard, and the most effective voice to speak against special provisions in our tax laws, is that of the tax bar. The time is ripe for organized action by those whose sole interest is the over-all fairness of any tax pattern. Such a group without any special interest could speak out against proposed legislation on the sole ground that it is designed to serve a special interest. When we pause to realize the potential good that could come from such concerned action, the support that could be given to those in Government and in Congress who grow weary of fighting special concessions, we realize the extent to which the tax bar is failing to meet an unprecedented opportunity for service. If then our concept of ethics includes the duty to act affirmatively when we possess special talents that would achieve unusual good for the public, then the greatest ethical problem in connection with tax legislation today lies at the feet of each member of the tax bar who seeks no special legislation but fails to take action for a concerted effort to defeat the continued requests for special legislative favors.

EDMOND CAHN: As we found last year, the best part of the proceedings begins at this point. We are fortunate in having a goodly number here, and, therefore, it is only fair to ask each one to make his comments as pithy as possible so that the others will be heard from, too. Without wasting more time telling people not to waste time, I will begin by calling on Dean Niles.

RUSSELL D. NILES: I am, of course, not a tax expert. I am an educator, and so my first reaction is this: I wish that all of our tax students could have been here tonight.

I have only one comment. I have often wondered why so many lawyers felt a real sense of personal loss in the death of Judge Robert Patterson, because, while he was a good lawyer, there are many lawyers as good; while he was a good judge, there are many others as good. He was a great soldier. He had certainly been a good public servant. He was a very likable and approachable man.

But I don't think that many of us had a feeling of personal loss and a real sense of depression when we heard of his death for any of these reasons. I think that somehow we felt almost intuitively that there was a sort of lawyer that we would all have liked to be. I think we feel that there had been less erosion in his case than in that of almost any lawyer we knew. There was a person who still possessed absolute integrity. I think that is probably why all of us felt that his loss was great.

I hope that we can learn somehow, either by symposiums like this or perhaps some day by telling our students of some of the great men of the law or some of the current figures in the law, to make them aware of their professional obligations, because I don't think that we have done too well at it in recent years, and I still think we have to find some ways of doing it.

EDMOND CAHN: I am going to call on Dean de Capriles, and then all academic distinctions will be ignored and we will go right around the table.

MIGUEL A. DE CAPRILES: I feel I have been subjected to quite an intellectual and emotional experience tonight, and it seems to me that the flow of the papers was extraordinarily good, because as questions arose in my mind they were successively answered by the papers; so I think very well of them.

I am troubled more or less in a general way by an old dilemma which seems to underlie some of the problems discussed tonight, and that is the problem of obedience to the unjust law. It seems to me that we are taking for granted, are we not, that the Socratic answer is still the right one?

The point is important in connection with Mr. Miller's discussion of special privilege, of which I think the tax law is becoming rapidly a disgraceful example. It is important in connection with Mr. Schachner's preliminary remarks about prohibition and the readiness of the public to accept the law. Just as a question mark, to what extent may it perhaps be at the root of a possible unethical behavior in lawyer-client relationships or lawyer-Treasury relationships?

J. P. WENCHEL: I am a little bit disturbed at the disturbance that seems to be around the table and which possibly generated the topic tonight, and that is the fear and the thought that there is something wrong with the tax bar, there is something wrong with the Bureau of Internal Revenue.

What has happened in the Bureau of Internal Revenue is a cycle. It is not the first time. We had the Couzens investigation before that. Back in the 1880's you had an investigation, and right after the Civil War you had an investigation. That was a very interesting investigation, because at that time and probably for the first time in our history the taxes were farmed out. Of course, there was a lot of money stolen. It is not going to make any difference whether the personnel are appointed by the President or appointed by the Civil Service Commission. People are always going to be people. There are going to be some crooks.

In my tour of duty and experience in the practice, there has been only one instance, and that was when I was in the Bureau, where an agent offered to settle a case upon a payment of money. And only one lawyer ever called me up, and within four hours he was before the United States Commissioner. Personally, in my outside practice I have never had any approach. As to the type of lawyer around the table tonight, you don't have to worry about him. It is the blackleg—and he was always in the profession. What are you going to do about him? He is on the fringe of society. All the meetings we may have I doubt will do him any good. It is the coming generation that counts. If you can indoctrinate them, then you will have the type of bar for which you are aiming.

I will give some free advice. Whenever I am called in a case, I get my own auditor and I get my own net-worth statement, and I don't depend on my client's net-worth statement or his auditor.

EMANUEL GORDON: I think the most significant statement I heard was Merle Miller's closing statement: that we all talk about the weather but none of us does anything about it. I think we all know what the standards of ethics are, and I think very few of us would disagree as to what the outcome should be in any particular case. We might disagree as to what the tendency to violate those ethics is in any particular situation.

Personally, I think that the situations Jerry Hellerstein gave as the particular cases in which any practitioner would refuse to go along with his client are not situations in which most practitioners would refuse to go along with their clients. I think the violations are far more widespread than any of us are willing to admit.

But I think the important question is: What are we going to do about it? I think the reason why so many practitioners aren't able to do anything about it is that these violations of ethics are like a malignant growth; if it only exists in a small portion of our community, then we are able to isolate it, the ill effects are limited, it won't spread too far; but the minute it begins to hit a substantial portion of the community, you have that competitive effect. If you won't do it, somebody else is going to do it. That is the attitude that leads to widespread breakdown of law enforcement.

I think that is the situation which faces the tax bar today. You do have a widespread breakdown of the observance of ethical standards which all of us would admit are right and proper and should be observed. The problem is: What can we, as a practical matter, do about it?

I don't think any of us are in a position to sit back and say, "It isn't me; it is the other fellow." I think it isn't so, because all of us know of particular instances in which there have been violations, grievous violations, where bribes were passed, and yet none of us has done anything about it. In most cases, perhaps, we could say that there isn't anything you can do about it. Two years ago whom could you have turned to as a practical matter if you knew some agent had taken a bribe? To the United States attorney, who was controlled by the same little group that played ball with the agent who took the bribe?

After all, the taking of bribes isn't an isolated incident where the agent simply takes the money from the taxpayer. In most situations it is a far more complicated thing, where the taxpayer goes to somebody who knows an agent or who knows his supervisor and the money is paid to the supervisor, who then splits it with the agent. The minute you begin to have that kind of organized group, it is very difficult to do anything about a particular case of which you have any information.

We have the King Committee, with which Bruno Schachner is now associated. I don't know that the King Committee is going to uncover or prosecute every single instance of malfeasance which comes to its attention, but how many of us have taken the trouble to notify people on the King Committee of instances about which we have information which they need? They may have a lot of rumors, but without the fact itself it is awfully difficult to investigate or do anything.

I think we ought to do a little soul-searching of our own and see what we have done to end the sort of practices about which we have information, instead of simply sitting back and saying, "Well, it is a nasty situation, but it is the other fellow; I am not doing it."

JESSE R. FILLMAN: I wasn't quite clear in Tommy Tarleau's remarks, which I thought were quite pointed, as to whether, in the case where information came to the lawyer after he had been engaged in conference, he was entitled to withdraw from the case, or whether he was duty-bound to reveal the information. Perhaps someone else here will clarify it for me.

With respect to Merle Miller's remarks, I feel very strongly on the subject that he was talking about, not particularly directed to legislation in so far as appearances at Washington are concerned. I served on the tax committee of a very distinguished bar association at one time in my career. I believe there are no members of that committee here. An issue arose that was so outstanding that I think I will comment on it. I wouldn't say it was untypical; it was just perhaps more pointed. The question was what the committee should recommend in respect to the contemplation of death. It seems to me there was a sound difference of opinion on that. Finally, one member of the committee said, "Let us ask for such and such, because we ought to ask for more than we expect to get."

I was shocked when no one in the committee took any exception to that approach. I was so shocked that I didn't do it myself. I think that that has been repeated more frequently in some of our bar-association groups and other groups of lawyers than we would care to admit.

HARRY J. RUDICK: First touching on Jesse Fillman's remarks, one of the things I prided myself on when I was chairman of the New York City Bar Association Tax Committee was that we did oppose special legislation of the kind that Merle was talking about. I am sorry to say that at that time that attitude was not typical of bar association committees generally.

I would like to touch on the ethics of the law. I understand that is reserved for next year.

EDMOND CAHN: We shall talk next year about the ethics of the Government in this situation. Tonight we are talking about the practitioner's ethics.

HARRY J. RUDICK: In a sense, the law is the practitioner, and vice versa. I don't think you can separate that completely from the ethics of taxpayers and tax practitioners.

Suppose the law is an ass. Do we have to slavishly respect it? Or if there is a means of going around, to take Jerry Hellerstein's example of the *Court Holding Company* case, why should there be two taxes if the company is going to dissolve? If there is a way of fixing it that there should be one tax, are we compelled to arrange it so that there should be two taxes?

Take another example. Suppose a man wants to sell his business to his brother. There is going to be a loss on the sale, but it is a bona fide transaction. The law doesn't allow that loss. Is the tax practitioner precluded from advising that man to sell that business to his brother's wife so he can get the deduction? I don't think so.

I think that you can't completely separate the two ethics. I believe they are intertwined. I gather from what has been said that the ethics that we are talking about here are not absolutes. They are relatives, like the mores and the morals that Jerry Hellerstein talked about. If that is so, ethics are a product of time and place.

Incidentally, I agree with Tarleau that this is not the worst of all possible times so far as tax morality is concerned. Certainly, so far as avoidance is concerned, avoidance is as old as taxes. Let me give you an example of how ethics are a product of time and place. In Switzerland there is a cantonal tax on your net worth as of the beginning of the year. Prior to 1940 nobody—literally nobody—in Switzerland ever declared his net worth in his annual statement. The tax officials knew that nobody declared his net worth, and so fixed the rates at a high enough figure to produce the revenue which was needed. If a new resident of Switzerland came to a Swiss lawyer and asked for his advice, should the Swiss lawyer tell him to declare his true net worth?

Mark H. Johnson: As I found very often when I served under Harry Rudick on the City Bar Association, he managed to anticipate what I was about to say. It is very much along those lines but with a little of this emphasis.

I think it has been mentioned before that what we are talking about is not very much the problem of the professors or of the lawyers who have a history of public service and of responsibility. If you are trying to establish a system of tax ethics, a criterion of tax ethics, that means something in weight, it is something that pretty much has to be built up from the bottom. That is where, let us say, 98 per cent of the taxes and the tax problems are being handled.

How you are going to do that, of course, is something else: education from above, the example from the leaders of the Bar, which I am sure have some effect. But—and this, I think, is Harry's point—to build up that criterion, that standard, from the bottom, you have to build it basically on a sound system of law and a sound system of administration.

The pressures come from a lot of directions. You have lawyers who are economically or spiritually marginal; you have confiscatory tax rates, silly tax laws, a tax system, for example, of revenue agents who have to come up with a deficiency (so why shouldn't you throw something to them in the first place?), a silly Court Holding Company rule where, if you take one rule, you come out one way and another, another. Those pressures are almost inexorable, and unless you eliminate them and build a sound system, I think you are always going to be faced with that problem.

JACOB RABKIN: I should like to address myself largely to Jerry Hellerstein's implied and direct accusations. I find that in this question of morality and ethics in the tax practice there are no different problems from those of deciding these questions in other courses of conduct. I think it is a question of partition into the permissible right and the forbidden left and the hazy, misty, or amorphous middle.

On the question of the permissible right, I am sorry that I have to be the first one to raise a dusty and musty old platitude, but I think as a lawyer I must. Just to paraphrase Dean de Capriles' remark, the problem is not one, as he puts it, of obedience to an unjust law; the problem is one of taking advantage of an unjust law.

I think that the tax lawyer owes it, as a primary duty to his client, to see that the client gets the full rights and benefits that the law allows. I refuse to plead guilty to the implied charge that we tax lawyers are engaged in a shady, knavish kind of business in which our stock in trade is a very fancy variety of intricate devices designed to unfairly shift the burden from our taxpaying clients. We are not the keepers, as somebody has put it, of Congressional conscience. So much for the right.

As to the extreme forbidden left, I have no difficulty with the examples posed by Jerry Hellerstein. I don't think any of us are going to condone the suppression of evidence, the manufacture of a purported intent, the perversion of a purpose, the pre-dating of instruments, the preparation of side agreements, or any of these invidious and disgusting kinds of practices.

I know—and I don't deceive myself—that very frequently we put wrong labels on these devices. We call them inventiveness, ingeniousness, creative tax-thinking, ingenuity. We know them for what they are, and we discard them. I dare say most of us spend a great deal of time persuading clients not to use these devices.

* The trouble I have is with this middle area, which hasn't been touched on, I think, directly. It is the area in which we unconsciously take advantage of the slowness and inefficiency of the administrative process. Just stop and think for a moment of the thousands of *Gregorys, Horsts, Cliffords, Towers* and others who did not pay the tax liabilities that these specific taxpayers did actually pay. There is a reason for it. Counterparts of these specific avoidance plans that I just referred to are presented to us daily. They are not tried. They are not tested. They are doubtful.

But there is a tremendous temptation to accept them, because the administrative process is long in developing a technique for overcoming a specific tax-avoidance device.

It is wrong to assume that the tax collector is in hot pursuit of every taxpayer. He isn't. He is far behind us. It is in this particular area in which we are tempted to accept untried schemes or devices, programs, and in which we hope for an element of its success because of the mathematical possibility that the administrative process will work either inefficiently or too slowly, where a tremendous amount of self-restraint on the part of the tax bar is required in order not to create this inequitable shifting of the fair load from your high-bracket taxpaying client to the low-bracket general taxpayer.

PAUL LITTLE: I might just inject one thought here. We might remember here that we are dealing with two-headed monsters rather than this monolithic character we call the tax practitioner.

There is a canon of ethics and a long professional history behind the lawyer, but the other portion of the tax-practitioner group is made up of accountants, who, it seems to me, should also be considering the problems that we have met here tonight for, and there should be some type of cooperation between them in order to see that similar standards are maintained by each; otherwise, we are trying to fill the bucket with a hole in the bottom.

JACQUIN D. BIERMAN: This whole problem of ethics is very interesting to me because of the fact that we are taking it out of its real context, discussing it as if it existed by itself without relation to the entire pattern in which it fits. You've got today an economy where there are bills required, pressures on the part of individuals to keep money after taxes, pressures on the part of the Government to collect the tax revenues that it needs. We have a tax system today whereby we are presumed to protect the taxpayers and the Government protects the revenue instead of, as a Congressional committee once said, also seeking to protect the taxpayers.

I have a feeling in this environment we have a laboratory situation that is highlighting this problem of ethics, and that in some sense, anyway, we are confusing the problem of tax ethics with the philosophy of what should be tax management.

My own feeling and reaction is that in the light of the changing conditions which require different approaches to the collection of revenues and certainly different approaches at the very low taxpayer level, there must be some consideration given to possibly a different way of enforcing the revenue, to take away from the tax-gathering authority the job of being simultaneously the collector, the prosecutor, and the judge. Until that can happen, until we can make moves in that direction, the only reaction that I can have is that you have to live within your own personal integrity and try to process the case as best you can.

LLOYD GEORGE SOLL: I have been in ready agreement with the fact that we have to teach all young people to be honest, and I am also in agreement with the various people who have spoken on the problem of interpreting their ethics in the light of the various pressures and the problems of achieving justice under what might be considered unjust laws.

My basic concern is with the reason for this very meeting, which is the recent scandals. My basic concern is that our tax structure can slide into what has been going on in some of the countries to the south and in Europe, the problem of "the bite." The Government comes along and extracts a bite, and the people kind of accept it.

I think the answer lies in more direct action, in terms of policing our government officials and possibly in even more direct action against the bribe-giver as well as the bribe-taker. It hasn't been called to my attention that any really affirmative steps have been taken against the bribe-giver.

JOHN F. COSTELLOE: When you find drunkenness, it is good to see if the man needs vitamins or a better home or a better job or something. I think we, perhaps, take a little too much on ourselves by trying to cure our ills with ethics. My own company has made payments of $6 to tax collectors for every $1 it has paid to common stockholders for ten years. I think on the individual level you will find the same ratio existing.

In a country where competitiveness and salesmanship and holding your trade secrets are things which are accepted and which are responsible in large part for our ability to take on a load abroad which is inconceivable in its charity, I believe perhaps the profession might borrow from business to give the people involved institutional safeguards that are not necessary in the trial of a boundary suit once every twenty years. This happens every day all the time. I think the profession might do well to borrow from commerce.

HENRY SELLIN: Macauley, in his *Life of Bacon,* not only points out that Bacon was convicted of taking bribes but that nobody was horrified. Nowadays, when someone is accused of bribe-taking, the entire community is horrified. I think that portends hope for the future.

FRANK McEVOY: Jerry Hellerstein's last example, where under a given factual situation the law is moot on the question, raises the question whether the taxpayer, through his tax practitioner, should make a disclosure of those facts in the return. I understand that a proposal has been made by the Government that, where such a situation exists, a full disclosure of those facts be made in the return, so perhaps if the tax practitioner does not tend to his ethical standards the Government may do it yet by statute.

GERALD L. WALLACE: I would just like to raise a question with respect to one of Tommy Tarleau's original statements. I may have misunderstood him. I would suppose that if an attorney generally, unless there is some special circumstance, learns of an understatement of income by his client, then, instead of its being his duty to disclose that fact to the Government, it would frequently, perhaps generally, be his duty not to.

I am not sure I caught all your facts. Are you discussing the statement prepared by the attorney?

THOMAS N. TARLEAU: Yes.

GERALD L. WALLACE: I would agree with you on that basis.
Referring to Jerry Hellerstein's last category, I have a good deal of question about the duty of a lawyer to disclose all of the facts in the case where there is bona fide and reasonable doubt as to what the law is. If the attorney is of the opinion that the Bureau's position is wrong, I shouldn't suppose he was under any duty to make a full disclosure of the facts for the purpose of inviting close examination.

BORIS I. BITTKER: I was particularly interested in both Mr. Hellerstein's and Mr. Rudick's remarks. I thought Mr. Rudick's pointing to the Swiss cantonal tax was an acute observation. Of course, it wasn't necessary to go quite that far afield, since the same, I think, is probably true of the Illinois personal-property tax, and while I don't want to make a public confession, we have a personal-property tax in Connecticut that isn't complied with as it should be.

Mr. Rudick's suggestion about the sale to the sister-in-law, I suppose, is all right, if you stop at that point, but, if you go on to add that the brother is putting up the money and the sister is to be a nominee, I suppose you are back where Mr. Hellerstein left us, and I haven't yet heard any really persuasive answer to those problems. They seem to me to be just as morally reprehensible as moral corruption, and more dangerous, because they are harder to detect.

I don't know how widespread those things are. I hope to hear more about that. I do know from questions that come to me from time to time from practitioners, that a good many members of the bar would go a long way in tolerating some of the things which Mr. Hellerstein suggested and which others here seemed to regard as entirely improper. I guess that is a pessimistic note to end on.

JEROME R. HELLERSTEIN: I am not entirely certain that there is such complete difference of opinion between Hellerstein-Tarleau and Rudick-Rabkin as there appears.

I think there was an overtone in some of the remarks that exaggeration and distortion of fact are permissible, which I regard as reprehensible. That this is widespread, I have no question—widespread among highly respectable members of the tax bar, not only the blackleg fringe.

Another thing I would like to press is that in the item of full disclosure I tried to make clear that I don't believe any of us regards that as our duty. My point is, I think, it ought to be our duty, and I think that we would all live happier lives, and I think there would be a fairer distribution of the tax results.

By the way, we would have a lot more business if there was full disclosure.

MERLE H. MILLER: I would like to get our discussion back to the self-analysis which I underwent last year when I was trying to prepare a paper for a New York University program and since which time the practice in our own office has changed tremendously.

I found that, on preparing that paper and trying to fit the things that we were doing into any canon of ethics or generally accepted practice, I was amazed at the things which I had been doing, which I thought were perfectly all right but which simply could not be justified.

After I gave that talk, a number of people asked me whether I was going to retire. In the light of the statement here about competition and so forth, I should report that it has been some nine months since then and we have tried out our higher code on our clients, and they seem to like it. I doubt very much whether there is anything to that competitive business. I think clients come to you to try out something, to see whether it is all right, and I think, if you tell them it isn't, that is the end of it, and I think they respect you more for it.

The most dangerous philosophy that I have heard expressed tonight was expressed by some of the most undangerous people here, and that is the philosophy that the law, being unfair, justifies something less than complete honesty or the highest ethics in our compliance with the law. That, I believe, is the most dangerous thing. I think there are men in jail today for justifying their actions on that ground. I know of no basis on which any lawyer can justify cutting any corner, evidentiary or otherwise, because he believes that the law itself is unjust.

EDMOND CAHN: I feel grateful to each and every one of you for your participation this evening, and I believe that the transcript of this session is going to be of genuine value to the profession, because we have heard a variety of views here which will start people thinking and make for self-examination. It isn't necessary that they end up by agreeing, but it is important that they start becoming aware of their duties and sensitive to them.

A man can only arrive at an answer that is honest in his own heart, and, if he doesn't agree with one or the other of us, it is still an answer that he is willing to commit himself to and be responsible for in his dealings. I think that is the first condition of the really ethical life.

3. Morality in Tax Planning

Merle H. Miller

Those who have come tonight expecting salty revelations are doomed to disappointment. Our subject concerns primarily the inanimate object of taxes and not the personal lives and idiosyncrasies of those who pay or concern themselves about taxes. The term morality is usually used in some connection with the sex life of homo sapiens. Tonight, however, we shall consider other aspects of morality, for there really is no sex in taxes notwithstanding the rate at which they have been multiplying, or the fact that some taxpayers have been heard to question the ancestry of some of our recent levies.

Morality for our purposes shall be the distinction between right and wrong. It is the word used to denote the quest of man for what ought to be. Morality is a sense that distinguishes man from all other creatures upon the earth, and the quest for a moral society is one of the greatest continuing forces in the world today.

We are not alone in pausing to consider morality in our professional life, or in our national life. In the midst of the greatest production of goods in our history, at a time when man has learned most about the control of the available resources, when physical forces have been found which outmode yesterday's perfection, men in all walks of life are pausing to consider whether there is something beyond guns, production and resources which go to make a nation and its citizens great. It is proposed that a two-year study be made of ethics in government. Irregularities which would have been regarded as commonplace a generation ago are rightfully scandalous to a more keenly developed sense of morality that prevails in the nation today.

A seventy-three year old man, who thirty years ago

caught a vision of the true force of morality in lives of men, today heads a movement which has accomplished wonders through no other media than an appeal to the moral sensibilities of men. Moral Re-armament has spread to eighty countries and is now regarded by many as the most potent challenge to Communism in the struggle for men's minds. It is distinguished from most organizations in that it is dedicated to the improvement of its own members, with each member working on himself. Its four absolutes of honesty, purity, unselfishness, love, are commonplace virtues with a modern application. Yet the already apparent effect of a number of individuals striving within themselves to be absolutely honest, absolutely unselfish, is little short of the miraculous. The halting of a three-year old strike of the National Airlines, the neutralizing of Communist leadership in British colonies, the integration of Europe as envisioned by the Schuman plan, and the recent Japanese Peace Treaty in San Francisco are all laid at the door of Moral Re-armament by the leaders most responsible for the success of these various enterprises. The story of Moral Re-armament is one of the most exciting chapters in world history, and give dynamic proof of the great underlying power of morality in our world today, or any time.

The linking of morality with our tax laws is something new in this country. The people who used the tax on tea as the spark to ignite a revolution and who had included in their Constitution a prohibition against any direct tax by their Federal Government were not likely to discuss morality and taxes in the same breath. The tax collector was an intruder, and if you could escape his clutches, you were in the same fortunate position as someone who had escaped smallpox or diphtheria.

It was only natural that the courts would reflect the public attitude of the time, and declare that the burden of proving a citizen's liability to his government was upon the government, and that the citizen was free to use any sort of device to avoid the tax so long as he stayed literally within the

---

[1] Look Magazine, October 23, 1951, p. 102.

letter of the statute.[2] But that was when taxes were mere nuisances and a citizen who was able to dodge a tax was not thereby given a considerable advantage over his neighbor.

Public Attitude Toward Tax Schemes.

But now taxes are too great a part of our business life to be treated so lightly. A taxpayer who by some device is able to dodge a tax will wind up with as great a competitive advantage over his neighbor as if he had cheated the neighbor directly out of a considerable sum. A man who can form a family partnership and reduce his taxes by ten thousand dollars can have automobiles, take trips and afford luxuries which his neighbor can not. A tax advantage obtained by some scheme, may more than offset the greater production efficiency of a competitor.

So there has come about a tremendous change in the public attitude toward tax manipulations. Last year the Department of Justice was able to obtain convictions in ninety-seven per cent of the cases in which it prosecuted taxpayers criminally for tax evasion,[3] despite the fact that each of those taxpayers had the right to a jury trial. Such a record would not be possible in the absence of an aroused public opinion against those who lie about the facts upon which their tax liability is premised. It is not popular today to be known as one who has pulled a clever tax scheme, whether or not it constitutes a criminal evasion. One of our largest meat packers decided of its own accord not to avail itself of what appeared to be an opportunity to cut its taxes $1,500,000 a year by sending its freight bills to its offices at Canada for payment thereby avoiding a tax on freight. Its decision was based in part on a feeling that such a loophole could not be permitted to continue to exist, and also that its public relations would be jeopardized if it were to resort to this method of avoiding taxes by a tech-

---

[2] United States v. Isham, 17 Wall. 496 (1873).
[3] Report of Commissioner of Internal Revenue for Fiscal Year ended June 30, 1950, p. 61.

nicality. At the present time, then, there is a moral consciousness of the general public with respect to our tax laws, and a genuine interest and wide-spread feeling as to what ought to take place in the determination of a citizen's liability to his government.

In the light of this public attitude Congress has been moved to act, both in closing loopholes and in removing inequities in our laws. Of the great volume of words and phrases which constitute the present internal Revenue Code, the portion measuring and leveling the tax could be condensed into a very few pages. All of the remainder relates to exceptions either in the interest of removing inequities against taxpayers, or in preventing undue advantage to some taxpayers because of assumed loopholes in the law. And when taxpayers have been particularly ambitious, Congress has not hesitated to act retroactively to remove an assumed advantage in the interest of keeping all taxpayers on a fair and equal basis.[4]

The Courts have a Conscience—for Taxpayers. It is the courts, however, who really have a conscience for those taxpayers whose sensibilities have become hardened through non-use. It might be said that it is not necessary for taxpayers to be moral about their tax liability—the courts will be moral for them. We have witnessed during the past twenty years the growth of court-made law which is to our tax law what equity was to the old common law. Formalities are no longer controlling, but may be completely or partially disregarded to the extent necessary to achieve a "right" result. The definition of a right result can be found nowhere other than in the moral sensibilities of the courts today.

Mrs. Gregory met every requirement of Section 112 in combining a tax free reorganization with a subsequent liquidation in order to obtain the distribution to her of certain property of her corporation at capital gain rates. There was no provision in the Code to prevent this result, and while the case was in litigation, Congress enacted an

---

[4] IRC § 129, added by Sec. 128 of the Revenue Act of 1943.

amendment to the Code effective for subsequent years which would close this loophole. But the United States Supreme Court found that although Mrs. Gregory had met every technical provision of the code, she nevertheless should be taxed as upon the receipt of a dividend since that was the ultimate economic result reached.[5] Where did the court find authority for what was the right result in this case? All prior decisions had said that so long as a taxpayer turned square corners and followed the literal provisions of the revenue acts, no other questions need be asked. The court found the answer in a moral sense of its members that such a result should not be permitted. This decision has been rightly regarded as a landmark decision in the new body of tax laws that have come into being in recent years.

The negotiable interest coupons which Mr. Horst delivered to his son, vested title in the son and the interest money subsequently received by the son was in his absolute right. The Code taxes people upon the receipt of income and since the coupons represented interest which was later received by the son, he would have been taxable upon that income under any literal interpretation of the Code. But the Supreme Court enunciated the doctrine that the man who owned the tree should pay the tax on the fruit even though he did not get it, and taxed the father on the subsequent interest payments received by his son, when the coupons were cashed.[6] Under any literal interpretation of the common law or our tax laws, that income should have been taxed to the son who received it, but the court felt that such a result ought not to be allowed under a system of graduated taxes. Its moral sensibilities had been disturbed, and it felt that any other result ought not to be.

All the law of the land holds that a trust, of however short duration, is a valid trust and serves to vest in the beneficiary the interest indicated in the trust instrument. The Internal Revenue Code prescribes how the income of a trust shall be taxed, without making any differentiation

---

[5] Gregory v. Helvering, 293 US 465 (1935).
[6] Helvering v. Horst, 311 US 112 (1940).

as to the length of the terms of a trust, the powers vested in the trustee, or the relationship between the grantor, the beneficiary, or the trustee. All of the applicable common and statutory law would tax to Mrs. Clifford the income from the ten year trust established by her husband. What law then was applied to tax that income to the husband? It could only have been the sense of right and wrong whereby the court felt that the technical niceties of a statutory and common law notwithstanding, Mr. Clifford should not be permitted to reduce his taxes in this manner.[7] If the distinction between right and wrong is the essence of morality, then that sense of morality in our courts is the only known factor accountable for the decision in the *Clifford* case.

One of the best examples of the effect on courts of the feeling of what ought to be, lies in the very controversial area of the sale of corporate assets. In the *Court Holding Co.* case,[8] the court found that a corporation should be taxed upon the sale of its assets even though it entered into no valid contract for the sale of the assets and was not in existence when the sale was effected. This result was reached because the court felt that taxpayers should not be permitted to reduce this obligation by merely changing the form of the transaction which had already been agreed upon.

But later the court realized that Congress itself had relied completely upon form in prescribing the tax liability on this type of transaction. If the assets were sold by the corporation and the proceeds then distributed to the stockholders, there would be two taxes, whereas if the assets were distributed to the stockholders and then sold by them there would be but a single tax. There is a general repugnancy about the impact of two taxes upon a single transaction so that the court came to feel less agitated about the efforts of individual taxpayers to comply with the form which Congress apparently allowed to result in only a

---

[7] Helvering v. Clifford, 309 US 331 (1940).
[8] Comm'r v. Court Holding Co., 324 US 331 (1945).

single tax. In the *Cumberland* case,[9] the court placed upon Congress the responsibility for discrepancies in this area, and left it for Congress to say whether there should be a single tax or a double tax on all such transactions. Because of a lack of conviction as to the overall fairness of a double tax, the court has shown a leniency toward form in this particular area that can not be counted upon to be extended into other areas. An even better example are cases involving the sale of stock to a third person immediately before redemption in the days when gain on the sale of stock was taxed as capital gain, but the gain on redemption was taxed as ordinary income. The courts being out of sympathy with such an arbitrary discrimination, followed the form of the transaction in those instances,[10] under circumstances where the form would have been completely disregarded with a taxpayer trying to avoid an impact of a different nature.

However the taxpayer may feel about any relation between morality and his tax plans, the courts are busy applying their own concept of morality to all tax questions, and in the process are writing a law more comprehensive and to the tax practitioner even more important than the Code itself. This body of law is as yet sketchy and will, of course, never be completely filled in. But in its present sketchy state, any tax practitioner who attempts to chart a course by merely taking into account the results reached in specific instances is disregarding the most important factor in our tax life today. Even though the result reached in a specific case may have no bearing whatever upon a proposed plan, in the ordinary manner in which legal authorities are applied, the salient fact is that the courts are saying at every opportunity that taxes are a very practical matter, and that any plan which will remove from a taxpayer the burden which he otherwise would carry, and which is being carried by his neighbors, will not be tolerated if the end result seems unfair. There is a sense of morality rampant in our courts today, ready

---

[9] United States v. Cumberland Public Service Co., 338 US 451 (1950).
[10] W. P. Hobby, 2 TC 980 (1943); Stanley D. Beard, 4 TC 756 (1945).

to take care of any omission of Congress, or any brilliant scheme of the most brilliant genius, which would result in an unfair dislocation of burdens of government which every citizen should share.

The tax counselor today must know the statutes and must recognize that Congress has been acting for a number of years with a very keen sense of awareness as to what is fair as between taxpayers and has sought to plug up any loopholes. He will not, therefore, attempt to jump through what appears at first glance to be a loophole. Even if he finds a loophole which long research fails to discount, he will realize that on a long term basis it will not last. Then the tax counselor today must be alert to the moral sensibilities of our courts and recognize that the decisions are but indications of a trend and do not delimit the farthest reaches of the trend. It is a hard time for tax practitioners, for as Chancellor Coke once observed, it would be better for a rule to vary according to the length of the Chancellor's foot than according to his conscience, for there is less variation in the length of men's feet than there is in the application of their consciences. In such a difficult situation, with the rules not delimited in this period of change, the wise tax counselor will not be afraid to apply in his daily conduct as a tax counselor, the rules of every day life which have been found useful and applicable in other fields. He will not hesitate to condemn a plan merely on the ground that it offends his own moral sensibilities and is, therefore, apt to be found deficient by a court that would have less desire to find the plan effective than would the tax counselor.

Role of the Tax Practitioner Today. The popular concept of a tax practitioner is not a very complimentary one. And doubtless many of those who are now active in this field have felt some compunction about devoting their lives to devising schemes for enabling people to dodge a levy that all should share. Most people think of us as having a bag of tricks that greatly reduces our clients' taxes and probably gets us out altogether on our own. At least that is what they think until they call upon us in a professional way and usually leave in amazement after being told that they really owe more than they thought they did when they came to see us. That is because the average layman has more faith in technicalities than does the tax practitioner who is supposed to deal in them.

So it is that many people who feel themselves doing worth while things today must feel sorry for us. In their eyes we toil not, neither do we spin—other than fanciful tax schemes to be later found invalid by the courts or declared retroactively ineffective by Congress. In their minds' eye they can see us as our grandchildren climb upon our knee and ask what we did in the great battle between the West and East. They can see us flush with shame, avert our eyes, and slowly mumble, "Grandchild, I spent my nights working out phony family partnerships, I developed my present literary style from dictating glowing minutes depicting reasons for not paying out dividends, and I wrote long instruments setting up tricky trusts so that those who came to me would not stand their full share of the tax load."

Every active tax practitioner knows that the popular concept is not the true picture. The tax practitioner today spends nine-tenths of his time killing schemes believed by the proponents to be new, but which were actually dead and buried many Revenue Acts and many decisions ago. As we grow old in the practice, this mortality rate bothers us less and less, and we come to suspect that the scheme is bad even before we have heard it. Once a man has become reconciled to the proposition that there is little new under the sun, this job of decimating someone else's brain child becomes rather perfunctory, and even loses some of its zest.

In killing poor tax schemes, the tax practitioner is rendering invaluable service to his country. A good man can kill more such schemes in a year than ten revenue agents could examine and settle in five years. He is not only saving his clients the costly experiences of following through on a dead plan, he is saving the government a great deal in manpower and is in general contributing greatly to the efficiency of our tax collecting system. A roll call of top flight tax practitioners would reveal a continuing counsel to taxpayers that prevents them from going off on screwy tantrums, diverting their energies into non-productive tax avoidance activities, to the great detriment of our productive system and our tax collecting system. The man who can kill off a bad tax scheme at its inception is contributing greatly to the well being of the country at large.

It is easy to kill off someone else's scheme, and it is easy to examine critically almost any proposal that would seem to give an unwarranted advantage to the taxpayer. But it is most difficult to maintain that critical attitude with respect to one's own creations. For when we start with a problem we want to solve, we are soon enmeshed in the same wishes which motivate our clients and we are thereby rendered easier to please with our own answers and less critical of the outcome. It is then that we are most apt to fit together the letter of the statute and the court decisions and come up with an answer that will satisfy everyone and everything, excepting the moral sense of the revenue agent and the court that will test it. It is at this point that many who will have been able to invoke the righteous indignation of a third party to kill off a flagrant tax scheme, will fall victim to a lack of moral sensibilities in testing their own brain creations. Infanticide is as abhorrent in the intellectual, as in the physical realm.

At this point a sense of morality is the best guide, even though it may prove to be a most troublesome one. Many clients are in trouble today because lawyers assumed that their own moral sensibilities were irrelevant as guides in determining upon a course of assumed tax reduction. Lawyers have long been taught that they owe a duty of making available to the client all of his rights under the law, however repugnant the ultimate outcome may be to the lawyer's own moral sensibilities. But now that morality is a part of our tax laws, it begs the question to assume that a client would obtain a result under the technical provisions of our laws if that result did offend moral sensibilities. Since morality has been accepted in our courts, a taxpayer can not afford to have a tax advisor whose sense of morality is less acute than that of the courts. Therefore, those who feel a call to apply to the practice of tax law the same standards of fairness, of right and wrong which they apply in their daily lives, should feel free to do so.

If tax schemes must meet a test of fairness as well as technical compliance with the Code, then tax practitioners should be as zealous in developing a sense of moral fairness as in acquiring a technical working knowledge of the Code. Since a sense of morality is something that can not be acquired merely for use in a particular set of circumstances and then abandoned until subsequent need arises, the tax practitioner will be constantly testing not only his tax schemes, not only his clients, but even himself to see whether his own actions and his recommendations fit in with a code of morality that will stand scrutiny.

Applying any such tests to daily conduct can bring about surprising and even frightening conclusions. Specific illustrations are always most effective, but they are most dangerous in a talk such as this. There is always the feeling that the man who selects the illustrations is hurling accusations at some one else, and if he selects one which applies to him, then he is met with the challenge that he should practice what he preaches.

This study together tonight can in no way be counted as a preachment by me, and I would regard it as most unfair if I chose as illustrations those sets of circumstances in which I might happen to be lily-white. Instead I have chosen instances close to home, being as surprised as you will be in many instances to find moral connotations involved. I present them more to illustrate the problem than to imply an answer, or even to seek any agreement on an answer.

Instances that May Try Men's Souls.

Section 811(g) provides that insurance will be included in the gross estate of a decedent to the extent that he has paid the premiums either directly or indirectly. A client comes in and inquires as to what would amount to an indirect payment of premiums. He says that he, of course, does not want his insurance included in his estate, and the members of his family who would be the logical ones to carry the insurance would be stripped of their resources if they undertook the burden of paying his premiums unassisted. He inquires as to the possibility of giving $3,000 a year to his son, with his son using $2,000 of the money to pay the premiums on his father's insurance. If that plan receives a frown, then he inquires as to whether he can give his son stock of the value of $60,000 which will yield an income more than sufficient to meet the premiums on the insurance. In the absence of any undertaking by the son to pay the premiums, but knowing the reason for the gift of the stock to the son is to enable him to pay the premiums, is the tax practitioner justified in approving that plan on the ground that there will be insufficient evidence to prove indirect payment even though he knows, because of the manner in which the question arose, that the son would no more think of letting the insurance drop, in the absence of his father's consent, than he would think of stealing the family silverware?

In the practice of criminal law, there is a well recognized distinction between what a lawyer may do for a client who is in trouble and what he may do in the way of manufacturing evidence to keep a client out of trouble. Suppose you were engaged in the practice of criminal law and one of your best retainers had just returned from an extended sojourn at the government's expense. Suppose he walked into your office and said that he would like to be in St. Louis the following Monday night. You might suggest that he had his choice of plane, train, or automobile, whereupon he would say that it was true he wanted to be there but that he might also want to be some place else at the same time and he was stopping in to inquire as to what constituted legal evidence that he was in St. Louis. You might suggest that a letter in his handwriting mailed in St. Louis at the time he wanted to be there, his entry into a double feature show under circumstances which caused the ticket seller and the usher to recognize and remember him, and his registering in a hotel with substantial tips to the doorman and the bellboy would be about as good as he would hope to do in the way of evidence and should be sufficient. If you thus advised him in the knowledge that he was establishing an alibi and was actually going to skip over to East St. Louis for a little special job in between the time when the hero first fell in love with the heroine and the time when they finally married after several intervening unrealistic spats and quarrels, then you would properly be a subject for disbarment.

But you are engaged in the practice of tax law and a client comes in complaining that the combined effect of the corporate tax and high individual income taxes leaves him practically nothing out of any dollars which he distributes as dividends. Having heard of Section 102, and even knowing it by number, he asks what will be regarded sufficient evidence to warrant the retention of the money by his corporation instead of paying it out to him as dividends. Thereupon you tell him that money retained for expansion, for new buildings, new equipment, has been held sufficient excuse to prevent the imposition of the tax under Section 102, provided the plans for expansion, and for the new equipment were sufficiently crystalized to convince the court that the plan existed other than in the mind of the taxpayer shareholder. Evidence of the plans for expansion would consist of architect's drawings, estimates by the builder, the taking of an option on land and the recording in corporate minutes of the intent to make the expansion. Whereupon he sets out to obtain drawings from an architect, an estimate from a builder, and an option at almost any price on the adjoining land, leaving to you the writing of the corporate minutes so that they will set forth accurately the true intent of the directors, as required by the most recent Tax Court decisions on the subject.

This is not to compare the felony of robbery with the accumulation of surplus to avoid imposition of surtax on shareholders. But if it is wrong for a lawyer to advise on the setting up of facts which will conceal the true intent of his client with respect to a criminal case, is there not a moral question when the lawyer does acts of a similar nature to cover an intent which, if disclosed, would lead to civil tax liability.

Then take the case of a man in the top brackets who owns some rental property. In looking for ways to organize his business activities so that he will pay the least tax, you suggest that an office building be first mortgaged and then transferred to a corporation that would assume the mortgage. The mortgage assumed would not be in excess of the tax basis of the property, so that you feel that there would not be an immediate taxable gain under Section 112(k). By this means you predict that the corporate income subject to the lower corporate rates may be used to pay off the mortgage, instead of being taxed to him at his higher surtax rates. Section 102 provides for a penalty tax on the undistributed income of any corporation formed or availed of for the purpose of avoiding the imposition of a surtax upon a shareholder. Was this corporation formed to prevent the imposition of the surtax on its shareholder? Is a lawyer warranted in recommending a plan on the ground that the motive which would vitiate it, cannot be proven?

Not so long ago it was true, and the courts are still saying in some instances, that the intent of a taxpayer to evade taxes is not to be considered. But now Congress has made the imposition of some taxes dependent entirely upon the intent of the taxpayer. In such a case is a lawyer who prides himself on disclosing all the facts, free to conceal the intent which is the most important fact? Or perhaps what is even more relevant to our present discussion, is a lawyer free to advise acts to reduce taxes which depend for their success upon the non-disclosure of the intent behind the acts? And when called upon to defend his client, is he free to contend that the intent was other than he knew his own intent to be?

Then there is the client who wants to be billed in such a manner as to obtain a deduction for the fee paid. If you have done a job of estate planning and he wishes you to bill his corporation, or to bill him for services in other matters, the answer is obvious and easy. If, however, he merely asks you to bill him for services rendered without indicating the nature of the services, the answer should be obvious, particularly if you normally set out the services rendered in your bill, but it is not an easy answer for the reason that it implies a mistrust of the client and, of course, will be neither understood nor appreciated by him. Then comes the instance where services have been rendered to both the corporation and the individual, and there is the everpresent temptation to lean heavily on the corporation and lightly on the individual in allocating the total amount of the fee. Even in the absence of taxes there would be an inclination to bill the business heavier than you would bill the individual, but when you realize that dollars are at stake for someone and the only practical curb to assure a correct result is your own conscience, it is sometimes most difficult to distinguish between your duty to obtain the lowest possible tax for your client through proper legal advice, and the temptation to reduce his taxes by a little practical aid in the manner in which you bill him for services rendered.

Our Duty to Our Government and Its Agents.

While considering the duty of the tax practitioner, in his daily work, what about aiding and abetting taxpayers in their suspicion, distrust and even animosity toward those who are writing and enforcing our tax laws. To the layman who can see only the apparent arbitrary application of a provision of the law in his particular set of circumstances, such an attitude is understandable. But the active practitioner who should be seeing the overall picture with its many insolvable problems, should be held to a higher degree of accuracy when he chimes in with his words of condemnation. The people who hear him, think that he speaks with authority and therefore give more weight to his pronouncements than they would to the ordinary citizen. So when he speaks of manifest inequities, of needless complications in our tax laws, and when he questions the motives of the agents who are applying those laws, his responsibility is greater. While the average lawyer in a damage suit might indulge himself in the luxury of agreeing with his client as to everything the client said about the opposing party, there is too much at stake for the tax practitioner to aid and abet clients in their misconceptions of our tax laws and those who administer them.

To the tax practitioner falls the duty of adding enlightenment and not compounding darkness. It is encumbent upon him to point out the intricacies of our laws and the different fact situations which have brought about those many complications. It is up to him to point out that the law could be condensed into a very few sections if it were not for the overwhelming desire to protect against inequities against taxpayers, and prevent undue benefits to other taxpayers. It is his duty properly to acquaint clients with the real character of the government agents who spend their lives in the thankless task of enforcing these laws. It is his duty to depict them as the human beings that they are, with commendable aspirations to do a decent and creditable job to the best of their abilities. And at this particular time it is important for him to speak out and place the results of the current King Committee investigations in their proper perspective against a background of 55,000 career workers who have performed a monumental task of collecting $300,000,000,000 in the very recent past.

This is a duty which the tax practitioner owes not only to his government but to himself. For unless he sees in the complexities in our statutes an effort by Congress to achieve equity for all taxpayers, unless he feels in the decision of the courts an overall purpose to state what ought to be the result in certain situations out of fairness to taxpayers, and unless he sees in each agent of the Bureau a human being intent upon carrying out a given task fairly to the best of his ability, the tax practitioner will be at odds with true reality, and therefore can not be doing the best job for his client.

We are engaged in a most challenging economic struggle. Before too many years will be answered the question as to which economic system is more efficient, that in which the properties are owned by the government and operated by government employees, or that in which the people own the sources of production, the factories, the distribution facilities, and from these sources of wealth chip in their share toward assembling resources to be used for the common defense and general welfare of the people. It is the system of taxation which supplies the very life blood of the government operating under the latter system, and today when such tremendous amounts must be raised, the system of taxation of necessity becomes an honor system. There is not available the personnel to police a taxing system against the wishes of the people and to assure honesty in the absence of an overwhelming moral consciousness on the part of the vast majority of the people. In this picture the tax practitioner plays a dominant and most responsible role. His attitude becomes the attitude of his clients, his basic honesty becomes their standard of comparison, his sense of morality becomes a guide to them, for they feel that others are abiding by the same high or low standard.

The tax practitioner then above all people has need of a highly developed sense of that morality which leads men to seek a fair and just apportionment of tax burdens to be carried. He needs this in order that he may read with proper appreciation the many provisions of the Code, and may construe properly the great body of equity tax law that the courts have been enacting in recent years. He needs a keen sense of morality for he will be more tempted than those in other fields to indulge in flights of fancy, and to set up fact situations which are not real, under the constant prodding of clients who have not had the benefit of an understanding of the overall tax pattern which should be the stock in trade of a tax practitioner. And lastly he owes a great duty to the country that has educated him, and made possible his present success. He must do his best to maintain in his fellow citizens a proper respect for the methods we have set up under a democratic system for the collection of each citizen's share to meet the present emergency. He must inculcate in each citizen a respect for the system, and a proper respect for the part which honesty plays in that system. It is an awesome responsibility. Pray God that we may have the moral caliber to meet it.

4. The Lawyer as a Tax Adviser
Randolph E. Paul

There is a story that a savage, on being asked what was the difference between right and wrong, answered: "It is right when I take my neighbor's wife, but it is wrong when he takes mine."[1]

Analysis of the ethical problems of lawyers as tax advisers has many of the fascinating and challenging qualities associated with exploration of a moral and legal frontier. One gets quickly to the borderlands of knowledge of the subject. I would guess that a fairly general ignorance upon the subject is partly in the realm of philosophy and partly a matter of application. Until recently[2] very few tax lawyers have given much thought to the ethics that should govern the practice of their profession. Moreover, tax law as a specialized field of practice is still in its comparative infancy. There is no venerable tradition to compel the adherence of the tax bar to fixed rules of behavior,[3] and there are very few illustrious examples in a short past to guide the lawyer's conduct. There has hardly been time to evolve a new creed to fit a rapidly developing group of ethical problems. Technical problems of the most baffling character have monopolized the capacities of tax practitioners who have used all their energies in trying to keep pace with the multiplying intellectual complexities of a vast modern product of the law.[4] Tax counselors have therefore lacked opportunity to develop a solid core of philosophy to serve as chart and compass when they encounter the ethical problems constantly arising to plague them in the daily round of their exacting work.

---

[1] VINOGRADOFF, COMMON-SENSE IN LAW 15 (1946).

[2] At the 1952 annual banquet of the *Tax Law Review* a number of leading tax practitioners read papers and participated in informal off-the-cuff discussions of ethical problems encountered in office counseling, in dealing with Treasury representatives, in tax prosecutions, and in lobbying for legislation. The discussion is reported at 8 TAX L. REV. 1 (1952). This discussion was a welcome and hopeful indication of a new interest in an important subject.

For a further discussion of problems facing tax advisers, see Darrell, *Some Responsibilities of the Tax Adviser in Regard to Tax Minimization Devices*, N. Y. UNIVERSITY, 8TH ANNUAL INSTITUTE ON FEDERAL TAXATION 983 (1950), reprinted in part in SURREY & WARREN, FEDERAL INCOME TAXATION CASES AND MATERIALS 67 (1953); Miller, *The Successful Tax Lawyer—His Character and Personal Relationships*, 7 TAX L. REV. 9 (1951); Paul, *The Responsibilities of the Tax Adviser*, PROCEEDINGS OF THE TAX INSTITUTE, UNIVERSITY OF SOUTHERN CALIFORNIA SCHOOL OF LAW 1 (1950); 63 HARV. L. REV. 377 (1950), reprinted in part in SURREY & WARREN, FEDERAL INCOME TAXATION CASES AND MATERIALS 72 (1953).

[3] Few fixed rules of behavior are applicable generally to the bar. The *Canons of Professional Ethics* adopted by the American Bar Association point out "that no code or set of rules can be framed, which will particularize all the duties of the lawyer in the varying phases of litigation or in all the relations of professional life."

[4] See preface to STANLEY AND KILCULLEN, THE FEDERAL INCOME TAX IX (2d ed. 1951).

The ethical problems arising in the life of tax practitioners are not simple, copybook problems. It is not possible, in ex-President Hoover's analogy, to make the rules controlling their conduct in practice "as clear as the Ten Commandments." Most tax practitioners will not countenance fraudulent conduct in any crude sense of that term. To a suggestion that a taxpayer may evade taxes by omissions or false understatements of income in his return, by deceptive overstatements of items of deduction, by fictitious entries in books of account, or by concealing assets from the revenue collector, most tax advisers will quickly make the blunt reply that they will not participate in a transaction involving such elementary misconduct. This type of situation rarely presents a serious problem for tax counsel. He knows that he should not have even an advisory part in any transaction involving methods of tax evasion which plainly cross the line of legality. His moral instincts and training forbid participation; in addition, he knows very well that participation will sooner or later end in disaster for his professional career. Tax evasion in this brutal sense of the term "evasion" is a risky game that cannot be won. As Chief Justice Vinson once tersely remarked when he was Secretary of the Treasury: "There is no future in it."

As a matter of fact, the morals of most clients are far above the level which would sanction unmitigated fraud of this variety, even if they were convinced that it would go undetected. Moreover, they are unwilling to take the risks involved in plainly fraudulent conduct, nor do they often present to their tax advisers proposals involving wilful attempts to evade or defeat tax liability. The ethical problems presented to tax advisers are of a more subtle character. Borderline questions are presented which usually have enough potential argument in their favor to furnish some basis for rationalization leading to a decision to act in the apparent immediate financial interest of the taxpayer.

Advising As To Potential Tax

Analysis of the ethical responsibilities of tax advisers may profitably start at the earliest point in the adviser's contact with transactions involving potential tax liability. The high tax rates in force since the beginning of World War I compelled the American taxpayer to beware of the tax implications in important personal and business transactions. Moreover, there is an increasing number of taxpayers whose past failure to consider the tax effects of impending transactions has brought sorrowful effects. These and other considerations have made long distance tax planning a first order of personal business, especially as advance analysis of tax effects may minimize the impact of high income and estate taxes upon a family group.

A taxpayer may desire to reduce the tax liability implicit in an existing distribution of wealth among the members of his family or to avoid unnecessary income or gift tax in connection with a divorce settlement. No prudent businessman enters into an important business transaction without consultation with his tax attorney before he crosses the Rubicon. The businessman may wish to avoid some hidden pitfall, or more affirmatively he may wish to reduce to the lowest legal minimum the taxes which may result from a business transaction into which he is about to enter. In this latter connection his objective may be to take advantage of the capital gain provisions of the Internal Revenue Code or to avoid so-called "double taxation" on a sale of property by a corporation which is about to be liquidated.[5] In these cases the taxpayer may have a specific plan in mind or he may have a general objective which needs implementation. The purpose of his visit to the tax attorney is to check whether a given course of conduct will produce unforseen tax liability or whether a foreseen liability may be minimized.

If a tax attorney is to handle this type of work capably, and the later work of representing clients before the Treasury and the courts in connection with transactions involving attempts to minimize tax, he must first organize his philosophy on the subject of tax avoidance.[6] A coherent philosophy is vital to a consistent and effective attitude. Some tax attorneys have a vaguely uncomfortable feeling, which does not always reach the point of consciousness,[7] that there is something "mildly unethical"[8] in the desire of taxpayers to minimize tax liability, and that it is at least a venial sin to give consideration to the tax consequences of future transactions. This is not so. The standards of tax law are external standards,[9] except in those instances in which the statute itself indicates that "purpose or state of mind determines the incidence" of the tax. "Moral predilections must not be allowed to influence our minds in settling legal distinctions."[10] There is no moral turpitude[11] and nothing sinister in arranging one's affairs so as to keep taxes as low as possible. As Judge Learned Hand has emphatically said: "Everybody does so, rich or poor; and all do right, for nobody owes any public duty to pay more than the law demands:

---

[5]See United States v. Cumberland Public Service Co., 338 U.S. 451, 454 (1950); cf. Commissioner v. Court Holding Company, 324 U.S. 331 (1945).

[6]Long ago I gave up an over-ambitious attempt to distinguish the terms "tax avoidance" and "tax evasion." PAUL, STUDIES IN FEDERAL TAXATION 12 (1937).

[7]HOLMES, COLLECTED LEGAL PAPERS, 169-171 (1920).

[8]Marshall v. Commissioner, 57 F.2d 633 (6th Cir. 1932), cert. denied, 287 U.S. 621 (1932); see also Commissioner v. Yeiser, 75 F.2d 956 (6th Cir. 1935).

[9]HOLMES, THE COMMON LAW 110 (1881).

[10]Id. at 148.

[11]See Eddy's Steam Bakery v. Rasmusson, 47 F.2d 247 (1931), rev'd on other grounds, 57 F.2d 27 (9th Cir. 1932), cert. denied, 287 U.S. 601 (1932).

taxes are enforced exactions, not voluntary contributions. To demand more in the name of morals is mere cant."[12]

Tax attorneys know very well that tax avoidance is "in the nature of mortals."[13] Certainly the courts have resigned themselves to the thought that it is almost universal.[14] There is nothing reprehensible[15] or illicit[16] in attempts to avoid by legal means some portion of the burden of taxation or in honest efforts "to reduce taxes to the minimum required by law."[17] Tax avoidance has been said to be "above reproach."[18] At the very least, it is a natural product, in terms of human attitude, of conditions requiring unparalleled contributions to the Federal Treasury. Justice Holmes expressed a personal attitude toward taxes when he said: "I like to pay taxes. With them I buy civilization."[19] His judicial attitude toward tax avoidance was a horse of a different color. "When the law draws a line," he said, "a case is on one side of it or the other, and if on the safe side it is none the worse legally that a party has availed himself to the full of what the law permits."[20] On another occasion Justice Holmes added the thought: "The fact that it desired to evade the law, as it is called, is immaterial, because the very meaning of a line in the law is that you intentionally may go as close to it as you can if you do not pass it. . . . It is a matter of proximity and degree as to which minds will differ. . . ."[21]

---

[12]Commissioner v. Newman, 159 F.2d 848, 850-51 (2d Cir. 1947), cert. denied, 331 U.S. 859 (1947). Judge Learned Hand dissented in this case, but the disagreement related to other matters involving the construction of a trust instrument. See, also, the opinion in Chisholm v. Commissioner, 79 F.2d 14, 15 (2d Cir. 1935), cert. denied, 296 U.S. 641 (1935), in which Judge Hand, speaking of the Gregory decision, 293 U.S. 465 (1935), stated that the purpose "merely to draft papers" and "in fact not to create corporations as the court understood that word" was "the purpose which defeated their exemption, not the accompanying purpose to escape taxation; that purpose was legally neutral. Had they really meant to conduct a business by means of the two organized companies, they would have escaped whatever other aim they might have had, whether to avoid taxes, or to regenerate the world."

[13]Wiggin v. Commissioner, 46 F.2d 743 (1st Cir. 1931).

[14]See Snyder v. Routzahn, 55 F.2d 396 (N.D. Ohio 1931).

[15]See Iowa Bridge Company, 39 F.2d 777 (8th Cir. 1930).

[16]The word "illicit" is used in Sawtell v. Commissioner, 82 F.2d 221 (1st Cir. 1936).

[17]In Charles E. Mitchell, 32 B.T.A. 1093, 1129, modified, 89 F.2d 873 (2d Cir. 1937), rev'd, 303 U.S. 391 (1938), the court speaks of "an honest effort to reduce taxes to the minimum required by law." See Standard Envelope Manufacturing Co., 15 T.C. 41, 49 (1950), in which the Tax Court conceded that "a taxpayer may give consideration to the tax consequences of transactions." See also Shoenberg v. Commissioner, 77 F.2d 446 (8th Cir. 1935); Commissioner v. Dyer, 74 F.2d 685 (2d Cir. 1935); United States v. Cummins Distilleries Corp., 166 F.2d 17 (6th Cir. 1948).

[18]Rands, Inc., 34 B.T.A. 1094, 1106 (1936).

[19]FRANKFURTER, MR. JUSTICE HOLMES AND THE SUPREME COURT 42 (1938). See also Holmes dissenting in Compania General De Tabacos De Filipinas v. Collector, 275 U.S. 87, 100 (1927); New York ex rel. Cohn v. Graves, 300 U.S. 308, 313 (1937); Frankfurter, dissenting, in Texas v. Florida, 306 U.S. 398, 431 (1939).

[20]Bullen v. Wisconsin, 240 U.S. 625, 630 (1916). See also Horning v. District of Columbia, 254 U.S. 135 (1920); Gregory v. Helvering, 293 U.S. 465 (1935); U.S. v. Cumberland Public Service Co., 338 U.S. 451 (1950).

[21]Superior Oil Co. v. Mississippi, 280 U.S. 390, 395 (1930).

Still less is there any requirement that the taxpayer choose the one of two available courses to the same final destination which will produce the greater tax liability. The taxpayer is always entitled to seek "such shelter as the law offers in an effort to escape," or "diminsh" the blow of taxation. Of course, he must always determine whether the shelter he accepts is really constructed of statutory material. But, to mix metaphors, if high taxes, like high water, make an old path unusable, the taxpayer is entitled to choose any new path his tax attorney charts in the course of a survey preliminary to entering upon a transaction. "To say that the old path must be blindly followed, that by-paths or new paths may not be laid out with proper strides within legal bounds, goes too far."[22] Different tax consequences may flow from different methods of accomplishing the same ultimate economic result. Taxpayers are plainly entitled to select the method which results in the lower tax liability.[23]

I do not mean to give blanket sanction to the many tax avoidance schemes that are constantly being presented to tax advisers.[24] Above all things, a tax attorney must be an indefatigable skeptic; he must discount everything he hears and reads.[25] The market place abounds with unsound avoidance schemes which will not stand the test of objective analysis and litigation. The escaped tax, a favorite topic of conversation at the best clubs and the most sumptuous pleasure resorts, expands with repetition into fantastic legends. But clients want opinions with happy endings, and he smiles best who smiles last. It is wiser to state misgivings at the beginning than to have to acknowledge them ungracefully at the end. The tax adviser has, therefore, to spend a large part of his time advising against schemes of this character. I sometimes think that the most important word in his vocabulary is "No;" certainly he must frequently use this word most emphatically when it will be an unwelcome answer to a valuable client, and even when he knows that the client may shop for a more welcome answer in other offices which are more interested in pleasing clients than they are in rendering sound opinions.

I am far from advising undue receptivity on the part of tax advisers to tax avoidance devices though I am dealing with the problem of

---

[22]See Member Goodrich's dissent in George H. Chisholm, 29 B.T.A. 1334, *rev'd*, 79 F.2d 14 (2d Cir. 1935), *cert. denied*, 296 U.S. 641 (1935).

[23]U.S. v. Cumberland Public Service Co., 338 U.S. 451, 456 (1950); see also, Wall v. United States, 164 F.2d 462 (4th Cir. 1947); Commissioner v. Gilmore's Estate, 130 F.2d 791, 795 (3d Cir. 1942); Riddlesbarger v. Commissioner, 52-2 U.S.T.C. 46,384, 46,390 (7th Cir. 1952); Stanley D. Beard, 4 T.C. 756 (1945).

[24]See Darrell, *Some Responsibilities of the Tax Adviser in Regard to Tax Minimization Devices*, N. Y. UNIVERSITY, 8TH ANNUAL INSTITUTE ON FEDERAL TAXATION 983 (1950), reprinted in part in SURREY & WARREN, FEDERAL INCOME TAXATION CASES AND MATERIALS 67 (1953); Paul, *The Responsibilities of the Tax Adviser*, PROCEEDINGS OF THE TAX INSTITUTE, UNIVERSITY OF SOUTHERN CALIFORNIA SCHOOL OF LAW 1 (1950); 63 HARV. L. REV. 377 (1950), reprinted in part in SURREY & WARREN, FEDERAL INCOME TAXATION CASES AND MATERIALS 72 (1953).

[25]PAUL, STUDIES IN FEDERAL TAXATION 99 (1937).

the tax adviser's attitude toward tax avoidance. Taxes have a statutory base; there is no taxation without legislation.[26] Every tax asserted by the Commisioner must be "authorized by Congress."[27] The question for the tax adviser is not what the law ought to be, but what it is or will become.[28] My point is that in deciding that question the tax adviser must put aside his personal notions of tax policy and make his most intelligent guess as to the meaning of a statute passed by Congress.

True, the tax practitioner must be careful not to put undue trust in the letter of the law; the policy of tax statutes is not always to be found in the literal meaning of the language employed by Congress.[29] The tax adviser must accept interstitial judicial legislation as one of the realities of life.[30] Legislative words are not inert, but derive vitality from the obvious purpose at which they are aimed.[31] But sometimes the words of a statute are too clear to be escaped; there is no room for construction; and there is nothing for the courts to do but to bow their heads and obey.[32] At any rate, the tax adviser need not worry about his moral position. It is not his function to improve men's hearts.[33] As Judge Frank has observed, the task of a lawyer is to win specific cases and guide clients to pleasant destinations.[34]

To accomplish this result, the tax counselor must divorce from his thinking all "mental prepossessions"[35] and think in terms of things, not words.[36] It is sufficient that his advice puts his client on

---

[26]As Judge Frank has wisely observed: "Income tax 'law' is not a matter of pure reason. It is a composite of constitutional doctrine and interpretations of changing statutory provisions each having its history." Choate v. Commissioner, 129 F.2d 684, 686 (2d Cir. 1942). See also, GRISWOLD'S CASES AND MATERIALS ON FEDERAL TAXATION 14 (2d ed. 1946), in which the author suggests to tax students that one should not indulge in "great thoughts about a tax problem unless the thoughts are firmly based on the controlling statute."

[27]Helvering v. Griffiths, 318 U.S. 371, 394 (1943).

[28]See Johnson v. United States, 163 Fed. 30, 31-2 (1st Cir. 1908), *later decision*, 170 Fed. 581 (1st Cir. 1909). See also, Stone, *The Common Law in the United States*, 50 HARV. L. REV. 4, 12 (1936).
Keifer & Keifer v. Reconstruction Finance Corp., 306 U.S. 381, 391 n. 4 (1939), quotes the *Johnson* case and cites Stone, 50 HARV. L. REV. 4, 13 (1936), and Landis, *Statutes and the Sources of Law*, HARVARD LEGAL ESSAYS 213 (1934). See, further, United States v. Hutcheson, 312 U.S. 219, 235 (1941); PAUL, FEDERAL ESTATE AND GIFT TAXATION 49, 81 (1942).

[29]See CARDOZO, THE NATURE OF THE JUDICIAL PROCESS 103, 113 (1921).

[30]*Id.* at 29. Courts do and must legislate, but "they can do so only interstitially; they are confined from molar to molecular motions." Holmes, dissenting in Southern Pacific Co. v. Jensen, 244 U.S. 205, 221 (1917).

[31]Griffiths v. Commissioner, 308 U.S. 355-58 (1939).

[32]See Morse Drydock Company v. Northern Star, 271 U.S. 552, 555 (1926); PAUL, FEDERAL ESTATE AND GIFT TAXATION 43 (1942).

[33]HOLMES, THE COMMON LAW 144, 148 (1881).

[34]FRANK, LAW AND THE MODERN MIND (1930) *passim*; Frank, *What Courts Do in Fact*, 26 ILL. L. REV. 645 (1932); Frank, *Are Judges Human?*, 80 U. OF PA. L. REV. 233 (1931); Frank, *Mr. Justice Holmes and Non-Euclidean Legal Thinking*, 17 CORNELL L. Q. 568 (1932).

[35]*Cf.* Brandeis, *The Living Law*, 10 ILL. L. REV. 467 (1911).

[36]HOLMES, COLLECTED LEGAL PAPERS 238, 282 (1920); DIXON, THE HUMAN SITUATION 60, 65 (1937). FAIRMAN, MR. JUSTICE MILLER AND THE SUPREME COURT

the safe side of the line drawn by the statute. Indeed, it is his positive duty to show the client how to avail himself to the full of what the law permits. He is not the keeper of the Congressional conscience.[37] In representing his client in a particular case the tax lawyer must take the law as he finds it. He is functioning as an adviser with respect to the meaning of a statute the policy of which has been or will be determined by properly constituted authority, and he is entitled—in fact, he is obliged—to help his client in the case he is handling.

At times he will be wise to discard some arguments, and he should exercise discretion to emphasize the arguments which in his jugdment are most likely to be persuasive. But this process involves legal judgment rather than moral attitudes. The tax lawyer should put aside private disagreements with Congressional and Treasury policies. His own notions of policy, and his personal view of what the law should be, are irrelevant. The job entrusted to him by his client is to use all his learning and ability to protect his client's rights, not to help in the process of promoting a better tax system. The tax lawyer need not accept his client's economic and social opinions, but the client is paying for technical attention and undivided concentration upon his affairs. He is equally entitled to performance unfettered by his attorney's economic and social predilections.

It may be added that in tax cases the protection of a client's rights is a sufficient job for most lawyers. It is not always easy to determine the policy of tax statutes,[38] and the private views of the lawyer may be at variance with Congressional policy. Even though the tax adviser is in violent disagreement, the client is entitled to an objective expression of views as to that policy.

These are the principles which guide me when I discuss with clients tax questions involving the minimization of tax liability. I do not hesitate to advise the client fully and frankly in choosing among "the oddities in tax consequences"[39] that emerge from differ-

---

197, n. 32 (1939), quotes a letter written by Miller in 1878 in which he said that he regretted that in the older American colleges "the student who takes the old regular Classical Course is a patrician, while the man who seeks the knowledge of *things* instead of the knowledge of *words* is a pleb." See also, Frank, *A Lawyer Looks at Language*, published in the appendix of HAYAKAWA, LANGUAGE IN ACTION 322 (1941).

[37]Paul, *The Responsibilities of the Tax Adviser*, PROCEEDINGS OF THE TAX INSTITUTE, UNIVERSITY OF SOUTHERN CALIFORNIA SCHOOL OF LAW 1 (1950); 63 HARV. L. REV. 377 (1950), reprinted in part in SURREY & WARREN, FEDERAL INCOME TAXATION CASES AND MATERIALS 72 (1953).

[38]See FRANK, COURTS ON TRIAL 302 (1949); PAUL, STUDIES IN FEDERAL TAXATION 176, 212 (3d Series 1940); *cf.* United States v. Klinger, 199 F.2d 645-48 (1952) as to nontax statutes.

Moreover, "Solicitude for the revenues is a plausible but treacherous basis upon which to decide a particular tax case. A victory may have implications which in future cases will cost the Treasury more than a defeat." Arrowsmith v. Commissioner, 344 U.S. 6, 11 (1952). See also Portland Oil Co. v. Commissioner, 109 F.2d 479 (1st Cir. 1940); Lewis v. Commissioner, 176 F.2d 646, 648 (1st Cir. 1949).

[39]U.S. v. Cumberland Public Service Co., 338 U.S. 451, 455 (1950).

ent methods of accomplishing the same ultimate result. I will do all I can to help the client reduce his tax liability to the lowest possible legal level or save him from a greater tax liability than his transaction needs to carry. This sometimes requires a substantial modification of an orginally proposed transaction and a consideration by the client of the question whether the modified transaction will sufficiently serve his business purposes. Modifications must have substance,[40] and the client may decide that the price he has to pay is more than the projected tax saving is worth. On the other hand, he may be willing to do what is required to place the transaction on the safe side of the line drawn by the statute. He is entitled to counsel which makes the outlines of his choice clear to him.

These problems frequently arise in the lives of tax attorneys when their clients seek to take advantage of the capital gain rate of tax, or when their purpose is to minimize the impact of taxation upon the family by a bona fide distribution of property to wife and children. When this happens to me, I take, as I see it, a statute the policy of which I do not personally favor; I even accept the policy of statutes which I have opposed. This is true, for example, of the stock option provision,[41] the family partnership provision,[42] and the percentage depletion provision.[43] In advising in connection with provisions of this kind,[44] I try to be strictly on guard against over-interpreting relief provisions; but I see no reason why in my role as tax adviser I should set myself up against Congress as the arbiter of tax policy. My assignment is simply to be careful that the client does not overstep the line of policy drawn in the statute as Congress has passed it and as the Treasury and the courts have refined that line in their interpretive regulations and decisions.

Guided by these principles I feel that I am justified in recommending to a client that he transfer some of his property to a trust for the benefit of members of his family with the object of minimizing the family tax burden. The client may express a natural desire to retain as much control over the property as he can without sacrifice of the objective of shifting the tax on the income from the transferred

---

[40] See Commissioner v. Court Holding Co., 324 U.S. 331, 334 (1945). *Cf.* United States v. Cumberland Public Service Co., 338 U.S. 451, 454 (1950).
[41] INT. REV. CODE § 130A.
[42] INT. REV. CODE § 3797 (a) (2); § 191.
[43] INT. REV. CODE § 114 (b) (3), § 114 (b). See PAUL, TAXATION FOR PROSPERITY 304 (1947).
[44] See the interesting comment made by Harry Rudick, 8 TAX L. REV. 1, 31 (1952), in referring to a taxpayer who wanted to sell his business to his brother. The sale would have resulted in a loss and was a bona fide transaction. However, it would have been disallowed because the sale was to the taxpayer's brother. See INT. REV. CODE § 24. Mr. Rudick asked whether the tax practitioner was precluded from advising his client to sell the business to his brother's wife so that he could get the deduction. Mr. Rudick undoubtedly had in mind that the brother's wife had sufficient funds to make the purchase and that she was not a mere nominee of her husband.

property. As I see it, my task is to help the client without letting him venture any further than necessary into unsafe territory. In doing so I will feel no moral qualms. The problem does not involve ethical issues. My client's objective is legitimate. I often resolve some legal doubts in favor of the Government so that the client has a reasonable margin of safety. This too is my duty, but I would be derelict in the performance of my responsibility if I failed, because of moral scruples or because of disagreement with the policy of the statute, to guide the client as far as he can safely go in the direction of his desire.

Keeping to the concrete, I may sanction a plan under which a corporation with a history of recent losses acquires a profitable business so that the profits and losses of the two businesses will offset one another. When I am consulted in such a matter, my assignment is to appraise conservatively the effect of a section of the Internal Revenue Code[45] which deals with this subject, but which may not apply to the particular facts of the case presented to me. In advising with respect to the transaction my sole concern should be whether the desired result can be safely achieved. It does not concern me that as a matter of policy it might have been better if Congress had passed a more comprehensive statute eliminating this tax saving opportunity. I frequently have to make a calculation of the risks involved in going forward with a proposed business deal. If I am not prepared to devote my undivided loyalty to the objective of gaining for the client every advantage offered by the law as it is written, I should tell him at the outset to go to some other lawyer whose allegiance to his interest will be less fractional.

Of course there are limits as to how far a tax attorney may honorably go in advising clients as to the tax effect of future transactions. He should not yield to a temptation sometimes presented when his client consults him with respect to the tax effect of a desired course of action. The suggestion may be that the contracts and other papers expressing the transaction disguise its real character so that a revenue agent will miss its tax impact when it is later presented as a consummated transaction. I hope that it is almost superfluous for me to express a lack of sympathy with all techniques designed to camouflage contemplated transactions in such a way as to conceal those parts of them which may provide the basis for an assertion of tax liability. The Government is a silent partner in all business transactions and is entitled to a fair view of those transactions so that it may assert its claim of interest. One may go further by saying unequivocally that attempts at misrepresentation border on fraudulent conduct. At least it is conduct unbecoming a tax attorney.

---

[45] INT. REV. CODE § 129.

It is easy to give illustrations of prevailing techniques of misrepresentation. One favorite device is to put a transaction into two contracts, one of which is to be shown to the Government's representatives, and the other of which is to be kept secret. This happened once in my experience in connection with a sale of stock to a buyer for about $5 million. Since the buyer had an option on the stock of about $3 million, it was obvious that $2 million was being paid for an agreement not to compete. A payment for this covenant would have been ordinary income and not capital gain. The seller insisted that this transaction be put in two documents, one which would recite the sale of stock for $5 million, and the other of which would provide against competition without mentioning any consideration. I felt obliged to refuse to be an adviser in this transaction. As a result, my client, who had recultantly agreed because of anxiety to procure the stock, went to another attorney who was willing to let the client do what the seller wished. The client never came to me with his subsequent problems.[46]

The ingenuity of fertile-minded clients and fringe tax advisers has devised many dubious methods of tax avoidance. The president of a family corporation may ask his lawyer if it is all right to minimize corporate tax liability by making his wife vice-president of the corporaton and paying her a substantial salary, even though she performs no services whatever for the corporation. Some businessmen, in an attempt to become members of what Life calls "the expense account aristocracy," may seek arrangements under which they receive a substantial fixed allowance for miscellaneous entertainment and promotional expenses greatly exceeding the amount they expect to spend for those expenses. The argument is usually made that others in the same business engage in similar practices. It is hardly necessary to say that this is no argument at all, yet it is one which appeals to some clients.

Representing the Client

We come now to a more difficult problem area. In the law generally the antagonists in controversies are private citizens. Here a lawyer's duty to his client is paramount and exclusive. The client has put a special trust in his lawyer; the lawyer owes the client a sacred duty. "The office of attorney does not permit, much less does it demand of him for any client, violation of law or any manner of fraud or chicane. He must obey his own conscience and not that

---

[46] Jerome R. Hellerstein mentioned a similar problem in 8 Tax L. Rev. 1, 4 (1952), when he spoke of the case of a client who on January 10, 1952, informed his tax adviser that he would like to sell his boat to a friend. The sale would have involved a taxable gain. If it had occurred in 1951, the gain could have been offset by capital loss carryover from 1946. The client suggested that the document of sale be predated to December 28, 1951, so that the gain might be reported in the 1951 return and the 1946 capital loss carryover used as an offset.

of his client." But a lawyer's devotion to the interest of his client must be entire and unadulterated. The lawyer owes his client "warm zeal in the maintenance and defense of his rights and the exertion of his utmost learning and ability."[47] He is not representing himself, but is acting vicariously. He must treat his client better than he treats other people. This may, indeed, as Charles P. Curtis has suggested,[48] involve lower standards of conduct toward outsiders than toward his client. No attorney in general practice can be intellectually impartial or maintain complete equilibrium of judgment; he is a partisan advocate. His first rule of conduct must be to protect to the full extent of his ability the position he is engaged to maintain.

In tax law the adversary of the taxpayer is his own, and the tax adviser's own, Government.[49] The tax lawyer is licensed to practice before the bar of the Treasury which is his opponent. It is sometimes urged that a taxpayer's citizen relationship to his Government is not comparable to that of a plaintiff or a defendant to his adversary in an ordinary law suit and that the citizen owes his Government and his neighbors the duty of paying his share of taxes as required by law. It follows, according to this argument, that tax lawyers, as ministers of law, cannot countenance or be accessory to an escape by taxpayers of their duty to their Government.[50] The conclusion of the argument is that the tax practitioner has a "dual responsibility." He must serve two masters.[51] He must be loyal to his client, but he is also duty bound to the Government to see that his client does not "avoid his just share of the tax burden except by positive command of law. . . ."[52] Almost invariably the proponents of this argument quote Holmes' aphorism: "Men must turn square corners when they deal with the government."[53]

The argument mentioned also develops the point that the responsibility of the tax lawyer in connection with the preparation of returns and in the conduct of a case within the Treasury lodges in

---

[47]CANONS OF PROFESSIONAL ETHICS, CANON 15. It has been suggested that lawyers are dedicated to a code of ethics which transcends the code of law. Hellerstein, *Ethical Problems of Tax Practitioners*, 8 TAX L. REV. 1, 5 (1952). Mr. Hellerstein quotes JAMES, THE PROFESSIONAL IDEALS OF THE LAWYER 4 (1925), who in turn quotes Henry Wade Rogers as saying: "A lawyer is unworthy of membership in the profession who would regulate his conduct solely according to what the law permits rather than what morality and honor require." But what about the lawyer's duty to secure for his client what the law permits? Should not his conduct be regulated by that requirement?

[48]Curtis, *The Ethics of Advocacy*, 4 STAN. L. REV. 1, 5 (1951).

[49]8 TAX L. REV. 1, 13 (1952); see also, Paul, *The Responsibilities of the Tax Adviser*, PROCEEDINGS OF THE TAX INSTITUTE, UNIVERSITY OF SOUTHERN CALIFORNIA SCHOOL OF LAW 1 (1950); 63 HARV. L. REV. 377 (1950), reprinted in part in SURREY & WARREN, FEDERAL INCOME TAXATION CASES AND MATERIALS 72 (1953).

[50]See discussion of Hellerstein, 8 TAX L. REV. 1, 4 (1952).

[51]See discussion of Tarleau, 8 TAX L. REV. 1, 10 (1952).

[52]Stone v. White, 301 U.S. 532, 537 (1937). See also, Helvering v. City Bank Farmers Trust Co., 296 U.S. 85 (1935); Burnet v. Wells, 289 U.S. 670 (1933).

[53]Rock Island, A. & L.R.R. v. United States, 254 U.S. 141, 143 (1920); see also, Cahn's discussion of the applicability of this maxim in 8 TAX L. REV. 1 (1952).

certain additional circumstances which are peculiar to tax controversies.[54] To a considerable extent Government representatives depend upon facts presented to them by the taxpayer. While the Government has every power to inspect taxpayers' records and examine the taxpayer and others who have knowledge of transactions needing scrutiny, this power is in many respects more theoretical than real. In the normal case even the revenue agent who makes an examination of the taxpayer's records cannot examine every item in those records; if he did, he would never finish his job. He must to some extent depend upon the taxpayer or the taxpayer's lawyer or accountant to make the relevant data or facts available. This control over the facts of a controversy by the taxpayer sometimes makes deception an easy matter for the tax attorney who is willing to take advantage of the Government.

Moreover, the lawyer of accepted reputation soon comes to find, and should be particularly conscious of the fact, that Government representatives sometimes rely to a marked degree upon his integrity. On occasion they accept without minute examination or meticulous scrutiny statements of facts presented to them by an attorney they trust. They may assume that statements presented comprise all the facts. In doing so they are to some degree depending upon the tax adviser's sense of candor and fairness. This tendency on the part of some Government representatives puts a load of special responsibility upon the tax adviser. Some clients are willing, sometimes innocently and sometimes deliberately, to trade upon their lawyer's good reputation. Lawyers whose word is their bond have a special obligation to be diligent in their analysis of the facts involved in tax controversies and scrupulously careful that their factual presentations to Government representatives fairly reflect the truth.

I have also heard the additional argument that since the success of the income, estate and gift taxes depends in such large degree upon the co-operation of taxpayers, an understanding by them of the revenue necessities of the country is inevitably required. Certainly it is true that the American federal tax system cannot rely solely upon enforcement; the maintenance of a co-operative public attitude is of the utmost importance to the success of that system. Between 80 million and 90 million returns pour annually into the Bureau of Internal Revenue. The Bureau employs only about 20,000 revenue agents, deputy collectors, and auditors.[55] These Bureau representatives manage to examine approximately 4 million returns each year, or less than one of every 20 filed. In that process each Bureau representative examines an average of 200 returns a year. Even a super-

---

[54] See Tarleau, 8 TAX L. REV. 1, 10 (1952).
[55] Paul, *Directions in Which Tax Policy and Law Have Been Moving*, 30 TAXES 949, 955 (1952).

ficial examination ordinarily involves checking many details reported on the return, conferences with the taxpayer, an examination of his personal records or books of account, and the preparation of a report on the examination made.

The more thorough examinations required in more complicated cases may entail such further activities as checking the taxpayer's business inventory, verifying his travel and entertainment expenses, interrogating business associates and parties to transactions with the taxpayer, and many other time-consuming activities. To be even reasonably sure that the taxpayer has not failed to report taxable income, or that he has not overstated his allowable deductions, the examining agent must check bank records, stockbroker records, and many other sources of information. No revenue agent can, or does, conduct 200 thorough examinations per year. Only a few taxpayers ever undergo a complete examination; as to the rest, there can be little more than a token, or spot-check, enforcement.

If tax advisers have special responsibilities of the sort described, the Treasury Department has been far from prodigal about their articulation. The Act of July 7, 1884, gives to the Secretary of the Treasury the right to prescribe rules and regulations governing the recognition of attorneys and agents representing claimants before his Department.[56] He may require that attorneys practicing before his Department show that they are of "good character and in good repute," and that they are "possessed of the necessary qualifications" to enable them to render valuable service and are otherwise "competent to advise and assist" claimants in the preparation of their cases. Under Circular 230[57] every enrolled person must conduct his practice "in an ethical and professional manner," and it is his duty "to observe the canons of ethics as adopted by the American Bar Association." Agents other than attorneys must observe the ethical standards of the accounting profession. When they accept a Treasury card evidencing their right to practice before the Bureau of Internal Revenue, enrolled attorneys also agree to obey a number of commands set forth in Circular 230, among which are the following:

> (c) Knowledge of client's omission.—Each enrolled attorney or agent who knows that a client has not complied with the law or has made an error in, or an omission from, any return, document, affidavit or other paper, which the law requires such client to execute, shall advise his client promptly of the fact of such non-compliance, error, or omission.
>
> (o) Preparation of financial statements.—Each enrolled person shall exercise due diligence in preparing financial statements for clients and in certifying to the correctness of the same.

---

[56] 23 STAT. 258 (1884). The administrative provisions of this statute have been changed by Reorganization Plan No. 26 of 1950, 64 STAT. 1280 (1950).
[57] Revised to December 7, 1951.

(t) *Production of records.*—No enrolled person shall neglect or refuse to produce records or evidence in any matter before the Treasury Department upon proper and lawful demand by a duly authorized agent of the Department, unless the attorney or agent has reasonable grounds to believe and does believe that the said demand is of doubtful legality; or shall otherwise interfere, or attempt to interfere, with any proper and lawful efforts of such Department or agent to procure such information.

(w) *Preparation of documents by enrollees.*—Each enrolled person shall exercise due diligence in preparing or assisting in the preparation of, approving, and filing returns, documents, affidavits, and other papers relating to Treasury Department matters, and in otherwise representing clients before the Treasury Department; and no enrolled person shall unreasonably delay the prompt disposition of matters before the Treasury Department by neglecting to answer correspondence, by unreasonably delaying the filing of closing agreements, by filing frivolous claims for refunds, or otherwise.

Do the above quoted requirements, in combination with the assumptions implicit in the structure of the American revenue system and the established procedures for the disposition of tax disputes short of resort to the courts, provide a standard of conduct different from that which binds the general practitioner representing clients in private litigations? Do they place the tax adviser in a position of "dual responsibility," which dilutes the supreme duty he owes to his client? Do the stated rules and assumptions demand more meticulous conduct than is required of attorneys when they try cases in the Tax Court or other courts having jurisdiction of tax cases? Many, of whom I am one,[58] have asserted that they do. Yet the answer to these questions is far from clear, and strict analysis requires admissions of doubt. This is not to deprecate the need of a high standard of ethics in the practice of tax law. The question is whether the standards applicable to the conduct of attorneys representing clients before the Bureau of Internal Revenue vary from those which are applicable to attorneys engaged in general practice, and place upon the former a responsibility on certain occasions to put the interest of the Treasury in a position paramount to the interest of their clients.

Those who urge a double standard of ethics have cited examples in their discussion of the ethics of tax practice. It is always healthy to test general propositions by getting down to concrete cases. In the *Tax Law Review* Symposium Mr. Hellerstein mentioned the case of Mr. Brown, an officer of a small closely held corporation, who wanted

---

[58]See Paul, *The Responsibilities of the Tax Adviser,* PROCEEDINGS OF THE TAX INSTITUTE, UNIVERSITY OF SOUTHERN CALIFORNIA SCHOOL OF LAW 1 (1950); 63 HARV. L. REV. 377 (1950), reprinted in part in SURREY & WARREN, FEDERAL INCOME TAXATION CASES AND MATERIALS 72 (1953).

to imitate the conduct of his neighbor, Jones, "a fine upstanding citizen." Jones, who made generous contributions to deductible charities, told Brown that he had had his personal automobile, which he never used in the business, purchased, owned, serviced and insured by his corporation.[59]

In the same symposium Thomas N. Tarleau presented two further questions.[60] One involved depreciation on property inherited by the taxpayer which, he told his adviser, had been converted to a business use shortly after its inheritance ten years before the taxable year. The property had been rented or held out for rent for a considerable period, and it was possible to show a substantial value on the date of conversion. The Treasury representative before whom the case was being argued on protest seemed to be convinced, and asked for some supporting information. In the course of assembling this information the lawyer learned for the first time that while the real estate was still held by the taxpayer, the building actually had been torn down prior to the taxable year. The question was whether the taxpayer's lawyer was required to suggest to the agent that the depreciation should be disallowed.

In another question presented by Mr. Tarleau, a taxpayer consulted his lawyer about the deductibility of certain European traveling expenses incurred on a trip made for the purpose of purchasing merchandise to be resold in the taxpayer's business. The items of expense for steamship and railroad fares, and the hotel charges and like items, appeared to be reasonable in amount. However, the lawyer's investigation uncovered the fact that the taxpayer's wife, who had no connection whatsoever with the business, had accompanied the taxpayer on the trip. The charges covered her transportation and hotel expenses. The question submitted was whether the lawyer was required to disclose to the Treasury agent that part of the traveling expenses was for the taxpayer's wife.

I doubt if any reputable tax practitioner would have any trouble with these cases. He would promptly tell Mr. Brown that the conduct of his neighbor, Jones, was highly questionable. He would unhesitantly advise the Bureau that the building had been torn down in a year previous to the taxable year and admit that his client was entitled to no depreciation whatever. Under the circumstances stated he would refuse to sanction the deduction of the wife's expenses on the European trip.

But, unfortunately, these cases do not help very much in the disposition of the question under discussion. I would guess that most reputable tax attorneys would not undertake to defend the

---
[59] 8 Tax L. Rev. 1, 7 (1952).
[60] Id. at 11.

proposed conduct of these taxpayers before the Tax Court or any other court. I would also be doubtful whether most attorneys in general practice would be willing to represent clients whose position on the facts was so indefensible as it was in these cases. The cases therefore furnish no basis for any firm rule that a tax adviser in appearing before the Bureau assumes some load of responsibility to the Government which is not present when he represents a client in private litigation.

We may perhaps find the answer to our question in some more difficult examples. Mr. Hellerstein submitted[61] a question involving the settlor of a trust, the income of which his tax lawyer was fearful might be taxable to him under the Clifford doctrine[62] and regulations.[63] However, the issue was in doubt. He also submitted a question involving interest payments on notes held pro rata by the stockholders of a corporation which might be attacked under the so-called "thin incorporation" doctrine.[64] In these two cases it was clear that the Bureau would decide the issue adversely to the client if the facts were brought to the Bureau's attention, though it was not clear what the result would be if the question went to litigation. Should the tax practitioner insist upon a full disclosure, advising the client to set forth in his return all the facts relating to the Clifford question? Should he advise the corporation to call attention in its return to the circumstances of "thin incorporation," so that the issue would not be overlooked by the Bureau? Or should the tax adviser resolve these questions in the taxpayer's favor and advise him not flag them in the return?

These questions are not easily answered. Mr. Hellerstein concluded that most tax practitioners would not advise disclosure, but would go along hoping "with some anxiety, but with no feeling of guilt, that the revenue agent would miss the item." "It is the ethic of the profession," Mr. Hellerstein regretfully concluded, that "the tax practitioner does not regard it as his duty to recommend full and fair disclosure of the facts as to items questionable in law."[65]

This may be true as to the particular illustrations given. The Clifford Doctrine, is a thicket of obscurity, and there is no yardstick for the measurement of the "thin incorporation" doctrine. There are, however, cases in which there is a clear duty of disclosure which most tax attorneys would respect. For instance, in spite of the *Textile*

---

[61]*Id.* at 8.
[62]See Helvering v. Clifford, 309 U.S. 331 (1940); see also, Eisenstein, *The Clifford Regulations and the Heavenly City of Legislative Intention*, 2 TAX L. REV. 327 (1947).
[63]U.S. Treas. Reg. 111, § 29.22 (a) -21; see Commissioner v. Clark, 53-1 U.S.T.C., ¶9217 (7th Cir. 1953).
[64]Schlesinger, *"Thin" Incorporations: Income Tax Advantages and Pitfalls*, 61 HARV. L. REV. 50 (1947).
[65]8 TAX L. REV. 1, 8 (1952).

* *Mills* decision[66] and the applicable regulation, there remains some chance that legitimate lobbying expenses are deductible. Yet I think most tax attorneys would refuse to sanction the deduction of lobbying expenses in a return without a complete segregation of the deduction so that it would automatically come to the attention of the revenue agent. At the other end of the spectrum, in some areas of the tax law the Bureau of Internal Revenue has adopted a policy of persistent litigation of questions which have been repeatedly decided favorably to taxpayers by the Tax Court and by the Courts of Appeal in several circuits.[67] Here the average tax attorney would, I think, advise a client that he need not flag an item in his return because his position was supported by a number of authoritative and carefully reasoned court opinions. Between these two poles many borderline problems constantly arise to plague tax advisers.

Similar problems confront the tax adviser in the presentation of the taxpayer's position within the Bureau of Internal Revenue on protest or before the Appellate Staff. Of course, a tax lawyer should respond truthfully to questions asked by Government representatives about the facts of the case he is presenting; "in his intercourse with those in authority . . . touching the performance of their functions, he is bound to exhibit truth, frankness, and integrity."[68] As Circular 230 indicates, he "must exercise due diligence in preparing financial statements for clients and in certifying to the correctness of the same." He should not "neglect or refuse to produce records or affidavits in any matter before the Treasury Department upon proper and lawful demand," unless he has reasonable grounds to believe, and does believe, that the demand is of doubtful legality. He should not interfere with any proper and lawful efforts of the Bureau to procure information Government representatives believe to be relevant to the Government's side of the case. He must exercise due diligence "in preparing or assisting in the preparation of, approving, and filing returns, documents, affidavits, and other papers relating to Treasury Department matters."

We have gone so far as to require a tax adviser to inform Government representatives as to points of fact which completely dispose of the taxpayer's case. We have also suggested the obligation upon tax attorneys to supply truthful answers to all questions asked by the

---

[66]314 U.S. 326 (1941); see the reference in Lilly v. Commissioner, 343 U.S. 90, 95 (1952), to the Supreme Court's acceptance in the *Textile Mills* decision of a Treasury Regulation which disallowed the deduction of "*certain* expenditures for lobbying purposes." (Italics supplied.)

[67]See, *e.g.*, Jones v. Herber, 198 F.2d 544 (10th Cir. 1952); Commissioner v. Guminski, 198 F.2d 265 (5th Cir. 1952); Hofferbert v. Anderson Automobile, 197 F.2d 504 (4th Cir. 1952); Commissioner v. Weisman, 197 F.2d 221 (1st Cir. 1952); Lela Sullenger, 11 T. C. 1076 (1948). The Bureau finally acquiesced in I.T. 4104, 23 Cum. Bull. 4 (1952).

[68]Trist v. Child, 88 U.S. 441, 450 (1874).

Government representatives. I certainly agree generally with Mr. Tarleau that tax advisers should "engage in open-handed dealing," and "avoid anything suggesting concealment or trickery."[69] But are they obliged "to reveal every fundamental fact which is pertinent to the issue under consideration?" What if the Government representatives fail to make a specific request for certain information in the possession of the tax attorney which is harmful to, but not dispositive of, a taxpayer's case? To what extent is the tax attorney obliged to volunteer information at such a time? Must he turn over every item of information in his possession irrespective of the effect of doing so upon his client's case? If the answer to this question should be in the affirmative, I am sure that we have found a substantial difference between the position of attorneys representing clients in private litigation and attorneys representing taxpayers before the Bureau of Internal Revenue.

I can give no definitive answer to the questions I have just asked. There are times when a failure to speak may be a misrepresentation. But I will venture the statement that most tax attorneys would rarely volunteer information under the circumstances stated. And I would be the last to condemn them for not doing so.[70] I would not know how to answer their argument that except where the rules of practice dictate otherwise tax proceedings in the Treasury are predominantly adversary proceedings calling for no higher ethical standards than those imposed upon attorneys engaged in general practice.[71] At times one encounters a revenue agent or a conferee who is genuinely interested in ascertaining the taxpayer's correct tax liability wherever the chips may fall. But this is the exception rather than the rule. Treasury representatives are subject to many pressures, and as a rule their conduct closely resembles the conduct of attorneys in private litigation. They put the most favorable face upon the facts supporting the Treasury side of the controversy, as taxpayers do upon

---

[69] 8 TAX L. REV. 1, 12 (1952).

[70] Samuel Williston would not condemn him. "The lawyer must decide when he takes a case whether it is a suitable one for him to undertake and after this decision is made, he is not justified in turning against his client by exposing injurious evidence entrusted to him.... [D]oing something intrinsically regrettable, because the only alternative involves worse consequences, is a necessity in every profession." Williston's autobiography tells of one of his early cases which illustrates the difficulties involved in this type of situation. Williston's client was sued in a financial matter. Williston at once went through his letter file painstakingly, sorting and collating it. As the trial approached, the plaintiff's lawyers did not demand to see the correspondence or ask for its production. Williston states that he did not feel bound to disclose the correspondence. At the close of the trial in the course of the remarks the Chief Justice stated as a reason for his decision a supposed fact which Williston knew to be unfounded. He had in front of him a letter showing the Judge's error. Williston says: "Though I have no doubt of the propriety of my behavior in keeping silent, I was somewhat uncomfortable at the time." WILLISTON, LIFE AND LAW 271 (1940).

[71] Tarleau suggests that the obligation "to avoid concealment or subterfuge does not go so far as to require counsel to furnish the Government with ammunition to defeat a taxpayer's valid claims." 8 TAX L. REV. 1, 12 (1952).

the facts supporting their side; and they argue, sometimes with considerable vehemence, that the precedents require a conclusion in favor of the Government. Certainly they are not, and do not pretend to be, acting as impartial referees.[72] I do not say that they should. They are servants of a Government which needs revenue badly, and they would be more than human if they were not at least a little partisan on behalf of that Government. All these considerations lead to doubt whether the tax attorney has a responsibility to the Treasury over and above the responsibilities enumerated in Department Circular 230 and those described in the *Canons of Ethics* which are incorporated by reference in that Circular.

Whatever special rules may apply to the conduct of a case before the Treasury, it seems clear enough that they cease to apply when a civil tax case reaches the litigation stage, either in the Tax Court,[73] the federal district court, or the Court of Claims. Like other "legal battles fought in a court room," these proceedings are "fights."[74] The parties, one of which is the Government, are in a law suit which does not differ in any essential respect from any other law suit. A judge is in charge of the trial, and counsel for both sides are functioning as advocates. The Government has full power to investigate the facts underlying its case. It may call witnesses to testify to those facts and it may cross-examine the taxpayer's witnesses. It has the advantage involved in a presumption of correctness for the deficiency letter and all findings made by the Bureau of Internal Revenue. The taxpayer generally has the burden of proof.[75] No special Treasury rules impose any inhibitions upon the conduct of his attorney. I do not see that the taxpayer's attorney has any obligation affirmatively to present facts hostile to his client's case. He may do so to minimize the impact of the adverse facts upon the judgment of the court if they should be presented by the other side. But here, again, the problem

---

[72]Here I have stated what I believe to be a fact of tax life noted by HORSKY, THE WASHINGTON LAWYER 138 (1952). Judge Learned Hand's statement quoted by Horsky from Fishgold v. Sullivan Drydock & Repair Corporation, 154 F.2d 785, 789 (2d Cir. 1946), aff'd, 328 U.S. 275 (1946), may not wholly support the conclusion stated since Judge Hand seems to refer to public officers "charged with the enforcement of a law," rather than the public officers "who must decide a dispute." Certainly Judge Hand's statement would apply, however, to attorneys appearing for the Government in the courts.

[73]The Tax Court Rules simply require that applicants for admission to practice be "of good moral character and repute, and possessed of the requisite qualifications to represent others in the preparation and trial of cases," and that practitioners "shall carry on their practice in accordance with the letter and spirit of the canons of professional ethics as adopted by the American Bar Association." The court may deny admission to, suspend, or disbar any person "who in its judgment does not possess the requisite qualifications to represent others, or who is lacking in character, integrity, or proper professional conduct."

[74]FRANK, COURTS ON TRIAL 26 (1949).

[75]Old Mission Portland Cement Co. v. Helvering, 293 U.S. 289, 294 (1934); Botany Worsted Mills v. United States, 278 U.S. 282, 289 (1929); United States v. Anderson, 269 U.S. 422, 443 (1926); Welch v. Helvering, 290 U.S. 111, 115 (1933). See also, Tax Court Rule 32.

is one of judgment, not of ethics, and the attorney for the taxpayer certainly has no obligation to present the other side's case. He may be obliged to submit to judgment against his client if he knows some critical fact which completely disposes of the case, but he is certainly not required to submit evidence which merely points in the direction of judgment for the Government.

There is general agreement among tax attorneys, I think, that no special rules apply to the conduct of criminal fraud cases. These cases are primarily criminal cases involving taxes and not tax cases involving criminal law.[76] The question is whether the taxpayer is to be charged with a crime. His liberty, as well as his property, is in peril. On the basis of independent investigation by its agents the Government is asking the question whether the taxpayer is guilty of wilful failure to report his correct tax liability. The facts leading to investigation are not usually facts disclosed in the taxpayer's return; indeed, they are usually facts not there disclosed. The Government rarely reveals the evidence upon which it proposes to base its charge; in fact, some Government attorneys seem at times zealous to preserve a degree of secrecy which will enable the Government to surprise the defendant at the trial of the case. Of course the Government has the burden of proving the crime beyond a reasonable doubt. But in assembling its proof the Government does not to any marked degree rely on representations made by the taxpayer's attorney; on the contrary, it specifically assumes the responsibility of gathering its own information. Under these circumstances the tax attorney owes the Government no duty beyond the obligation not to present what he knows to be untrue. His duty to his client is undivided and he need not disclose any information not to his client's advantage. This type of case may even present a duty to advise the client not to co-operate with the Government, but to place upon the Government the whole burden of investigation. Under the Fifth Amendment to the Constitution a fraudulent taxpayer cannot be compelled to be a "witness against himself."

Another question sometimes arising in the doubting minds of tax attorneys is whether they are free at all stages of a tax controversy to make legal arguments in which they do not sincerely believe. Should they discard arguments that do not persuade them and restrict their advocacy to the arguments they personally believe to be sound? Some will say that the question is academic because of the propensity of lawyers to achieve convictions on the side of any cause in which they are engaged. Brandeis once said that "the lawyer is not often harassed by this problem partly because he is apt to believe at the time in most of the cases he actually tries, and partly because he either abandons or

---

[76]Schachner, *Ethical Problems of Tax Practitioners*, 8 TAX L. REV. 1, 15 (1952).

settles a large number of cases he does not believe in."[77] But this capacity for "self-sown sincerity"[78] is not unlimited, and the question I raise needs an answer.

In its most acute form this question arises in criminal cases in which the lawyer is representing a client he knows to be guilty.[79] But the same essential question may confront the tax lawyer representing a client who in the belief of the lawyer owes the tax asserted by the Government. The same question arises in a reduced degree when several arguments present themselves to the mind of the tax lawyer, some of which he believes to be good arguments and some of which are unconvincing to him. Should he cast aside the arguments which do not persuade him, and urge upon the Treasury and the courts only those in which he does believe?

The classical solution of this problem was suggested a long time ago by Dr. Johnson. Boswell asked Johnson what he thought of "supporting a cause which you know to be bad." Johnson answered:

> Sir, you do not know it to be good or bad till the Judge determines it. I have said that you are to state facts fairly; so that your thinking, or what you call knowing, a cause to be bad, must be from reasoning, must be from your supposing your arguments to be weak and inconclusive. But, Sir, that is not enough. An argument which does not convince yourself, may convince the Judge to whom you urge it: and if it does convince him, why, then, Sir, you are wrong, and he is right.[80]

My answer would be to much the same effect. A tax lawyer's judgment may dictate that it would better serve his client not to present an argument which will do worse than fall flat by implying that he has no better argument. But ethics do not require him to discard any arguments. As I have indicated, once he has taken a case, the tax lawyer is obliged to present arguments even though they may contribute to tax avoidance or conflict with his own notions of what the law should be. Equally, he had better not cast away an argument just because it is not convincing to him. That may be the very argument which would persuade the Government representative or a judge to decide the case in his favor. It is no objection to an argument that the lawyer has to put his tongue in his cheek when he presents it; "a lawyer is required to be disingenuous."[81] Advocacy requires a certain capacity for insincerity. A tax lawyer need not believe in every argument he presents. In the first place, he may not know whether or not it is valid, or what he thinks he knows may be

---

[77] Brandeis, *The Opportunity in the Law*, 39 AM. L. REV. 561 (1905); LLEWELLYN, THE BRAMBLE BUSH 154 (1930).
[78] Curtis, *The Ethics of Advocacy*, 4 STAN. L. REV. 1, 14 (1951).
[79] *Ibid.*
[80] 2 BOSWELL, THE LIFE OF JOHNSON, 47-48 (Hill ed. 1887).
[81] Curtis, *The Ethics of Advocay*, 4 STAN. L. REV. 1, 9 (1951).

wrong; Omar Khayyám anticipated tax law when he observed: "a hair perhaps divides the False and True." In the second place, an advocate is engaged to dissemble, to pretend; the legal profession and our prevailing system of advocacy make a virtue of some capacities which may on other occasions be vices. The tax lawyer would be breaching his duty to his client if he indulged a sensitivity of conscience which has a higher place in other contexts than it has in a system of law which acts "under the impression that truth is best discovered by powerful statements on both sides of the question."[82]

Representing Broader Interests

As I come to the end of this inconclusive discussion of the ethics of tax advocacy, I find myself wanting to be sure that the reader does not misunderstand my attitude upon one point. I have argued that a tax lawyer should be careful not to let his private notions of fiscal policy intrude into work for a client on a tax case except as his knowledge of policy considerations may help him the more intelligently to represent the client. But I do not want anyone to infer from this discussion that I object to participation by tax advisers in efforts looking to the improvement of tax law. I feel strongly to the contrary. To me it is one of the tragedies of the time that tax advisers do not use more generally for their Government, as well as for their clients, the special knowledge their education and experience have bestowed upon them. I think that they should use this knowledge actively, affirmatively ,and even aggressively. The country most sorely needs the contribution they are so well qualified to make to the serious problems the Government faces at home because of its obligation to take a leading part in international affairs.

The tax adviser is not disqualified from activity on this front because he represents taxpayers. The shoe is on the other foot. The representation of taxpayers gives to tax advisers the experience that theory always needs if it is to ripen into maturity. It teaches them what will work in practice, as distinguished from what looks good on paper. It enriches the whole outlook of tax advisers, and makes their advice to their Government more realistic and dependable. It makes them all the more qualified to express a constructive opinion about what is wrong with tax law and what should be done to improve the tax system. On the other hand, it is necessary to be on guard against a tendency to assume that what is best for clients is best for the United States. Much representation of clients sometimes makes lawyers captives of their clients' opinions, and an analysis of many tax betterment proposals from tax lawyers quickly reveals that the

---

[82]*Ex parte* Lloyd, Nov. 5, 1822, Montague's Reports 70, quoted in MacMillan, Law and Other Things 182 (1937). See also, Lecky, The Map of Life, Conduct and Character 119 (1889), quoted in Curtis, *The Ethics of Advocacy*, 4 Stan. L. Rev. 1, 12 (1951).

lawyers are promoting the special interests of their clients. A tax lawyer needs to preserve an independence of outlook, unclouded by prejudices acquired from his clients. His clients do not always know what is good for them, and there is a sense in which what is good for the United States is good for clients.

No doubt some tax lawyers feel constrained to abstain from activities on behalf of a better tax system because they think that their clients may object.[83] Clients have no right to object if the tax adviser handles their affairs competently and faithfully and independently of his private views as to tax policy. They buy his expert services, not his private opinions or his silence on issues that gravely affect the public interest.

I suspect that the thinking of some tax advisers exaggerates the objections clients have to activities on behalf of improvement in the tax system. It is true, as Adams once observed,[84] that taxation is "a group contest in which powerful interests vigorously endeavor to rid themselves of present or proposed tax burdens," and that "class politics" is of its essence. But more and more in recent years there has developed in businessmen, and that wealthier segment of the population which furnishes tax clients, a realization of the need of more expert attention to the tax problems than can come from persons within the Government. It is one encouraging sign of the times that taxes have captured the interest of a wide public. Sometimes that interest expresses itself in pressure politics and propaganda,[85] and attempts to advance the cause of the few at the expense of the many. But objectivity is also spreading its more wholesome influence. At least, it is no longer a mark of condemnation of a tax adviser that he serves his country on the tax front.

---

[83] See Gerhart, *The Compleat Counsellor: The Ideal of the Fully Accomplished Lawyer*, 35 A.B.A.J. 975, 978 (1949).

[84] Adams, *Ideals and Idealism in Taxation*, 18 AM. ECON. REV. 1 (1928). *Cf.* Griswold, *The Blessings of Taxation: Recent Trends in the Law of Federal Taxation*, 36 A.B.A.J. 999, 1002, 1057 (1950).

[85] BLOUGH, THE FEDERAL TAXING PROCESS 31, 44-5, 447-448 (1952).

5. Responsibilities of the Lawyer in Tax Practice
Norris Darrell

MR. PHILIP C. JESSUP, JR. (President, Harvard Student Bar Association): On behalf of the Harvard Student Bar Association, I would like to welcome you to the first of a series of five talks on "Lawyers' Problems of Conscience."

I would also like to thank Mr. Darrell for taking time off from a very busy schedule to talk to us on the "Responsibilities of the Lawyer in Tax Practice", after which he has consented to answer any questions there might be from the floor.

Dean Griswold has consented to talk to us a few minutes on the general subject of our series, as well as to introduce our distinguished speaker.

DEAN ERWIN N. GRISWOLD: One of the problems with which law schools have struggled for a long time is instruction in the area of a lawyer's responsibility in practice. I didn't say anything about legal ethics, although that is certainly an important part of the area.

Practitioners have long complained about the law schools because they haven't done more work in that area. The law schools, while recognizing the problem, have said, "It is no answer to give a course in legal ethics, as such a course tends to become instruction in how far you can go without getting caught." So the law schools have fallen back—I don't think in default, but as the best they have been able to do in general—on the defense which is typified by the statement I so often hear from older alumni, that there never was a better course in legal ethics than any course with Dean Ames. And yet that doesn't do the job. Dean Ames isn't here any more anyhow, so we can't quite rely on that.

It was in that setting that the Harvard Student Bar Association, on its own initiative, came up with the idea for this series. I like that very much because most of the good things that are done around here are done on student initiative. I think it is one of the great things about this school, that it does encourage and develop and stimulate opportunities for not merely setting up initiative, but carrying it into effect. I can only say that when the idea was proposed—and I think the officers of the Association will agree—it was enthusiastically supported by the administration of the school, and particularly by Vice Dean Hall, who has worked very closely with the committee in the development of this program. The program seems to me to be an excellent one, and one which should do a great deal towards making available to students in the school some of the facts and considerations which bear upon the extraordinarily difficult problems that can be encountered in this area.

We have an excellent program altogether, and we are very fortunate indeed in our first speaker whose topic is "Responsibilities of the Lawyer in Tax Practice."

Mr. Darrell is another one of those proofs of the statement which can be made that most of the big New York lawyers didn't come from New York, for Mr. Darrell is a country boy. Some 25 years in the big city may have done something to modify the sturdy stock, but he came from Minnesota and was a graduate of the Minnesota University Law School. He then went to Washington for two years as Law Clerk for Mr. Justice Butler, and I dare say that his experience during those two years may well have contributed materially to the subject on which he is going to talk to you this afternoon, for Mr. Justice Butler, conservative as he may have been and tied to his past as we all are, was nevertheless a very sterling character who knew very clearly the difference between right and wrong and didn't hesitate to put that knowledge into practice. I suspect that a young man working for two years with Mr. Justice Butler may well have learned a great deal about what lawyers ought to do.

After that, Mr. Darrell went to New York. He had a broad and varied experience in different types of work, as I think is perhaps wise. He didn't become a tax lawyer until he had attained years of discretion. In the last fifteen years, he has become one of the outstanding tax lawyers of the country.

I will say only one more thing about him before giving him a chance to talk, for he is the one you want to hear, not I. He is one of the relatively few tax lawyers in my experience who, though eminently successful, have retained completely their objective viewpoint. He is able to produce results for clients; the evidence is plain as to that. But he has not sold his soul. He has not sold his own independence. I think we should all remember the high traditions of our profession, under which though we do sell our aid and advice, we remain individual counsellors. A lawyer who goes too far in identifying his own views with those of his client may do disservice both to the client and to himself. That Mr. Darrell has not done, and that capacity of his seems to me to make him especially well qualified to talk to you this afternoon on the subject of the day. Mr. Darrell.

Mr. Norris Darrell: Dean Griswold, Mr. Jessup and members and friends of the Harvard Student Bar Association. I have always had the highest regard for the ability and integrity of Dean Griswold, and I would never have thought him capable of enlarging upon the truth, but as I listened to his introduction I began to wonder. However, I thank him for it and I like the human generosity that it suggests.

I would like, also, to commend the Student Bar Association for undertaking this series of talks. As Dean Griswold has said, too little attention is paid to the subject of a lawyer's responsibilities, both in the law school and indeed outside of the law school. I suppose it has been generally assumed that a gentleman naturally understands the moral code and knows instinctively how to apply it. But this, I think, overlooks the possibility that education is needed in order to see and to understand the moral, ethical and social implications of any given act or conduct, and I am sure—as this gathering indicates—that the student body will give the series the support it deserves.

It seemed rather significant to me that the tax lawyer's problems should have been selected as the opening subject of these talks. This couldn't have happened 25 years ago, and I suppose it reflects the growing importance of that field. As a matter of fact, I have never liked the phrase "tax lawyer". Somehow it suggests a qualification upon the term "lawyer". After all, a tax lawyer is a lawyer first, with all that that implies. He is not simply a tax man who happens to hold a legal degree.

Now I don't intend to discuss with you the obvious. I am not going to say I am against sin. Fraud, crime and influence peddling, of which one hears so much today, are outside my topic. The current investigation going on today in Washington is an important, outstanding and much needed development. The relaxing moral standards now being disclosed are not only deplorable; they are dangerous. Our citizens are now widely asked to pay undreamed of taxes. An effective income tax system depends upon honest self-assessment. If the public believes that influence peddling and favoritism abound in government, large segments, in anger, are likely to refuse to cooperate. That is the sort of thing we have heard about in some countries abroad.

But one of the students here—having in mind no doubt these daily reports of tax scandals and Treasury purges—said to me that you would like to hear, especially, just how responsible you can expect your brothers at the bar actually to be, in spite of their fine words. Does this sort of conduct really permeate deeply into the Treasury administration and the tax bar? As you read the papers, please remember this: only the bad, rarely the good, constitutes news. Though all too many examining agents and revenue officials at the very bottom and very top may need cleaning out, the vast bulk of revenue officials with whom tax lawyers deal are career men. They are proud of their jobs and they deeply resent attempts at political influence or pressure, to say nothing of suggestions of bribery. Members of the tax bar know this and for this reason, as well as for the sake of their own reputations, few active tax practitioners of any standing would dare indulge in these things, even if they had no moral compunction about it. I suppose my experience in this regard is typical. I have no firsthand experience in regard to attempted bribery. Both bribe-soliciting agents and bribe-offering taxpayers know better than to disclose their vice to reputable counsel. Fortunately, most clients do not traffic in such stuff. As to influence peddling, well, perhaps I have run into that. In my experience, however, this is a field—perhaps I should say field day during recent years—for politicians and not tax lawyers. If the client insists on pursuing the influence route—which incidentally is generally unsuccessful—reputable counsel usually withdraw for their own protection. Few competent tax lawyers fail to realize the dangers of these associations and the futility of indulging in these things. Indeed, if my knowledge and experience are any guide, reputable members of the tax bar are rarely tempted,—and these are not merely fine words.

Now let us turn to some of the problems of an ethical nature which the lawyer faces in his everyday tax practice. At the outset let me say that in his relations with both clients and government, as elsewhere in life, common honesty is Cardinal Rule No. 1. A lawyer is many times tempted to tell half truths or hide important information pertaining to issues in dispute. While he owes no duty to do the government's job for it, he does owe a duty to come clean on a particular issue when he purports to do so.

First a word about fraud cases. Defrauders, repentant or otherwise, are entitled to counsel and the lawyer in tax practice may properly represent them in their legitimate defense or in making full disclosure in an effort to arrive at the best possible settlement. Some lawyers dislike this type of practice, but that is a matter of personal taste. Yet even a lawyer normally rejecting this sort of practice may get into the periphery of it. Suppose a client comes to you in confidence and says his firm has just discovered that the retired treasurer—a nice old gentleman—had falsified the records to save the firm taxes. They had just found out about it, and it has been stopped, and what should they do? You will advise, of course, that they should make full disclosure and pay up what is due. Suppose, after consideration, they come back and say they've decided not to make full disclosure because they think the issue is dead and gone and is unlikely to be discovered, and they wish to avoid getting the nice old treasurer into trouble. Seeking no more advice from you on that question, they ask you to advise them on a proposed pension plan for employees, and also to get a ruling from the Treasury Department on it. Can you do that?

If you are in a position to pick and choose clients you might choose not to represent a company in the position of an unrepentant defrauder, but if you are not so fortunate I know of no moral or ethical reason why you may not represent the company as to the pension plan. Of course, you cannot disclose the fraud to the government because that would violate your professional duty. The fraud was a past and not a continuing one, and knowledge of it was communicated to you in your professional relationship and it is a confidential communication. You can even undertake to seek a ruling as to the tax status of the pension plan, but if, in so doing, it is or becomes necessary to submit to the government past financial statements known by you to be incorrect because of the fraud, then I think you must not accept the assignment or must withdraw; you clearly cannot have anything to do with furnishing false information to the government. Can you then explain to the client why you are withdrawing and recommend another lawyer innocent of your knowledge? Here opinions may differ. I would hesitate to go that far.

Now, let us leave fraud and look at some everyday problems. Perhaps the lawyer's most important everyday tax problem, long antedating the tax return, has to do with facts. Facts are grist for his mill in grinding out tax advice. True facts are elusive and difficult to dig out; clients, consciously or unconsciously, seem to be adept at obscuring the relevant and emphasizing the unimportant. Only last week I was asked for an opinion on the sale of preferred stock which had been issued as a dividend the preceding year; I asked whether the preferred stock was to be redeemed shortly, as that would make a very great difference in determining the seller's possible tax liability, and I was assured that there was no plan for redemption. On close questioning and examination of the actual facts, however, it soon became apparent that there was a great probability that the stock would be redeemed; no purchaser would pay the price proposed to be paid for the preferred, unless he was counting on getting the redemption premium within a short time. You have to be very careful about the facts clients give you, and you have to look into the situation hardheadedly. All too frequently the suggestion is made about ignoring an unwritten understanding, tearing up a paper, pulling a page out of a book, because "no one will ever know." No doubt, lawyers do not always know when this happens but it should not be necessary to say that they must not countenance it.

Once a lawyer gets his evidence, he often faces a difficult task in interpreting it. Tax lawyers spend lots of time looking at transactions to see whether they are colorable or actual. Jeremy Bentham once said that law is the art of being methodically ignorant of what everyone knows. Now it is fatal for a tax lawyer to practice that art. He must not be diverted by form. He must ask himself, "However alluring this may appear, what is it really? Is this something that looks different from what it really is?" If it is, he had better forget it.

Of course, Congress sometimes makes the mistake of providing different tax consequences for accomplishing the same result by different methods. In such event there is no objection to taking advantage of it, but you must know what you are doing. It is unethical, however, to set up a transaction to make it appear to be what it isn't, to fool someone. All the facts which are pertinent should be spread on the record.

It is not normally the lawyer's function to prepare tax returns, but frequently if he engages in tax practice he is consulted about them. What advice should he give about reporting doubtful but arguable points in a tax return? If he believes that a certain item is not income, he may properly advise that the client is not required to report the item as income. But he should advise the client to call attention to the facts by rider if he believes the government would probably seek to tax it. Suppose, however, the crucial issue were one on which there were many court decisions uniformly in his client's favor but as to which the government bullheadedly simply hadn't yet given up. In that situation, he might be justified in not reporting even by rider; but, by and large, wherever there is an item in doubt which might be considered taxable by the tax authorities, it should be disclosed somewhere, even though it is not actually reported as involving taxable income.

Clients sometimes ask advice about returns previously filed. Suppose a client confidentially asks you as his lawyer for legal advice concerning a clearly taxable income item which he inadvertently omitted from his income tax return for the preceding year, with the preparation and filing of which you had nothing to do. Your advice should be to file an amended return or otherwise report the omission. If the client were a corporation or other taxpayer subject to annual audit, it might be sufficient to put a note in the file to be submitted to the examining agent when he comes in to audit. If the client refuses to heed this advice, your responsibility would cease. The attorney-client privilege would appear to prevent you from turning informer; and this would probably also be true if the omission had been deliberate and fraudulent assuming the fraud was a past and not a prospective one, disclosed to you in confidence.

Assume the facts were the same, except that the income tax return had been prepared and certified by you or in your office, and the client refuses to authorize you to disclose the information he has given you. This opens up a number of perplexing questions as to which there is little direct precedent. With lawyers increasingly encouraged to enter the tax return field, these questions become more important, involving as they do the extent to which the attorney-client privilege is sacrificed, and the lawyers' rights and duties affected, by undertaking this type of work.

The privilege does not apply to information received and advice given outside the scope of professional employment or to matters handled in a capacity other than professional. Communications with accountants, for example, are not privileged, except where the privilege is granted by statute. Services in connection with the preparation of a tax return may be deemed services of a ministerial or accounting nature rendered in a capacity other than professional. Conceivably, the answer might be influenced by whether or not the preparation of the return was purely incidental to or inseparable from legal consultations and advice, or by whether the lawyer prepared the return or clerks or accountants in his office, or by whether the lawyer is also a certified public accountant or especially experienced in accounting matters. But, even though communications between attorney and client in connection with the preparation of a tax return were to some extent deemed to be within the scope of professional employment—i.e., incident to the seeking and giving of legal advice, the privilege would nevertheless seem inapplicable to information thus furnished which is authorized to be reflected in a tax return intended to be filed with the tax authorities, since such information was not intended to be confidential.

In the case just put, the determination of whether you are at liberty to notify the government of your client's error, if he refuses to correct it, is a difficult one. Assuming you could work your way through to the conclusion that the privilege does not apply and you are free to disclose, what then would be your duty? May you wash your hands of the matter? Or, the return having been certified by you or your office, should you not disregard your client's request and report the omission to the proper authorities? The answer may not be easy, the return having been honestly prepared; but notification of the error seems more in keeping with a lawyer's high responsibilities; of course it would be more desirable from the standpoint of his self protection. To say the least, the situation of a lawyer taking on the preparation of tax returns is fraught with the possibility of embarrassment.

Suppose that, on reviewing your client's income tax return for a prior year you find he made two unrelated mistakes, one favorable to him and the other favorable to the government, both honestly made. He asks you to do what you think best in his interests. Would it be proper to raise the favorable item and remain silent on the unfavorable one? It is of course difficult to be categorical where the balance of considerations depends so much upon the particular facts. But, broadly speaking, the question should probably be resolved this way. If you were then preparing the return in the first instance, would you feel bound to disclose the unfavorable item? If so, there seems little justification for not pointing it our later when the favorable one is raised. If you should conclude that omission of the unfavorable item, although involving some risk, was not clearly a mistake and need not have been reported, would it be appropriate to postpone the filing of the refund claim until just before expiration of the statute of limitations, so that, if the government discovered and raised the unfavorable point upon investigating the claim, it could do no more than offset the claim? The answer may depend upon the particular facts and the degree of doubt the unfavorable item involves. But there are situations where, as a precaution, this procedure would be appropriate. Yet, where omission of the unfavorable item represented a clear error, I believe that to pursue this course would be too sharp a practice.

I had an opportunity last night to look at the mimeographed questions which were prepared by the student committee and distributed among you. As they bear on the problems I have just been discussing, I thought it might be interesting to take them up at this point. I do so with some hesitation, however, because in this room there are some tax lawyers of greater distinction by far than I possess. If they disagree with anything I say, I would like them to speak up.

Question 1: "*A*, a resident of Massachusetts, owns 100 Missouri Pacific Railroad First Mortgage 5% bonds upon which interest was defaulted about 1933. In 1944 Railroad began to pay interest at the rate of $50 a bond a year in exchange for the defaulted coupons. The Treasury Department issued Regulations in 1944 stating that the $5,000 *A* received was not taxable income but was to be used to reduce his cost basis. A decision of the Supreme Judicial Court of Massachusetts in 1947 held that such payments were subject to Massachusetts income tax. Should *A*'s lawyer advise him to file amended Massachusetts returns for 1944, 1945, 1946?"

As to those years, it does not appear whether the statute of limitations is a bar to an additional assessment. It does not appear that any fraud is involved. Certainly, if the statute of limitations has not run, the advice should be to file amended returns and pay up. If the statute of limitations has run, I don't think the lawyer can justify insisting on the client paying up if there was no fraud, and it was a purely legal question decided in 1947 contrary to the Federal law.

I had a client—a wonderful old gentleman from upstate New York— whom I advised in a case involving peculiar circumstances. His son was a specialist on the stock exchange and one day, being a specialist, he had an opportunity to make $30,000 in security transactions. He didn't want to do it for himself and he did it for his father. His father thought that he was getting a gift. Years later, after the statute of limitations had run, it turned out that nobody had reported that income. The father came to me about it to have the situation cleared up. I told him I would see what I could do. I invited the government in and they investigated through a special agent who wrote a report that there was no basis for a fraud charge. I then went to the Revenue Agent in Charge and offered to pay up but asked that interest charges be waived because assessment was barred by the statute of limitations, no fraud having been involved. The Federal Revenue Agent in Charge said we had to pay the interest too; if we didn't, he'd bring fraud charges anyway. The State authorities, on the other hand, to whom a similar offer was made, thanked us very sincerely for offering the principal, and said they would be delighted to waive the interest.

Turning now to the year 1947, it seems clear that the advice should be to report the income. If *A* refuses to follow the advice, I don't believe the lawyer has any right to file a return for him. But if *A* is continuously dodging taxes and not paying attention to your advice, it would be better not to represent him. It would seem to me that there is little justification for not at least disclosing the item.

Let us look at Question 2: "*B* has received $10,000 under circumstances which make it practically a gift. His lawyer honestly thinks it is a gift on the basis of reported decisions. However, the Income Tax Regulations clearly state the $10,000 is taxable. What advice may the lawyer give to *B*? Should the return make no mention of the $10,000 at all with the hope that it will never be discovered? Or should the lawyer attach to the return a statement of the $10,000 and his reasons for considering it not subject to tax?"

The lawyer has of course a double duty: a duty to do his best for the client and not to bring the lightning down upon him, and a duty to live up to his professional responsibility. In some situations, failure to report the item might be justified. But normally I think he should advise the client either to report the item as income or, if he were willing to assume a possible risk of penalty for intentional disregard of the regulations (if the regulations themselves covered the matter), to call attention to the item by rider attached to the income tax return or, failing that, to file a donee's gift tax information return. If the client refuses to do any of these, the lawyer's duty is done, assuming of course he is not responsible for the preparation of the tax return and that under the facts failure to disclose would not constitute a fraud or crime.

Question 3: "*C* conveys Blackacre worth $100,000 to son *S* upon his lawyer's advice, to simplify probate of *C*'s estate. The deed is recorded. *S* reconveys by a deed to be recorded only if *S* dies before *C*. *C* predeceases *S*. Should the lawyer advice *C*'s executor that Blackacre is part of *C*'s estate upon which estate tax is due?" In my opinion, the lawyer should advise the executor that the property should be included in the decedent's gross estate, or the transaction at least reported in the estate tax return by rider, because, though the only deed of record is the one to *S*, the two deeds may have been part of one transaction amounting to a gift by *C* to take effect in possession or enjoyment at death.

"S insists that the executor omit the $100,000. Is the lawyer bound by the attorney-client privilege to remain silent, or should he act by informing the Internal Revenue Bureau, or file his idea of a proper return?"

The lawyer is of course bound by the attorney-client privilege to remain silent unless the privilege is waived or the executor's proposed action would be criminal or fraudulent. Could you reasonably conclude on these facts that what the executor proposes to do would amount to fraud? Remember, a lawyer is not free to disclose confidential information concerning a contemplated crime or fraud unless he is reasonably sure of his facts. If you conclude it would amount to fraud, is it your duty to inform the Treasury, the attorney-client privilege then being inapplicable, or would you feel it sufficient simply to withdraw as counsel for the executor, there being no Treasury regulation requiring you to become an informer?

* Curiously enough, one of the few tax cases involving the attorney-client privilege had to do with just such a factual situation as this. The executors were the son and the decedent's lawyer, who later resigned. In addition, the son, though not present when the decedent and the lawyer worked out the arrangement, was later brought in simply to be told what was intended to be done and to sign his deed. And it was established that when the plan was devised and carried out, the possibility of avoiding estate tax was not considered or desired.

What happened there was this. The son filed an estate tax return excluding the property. The decendent's lawyer refused to execute it but, before resigning, filed a return on the same day in which it was stated that the property had been transferred in contemplation of or intended to take effect in possession or enjoyment at or after the decendent's death. The case was taken to the Board of Tax Appeals. On the lawyer's testimony the Board held the property taxable as a transfer intended to take effect in possession or enjoyment at or after death. The Circuit Court of Appeals, over one dissent, reversed, holding that in the absence of the lawyer's testimony, which was disputed, there was no evidence to support the Board's decision and that the lawyer's testimony was inadmissible because it was a communication protected by the attorney-client privilege, the privilege not having been waived by the decedent and the confidential character of the communication not having been lost by virtue of the son's slight participation.

The case was an unusual one, any original tax avoidance intent being entirely eliminated. Had the facts been somewhat modified, a different result might have been reached.

Cases of this sort always present difficulties. There is one pending in the New York courts now, where a father wanted to save taxes and he sold his brother a very valuable property for a much lesser sum. The brother, it is believed, was supposed to account to the wife and children, but after fifteen years the family discovered he really wasn't going to do so, so they commenced litigation in the courts, the latest decision being in favor of the children. I doubt that the father contemplated such troubles when he set up the tax saving arrangement.

Question 4: "E died in Texas leaving an estate valued at $20,000,000, all but $45,000 of which is located in Texas. A cottage worth $20,000 and a bank account of $25,000 are in California where E has spent nine months of each of the past ten years. Should his lawyer forget the California assets to avoid California estate taxes, since he is fairly sure that California courts will consider E a citizen of California? The lawyer knows that Texas will collect estate taxes. Would it make any difference if the lawyer is opposed to the principle of two states collecting estate taxes?"

Well, the lawyer's prejudice might make a difference in what he advises, but it shouldn't. The facts in the case suggest that California has a really legitimate claim to residence, and I think if the lawyer cannot satisfy himself that any claim by California would be unfounded, it would be his duty, after pointing out the legal and practical situation as to enforcement of any claim by California, to advise raising the question with California and getting it settled.

I have had a case of this nature. However, the decedent had spent much less time in the Western State, and all he had there when he died was a bank account of a few hundred dollars. After long deliberation, we decided there was no real basis for a claim by the Western State. We were advised that we might avoid a lot of red tape, and possible difficulties and expense, if we did not file a return and did not try to collect the money; it might cost more than that to resolve the matter. We followed that advice. We have had many letters since, from people in that State, offering to tell us about the money if we would share it with them!

The responsibility of lawyers in respect to taxes of governments of domestic States other than their own, and in respect of foreign governments, suggests questions in a seemingly uncharted field. Can a lawyer say he owes no duty to any State other than his own; that collection of taxes by another State is its business; that if it has a claim against assets beyond those within its jurisdiction it must sally forth and assert it; and that the lawyer's duty is limited to meeting that claim fairly and truthfully only if raised? If this be not so, is there any rational basis for a different answer where the out-of-State assets are in Canada, or France, or some other foreign country? I cannot give you positive answers. Whether irrationally or not, there is no doubt a general tendency to feel a lesser sense of responsibility to such governments than toward one's own State and Nation.

Question 5: "F has kept two sets of books for years, but realizing that the complicated government regulations require legal talent, he hires a lawyer. The lawyer is asked to manage all subsequent financial transactions. What should be his attitude and advice to F regarding the earlier fraud?"

Well, obviously, his advice should be to disclose and pay up what is due.

"If F refuses to file a late return and pay the penalties, should the lawyer act for F, provided F will act honestly in the future?"

I think I have discussed that question in my earlier remarks about fraud cases.

So much for the specific questions. Let's turn to the most common contact lawyers in tax practice have with government officials. This is in connection with tax settlement negotiations, seeking rulings, and the like. The lawyer's duty is to see that the full basic facts are given on all issues in dispute or on which a ruling is requested. He is entirely free to present the facts in the way calculated to appear most favorable to his client's position and to argue for the most favorable interpretation of the law. But he must not be tricky, and must avoid any misrepresentation of facts pertinent to the issue. The client having acted honestly, the lawyer may support his position even though it is arguable. And he has no duty to call attention to unrelated weak points the government has overlooked. However, weak spots should be taken into account in appraising the desirability and terms of settlement, for the weak points may be injected later.

The same standard is required in tax litigation. You must not ask the government, for example, to stipulate facts theretofore assumed to be true but which your investigation discloses to be inaccurate. This would not only be improper but also unwise.

In my experience, one of the things leading practitioners are most careful about is this question of reliability and integrity. The responsible lawyer must always be on the watch to avoid getting into a position where he can be criticized for a lack of frankness and honesty as to matters under consideration with the tax authorities. Many times revenue officials have said what a great help it is when they can deal with lawyers they trust, who present facts and arguments fairly and competently, carefully avoiding misleading factual statements and half truths. Nothing is more valuable to the lawyer—nothing is more helpful toward a favorable, expeditious settlement of a disputed issue—than so conducting himself that those on the other side can believe in his integrity and confidently rely on his word.

Thus far I have been talking about practical matters of common honesty. The responsibilities of the lawyer in tax practice go considerably beyond that. The lawyer entering the tax field, as in any field, bears a heavy responsibility to be adequately equipped to guide his clients wisely and well. He must master his technical tools, and know how to find and interpret facts. He must be well prepared before he advises, and he must be able to face up to and not shrink from decision. To be sure, this involves much conscientious digging and, even so, a good lawyer can make mistakes. But with taxes as high as they are today, there can be no excuse for professional carelessness or for frustrating appropriate and desirable action because of lurking fears, born of confusion.

Clients are usually honest innocents who must be guided not only away from transactions which are questionable because unwise or merely colorable but around pitfalls that abound in seemingly valid and reasonable family and business affairs. Their fate rests in the hands of counsel perhaps to a greater degree than they themselves may realize. I might illustrate this point with a story.

Some twenty years ago, a promising business executive sought advice about a proposed employment contract containing a stock purchase option. He was told the law was not settled but as the law was developing he would probably be taxable on the excess of the value of the stock over the option price at the time he exercised the option, and he was advised against entering into the contract. Displeased with this advice, he secured a favorable opinion from another lawyer, and on the basis of that opinion he went ahead. Years later, he found himself in court, the principal in one of the early stock option tax cases. He had assigned the option to his wife, who exercised it, and the government asserted a very large tax against him. Meanwhile, his situation had changed and, when the court decision went against him, he took out a gun and shot himself!

Tax considerations are important. But the lawyer in tax practice must never lose sight of the fact that the tax consideration is only one of the many factors that must be taken into account in determining the desirability of any proposed action. He should see to it that all aspects of the matter are put before his client in the proper light so that the client will be guided toward a wise decision. Saving money is not the only end or only satisfaction in life. Ill-considered action to escape taxes may prove as tragic in modern times as was the action many years ago of King Lear. I frequently find this a handy illustration. King Lear, you will recall, seeking to escape responsibilities, made the grave mistake of turning over his Kingdom to his seemingly more loving daughters. Of course the client in the last analysis must make his own decision, and may decide as did King Lear against the advice of wise counsel. But the point is—and this should be emphasized—he should not be led to discolor his real desires and neglect his best interest by overemphasis on tax savings.

What I have said is not inconsistent with recognizing that a lawyer may quite properly help a client arrange his affairs so as to keep taxes down. The courts have repeatedly emphasized this, the most refreshing recent judicial utterance on this point being this quotation from Judge Learned Hand:

Over and over again courts have said that there is nothing sinister in so arranging one's affairs as to keep taxes as low as possible. Everybody does so, rich or poor; and all do right, for nobody owes any public duty to pay more than the law demands: taxes are enforced exactions, not voluntary contributions. To demand more in the name of morals is mere cant.

To be sure, as Justice Holmes once observed, taxes represent the price one should be happy to pay for our civilization. That is entirely true. One should not be too pessimistic over having to pay high taxes. It would be much better to say with Kettering, "How fortunate it is we don't get the quantity of government we pay for." Justice Holmes was of course talking about the taxes one owed. It is for the government to determine what taxes should be paid and in what circumstances. As Judge Hand said, it is mere cant and sheer nonsense to say one should pay more than the law imposes or that something is wrong with trying to keep one's tax liability down. Unfortunately, the terms "evasion" and "avoidance" have been much abused even by the courts. To infer that there is something morally wrong with avoiding tax in a legitimate way, there being no fraud, deceit or make-believe, is pure hypocrisy.

Senator Pat Harrison was fond of using this illustration. If there are two bridges across a river, one a toll bridge and the other free, both leading to the same destination, there is no moral reason whatsoever why the traveler shouldn't choose the free one. If the law permits a taxpayer to arrange to make a profit in such a way that it is taxable as capital gain and not as ordinary income, there is no moral reason whatsoever why he shouldn't do it. If, by judicious use of gifts and the marital deduction in estate planning, a taxpayer can save taxes, thereby leaving more for his heirs than if he had simply willed them the property in the old-fashioned way, he would be foolish not to do it.

But what I have said must not be taken too loosely. The lawyer in tax practice must not develop too heightened a sense of cleverness. He should be resourceful but should realize that clever tax schemes should be weighed with caution and must not be indiscriminately applied. Here, judgment becomes more important. Cleverness is not competence. The too-clever, overly-enthusiastic tax planner is likely to be either a limited or an irresponsible man. The vision and foresight of such men is likely to be so clouded that it may be said, with Josh Billings, that the trouble with them is not what they don't know, but that they know so much that ain't so.

The too-smart tax planner is likely to overlook that the history of the tax statute is like a military armament race. History shows that each new military invention is inevitably succeeded by a better and more formidable counteracting weapon. So too is the loophole race between government and taxpayer. As a statutory loophole is discovered and comes into wide use, Congress steps in and closes it. Usually, it doesn't pay therefore to set up a program where the advantage depends upon the continuance of a loophole. An insurance trust to pay premiums on one's own life insurance, for example, may have seemed a smart tax saving idea originally, but when Congress made the insured liable for tax on the trust income, and the insured couldn't use the trust income to pay the tax, some taxpayers found themselves in a pretty tough fix. The difference between the lawyer who encourages grasping at trick loophole opportunities and one who says "Go slow; look ahead," is the difference between the lawyer who wants to keep his client always and the one-shot, in and out, hit and run, adviser.

The too-smart tax planner is also likely to overlook the function of the courts in tax laws. The courts, as you know, have developed exceedingly broad guiding rules of statutory interpretation. Influenced by the necessity of dealing with bold tax schemes neatly fitting the Congressional language but not the intent, the courts have gone far in interpreting tax statutes in the light of and in order to effectuate overriding Congressional purpose. Now if the courts have power to make such broad rules they have the power to expand them and even make new rules to prevent results under the tax law which they think improper. Any tax plan simply jigsaw-cut to the present state of articulated tax law may therefore be unsafe.

This being so, it becomes apparent that considerations of moral and ethical propriety and legal effectiveness in tax planning often shade into each other. A foul-smelling viscerally objectionable plan is likely to be adjudged ineffective. This eases the lawyer's problem of conscience by converting many moral problems into legal ones. As with the perfume smeller or the wine taster, a finely developed sense of smell or taste is not likely to be possessed by those who are insufficiently educated to know what is good. Colorable schemes, legitimate on their face, often lead to harsh law and endless litigation, sometimes dragging valid arrangements into the mess. A question of ethics may be involved in furthering an arrangement which, though seemingly valid, is factually colorable and artificial. Apart from whether such a scheme would be practically effective, the lawyer has, I suggest, an affirmative professional responsibility to discourage abortive tax plans of this sort in the interest of avoiding unduly harsh remedial legislation, of relieving the administration and the judiciary of undue burdens and of making the tax system work.

If time permitted, I would devote a few moments to the practical and other reasons why it is desirable for a lawyer in tax practice to try to develop a sympathetic, at least non-antagonistic, attitude toward the interests of the public and the legitimate needs of the revenue. I would also dwell a little bit upon his duty to help his clients understand the public policy reasons underlying the tax rules affecting them in order that they may better understand the moral implications of what they do and develop broader and more farsighted judgments as to their own long-run interests. The lawyer bears a heavy responsibility here, for his standards may become the guiding standards for his clients. In educating clients, the lawyer needn't talk in loose terms of moral values. Hard-headed, realistic considerations are more effective and more sensible. The client will usually comprehend if the rational basis for the law is explained to him and if the true nature and implications of what is proposed are made clear as well as the possible consequences. He will get the point; and if he doesn't get it, a few choice comments, added for seasoning if appropriate, about the consequences of a fraud charge might be very effective. It is always comfortable to have practical justification for long-range wisdom and high conduct.

My final point is one which I am sure has arisen in your minds. It is this: must a lawyer in tax practice always act consistently with the client's immediate best interests, irrespective of the public interest? Some lawyers, as Dean Griswold pointed out, so identify themselves with their clients at all times that their respective interests seem indistinguishable. There is no duty to do this; indeed, I should say the best and most competent lawyers do not. It goes without saying, of course, that a lawyer must not use knowledge gained in a professional relationship to hurt his clients. He cannot, while purporting to represent a client in accomplishing a specific objective, try underhandedly at the same time to defeat it. If he undertakes to represent a client on any matter, he is duty bound, within the limits of propriety, to do the best he can for the client, and he must not be halfhearted or negative about it if he undertakes the matter at all.

The lawyer is an essential cog in our system of government—a government of laws, not men. His professional work is an essential part of the process of orderly administration of justice under that system. He may properly contend in particular cases for results which he believes authorized by law, though he would not have permitted them had he been the lawmaker. He may properly aid a client in taking advantage of legitimate tax saving loopholes, though he would close them if he made the law. It is perfectly proper to do this—Congress may deliberately have intended to permit; if not, it is for Congress to change it.

But this does not mean that the lawyer must be a slave of his client or must trim his views and adjust his extracurricular activities to fit the client's sail. The lawyer is first of all a citizen. He does not lose his rights and obligations of citizenship by joining the legal profession. He is entirely at liberty to speak out as a citizen at appropriate times, and to use his special knowledge and experience in the public interest in order to make tax law more fair, equitable and workable, whatever the immediate effect upon his client's pocketbook may be. Indeed, many lawyers feel this is not simply a right, but a duty.

Fortunately, such independence appears not to harm the lawyer's professional tax business. It may actually help him keep an open mind and be better informed; and in the long run it may make for better judgment. Clients usually understand this and often feel better protected when represented by such a man. They respect independence of mind and normally, do not demand the soul.

When I was in law school I was concerned over whether one's conscience or usefulness to his fellow citizens would in any way be impaired by becoming a member of the bar. I am happy to report, after more than 25 years of active practice, that the answer in my opinion is "No." Instead of being impaired by professional practice, I think the legal profession's awareness of moral, ethical and social implications—and the capacity of its members to understand the full consequences of any particular action and its effect upon the public interest—are on the whole, with all the admitted inadequacies, more developed, sharpened and alerted than can be said of citizens generally.

Honorable participation in the orderly administration of justice is the source of great pride and satisfaction to the practicing lawyer, whether he engages in general practice or in a so-called specialty or both. And I venture to say that even greater satisfaction is likely to flow to him who, in addition, seizes upon available opportunities to participate as a citizen in the never-ending search for means of advancing the public welfare, through placing at its service his special talents and experience.

I can do no better in closing than to restate this thought in the words of Mr. Justice Holmes:

Law is the business to which my life is devoted, and I should show less than devotion if I did not do what in me lies to improve it, and, when I perceive what seems to me the ideal of its future, if I hesitated to point it out and to press toward it with all my heart.

I thank you.

Discussion

Dean Griswold: I have long thought Mr. Darrell should have been a law professor. He has surely demonstrated it this afternoon for he talked precisely 50 minutes.

Now there may be some of you who would like to put some questions, and I will act as interlocutor, or allow Mr. Darrell to deal directly with you, whichever he prefers. Will you please speak clearly so all can hear.

From the Floor: What is a tax lawyer's responsibility as to law if he has a case in progress, and another case comes along which overrules the first case. Is he under an obligation to cite both?

Dean Griswold: Remember that the other client is always the government in that case. The question is, what is the duty of the lawyer with respect to citing authorities which are against him?

Mr. Darrell: I would say that the easier part of your question relates to the lawyer's duty to cite reversals. Of course the lawyer shouldn't cite a case that has been overruled or reversed without disclosure of what happened. Actually, the government is pretty well equipped to check up on that, so it would be foolish if he failed to disclose. As to his duty to cite other cases clearly pertinent but harmful to his case, I think it is better to come out with all the authorities in point and to do one's best to distinguish them. Normally it is better practice to recognize the weak points and argue from there; usually, before one is through, the weak points will be brought out.

FROM THE FLOOR: This may be unrealistic, but assume there is a transaction which is absolutely safe from discovery and a little bit shady; in a hardheaded way you try to convince the client it is going to be found out but you are unsuccessful; you feel it is unethical and the client feels it is ethical; what is the duty of the lawyer?

MR. DARRELL: It is difficult to be categorical where you don't have the precise facts, but if you were the lawyer and a client wanted to do something that you think is colorable—that borders on fraud—you should have nothing to do with it. If it is shady and wrong, it is very, very clear that the lawyer should have nothing to do with it and should do his very best to prevent it. If the transaction would amount to a fraud on the government, there is a real question whether the lawyer, even though he advised against it, could properly simply stand by silently and watch his client committting it.

FROM THE FLOOR: Suppose you are a lawyer and you don't have enough clientele so that you can refuse that man. He refuses to follow your advice in reporting an item of income. Would you continue to advise him?

MR. DARRELL: There, again it is difficult to be categorical. I think there are lots of clients who are not fraudulent minded, but just a little misguided. You may represent them hoping that in the course of time your guidance and influence will be felt, things will clear up and they will be more satisfactory clients. There may come a time of course when you shouldn't go on any longer. But you do not have to throw out a client because he has made some honest mistakes. If you tell him that a certain doubtful income item should be reported by rider and he says in good faith, "No, it is not income; I am not going to do it," and you can't persuade him to do it, that is the extent of your duty and you are not required to stop representing him.

There are, you know, other types of clients, and I might mention one. It is a true story. There came into one of the large New York law offices—not ours—a woman who wanted some advice about a plan to give away a large sum of money. She presented her problem to the lawyers and they made an appointment for her to come down the following week. When she arrived, four lawyers were present, including the firm's top tax specialist, and they started to dissect the problem in a very learned way. As they were explaining to her that if she would make the gifts in installments she would save substantial income taxes, she interrupted and said she didn't intend to do any such thing; she intended to give her money away and wanted the government to benefit too.

DEAN GRISWOLD: Can I vary the last question a little bit? Suppose you were retained, not merely to advise the client on this particular matter, but to prepare his tax return. Suppose you find this matter and tell him it should be dealt with by rider and he says nothing doing. What do you do then? You are required by regulations to sign the return.

MR. DARRELL: I wouldn't sign the return. I would take the consequences.

DEAN GRISWOLD: In other words, there is a distinction between legal advice and the matter of actually filing a return.

MR. DARRELL: Entirely so.

FROM THE FLOOR: When a lawyer sends in a return which he has prepared and signed for a client, and then he finds out there is an item which the client did not report—say an item of ten thousand dollars—what is his duty?

MR. DARRELL: The lawyer has prepared his return. It has his certificate attached to it and he files it, and he discovers while it is pending before audit that there was some item omitted, but not fraudulently omitted; just a mistake—

FROM THE FLOOR: Now the client does not want to file an amended return.

MR. DARRELL: I am glad I don't have that problem, but I would be very much disturbed if he didn't file an amended return. I would at least see to it that the information was brought to the attention of the revenue agent when he comes in to audit, and I would try to get the client to do it unless the audit takes place in my office.

FROM THE FLOOR: A taxpayer has been engaged in fraudulent practices in the past but would like to make a new start, so he comes to you for tax advice. You tell him he has to disclose, but if he discloses, the penalties in back taxes are going to be such that he will be ruined. It is either a question of being honest in the future and not disclosing past practices, or disclosing the past and accepting financial ruin. What is your duty here?

MR. DARRELL: If you are satisfied that he is now an honest man and you don't have to do anything that makes use of false information which is based on the past fraud, then I suppose if you want to you can represent him in legitimate matters. You are not at liberty to report the fraud assuming knowledge of it came to you in professional confidence. The trouble is, you don't know when the knowledge will plague you; as in the example I gave earlier, a question may arise of your filing statements of your client's worth and because of the fraud net worth may not be what the records say. There is where your problem would lie. If a man has turned over a new leaf, I don't think he should be denied counsel, but I do think that you have to be awfully careful.

FROM THE FLOOR: What difference would it make if the statute has already run?

MR. DARRELL: If the statute has run on the liability, and the lawyer satisfies himself that it was only an erroneous omission and not fraudulent, there is no duty on the part of the lawyer to insist that the client pay up. The duty of the lawyer is to tell him what the law is and let the client decide himself whether he will take advantage of the statute of limitations. You realize, of course, that the statute of limitations works both ways—in favor of the government, and in favor of the taxpayer. The government doesn't waive the statute of limitations when an overpayment is involved and there is no legal duty that I know of to urge a client to report and pay up some past liability discovered after the statute of limitations has run.

DEAN GRISWOLD: Don't forget, however, two things just by way of statement of the law. If the omission was fraudulent, there never is any statute of limitations; and if the error was one of omission and amounted to 25 per cent, then the statute of limitations is five years and not three years.

MR. DARRELL: I'm glad you brought that out.

FROM THE FLOOR: I would like to know how far a tax lawyer can go in going to the legislature and trying to influence them in favor of a client.

MR. DARRELL: Well, some lawyers are pretty good at legislative matters and others don't do it at all. I think that a lawyer is free, if he discloses whom he represents, and files a proper lobbying law report if required, to try openly and frankly to persuade legislators to back a bill for his clients. I think it would be improper to take a retainer to go down and try to influence the legislators to do a particular job, and lead them to believe that you are doing it as a citizen. The interest must be disclosed. If it is, then I think it is legitimate as long as you don't go beyond propriety.

DEAN GRISWOLD: To put it in its clearest form, the appearance of a lawyer before a legislative committee hearing on behalf of a client is surely proper professional activity.

MR. DARRELL: Yes. And no lobbying law report is required for that.

FROM THE FLOOR: In the case of a lawyer who represents a man who has turned over a new leaf, is it conclusive that the lawyer should not disclose any prior fraud that may have been committed?

MR. DARRELL: Where in the course of a professional relationship a lawyer is told in confidence by a client of a fraud that the latter committed in the past, the lawyer has no right whatsoever to disclose to the government or anyone else the knowledge he thus gained. That is an important ancient rule. If the professional privilege did not exist, clients would be in jeopardy in consulting lawyers. The privilege was designed to make it possible for clients freely to take up their problems with lawyers. The privilege does not apply, as I said earlier, to contemplated frauds and crimes.

FROM THE FLOOR: Suppose that a committee for a tax reform comes around and gives you a petition to sign with them to urge Congress to change the statutes—a very much needed reform—but you realize that it will cut the legs out from under three or four of your clients that you have right now. What do you do then?

DEAN GRISWOLD: The question in substance is that a body of public-spirited citizens want you to join with them in urging a particular reform in the tax law which you believe in but the adoption of that reform would very seriously adversely affect some of your clients? What do you do?

MR. DARRELL: If you believe the proposed reform would be a good thing, you certainly are free to join in urging it, and many lawyers would do so without thinking of clients' views. But if in your special situation it would get you into difficulties with your clients if you publicly joined in the appeal, you are not required to forget the client problem and to go ahead nevertheless; your name attached to the appeal might not be that important. In other words, on balance, you might fully justify remaining silent. I would certainly say, however, that the lawyer ought to try to participate in those things which he thinks are useful in the public interest, and I don't think that clients, generally, take offense.

DEAN GRISWOLD: I would like to say just one final word. I am not sure that I will put it into the best form, but I have particularly liked Mr. Darrell's presentation of these problems because he has shown that they are problems, that they are very difficult matters and that there are no clear, simple and easy answers to them. He has not painted these things as being black and white. He has not said, you can do this and you can't do that and the line is clear as to which side you are standing on. But he has shown that as you get close to the line, it becomes very difficult and in many situations—I think he would agree with me—you can't lay down a general rule but you must undertake to be prepared to decide that particular question when it arises. In many discussions of these questions I have heard lawyers say, "Oh well, if there is the slightest question about it, you musn't touch it at all. You can't have anything to do with it if anybody will conceivably raise any question about it." That has always seemed to me to be dodging the issue. I think in many of these cases where the question is raised it means you must be awfully careful to give full thought and full consideration to the question and then to resolve it as you think it should be resolved. Mr. Darrell, do you want to make any rebuttal to that?

MR. DARRELL: I agree with you one hundred per cent.

DEAN GRISWOLD: On behalf of the Student Bar Association and the audience in the room, I want to extend very great thanks to Mr. Darrell for his excellent presentation.

6. Conscience and Propriety in Lawyer's Tax Practice
John M. Maguire

Honorable lawyers have no occasion for personal perplexity with respect to breaches of professional rectitude so great as to call for severe discipline. Such conduct is obviously bad. But these same practitioners dealing with revenue officials in behalf of taxpayer clients would welcome much more authoritative guidance than they have had on delicate, though often commonplace, matters of conscience and propriety. Lack of this guidance cannot, of course, be attributed to scarcity of occasion. We scan no untrodden area, but rather one bewilderingly criss-crossed by lawyers' tracks, ancient and modern. Every counselor who advised a client to avoid the old general property tax on intangible investments by shifting his funds into exempt bonds over tax-day,[2] or who planned and executed a quick, concealed transfer of taxable assets from an obvious taxpayer to one unexpected and unpursued,[3] had to make a moral determination first. Nowadays, with our prodigious burden of taxation sustained in its

---

[1] The title above is meant to indicate a discussion of problems of such professional behavior as does not, even at worst, become punishable as violative of law, that is, the questions raised are those properly considered by Ethics Committees of bar associations rather than by Grievance Committees involved in administration of sanctions for illegality. *See* Drinker, Legal Ethics 30 *et seq.* (1953), with special reference to the difference of opinion remarked at 48 nn. 38, 39.

This paper purposely avoids chokingly profuse documentation, that bane of much contemporary legal writing in the United States. Setting out the thesis that we do not now have the answers, it is meant to be provocative instead of definitive. Provocation works better when short and sharp.

[2] Shotwell v. Moore, 129 U.S. 590 (1889), by main force and awkwardness, steam-rollered an attempt at this sort of "window-dressing," but there was a pointed dissent taking the ground that the Court had to deal with "a question of law" and not one of high-minded citizenship. This dissent indicates why the courts cannot in the immediate connection give the legal profession all the advice it needs. He would be a poor lawyer indeed who confined his professional advice to the strict limitations of legal enforceability.

[3] *See* Sears v. Nahant (a situation tenaciously litigated in various aspects), 205 Mass. 558, 91 N.E. 913 (1910); 208 Mass. 208, 94 N.E. 467 (1911); 215 Mass. 234, 102 N.E. 491 (1913); 215 Mass. 329, 102 N.E. 494 (1913); 221 Mass. 435, 109 N.E. 373 (1915); 221 Mass. 437, 109 N.E. 370 (1915); and dismissals for want of jurisdiction, 248 U.S. 542, 543 (1918). The brief for the taxing officials in the earliest of these cases charges that the taxpayers ". . . deliberately undertook to evade taxation . . ." and makes remarks about "hocuspocus." Much further technicalism on both sides peeps through the records and briefs covering later stages of the controversy.

largest aspect—the income tax—by a system of voluntary compliance,[4] these lawyers' determinations come portentously thick and fast.[5] We need a proper pattern for them.[6]

No comprehensive pattern is going to be pricked out by judicial decisions. Save in proceedings specifically aimed at bar discipline, on charges which if substantiated will have arisen from indefensible misconduct, the courts have other obligations to meet. They wisely refrain from gratuitous collateral sermonizing. Here is an illustration.

The setting for *Baldwin v. Commissioner*[7] was consultation between an elderly California lady and her lawyer about the disposition of her estate, including some real property in Texas. The lady wished this realty to go to her son. The lawyer advised, and she agreed, that for the purpose of saving probate inconvenience and expense respecting the Texas holding and *not* with any desire or intent to evade federal estate tax, the lady should make and record a deed of gift to the son, who should at the same time execute a donative reconveyance. This reconveyance was not to be recorded unless the son predeceased his mother. The transaction was so set up, the lawyer holding the second deed. The mother predeceased the son, the lawyer returned the second deed to the son, and the son destroyed it.

In her Will giving the bulk of her property to the son, the mother designated lawyer and son as co-executors. They both qualified. About one year later the son filed an estate tax return which the lawyer refused to sign because it did not report the second deed; it did report the first deed, stating that the transfer was neither in contemplation of death nor intended to take effect in possession or enjoyment at or after grantor's death. Nearly six months after the filing of this return, the lawyer filed a separate estate tax return for the de-

---

[4] The present federal system of current individual income tax payment and withholding has in this connection done little more than transfer the obligation of compliance from one taxpayer to another.

[5] CAHN, THE MORAL DECISION 164–175 (1955), soberly indicates the portentous quality of these determinations by client and legal adviser.

[6] *Ethical Problems of Tax Practitioners*, 8 TAX L. REV. 1–33 (1952), discloses by the give and take of open discussion among highly competent tax law practitioners something of the diversity and uncertainty of view now prevailing. Another stimulating reference, less easily available, is a discussion of tax morals and manners in the pamphlet entitled LAWYERS' PROBLEMS OF CONSCIENCE 1–23 (1953; Harvard Student Bar Association, American Law Student Association). For convenient brevity, the first of these titles is hereinafter referred to by name of speaker and the second as PROBLEMS OF CONSCIENCE. *See too* Miller, *Morality in Tax Planning* in NEW YORK UNIVERSITY TENTH ANNUAL INSTITUTE ON FEDERAL TAXATION 1067 (1952); and Paul, *The Lawyer as a Tax Adviser*, 25 ROCKY MT. L. REV. 412 (1953).

[7] 43 B.T.A. 183 (1940), *rev'd*, 125 F.2d 812 (9th Cir. 1942).

cedent, reporting both deeds, stating that the decedent mother had received all the income from the Texas property until her death, and asserting that decedent had made a transfer in contemplation of or intended to take effect in possession or enjoyment at or after her death. More than two and one-half years after filing the separate return, the lawyer resigned as co-executor.

In consequent litigation of an estate tax deficiency before the Board of Tax Appeals, the lawyer as the Commissioner's sole witness gave vitally important testimony as to his dealings with the mother. The Board held that there had been sufficient disclosure to the son, with the mother's consent, of the client-lawyer communications to remove the usual seal of secrecy, that the lawyer's testimony was properly receivable, and that the Commissioner's position was sound. This result the Court of Appeals reversed in a split decision, the majority reasoning that son as well as mother had been a client, and was entitled to enforce the confidential communication privilege as against the Commissioner, a stranger to the negotiations. There being no testimony other than the lawyer's to support the Board's decision, it fell. The dissenter argued that the separate estate tax return filed by the lawyer, which return had been admitted in evidence without objection or restriction, supplied adequate evidential underpinning for the decision of the Board.

The alert reader will observe that this case fairly bristles with questions of lawyers' proper behavior. These questions become prominent points of reference in the following discussion. Not one of them required an answer to meet the issues directly presented for instant decision. Reasonably enough, not one of them is explicitly stated, let alone resolved. The Board and the Court stuck strictly to their knitting. Such restraint is regularly practiced in judicial and quasi-judicial proceedings. Hence the paucity of relevant precedent from this quarter.

Consequently, we are thrown back upon the Canons of Professional Ethics which are in some respects pointedly specific and in others very generalized;[8] such complementary rules of behavior as Circular 230;[9] and interpretative applications, largely unofficial, of

---

[8] The reference here is, of course, to the Canons adopted and maintained by the American Bar Association, which have become fundamentally influential throughout the whole United States, locally as well as nationally. It is common professional knowledge that these Canons are now undergoing careful scrutiny at the hands of a Special Committee of the American Bar Foundation. With respect to this reappraisal an illuminating statement appears in 41 Mass. L.Q. No. 3, 33 *et seq.* (1956).

[9] Title 31, Subtitle A, 31 C.F.R. §§ 10, 12, and 13 (1949), CCH ¶¶ 45,801 *et seq.* (1957). It is worth noting that this set of rules for enrolled Treasury attorneys and agents in section 10.2(z) requires each attorney to observe the A.B.A. Canons of Ethics.

these Canons and rules.[10] Further discussion in this paper draws freely upon the most easily accessible collections of interpretative applications, namely, the published Opinions of the American Bar Association's Committee on Professional Ethics and Grievances [11] and the published Opinions of the Committees on Professional Ethics of (1) The Association of the Bar of the City of New York, and (2) The New York County Lawyers' Association.[12] In carrying the discussion forward it is important to set up a simple outline, and that step is now essayed.

FUNDAMENTAL PRINCIPLES OF THE CANONS OF PROFESSIONAL ETHICS

As the Canons now stand they are 47 in number. The principles illustrated are far less numerous, and some of these principles are irrelevant to our immediate purpose. To begin with, tax controversies which have passed beyond the ordinary administrative stages and are in the hands of the courts present few if any ethical problems differing from those encountered by trial lawyers generally.[13] In the instant connection we may let this common ground take care of itself.[14]

---

[10] The term unofficial in the text is meant to signify that most of the specific interpretations are issued by bar association committees rather than by governmental authorities, either judicial or administrative. Relevant published Treasury rulings on practice before that Department are few indeed. *See* the closing references in note 32 *infra*.

[11] These Opinions have been embodied from time to time in a series of cumulative compilations, the latest of which has appeared in 1957. It contains 291 Opinions and 295 briefer Decisions. While the 1957 compilation appeared too late for use in preparation of this article, the numbering of Opinions remains constant and the references carried by the present footnotes are therefore adequate. The Decisions had been previously published in DRINKER, *op. cit. supra* note 1, at 283–303 (Appendix A), and references to this collection of them are given herein.

[12] The latest publication of these Opinions is in a well-edited volume by The William Nelson Cromwell Foundation, LEGAL STUDIES (1956). The total number of published Opinions, running into 1955, exceeds 1,200; some are joint Opinions of the two Committees. The *Harvard Law Review* contains a penetrating review of this book by Paxton Blair, Chairman of the Committee on Professional Ethics of the New York State Bar Association, whose analysis and citation are broader and more detailed than those of the present writer with his more limited purpose (70 HARV. L. REV. 1120 (1957)). Drinker lists Opinions and collections of Opinions by other bar associations. These the writer has not pursued beyond Drinker's occasional citations of them (DRINKER, *op. cit. supra* note 1, at 32, 410–415, 435–436). References herein to the Opinions from New York are initialed A.B.C.N.Y. or N.Y.C.L.A. to indicate committee authorship and give serial numbers, pages of the compilation cited in the first sentence of this note, and dates.

[13] The term "courts" in this connection includes such tribunals as the Tax Court of the United States. Paul, *The Lawyer as a Tax Adviser*, 25 ROCKY MT. L. REV. 430–433 (1953), is in accord with the statement of the text above.

[14] This sidelines Canons 1–3, 15 (in large part), 17–21, 22 (in large part), 23, 24, 30 (in part), and some portions of other Canons.

Nor need anything be said here about the lawyer's peculiar obligations in defense and prosecution of criminal cases;[15] problems relating to the fixing and collection of fees;[16] conflicting interests and related considerations;[17] or a number of miscellaneous occasions for circumspection.[18]

The remaining Canons upon which the paper does touch suggest four groupings of problematical situations. To some extent the groupings overlap, but it is worthwhile to specify them and to follow the specification as a working outline. First, the lawyer must not stir up strife and litigation.[19] Second, the lawyer must not advertise for business or pursue practices related to advertisement.[20] Third, the lawyer must be faithful to the obligations he assumes.[21] Fourth, the lawyer must not practice deceit or connive at its practice.[22]

Inciting Litigation

"It is disreputable to hunt up ... causes of action and inform thereof in order to be employed to bring suit...." Thus Canon 28 in part. But suppose a lawyer in the course of a civil suit discovers that a corporation is liable for back taxes which have not been levied against it, of which taxes the county attorney is ignorant but which it is the county attorney's duty to collect. We must remove one complication by assuming that the corporate taxpayer is not and has not been the lawyer's client. Even so, the case is not simple, for a duty to the public pulls against unquestioning compliance with the general

---

[15] Canons 4 and 5.
[16] Canons 12–14, 34 (the last in part).
[17] Canons 6, 10, and 11; cf. 38.
[18] Canons 7 (poaching upon other lawyers' employments); 25 (respecting customs and practices of bar, etc.); 31 (discretion to refuse retainers); and 36 (limitations upon advocacy and other employment after retirement from bench or other public post; cf. Circular 230, § 10(a)(2), (3)).
[19] Canons 28 and 42 (agreement to pay or bear litigation expenses).
[20] Canons 7 (encroaching upon professional employments of others); 8 (duty to give restrained and pacific advice as to merits of clients' cases); 27; 28; 34 (division of fees with non-lawyer improper); 35 (impropriety of drawing business through intermediaries); 40 (improper for lawyer to agree with publisher of his articles upon law to advise inquirers respecting their individual rights); 43 (publication of lawyer's name in law list); 46 (notice to local lawyers of willingness to associate in particular branch, etc.); cf. 45 (applicability of Canons to specialists); and 47 (use of lawyer's services or name to further unauthorized practice of law). See also Circular 230, § 10.2(l), (v), especially the latter.
[21] Canons 15, 30, 31, 37, and 44; cf. 16. This is a field of great doubt and difficulty.
[22] Canons 9, 15, 22, 26, 29, 32, 33, 39, and 41. Application of these Canons is full of doubt, difficulty, and complexity. See too Circular 230, §§ 10.2(d), (p), and 10.10(b)(3), (4), (6), (8), (10), (12), (13).

prohibition of the Canon. An Opinion [23] rendered upon this problem says that it is the lawyer's "professional and private privilege, and rather his duty to give the information to the [responsible] authorities," but he may not properly seek [or accept?] employment in the job of collection. This seems neatly to split the difference between silence and solicitation.

Now take the converse problem—an attack, reasonable and in good faith, upon the validity of a tax. A lawyer has a client against whom the tax is being asserted, but the amount involved is so small as to make a solitary battle by this client at best a Pyrrhic victory. The lawyer knows that the same tax affects many other persons and envisions, primarily for his own client's benefit, a test suit sustained by moderate contributions from a number of affected taxpayers. How far may the lawyer go in organizing a mass attack? Again we face a situation which is not simple. It is as important to protect the citizenry from improper fiscal impositions as to insure full collections of proper levies by the Government. Moreover, this is a case in which sundry obvious considerations encourage prosecution throughout by the lawyer who initiates tax resistance. A situation substantially parallel came up for an Opinion,[24] and gave real difficulty. The upshot is gingerly approval of the effort to form a coalition, the client to take the greatest, and the lawyers the least, possible share in the effort, and the proposal to be couched in most restrained

---

[23] Opinion 87, A.B.A. (Dec. 2, 1932), mentioned in DRINKER, LEGAL ETHICS 66 n.47 (1953). *See also* Opinion 252, N.Y.C.L.A. 669 (1927), involving discovery of an unclaimed tax deduction, notification of responsible counsel, and request for a fee.

A problem superficially different, but fundamentally related, arises when an expert on taxation delivers a lecture or publishes a technical article dealing with some portion of his field. Dissemination of true understanding to legal professionals and lay taxpayers is commendable; twisting the dissemination into incitement of litigation is bad; and a deliberate bid for business attached to such dissemination is disreputable. *See* Opinion 92, A.B.C.N.Y. 42 (1928–1929) (no professional impropriety in organizing and operating a "Tax Institute" as an information and education service); Opinion 666, A.B.C.N.Y. 384 (1944) (lawyer publishing articles on taxation in a trade magazine must not answer questions of subscribers about their personal interests); Decision 228, A.B.A., DRINKER, *id.* at 295 (radio answers to specific legal questions); and Opinion 367, N.Y.C.L.A. 755 (1941) (Lawyer familiar with income tax law may not properly solicit opportunity to give instructive lectures thereon, either for pay or gratuitously). Does this make it a matter of delicacy to accept a retainer from a client who comes to a lawyer because of hearing him lecture or reading his published articles? *See generally* DRINKER, *id.* at 263–265.

[24] Opinion 586, A.B.C.N.Y. 330 (1941). Under the particular circumstances the taxpayer and 37 others were at least morally entitled to a refund of New York transfer taxes, but special legislation was necessary to make refunds practicable. Hence the composite effort was to be legislative **rather than litigative**.

terms. Since this sort of ways and means problem may arise in other connections than that of taxation,[25] the approach to its solution might well be standardized by an addition to the substance of Canon 27 [26] or Canon 28, or both.[27]

Advertising, "Feeders," and Related Devices

While the primary reason for prohibiting incitement of litigation is surely desire to maintain a friendly and pacific community atmosphere, a secondary reason must be the sustaining of professional dignity. Unquestionably a motive for incitement will always be personal gain to lawyers who flourish by serving in the quarrels of others. Thus incitement tends to become a strong-armed self-advertisement, and its mention leads to consideration of the opening assertion in Canon 27: "It is unprofessional to solicit professional employment by circulars, advertisements, through touters or by personal communications or interviews not warranted by personal relations." The sentence just quoted is followed by condemnation of indirect advertising through self-laudation, but the whole passage suggests reasonable limitations upon its prohibitions. If lawyers sedulously hid themselves, their calling, and their capabilities from public knowledge, highly necessary expert services would be hard to come at, and the profession might perish through malnutrition.[28] The Canon indeed goes on with helpful specification as to permissible professional cards, acceptable contents of identifying items in reputable law lists,[29] and traditional specialities allowed to be pub-

---

[25] Opinion 717, A.B.C.N.Y. 430 (1948), for instance, deals with a statutory interpretation situation involving claims against a municipal corporation. The Committee, strongly feeling the need of caution, declined to approve the proposed solicitation on the showing made. *Cf.* People v. Ashton, 347 Ill. 570, 180 N.E. 440 (1932), cited by the Committee.

[26] This is the Canon disapproving direct or indirect advertising, with carfully limited exceptions.

[27] Of course no cut-and-dried formula can be prepared for universal application, but statement of the common factors of difficulty and the criteria for handling them would be useful. Opinion 586 is scarcely comprehensive. A cautious reader considering it could reasonably remain in doubt as to the permissible degree of persuasion with regard to letting counsel for the initial client take control of the collective proceeding.

[28] It would be a ludicrous falsehood to assert that lawyers refrain from all efforts to attract clients. One of the first questions likely to be asked a job-seeking law school student or graduate is as to his prospects of bringing business. Drawing the delicate distinctions between proper manifestation of capability and improper solicitation is a fairly constant problem in all types of practice and therefore need not be specially discussed here. For a helpful presentation of the general principles of what may be called publicity conduct by lawyers, consult Opinion 375, N.Y.C.L.A. 762 (1947) (joint Opinion with A.B.C.N.Y.).

[29] Contrast the censure of disreputable law listing by Canon 43.

licly indicated.[30] These specialties do *not* include taxation,[31] which seems distinctly questionable. Half a century ago any lawyer worthy of the title could adequately deal with most tax problems. This is no longer true and in no other field of the law can fumbling cause more grief to clients or, it may be added, to governmental authorities.

The announcement, professional card, letterhead, and office door problem also takes intricate twists and turns because of the intermingling practices of accountancy and law in matters of taxation. Some of these complexities seem highly formalistic,[32] but the documentary difficulties are symptomatic and questions are raised at a fundamental level by doubts as to propriety of simultaneous active connection with both professions.[33] The risk commonly urged is im-

---

[30] Admiralty, patents, and trademarks. Opinion 788, A.B.C.N.Y. 482, 483 (1954), and Opinion 375, N.Y.C.L.A. 762, 764 (1947) (joint Opinion with A.B.C.N.Y.), add copyrights. *See* note 31 *infra*.

[31] The following Opinions are related to the non-inclusion noted by the text, but the publicity considered by some of them would have been of an improper type for use by a specialist even in the branches of practice stated by note 30 *supra*. Opinion 260, A.B.A. (June 9, 1944) (improper for lawyer to advertise that he has tax service in his office); Decisions 89 and 101, A.B.A., Drinker, *op. cit. supra* note 23, at 288 (free copies of revenue laws; free tax returns); Opinion 387, A.B.C.N.Y. 206 (1936) (improper to circulate card announcing lawyer as tax counsultant for reducing estate taxes and procuring refunds); Opinion 543, A.B.C.N.Y. 304 (1940) (improper to send local bar multigraphed letter stating specialization in various subjects including taxation); Opinion 581, A.B.C.N.Y. 327 (1941) (improper for lawyer to set up and publicize to other lawyers an income tax service); and Opinion 772, A.B.C.N.Y. 467 (1952) (improper for New York lawyer to include in letterhead statement of association with Florida firm for purposes of tax practice). Contrast early Opinion 195, N.Y.C.L.A. 629 (1921) (matter of personal taste only in lawyer's use of card stating he is income tax consultant). *Cf.* Opinion 445, N.Y.C.L.A. 828 (1955); Opinion 375, N.Y.C.L.A. 762, 764 (1947) (joint Opinion with A.B.C.N.Y.) (professional announcements by lawyers returning from government service to private practice *and sent only to other lawyers* may state particiular branches of practice: ''. . . still predominantly informational . . . lawyers . . . not substantially influenced to employ other lawyers by announcements or impressed by their implications.''). *Accord*, Opinion 788, A.B.C.N.Y. 482, 483 (1954). Opinion 393, N.Y.C.L.A. 781 (1950), deems such characterizations as ''tax specialist'' improper if circulation is not restricted to other lawyers. *See* comment in Drinker, *id.* at 242–245.

[32] *E.g.*, Opinion 437, N.Y.C.L.A. 822 (1954), where a man who was both lawyer and certified public accountant and had been using two separate letterheads and two separate sets of professional cards to segregate the professions, wished to simplify his life by putting the whole story on a single letterhead and a single card; his proposal was disapproved. This opinion was influenced by Opinion 434, N.Y.C.L.A. 819 (1954), presenting a like problem with elaborations, two members of a firm being involved. More serious questions of this general type appear in Opinion 738, A.B.C.N.Y. 444 (1949); Opinion 742, A.B.C.N.Y. 447 (1949); and Opinion 445, N.Y.C.L.A. 828 (1955). *Cf.* statements by the Treasury Committee on Enrollment and Disbarment presented in CCH ¶ 45,839.075 and .26 (Supp. 1957).

[33] Opinion 272, A.B.A. (Oct. 25, 1946) is not entirely convincing. It takes the stand that a lawyer who is also a certified public accountant may not hold himself out as practicing accountancy in the same office where he practices law; the majority of the Committee go the length of saying that such a lawyer may not, even in separate offices, practice both pro-

proper use of contacts with accountancy clients as a "feeder" device for the lawyer. But other risks chime in. The footnotes indicate that serious uncertainties in this connection call for clarification.

Fidelity to Professional Obligation

The lawyer's duty to discharge unwaveringly his professional obligations is the third item. A connection has already been noted between the duty to refrain from stirring up strife and the duty to eschew self-advertisement, respectively the first and second items. The two are to a considerable extent conjunctive and complementary. The third item bears an exceedingly close relation to the following and final item—the duty to steer clear of deceitful conduct. But this time the relationship is largely disjunctive or opposed. That is,

---

fessions at once because of the feeder potentialities of accountancy. Opinion 388, N.Y.C. L.A. 775 (1950) would permit the New York office door of two lawyer-certified public accountants to bear a legend announcing both professions. But Opinion 434, N.Y.C.L.A. 819, 820 (1954) weakens this by asserting that such legends in such a city are unlikely to attract persons to enter; if so, why waste the paint? *Cf.* DRINKER, *op. cit. supra* note 23, at 224–225, and note 31 *supra*.

It is easier to sympathize with disapproval of service to clients by lawyers in partnership or other association with accountants, investment counsel, and so on, *who are not lawyers*. Opinion 234, A.B.A. (Feb. 21, 1942), Opinion 239, A.B.A. (Feb. 21, 1942), and Opinion 269, A.B.A. (June 21, 1945) are severe to the point of demanding that lawyers who maintain such associations withdraw from law practice. *See further* Opinion 412, A.B.C.N.Y. 218 (1937); Opinion 484, A.B.C.N.Y. 264 (1939) (no full answer to inquiry because questions of law involved); Opinion 201, N.Y.C.L.A. 634 (1922) (mentioning the arguments of improper fee-splitting and affording opportunity to laymen to give legal advice); Opinion 343, N.Y.C.L.A. 733 (1938) (fee-splitting with accountant admitted to practice before Tax Court); Opinion 344, N.Y.C.L.A. 735 (1938) (combining some elements of Opinions 201 and 343 *supra*); Opinion 398, N.Y.C.L.A. 785 (1950) (joint Opinion with A.B.C.N.Y.) (lawyer-certified public accountant in partnership with non-lawyer); Opinion 399, N.Y.C. L.A. 785 (1951) (situation like that of Opinion 398, except that partner is certified public accountant; nevertheless disapproved because partner under different standards and subject to different discipline in different tribunal); Opinion 427, N.Y.C.L.A. 811 (1954) (lawyer member of certified public accountant firm); and Opinion 445, N.Y.C.L.A. 828 (1955) (association of lawyer-certified public accountant with non-lawyer-certified public accountant). *In re* Rothman, 12 N.J. 528, 97 A.2d 621 (1953), cited by Blair in 70 HARV. L. REV. 1125 n.36 (1957), is an important and detailed discussion, developing dissent.

Cf. Opinion 544, A.B.C.N.Y. 304 (1940), where the letterhead of a lawyer and a certified public accountant, who were in partnership, announced that they were tax consultants. No necessary impropriety was deemed involved, but lawyer's practice and office in that capacity should be separate and without feeder connection, which probably meant that the lawyer must refuse as law clients persons who consulted the partnership for tax advice. Interestingly comparable situations are discussed in Opinion 614, A.B.C.N.Y. 350 (1942), disapproving on numerous grounds plan involving occasional recommendation to accountant's clients of joint retention of himself and a lawyer in whom the accountant had confidence; and Opinion 738, A.B.C.N.Y. 444 (1949), saying that no problem of professional ethics arises from a lawyer's point of view if an accounting firm, without his solicitation or agreement, recommends his retention to its clients.

the lawyer's commitment to battle for his client through thick and thin, by every effective means, should definitely be held within bounds by the requirement of straightforward probity. The resulting pull and haul of opposing impulses makes for most painful perplexities in tax practice.

Of course many manifestations of devotion to full rendition of legal duty involve no such torturing conflict of decision between moral principles. The high professional conscience which led the late Randolph Paul across the threshold of death in the very act of presenting his honest views to a Congressional committee was unclouded by counter-considerations.[34] Less dramatically, but with equal clarity, a lawyer, whose accounts an Internal Revenue agent is auditing, must decline to permit such examination of a special account for escrow funds as would disclose the content of confidential communications from clients.[35] In matters of taxation the lawyer is often doubly charged, owing fidelity both to client and to Treasury. He should, for example, "... exercise due diligence in preparing ... returns ... and other papers relating to Treasury Department matters. ..."; and he should not "... unreasonably delay the prompt disposition of matters before the Treasury Department. ..." by dragging his feet or interposing frivolous obstacles.[36] Again, he is told that he should, despite the unpleasant nature of such action, give on due request "... any information which he may have concerning violations of the [Treasury] regulations ... or of the occurrence of any acts or omissions which would be grounds for suspension or disbarment, *unless said information is privileged."* [37]

The italicized words at the end of the preceding quotation correctly suggest that it is really impossible to go very far in discussion or even description of the present item without drawing in some opposition of duties and specifically an opposition to frank disclosure. Thus the next item is foreshadowed. But before moving to that item, one brief specification of an unanswered question:

In our federalized aggregate of numerous governments, how far across political borders does the lawyer's duty run? Referring back

---

[34] This reference to Randolph Paul would be incomplete without the added statement that of all legal tax experts in the United States none stood higher than he on insistence that his clients should maintain thoroughly honorable attitudes toward the Government. In the words of Canon 16, he would firmly prevent them "... from doing those things which the lawyer himself ought not to do...."

[35] Opinion 413, N.Y.C.L.A. 800 (1953).

[36] Circular 230, § 10.2(w). A reciprocal attitude on the Treasury's part is presumably taken for granted.

[37] Circular 230, § 10.2(d); emphasis added.

to the *Baldwin* [38] case, the reader will remember that both lawyer and original client were Californians, while the real estate which furnished the groundwork of dispute lay in Texas. The California lawyer's probate avoidance scheme involved the possibility of Texas tax-dodging. Had the interests of the Lone Star State a legitimate call upon his conscience? A reported discussion involving the *Baldwin* problem did not take up this exact question, but did stir something related. The supposition was of a decedent who might be held domiciled in either Texas or California and who had much property in the former state and comparatively little in the latter. Would it be proper for a Texas lawyer, advising personal representatives reconciled to a determination of Texas domicile, to recommend simple abandonment of the California property to avoid all risk of a *Dorrance* outcome? The discussion leader [39] believed that unless the lawyer convinced himself of the unreasonableness of any domicile claim by California, he had a duty to advise raising the question with California and getting it settled. But this, said the leader, is a "... seemingly uncharted field. ...", with possibly reasonable variations of attitude between obligations to sister states and to foreign countries.

Deceit or Contribution to Deceit

(1) An estate tax problem. Discussion may now turn in earnest to the *Baldwin* case. On the facts found, and especially with the form of the federal estate tax return in mind,[40] the lawyer might well conclude that the son's return was improperly deceitful. What was the lawyer to do about it? Under Canon 16 and Circular 230, the very least he could do was to point out the ethical connotations of the son's proposal and refuse to participate.[41] If the son persisted, Canon 44 [42]

---

[38] *See* pp. 28, 29 *supra*.

[39] LAWYERS' PROBLEMS OF CONSCIENCE 10–12 (1952), the discussion leader being Norris Darrell. *Cf.* note 6 *supra*.

[40] This may as well be considered in the light of current Form 706, Schedule G, and Instructions.

[41] The reference in Circular 230 is to § 10.2(c), which, rather significantly, requires an enrolled attorney "... who knows that a client has not complied with the law or has made ... an omission from, any return. ..." to "... *advise his client* promptly of the fact of such noncompliance ... or omission." (emphasis supplied) What bearing do the emphasized words have upon the lawyer's disclosure in his dissenting return? Was the son a client? The Court of Appeals for the Ninth Circuit decided that he had once been one. *Cf.* the elaborate prohibitions in § 10.10(b)(3), (6), (12), and (13) of Circular 230 against *participation* by an enrolled attorney in filing, preparation, or approval of a falsified return or other document.

[42] This Canon, while stating that an attorney may not withdraw from an employment once assumed, except for good cause, permits withdrawal in case "... a client insists upon an unjust or immoral course. ..." The timing of the resignation here involved raises a serious question whether it was too long delayed. *See* p. 29 *supra*.

probably sanctioned the lawyer's withdrawal from responsibility by resigning his executorship. It can be argued that he had become bound in honor to the dead testatrix to stick with the ship, but this seems scarcely convincing. The son having become the dominant party in beneficial interest, and seemingly the only person affected by the outcome of the litigation, a living hand had replaced the dead hand, at least with respect to a matter about which the mother most likely never thought seriously.[43]

But the lawyer went beyond resignation. He elected to make disclosure by filing the separate dissenting return. This was an extreme step. The situation involved a highly debatable issue as to whether the content of the consultations between mother, son, and lawyer was sealed in secrecy as a set of privileged communications. The lawyer may have felt that by accepting appointment as executor he became obligated in law or conscience to the Treasury to present what he regarded as a truthful estate tax return. Or he may have considered that the son had so misapplied the possibilities of the situation as to fall within the principle of the familiar doctrine that privilege fails when legal service is sought or obtained to enable or aid a client to commit a crime or tort.[44] Yet the ultimate decision of the case sustained the claim of privilege, and bar association committee Opinions suggest grave doubt as to the propriety of disclosure.[45]

---

[43] Conceivably the lawyer might have sought to have the son removed, but this action scarcely seems suitable.

[44] *See* what substantially amounts to a codifying restatement in UNIFORM RULES OF EVIDENCE, Rule 26(2)(a). While a lawyer, to whom a client in seeking legal advice confidentially reveals his past crime, may not break this confidence unless the breach is necessary to protect himself against a subsequent false accusation by the client, the lawyer is under no such restriction as to the client's statement of intention to commit a future crime or continue a wrongful course of action. Opinion 202, A.B.A. (May 25, 1940). This is in part a simple application of the clear wording of Canon 37. The judges handling the *Baldwin* case made no reference to this Canon or to the recently rendered Opinion.

[45] Opinion 274, A.B.A. (Oct. 25, 1946) (wife in divorce proceedings originally told her lawyer a falsehood as to the date of husband's desertion, but later told the lawyer the truth and asked him to abandon desertion as a ground for divorce; lawyer neither bound nor permitted to reveal the later disclosure, despite the fact that it opened husband to prosecution for perjury in escaping military draft). Opinion 287, A.B.A. (June 27, 1953), reported in 39 A.B.A.J. 983 (1953), involves two situations. The first is another divorce case in which the husband informed his lawyer that he gave perjured testimony as to date of desertion and in consequence was being blackmailed by the wife. On this the Committee split; five members ruled that the lawyer should urge his client to disclose the truth, and decline to represent him further if he refused, but should not himself make disclosure; two members felt that the lawyer might have to disclose. The second case involved a lawyer's duty to speak up when he knew from his client that the latter had a criminal record and heard the record clerk tell the opposite to the judge who was about to sentence the client. The Committee considered several varied aspects of this general situation and again split; the majority was against the lawyer's disclosure, urging circumspection of language even in case

Another angle is worth mentioning. Any practitioner caught in this kind of tangle realizes all too painfully the involvement of his reasonable personal interests. The public is censorious of lawyers, and bitter comment and loss of standing may easily result from action which can by any stretch of reasoning be considered an officiously voluntary breach of professional confidence.[46] In the instant case the lawyer might justifiably assume that the son's estate tax return would receive careful scrutiny and investigation. Action of that sort is much more a matter of course in connection with estate tax than in connection with income tax, and abstention of the lawyer from signing the return, particularly if coupled with his resignation as executor, was well calculated to arouse suspicion. Hence, it may be strongly argued that the lawyer would discharge fully his obligation of honesty in disclosure if he maintained silence unless and until questioned by Treasury representatives. Furthermore, if that questioning occurred, the lawyer would commit no deceit and would seem laudably to protect the confidential communication privilege by responding that he was in doubt as to the propriety of disclosure but would promptly obey a court order.[47]

(2) Income tax problems. Turn now to federal income tax for suggestion of further doubts with which the lawyer must wrestle in this branch of practice. Change the position of the persons involved so that discussion deals with lawyers as taxpayers' advisers and champions only, and not with lawyers in the common but equivocal posi-

---

of direct questioning by judge. The Opinion should be read carefully, since it covers additional points. As to the second case, see ANNUAL STATEMENT [1953] OF GENERAL COUNCIL OF THE BAR (ENGLAND) 21.

[46] One of the most famous examples of the risks which beset a lawyer with respect to reconciling candor, advocacy, and preservation of confidence is found in the *Courvoisier* murder case. See SHARSWOOD, LECTURE ON PROFESSIONAL ETHICS 40–41, 107 *et seq.* (1854), reprinted in 32 A.B.A. Rep. 103, 183 *et seq.* (1907). Here an eminent counsel, Charles Phillips, began his defense of the accused in an English murder case believing his client innocent and cross-examined at least one witness with a view to suggesting that either the witness or another person might have been the killer. At a later point in the trial the defendant admitted his guilt to Phillips, yet expressed expectation that Phillips would defend him "... to the utmost." Following the advice of no less a person than Baron Parke, Phillips did continue the defense, but according to his earnest contention, backed up by the word of several discerning observers who attended the trial, neither asserted his own belief in Courvoisier's innocence nor intimated that any other was guilty. Nevertheless, he was for years suspected and accused of having done the reverse. *Cf.* DRINKER, LEGAL ETHICS 141 n.16 (1953).

[47] Consider Circular 230, § 10.2(t), asserting the duty of enrolled attorneys to produce records and evidence upon proper and lawful Departmental demand unless they reasonably believe "... that the said demand is of doubtful legality...." *Cf.* Opinion 287, A.B.A. (1953).

tion of the attorney who has become an executor or trustee. Start with initiation of the client-lawyer relation.

(a) Retainer and preliminary shaping of the situation. It is plain enough that if a would-be client approaches a lawyer with a tale of past misconduct in relation to taxes, or proposal for future tax-saving schemes, the lawyer may refuse employment unless satisfied with both behavior and attitude.[48] When the lawyer accepts employment and has really been let in on the ground floor, so that he can advise about conduct to be pursued for the purpose of minimizing tax liabilities, he ought to avoid arranging anything like a mere masquerade. Familiar examples turn up constantly, *e.g.*, directing specially vivacious behavior by an elderly, wealthy man preparing to make a transfer which may be challenged as having been in contemplation of death, or drafting persuasive records, contracts, etc. in connection with a retention of corporate earnings which may be attacked as an improper accumulation of surplus.[49] Standards in such matters must allow for much play in the joints. The distinction between collecting and preserving evidence, on the one hand, and faking evidence, on the other,[50] cannot be sharp and categorical. Norris Darrell suggested a useful wording when he warned against nurturing and exercising "... too heightened a sense of cleverness."[51] Another serviceable test is put in terms of normality of behavior—plans calling for marked departure from the tried and conventional require many grains of salt.[52]

(b) Candid disclosure in returns and related procedures. Consider a succession of situations respecting the tax return of a client whom the lawyer has accepted. First, suppose it is clear to the law-

---

[48] Canon 31 puts this emphatically, of course in general terms. If a lawyer knowing facts which make him unwilling to act for a client can suggest another lawyer who does not know these facts, ought he to do so? It has been said that here opinions differ, but to the writer this sort of playing upon ignorance-is-bliss seems quite improper. PROBLEMS OF CONSCIENCE 5 (1953).

[49] Both these situations are interestingly discussed in a Monograph by MACKINNON, PROBLEMS OF ETHICS AND GOOD PRACTICE OF TAX LAWYERS 33 *et seq.* (1956). This was prepared, and later discussed by experts, in connection with the work of the American Bar Foundation (*see* note 8 *supra*) but is unfortunately not readily available. Otherwise frequent reference to it would be rewarding. In the immediate connection this Monograph quotes on the corporate question remarks by Hellerstein in *Ethical Problems of Tax Practitioners*, 8 TAX L. REV. 4, 6 (1952). *Cf.* note 6 *supra*. See also Miller, *Morality in Tax Planning* in NEW YORK UNIVERSITY TENTH ANNUAL INSTITUTE ON FEDERAL TAXATION 1077–1081 (1952).

[50] For instance, misdating checks or bills of sale.

[51] PROBLEMS OF CONSCIENCE 15 (1953). *Cf.* Rabkin, 8 TAX L. REV. 28 (1952); Miller, *supra* note 49, at 1075; Paul, *The Lawyer as a Tax Adviser*, 25 ROCKY MT. L. REV. 416 *et seq.* (1953).

[52] In many applications this becomes a paraphrase for the familiar "business purpose."

yer that a certain item of income should be included, but the client is perfectly immovable and refuses to put it in. If the lawyer is doing no more than advising, with the actual making of the return referred to the client himself or some third person, there is respectable authority for the position that giving the disapproving advice is enough. The lawyer need not part company with the client; still less is he obliged or even free to make disclosure to the Internal Revenue Service.[53] If, however, the lawyer is to prepare the return, sign it, and thus take responsibility for the correctness of its content, he reaches a breaking point. He must not participate.[54]

Second, suppose the return has been prepared and filed with no shadow of bad faith on the lawyer's part, but he discovers, perhaps by communication from the client, on the eve of conference with an examining Internal Revenue Agent, that the client has engineered an unmistakably improper omission of an item of income or inclusion of a claim for deduction. What about client-lawyer confidential communication privilege?[55] Would the problem become peculiar and specialized if the client invoked the lawyer's aid because the Treasury was questioning a particular aspect of the return—whether there had been devotion to business purposes of a building, originally residential, on which depreciation was claimed; or business nature of a trip for the expenses of which the taxpayer sought deduction—and the lawyer's painful discovery had to do with another aspect? Seemingly the answer to this question is negative.[56]

---

[53] Darrell in PROBLEMS OF CONSCIENCE 20 (1953); DRINKER, *op. cit. supra* note 46, at 138 n.31, citing Cleveland and Michigan Opinions.

[54] *Ibid.* This is plain as a pikestaff under Circular 230, § 10.10(b). Here sounds an echo of the *Baldwin* case (pp. 28, 29 *supra*) with the complication of co-executorship somewhat watered down but still significant.

[55] Tarleau in *Ethical Problems of Tax Practitioners*, 8 TAX L. REV. 13–14 (1953), expressed doubt as to the existence of a client-lawyer privilege when the latter discovers that the former has furnished misinformation for inclusion in the return. Observe that the misinformation was not intended to be kept secret but to be revealed, though not, of course, along with admission of its falsity. Is the situation to be handled differently if the client suppresses relevant information which the lawyer later digs up? *Cf.* Opinion 287, A.B.A. (1953). With all due respect for proper hesitation to break silence respecting a client's communication, it is not so easy here as it would have been in the *Baldwin* case to salve a lawyer-like conscience by significant but less radical action. The Service may never find out, for instance, that the lawyer withdrew, if that is all he does. Mr. Darrell, taking the problem very seriously, would try his hardest to make the client file a proper amended return and, failing this, would apparently in some fashion bring the matter to the attention of the Revenue Agent if the audit took place in the Darrell office. Darrell in PROBLEMS OF CONSCIENCE 20–21 (1953).

[56] Tarleau, *supra* note 55, at 11–12, where the different aspect, it should be noted, had direct bearing upon the disputed item. *See also* Fillman, *id.* at 26, asking whether withdrawal by the lawyer is enough, without disclosure of the truth. And consider the further

Should distinctions be drawn according to whether (i) the lawyer knew nothing about the return before the client asked for his services in connection with audit, (ii) the lawyer had advised the client about the original preparation of the return, or (iii) the lawyer had prepared and therefore signed the return? This last question raises very pointedly a sub-question: How far and under what circumstances may the lawyer protect that precious professional property, his reputation with the Service for honesty and candor?[57]

A common variant on the foregoing series of elemental problems is encountered when client and lawyer have to deal with an item bearing debatable tax consequences. The two reasonably believe or at least hope that those consequences would be decided favorably to the taxpayer in a last-ditch fight, but the lawyer at least knows only too well that full and frank description will result in an unfavorable administrative ruling. Once again we are out of the realm of categorical imperatives[58] and rather uncomfortably removed from authoritative advice. This is not a situation in which any lawyer at all awake to the broader considerations of costly modern organized society should feel entirely easy if, in behalf of the immediate interest of a taxpayer client, he holds the cards tight against his wishbone and plays to the limit the game of *caveat fiscus*.[59]

But few practitioners of tax law could truthfully deny that they have often and rather artfully done something very much on this order. In public discussion, one fears, there are more words of conscientious subservience to the idea of open returns openly arrived at than unpublicized practice justifies in fact.[60] Certainly reticence is

---

complication raised by discovery of two unrelated mistakes in the return, one harming the Treasury and the other harming the taxpayer. May the latter conscientiously be revealed and its correction pressed without disclosure of the former? Is the lawyer's responsibility lessened by the fact that the Service would thus be invited, and very likely led, to make a thorough investigation? Darrell in PROBLEMS OF CONSCIENCE 8 (1953).

[57] PROBLEMS OF CONSCIENCE 20 (1953); Tarleau, *supra* note 55, at 13; Paul, *supra* note 51, at 423; *see* pp. 45, 46 *infra*.

[58] Hellerstein, Gordon, Rabkin, McEvoy, and Wallace in *Ethical Problems of Tax Practitioners*, 8 TAX L. REV. 8–9, 24–25, 28, 30–31, and 32 (1952).

[59] CAHN, THE MORAL DECISION 164–175 (1955), dealing with a case in which a good court split as to whether cheating the whiskey tax laws was "a crime involving moral turpitude," argues cogently for a graver view of this kind of thing. And note the high percentage of convictions in tax fraud cases. Miller, *supra* note 49, at 1069. *But see* State v. Evans, 94 So.2d 730 (Fla. 1957), a bar discipline case in which both majority and dissent argue that filing false and fraudulent federal tax returns is a crime not involving vileness or baseness in any shocking degree.

[60] "The tax practitioner does not regard it as his duty to recommend full and fair disclosure of the facts as to items questionable in law." Hellerstein, *supra* note 49, at 8. Paul, however, (*supra* note 51, at 427–428) expresses the belief that with respect to such a certainly challenged deduction as that of lobbying expense most tax attorneys would insist

not always blameworthy, as where the Service "... has adopted a policy of persistent litigation of questions which have been repeatedly decided favorably to taxpayers by the Tax Court and by the Courts of Appeal in several circuits." [61] And so, perhaps, in many instances where Service, Courts, and Congress have allowed the law in action to become "... a thicket of obscurity....," [62] it is not wondrous wise to risk getting your eyes scratched out. But on this elemental yet murky problem, where articulate standards would be welcome, everything has been left to implication and generalities.[63]

(c) Atmosphere of negotiation. As the preceding paragraph implies, one matter of pervasive importance on which clear declarations of principle would be useful is the general attitude properly to be taken in dealing with representatives of the Service. A number of factors, frequently and angrily mentioned, offer temptation for adopting an attitude quite the reverse of companionable. The fundamental ground for this temptation is belief that our present scheme of taxation, most particularly as evidenced in federal income tax, is essentially insincere. Steeply graded progressive rates are, it is said, concessions to ignorant popular clamor and shockingly uneven in actual application because the legislators, secretly conceding their undue harshness, have honeycombed them with termite borings of special alleviation.[64]

Coming down to particulars of administration, we have the constantly denied, but even more constantly repeated, assertion that Revenue Agents are instructed, or at least reasonably led to believe, that their hopes of promotion rest upon ingeniously exercised ability to turn up deficiencies. Still, in administrative particulars all lawyers know well enough, and most of them obey, Canon 9 which says that they "... should not in any way communicate upon the subject of controversy with a party represented by counsel. ..." This, they realize, is to prevent imposition by the expert upon the inexpert.

---

upon complete and prominent segregation of the item. And *see* Darrell in PROBLEMS OF CONSCIENCE 6 (1953).

[61] Paul, *supra* note 51, at 428.

[62] *Id.* at 427.

[63] Observe particularly the careful reservations of Circular 230: "... unless said information is privileged." (§ 10.2(d)); "... has reasonable grounds to believe and does believe that the said demand is of doubtful legality...." (§ 10.2(t)); "... false Federal income tax return ... knowing the same to be false." (§ 10.10(b)(3)); etc. Bar association Committee Opinions give no direct help.

[64] *See* Surrey, *The Congress and The Tax Lobbyist—How Special Tax Provisions Get Enacted*, 70 HARV. L. REV. 1145, 1149–1151 (1957), a careful, temperate, and thoroughly informed article. Consult also BLUM AND KALVEN, THE UNEASY CASE FOR PROGRESSIVE TAXATION (1953).

Yet in federal tax practice they frequently hear of, and sometimes experience, descents by Revenue Agents directly upon clients whose representation by counsel has been brought home to the Service. The Revenue Agents, to be sure, are presumably in these cases not members of the bar and so technically beyond the reach of Canon 9. The abuse, however, is exactly the same—risk of imposition by the expert upon the inexpert.[65]

Set this, and much more along such lines, in the general framework of Anglo-American traditional tax dislikes, and it is no wonder that there is strong talk of fighting the fire of imposition with the fire of reticence by being truthful but not frank, yielding facts only in driblets under pressure. A vitriolic critic of our present revenue system quotes this from an anonymous Delaware lawyer: "The practice of tax law these days requires the constant taking of anti-emetics."[66] It remains to the credit of reputable tax specialists, however, that they refuse in serious open discussion to accede to contra-governmental principles of this sort.[67]

For this refusal there is a specific, although as yet inadequately gauged, reason. The private lawyer in a tax controversy realizes that on the other side are his Government and the community of which he is a member. More voices than one have pressed upon him a sense of double responsibility,[68] even though the public interest side of his obligations has not been prodigally articulated.[69] So, while in ordinary litigious controversy the bar has been told that it is entitled and perhaps required to take a tough, unyielding attitude with respect to revelation of distasteful evidence,[70] there may be a call for less

---

[65] In this connection it is worth considering the cases, not yet systematically grouped and developed, where suppression of evidence obtained by Internal Revenue personnel has been sought on the ground that unfair methods were used. *E.g.*, United States v. Wheeler, 149 F.Supp. 445, 448 *et seq.* (W.D.Pa. 1957). *Cf.* Decision 250, A.B.A. in DRINKER, LEGAL ETHICS 296 (1953), stating that it is improper for an insurance company to interview the mother of an injured child who is represented by counsel.

[66] Hawley, *Morality vs. Legality*, 27 PA. BAR ASS'N Q. 230, 235 (1956); this article enjoys the extraordinary distinction of having been reprinted in the Saturday Evening Post, July 14, 1956, p. 27.

[67] Consider the whole tone of the discussions referred to in note 6 *supra*.

[68] One example of many was furnished by Tarleau in *Ethical Problems of Tax Practitioners*, 8 TAX L. REV. 10–14 (1952).

[69] The phrasing is borrowed from Paul, *supra* note 51, at 421–425, especially 424.

[70] Instance after instance can be adduced. WILLISTON, LIFE AND LAW 271–272 (1940) (refraining from correcting judge's statement of fact, although Mr. Williston did and his opponents did not know the truth); Opinion 309, N.Y.C.L.A. 708 (1933) (not improper to refrain from revealing presence in court of eye witness vital to case of client's opponent, a three year old child. DRINKER, *op. cit. supra* note 65, at 285 n.42, questions this opinion); *cf.* Opinion 307, N.Y.C.L.A. 706 (1933) (not improper to refrain from warning witness whose testimony would be helpful to client that witness by testifying may expose himself

strictly partisan behavior when tax disputes are handled. This line of thought, familiar through much reiteration, is emphasized by knowledge that the official enforcement personnel could not possibly make our burdensome and complex revenue system work without a high degree of acquiescence and cooperation from taxpayers and their experts. An authoritative statement of sound criteria in this connection is long overdue.

(3) Advocacy of legislation. Since taxation in the large, and to an increasing extent in detail,[71] depends upon statute, it is inevitable that tax lawyers are requested to make legislative appearances. Here all hands agree that whenever such a retainer is accepted there must be the utmost frankness as to interests represented.[72] There seems further to be a marked tendency to deny lawyers testifying before legislative committees the same representative impersonality accorded counsel in ordinary trial of cases.[73]

Conclusion

This discussion began with an assertion that the legal profession has not received adequate marching orders or advice as to its proper attitudes and conduct in a number of commonplace situations produced by tax practice. It is submitted that the footnote documentation bears out the assertion. As to forbidden incitement of litigation, anti-ambulance-chasing analogies are in some degree emphatically

---

to prosecution). *See also* notes 44, 45, and 46 *supra*. As to disclosure of unfavorable law as distinguished from unfavorable facts, *see* Opinion 280, A.B.A. (June 18, 1949), reported 35 A.B.A.J. 876 (1949); Darrell in PROBLEMS OF CONSCIENCE 19 (1953); *cf.* Decision 18, A.B.A., DRINKER, *id.* at 285. And consult ANNUAL STATEMENT [1953] OF GENERAL COUNCIL OF THE BAR (ENGLAND) 20.

[71] The 1954 Code is a wholesale surrender to the practice of stuffing the statute with detail.

[72] Darrell in PROBLEMS OF CONSCIENCE 22 (1953); Miller in *Ethical Problems of Tax Practitioners*, 8 TAX L. REV. 20–21 (1951). *Cf.* Decision 20, A.B.A., DRINKER, *op. cit. supra* note 65, at 285, which is ambiguously reported and may mean nothing more than that a lawyer who is himself a member of a legislative committee should disclose his interest in pending legislation.

[73] Miller in *Ethical Problems of Tax Practitioners*, 8 TAX L. REV. 20 (1952) (improper to lobby in behalf of a client for legislation in which lawyer does not himself believe). The very fact that everybody who participates in presentations before legislative committees or commissions is commonly called a ''witness'' points in this direction. Suppose a lawyer believes in the validity of pending legislation which will harm the immediate interests of a client. Is the lawyer free to advocate passage? Darrell in PROBLEMS OF CONSCIENCE 22–23 (1953), answers affirmatively but adds that the lawyer is free to hold his peace as well. Smith, moved by the obligation of fidelity to clients, either present or past, doubts the lawyer's conscientious freedom of advocacy in the situation suggested. PROBLEMS OF CONSCIENCE 42 (1953).

sound. A man run down by a motor vehicle knows he has something to complain about. Yet the enterprising lawyer is forbidden to bustle up with proposals of monetary balm. Many a promising potential taxpayer client may not know that he has been technically hurt unless somebody better versed respecting revenue law tells him. All the more, then, under such circumstances there is no proper room for stimulating legalistic inducement. But only a step beyond the obvious lie debatable cases, with little guiding authority.[74]

As to unprofessional advertising and kindred activities or relationships, we find much more documentation.[75] But we also find here some questioning whether the Canons in existing form are a proper answer to modern needs and whether their interpretation may not have been on some occasions too technically niggling.

The demands for professional fidelity to clients' interests and for avoidance of deceit appear as frequently conflicting forces.[76] Their acceptable resultants have been all too little manifested.

We have indeed, then, sound reason to try for a better set of steering directions. The writer ventures two suggestions, neither of them startlingly original:

First, a suggestion for systematic individualized approach. It may well be reckoned that the lawyer who went through such a harrowing experience in the *Baldwin* case was never caught by that snare again. If on any other occasion he gave similar conveyancing advice to a client, he very likely accompanied the advice with explicit statements as to what he would consider his duties of disclosure and silence in connection with tax controversies. If the client balked, the lawyer's plain path to safety was withdrawal from the transaction.

Since the *Baldwin* facts and opinions have been published for all to read, the rest of us need not risk like doubt and peril even once. And since any lawyer to be worth his salt in modern American taxation must have developed with growing experience a wise practice of constructive imagination, there is nothing to prevent him for himself or his firm from framing a code of conscience with respect to tax procedures. Even without more than long-range self-interest in mind, such a code will rise considerably above minimum legality and minimum ethical level. The framer, if he is wise, will sedulously arrange for preservation of what has been termed above a precious professional property—justified reliance upon his probity by the Service.

---

[74] *See* pp. 31–33 *supra*.
[75] *See* pp. 33–35 *supra*.
[76] *See* pp. 35–45 *supra*.

As a matter of fact, it is perfectly clear that plenty of lawyers' consciences operate independently of materialistic self-interest.[77] Nor are clients unmoved by similar impulses. According to one practitioner who deliberately stepped up the practice of his own office, "... we have tried out our higher code on our clients, and they seem to like it."[78]

Second, there might perhaps be a systematic group approach. Available evidence does not hold out lively hope for any rapid assemblage of a code of tax practice conscientiousness through the work of established bar association Committees on Professional Ethics. With more than 40 years of federal income tax experience in their background, and a far longer experience of taxation in general, these groups have produced exceedingly few Opinions or Rulings which really illuminate the dark recesses of our field.[79] This is said in no carping spirit. Members of these Committees are not normally tax experts. That portion of the bar which specializes in tax matters has become more and more sharply aware of increasing peculiarity in its practice. Not only has growing complexity made the subject-matter largely unintelligible to the non-specialist, but the interrelationships, habitudes, and conventions of the field are unique.[80] Hence, these specialist practitioners feel comparatively slight incentive to refer their conscientious doubts to Committees on Ethics having general jurisdiction.

What they have done with significant recent frequency is to talk over doubts and worries among themselves.[81] What they might enthusiastically welcome would be a specially skilled and accessible Ethics Committee, specifically, perhaps, within the framework or drawn from the membership of the Section of Taxation of the Ameri-

---

[77] Take collectively the expressions of opinion listed in note 6 *supra*. None of them is mealy-mouthed, but all show conscientious sensitivity.

[78] Merle H. Miller in *Ethical Problems of Tax Practitioners*, 8 TAX L. REV. 32 (1952).

[79] The index of DRINKER, LEGAL ETHICS (1953) contains no heading "Tax" or "Taxation"; the index of the recent valuable collection of New York Opinions described in note 12 and gratefully used in this investigation does mention tax specialists, but almost exclusively in the context of notes 30 *et seq. supra* which do not treat the really engrossing problems of tax practice.

[80] To be sure, taxation fills one of the oldest and most important niches of administrative law and therefore comes under a broadly inclusive heading. Theoretical classification and practical operation, however, are entirely different matters. A public utility or labor law expert would be staggered by the technique of tax procedure and vice versa.

[81] The text and notes of this paper sufficiently indicate both solo exposition and multiple discussion. But more goes on than is embodied in occasional writings and fitful meetings. The Boston Tax Forum, to which the writer belongs, meets regularly throughout the most active part of the lawyers' year. Scarcely a meeting passes without discussion of some point of conscience. Like organizations can be found in other cities.

can Bar Association. Such a proposal calls for cautious handling. It carries a hint of secession and suggests the risk of rivalry and dissent in relation to a valuable body of ethical precept already built up. Bickering over a topic on which there should be the closest possible harmony would be most unfortunate.

But two obvious factors suggest the desirability of segregation. To begin with, the Canons of Professional Ethics are directed principally, though not entirely,[82] toward lawyers' duties in connection with judicial controls. The persistently peculiar problems of taxation, as explicitly indicated above,[83] have to do with administrative controls, relationships, and procedure. Secondly, tax specialists in their most important relationship with the Treasury are subject to the somewhat distinctive code of conduct embodied in Circular 230. With respect to professional ethics this Circular makes two sets of demands: (1) it embodies by reference the standards of the Canons of Professional Ethics;[84] and (2) its own special provisions imply an obvious, if somewhat haltingly and enigmatically expressed, view that the enrolled Treasury attorney owes, when dealing with revenue matters, important additional obligations.[85] The full connotations of demand (2) urgently need to be spelled out.[86]

So far as the American Bar Association is concerned, it seems reasonably clear that the Committee on Professional Ethics and Grievances as now functioning cannot properly be charged with the job. Specialized training and acquaintance with masses of specialized materials are required. Might not an appropriately empowered Committee within or drawn from the Section of Taxation, quite contrary to being a harmful rival, prove a helpful and constructive supplementary agency?

---

[82] Note Canon 26, headed Professional Advocacy Other Than Before Courts. With eminent propriety this requires such advocacy to be open and aboveboard; that generality alone, however, comes nowhere near covering the conscionable aspects of administrative procedure.

[83] *See* pp. 43–45 *supra*.

[84] Circular 230, § 10.2(z).

[85] *Id.* §§ 10.2(c), (d), (e), (g), (i), (j), (k), (l), (m), (n), (p), (t), (u), (v), (w), and 10.10(b) *passim*. Some of these provisions seem repetitive of the Canons, but others are not.

[86] And in the long run made definitely authoritative by rewording the Circular.

7. The Tax Practitioner's Duty to his Client and his Government *Norris Darrell*

It has been said that nothing is often a good thing to do and always a clever thing to say. It may well be that nothing *would* have been the best thing for me to do today, or at least to *say* on the subject I am asked to talk about, for gentlemen instinctively dislike talking about duties. Moreover, some may think it sufficient to sum up the matter simply by quoting Lord Reading's well known remark that as a lawyer gets on he gets honor and as he gets honor he gets honest. I may therefore have been unwise in understanding this assignment, but I want you to know I do so in the mood of Thomas Huxley when he prayed: God give me strength to face a fact though it slay me.

My subject today encompasses matters of conscience and propriety in relation to the professional tax practitioner's multiple responsibilities — his duty to his client, his duty to his conscience, and his duty to society, including his Government. These responsibilities, of course, include the duty to give whole-hearted devotion and competent attention to the client's interests and to avoid representation of conflicting interests; the duty, subject to limited exceptions, to preserve the client's confidences in connection with legal consultations; and, of particular importance here, the duty to refrain from over-zealous conduct on behalf of the client not in keeping with high professional standards and good conscience and to advise against and refuse to assist in wrongful or improper acts.

In addition, in my view certain social responsibilities should be

Editor's Note: Mr. Darrell's article is based on an address delivered on September 28, 1960 during the luncheon session of the Tax Section of the State Bar of Michigan at the Michigan State Bar Convention at Grand Rapids, Michigan, and on another address delivered at the dinner session of the New York University Institute on Federal Taxation in 1958, subsequently published in New York University Seventeenth Annual Institute on Federal Taxation (Matthew Bender & Company, Inc., Albany, N. Y., 1959) at p. 1 under the title Conscience and Propriety in Tax Practice.

added: the duty to help make our self-assessing income tax system work; and the duty — if I may be permitted to call it that — to lend under appropriate circumstances one's special talents and experiences to the never-ending search for means of improving that system in the public interest.

In attempting to deal with so broad an area, one can talk in a rather general way, or one can attempt to deal with a large part of the subject as I propose to do by taking up borderline questions in a practical fashion through a series of hypothetical illustrative cases.

However, this method has its problems since it is easier to generalize than to provide ready practical answers in concrete situations. Moreover, in attempting to deal specifically with practical problems in this area, one runs the risk of creating an unrealistic impression. I hope I shall be able to avoid these pitfalls. My purpose is more to direct thought and attention to difficult questions and to stimulate exchanges of views thereon than to provide positive answers; and such answers to unsettled questions as I may suggest are put forward tentatively and subject to change after further reflection and discussion.

Indeed, to speak too positively and precisely about what one should do on facts sketchily drawn might well be misleading, since a variance in a fact here and there might change the color and shape of the problem and justify a different conclusion. Moreover, in hypothetical cases the human element tends unrealistically to be ignored. In the last analysis, the lawyer must consider each situation as it arises, evaluate all the factors pertaining to it, and make his own decision; and what he may decide in good conscience in one situation may conceivably differ from the decision he may properly reach in another, though at first blush the two might superficially appear to be comparable. With this caveat, I turn first to general advisory problems.

General Advisory Problems

Perhaps the most important everyday ethical problems of the lawyer in tax practice, long antedating the tax return, have to do with general advisory matters. In principle we surely all agree on this: the lawyer's responsibilities include the obligation to make every reasonable effort to equip himself to advise and represent clients wisely, and he must have the stamina and sufficient detachment to tell them the truth.

Clients are for the most part reasonably honest innocents who must be guided not only away from transactions because unwise or merely colorable, but around tax pitfalls that abound in seemingly valid family and business affairs. Their fate rests in the hands of their tax advisers, perhaps to a greater degree than they themselves may realize. The tax adviser bears a heavy responsibility here, for his standards may become the guiding standards for his clients.

In ancient Rome, Coriolanus, in explaining to his mother why he would not modify his attitude to gain the support of the crowds in the market place, is made by Shakespeare to say: "Know, dear mother, I would rather be their servant in my way than sway with them in theirs." Such is the spirit I am talking about. Now for some cases.

I.

A corporate client consults you on the following proposal. Having learned that another corporation is about to pay $100 per share of dividend arrearages on its preferred stock, it proposes to purchase some of the preferred cum-dividend at $250 a share, receive the dividend of $100 per share, and then sell the preferred ex-dividend at $150 per share, a transaction expected to net zero results apart from the tax consequences but to produce a tax saving of between $17 and $44 per share through operation of the dividend received deduction and the short-term capital loss deduction provisions of the 1954 Code or, possibly, if it is a dealer, the ordinary loss deduction provisions.

The client points out that, even though the purchase price of the preferred cum-dividend is run up because of the tax saving opportunity so as to produce a net loss on the transaction, but for the tax consequences, the tax savings would still make the transaction worthwhile. He wants your advice as to how long he should hold before selling, as he does not wish to hold beyond the point necessary to obtain the desired tax results.

This case of course suggests problems relating to the familiar phrases "business purpose," "transaction entered into for profit," and "transaction entered into solely for tax purposes," upon which it is your duty to be well informed. It invites careful consideration in particular to the principles recently expounded by the Supreme Court and other courts with respect to transactions undertaken solely to acquire tax deductions.

Nevertheless, while one might have no stomach for promoting or encouraging tax schemes of this sort, or might question the long-range wisdom of burdening or abusing the dividend received deduction, and might be particularly concerned over the effectiveness of the plan where the only possible profit is through the tax differential, would it not be perfectly proper from an ethical standpoint for you to pass on the tax effectiveness of such a plan, as requested, and to advise to the best of your ability as to the tax risks involved, the importance of running a reasonable risk of stock ownership, and the advantages or disadvantages of holding the purchased preferred for periods of varying lengths? After all, the opportunity to utilize the dividends received deduction was created by Congress and, even after the recent legislation [section 246(c)] there may still be room for utilization of plans of this sort. Yet, conceding that you may so advise, may you not be charged with a public duty to try affirmatively to discourage the use of pure tax gimmicks that can produce no profit except one that flows from an unintended operation of the tax statute?

II.

You are consulted about a proposed family partnership between husband and wife, valid in form under the laws of the State, but to be operated on the unwritten understanding, which may never be discovered, that the husband will continue to control the property and manage the partnership, that the wife will pay family bills out of her share of the profits, and that the wife will hold her interest subject to his control, even to the point of returning it to him should he need it. What should your attitude be?

Schemes such as this often lead to harsh law and endless litigation, sometimes dragging valid arrangements into the mess. A question of ethics is clearly involved in furthering arrangements which, though superficially appearing to be valid, are factually colorable and artificial. Can we not go further and say that, apart from whether such a scheme would be legally or practically effective, there is an affirmative professional responsibility to discourage abortive tax plans of this sort in the interest of making the tax system work and of relieving the administration and the judiciary of undue burdens?

III.

You are consulted about a corporate reorganization or readjustment, the tax consequences of which may depend upon the existence of a good business purpose, or at least upon the existence of a purpose other than saving taxes. You know that the client is tax conscious and that a tax advantage is an important consideration. Is there any moral objection to your canvassing and seeking to develop with the client all possible nontax reasons that could fairly be given in support of the transaction? And can you properly suggest modifications of the plan to strengthen it from this standpoint?

The same sort of problem arises when clients are concerned over and seek aid in buiding up a current record that will enable them to put their best tax foot forward with respect to potential liability for accumulated earnings tax, or potential contemplation of death treatment of a gift, or the possible application of section 269 or, indeed, any situation where tax liability may depend upon motive or intent or upon existence of a business as distinct from a personal or purely tax purpose.

Obviously, it is improper to build a house of cards, to manufacture evidence; reasons given must be genuine, and the lawyer must search his conscience and be extremely careful to avoid misleading camouflage. But you would feel free, would you not, to advise on the law, the factual record, and possible amendments to the plan that would strengthen the tax position?

Purposes and motives are often by their nature elusive, and experience shows that clients often need help in thinking out and articulating their own real objectives. But, do you not agree that one must be very careful to avoid feeding motives into a tax-conscious client's mind? In the zeal of the undertaking, it is very easy to cross the dividing line without recognizing it, and we tax practitioners may not always tread carefully enough in these matters.

Tax Return Problems

Lawyers engaged in tax practice are often confronted with problems of another type — problems relating to tax returns. These may arise in a variety of situations, as illustrated by the following.

I.

A client confidentially asks you for legal advice concerning a clearly taxable income item that he inadvertently omitted from his income tax return, filed six months previously, with the preparation and filing of which you had nothing to do.

Should not your advice be to file an amended return, or, if the client were a corporation or other taxpayer subject to annual audit and were not concerned over the running of interest, to put a note in the file to be submitted to the examining agent when he comes in to audit? If the client refuses to heed this advice, does not your responsibility cease?

The attorney-client relationship would appear to prevent you from turning informer, and Treasury Circular No. 230 does not require you to become one. Indeed, this would be true even if the omission had been deliberate and fraudulent, if it be concluded that at the time of the disclosure the fraud was a past and not a prospective or continuing one, disclosed to you in confidence.

II.

Assume the facts of the preceding case, except that in connection with your work as legal adviser to the client on tax matters, the income tax return had been prepared and certified by you or in your office, and the client refuses to authorize you to disclose the information he has given you.

The privileged communications doctrine does not apply to information received and advice given outside the scope of a lawyer's professional employment or to matters handled in other than a legal capacity. Communications with accountants are not privileged, except where the privilege is granted by statute.

Are services in connection with the preparation of a tax return within the scope of a lawyer's professional employment, or are they services of a ministerial or accounting nature rendered in a nonlegal capacity? In my view, if the preparation of the return is incidental to legal consultation and advice, communications in connection therewith should be deemed privileged.

Lawyers customarily prepare documents — contracts, deeds, trust instruments, etc., — in connection with and incidental to their legal work; and the preparation of tax returns, though a proper function of the accountant, is also within the lawyer's field because of the legal questions normally involved in their preparation. However, if you were also a qualified accountant, the answer might be influenced, in states where the privilege is not extended to accountants, by whether you were retained in a legal capacity or simply to prepare tax returns and handle audits in the capacity of a qualified tax accountant.

But, even though confidential communications between attorney and client in such situations are privileged, it has been held that the privilege is inapplicable to information supplied for inclusion in a tax return intended to be filed with the tax authorities, since such information — unlike information furnished as the basis for legal advice — is not intended to be confidential.

Here, you received the information in your legal capacity subsequent to the filing of the return and the privilege applies. Accordingly, you are not free to disclose the information furnished against the client's wishes; and, if you cannot obtain his consent to disclosure, you would face the question whether you should refuse to represent him on audit of the return, or whether to do so would violate your duty under the canons of ethics not to withdraw to the client's detriment except for good cause. Your answer no doubt will be affected by the facts of the case in the light of past experiences with the client. In some cases it may not be an easy matter to decide unless, in keeping with your professional responsibilities as well as your self protection, you can succeed in obtaining his consent to the correction of the omission.

III.

On reviewing your client's income tax return for a prior year, you find he made two unrelated apparent mistakes, one favorable to him and the other favorable to the Government, both honestly made. He asks you to do what you think best in his interests. Would it be proper to raise the favorable item and remain silent on the unfavorable one?

It is of course difficult to be categorical where the balance of considerations depends so much upon the facts. But, broadly speaking, would you agree that the question should be resolved this way: would you have felt bound to disclose the unfavorable item if you had prepared the return in the first instance; if so, is there any justification for not pointing it out later when the favorable one is raised? If you should conclude that omission of the unfavorable item, although involving some risk, was not clearly a mistake and need not have been reported, would it be appropriate to postpone the filing of the refund claim until just before expiration of the statute of limitations, so that, if the Government discovered and raised the unfavorable point upon investigating the claim, it could do no more than offset the claim? The answer may depend upon the particular facts and the degree of doubt the unfavorable item involves. But, are there not situations where, as a precaution, this procedure would be appropriate? Yet, is there not common agreement that, where omission of the unfavorable item represented a clear error, to pursue this course would be too sharp a practice?

IV.

A client engaged in the manufacturing business submits to you for review and approval a federal income tax return reflecting the taxable income of the business, together with a letter from the client's regular auditors stating that in their opinion the return properly reflects taxable income, except that certain expenditures have been taken as current expense deductions which they consider should have been capitalized.

The client concedes that these items are clearly capital in nature but desires to claim them as expense deductions in the hope that, buried in a long list of items, they will not be discovered on audit or, if discovered, will be available to concede in order that the field agent might find an additional tax, which the client believes he would consider a mark to his credit and thereby reduce the likelihood of other unfavorable adjustments. What should you advise?

Is it not clear, there being no doubt as to the law, that you should not advise or encourage action on the basis of what the client may get away with — on the basis of what may slip by on audit, or be available at that time to concede? Indeed, should you not try to discourage the client from reporting on that basis? The practice of deducting items known to be non-deductible is one that I consider quite questionable and that, I regret to say, would be less appealing if the Service through its field agents could convince taxpayers that it does not pay.

V.

You represent the executor of an estate, the assets of which are situated in Michigan, where the decedent long lived, with the exception of a small bank account in California, where the decedent spent a substantial part of his declining years and died. Michigan is certain to regard the decedent as domiciled in Michigan, and there is some possibility that California might assert that his domicile was there, if the question were raised.

If proceedings were instituted to collect the California assets, the question might be raised, and the cost of the proceedings, even though successful, might well exceed the California assets. You are asked to advise whether it would be proper simply to abandon the California assets and do nothing about a possible California claim.

Assuming you are satisfied that any claim of domicile by California would be unfounded, would you not be justified under these facts in abandoning the California assets and making no report to the California tax authorities? If the facts were such that you believed the decedent's last domicile might reasonably be found to be California, would you not feel differently; would there not then be a duty; after pointing out the legal and practical situation as to enforcement and collection of any claim by California, to advise raising the question with California and getting it settled?

On the other hand, can you say you owe no duty to California; that collection of its taxes is its business; that, if it has a claim against assets beyond those in California, it must sally forth and assert it; and that your duty as a Michigan attorney is limited to meeting that claim fairly and truthfully only if raised?

Would your answer to the preceding questions be different if the decedent's California property had been such that California law required the filing of an inheritance tax return regardless of domicile? Should you not then advise the executor to file such a return even though the domicile question might be raised?

Finally, is there any rational basis for a different answer to any of these questions where the out-of-State assets are in Canada, or France, or some other foreign country?

The responsibility of lawyers in respect to taxes of foreign governments, and governments of domestic states other than their own, suggests questions in a seemingly uncharted field. Whether irrationally or not, there is no doubt a tendency to feel less sense of responsibility to such governments than toward one's own State and Nation.

Post Audit Problems

The most common contact lawyers in tax practice have with government officials is in connection with post audit problems, tax settlement negotiations, and litigation. In seeking the most favorable interpretation of the facts and the law applicable to his case, the lawyer can deliberately present the facts and legal precedents in the way calculated to appear most favorable to his client's position, but he must avoid trickery, misrepresentation of fact or law, and concealment of material matters relating to any issue under consideration. Sedulous though he must be in these latter respects, he need not lean over backward to help the Government's case. On this, all of you will no doubt agree.

I.

In preparing a protest for your client against an asserted additional income tax liability for an earlier year, you discover an unrelated weak point in your client's case that the Government has overlooked. He took a deduction for a legal fee for services in a gift tax case, whereas, though it was deductible under a federal District Court decision, an earlier Tax Court decision, affirmed on appeal but not yet reviewed by the Supreme Court, held it was not under the then existing statute. What should you do?

Of course, a weak spot such as this should be taken into account in appraising the desirability of filing the protest and the terms of any settlement, for the weakness may crop up later. But, if the Government overlooks it, and it could have been discovered from a careful examination of the record or by normal inquiry, do you not agree that there is no duty to call the matter to the Government's attention or to urge the client to do so? If the Tax Court decision had also been affirmed by the Supreme Court, would you not then hesitate to protest the disputed point without disclosing this item?

II.

You are retained to prepare a brief for submisison to a court on an unsettled federal tax question. You find clearly pertinent federal tax decisions, some of which might be harmful to your case. You also find an obscure but well reasoned state court decision that might hurt you, and a British court decision of the same sort. Finally, you encounter a line of federal court cases, not pertinent to the Government's present theory in your case, but which might suggest to it a different approach that might prove harmful. Are you obliged to cite all cases you have found that might be harmful to your position?

Would you not say that all considerations dictate that federal tax decisions clearly pertinent should be cited? Would you not agree that as an ethical matter, citation is not required either of the state court and British decisions, even though other unrelated decisions from those jurisdictions are cited? Would not the answer be the same with respect to the potentially harmful federal tax decisions unrelated to the Government's theory of the case, particularly if you can conclude that these decisions are not clearly ones the court should consider in deciding the case? Would you not feel somewhat less responsibility with reference to this last proviso if the brief were for submission to the Internal Revenue Service and not to a court?

The opinion by Chief Justice Vanderbilt in the New Jersey case of *In re Greenberg*, 15 N.J. 132 (1954), a disciplinary proceeding, contains an interesting discussion of the lawyer's responsibilities to the courts in this regard. But, whether the lawyer's obligations to the Internal Revenue Service are as strict as those he owes a court has not been clearly established. But surely he owes no duty to inform it of its own rulings and other administrative decisions.

III.

You have a Tax Court case involving a large business expense deduction issue. A lazy examining agent accepted, without checking, your client's figures as to the amount of the expenses your client paid. The 90-day letter, accepting these figures, is based on the legal ground that the item was not a deductible business expense but a capital expenditure, though the amount of the expenditure is technically put in issue.

During your preparation for trial, you discover there is very real doubt as to the actual amount expended by your client, and you believe it would be extremely difficult to prove the amount claimed if you attempted to do so through witnesses at the trial. What should you do?

Government counsel frequently rely upon the findings of the revenue agents. May you properly ask Government counsel to stipulate the facts accepted by the examining agent, without calling attention to what you know? Do you not agree that this would be clearly improper? Would it not be preferable to arrange with your opponent for a joint investigation into the facts in the hope of arriving, by compromise if necessary, at an agreed statement of facts?

IV.

The executors of an estate of a relatively youthful but wealthy former client retain you to defend against an asserted additional estate tax liability based on a claim that certain inter vivos gifts to the decedent's daughter, slightly less than three years before his accidental death, were made in contemplation of death. You had advised the decedent in connection with the gift, and had explained to him the potential income and estate tax savings from the gift. The decedent then had told you privately and confidentially that, while he wanted to save income taxes and provide some income for his daughter, he did not expect to live very long in view of his family history and that he was primarily interested in the potential saving in estate taxes on his estate. The decedent had not discussed with you what you might say should a question later arise. What should you do?

Is it not clear that you cannot tell the whole story because you cannot disclose what you learned from the confidential communication with your deceased client? This being so, would it not be improper to present arguments in support of the nontestamentary motives while remaining silent as to the testamentary motives?

In these circumstances, since you cannot properly make full disclosure of pertinent facts within your knowledge, should you advise the executors to consult other counsel or should you advise them to concede liability? May you not properly explain the situation to the executors and, if in your opinion the gift was in fact clearly made in contemplation of death, recommend that liability be conceded, otherwise that other counsel be consulted?

Fraud Problems

Defrauders, repentant or otherwise, are entitled to counsel, and the lawyer in tax practice may properly represent them in their legitimate defense or in making full disclosure in an effort to arrive at the best possible settlement. Some lawyers are not experienced in this type of practice. Yet, even such lawyers may get into the periphery of it.

I.

The president and controlling stockholder of a corporation that he has caused to engage in deliberately fraudulent under-reporting of income in the past would now like to make a new start and comes to you for legal advice. If the past fraud is disclosed, the back taxes and penalties technically due are likely to ruin him and the corporation financially, so that the alternatives, as he sees it, are to disclose the past fraud and face practical financial ruin or to remain silent and in business, but be honest in the future. What should your advice be?

Does anyone doubt that under the canons of ethics and Treasury Circular No. 230 you should advise him to disclose and pay up what is due, whatever the consequences? But may you not properly explain to him at the same time the current policy of the Internal Revenue Service with respect to voluntary disclosures and the treatment he may receive upon such disclosure, the possibility that the voluntary disclosure policy of the Service might some day be more lenient, and the probable consequences if before any voluntary disclosure the Service itself should discover the fraud?

This advice having been given, the president returns and informs you he really intends to turn over a new leaf but has decided not to have the corporation make disclosure. Seeking no further advice on the fraud question, he asks you to advise the corporation on a proposed corporate transaction and also to obtain a ruling on it from the Service. What is your duty here?

Is it not clear that you must remain silent as to the fraud? Since the fraud was a past and not a continuing one, knowledge of which was confidentially communicated to you in your professional capacity, its disclosure without the client's consent would seem clearly to violate your profesisonal duty. But, knowing of the fraud, can you advise the corporation on the proposed corporate transaction?

A lawyer in a position to pick and choose clients might decide not to represent a client in the legal position of an unrepentant defrauder, but is there any ethical reason why you should not do so here? Believing that the corporation and its president will act properly in the future, would you not feel free to represent the corporation on these new matters if you wished to do so?

Suppose, however, that if you undertook to seek the Treasury ruling it would be pertinent and necessary to submit to the Service past corporate financial statements, the only statements available being known by you to be incorrect because of the fraud. Is it not clear under Code section 7206(2) and Treasury Circular No. 230 that you cannot undertake that assignment? After explaining to the client why you cannot do it, would you not hesitate to go so far as to suggest another lawyer innocent of your knowledge? And, if another lawyer were retained and were to ask you why you withdrew, must you not withhold your reason?

Lobbying and Influence Problems

I.

Your services are sought for the purpose of engineering tax legislation through Congress for the benefit of the client. May you properly undertake that assignment?

Apart from the question of personal taste or suitability for such matters, I am confident you will agree with this: acceptance of such a retainer is entirely proper under the canons of ethics if you comply with the lobbying law and do not conceal your relationship or use improper influence. But, if you accept the retainer, you should affirmatively disclose your status to those whom you seek to persuade.

II.

The client whom you are representing in a federal tax case proposes to pursue the influence route and wants to retain in the case an out-and-out politician-lawyer, clearly not qualified to help on a technical basis, in an effort to influence a favorable settlement through high level contacts. What should your position be?

Normally, should you not first endeavor to dissuade the client by pointing out to him the dangers of such associations and the probable futility of indulging in such things? If he persists, would you not, in the absence of special circumstances, normally feel obliged for your own protection to withdraw from the case? And would you not normally withdraw even though, in the then existing climate of things, you cannot be too sure that, however unlikely, the politician-lawyer would not somehow produce a better result than you might be able to obtain?

Fee Problems

I.

During the year you rendered legal services to an individual client the fees for which will be partly deductible by him (because they pertain to his investment or business affairs or tax advice) and partly not deductible (because they relate to the execution of a will or some other personal matter). How far can you go in loading the fee for the deductible items and lightening the fee for the others?

A lawyer does not work by the clock, and his fees are dependent on many factors, including the time spent, results accomplished, the importance, novelty and difficulty of the matter, custom, and the client's views. He may at times even work without fee. It seems clear that he need not automatically apportion his total charge according to the relative hours spent on all these matters and that he is fully entitled to differentiate on the basis of the above factors, including the factor of tax deductibility.

But, would you not say that, whatever you may charge in respect of the nondeductible items, you should not be influenced by the tax consideration to the extent of charging more for services in respect of the deductible items than can fairly be justified therefor? The Government thus far usually accepts the lawyer's word as to the allocation of his fees; it would be most unfortunate if the time should ever come when his word will not be acceptable.

II.

Your client, suspecting that he might dislike any allocation you might make, requests that you simply bill him for services rendered, without description or itemization of any kind, thinking that this might serve him better. Would you see any objection to your doing this?

Your answer may be influenced by whether this would be a departure from your general custom, or your prior custom with the client, or by whether you knew or suspected what he had in mind. But, generally speaking, is not the ethical problem here simply one of avoiding any statement that would mislead the ordinary examining agent and deter him from inquiring into the facts? Or, have you an affirmative duty beyond that? This type of problem may be more acute where a large part of the services was rendered to a controlling corporate stockholder who desires the corporation to be billed.

Problems of Public Responsibility

I.

Your client informs you that, in connection with the audit of his income tax return, the examining agent has distinctly suggested that he would concede a disputed item and close the case if the client would hand him a round-trip ticket to Florida, and he asks you whether he should simply decline the suggestion or report to the authorities.

Is it your duty to advise the client to inform on the agent and to co-operate in efforts to trap him if requested to do so? Assuming you so advise in the belief that it is a public duty to do so, and that the client refuses to act himself, but waives any attorney-client privilege, is there then an affirmative duty on your part to report to the agent's superiors? Would the answer be the same in the unlikely event that the agent made the suggestion directly to you?

If your answers to these questions are in the affirmative, as I believe in crystal-clear cases they should be, do tax practitioners generally perform such duty? Is this essentially a matter of one's own sense of social responsibility, or is it more than that — a matter of professional responsibility as I am inclined to consider it? No rule or regulation apparently requires reporting of fraudulent or criminal suggestions, however clear, but without the co-operation of taxpayers or their advisers the policing of tax administration would be most difficult.

II.

A body of public spirited citizens asks you to join with them in signing a petition urging upon Congress a reform in the tax law that you believe to be much needed but that, if adopted, might seriously adversely affect some of your clients. What should you do?

Would you not consider yourself free to join in urging the reform, if you believe in it and it would not conflict with your duty to any client in any matter in which you have been retained? On the other hand, even though there were no such conflict, might you not properly conclude that you would be fully justified in remaining silent, if you believe you would get into difficulties with one or more clients by joining in the appeal; the importance of lending your name to the appeal might not outweigh the damage to your client relationships. I feel sure you will agree, however, that, generally speaking, a lawyer ought to try to participate in those things that he thinks are useful in the public interest; and ordinarily clients do not take offense at this.

Closing Observations

May I conclude with a few general observations. I question the notion that, where his adversary is the Treasury, the lawyer need give less than full devotion to his duty to his client because of a larger duty he owes to the Government or his fellow citizens. I believe the lawyer surely owes no less devotion to his duty to a taxpayer, who is his client, than he owes to a criminal whom he undertakes to defend. Both are entitled to full legal representation.

Yet, with respect to ordinary, everyday, administrative tax practice, especially where a crystallized controversy headed for the courts is not involved, there may be differences in shading or degree. The questions here are perplexing, and the area is one especially in need of further study and clarification.

It may be suggested, on the one hand, that the obligation of candor and fairness, involving the disclosure of distressing things, should be more strict and rigid when it runs to a court — a judicial umpire whom not even silence should be permitted to mislead — than when it runs to the Treasury which through its representatives of varying attitudes and qualifications is in the equivocal position of investigator, claimant, and administrative judge. On the other hand, it may be thought that this obligation of the lawyer should be at least as, if not more, strict and rigid when he is facing the Treasury, the thought here being that a tax matter is not simply a matter between taxpayer and Treasury but between taxpayer and the Treasury and other taxpayers.

To be broadly categorical about this, one way or the other, seems inappropriate because circumstances, settings, and opposition attitudes vary widely, and these may affect the extent of the lawyer's obligation.

But one thing I should like to emphasize. It may well be that some day persons performing so vital a function as those of the tax practitioner in the operation of our self-assessing, national, income tax system will more generally recognize, as I believe they should, and as many already do, that their work is affected with the public interest and, leaving aside responsibilities to clients with respect to issues joined in battle, will more freely accept a high level of responsibility for leadership in the co-operative effort necessary to the successful operation of the system. Such co-operation may be vital if the system, which is dependent for enforcement primarily upon voluntary compliance and not police state methods, is to survive as other than a deplorable muddle, destroying the moral stamina of our citizens by teaching or stimulating them to cheat.

If this be so, it means that the tax practitioner, while continuously struggling to keep his own tax house strictly in order, must try to develop qualities of leadership and help to educate and influence clients to conduct themselves in their tax affairs as honorably and ethically as the adviser would himself act under similar circumstances.

In most taxpayers, ourselves included, there is a tendency toward a little larceny when it comes to taxation, though none of us would think of stealing a cent from or deliberately hurting our friends. This natural tendency is nurtured whenever tax officials, also human, seem to act in an overzealous and partisan fashion, and it thrives in an atmosphere of distrust of the fairness of the tax law. For these if for no other reasons, may not the tax practitioner be charged with the further duty I mentioned at the outset, namely, a duty to do what he can to help make the tax law more fair, practical, and equitable, and to improve its administration?

I have the impression that during recent years there has been a considerable improvement in the tax practitioner's sense of public responsibility. The increased attention at tax practitioners' gatherings to ethical problems in tax practice indicates to me a growing interest in such problems. The increasing number of lawyers in tax practice who give time and energy toward helping improve the technical provisions of the tax law and its administration, and who try to do so dispassionately, indicates to me a growing sense of duty to society. It must be conceded, however, that in these respects there is much still to be desired, and further that with rare exceptions lawyers who specialize in taxation have not individually in their private capacities stepped forward to exercise notable leadership in informing or guiding the public on broad controversial questions of tax policy. It may be that this is largely because such lawyers have been so preoccupied with the ever increasing technical intricacies of modern taxation that they not only have become accustomed but feel compelled to devote themselves to tax techniques at the expense of broad tax policy. It may also be partly because the organized bar wisely tries to avoid taking sides on controversial tax policy questions not within the lawyer's special competence. But, perhaps the day will come when the individual lawyer in the tax field will find it possible, as a community leader, to render a more useful service in the larger area not unlike that of his professional brethren who in the past individually contributed so much to the development and understanding of our National Constitution and the intelligent solution of the political problems of their day.

Recent signs of progress toward recognition of greater public responsibility on the part of lawyers generally are not lacking. The large 1958 Conference at Arden House on continuing legal education for professional competence and responsibility about which you may well have heard, and the smaller 1960 meetings at Le Chateau in the Savoy Hilton Hotel in New York, about which you may not have heard and out of which has come a plan for promoting a new organization, since created but not yet implemented, entitled Council on Education of the Bar for Public Responsibility, indicate a reawakened professional interest in developing qualities for public responsibilities in lawyers generally.

It is hoped that these and other initial steps will lead to a challenge, and an opportunity for larger service, that the bar, including members specializing in tax practice, will strive to meet.

8. Responsibility of the Tax Adviser
Thomas J. Graves

Many of the tax institutes conducted during the last year have presented serious discussions of the responsibilities of the tax adviser. There has been so much discussion that the casual observer could not be blamed for misjudging its implications and perhaps being led to a false conclusion that the observance of ethical standards by lawyers and certified public accountants leaves much to be desired. While we know that the professional adviser undertakes a heavy burden when he engages in Federal tax practice, and we feel the need to weigh that burden from time to time in order to be sure it is thoroughly understood, we should be careful that these discussions do not create misconceptions as to our acceptance of the standards of responsibility under which we operate.

If the nature of this responsibility seems at times to be difficult to define, it is because of the complexities that stem from the conflicting interests of those served by the tax adviser. His primary responsibility is to his client, whose interests must be protected. At the same time, it is essential that he and his client deal fairly with the public, whose interests are embodied in the tax-collecting machinery of the Treasury Department. Since the taxpaying objectives of the client are likely to be in conflict with the tax-collecting objectives of the Treasury, it should be apparent that the problems of meeting this burden of responsibility may not result as much from a failure to develop workable standards of practice as they do from the natural frictions caused by the conflict of adverse interests. In addition, the practitioner has another responsibility — to his contemporaries (and to himself) — to discharge his duties in such a way as to bring credit to his profession and enhance its position in our society.

Responsibilities may be misunderstood

Unfortunately, the nature of these responsibilities and the problems faced in meeting them are not always understood. There are some who seem to blame all of the problems of the tax system, of which there certainly are many, on the tax adviser — the CPA and the attorney who engage in tax work. For example, in a speech before the Senate on May 26, 1961, Senator Douglas said:

> We all know that our present tax system has so many loopholes or "truck" holes that certain favored groups are able to escape taxation on large parts of their income. These exemptions are steadily widened by legislation and perhaps even more by the rise of two well-paid new professions, namely tax lawyers and tax accountants. These gentlemen help citizens avoid and, in some cases, evade the payment of taxes which in all good conscience they should pay. A bewildering variety of tax "gimmicks" and arguments are developed with which the revenue officials and the courts are either unable or unwilling to cope. All this has been sanctioned by sage counsel which I have heard promulgated from this body, and from even more august quarters, that it is a patriotic duty for a citizen to pay as little taxes as possible.

This is typical of comments that appear from time to time. While they do not suggest that the adviser is legally wrong when he helps a client reduce his tax burden, they imply that there may be something morally reprehensible about his activities.

There are others who, with the best intentions, seem to suggest that if the tax practitioner will meet his responsibilities resolutely and with an unwavering enthusiasm to seek the best solutions in the interest of all concerned, he will create such an aura of fairness and reasonableness in the operation of the tax system as to make it acceptable to those who are now rebelling against it. This approach would have the tax adviser reach out for a responsibility to make the tax laws work. It has validity, but it fails to recognize that he bears only a part of the burden of a system that is creating irresponsibility largely through its frustrations and inequities.

If our tax system is not working as perfectly as its creators and administrators would expect, a great deal of the blame can be laid to the grotesque law they have created and to overly competitive administration of that law in the past.

Problem of taxpayer integrity

It is time to consider the possibility that the problem of tax evasion is not so much one of inadequacies or imperfections in the standards of responsibility observed by tax advisers as it is an indication that normal standards of integrity are not being observed by taxpayers in their response to their tax obligations. If the increasing recognition by the press and by public commentators of "tax cheating" can fairly be said to indicate that "cheating" has become a serious problem in recent years, it should be recognized that this development may reflect a public attitude that seems to apply a different standard of integrity where questions of taxation are involved. Our people normally are honest and law-abiding. If there is evidence that they are departing from their normal habits when discharging their tax obligations, perhaps more attention should be given to the reasons.

The enforcement problems with which we are concerned may be mere symptoms of the development of a situation in which normal moral sanctions are not being applied to deviations from appropriate standards of propriety. Thus, in discussing the responsibilities of the tax adviser (as important as they may be), we may be concentrating on what is only a small part of a more basic problem — an increasing lack of confidence in the fairness of our tax system.

Perhaps this is unavoidable when tax rates go as high as they are today. The trend is likely to continue, however, unless we reverse it by revising the tax structure, which is viewed by so many as being oppressive, and by avoiding any tendency to overly aggressive administration of that structure. Real tax reform would probably do more than anything else to reduce the problem of tax evasion.

It is heartening to see that while Commissioner Caplin has taken the lead in examining problems of integrity and responsibility, he also has given attention to the importance of evenhandedness in the administration of the Internal Revenue laws. For example, in a recent message to all audit personnel of the Service he stated:

> . . . a reasonable, practical, common-sense approach is not inconsistent with a vigorous, effective enforcement program and, in fact, will go far toward increasing confidence of the taxpayer in our administration of the tax laws. . . .
> Our attitude should be one of proper and reasonable appraisal of the merits of the issue. We must not allow our decisions to be unduly influenced by the potential tax adjustment involved; we should never adopt a superior attitude; nor should we take advantage of the taxpayer's technical ignorance.

This approach is to be applauded. The Commissioner is doing his best to change attitudes of long standing. We all hope that he succeeds.

Role of the tax adviser

At the same time the tax adviser has an important role to play in maintaining public confidence in the tax system and in raising the level of integrity of the public in its compliance with the tax laws. He can do this by observing appropriate standards of responsibility in conducting his tax practice. He can do it also by helping taxpayers understand the difference between what is right and what is wrong. Certainly a well-advised taxpayer is more likely to observe good standards than one who is ill-advised and, being uninformed, feels himself free to take refuge in his own subjective views of what the law might be.

The frequent discussions of the responsibilities of the tax adviser may have created the impression that our standards of responsibility are inadequate. That certainly is not the case. As far as certified public accountants are concerned, while some of the rules they observe may need interpretation for the sake of clarity and emphasis, there should be no question as to their adequacy.

Even some CPAs have confused this need for further clarification with an assumption that existing rules do not provide guides to the resolution of problems that arise in the day-to-day conduct of our work. They have so emphasized the possible improvements as to imply that the level of the standards applicable to tax practice may be too low. For example, there has been concern with the obvious inapplicability to tax practice of those portions of the Code of Professional Ethics of the American Institute of Certified Public Accountants that deal with the examination and presentation of financial statements. Actually, the requirements of the tax return jurat and the rules governing practice before the Treasury Department (Circular No. 230) set standards for the enrolled practitioner that are at least as stringent as the standards set by the Code of Professional Ethics.

There is no real question whether our Code applies to tax practice. It does. However, there is no evidence of an intent to apply to tax work those rules that were designed to deal with the problems of accountants' reports on financial statements. Thus, there should be no question of a failure to observe the Code of Professional Ethics when a CPA does not express an independent opinion as to the conformity of a tax return with generally accepted accounting principles.

It seems evident that a tax return is not a financial statement in the sense of our Code and was never intended to be so regarded. An income tax return is exactly what its name implies — a return of information as to income that has been used as a basis for the self assessment of tax on the person who makes it.

Basic Areas of Professional Responsibility

What are the responsibilities that a certified public accountant undertakes when he engages in tax practice? It would be helpful to get an understanding of them before considering specific rules.

Responsibility to clients

A CPA's primary responsibility is to his client. He must see to it that his client pays his proper tax under the law, but no more than that. While a taxpayer has a moral obligation to support his government, the specific provisions of the tax law are not derived from moral law, or even from the law of equity. They were devised by Congress and they can be changed by Congress if they do not serve their purpose well. No taxpayer is charged with a responsibility, either moral or legal, to accept more of a burden than has been laid upon him by Congress. In determining the extent of his burden, it is clear that the taxpayer has the right to resolve questionable points in his favor.

This means that a CPA should assist the taxpayer-client in his tax affairs as a protector of his interests. In this respect the traditional independence of the CPA is tempered in his tax work by his primary responsibility to his client. He must observe the same standards of truthfulness and integrity as he is required to observe in any other professional work, and he must be independent in the sense that he is not swayed from those standards. But he is not expected to approach uncertain tax questions with the same lack of bias that he must apply in expressing an opinion on the fairness of presentation of a financial statement.

A CPA is under no obligation to act as though he is an arm of the Government. In fact, the workings of our tax system are such that the taxpayer would be denied needed assistance if his advisers were to attempt an independent resolution of all issues in which the interests of the taxpayer and the Government are adverse.

Responsibility to the public

The CPA is very conscious of his responsibility to his client. Yet, at times in his tax work, this responsibility seems to conflict with his responsibility to the public, represented for this purpose by the Treasury Department and the Internal Revenue Service in their administration of the Internal Revenue laws. Actually there should be no conflict. In doing tax work for his client, the CPA has a clear obligation to observe the requirements of the Internal Revenue laws and regulations. This means that he must accept the responsibility imposed upon him by the jurat on the returns he prepares and, if he is an enrolled agent, he must observe the Treasury Department's rules of practice.

His own Code of Professional Ethics requires the CPA to bring the highest moral standards to his activities in the tax field. When he is charged with "maintaining high standards of personal conduct" and with avoiding "an act discreditable to the profession," he has the obligation to be governed by general moral principles as well as by the sanctions of the special rules that cover his activities. Thus it seems clear that he must observe not only the letter but also the spirit of the Treasury's rules of practice.

Responsibility to profession

In a sense a CPA's responsibility to the public is the same as his responsibility to his profession and to himself. There is more to being a member of a profession than just being competent and winning public recognition of that competence. The essence of a profession is dedication to responsible service to others. The professional man has a responsibility to his fellows to maintain the highest standards of morality and integrity in his professional activities.

SPECIFIC GUIDANCE IN TAX WORK

Obligations imposed by tax return jurat

In the CPA's preparation of Federal income tax returns, next in importance to his own Code of Ethics is the obligation, accepted by the preparer in signing the tax return jurat, to state that the return is "true, correct, and complete" to the best of his knowledge "based on all information of which he has any knowledge."

In attempting to measure this obligation, the really significant question is what is meant by the word "knowledge" when used in this context. In other words, is information of which the preparer has any knowledge limited to the information furnished him in response to his specific questions, or does it include also the possible implications of that information and of other information that has come to his attention? When the preparer has reason to believe that the facts are not complete or not what they seem, but does not actually know that this is the case, is he under an obligation to make further inquiries?

The CPA's answer to these questions seems obvious. Although he is not required to make an audit, an informed evaluation of the implications of the available information certainly is his ethical responsibility. He may not have to investigate everything that is furnished to him, but he is obliged to make reasonable inquiries if he has any reason to believe that the available information is not "true, correct, and complete." Good practice requires that the word "knowledge" of the jurat be interpreted in this way.

The deduction of business expenses of the individual taxpayer provides examples of how this interpretation should be applied. If he is guilty of a deliberate misstatement in providing information for his return, it is clear that the misinformation cannot be used. The same would be true of arbitrarily increased deductions designed to permit some disallowances and still leave him an acceptable net allowance.

On the other hand, where the taxpayer proposes the deduction of a blanket or round amount, substantiation may not be possible. Good tax practice would require inquiry by the CPA into the circumstances that would indicate the propriety of the claimed expenditure. If the inquiry results in a satisfactory explanation, there would be no basis under present rules for the CPA to refuse to include the information in the return he is preparing. This is particularly true where there is reasonable secondary evidence available.

There should be no implication that the CPA is under an obligation to investigate and verify the authenticity of all information furnished him for inclusion in a return. It should be made clear, however, if it is not clear now, that he is not warranted in ignoring indications that something might be wrong with the figures given to him.

The CPA cannot turn away and deliberately fail to recognize the obvious implications of the things he sees. That is what Circular 230 means when it refers to "due diligence." Strict observance of the spirit of the existing rules is all that is needed to solve any problems as to the standards to be observed in tax practice. There is no real room for subjective rationalization.

Rules of practice before the IRS

Treasury Department Circular No. 230 states the rules governing the practice of enrolled agents before the Internal Revenue Service. It presents a statement of duties and restrictions for enrolled attorneys and agents, including a listing of thirty-one specific forms of disreputable conduct. The prohibitions of the Circular are stated clearly and cover the full range of problems of responsibility that might arise in the conduct of a CPA's tax practice. As a body of rules they leave little to be desired. The problem seems to lie in the infrequent occasions when they are ignored and, to some extent, in the excessively subjective way in which some practitioners may attempt to interpret them.

Although preparing returns and furnishing information at the request of Internal Revenue agents are not considered practice before the Service (10.2(b)),[1] and enrollment is not necessary for either of those activities, enrolled agents and attorneys who do prepare returns are subject in their performance of that work to the duties and restrictions prescribed by the rules of practice and to all the prohibitions against disreputable conduct. A violation of the rules subjects the enrollee to possible reprimand, disbarment, or suspension from practice before the Service.

The impact of these rules can be illustrated best by explaining their application to a few typical problems.

1. *Diligence as to accuracy (10.24(a))*. One of the rules requires that the enrolled agent exercise due diligence in preparing or assisting in the preparation of returns. The first impression might be that this conflicts with our understanding that the jurat does not require a detailed investigation of information included in a return on the basis of the knowledge of the preparer. It is evident from a careful reading of the due diligence requirement, however, that the diligence is to be applied to the preparation of the return and not in an investigation of the knowledge furnished by the taxpayer.

This interpretation is supported by the language of the third of the listed acts of disreputable conduct, which is the preparation of a false Federal return if there is knowledge that the return being prepared is false. This concept, the "knowledge" of the preparer, is found throughout the Rules of Practice. It is the key to their interpretation. As in the case of the tax return jurat, an absence of direct "knowledge" does not permit ignoring indirect indications that information presented by a taxpayer may be false or misleading.

[1]This and similar succeeding references are to paragraphs of Circular No. 230.

2. *Willful failure to follow regulations.* Since the income tax regulations may have the force of law, willful failure to observe them in the preparation of a tax return may constitute the preparation of a false return. It is common practice, however, where there is a basis for contending that the regulations themselves are not valid, to take a contrary position and disclose that position in the return prepared. While this is an accepted practice and should not result in the assertion of a negligence penalty, the disclosure is essential if a charge of willful failure to follow the regulations is to be avoided.

It is not necessary to reveal every possible point of difference in interpreting the tax effect of facts that are the basis for positions taken in a return. This is true also of an unsettled question of law if the Code and regulations do not specify the appropriate treatment. Where there are unsettled questions of this type, the related accounting data may be placed in the return in a normal way. For example, where a deduction is claimed for repairs that possibly could be subject to a capitalization, if there is a reasonable factual basis for concluding that the expenditures actually are deductible, there is no obligation to list questionable items separately or to include a description of the circumstances in the return.

On the other hand, deliberate hiding of an item that might be questioned suggests an element of falseness in the representations made. Certainly questionable repair expenditures should not be removed from their normal place in the accounts and included with some other item to enhance the possibility that they will not be reviewed. Hiding and mislabeling may be as serious an infraction of the rules as deliberate filing of false and misleading information (10.51 (b)(9)).

3. *Failure to sign (10.51(b)(14)).* If a false return is prepared, the failure of the preparer to sign it will not help him avoid the rules. Advising or aiding in the preparation of a false return is also an act of disreputable conduct. In fact the regulations as to procedure (1.6065-1(b)) require that the preparer sign a return prepared for a taxpayer for compensation or as an incident to the performance of other services.

What is the position of a practitioner who prepares a draft of a correct return for his client and makes it available to the client, knowing in the course of the preparation that the client intends to take the correct draft and revise it, falsifying some portion of the information that will be filed? Regardless of any rationalization, if this is done it too would seem to constitute aiding in the preparation of a false return.

4. *Knowledge of client's omissions (10.23).* A difficult problem may arise when a return has been prepared and filed in good faith but it develops later that there was an error or omission that affected the tax liability. If this happens, the enrolled agent has a responsibility to advise the client promptly that the return was wrong. However, he is not required to advise the Internal Revenue Service. In fact, advising the Service would violate the confidential relationship between a CPA and his client and would be contrary to Rule 1.03 of the American Institute's Code of Professional Ethics.

Most taxpayers will want to correct errors, either immediately or when the return is examined by an agent. Where the taxpayer decides to avoid correction, however, and where the error or omission is material, even though not intentional, the CPA should consider withdrawing from the engagement. Of course, if a CPA finds that a taxpayer's error was intentional, he should advise the taxpayer of the possibility of criminal prosecution and should suggest that he consult an attorney immediately.

Suggestions for the Future

What should CPAs do to clarify and emphasize the standards of the profession in the tax field?

Perhaps our main failure is that we have not made sufficiently clear our unqualified acceptance of the implications and requirements of the tax return jurat and the rules of practice, as well as our own Code of Professional Ethics. Our professional organizations have been unusually successful in delineating our responsibilities in other areas of our practice, but there is little in our literature that indicates our general acceptance in tax practice of the approach I have described. Yet it is clear to me from my discussions with certified public accountants throughout the country that they do subscribe unqualifiedly to these principles.

It would be helpful if the American Institute of Certified Public Accountants would develop formal interpretations of some of the requirements of the jurat and of Circular No. 230. While they are not our rules, in the sense that we did not prepare them, we must observe them in our tax practice. Our subcommittee on responsibilities in tax practice has been working at this task for some time. It should not be unreasonable to expect that in the near future we will have authoritative statements of the standards of inquiry, disclosure, and performance to be applied by CPAs in tax practice.

Another constructive step would be to change the form of jurat so that it would reveal to the Internal Revenue Service the extent of the work done when information is collected for the preparation of a return. Such a jurat might read:

> I declare under the penalties of perjury that this return (including any accompanying schedules and statements) is, to the best of my knowledge and belief, a true, correct, and complete return, based on all the information of which I have knowledge. Information included in the return was obtained in connection with (check one):
> _____ An examination of the accounting records of the taxpayer in accordance with generally accepted auditing standards;
> _____ A limited examination of the accounting records of the taxpayer;
> _____ Information furnished by the taxpayer or obtained from the accounting records of the taxpayer without audit.

The Institute's committee on Federal taxation suggested this type of jurat to the Internal Revenue Service in 1954 but it was not adopted, apparently because of the opposition of other groups. The committee is studying this suggestion again. If it is renewed, and if the Service still is unwilling to adopt it, consideration might be given to changing our Code of Professional Ethics to require similar disclosures on all tax returns prepared by CPAs.

9. Does the Tax Practitioner Owe a Dual Responsibility to his Client and to the Government? — The Theory   *Mark H. Johnson*

Almost any practicing lawyer's instinctive reaction to this question is a fervent "No." Since I do not pretend to be anything but an old-fashioned lawyer, that is my own answer, even after considerable thought. Nevertheless, I believe that the question is worth a great deal of thought.

Several respectable and responsible persons have lately been asking some disquieting questions. Are we sentimentally defending an outworn morality with anachronistic shibboleths? Or, worse, are we cynically defending a code of convenience as the product of sacred professional obligations? We owe it to ourselves, as well as to the community, to reexamine some basic attitudes which we have come to take for granted, in order to see whether they have any basic validity.

It is appropriate that today's session began with the question of *taxpayer* morality, because an understanding of the taxpayer's own obligations necessarily precedes any analysis of his adviser's. The basic starting point is our system of self-assessment and voluntary compliance, which everyone seems to agree is worth preserving and fostering. Voluntary compliance, in turn, must be backed up by a system of effective enforcement; so that each taxpayer is confident that his neighbor is also paying his own fair share of the total tax burden. Both voluntary compliance and fair enforcement must be built upon a code of law. It is obvious that compliance, by its very nature, cannot be predicated upon some vague concept of equity or fairness. No taxpayer can be asked to pay a tax which he considers to be "fair" under some abstract code of morality. An absolute requisite is a rule book—a written set of rules whose meaning is reasonably clear and explicit. Conversely, the existence of a rule book is the only assurance we can ever have for a fair *enforcement* of our tax system. The alternative to a rule of law is, as always, a rule of men; and if we give to our tax collectors the duty, and the power, to collect *their* concept of a "fair" or "reasonable" tax, we are inviting the pattern of extortion, bribery, and political favoritism which is so common in other corners of the world.

Now, ideally, the rule book should itself be completely equitable; it should not create favoritism or discrimination among different classes of taxpayers who are really similarly situated. Even more important, however, there should be clear and explicit rules to assure that all taxpayers who are obviously in the same class should be taxed alike. But, as our economy grows more and more complicated, and as the government's share of our income and wealth grows greater and greater, these clear and explicit rules become more and more a lovely dream. The process is familiar enough to all of us in this room: the equitable exemption here, the loophole-closer there, and the statute proliferates into a labyrinth in which the average citizen is lost.

It is here that we can shift our focus from the taxpayer to his adviser, because it is precisely here that the political role of the lawyer and the accountant becomes clear. Subjectively, of course, the professional tax expert is simply trying to earn his living by helping his own particular clients—by explaining the intricacies of the law, by advising courses of action and predicting the results, and by fighting for his client's rights if the tax collector disagrees. The by-product of this activity, however, is a remarkably coherent, uniform, and equitable body of law. Let me emphasize that this last statement is meant without any irony or sarcasm: we *do* have, contrary to periodic campaign oratory, a remarkably coherent, uniform, and equitable tax system. I know full well that many of us here could write a frightening list of traps for the unwary and of loopholes for the sophisticated. But those lists are formidable only in close-up; if we step back and view them in perspective, we see that they are just little bumps and scratches on a pretty smooth landscape. And our own system is as good as it is, primarily because we have a body of experts upon whom our citizenry relies.

But why, someone may ask, do we not instead concentrate on getting a better Treasury Department? Surely, if we would give our underpaid officials a reasonable fraction of the fees earned by our more successful private practitioners, we could count upon a superb group of intelligent, informed, and dedicated public servants. Could we not collectively, through our government, finance such a group, and thus buy for ourselves a truly fair and uniform tax system without all the wasteful uncertainty and controversy of our present system?

I realize that no one in this sophisticated audience would ask that naive question, but a couple of years ago I had to answer very nearly that question to a group of earnest and intelligent tax administrators of a foreign country which was trying to emulate our own system. The question went something like this: "Tax collection is the very lifeblood of a government. We now have a democratic tax system which is practical and equitable. We are staffing our tax offices with the ablest young people in the country, and we are giving them an intensive education in the tax law. We are writing fair and reasonable regulations, and we are doing our best to make our system work right for everybody. Why, then, should we encourage an outside group of accountants and lawyers who will argue with us, and confuse the issues, and upset everything? What has the government to gain by even tolerating such a group? Why do *you* do that in the United States?"

It took a while for the answer to come to me, but then it was crystal clear. I had to say, "Because the people don't trust you." The difference, actually, is between the people collectively as a citizenry, and the individual citizens as separate taxpayers. Collectively, the people may be convinced that they have elected an efficient and fair-minded administration; they may even believe that the administrators are paragons of intelligence, industry, and virtue. Individually, however, each taxpayer knows that he has an interest adverse to that of the government; he knows that the government, as the representative of the collective taxpayers, must often take a position to his own individual detriment. He knows that, if he is to assert his own rights, he cannot ask the advice and assistance of a person whose first loyalty is to the government.

All of us here can think of hundreds of areas of potential conflict in something as inherently complex as an income tax. Let us take one simple example. John Doe estimates that he spent at least $1,000 last year on business entertainment, but he has receipts and records for less than half. The revenue authorities have decided, because of widespread cheating on these items, that the best public policy is to disallow all expenses which are not specifically proven. What is Mr. Doe to do? If he asks advice at the revenue office, he will probably be told to deduct what he has receipts for. He may even get a polite explanation for that advice. Now, John Doe may sympathize with the Commissioner of Internal Revenue, but he wants individual justice. He wants advice from someone who is worried about *him*, not about an over-all enforcement problem. And so he goes to his own expert, who sifts the facts and advises him that he can reasonably prove about $850 of expenses; and the expert's advice is to deduct $850. The taxpayer in this case will likely follow that advice, in the knowledge that this is the *right* thing to do, and with the further comfort that he will have a responsible advocate if he is challenged.

There are, of course, several obvious alternatives. He may deduct $1,000 on the theory that this is what he *believes* to be right, and on the chance that his return will not be examined. Or he may deduct $2,000 on the theory that a revenue agent will be satisfied with a 50% disallowance. Or he may deduct $5,000 on the theory that he can afford to bribe the revenue agent and still come out ahead. Now all of these alternatives are sometimes adopted—occasionally, I am told, even with the advice or consent of an expert. But at least the last of these alternatives is, I believe, relatively rare. There are other countries, however, where that alternative is the accepted norm. And, inevitably, those are the countries which lack the tradition of legal advice for tax liabilities.

Whether it is by instinct or by tradition I do not pretend to know, but most taxpayers seem to be satisfied to pay their correct tax, *provided* they are satisfied that they are not paying a cent more than they have to. Moreover, there seems to be a certain psychic satisfaction in being able to *do* something about one's tax liability—to take advantage of some election or choice, or to reduce the tax by some advance planning. When the low-bracket taxpayer complains of the rich man's "loopholes," he is not really dissatisfied with the relative over-all tax rates; he is envious of the rich man's supposed maneuverability, and he has a kind of claustrophobia in his own tax trap. Parenthetically, I may note that for this very reason I have come to suspect the psychic validity of our short-form returns and standard deductions: I wonder whether it is not worth the trouble to give even the low-bracket taxpayer the satisfaction of specific deductions.

At any rate, then, the average taxpayer is willing to pay the tax imposed upon him by law, provided that he has the benefit of all doubts and of all choices. If he can receive expert advice which he trusts, he will follow that advice. If he does not, he will use a do-it-yourself kit of his own. It is this latter prospect at which we should all shudder—not as tax experts who will be done out of fees, but as citizens facing the breakdown of our voluntary compliance system. It is vital for us to distinguish between tax avoidance under a system of respectable expert advice, and the wholesale tax evasion which would be accomplished by a skeptical and unadvised citizenry. Right now, all the highly publicized tax avoidance gadgets amount to a narrow strip of gray between the accepted blacks and whites of the law. That small blemish on the purity of our tax structure is indeed a slight price to pay for keeping the black and the white as separate as they are; the alternative could be one large smudge of dirty gray.

Since the absolute condition to a taxpayer's compliance is his confidence in his expert's advice, the whole community has a stake in instilling that confidence. First, we must see to it that there is an adequate supply of experts. We should do our best to make sure that they are *real* experts, and not hacks and quacks. We should try to increase the undergraduate tax schooling for lawyers and accountants, and we should make available the best and most extensive postgraduate courses, lectures, and institutes that we can devise. Then, from the opposite direction, we should make strenuous efforts to keep the tax law within the bounds of comprehensibility. It is too late now even to hope for a code which the average business man can cope with, but at the very least we should stop writing statutes that even genuine experts cannot be sure they understand. And, finally, and most important, we must assure the taxpayer that the advice he gets is being directed to his own best interest. He must feel sure that he is not getting the advice of a conscientious revenue agent, nor even the advice of a conscientious Tax Court judge. He must know that he is getting the advice of his own counselor and advocate. He must know, in other words, that his adviser is in his own corner, and is not in the middle of the ring as a referee. Only then can the taxpayer be expected to be trustful enough to throw away his own tip sheets and stifle his own protective instincts.

If that is the kind of advice that the taxpayer is entitled to expect, then that is the kind of advice that the adviser is obligated to give. After all, professional ethics are largely a matter of honesty, and honesty in turn is a matter of performance in accordance with one's promises and representations. If the lawyer or accountant is either expressly or impliedly promising to the client an undivided loyalty, then his only ethical conduct is to give that loyalty.

How does that loyalty express itself? In an area as subtle and complex as this, it is hard to fix boundaries. Perhaps, at least at this stage, the most useful approach is the empirical; it is therefore likely that the specific cases which are to be discussed in the balance of this program will delineate the problems more meaningfully than do the generalizations of this paper. In any event, however, let me state what I conceive to be the minimum components of the loyalty that we owe. Surely, we must give our client the benefit of all reasonable doubts on the facts and the law. We of course should communicate to him our expert evaluation of all reasonable doubts, so that he will be prepared for all contingencies. But, once we are honestly convinced that he has a reasonable basis for an advantageous position, we can counsel and advocate that position without first satisfying ourselves that we would accept that position if we were a revenue agent. That kind of schizophrenia is not demanded of a lawyer in any other branch of law, and it should be no different in the tax law. By the same token, if we believe that the taxpayer's position depends upon a correct, or even reasonably tenable, interpretation of the law, we do not have to provoke controversy by advertising the grounds on which it might be attacked. We do not owe the tax collector a law review article as a footnote to any debatable item on a tax return.

When we get to the question of fact disclosure, however, we come to more difficult ground. This question arises most often in examination or conference, and we have all had to search our souls in borderline cases. There is often a thin line between nondisclosure and misrepresentation. If the effect of presenting one item of evidence and concealing another is to make a substantial misrepresentation of the relevant facts, there is of course no lawyer-client loyalty which excuses the fraud upon the government. On the other hand, when the lawyer believes that his essential facts are clearly supported by the weight of all the evidence, does he have to volunteer every scrap of fact which might make his case more difficult? There are borderlands here where every lawyer is ultimately alone with his own conscience.

A recognition of these boundaries, however, is far from an acknowledgement of a professional responsibility to the government. I am not retreating from undivided loyalty to my client, and I am not accepting a professional obligation to the government, when I say that I will not commit a fraud for my client. This, it seems to me, is simply a matter of my dignity and pride as a lawyer. I would hate to think that this is considered some special obligation of the *tax* lawyer. I am sure that our colleagues in other branches of the law would subscribe to as much holiness as that.

Unless we are just playing with words, the undivided loyalty which the lawyer owes his client is inconsistent with any reliance by the government upon his fiduciary obligation to itself. There is still the question, however, of whether the government can, or ought to, change the rules of the game: may it initiate a policy of reliance, and thereby impose an obligation for the lawyer to itself which proportionately diminishes the lawyer's obligation to his client? This brings up the much publicized proposal for "certified" tax returns which would acquire some kind of presumption of honesty and accuracy for the purpose of examination. Such certification would be made by a lawyer or accountant in good Treasury standing, and would amount to his own endorsement of the items on the return.

This question raises another which I have thus far managed to brush under the rug. Are lawyer and accountant in the same position on the over-all question of client responsibility? If there are differences, we must take them into account, because we cannot treat the tax adviser problem solely from the lawyer's standpoint.

I gather that the concept of a certified tax return has met with a sympathetic response in some accountants' circles. It bears a deceptive similarity to a certified financial statement for credit purposes, and it would extend the accountant's impressive function of certification. Actually, however, this procedure would merely highlight the accountant's equivocal position as counsel and advocate under our present tax procedures. Frankly, this aspect of the problem has always seemed more important to me than the question of technical competence, and I have never heard a satisfactory delineation of the problem from any accountant.

It is easy for a lawyer to adopt an undivided loyalty to a client; for better or for worse, that is his professional tradition and obligation. The accountant's tradition is quite the opposite: he is proud of his "independent" status as a certifier of statements. In the exercise of this function, he is the adversary of his client, and his liability is to the creditors who rely upon him. Of course, he is paid by the client, and his certification is ultimately in the client's interest, but he trusts his client at his own peril. In this respect, the accountant is more policeman than counselor. The accountant's advisory function, which for a long time was quite secondary, blossomed into a major activity with the growth of the income tax. In some instances, this conversion has been very marked: the accountant is often the client's confidant as the lawyer is not. But even in these cases the relics of the past may intrude. Will the accountant always prepare a tax return in the client's best interest, if he knows that he must certify a statement of the tax liability which has a substantial possibility of being an understatement? Even when the accountant himself is willing to cast himself unambiguously in the role of counselor, the law itself refuses to recognize the completeness of this role; for example, most states reject all rules of privilege for confidential communications between client and accountant.

With this background, it is not surprising that the accountant sometimes thinks of himself as an adjunct of government. Some of the more august members of the profession, perhaps taking their cue from their British chartered cousins, express indignation at the challenge of a tax return which has their signature. They, of course, would be the ones to welcome a "certified" return. I do not pretend to know the solution which the accountants should work out for themselves. Frankly, I cannot imagine how they can ever logically reconcile their contradictory functions of certification, counseling, and advocacy. But I do believe that as tax advisers the accountants will best serve their clients individually, and the community collectively, if they adopt the lawyer's approach of an undivided loyalty. The certified tax return, or any kindred device which tends to split the professional obligation, would be a step in the wrong direction.

Are all the practitioners then to be limited to the role of anti-government adviser and advocate? I have heard the complaint that this leaves us as "tax mechanics," and deprives us of our participation in the architecture of the law. First, by way of demurrer, it can be pointed out that this is more than a minor function in the shaping of the law. Traditionally, our common law has been distilled from the arguments of opposing counsel; and even a statutory system like the tax law has in the United States developed its underlying concepts through the adversary system in our courts of law. Whether or not we like the elaborate system which we now live under, we must recognize that it has been achieved primarily under the stimulus and pressure of the private practitioner.

Nevertheless, most of us feel that a professional career devoted solely to clients' interests is not quite enough. Our shaping of the law in that employment is too accidental and sporadic to be entirely satisfying. The socially conscious person begins to wonder if he is not living for bread alone, and he worries that his abilities are often twisted toward ends which he knows are not the most desirable for the community at large. Must the reformer instinct be constantly thwarted so long as we remain in private practice? Is there no way in which our expertise may be directly employed in the public interest? In a field as vital and as complicated as taxation, the legislators, the administrators, and the judges all desperately need the unbiased help of those who understand the problems from the taxpayers' point of view.

The answer is that we have numerous avenues for disinterested public service. Teaching, writing, and lecturing are available to many. An even wider opportunity is through professional organizations such as bar associations and accountants' societies. Here the professional is privileged to work singlemindedly in the public interest. Perhaps his focus is simply on making life easier for himself by helping create a more consistent and more predictable pattern of law. And inevitably his concepts of right and wrong are colored by his experience and his environment. Nevertheless, these reflect his true moral standards, and they are a proper part of any personal crusade which he enjoys waging. Some lawyers and accountants make the mistake of bringing their clients' cases with them to association meetings. Apart from the question of ethics, this is the wasting of an opportunity for self-expression. It is generally accepted that no client buys a lawyer's time at a bar association meeting. I have known many instances of lawyers (including myself) who have advised clients how to take advantage of a loophole, and have then worked in the bar association to change the law so that the loophole would no longer exist. Nor is this a matter of expiation for guilt. It is simply a question of what hat we are wearing at the moment. When we are wearing the hat of counselor and advocate, it is not only our right, it is our duty, to advise the client in his best personal interest, and to fight for his rights under the law. But, when we are wearing the hat of a professional organization which purports to act in the public interest, it is wrong to allow a client's interest to interfere with a clearly sensed public need.

So long as he keeps his hats clearly distinguishable, the practitioner need have no fears of schizophrenia, nor does he need to apologize or to expiate. In both capacities he is serving a purpose for which our political and economic structures have a great need. It is indeed important to define ethical limits, but let us not confuse the issue by asking him to wear two hats at the same time. Let us never forget that the private tax practitioner's basic obligation is to his client, and that our entire tax system depends upon the taxpayer's confidence in the fulfillment of that obligation.

10. Does the Tax Practitioner Owe a Dual Responsibility to his Client and to the Government? — The Practice
Milton Young

May I preface what I am about to say with a self admonition not to be hypocritical, theoretical or pontifical.

Any discussion of a subject as delicate as "The Tax Practitioner's Dual Responsibility" requires a rather precise definition of terms.

A "dual responsibility" does not necessarily mean a conflicting one. It may be as compatible as the doctor's responsibility to his patient and to his hospital.

Since we do not practice our profession in a vacuum, every responsibility stems directly or indirectly from our relationship with clients. Thus, the tax practitioner has a responsibility to his clients to keep himself well-informed as to the techniques of his profession.

Certainly, here there is no offensive duality unless one is to read only cases decided in the taxpayers' favor.

The tax practitioner has a responsibility to his clients to counsel and guide the young lawyer in his office.

Surely, in introducing the young lawyer to the proper

standards of ethical behavior there is no conflicting duality. Indeed, one might argue that those who teach tax law assume the heaviest responsibility of all—to guide and to shape the morals and the attitudes of the Bar to be.

Here, there is no objectionable duality but one responsibility—to inculcate in the student knowledge and character. Yet students who receive the same teaching may emerge in diverse professional capacities—some in private practice and others in Government service.

I suppose the question, in the context of the announced subject, is simply this:

In our day-to-day relationship with clients, how shall we conduct ourselves, bearing in mind that the operative facts will always be subject to disclosure?

The assumption of a full revelation of the facts is essential to any intelligent discussion of the problem. To rely on the "no audit" ostrich approach is to evade the issue.

When we are faced with a tax "gimmick," such as the bond purchase plan where the taxpayer is neither a true owner nor a true debtor, the tax practitioner should trust his instinctive reaction of distaste. Not only may this reaction have a sound moral basis, but usually it is a correct forecast of the effectiveness of the plan itself.

Mr. Norris Darrell put it well in an early article when he said,

> "A foul-smelling viscerally objectionable plan is likely to be judged ineffective."

* Mr. Louis Eisenstein, in a recent lecture, emphasized the fact, and I agree with him, that morality in taxation is a two-way street.

He argues that there is nothing unethical in taking advantage of statutory ambiguity because he says "the Government does precisely the same without any qualms." An example of administrative irresponsibility is the manner in which the government has interpreted the collapsible corporation section.

Is the attitude of some in tax matters, a symptom of a national malady, that of talking out of both sides of the mouth on ethics and morals?

An educator recently said,

> "We tell our child to respect authority while we disparage our public officials. We tell him to obey the law while we attempt to bribe a policeman or fix a ticket. We tell him to be decent and honest and, above all, upright—while we cheat on our income tax. We stress the importance of scientific and academic achievement and then make millionaires of our entertainers and paupers of our professors."

It seems to me that we have a continuing responsibility to our clients and to all citizenry, hence the Government, to maintain a dignity and a decency in our professional conduct.

We should establish our own criteria of behavior rather than follow those of the client, particularly the client who may be indifferent to the means, persistent about the ends, and generous in payment. Yet, we may discharge this role of arbiter on ethics and still be the practical counsellor.

Let us examine a few specific cases:

1. Your client owns stock in a corporation whose only asset is a building. The corporation was formed many years ago with $500 capital. The building today has a fair market value of one million dollars. Its adjusted cost is very low. He consults you about the possibility of liquidating the corporation to take advantage of a higher depreciation deduction. He would like to avoid the immediate payment of a capital gains tax of a quarter of a million dollars.

You suggest that your client sell the stock of the corporation to his two adult sons, who will pay him one million dollars, the fair market value of the stock, at the rate of a hundred thousand dollars a year for the next ten years. After the sons have acquired the stock, they might liquidate the corporation. Since they carry the stock at a cost of one million dollars, and since the property's worth at the time of liquidation is one million dollars, there is neither gain nor loss to them.

For depreciation purposes, they may depreciate the building on that portion of the million dollars attributable to the building itself.

The father will realize a capital gain of one hundred thousand dollars in each of the following ten years.

Is this proper tax planning? It is.

Has a tax practitioner recognized his dual responsibility to his client and to the Government? He has.

But suppose that after your conference the client in fact does the following without, of course, advising you: He goes through the motions of a sale of the stock to the sons and the corporation is liquidated. The father then causes the sons to immediately execute a deed back to him, without recording it. Rents are collected and retained by the father, who instructs the sons to treat the rents as their own income each year. In effect, the father has parted with nothing.

Here, there has been a failure to discharge responsibility not on your part in suggesting a plan but on the part of the client in perverting it.

2. Let us go on to the client who wishes to "die smart." He would like a will which would achieve the maximum estate tax savings with respect to non-community property. You explain that if his will were to contain an outright bequest to his wife or one in trust with income payable to her for life with a power of appointment, the taxable estate may be reduced by as much as one-half; which pleases the client no end.

He comes back to the "power of appointment" and

asks you what it means. You explain that upon the wife's death she may designate who shall take the principal of the trust.

He asks,

"Does this include my successor?"

You say,

"Yes, she may leave it to a second husband. She may leave it to children of another marriage. She must be able to leave it to anybody she pleases."

So the client asks you to draw a contract whereby the wife will agree now never to exercise the power of appointment but rather to permit the property in trust to pass in a manner designated in the husband's will. For the purpose of this discussion, we will assume that the agreement is binding in the particular jurisdiction where drawn by reason of the consideration passing upon its execution.

Now, we have three problems.

Is there any ethical impropriety in drawing the agreement, the so-called side agreement?

My answer is "Yes." It is being drawn to frustrate the law. Obviously, if the intention is to limit the exercise of the power of appointment, the will should so provide. The simultaneous existence of a will and the agreement emphasizes the intention to limit the power and retain the tax benefit. Since this cannot be done except by surreptitious concealment of the agreement, participating in its drafting and execution is improper.

The second problem may arise upon the husband's death, when you are retained as counsel for the executor in the preparation of the estate tax return and learn for the first time of the arrangement. Should you claim the full marital deduction, knowing that if the Internal Revenue Service learns about the existence of the agreement, it will disallow the deduction?

It seems to me that you have a duty to tell the executor that the estate cannot claim the marital deduction without disclosing the agreement. If the executor refuses, you should not continue to be attorney for the estate.

Let us examine the third situation:

You had nothing to do with the agreement. You had nothing to do with the tax return. You are retained as tax counsel in the audit of the estate tax return and you learn, for the first time, of the will and the side agreement.

Are you under an affirmative duty to tell the Internal Revenue agent of the agreement if you remain in the case? My answer is "Yes." I believe that you should tell your client what you propose doing and, if he disagrees, you should resign as counsel.

3. Let us consider the case of the "tardy" taxpayer. He proudly proclaims to you that three weeks ago he sold property at a handsome profit. He has vaguely heard about some law which limits the tax upon the gain to one capital gains tax.

You say, "You mean that you own the stock of a corporation which sold property at a gain?"

He says, "Yes."

You say, "Well, I am sorry. There is such a law, but you have failed to comply with it."

At this point, have you discharged your responsibility to the client and to the Government? You have not.

The conversation might be:

"Are you the sole stockholder of the corporation?"

"Yes, I am."

"Tell me what you proposed to do when the property was sold."

"I told you, all I intended to do was to pocket the proceeds and no longer use the corporation."

It seems to me that under the facts the client may well

have complied with the requirements of Section 337. It is not necessary to pretend that a "meeting" of one stockholder was held, and prepare "minutes" reflecting a meeting that never took place.

All the lawyer need do is draft an affidavit for his client stating, in effect:

> "I am the sole stockholder of X corporation. It was my intention that the corporation sell its property and for me thereafter to receive the proceeds of the sale and all other corporate assets and liquidate the corporation."

Let us make it a little tougher, however.

Again, the client tells a story of the sale of the building and again you ask, "Are you the sole stockholder?"

"No, there are three of us, my sister in California, my brother in Florida and myself in New York.

"My brother in California told me that, 'When we sell the property, let us keep the money in the corporation and buy another piece of property.' My sister in Florida told me that, 'I will do whatever you two decide.'

"I wanted to obtain the proceeds of the sale and liquidate the corporation."

Under those facts, the attorney may not take the position that there was a plan of liquidation prior to the sale.

4. A client in the 90% bracket has a contract to buy a building. After holding the contract for two or three months, he learns that he may sell it at a profit of $20,000, and consults you.

If he sells the contract he will enjoy a short-term gain, the Government will receive $18,000 and he will retain $2,000.

He asks what can be done under the circumstances. You suggest that he form a corporation (or use an existing corporation, if he has one), to which he tranfers the contract. That corporation may engage in the sale, enjoy the same short-term gain of $20,000, and pay a corporate tax of $6,000.

The advice is sound depending upon future corporate conduct.

If that corporation thereafter continues to be a real entity using the fruits of the sale for real estate investments or the like, I think the plan is proper.

If, on the other hand, the corporation receives the proceeds of the sale and merely awaits the passage of months before liquidating, the plan is defective.

5. Finally, we have the client who has an old master, for which he paid $3,000. He has owned it perhaps a year or so. Two reputable galleries have appraised the painting at a fair market value of $20,000.

He consults you about a gift of the old master to a university. You examine the appraisals and are satisfied as to their validity. You explain to your client that he may deduct $20,000, regardless of the cost of the painting on his income tax return, subject, of course, to the charitable limitations.

He is followed by a client who tells you the following story:

"I bought a painting yesterday for $500. I am giving it away to a charity, and I have an appraisal of $5,000."

You ask for more details about the transaction.

"Well, there was an ad in the paper by a gallery which read 'Paintings for sale. Appraisals freely given.' I called the gallery and they told me they had a wonderful painting for me for $500, and would immediately give me a $5,000 appraisal. The gallery had earmarked the painting for a receptive institution."

You ask the client, "Have you seen the painting?"

"Oh, no."

"Do you know the name of the institution?"

"Well, it is on the bottom of the letter."

All that happened was a telephone call, a payment of $500, and the receipt of an appraisal for $5,000, followed a week later by an acknowledgment from the "donee."

Obviously, the second course of conduct is wrong and the the tax practitioner who endorses this sort of transaction is not discharging his responsibility to his client and, therefore, to his Government.

The responsibility of the tax practitioner to his client and to his Government is an ever-changing one. What is right or wrong today may differ from the proprieties of yesterday.

Mrs. Gregory may have been properly advised to form and immediately liquidate a corporation for the sole purpose of effecting a reorganization. Today, a tax practitioner would hardly counsel a Gregory pattern.

Reputable taxpayers of thirty-odd years ago were advised to sell assets to members of their family in order to establish losses. In other cases, appreciated assets were transferred to foreign dummy corporations, which would effect the sales. Taxpayers would buy and sell securities simultaneously to establish losses and yet preserve their ownership. None of these devices are now acceptable.

Does the tax practitioner owe a dual responsibility to his client and to his Government? Indeed he does—a triple or quadruple responsibility, if you will—all calculated to help discharge his duty to the client.

First, the practitioner owes a responsibility to be proficient in his skills and ethical in their application.

Second, he has a duty to appraise a suggested course of conduct to see that it is neither technically unsound nor morally repugnant.

How happy is the partner whose family partnership had no economic or tax reality? His was a double punishment, for not only did he have to pay a tax on the income attempted to be channeled to another, but he could not properly recapture the income as well. How happy is the client who bought a yacht for a half million dollars on the advice that all of its operating expenses would be deductible whether or not he flew a flag on which the numerals 1040 were emblazoned? Not only did he have to pay taxes on the disallowance of the expenses but he is now faced with an indifferent market—there are few yacht owners who will pay a half million dollars without a tax benefit.

In this appraisal process the tax practitioner is discharging a responsibility to his client and to his Government, as well, if, by "Government," we mean not a detached entity hostile and unrelated to the client, but the representative of all taxpayers, including the immediate client.

Third, it seems to me the tax practitioner has a responsibility to help evolve a workable system of taxation.

For example, when clients overwork certain techniques of corporate liquidations, all liquidations are affected. Thus, it was not unusual at one time to liquidate corporations which built one-family houses prior to the sale of any of them. But Congress stated that due to the one-family house builder and the canny motion picture producer, it was compelled to adopt the collapsible corporation section. Yet the law affects persons who use corporations for other than tax reasons and find that they must treat as ordinary income, the gain on the sale of stock or upon liquidation.

Gifts of appreciated property to charity are proper and serve a social as well as a tax purpose. Yet when a false appraisal is used, it precipitates Congressional inquiry which may change the rules of the game so that all donors, including the ones acting in good faith, may have to pick up a gain on the gift of appreciated assets.

The law today properly permits the purchaser of real estate to use as a basis for depreciation the allocated cost of the property, even though part of the cost is reflected by a purchase money mortgage. But when purchase money mortgages are artificially inflated, so that the total "cost" is far in excess of real fair market value, a re-examination of the rules of the game may follow. The result may be another unfair wholesale change.

I promised not to be hypocritical. Have I advised clients to depreciate property on the basis of cost, including a high purchase money mortgage? Of course I have.

Is the client concerned about other taxpayers who may lose the benefit? Not in the least. But upon reflection, he may hesitate about a transaction whose only attraction is the tax benefit, particularly if the tax benefit may disappear within a short time—and we should encourage that hesitation.

The tax practitioner has the responsibility, above all, to walk upright. Thus may he discharge his multiple responsibilities to his client, to his Government and to himself.

11. What is Good Tax Practice: A Panel Discussion
H. Brian Holland, Chairman

Introduction

CHAIRMAN HOLLAND: Before starting the discussion, I should state, I think, that any views expressed by Mr. Hauser or Mr. Barron are their own personal views and do not necessarily represent the official views of the Internal Revenue Service. To what extent the Internal Revenue Service has official views in the area we are going to talk about I really do not know! You might think, as long as the Commissioner himself is here, that if he fails to express disagreement with anything that Mr. Hauser or Mr. Barron might say, it should be taken for granted that he agrees with everything they say. But I do not think it will be quite fair to assume that. So far as Mr. Caplin is concerned, I do not think that I need to wave any red flags as to the official or unofficial nature of anything he might say. I am sure he can take good care of himself in that respect!

To get the ball rolling, I would like to bring up this question and see what the views of the members of the panel, particularly those who are in private practice, may be with respect to it.

The Tax Practitioner—a Dual Obligation

The Commissioner in his talk indicated that perhaps accountants and lawyers dealing with tax matters had some greater degree of responsibility to be objective in their advice to clients than would be the case if they were not dealing with tax matters, but were dealing with situations in which the opposite party, or the other party in interest, was not the government but was a private citizen.

Mr. Mintz, would you care to express any views on this?

MR. MINTZ: I would like to start out with a disclaimer somewhat akin to the one that you made for Dean Barron and Crane Hauser. Anything I say today represents my own views and not those of my clients.

One Client, One Loyalty

The answer to the question is not easy. There certainly are divergent answers to it. I am confident, from the things I have heard practitioners say at other tax institutes, and some of the comments I have read, especially in recent months, that a sizable segment of the tax bar at least—and I am sure that a good many accountants and CPAs could share this view—believes that there is no such thing as dual loyalties in the tax field, their view being that the practitioner owes undivided fidelity to his client. As a matter of fact, I think that very language, "undivided fidelity" or loyalty or some language akin to it, is in the canons of ethics of the American Bar Association.

* This same group of practitioners would, I think, say that so far as Circular 230 is concerned, it merely specifies with some considerable particularity—listing, I think, as many as twenty-five or thirty specific instances—the ethical requirements that the practitioner is required to live up to if he wants to retain his Treasury card. But this group of practitioners, whose view I am now describing, would say that that specification is merely an implementation or an elaboration of the Canons of Ethics of the respective professions, of law and accountancy. While it adds detail, it does not change the underlying responsibility that the practitioner has to his client in any kind of controversy, whether it is a controversy with the government or with a private party or is no controversy at all. And these people would stand on that concept—you can serve only one client at a time.

Obligation to State

Another group—and I would guess that it might be a considerably larger group—would say that there is something special and peculiar about practicing in the tax field, and they would presumably base that on several concepts. One is that we have a system of self-assessment and that if it is going to be made to work it cannot work in a purely adversary context.

I think they say also that, to the extent that there is an opponent, it is always the same one, the sovereign, and that you just cannot treat the sovereign in the same way that you would an adversary in a purely civil adversary circumstance.

I think they also point out that you weight the score too heavily against the government if you give all the facts to one side and you give none of the facts to the other side, namely, the Treasury, except such facts as it can ferret out by an expensive investigative procedure, bearing in mind, too, the very small, if not minute, percentage of cases that are ever audited.

So this group of practitioners would emphasize the fact that all the facts are in the taxpayer's possession and he has to go to some lengths to share them with the Treasury Department.

This same group would add as a final fillip to this argument the fact that you cannot practice before the Treasury Department except as a member of the Treasury Bar, or, if you are not a lawyer, nevertheless you have to get a Treasury card, and that certain special sanctions are attached to this and that at least it demands a higher duty of disclosure than you might have to your private adversary.

Minimizing Adversary Posture

Midway between these groups is a moderate and intelligent group, of which I, of course, am a member. The members of this group would say, I suppose, that you really do not have to determine whether these are purely adversary proceedings or not, or at what level they may become adversary even though they may not be at the beginning. They say that you are never really up against the gun to determine whether the practitioner does have dual responsibilities, that is, one set of responsibilities to his client and another set to the government, but that it is just good business for you, for the client and for the government to try to minimize the adversary aspects just as much as possible, and to increase the disclosure aspects just as much as possible, and thereby to improve relationships among the three of you as much as possible.

Dangers of Tax Avoidance as Tax Practice

They would say, for example, that on seriously troublesome tax avoidance devices, the kind that even though lawful makes our stomachs squirm, it is just not good tax practice or good tax business to engage in them, because a number of things may happen. The legal tax gimmicks of today, the ones that you are reasonably confident the courts will approve today, may be the very ones that the courts are going to rebel against within a few years even if the law is not changed. You have to envision not what the courts would do with the problem today, but what they will do with your problem if you let your client engage in this extreme kind of tax gimmick. You have to predict what the courts will do three or four years from now after they have had a long series of these and their stomachs have turned in the process.

If you and your client get in the habit and achieve the reputation of being on the borderline of each new tax idea, each tax gimmick, each piece of extreme tax avoidance, the attitude of the administrators in the audit of your client's returns is going to be drastically different from what it would be in other circumstances.

There are a number of other factors that clients have to take into account before they engage in tilting with the Revenue Service. If the client is in a business that serves the public directly, occasionally the public will rebel against the tax reputation of the company or the individual from whom it buys goods or services.

Dual Responsibility

For all these reasons, I have somewhat the feeling that we engage in a mere academic exercise when we discuss the degree to which there is this dual relationship that we should or should not honor.

In summary, I would say that it is in our best interest to act as if there were a dual responsibility.

CHAIRMAN HOLLAND: Do you know which of these positions your clients take?

MR. MINTZ: I would say that it depends on the client. Those of them who are sufficiently introspective, I suspect, if they submitted themselves to a self-analysis, would come up with a position not greatly different from this one.

Duty to Explain to Client

CHAIRMAN HOLLAND: If you do take the position that there is some degree of dual responsibility, do you think that it is the duty of the tax practicioner to explain that to the client?

MR. MINTZ: I do not think you can explain it to them as an empty exercise in legal philosophy. I think what happens is that some time after the client relationship is established a problem will arise and you have an opportunity to have this kind of intellectual interchange with him. Sometimes the relationship breaks up as a result of it.

CHAIRMAN HOLLAND: I think it would be interesting to hear from Mr. Shaw, who is a certified public accountant, if he has any views on this.

Limitations on Dual Responsibility

MR. SHAW: I do not feel I have a dual responsibility. I believe that my responsibility to the government, to the

Internal Revenue Service, is that I must prepare an honest return that will disclose all material facts. I think I also have a responsibility to the Revenue Service not to take extreme positions just to squeeze every nickel out of the case for my client and thus put the government authorities to an undue amount of time and effort and trouble to settle the case.

Beyond that I am going to be in my client's corner. I am going to prepare an honest return which I think is proper, and disclose all material facts. Then I am going to stand by that return, and in any controversies that arise with the government, I am going to be on the side of my client. I am going to be like the second in the ring in the prizefight. I am in the corner of my fighter and I am not the referee in the middle of the ring.

Accountant in Tradition of Third Party Responsibility

Mr. Icerman: What we are talking about here is a matter of attitude, and it seems to me that the accountant traditionally is not brought up in the sense of the adversary or advocacy climate as is the lawyer. He has a responsibility to his client but he also has a responsibility to third parties and he must maintain some independence of judgment and attitude. This would probably allow him to accept the concept of dual responsibility more readily than the attorney, because to him perhaps the government is merely another third party that he has a responsibility to in preparing returns and doing his client's business with the government.

Mr. Shaw: Mr. Icerman, do you feel that this dual responsibility that the C.P.A. has extends beyong the point that I indicated?

Mr. Icerman: I think that there is a dual responsibility. Here I am speaking my personal views. I certainly do not feel I am speaking for the profession as a whole. In the first place, most of my clients, practically all of them I would say, do not regard the government as an adversary. In filing a return, during the administrative process, most taxpayers with whom I am acquainted do not feel that it is their job to get every dollar that they can for themselves and that the government's job, on the other hand, is not to get every dollar that it can for itself. I think that I reflect that position.

CHAIRMAN HOLLAND: I think you have a very well trained stable of clients, Mr. Icerman!

Obligation of Practitioner to Himself

MR. HAUSER: I want to add a footnote to what Mr. Mintz said. First of all, I want to state that I am a member of the moderate intelligentsia, just as Mr. Mintz is.

The point I think should be made is that perhaps there is a triple responsibility, a third responsibility, which is the responsibility of the lawyer to himself, of the accountant to himself, that his reputation is quite important. Since I have been in the Revenue Service, I have become increasingly aware of the amount of knowledge that the people in the Service have of the outside practitioners. This is true not only in the District and Regional offices, but also in the National office. Frequently we hear: "So-and-So is coming in on a ruling today," and someone will say, "Don't believe a thing he says, or be sure you get it in writing!"

I do not think this is simply a matter of ethics. This is a matter of dollars and cents to the practitioner. It is very important that you treat the government fairly, simply because that is the only way to maintain your professional standing and serve your clients.

MR. BARRON: Mr. Mintz beautifully presented the philosophical basis for setting a framework for dual responsibility. I think that there is a very practical reason for this responsibility. As a footnote to the administrative process, I say that all professional people are charged with knowing the difference between an administrative process and the judicial process. We have tried to convey to our 13,000 Revenue Agents and office auditors the need to take a fair and reasonable approach in dealing with taxpayers.

Service Need for Fair and Reasonable Attitude

This language perhaps is susceptible to some attack. I would like to defend it by saying that we have so many fact determinations to make—about 90% of our work is fact determination in the audit process—that we need, as we are gathering the various evidences looking usually to ultimate fact, to take a fair and reasonable attitude. I will say, very frankly, that if the examining officer is met with an adversary climate, he will very likely respond in the same measure; or, even worse, he may intiate an attitude of this type on his own. This is the problem of the psychological bias against taxpayers, which can develop over a period of time by working on returns that have potential issues.

Our general thrust, as you know, is to pick returns that we feel merit examination. This is another way of saying we think there is a potential issue. This is not uniform, but it is a general philosophy, and it tends to avoid selecting returns where there does not seem to be much need of examination. The other side of the coin is that examining officers are constantly exposed then to potential issue situations, and the psychological bias against taxpayers and practitioners can develop.

We try to offset this through articulation from the National Office, through group indoctrination. It is a very difficult process, and I say that the practitioners can contribute to the non-adversary climate if they will bear in mind this fair and reasonable approach that we are trying to inculcate in our people.

Taxpayer Duty to Other Taxpayers

MR. CULVERHOUSE: I would like to add another facet to the dual obligation, to the triplicate and now to the quadruplicate. I believe there is a duty from taxpayers to other taxpayers. Merle Miller expressed it very adequately here several years ago, that the taxpayer under a self-assessment system has a right to believe that the same standards are being applied to all other taxpayers, and when the taxpayer loses confidence, if he feels that it is not being done that way, the problem begins to set in, a breakdown of the self-assessment system. So I think that we do have more than just a dual obligation as a practitioner. I think that the taxpayer owes a duty to other taxpayers.

MR. HAUSER: I think we need somebody on this panel to take an unreasonable attitude!

Position Contrary to Ruling: Disclosure

Mr. Culverhouse: I would like to ask Mr. Shaw what he means by the preparation of an honest return with full disclosure of the facts. Let us assume that the Treasury has issued a regulation or a ruling, either one (I put them in the same status and perhaps you will take exception to that) and there has been litigation pending or decided that perhaps challenges the validity of the rulings and regulations as being erroneous.

In preparing the return, would it be proper, would it constitute an honest return, if you were to take a position contrary to that of the Treasury rulings or regulations without full disclosure? Under your statement I believe you said that an honest return requires a full disclosure of the facts.

Mr Shaw: I think an honest return would call for a disclosure in a situation like that.

Chairman Holland: Does anyone feel differently about that?

Mr. Culverhouse: I think that you would have people taking exception to this. I have heard it argued quite extensively, that you do not owe a duty to perform the audit for the Revenue Service, and that by doing this you would in effect be performing an audit for them and immediately starting litigation. They say, "Well, we have a right to determine in our own minds what are the correct taxes."

Risk of Negligence Penalty

Mr. Hauser: If you had a regulation involved, you might be in an unfortunate position as regards the negligence penalty if you did not disclose it. Under some of the cases you might have the negligence penalty even if you did disclose it. We do not know what the word "rules" means in the statute, whether that encompasses rulings or not. But this is something that probably has to be litigated in the future.

You always have to keep the negligence penalty in mind when you are deciding whether you want to disregard a regulation or not.

Does Disclosure Negate Negligence?

Mr. Shaw: Do you think a mere disclosure of the fact that you are not following the regulation will excuse the taxpayer from the penalty?

Mr. Hauser: It does not, under a couple of decided cases. I do not know what the future holds.

Chairman Holland: In other words, you are suggesting that maybe you not only have to disclose the item, but you actually have to take it into account in computing the taxable income, pay the tax and then litigate?

Mr. Hauser: Yes.

Mr. Culverhouse: I would take exception with that.

Mr. Icerman: I, too!

Mr. Culverhouse: In preparing the return, if you made a disclosure but resolved the question in your client's favor, it would be most difficult for me to imagine a jury or a judge imposing a negligence penalty.

Mr. Icerman: It seems to me that our whole system is based upon self-determination and that under such a system a taxpayer should be allowed to raise an issue. He should not be bound to put in something in his return that he does not believe is correct and then go through the expensive and difficult process of getting a refund. As long as we have a self-initiating system, the taxpayer should be allowed to raise an issue in his own return.

I do think that there should be some disclosure, but I do not feel, however, that it is necessary to write a letter along with the return and say that in such and such a case the taxpayer won on this issue although the regulations provide otherwise, and go into great detail. But it seems to me that the item in question should be put in a place where the Internal Revenue Service can be put on notice that it is there.

Mr. Hauser: I am not taking a position on the point; I am just stating that there are a couple of cases which so hold, that a person has to worry about it.

Chairman Holland: In other words, it is not really a question of what the law should be but what the law is?

Mr. Hauser: Yes.

Distinction Between Ruling and Regulation

Mr. Shaw: In other words, do you mean that the taxpayer would be penalized if he ignored, or took exception to, a regulation, but he would not be penalized if he did not follow a Revenue Ruling such as 62-92?

MR. HAUSER: There has been no litigation regarding the negligence penalty as applied to failure to follow rulings. There have just been a couple of cases that held, in the failure to follow regulations, that even though the taxpayer did disclose his failure to follow, he would still be liable for negligence purposes.

Disclosure Should Negate "Willful"

COMMISSIONER CAPLIN: I would like to add one comment to what Mr. Hauser said. There may be a case, with which I am not familiar, which holds that the negligence penalty would apply even if the taxpayer discloses in his return that he is not following the regulations. But this does not mean that we have to follow the case administratively. It would require the initiative from us to impose a negligence penalty. And while I am not prepared today to make a definitive decision on this, I say that instinctively I would be against imposing a negligence penalty if a person made a full disclosure.

MR. MINTZ: I would expect the law ultimately to develop that way. As I recall, the statutory language of the 5% negligence penalty is "a willful disregard of rules and regulations," and I do not think there has been a willful disregard in the statutory sense if there has been a disclosure.

MR. BARRON: I think it is most important that we realize that the assumption under which we are operating is that returns are prepared in accordance with the rules and regulations. We are today using manpower to visually scrutinize a segment of some sixty million returns. Obviously, it is a tremendous job to scrutinize all of these returns effectively. Of course, on the other side of the coin is the possibility that if the taxpayer makes a disclosure it will be caught, and if he does not, it will not be. But I cannot believe that this issue should turn on such a possibility, although it has its practical aspects. I feel, from a professional point of view, that we would have to say that there is a duty here to disclose.

Mr. Shaw: Do you feel that duty is as applicable to revenue rulings and lesser pronouncements as it is to regulations?

Mr. Barron: Yes, I do. I would not distinguish between the two.

Duty to Educate Clients

Chairman Holland: I would like to get away for a moment from this question of disclosure, and refer to a somewhat broader question that was brought to my mind by Mr. Icerman's statement to the effect that he did not think that his clients for the most part were anxious to squeeze the last dollar out of their tax returns.

I am sure that that is not a completely universal attitude on the part of clients. It seems to me that where this attitude exists, it must reflect to a considerable extent the attitude of the clients' tax counsel.

In that connection, I am wondering whether it may not be a very important part of the responsibility of a tax adviser to explain to clients the reasons for rules which may have been laid down by court decisions, or by regulations, or have just grown up as a matter of practice, which to the uninitiated client may seem arbitrary and unreasonable. I think that, when the client exclaims and protests against some rule that in the mind of the tax adviser is perfectly well settled, it is very easy for the adviser to curry favor with the client by saying, "Oh, sure, but, after all, the whole revenue law and the administration of the revenue law is pretty arbitrary anyway, and what can you expect?" and so on. The client then goes home thinking that his adviser is a pretty smart, sympathetic sort of fellow. But in the long run I wonder whether it does not make for better understanding of the tax laws, less friction between the public and the tax administrator, to explain these things to the client and explain the reasons for some of these seemingly arbitrary rules?

Does anybody have any thoughts on that?

Mr. Barron: I would like to make this one observation. The canons of legal ethics have a rule under which members of the bar are charged with supporting the decisions of the courts and generally speaking up affirmatively for the court position against criticism. I think that there is a parallel here to Circular 230 in terms of responsibility in the administrative process.

Good Ethics and Good Business

MR. CAPLIN: Like many other things in this area, you do not even have to approach this from the standpoint of standards of conduct or ethics or morality. It's just good business from your own standpoint.

In my prior law practice, and over the past two years in Washington, I have had an opportunity to view different types of practitioners, different types of conduct in negotiations with government. The fellow who pounds the desk and talks about arbitrary government may make a very nice show for his client and the client may puff with pride, but he does not necessarily bring home the bacon. On the other hand, the man who understands the problem of the fellow on the other side of the table, tries to be reasonable about it, tries to help him solve his problem, and tries to cooperate, frequently—and I think most of the time—does eminently better than the first chap I described.

The same is true for clients. Exercising restraint is going to strengthen relationships with the examiner of his tax returns. Maybe your zealousness wins this little battle today, but, thinking in terms of the long haul, you may have lost an awful lot in the process.

MR. MINTZ: Mr. Holland, I certainly agree with you. I do not think it ever pays to let your client get truly mad at the Internal Revenue Service. It does not serve any purpose.

I had one illustration of that. A client was subjected to a rather vigorous examination. As the revenue agent left the premises on the last day after a long audit, he said very airily to the taxpayer, "Well, we didn't leave you very much, did we?" The client just stopped filing returns for the next five years! It was a rather extreme reaction. We did manage to keep him out of jail, but just barely.

Responsibility in Tax Planning

CHAIRMAN HOLLAND: What about the responsibility of the tax adviser in connection with tax planning? I have quite often run into situations where a client comes in and says, "My neighbor, Joe Doakes, who goes to such-and-such a law firm, was telling me yesterday that his lawyers dreamed up a wonderful scheme whereby he could save thousands of dollars in taxes without risking anything. Why don't you consider setting up a scheme like that for me?"

The Gimmicky Scheme

Let us assume that the scheme is one which, when you look into it, is very likely all right, so far as the language of the statute and the regulations is concerned. You think that quite possibly you could get away with it. But, on the other hand, it is the kind of a scheme that, depending upon your own point of view, is somewhat repugnant to you. Do you have a duty under those circumstances to try to dissuade your client from going into this kind of gimmick?

MR. ICERMAN: I read or heard a little statement about the stock market that I use in talking to people about tax saving schemes—the bulls get some and the bears get some, but the hogs don't get anything at all!

CHAIRMAN HOLLAND: This is not always true, unfortunately!

I think that perhaps this has been touched on to some extent in the earlier discussion, but pinpointing the problem in this way, would anybody care to express any views on it?

Dissuading Client: Need for a Look Ahead

MR. CULVERHOUSE: I would think that the better procedure would be to speak to your client. If you think this is what we would call a slick gimmick, or a scheme which certainly would be repugnant to a sense of fair play, you should explain to him that eventually this will come home to roost somewhere in unfavorable circumstances.

Although you may lose this client by attempting to dissuade him from going into a scheme, you would in the long run enjoy your practice more by being able to do the constructive work that you believe in.

MR. MINTZ: I think we should add, however, that as a matter of strict ethics there is no reason why, in the circumstances that you have just assumed, if you wanted to you could not go forward and help the client put the plan into execution. It may be more a matter of personal taste with you than it is a matter of ethics.

In Terrorem

MR. HAUSER: I think a lot of it depends on whether it is the type of tax gimmick that is simply a matter of something missing in the statute or whether it is the type that involves some sham or window dressing to make it work. I think you should always approach this sort of thing from the standpoint: first, that your client's return is going to be examined; and, second that he may have to sit on the witness stand and explain what his business purposes were in entering the deal. I think you are likely to have a very different attitude when you think from that standpoint rather than from the standpoint of, "Well, my client is in such-and-such a tax bracket. The chances are three to one that he won't be examined," something along that line.

MR. BARRON: Mr. Holland, I would like to add a point here. I think that this is a real challenge to the competency of the tax practitioner in the sense that he must look way down the road and make a judgment as to what is the likely outcome of the scheme, not only in terms of the Revenue Agent, but also of the administrators in the Internal Revenue Service, the tax policy people at the Treasury level, and ultimately the Congress, as well as the courts. He is going to have to make these judgments at a very early time. The experience we have had with tax savings gimmicks and other unique devices points the way, and I think it gives the adviser a foundation from which he can make some of these judgments in terms of what is ahead.

The "Livingston" Deal

MR. CAPLIN: This group met this morning, not to rehearse any questions and answers, but to explore the pattern to be followed. I think at least three people on the panel said that they had been exposed to a "Livingston" type of interest deduction case in the stage of a client asking whether this was a plan that ought to be followed. At that time a private ruling was being widely circulated around the country and there were hundreds of people involved in this.

I think the three practitioners here said that they had turned down the plan despite this apparent evidence that it would bring a tax deduction. I do not know whether this was an ethical reaction, or a practical reaction. They did not like the looks of it; they applied the smell test to it, and they just did not want to give it their blessings.

Practical Reasons for Being Ethical

Frequently we will find ourselves pretty good tax advisers if we limit ourselves to some of the more traditional views. Many people regard a tax adviser as somebody who, when he is not seeing clients, spends all his energies studying the Code, looking for tax crevices. But indeed, I think the tax law is so complex and so involved that there is an enormous amount of room for giving good, sound, solid advice which in the long haul is going to stand up rather than to risk your reputation and your client's money on some of these borderline skimpy arrangements.

CHAIRMAN HOLLAND: I think very often where you have an adverse ethical or, if you like, visceral reaction to something of this kind, it is not too difficult to find very practical reasons for backing up your visceral reaction. I think perhaps that is what the Commissioner is suggesting, that in many of these situations, what seems all right today is very likely to turn out to be not all right when it really comes to a showdown. I think that perhaps one of the greatest assets of an experienced tax practitioner is a feel for that sort of a thing, a feel for the sort of thing that in the long run is not going to get by, although at the moment it may seem to be all right.

Finding Proper Motives for Plan

I think a related question, which arises perhaps most often under sections of the Code that involve matters of purpose or motive, subjective factors, is the extent to which the tax adviser can properly suggest to his client reasons for doing what he wants to do which will not fall foul of the statute. You can think of some obvious examples.

Loss Corporation

Cases involving or potentially involving section 269, where you have an acquisition of another corporation for the primary purpose of avoiding the tax are common. The client comes in to you and tells you very frankly that he has a nice looking loss corporation around the corner which he would like to take over and asks you whether he is going to be able to get the benefit of the loss.

Is it proper for you to suggest to him that there might be very good business reasons for his acquiring the corporation even though in the back of his own mind the principal reason for acquiring it is the hope that he will get the benefit of the tax loss?

It seems to me that this is quite a difficult area because you run the risk, on the one hand, of suggesting reasons to the client which may not exist. On the other hand, it seems to me that you have a right, if not a duty, under appropriate circumstances, to point out to him that there may be very excellent business reasons for his doing this, entirely apart from tax considerations. Does anybody have any comment on this?

MR. HAUSER: I think you will have to give him a lecture, as was done in "Anatomy of a Murder."

MR. MINTZ: If you follow that analogy, make sure you give him a lecture before he tells you what his motive was!

Contemplation of Death

CHAIRMAN HOLLAND: The same sort of situation could arise in connection with gifts which are potentially gifts in contemplation of death. The client may have good living reasons for making the gift, or he may not. Is it proper for you to prepare memoranda, take photographs of him out swinging a golf club, and that sort of thing, to prove that he had no expectation of dying at the time he made the gift?

MR. ICERMAN: It seems to me that some testimony in that area is not improper. After all, when this issue comes up, he is not going to be able to testify for himself. You have to prepare in advance for that sort of thing.

Propriety of Making Suggestions

MR. SHAW: Mr. Holland, is your question, really, should he help the client, should he assist the client in fooling the government? Is that your question?

CHAIRMAN HOLLAND: My question perhaps is when can or could it be said that he was assisting the client in fooling the government?

MR. SHAW: When the reasons he is putting down on this memorandum are just invalid, are just artificial.

CHAIRMAN HOLLAND: But you do not think that there is anything improper in suggesting that there may be good reasons for doing it?

MR. SHAW: No, I do not, because the client may have completely overlooked some good business reason for needing this loss corporation, and, if he has, then let us get it down and make the best we can of it.

Preparing the Record

MR. BARRON: It is very important that we have documentation. This is particularly true in respect to the revenue agent's work that is going to be done at a later time. If we do not make records of pertinent factors at the time that this is taking place, obviously we are not going to be in a position to demonstrate to him what the situation was at the time.

I think we could certainly subscribe to the view that we do not want to manufacture things that have no substance; but it seems to me proper to articulate what we really think does exist but may not be expressed.

CHAIRMAN HOLLAND: I think that is right. Of course, this situation quite often arises sometime after the fact, too. Then you have perhaps a somewhat different problem of trying to reconstruct reasons that motivated the client perhaps three or four years ago. I think that perhaps is even more difficult. It is more difficult to make sure that you stay on the right side of the line in that kind of a situation.

MR. HAUSER: In connection with this establishing the state of mind of the client, some practitioners have indicated that, in a situation where everything hinges on whether a principal purpose of tax avoidance was present although there were business considerations, it would be necessary in preparing the documents, to include in them a recital of tax motivation, if the tax motivation was part of the considerations in making the deal.

I think that is an unrealistic requirement, I do not really think the Revenue Service is so naive as not to get the idea that there are some tax avoidance considerations present in these cases. I just think that it is too extreme to require the practitioner to do this.

Tax Return Preparation

CHAIRMAN HOLLAND: We might perhaps get away from this somewhat general area now and come down to more specific problems. I have in mind some of the problems that arise in connection with the preparation of tax returns. We have already mentioned some of the disclosure problems that come up.

Substantiation: Lump Sum T & E

What about substantiation problems? I suppose this is perhaps more in the accounting field, generally speaking, than in the legal field, but to what extent should an accountant feel obligated to check into or verify deductions, entertainment expenses and things of that kind? Do you have any thoughts on that, Mr. Shaw?

MR. SHAW: Under the new rules that are going to exist after December 31st next, as far as traveling and entertainment are concerned, we are not going to be able to accept round figures. We are going to have to require supporting evidence for everything that is susceptible of being supported. For instance, club dues and club charges plus some explanation of why they have been incurred. Hotel bills and other types of expense that lend themselves to support of some kind. We may have to accept without any evidence charges for taxi fares and things of that sort, but it seems to me that as far as the expense is susceptible of support, then we have to insist on seeing that support before we permit the deduction to be taken.

MR. CAPLIN: Incidentally, Mr. Shaw, there is a $10.00 *de minimis* rule in the proposed regulations on T & E. As you know, on any particular expenditure, up to this amount, if you have made the appropriate diary entry, that would be sufficient.* The one major exception to documentation, such as cancelled checks, receipts, and the like, is when you have a casualty or fire which has destroyed all these records. Under those circumstances, the District Director has the discretion to permit a reconstruction.

Of course, the problem as I see it, and I believe somebody raised this question here at another session, is: "To what degrees must the preparer of the return go in determining that there is adequate documentation as required by the statute?" The statute very strictly says you must account for amount, time, place, business purpose, business relationship, et cetera. Can you prepare a return under these new rules without satisfying yourselves that the statute has been met?

MR. SHAW: I think that you would need to satisfy yourself and do what is called for by these new regulations that were issued yesterday, I believe, in connection with T & E. Not only that, but you should have data in the working papers to support the situation if ever you are questioned at some time in the future when the return is examined.

Reliance on Client

MR. CAPLIN: Let me ask you another question. What about this year's return? Suppose you are given a $10,000 blanket figure on T& E, can you accept that $10,000 figure and put it in the return and be satisfied?

MR. SHAW: I cannot believe anyone would incur $10,000 of expenses without having a fair amount of support for having spent that money, and if someone came to me and said he had spent $10,000, without any support whatever, I would find it hard to believe him and still harder to go through and prepare his return.

As far as 1962 is concerned, though, if I got some support, maybe $5,000 or $6,000 of support out of the $10,000, and the explanation I got for having no support for the remainder was reasonable, then I would be prepared to take

---

* *In the final regulations, an item of T & E expense (other than for lodging) less than $25.00 does not require a receipt.

that $10,000 deduction in the return, setting it out for what it is described to be by the client and I would also warn the client that he is very likely to be challenged on it and possibly that a good portion of it will be disallowed.

Mr. Icerman: To get back to the comment about the rules for next year which require substantiation, I do not believe that I am going to ask every client for whom we deduct travel and entertainment expenses to bring substantiation to our office before we will take any deduction. The government is not going to do this. They are not going to examine every tax return that is filed in the United States which has a deduction for travel and entertainment, and ask for substantiating evidence.

On the other hand, it seems to me that our duty is to explain to our clients what the rules are and at least to have some affirmative statement from him to the effect that these deductions are supportable in accordance with those rules. I do not feel I can ask my clients to bring in this supporting evidence or say that I will not deduct the expenses. I feel that we are entitled to believe our clients, for one thing, and that if they say that they have the supporting evidence, then it seems to me that is acceptable.

On the other hand, any experienced practitioner should be able to smell out situations which are not what they appear to be on the surface. I do not think we are privileged to refrain from asking the obvious questions. If there seems to be a doubt as to the substantiation, then it seems to me we are required to go into it further.

Round Sum T & E

Mr. Shaw: Suppose a client told you that he had spent around $3,000 of expenses during 1963, when these new rules come into effect. He wants to deduct that in the return and he has supporting evidence somewhere in his files. Would you just go ahead and deduct the $3,000?

Mr. Icerman: I think I would ask him a few questions about that before I would. I would not go so far as to say that we would require supporting evidence from every person for whom we were going to deduct travel and entertainment. That is what I thought you said.

Mr. Shaw: I pretty well said that.

Mr. Icerman: And I just took issue with that statement.

Mr. Shaw: In connection with this example I have just given of the $3,000, which is a round amount, and your client—

Mr. Icerman: I am always suspicious of round amounts, and I would never deduct that $10,000 you said you would deduct!

Mr. Shaw: Let me get back to that $3,000 for just a moment. It would seem to me that in requiring the client to bring in his evidence to support this $3,000, I am doing him a service because if he is going to find it difficult or awkward to bring it in now, he is going to find it doubly so two years from now when the Agent comes in and demands the detail.

Mr. Icerman: I did not say I would never do so. I said that I would not always do it. It seems to me when you have a round amount, and if this $3,000 is quite large for the activity that the person is engaged in; that you would have a perfect right to ask questions and ask for some evidence. But if the items are $342.97 and you ask him whether he has bills and supporting evidence, and you explain to him what is required, and he says, "Yes, I have," I do not believe I would say, "Well, go home and get them."

When Documentation Demanded

Mr. Caplin: Let us make it hard for Mr. Shaw. Suppose his client says that he has the documentation for $3013.52, will that be enough?

Mr. Shaw: Are we talking now about 1963 or 1962?

Mr. Caplin: 1963.

Mr. Shaw: I would say to the client, "In your own interest, bring in the evidence of the $3,013.52. I will look it over, and will tell you what I think of it before we claim the deduction, and having satisfied myself that it is proper, will ask you to put it carefully away in your files and save it for the revenue agent if and when he comes in." That would be my advice to the client.

Mr. Culverhouse: Perhaps I did not understand you correctly when you stated that you were not completely satisfied with the deductibility of this item. You would so advise him and then he would claim it. But you would have been on record with your client that this may be disallowed. Did I understand that correctly?

MR. SHAW: I was talking about 1962 then. I think the rules are going to be much tighter in 1963. In 1962, if the client, without complete support, satisfied me that he spent this amount of money, I would go ahead and claim it in the return and I would tell the client that in the absence of adequate support, he may very well get a portion disallowed on examination.

MR. CULVERHOUSE: But you would have satisfied yourself first that in your opinion he was entitled to the deduction?

MR. SHAW: I would do that, yes. I would have satisfied myself before I would take the deduction.

Lump Sum Charitable Deductions

CHAIRMAN HOLLAND: Of course, to the extent that this matter of T & E is now, or is going to be, governed by the statute and the regulations, we get away from the general problem, I think, of the responsibility of the preparer of the return. What about this general question: For example, suppose the taxpayer tells you that he has $25,000 of charitable deductions and may or may not give you a list of them. Is there any necessity for going behind that statement or do you just put $25,000 in the return?

MR. SHAW: No. I just would not listen to putting $25,000 in the return. Surely, cancelled checks and letters of gratitude and acknowledgment will be available if that is a valid $25,000 expense or charitable deduction. How could you believe a client that merely said, or merely made the statement that he spent $25,000 in charitable contributions but did not have anything to support it?

CHAIRMAN HOLLAND: In other words, you would ask him to support it?

MR. SHAW: I would insist that he support it.

CHAIRMAN HOLLAND: Would it make any difference if it was $1,000 instead of $25,000?

MR. SHAW: Even $1,000, I find it hard to believe that that had been handed out in cash without any evidence from the recipients of the gifts having been made. So even $1,000, I do not believe I would be ready to deduct in the return without support.

Canada Requires Proof

Mr. CAPLIN: Just to show that things are not so terrible down here, I had the pleasure of visiting the Inland Revenue Service up in Canada and watched how they handled returns. I was rather surprised to notice very bulky returns. Many of them were small returns in terms of the dollar amount that was reported. Yet they require that there be annexed to the returns receipts of charitable contributions, actual church receipts and other organizations. A rather interesting suggestion!

Mr. BARRON: Mr. Holland, before I make any comment on this thing, it seems to me that my views are offered in light of the caveat announced by you at the outset.

This is an area where professional judgment really must come into play. During the busy season when you are working at a tremendous pace, you will be forced on occasion to work from the taxpayer's figures. As a consequence, you come to the question of what credibility you can place in your client. How well do you know him? What has been your experience with him? All of these things come into play in terms of the inquiries that you are going to make.

Under the new T & E statute, in the first go-around, professional judgment is going to indicate a need to indoctrinate the client, to bring him into complete knowledge as to what the requirements are. Ultimately, at subsequent periods it may reach a point of reliance in the sense that this is just one other fact this is necessary in establishing a particular deduction.

Officer-Use of Corporate Facilities

CHAIRMAN HOLLAND: Again, in connection with the preparation of returns, what do we do with the situation of the stockholder officer of a closely held corporation who uses the corporation's automobile, or nowadays perhaps it is airplane, for his personal use? You being the preparer of the return may know enough about the facts to feel quite sure that when the agent comes in and starts looking around he is going to claim that the value of that use represents income, possibly compensation, more probably dividend income to the individual. Does anybody ever report that in the individual return as income?

Mr. Icerman: I can tell you what we are doing about it now. I must confess that until the last two or three years we paid little attention to this. We thought that it was de minimis. We now have them give themselves a raise in salary and then we have them pay back to the corporation a modest sum per month for the personal use of the company car.

Mr. Caplin: Of course, that might solve the whole T & E problem if you just had additional compensation and forgot all those rules!

Mr. Shaw: I think materiality is an important factor in this connection. A company yacht would be very much more something you would want to take issue with and perhaps eliminate a big chunk of the deduction for, than you would be concerned about a company car being used to bring down the President to the office each morning.

Mr. Icerman: The cases I am speaking about were cases where we have had disallowances of part of the use of an automobile on the grounds that the company officer not only drives it back and forth to work but for other personal affairs.

Return Does Not Require Report of Automobile

Mr. Mintz: There is a line on the return which requires a disclosure to be made about the use of a hunting lodge, a yacht or similar facility. Is an automobile a similar facility? In other words, is there not a possibility that you are required to make disclosure?

Mr. Icerman: I think one of the people with the Service ought to answer that!

Mr. Barron: I don't think, Mr. Mintz, that we had in mind automobiles when we used that "yacht, hunting lodge and similar facilities." It may be applicable, but I do not think we particularly had it in mind, although the Commissioner might contradict me there.

It seems to me that the use of company autos for personal purposes is a very interesting area in the sense that it gets the C.P.A. or the lawyer into an area where they are charged with being policemen. It is a difficult area. I feel it is very well covered by the rules of ethical conduct, to the effect of a need to inform the client in the event that he won't go along with adjustment. But there is a point beyond which the accountant cannot go in discharging his duty.

Mr. Shaw: If the Service wants to make an issue about the use of these automobiles for personal purposes, would it not be good to bring that out in the question that is on the return form instead of restricting the question to hunting lodges and yachts, and so forth?

Mr. Barron: I think it is not subject to argument that if we want to cover this, we should be specific, and I am sure that it will be given consideration.

Mr. Hauser: The "other facilities" are meant to cover a fishing lodge; is that right?

Mr. Bannon: Yes.

Inconsistent Taxpayers' Positions

Chairman Holland: Here is another question that has been suggested in connection with the preparation of tax returns. In the case of related taxpayers who in their own interests assume inconsistent positions, for example, an employee receiving a Christmas gift from his employer takes the position that it is a gift, and not reportable; the employer takes the position that it is compensation and, therefore, deductible. What is the duty of the preparer of the return, assuming that he prepares both returns? Does anybody have any thoughts on that?

Mr. Mintz: Just as a first impression, without having thought it through before, I suggest that he need not label it or red flag it in any way. This is a peculiar area. We all know of cases in which gifts to a recipient properly constitute business deductions to the payor.

I would hate to think that these two people would be less well served by the fact that they had one accountant or one lawyer preparing their return than if they had two. They are separate taxpayers. I would think that if the preparer felt that in each instance he was resolving the doubt reasonably in favor of the particular taxpayer whose return he was preparing, it would be all right for him to prepare them on an inconsistent basis on these particular facts. If we were not dealing with a gift-compensation issue, I would probably feel differently.

"Gift to Widow"

Mr. Shaw: Mr. Mintz, I have a question there. Suppose this is not just a question of a Christmas gift, but it is a payment of $10,000 a year or $20,000 a year to the widow of the former President. The company takes the deduction. You prepare the returns of both parties. Would you feel equally at ease in omitting any reference to the fact that you are not picking up this $10,000 on the widow's return?

Mr. Mintz: It might depend on when I was asked to do it. Certainly, during the period when the Revenue Service, in outstanding rulings, permitted that very specific situation, I would have no trouble in signing both of them, depending on specific facts.

Mr. Shaw: I am speaking of today, though. What would be your position today with a problem like that?

Mr. Mintz: It might well be different.

Refusal to Prepare Both Returns

Chairman Holland: Do you think there is anything to be said for the thought that perhaps the preparer should refuse to prepare both returns?

Mr. Mintz: Or refuse to prepare one of them.

Chairman Holland: Perhaps that is the answer.

Mr. Caplin: Next year deductibility of a business gift will be limited to $25.00 per person. This will eliminate many of the problems.

Mr. Shaw: Mr. Caplin, will that apply to payments to widows also?

Mr. Caplin: It will depend upon the factual background. If it is a "pure gift" under section 102, the $25.00 limit will apply.

Mr. Hauser: We are hoping the Supreme Court will speak upon the question again. We have application for certiorari up on two or three cases for a little more elucidation.

Conflict of Interests

Mr. Culverhouse: Mr. Mintz, would your position be

the same in the event you were limited to two parties in the contract of purchase and sale of a business and you had the question of allocation of the purchase price to good will?

Mr. Mintz: There you get into, I think, perhaps a squarer question of conflict of interest, and I think most people would feel very uncomfortable about representing both in that circumstance even if they each knew of your representing both and with awareness of it told you to go ahead.

Mr. Culverhouse: Then removing the conflict of interest, Mr. Shaw, if you were the accountant for both parties and the contract was negotiated without an allocation, and assuming further that you have been in on the negotiations and heard the discussions, what would your position be in the preparation of the returns?

Mr. Shaw: I would try to decide in my own mind whether an allocation should be made, whether part of it was for a non-compete agreement. Is that the sort of thing you have in mind?

Mr. Culverhouse: Yes.

Mr. Shaw: If I were satisfied under all the facts, after looking into the thing thoroughly, that an allocation should be made, then I would want to prepare the return of each party on that basis.

Material Error in Prior Year

Chairman Holland: Here is another question that comes up in connection with the preparation of returns.

Suppose that within the course of preparing a return for the current year, you find that a material error has been made in a return for a prior year. Do you have any duty to insist that the client file an amended return for the prior year? If he refuses to do so, do you have any obligations to decline to represent him any further? Does anybody have any views on that?

Mr. Icerman: I would speak to that. Once in a while clients make mistakes. As a matter of course we prepare amended returns for them and say, "You owe some more money for last year," and usually that takes care of it. I do not think that most people are interested in gypping the government out of a tax which they really owe. I think our clientele has confidence in us so that if we say they owe more tax they pay it. We had a case just like that about a month ago. A client was selling some lots on the installment plan and he fouled up his reporting on the payments. When we did his return for 1962, we found that there were errors in the 1960 and 1961 returns, and we prepared amended returns. He lives out of town. We sent them to him and he sent them in.

If Client Refuses to Correct

MR. SHAW: Mr. Icerman, would you care to express your views as to what your position would be if the client, having made an innocent mistake and left out $10,000 of income from his 1961 return, just refused to file an amended return when you came in to prepare the return for the subsequent years?

MR. ICERMAN: It is hard for me to imagine that sort of thing, but if it were actually done and he refused, he would have to get himself a new "boy."

MR. SHAW: You would not prepare the return under those circumstances?

MR. ICERMAN: No.

MR. SHAW: Even though the prior omission was completely innocent?

MR. ICERMAN: No.

CHAIRMAN HOLLAND: Suppose that the statute of limitations had run on the earlier year?

MR. ICERMAN: You people want a person to stick his neck out and then when you get it out, you want him to stick it out further and chop it off!

CHAIRMAN HOLLAND: A purely academic discussion!

MR. ICERMAN: It seems to me that if you owe somebody money, you ought to pay it. I do not care whether it is Uncle Sam or somebody else.

MR. SHAW: I agree with that a hundred percent, but I am just raising the question of what you can do if the client insists that he is not going to file an amended return.

MR. ICERMAN: It seems to me that the basis upon which you work with people is to a considerable extent that of mutual confidence and trust. If this error and refusal to pay was of such gross nature that it lessens or destroys your trust in your client, then I do not think you have any business representing him in any way.

Mr. Shaw: I think that is a very sound statement.

Circular 230 Does Not Require Action

Mr. Mintz: Oddly enough, I think some lawyers would have answered it just the reverse of what you two have agreed upon. They would say—and I gather up to this point they would be with you, Mr. Shaw—if an error is discovered in a prior year's return, certainly under Circular 230 the duty is upon the practitioner to bring it to the attention of the client and to recommend that the client disclose the fact and pay up the amount of the error. Circular 230 says nothing about what the practitioner should do if the client refuses to follow the recommendations.

Mr. Shaw: I just wish that Circular 230 could be amended to cover that situation. It leaves that important point unanswered.

Mr. Mintz: The answer from there on is not clear and we are left to our own devices. I gather that some lawyers, many lawyers perhaps, would have answered the question in the same way Mr. Icerman did. If the client refused to follow the advice the lawyer would give up the representation, if for no other reason than the fear perhaps that in some future year, in a continuing representation, the lawyer would be placed in the embarrassing position of having in effect built on that prior error. He, therefore, has been professionally compounding it, and he would feel, or a good many lawyers would feel, that the client, in refusing to follow the advice, was failing to act reasonably. If the prior dereliction was of a fraudulent character, the lawyer might well say that he might be asking too much of his client if he asked him to go in and submit himself to a possible criminal conviction. The lawyer would then again be faced with whether he should give up the representation.

This kind of client, having engaged in one fraudulent transaction, might well engage in another. Yet, I think a good many lawyers in that second case would think that the client was acting reasonably in failing to go in and subject himself to possible criminal jeopardy. The lawyer might thereafter, thinking the client had reasonably rejected the recommendation that he bring to light his dereliction, continue to represent that man, keeping his eye on him, of course.

PANEL DISCUSSION

Voluntary Disclosure

MR. CAPLIN: You brought up a point, Mr. Mintz, that suggests a question that I might anticipate.

The decision to expose this chap to possible criminal prosecution—by suggesting that he go in and report this income—gets into the area of voluntary disclosure.

As you know, the Service established a voluntary disclosure policy only for seven years, between 1945 and 1952. During that period, the Service guaranteed that if anyone made a full disclosure of all the pertinent facts before an investigation had begun, and made arrangements to pay the tax and the penalty and the interest, there would be no criminal prosecution. Civil fraud penalties and interest were paid, but there was no criminal prosecution.

You will also recall that in 1950 and 1951 there were congressional investigations. At that time the King Committee stated that the voluntary disclosure policy had led to many abuses on the timeliness and other facets of the disclosure, and recommended strongly that it be revoked. The policy was revoked in 1952.

Today, if this client of yours, under those circumstances, just walked into the room, made a full disclosure and was willing to make arrangements for payment of the full tax, interest, and penalty, there would be no guarantee that he would not be prosecuted.

Whether or not to recommend criminal prosecution is entirely discretionary today. But as a practical matter, in the absence of complicating circumstances, criminal prosecution is rarely recommended in a true voluntary disclosure case. To assure that this policy is being uniformly applied nationwide, for the last six months alleged voluntary disclosure cases with criminal recommendations must go to the Chief Counsel in Washington for centralized handling. I do not know if Mr. Hauser has received such a case, have you?

MR. HAUSER: One.

When Is Disclosure Voluntary

MR. CAPLIN: Questions often arise under an alleged voluntary disclosure, and many of the voluntary disclosure cases get quite sticky: an investigation may have previously begun, the disclosure may have been inaccurate. A case was argued before the Supreme Court the other day on these very issues, and everybody is watching for the results.

Mr. Mintz: Would it be proper to ask Mr. Hauser what he did with that one case?

Chairman Holland: I was just going to ask him, but I did not quite dare!

Mr. Hauser: It is under active consideration. We sort of feel in the National Office at times that a true voluntary disclosure is really a myth. You just do not get very many of them.

Mr. Caplin: I make one type of exception to that. Within a six-month period we had several hundred past discrepancies of the sort that Mr. Shaw is talking about reported to us. Over $2,000,000 were turned over to us by people who wanted to get their past records straight. This followed a speech about automatic data processing made down in Atlanta! Some of these cases went back to 1918. Although some of them have been very small, one was over $100,000. I do not know of any of those cases that involved a recommendation for criminal action. It could happen; I do not want to give you the impression that it could not happen, but I think in making your judgment you ought to weigh all these factors.

One of the problems is that it is very difficult to get a jury conviction where there has been a true voluntary disclosure.

The American Bar Association has submitted briefs on this subject and has had some discussions with us in which members of the Treasury Department and the Department of Justice have participated. The ABA is urging a reinstatement of the old voluntary disclosure policy. As of the moment, there is nothing to indicate that we will reinstitute the old policy. We may articulate in greater detail the existing policy, which is a discretionary one.

Chairman Holland: I suppose in making a disclosure, a taxpayer may very well have in the back of his mind the possibility that some day the Revenue Service is going to catch up with him, but I do not think that this should necessarily prevent his disclosure from being regarded as a voluntary disclosure.

Mr. Caplin: The chief question is whether or not an examination had already been set in motion. If the taxpayer comes in before an investigation has been set in motion, then this would technically come within the voluntary disclosure concept.

Social Relations with Internal Revenue Agents

Chairman Holland: Getting away entirely from this area for a moment, it might be pertinent to bring up the question of how far it is permissible to go in relations with internal revenue agents or other Revenue Service personnel in the matter of socializing or entertainment or buying lunches and things of that kind. I do not know whether the Commissioner wants to speak to this or whether he would rather have members of the panel talk about it.

Mr. Caplin: I would prefer at this time to defer to the members of the panel.

Mr. Mintz: May I just call attention to one of the canons of ethics that we referred to this morning. I think Dean Barron brought it to our attention, and he may still have it, because I think that, while it refers specifically and only to the case of the relations between members of the Bar and judges on a court before whom they appear, its language is in my opinion very appropriate for this discussion. Mr. Barron, do you still have that?

Mr. Barron: Mr. Mintz, I do not have my copy with me. It is No. 3, as I recall, of the Canons of Professional Ethics for Lawyers. In essence, it provides that there should not be any undue social attention to judges that would be subject to misconception by the public or other members of the Bar. I think that Mr. Mintz's observation is very pertinent, in the sense that this has applicability in our own situation as it relates to Revenue Agents. It is more of a question of "will it be misconstrued that a practitioner has an undue social relationship," and I emphasize the word "undue" and leave it to the specific rules that we have within the Service that are addressed to revenue agents and examining officers on their conduct. But I think the professional man will have to make his own judgment as to how far he would go.

Mr. Culverhouse: In my opinion there is more to be lost both by the practitioner and the Revenue Service by a sanctioned program of fraternization between the practitioners and the agents. I think the taxpaying public would be misled. I think that some practitioners would be taken advantage of by the fact of their association. I think that your best rule of thumb to go by would be that it should be a very minimum. Certainly, if you have neighbors, old friends with whom you were in the service, there is no reason for cut-off of friendship. But I think that the public display of fraternization and socializing should be at the extreme minimum, and I believe it is to the practitioner's benefit that it be kept that way.

Lunch During Examination

Chairman Holland: I would think that that was probably quite clear, but what about the very practical, perhaps minimal, but nevertheless practical question of the revenue agent who is in your client's office working over his returns. Comes lunchtime; the client has a lunchroom. Is it all right to let the client buy the agent a lunch or is that going too far?

Mr. Caplin: I would not have any problem with that, Mr. Holland. I remember a particular audit in my former practice where the revenue agent was so meticulous he would not go down to the cafeteria in the company's premises to have lunch with us. I felt it was going much too far. It seems to me that lunch under those circumstances certainly is not going to influence a man's decision, and I think this has an awful lot to do with it. Much depends on common sense and good judgment. Would this particular activity likely influence the man's decision? Would it give the appearance to others that it might indeed be likely to influence his decision? I think it is one thing to have a sandwich together in an office or to go downstairs in a little restaurant in the building; and another thing to go up to a place like the 21 Club and have a couple of drinks before you go on to finish the audit.

I think you get visceral reactions to these different situations. Where an individual gives the impression in the community that he is chummy with revenue agents or entertains a small group of agents at a hunting lodge or his home—you get into an area where all of us would have our ears go up and we would feel it is not right. But certainly there is no problem with the simple type of situation you describe, or the situations described by Mr. Culverhouse.

We have rules of conduct which state these principles broadly. What we are trying to do internally, as I mentioned at the outset, is within each district to develop some clear idea among our agents, revenue officers and others on what would be proper from their standpoint.

Congressional Intervention

There is one other point that I would like to discuss, Mr. Holland, because it was raised in a Washington tax letter the other day. We read these things, too! It raises the question of the propriety in a pending case of seeking congressional intervention.

CHAIRMAN HOLLAND: Does anyone want to speak to that?

MR. MINTZ: I certainly try to discourage it whenever I am asked. I think it is again bad business from a number of viewpoints. I do not think it works. I think it is likely to have an antagonistic effect rather than a helpful effect on the decision maker, whether he is in the Revenue Service or the Treasury or any government agency, the feeling on their part that they may be pushed around, and that if you had a good case on the merits, you would not have to run to your Congressman.

In addition, for a very selfish reason, I do not think it is good business for us to encourage that kind of activity on the part of our clients. If congressional intervention will assist them, they do not need our professional help; they can get somebody who is close to the Congressman. Therefore, for a variety of reasons, I would be very much against it.

MR. CULVERHOUSE: I would have to second that. Invariably it has been my experience that where the client, against your advice, solicits Congressional intervention, that if the case is successful (many times the ruling perhaps has already been into review status approving it), the client feels as though it was the Congressman who got it for him, and not you as the practitioner.

Mr. Caplin: I would like to state categorically that the news letter was absolutely wrong in the statement it made the other day. It said that it would be advisable for you to have the individual or corporation procure Congressional intervention in getting a ruling in the Internal Revenue Service, with particular reference to charitable foundations.

* We will be publishing on November 19th, as you know, new procedures on ruling applications. We make clear there that rulings are passed upon in order of receipt unless the taxpayer gives good and sufficient reasons why he should be given priority over another taxpayer. I think this is essential to the fairness and reasonableness of the whole ruling process.

Most Congressmen understand this completely, and most Congressmen, if they are asked to intervene for a constituent, will merely send a letter over and ask for a status report. They are concerned about the proprieties of their inquiries just as we are.

The people in the Internal Revenue Service are very sensitive to this. Since 1952, the Internal Revenue Service has been operating on a completely Civil Service basis in order to eliminate political intervention in appointments and ultimately in policy.

This Administration has been meticulous about this concept. The truth of the matter is if there is such a letter, if there is any call, this is spread all over the record and there is a tendency for people to react with extreme care to make sure no preference is given.

QUESTIONS AND ANSWERS

Limits on Dual Responsibility

Question: Does not dual responsibility end with the preparation and filing of the return or other disclosure? Is not the practitioner of necessity the adversary of the Agent who is bound by the black-and-white interpretations of the Service concerning the law?

Mr. Mintz: I do not think I can agree that the lines are drawn as precisely as that. I think that there is an equivocal relationship all the way up, almost until the time you get into the courtroom. There it is truly adversary.

But prior to that time, and looking at the role of the agent itself, most practitioners are not sure what the role of the agent is. I am not even sure that the Service is certain what the role of the agent is. There are certain prescribed rules as to what the agent can and cannot do. Under the outstanding mimeographs, as I understand them, he is supposed to be an investigator, a finder of the facts. If he uncovers any facts which disclose or suggest a possibility of additional tax liability, he is to bring it to the attention of the taxpayer. If the taxpayer doesn't agree, he is supposed to go up to the Group Chief and then to the Appellate Division.

Some agents act that way, but I think perhaps the more experienced ones, certainly the more aggressive ones, go beyond that and try to settle issues. I really think that the Service is well served by having that attitude, because I think we all benefit if these controversies are settled at as early a level as possible.

I have seen many agents who do try to send up only those issues that they think, on an objective basis, deserve to be considered by the Group Chief or the Appellate Division. Other agents, once they know that they are not going to settle the controversy with you, will try to uncover as many issues as they can in a subjective, non-objective way, feeling that they have to give the Appellate Division a considerable amount of horse-trading material.

I would say that the adversary nature of the proceedings will begin very early with that kind of agent, whereas with the first kind it will not begin at all.

Is Taking Advantage of Technicalities Justified

Question: While honesty and ethics indicate that accurate disclosure of facts to the Service is essential, how can the tax practitioner do otherwise than take every technical advantage possible for his client when the tax law itself is so full of traps for the unwary? For example, the taxpayer who makes an installment sale with no payment until the next year and then is stuck with the full tax without any money from the sale to pay it. Since the tax law frequently is technically unfair, why should the taxpayer ever forego a technical advantage? It should be a two-way street.

Mr. Caplin: I gather the thrust of that inquiry is whether because of some unfairness of the statute, the tax practitioner is justified in doing something which he does not basically feel is completely ethical, completely in accordance with his own normal standards of conduct.

I think it is pretty hard to justify improper action on your part, or on my part, merely because of some wrong in the law. This touches on the whole question of paying taxes. You may not like a particular program of government, and the question arises whether you should only pay 65% of your tax because 35% of the program is against all of your desires and all your wants. In a democracy, however, the only proper and sensible way to go about this is to see if you can get the law changed and not to commit another wrong in retribution. I find it very difficult to justify improper practice on my part because of an error or a bad statute.

Chairman Holland: Of course, I would take it that a good deal depends on what the question means by "taking every technical advantage possible." If this goes so far as to suggest that facts should not be fully disclosed, it seems to me that that is rather different from a technical advantage.

Mr. Caplin: Yes. As I read this question it seems to justify playing it pretty close to the line. Certainly if there is a legitimate deduction and this is within the spirit of the statute, by all means claim it. But I think the question would not be put unless there was some additional implication.

Ethics of Not Answering Questions on Return

Question: What is the effect of a failure to check the answer to various questions on the tax return, such as the 1963 question on T & E? What are the ethical problems involved?

Chairman Holland: I suppose the purport of that question is whether it is proper for a preparer of a return simply to ignore and fail to answer a question, the answer to which might be embarrassing or disadvantageous to his client?

Practical Danger: Invites Examination

MR. SHAW: I would think that the failure to answer a question such as that means that you are filing an incomplete return. A year or two ago there was a similar question in connection with T & E and the Revenue Service issued a pronouncement regarding its audit if these questions went unanswered. I think the Service's position was that the return would be accepted but that there would be a greater likelihood of examination if these questions remained unanswered. I would think that would still be true with the present returns.

CHAIRMAN HOLLAND: When you say you think that that would be an incomplete return, are you suggesting that it might be incomplete to the extent of being no return at all so that the statute of limitations would not begin to run?

MR. SHAW: No, I would not go that far. I think it would be accepted as a return, as an incomplete return, but I think the Revenue Service, would be likely or more likely to make an examination of a return which left questions unanswered.

CHAIRMAN HOLLAND: In other words, you think the failure to answer the question would spotlight it and make it almost inevitable that the Agent would come and investigate that particular area to which the question related?

MR. SHAW: Make it more likely, I would say.

MR. HAUSER: This would be incomplete.

MR. CULVERHOUSE: I do not believe as a practitioner that you could file or subscribe to a return if the answers were not made.

MR. ICERMAN: Sometimes these questions are like the one, "Did you stop beating your wife?" You cannot answer them yes or no in a little box. It seems to me if you cannot answer it that way, you should attach some sort of explanation. I do not think you could let the question be completely ignored.

Effect of Unanswered Questions on Automatic Data Processing

MR. CAPLIN: This is something that we have been talking about a great deal, particularly as we move into a data processing age and as we are requesting practitioners to file complete returns.

Down in Atlanta, for example, about two-thirds of the business returns filed over a year ago were deficient—some had almost a blank first page with just a summary figure and exhibits annexed. This creates a tremendous job in a data processing system, where you have key punch operators on a belt line basis key punching materials on returns. They just do not have the expertise and lose a great deal of time in going through all these exhibits. As a result, what we would have to do is to install a special desk of specialists to perfect these returns.

We will undoubtedly be running into this more and more as the data processing system moves throughout the country. But we have had meetings with practitioners in Atlanta this past year on their first data processing filing. After these meetings and discussions and clarifications, two-thirds of the returns were perfected. All the answers were filled out. One-third were unperfected.

We do not want to be in the position of rejecting returns and taking the position that the Statute of Limitations has not run. But again with the extreme capabilities of data processing and our ability to use this information effectively, we are going to be making requests about filling out all items in returns and answering all questions. There has been some examination of whether there is a negligence penalty involved or whether it is to be treated as an incomplete return.

We are talking only about small percentages of returns in terms of these unanswered questions. Most people answer them, and most people feel that if they answer them, others should answer them too. Certainly the suggestion that blanks would be more likely to invite an audit is not a wild one.

Quantity and Kinds of Audit

CHAIRMAN HOLLAND: Here is a suggestion perhaps, or suggestion coupled with a question, which I think perhaps the Commissioner might want to say something about. If he does not, he does not have to, of course. It reads this way:

Question: Generally, the best cure for the marginal gimmick, the "My neighbor does it, why can't I?" type of scheme, is a good examination by a Revenue Agent. Many taxpayers are never examined. With the data processing and taxpayer numbering system, is any consideration being given to checking the return of every taxpayer at least once in his lifetime Even if it takes ten or twenty years to get around to him? If every individual could be examined at least once rigorously before he is thirty years old, you would have a good taxpayer for the next thirty years.

Mr. Caplin: This touches on a number of the programs that we have been talking about and in part have instituted within the last year. It goes to the question of quality audit, what is meant by that. It also goes to the question of our selection of returns. What we have been trying to get across to our own people is that we are eliminating all statistical dollar goals or quotas in evaluating our agents. We want to eliminate the abuses inherent in such a system and to eliminate what can be a hasty examination.

We have prohibited accumulating such statistical data on an individual agent for the purpose of evaluating him. And this has had a sharp impact on our performance. We have tried to make clear to all our professional people that a quality audit, as we describe it, is not a C.P.A. audit, it is a special type of tax audit which involves taking sufficient time to identify substantial tax issues or to make a contribution to better compliance.

It does not involve a detailed audit in every case; it is a selective concept. If the Agent comes in, and after making certain preliminary checks feels that a return has been prepared well and it satisfies him, based on his experience and judgment, then no further examination is needed and he should move on.

A quality audit in this sense does not mean unncessary paper reports. All we require is sufficient documentation to permit an intelligent review. There has been over-reaction by some of the agents who felt that they had to have a detailed examination and detailed report in every case. But I believe that we have succeeded in correcting this. Current reports from the field indicate that a good balance is being attained.

Taxpayer Compliance Measurement Program

On the question of selection of returns, we have experimented with a random selection in most categories of income. We have done that on a partial basis this year. For next year, we are planning something that we call TCMP, Taxpayer Compliance Measurement Program. This will be a scientific sampling of returns at all levels. It is scheduled for our new audit program for returns to be filed this current year. The 1962 returns will be brought into this Taxpayer Compliance Measurement Program to carry out the very philosophy that is suggested in this question.

I think you have to recognize certain practical problems we have. In the past our entire return examination was focused on the so-called most productive returns, returns which per man hour were expected to produce the most direct enforcement dollars. In our presentations to Congress for annual appropriations, there very frequently is an inquiry into our results in increasing direct enforcement dollars. This has been used as a crude measurement of the Service's effectiveness.

If you look at the hearings during the past two years, you will see the shift in philosophy which we have been presenting to the Congressional committees. We are not looking solely at the productive returns. We are looking into the abuse areas too. Our examination in the charitable foundation field for example is going to be substantial in 1963, although we know that per hour expended it is not going to produce as many enforcement dollars as might be produced by other examinations. But our philosophy is that this broad audit program—looking at the abuse areas and giving taxpayers at all levels an understanding that somewhere along the line their returns will be examined—will make better taxpayers out of all of us and will contribute to better compliance. This I believe is the key to good tax administration.

In the perfect tax system we would collect everything through voluntary reporting and withholding. There would then be nothing to collect through our audit process or other direct enforcement programs. Of course, this is too much to hope for—although it remains as the millenium for all tax administrators.

Tax Return Is not Tax Paying Document Only

Question: The Internal Revenue Service is not giving

anything that is not shown on the return. Why then should we not take everything that is possible to get within the legal fringes?

MR. BARRON: I think that one of the first things that occurs to me here is that I think it is pretty generally understood that we have instructions outstanding in depth on this: if there is a credit item, an over-assessment factor in the return, that we want the agent to recommend the over-assessment be allowed. Of course, the examining officer necessarily is dealing with transactions that have already transpired; they are fixed and there will need to be a clear basis for a change, just as I hope there will be a clear basis for a change on the deficiency item.

Treasury Personnel as Return Preparers

Question: Are the government personnel who prepare returns for taxpayers going to demand that the taxpayer furnish full supporting evidence before they prepare the returns?

MR. BARRON: I would be able at this time only to give my personal view. I think it does not differ materially from what we discussed in relation to the professional man. We find it very difficult, frankly, in preparing returns for taxpayers, to deal with boxes of invoices. In fact, we make a point to try to avoid getting into this type of preparation taking into account the real need on the part of the taxpayer.

Extensions of Time for Filing Returns

Question: What is the prospect of modification of the Service's policy as regards granting of extensions for filing individual income tax returns?

My primary concern is the failure to consider work load of the practitioner a valid reason for granting such requests. Just in passing, my personal feeling is that inasmuch as the government has the bulk of the tax involved either through withholding or estimated taxes, an impossible burden is being placed upon practitioners doing quality work by crowding all individual work into an effective seventy-five day period.

Mr. Barron: In my personal view, the solution of this is not necessarily contained in changing the rule relative to granting extensions, because this was very carefully considered.

It seems to me that if, as professional people, you feel that it is desirable, and certainly it appears to me to be reasonable, recognizing the difficulty of crowding all your work into a short period, that you should seek the use of fiscal year filings or, if this is not satisfactory, that through the professional organizations an effort could be made to obtain filing on a different basis than April 15th, such as an alphabetic filing throughout the course of the year. If this sort of proposal were to come in, I know it would be given serious consideration by the Treasury Department.

Mr. Caplin: I might add that extensions of time have not been considered cavalierly. In several sessions with the Commissioner's Advisory Group, we canvassed this issue quite carefully. It is not just a question of our obligation to people who go to great trouble to file on time. We have found that extensions of filing time create many internal problems. First we have the question of equity to other people. Second, we find that a number of delinquencies are created. Third, it has an impact on the Treasury receipts and estimates for budgetary purposes. In addition, it affects our hiring policy for temporary personnel. It has been a pretty tough question. Mr. Barron, let me ask you this: In the Philadelphia region, what latitude do your District Directors have in granting extensions?

Mr. Barron: As I understand, Commissioner, we have the specific requirements now, and in the main our people are trying to adhere to the requirements and seeing that there is the proper justification for granting extension. There have been some failures called to our attention, but these are the human failures of the personnel that are handling the extension requests. In the main we are trying to adhere to the requirements, and we are not receiving any complaints on this from the practitioners.

Mr. Caplin: We have established liaison groups throughout the country for both lawyers and accountants, and this is a subject which I think might properly be raised with the District Director in each district: To what extent is his interpretation consistent with interpretations in other parts of the country?

We find that there is some variation. We are striving for greater uniformity here. We have had favorable cooperation from most practitioners, and we hope to clarify our position for the 1962 filing on a nationwide basis.

CHAIRMAN HOLLAND: I would like to thank the Commissioner and Mr. Hauser and Mr. Barron particularly, as well as the other members of the panel for coming here and enlightening us on some of these difficult questions.

12. Professional Responsibility in Federal Tax Practice
Boris I. Bittker

Foreword

For many years, Professor Boris I. Bittker, of the Yale Law School, has been a distinguished leader among academic tax lawyers in this country. His casebook on Federal Taxation is well-known, and his book on Federal Income Taxation of Corporations and Shareholders has shed much light into dark and difficult places in our tax law. It was therefore most appropriate that Professor Bittker was invited by the New York University School of Commerce to give these lectures on "Professional Responsibility and Federal Tax Practice."

The modern Federal income tax has been with us now for more than fifty years. Inevitably it plays a large role in the conduct of business affairs, and as the economy develops it affects directly and more substantially more and more individuals. It is plain that this system could never work effectively without the active participation of members of the accounting and of the legal professions. In many cases, they must not only participate, they must cooperate together.

At various times in the past there have been controversies between lawyers and accountants about their respective roles in the tax field, and occasionally these controversies have become rather bitter. It is clear, though, that the great professions of law and of accountancy must work together, not only in the public interest but also in their own interests. It was for this reason that the National Conference of Lawyers and Certified Public Accountants was established some fifteen years ago, by joint action of the American Bar Association and the American Institute of Certified Public Accountants. Through this Conference, many matters of potential controversy have

---

*These lectures were delivered at New York University in April, 1965, in the Ford Distinguished Lecture Series, sponsored by the N. Y. U. School of Commerce under a grant by the Ford Foundation.

been considered by representatives of the two professions, and, for the most part, serious difficulties have been avoided.

* The great achievement of the National Conference was the formulation of the Statement of Principles, to which Professor Bittker refers in his second lecture. It is true that this Statement speaks in rather general terms; and it is true that some of its provisions may not be very readily enforceable. But, it may be observed, they are not intended to be enforced, but to be observed. Through the Statement of Principles, the two professions have declared that lawyers are not to practice accountancy, and that accountants are not to practice law. It is true that there is a great overlap of the fields of the two professions, particularly with respect to taxes, and it is true that the questions which arise, like all questions worth considering, are questions of degree.

Nevertheless, experienced practitioners find that it is wise to stick to their own profession. When a question arises which involves matters well within the sphere of the other profession, it is best to bring a practitioner of that other profession into association on the case. Thus, if a lawyer has a case, whether before the Treasury or in the Tax Court or the regular Federal Courts, involving L.I.F.O. inventories, or a complicated matter of the investment credit, he should bring a certified public accountant into the case. And if an accountant has a matter involving substantial legal questions, he should associate a lawyer with him. Experience has shown, in many matters, that a team of a well qualified lawyer and an experienced certified public accountant can give the client far better service than either one could alone.

Thus, if I were to add anything to what Professor Bittker has said in these lectures, it would be to stress the importance of cooperation between the two professions, and the desirability that members of each profession recognize their own limitations, and call in a member of the other profession whenever the matter involves serious questions which are primarily within that profession's competence. As I have tried to indicate, it is not, it seems to me, a question whether such cooperation can be enforced, but rather that such cooperation is so desirable, and essential if best service is to be given and controversy is to be avoided, that it behooves every practitioner to see that he does not, in his own work, move too far into the area which is the special province of the other profession.

As Professor Bittker points out, this is especially true with respect to the planning of future transactions. There, it is extremely difficult to see that the lawyer can properly deal with matters that are essentially accounting questions, or that the accountant can properly deal with questions which involve real questions of law, even though accounting questions are involved, too. But this is likewise true where the questions arise with respect to past transactions. In all areas, it seems to me, lawyers should be scrupulous not to deal with questions which are essentially matters of accounting, and accountants should be equally scrupulous not to deal with matters which involve genuine and substantial questions of law, even of tax law. This should be done not as a matter of enforcing a code, but because the two professions are truly professions, and all members of either profession should want, on their own motion, to act in accordance with proper professional standards.

The question of the independence of the accountant, to which Professor Bittker refers at the close of his third lecture, is one which has long troubled me. One of the great things about the accounting profession, one of the things that makes accountancy a profession, is its independence. Yet, in the rush to move into "tax practice," a considerable part of this independence has been lost. As the accountant becomes an advocate, his independence is inevitably compromised. There are some signs that the accounting profession is concerned about this, and it would be fine if the problem could receive the extended consideration by the proper bodies of the profession which it seems to merit.

There is room in the tax field for both lawyers and accountants. There is, indeed, need in the tax field for both lawyers and accountants. Both professions should work together, and both should seek to develop and maintain the highest standards of professional responsibility. For Professor Bittker's important contribution to this end, we should all be grateful.

Erwin N. Griswold

Harvard Law School
Cambridge, Massachusetts
July, 1965

I. Professional Responsibility in the Preparation of Federal Income Tax Returns

Although the term "professional responsibility" has been appearing more and more frequently in the title of articles in professional journals, and of speeches at professional meetings, I am not aware of any definition of the term that is accepted as authoritative, or even of any informal attempt by an author or speaker who has used the term to define it. In view of this widespread, though not explicit, recognition of the dangers of competing with dictionary-makers, I too will eschew a definition. Lest I be accused of cowardice, or of having employed so vague a title for my lectures that neither the audience nor the payroll department of New York University will know whether I have delivered what I contracted to produce, however, I will at least suggest that the term "professional responsibility" is broad enough to embrace the standards of competence and integrity that emanate from courts and other governmental agencies, from professional societies, from professional traditions, and from the professional man's own conscience, and which serve to guide us in the discharge of our professional undertakings. The term has also come to be used to characterize—although I do not intend in these lectures to discuss — the professional man's concern for improvement or reform of the statutory law applicable to his field, and for the quantity and quality of professional service available to persons who are poor or otherwise disadvantaged. Although I am under no illusions as to the vagueness of the boundaries I have just suggested, I doubt that a more precise description of the area is possible, or necessary.

In grappling with this vague but nonetheless challenging and important subject, I will address myself primarily to its manifestations in the federal income tax field. I do not think that "professional responsibility" takes on a wholly distinctive coloration when viewed in the light of federal income tax practice, but by thus narrowing our angle of vision, we may be able to sharpen our focus, though I fear that fuzziness is inherent in the subject. In furtherance of my aim, I will discuss this evening the principal problems of professional responsibility that, to my mind, arise in connection with the preparation of federal income tax returns; in the two subsequent lectures, my concern will be with professional responsibilities in representing taxpayers before the Internal Revenue Service and in advising taxpayers in planning business transactions.

On turning to the relationship of professional responsibility to the preparation of federal income tax returns, we should perhaps note first that the Treasury Department requires a person who prepares a return for a taxpayer "for compensation or as an incident to the performance of other services for which [he] receives compensation" to verify the return under the penalties of perjury (Regs. §1.6065-1), but that the Treasury does not require him to satisfy any standards of educational achievement, professional or occupational experience, or personal behavior. The Treasury's enrollment procedure, under which its Director of Practice regulates admission to practice before the Internal Revenue Service and disciplines enrolled attorneys and agents whose conduct is found wanting, is not applicable to the preparation of tax returns.[1] Although it is easy to see why a person who assists a neighbor in the preparation of a tax return as a friendly gesture is not required to meet any enrollment or licensing requirement, there is less justification for exempting persons who engage in the business of preparing tax returns for compensation, some of whom promise that they can generate refunds for their clients or "guarantee accurate preparation of every tax return," all for as little as $5. There have been enough recent abuses in this area to suggest that a licensing or enrollment procedure ought to be considered seriously by the Treasury and Congress.[2]

[1] Treasury Department Circular 230, 1964-2 C. B. 877, §10.2(b). The exemption of "preparers" may be based on the theory that they are not engaged in "representing claimants" before the Treasury within the meaning of 23 Stat. 258 (1884), 5 U.S.C. 261 (1958), which is the principal statutory foundation upon which Department Circular 230 rests.
Although "preparers" are not required to meet the enrollment requirements, §10.24(a) of Dept. Cir. 230 provides that an enrolled practitioner "shall exercise due diligence in preparing or assisting in the preparation of, approving, and filing returns, documents, affidavits, and other papers relating to Internal Revenue Service matters," and fraud in preparing a return is made a ground for disbarment or suspension by §10.51(b)(3).

[2] For instances in which practitioners have manufactured deductions and credits on a wholesale level for their clients, or have failed to send the clients' remittances to the Internal Revenue Service, see United States v. Barnes, 313 F. 2d 325 (6th Cir. 1963); United States v. Herskovitz, 209 F. 2d 881 (2d Cir. 1954); Newton v. United States, 162 F. 2d 795 (4th Cir. 1947); United States v. Edwards, 230 F. Supp. 881 (D. Ore. 1964); see also Fulton v. Commissioner, 14 T. C. 1453 (1950), describing the practices of a practitioner who specialized in preparing fraudulent tax returns for airline pilots.
A licensing system would not eliminate all fradulent practices, but it could discourage misleading advertising and fly-by-night operations. The New York Times recently reported that landlords are sometimes reluctant to rent temporary space to companies engaged in preparing tax returns because some leave without leaving a forwarding address, with the result that the landlord is badgered by the company's disappointed clients. New York Times, Feb. 14, 1965, §8 (Real Estate), p. 1, col. 3.
According to the Internal Revenue Service, 86.2 percent of Forms 1120 (corporate returns) filed for 1956 and 48.3 percent of Forms 1040 (individual returns) for 1961 contained a "preparer's" name.

If federal standards were to be established for persons who prepare tax returns for compensation, of course, it would be necessary to decide whether the regulatory scheme should extend to those who perform such services as an accommodation to their customers, but without making a separate charge. In small towns and rural communities, for example, many taxpayers depend on bank tellers, insurance and real estate agents, stock brokers, and others for assistance in the preparation of their tax returns, and it may be that this network of laymen performs a socially useful function. On the other hand, the increasing complexity of the Internal Revenue Code, in a society with 28.3 million taxpayers reporting more than $5,000 of adjusted gross income and with 26.5 million taxpayers who itemize their deductions rather than use the optional standard deduction, suggests that we may have been assuming without sufficient study that federal standards of training, experience, or integrity are unnecessary.

In raising this issue, I do not mean to suggest that persons who engage in the preparation of federal income tax returns are immune from state laws and regulations governing the practice of law or accountancy. In the leading New York case on the right of an accountant to give federal income tax advice, the court said:

> The preparation of an income tax return is not primarily a matter of law and generally and mainly is not a matter of law. It may usually be prepared by one having no legal knowledge, from instructions prepared for lay consumption, or by one having only incidental legal knowledge. A taxpayer should not be required, therefore, and is not required, to go to a lawyer to have a tax return prepared. It is a practical, reasonable and proper accommodation to business men and the accounting profession not only to permit accountants to prepare tax returns but to permit them, despite the risks involved, to assume jurisdiction of the incidental legal questions that may arise in connection with preparing tax returns.[3]

It is not clear whether the court would have been equally tolerant toward the preparation of returns by persons other than accountants and lawyers, or if the legal question was of more than incidental importance to the taxpayer's liability. If the taxpayer's right to file a joint return was in doubt because the legality of his marriage was uncertain, for example, I question the right of a non-lawyer to resolve this question on his own, even under this dictum in the *Bercu* case. Some other states seem to have adopted a more restrictive view than

---

[3] Re New York County Lawyers Assoc. (Bercu case), 273 App. Div. 524, 537, 78 N. Y. S. 2d 209, 220 (1948). See also Lowell Bar Ass'n v. Loeb, 315 Mass. 176, 52 N. E. 2d 27 (1943) (layman may prepare simple returns for compensation).

New York's of the right of non-lawyers to resolve even those legal questions that are incidental to the preparation of tax returns.[4] A few states, moreover, have attempted to restrict the business of preparing tax returns to accountants, or certified public accountants, and lawyers; but these efforts have met with little success so far.[5] Even if state regulation of this area were less sporadic, it could hardly achieve the national uniformity of standards that seems appropriate to a national problem.

Even though the Treasury does not regulate the qualifications of persons who prepare income tax returns, and without regard to whether this activity constitutes the practice of law or accountancy under state law, the attorney or accountant who prepares a return for a client ought, in my opinion, to be held to the professional standard of competence that governs his other work. If the attorney or accountant makes an error, in other words, he should not escape responsibility for it because the same error might have been made by a lay preparer of similar returns. The client, after all, chose to engage a professional rather than a layman, and he is entitled to the skill that is reasonable and customary in the practitioner's calling. The issue is professional malpractice, not a layman's negligence.

Of course, the attorney or accountant is not an insurer. The mere fact that the client is required to pay interest or a penalty because his return was erroneously prepared,[6] or that he is unable to recover

---

[4]Gardner v. Conway, 234 Minn. 468, 48 N. W. 2d 788 (1951); State Bar Ass'n of Conn. v. Connecticut Bank & Trust Co., 145 Conn. 222, 140 A. 2d 863 (1958); Agran v. Shapiro, 127 Cal. App. 2d Supp. 807, 273 P. 2d 619 (1954).

[5]Courts have normally shown a reluctance to enforce state legislation which restricts the business of preparing tax returns. State v. Bookkeepers Business Service Co., ... Tenn. ...., 382 S. W. 2d 559 (1964); Moore v. Grillis, 205 Miss. 865, 39 So. 2d 505 (1949). In reverse fashion, a judicial attempt to restrict the preparation of complex tax returns to attorneys was thwarted by the state's legislature. Thus, Rhode Island Bar Association v. Libutti, 81 R. I. 182, 100 A. 2d 406 (1953), which enjoined an accountant (who was not a CPA) from preparing tax returns in which the income was more than $5,000 a year, was over-ruled by Gen. Laws R. I. §11-27-(7) and (9), (1956).

Some states allow, while others forbid, the preparation of tax returns by persons who are not CPAs or attorneys. Compare Cal. Bus. & Prof. Code §5051 (as interpreted by 10 Ops. Calif. Atty. Gen. 41, this statutory provision limits the preparation of tax returns by persons not licensed to practice public accountancy) with Mass. Ann. Laws ch. 112, §§87A-87E, as amended in 1963 (which exempts the preparation of tax returns from control as part of the practice of accountancy).

In 1944, the National Conference of Accountants and Lawyers (a joint ABA and AIA group) expressed the opinion that "the public will be best served if income-tax returns are prepared either by certified public accountants or lawyers." 76 ABA Reports 699 (1951).

[6]The fact that the taxpayer is required to pay a deficiency with interest does not, by itself, mean that he has suffered a loss. He has had the use of "the government's money" in the interim, and that may have been worth as much as the interest he must pay.

an overpayment of his taxes resulting from an error that is discovered after the statute of limitations has run, does not mean that the attorney or accountant who prepared the return failed to meet the required standard of professional competence. Many issues are so unclear that the practitioner cannot be expected to provide more than an educated guess; the client may so limit the scope of the practitioner's investigation, possibly in order to reduce the cost of preparing the return, that he has only himself to blame for the error; and there may be circumstances in which the ordinary practitioner cannot properly be expected to perceive a latent tax problem of a novel or complex character or even to recognize that the client should be advised to consult a more experienced specialist.

Defenses of this character may fail to excuse the error committed by the attorney or accountant in preparing his client's tax return, however, and he may then be properly held liable for his client's loss. There is a line of cases in which accountants have been held liable for failing to discover, in the course of auditing a client's records, that an employee has been embezzling the client's funds; although the accountant is not held absolutely liable like a surety company on a fidelity bond, he must display a reasonable level of alertness and competence in discharging his professional undertaking.[7] A similar obligation of professional competence seems to me applicable in the preparation of a client's income tax returns.[8]

I fully recognize that the Internal Revenue Code is longer than the Ten Commandments, and that, despite its length, it persists in leaving many questions unanswered. Does this entitle the accountant who undertakes to prepare a client's federal income tax return to disclaim any responsibility for errors on the ground that he is not a Philadelphia lawyer? Judge Learned Hand once said:

> In my own case the words of such an act as the Income Tax, for example, merely dance before my eyes in a meaningless procession: cross-reference to cross-reference, exception upon

[7] See e.g., Maryland Casualty Co. v. Cook, 35 F. Supp. 160 (E. D. Mich. 1940); National Surety Corp. v. Lybrand, 256 App. Div. 226, 9 N. Y. S. 2d 554 (1939); Dantzler Lumber & Export Co. v. Columbia Casualty Co., 115 Fla. 541, 156 So. 116 (1934); City of East Grand Forks v. Steele, 121 Minn. 296, 141 N. W. 181 (1913); see also note 8 infra.

[8] For the few reported cases in this area, see Lindner v. Barlow, Davis & Wood, 210 Cal. App. 2d 660, 27 Cal. Rptr. 101 (1962); Bancroft v. Indemnity Ins. Co., 203 F. Supp. 49 (W.D. La. 1962); L. B. Laboratories, Inc. v. Mitchell, 39 Cal. 2d 56, 244 P. 2d 385 (1952); Rassieur v. Charles, 354 Mo. 117, 188 S. W. 2d 817 (1945).

For the proper tax treatment of the damages collected by a client from his tax adviser, see Clark v. Commissioner, 40 B.T.A. 333 (1939); Rev. Rul. 57-47, 1957-1 C.B. 23.

exception — couched in abstract terms that offer no handle to seize hold of — leave in my mind only a confused sense of some vitally important, but successfully concealed, purport, which it is my duty to extract, but which is within my power, if at all, only after the most inordinate expenditure of time.[9]

Can the practitioner who is charged with having made a mistake recite these words, and express his wholehearted agreement with them?

The proper answer to these understandable questions, in my opinion, is that the complexities of the Code must be taken into account by the courts, professional societies, and others in fixing the standard of professional competence, but that they do not make it impossible to establish a standard. To the contrary, because it is these very complexities that bring a taxpayer to the office of his attorney or accountant, the practitioner must either limit his responsibility by candidly informing the client of his deficiencies, or else assume his professional responsibility — which depends in part, of course, on the standards of the profession to which he belongs — like a man.

Turning from the practitioner's professional responsibility to his clients when preparing federal income tax returns to his responsibility to the United States, I should first remind you of the requirement, which I mentioned earlier, that a tax return must be verified under the penalties of perjury not only by the taxpayer, but also by any person who prepares it for the taxpayer either "for compensation or as an incident to the performance of other services for which [he] receives compensation." Except for a statement in the Treasury Regulations that "[a] person who renders mere mechanical assistance in the preparation of a return . . . as, for example, a stenographer or typist, . . . is not considered as preparing the return,"[10] the Internal Revenue Service has not publicly explained the term "preparation." In most instances the term is not difficult to apply, but there are a number of peripheral problems on which an official announcement would be helpful.

In the absence of an official explanation, the Committee on Federal Taxation of the American Institute of Certified Public Accountants recently undertook, in its first Statement on Responsibilities in Tax Practice, to set out its understanding of when a certified public accountant is, and when he is not, the "preparer" of a tax re-

---
[9]Hand, Thomas Walter Swan, 57 Yale L. J. 167, 169 (1947).
[10]Treas. Regs. §1.6065-1(b).

turn. Some of the Committee's conclusions are debatable,[11] but it is unquestionably helpful to have this thoughtful expression of opinion on these borderline questions. At the same time, however, it seems to me that the task of interpreting the two brief sentences in the Treasury Regulations on this subject ought not to rest so completely on private shoulders. Of course, the Internal Revenue Service cannot be expected to anticipate all possible problems of interpretation in this area, any more than in others; but I see no reason whatsoever why the Service should not issue announcements on some of the recurring issues, such as whether the preparation of a capital gains, business income, or similar schedule by an accountant, to be incorporated as part of a return prepared in other respects by the client, imposes on him the obligation to sign as "preparer."

Quite aside from problems of interpretation, the legal effect of the requirement that the preparer of a return must verify it under the penalties of perjury is unclear. A person who knowingly prepares a fraudulent tax return can be prosecuted for violation of any of several criminal provisions, whether he signs the return or not, and this is true even if he is not compensated directly or indirectly and hence is not required to sign the preparer's declaration.[12] Moreover, a tax adviser or practitioner who participates in a client's plan to evade federal taxes may be prosecuted even if he has nothing to do with the fraudulent return itself — for example, if he prepares a false set of books and records, advises the taxpayer on a method of concealing his income, or makes a false statement to a revenue agent after the return is filed. Because the Internal Revenue Service has such a panoply of criminal weapons at its command, the requirement that the "preparer" of a return must sign it under the penalties of perjury — though it adds one more weapon if he does not believe the return to be true and correct as to every material matter[13] — hardly seems necessary to the vigorous enforcement of the revenue laws. It may

---

[11] J. Accy., October, 1964, p. 65. The Statement, provides, *inter alia,* that a CPA should sign the preparer's declaration even if he does not prepare the return for compensation, admitting that this admonition "goes beyond the scope of the Regulations." Although the laudable purpose of this departure is to aid in the establishment of uniform standards of responsibility, I should suppose that the Treasury ought to have the last word on the scope of its own rule.

The background of the AICPA Statement is described in Witschey, Responsibilities in Tax Practice, J. Accy., Sept. 1963, p. 65.

[12] Int. Rev. Code of 1954, §§7201 and 7206(2). In addition, the general conspiracy statutes are applicable. 62 Stat. 698, 701 (1948), 18 U. S. C. §§286 and 371 (1958).

[13] Int. Rev. Code of 1954, §7206(1).

well be, therefore, that the principal function of the preparer's declaration is not to impose an additional criminal sanction on him, but to remind him in a formal way of the responsibility he is assuming when he prepares a return, and to provide a convenient method of proving at a later time that he was privy to the return should it be found to be fraudulent.

Aside from criminal responsibility, does the practitioner incur any civil liability for the fraudulent preparation of a federal tax return? Although I know of no cases in which the United States has sued a practitioner for any loss suffered as a result of his preparation of a fraudulent return, I do not see any insuperable legal barrier to such a suit. The leading New York case on the civil liability of accountants, *Ultramares Corp.* v. *Touche, Niven & Co.*,[14] involved the liability of an accounting firm that certified a balance sheet for a client with knowledge that it would be used to obtain credit from banks and other lenders. The accounting firm was sued by a creditor for the loss suffered when the borrower became bankrupt, it having been discovered that the balance sheet included a large amount of fictitious accounts receivable. The decision is best known for its discussion of the accountant's liability for negligence, an aspect of the case that I will discuss shortly, but the court also dealt with the plaintiff's alternative claim that the accountant's certificate was false in certifying that the balance sheet corresponded with the books of account. As to this allegation, the court found that a jury would have been justified in finding as a fact that the certificate was untrue, because the receivables in question were not recorded in the client's journal or memo voucher book. A fraudulent certificate, the court made clear, would impose liability on the accountants for the loss suffered by the creditors. I see no reason why this part of the *Ultramares* decision should not be applied to an accountant's participation in preparing a fraudulent federal income tax return. If I am right, he could be held liable to the United States for any loss attributable to its inability to

---

[14] 255 N. Y. 170, 174 N. E. 441 (1931).
For comprehensive discussions, see Levy, Accountants' Legal Responsibility (1954); Levitin, Accountants' Scope of Liability for Defective Financial Reports, 15 Hastings L. J. 436 (1964); Hawkins, Professional Negligence Liability of Public Accountants, 12 Vanderbilt L. Rev. 797 (1959); Annotation, Liability of Public Accountant, 54 ALR 2d 324. See also Ready, Legal Liability of the Tax Practitioner, J. Accy., June 1964, p. 41.

collect the tax deficiency from the taxpayer himself when the fraud is discovered.[15]

The possibility that knowing participation in the preparation of a fraudulent return will subject the practitioner to civil liability for the government's pecuniary loss may seem unimportant in view of the much more drastic criminal responsibility that is attached to his misconduct. I turn, therefore, to a question of more frequent concern: if the practitioner's conduct is negligent (as judged by standards that I will discuss a little later) but not fraudulent, can the United States hold him responsible for a tax deficiency that cannot be collected from the taxpayer who is primarily liable for it? To be more specific, let us assume that a practitioner is supplied by a client with his books and records, from which a correct tax return could be prepared, but that the practitioner, working in haste or relying on a lazy or inattentive junior, fails to pick up several items of gross income that are recorded in the books of account. If the tax deficiency cannot be collected from the taxpayer when the error comes to light because he has become insolvent or the statute of limitations has run, can the practitioner be held liable to the United States because of his negligence in preparing the return?

In the *Ultramares* case, where the plaintiff alleged that the accountant was negligent — as an alternative ground to the claim that the certificate was false — the court was unwilling to hold the accountant liable for negligence (as distinguished from fraud) in preparing a financial statement where he did not have fair notice in advance of the third persons who might rely on it and of the amounts they might lend or invest. The court's reluctance stemmed from a fear that "a thoughtless slip or blunder . . . may expose accountants to a liability in an indeterminate amount for a indeterminate time to an indeterminate class." Because the financial statement in *Ultramares* was prepared "primarily for the benefit of the [client] . . . and only incidentally or collaterally for the use of those to whom [the client] might exhibit it thereafter," the court held that the accountant could be held liable only for fraud, and not for negligence. Unlike the financial statement in that case, however, a federal income tax return is prepared with advance knowledge of the use to which it will be put by the client, so that the practitioner could be held liable for negligence without exposing him "to a liability in an indeterminate

---

[15]The concept of a "loss" implies, of course, that the amount properly payable could have been collected if an honest return had been filed. If the financial condition of the taxpayer (and of his transferees, if any) was as bad when the return was filed as when his fraud was discovered, the United States would not have suffered any "loss."

amount for an indeterminate time to an indeterminate class." For this reason, the *Ultramares* case would not be inconsistent with imposing liability on the practitioner for loss incurred by the United States because of a negligently prepared tax return.[16] If such liability were to be imposed, the determination of negligence would of course have to take account of the practitioner's professional status, since an accountant could not be properly held to the same standard of skill in interpreting the Internal Revenue Code as an attorney, nor could an attorney be expected to perform accounting functions like an accountant; and, as I will suggest later, the terms of the agreement between the practitioner and his client would also be relevant in deciding if the practitioner was negligent in performing the services for which he was engaged.

The principal argument against imposing any civil liability of the type I have been discussing must rest on an assertion that the Internal Revenue Service, in auditing income tax returns, does not place any reliance on the fact that a return has been prepared and verified by a professional practitioner. It is of course clear that our federal self-assessment system presupposes that the government will rely to a considerable degree on the income tax return as filed in deciding which returns to select for office or field audit, as well as in deciding what items should be subjected to further scrutiny in respect of those returns that are selected for audit. Thus, the return is prepared and filed with the intention and expectation that the government will rely upon it. Even so, it is possible that the practitioner's verification is not intended to have, and in practice does not have, any effect beyond what is inherent the taxpayer's own verification of the tax return. Put another way, this point is that the government necessarily relies on the taxpayer's statements (including his omissions), but that arguably it does not place any additional reliance on the fact that the return was prepared for the taxpayer by an accountant or other practitioner and was verified by him. In the *Ultramares* case,

---

[16] In Glanzer v. Shepard, 233 N.Y. 236, 135 N.E. 275 (1922), a third party sued public weighers for negligence in weighing bags of beans. The public weighers were hired by the seller; the plaintiff was the buyer who had purchased the beans on the basis of the defendants' statement of their weight, which subsequently was discovered to be incorrect. The court allowed the plaintiffs' suit:

The plaintiffs' use of the certificates [of weight] was not an indirect or collateral consequence of the action of the weighers. It was a consequence which, to the weighers' knowledge, was the end and aim of the transaction.

Although losses to third persons as an "indirect or collateral" consequence of the preparer's error in preparing the tax return would not be within the rationale of *Glanzer* v. *Shepard,* they would be actionable if the standards of the *Ultramares* case were violated. A purchaser of a corporation's stock, for example, might be injured if the corporation's tax liabilities were greater than reported or reflected on its balance sheet.

and in other cases in which accountants have been held liable to third persons for losses resulting from financial statements that were negligently or fraudulently prepared, the injured third persons relied on the statements in making loans or investments, and their reliance was expected when the statements were prepared.[17] If reliance by the Internal Revenue Service on the practitioner's verification of a return is not to be anticipated, or if in fact it does not occur, the case for holding the practitioner liable for negligence is unquestionably weakened.

Closely related to the possibility of a practitioner's civil liability to the government for negligence in the preparation of returns, but of independent interest as well, is the propriety of uncritical reliance on information submitted to the practitioner by his client. When the amounts involved are material, either in absolute or in relative terms, and they could be verified by an examination of the client's books and records, is the practitioner warranted in foregoing any verification and relying solely on the information as submitted? If the client is unwilling to submit his books and records for examination, because he does not wish to pay for a full-scale or even a limited audit, does the practitioner have a professional obligation to note on the return that he did not go behind the information submitted by his client? If the client's books and records are incomplete, or if he has none at all, is there an obligation to test the validity of the information submitted by the client by a net worth and expenditures study for the taxable period involved? If the practitioner does not make such a study, and confines himself to the information submitted, should he indicate this fact on the return? When the client submits figures that are obviously estimates, should they be so labelled?

I wish that I could provide answers to these questions that you

---

[17] The governing principle is summarized by Restatement of Torts, §552 (1938):
> One who in the course of his business or profession supplies information for the guidance of others in their business transactions is subject to liability for harm caused to them by their reliance upon the information if
> (a) he fails to exercise that care and competence in obtaining and communicating the information which its recipient is justified in expecting, and
> (b) the harm is suffered
> (i) by the person or one of the class of persons for whose guidance the information was supplied, and
> (ii) because of his justifiable reliance upon it in a transaction in which it was intended to influence his conduct or in a transaction substantially identical therewith.

A recent discussion of this area may be found in Gediman v. Anheuser Busch, Inc., 299 F. 2d 537 (2d Cir. 1962), holding an employer liable to the estate of an employee for giving faulty advice to the employee regarding an election under its employee pension plan.

and I could regard as authoritative, but I cannot. The best I can do is to offer a few suggestions, and to express the hope that our professional associations, educational institutions, and the Internal Revenue Service itself will address themselves to these issues more directly and systematically than they have in the past.

Let me say, first, that I think that the fundamental issue is *disclosure*. If the practitioner merely accepts the figures submitted by his client (having no reason to believe that they are false), inserts them on the proper line of the tax return, and applies the tax rate schedule to the resulting total, I do not think he can be properly criticized if he adds to his signature as "preparer" the fact that he relied on information submitted to him. Even if the practitioner is a certified public accountant, I do not think he has a professional obligation to insist upon an audit before preparing a tax return; he is performing a useful function, it seems to me, in applying his professional skill to the information submitted by the client when he decides whether the items as estimated and described by the taxpayer are taxable, deductible, depreciable, and so on. In some instances, he may be called upon to exercise little or no judgment, and his functions may be limited to multiplying taxable income by the applicable tax rate and seeing that the taxpayer's social security number is entered in the right place. These are modest functions, but they take on great importance in a system that requires more than 65 million taxpayers to file returns each year; and I see no reason why taxpayers who are intimidated by these clerical tasks should not have them performed by an accountant or attorney rather than by a friend or fellow employee.

To be sure, Department Circular 230 provides in Section 10.24(a) that an enrolled practitioner must exercise "due diligence" in preparing or assisting in the preparation of tax returns, but I do not think that the practitioner violates this requirement when he accepts a limited engagement, involving no more than classifying or organizing data supplied by his client, or computing the tax due on unaudited estimates. Within this engagement, the practitioner must of course exercise due diligence in order to comply with the Department Circular; but to require more would mean that the Treasury's practice rules have supplanted the client's traditional freedom to fix the scope of the professional engagement, and I see no warrant for concluding that this was a purpose of the Treasury's regulations. Similarly, it seems to me that if civil liability to the government is to be imposed on the practitioner for negligence in the preparation of a return, along the lines I suggested earlier, the care required of him must be judged in the context of his professional engagement; his obligation to the United States is inexorably linked to the obligation he has undertaken at his client's behest.

In addition to requiring the practitioner to exercise due diligence in preparing returns, the Treasury rules (Sec. 10.24(b)) require him to exercise due diligence "to determine the correctness of representations made by him to the Internal Revenue Service." Does this preclude acceptance of the client's oral estimates or other unverified data in preparing a tax return? Assuming that this requirement is intended to apply to tax returns (as distinguished from oral statements and other material emanating directly from the practitioner), I am inclined to think that the only "representation" on the tax return that is "made" by the practitioner is that he prepared, or assisted in preparing, it. The amounts set out on the return, it can be plausibly argued, are representations made by the taxpayer himself rather than by the practitioner who prepares the return. If this line of thought is correct, the practitioner is not obligated to exercise due diligence to determine the correctness of amounts submitted to him by his client; his obligation is the more modest one of refusing to accept figures that he knows or has reason to believe are false.

If my conclusions so far are correct, then, the practitioner is warranted in accepting the limited professional engagements I have described, in which his contribution to the preparation of his client's tax return consists of computing the tax liability on the basis of data or estimates submitted to him. Does he have a professional obligation, when his role is thus restricted, to note on the return that he has relied on information submitted?

One might argue, I suppose, that the absence of a disclosure cannot mislead the Internal Revenue Service because it does not in any event assume that the practitioner has independently verified the figures used in preparing the return; thus, he need not inform the Service of what it already knows. The difficulty with this argument is that we do not really know whether the audit division of the Internal Revenue Service makes this assumption or not; nor am I aware of any reliable information on the extent to which practitioners rely without examination on the information submitted by their clients without noting that fact on the return. So far as custom is concerned, there may be a difference between the practices of certified public accountants on the one hand, and lawyers on the other; I should suppose that most lawyers would feel that they were not equipped by training or experience to go behind the information submitted by their clients as to items of gross income, cost of goods sold, inventory values, etc., though for some items (e.g., the basis of stock after a corporate reorganization) they might ordinarily accept professional responsibility. Similarly, it may be that the Internal Revenue Service in selecting returns for audit or in determining what items to examine on returns already selected, bases its decisions in part on the professional status of the "preparer."

In deciding whether a practitioner ought to disclose his reliance on information submitted by the client, moreover, a distinction might be made between those items that are commonly estimated because difficult to verify, and those that can usually be determined with accuracy. An example of the former is the amount of state sales taxes incurred by individuals on purchases for personal use or consumption. Some extraordinarily precise taxpayers may keep reliable records of such expenditures, but most of us do not; and since this fact is well known to the Internal Revenue Service, it can hardly be misled if a practitioner relies on his client's estimate without disclosing this fact.

In suggesting that the practitioner's duty to disclose that he has not verified the information submitted to him by his client is intimately related to the still-unknown extent of the Internal Revenue Service's reliance on the practitioner's role, I do not mean to imply that this relationship is wholly static. Even if it were found that the Service today assumes that practitioners do not ordinarily attempt to verify their clients' representations, some practitioners or the Internal Revenue Service itself might wish to effect a change in this practice. From time to time, we hear it suggested that the Internal Revenue Service ought to accept without further verification a tax return prepared by a qualified professional.[18] Certainly a first step in any such trend would be to require the professional either to assume responsibility for verifying the information submitted by his client, or to state unequivocally that he cannot vouch for the figures used in preparing the return. Although I myself think that proposals for acceptance of tax returns solely on the certification of a practitioner are open to serious objection, as well as visionary, I think it is quite likely that the professional status of the preparer of a return will have some influence on the way it is treated by the Internal Revenue Service, even if in theory this is supposed to be a neutral circumstance.

In a recent survey by Elmo Roper, commissioned by the Amer-

---

[18]The British practice is described by Wheatcroft, Ethical Restraints on Tax Practice in Great Britain, J. Accy., Feb., 1961, p. 59.

ican Institute of Certified Public Accountants, 48 percent of the businessmen interviewed expressed the view that an accountant's signature on a tax return meant that he "verified the information and took responsibility for its accuracy"; although a substantial number of these respondents may have been merely recording their belief that their own accountant took this kind of responsibility for the return's accuracy, the answers suggest that a significant number of businessmen may be confused about the accountant's usual responsibility as a preparer of tax returns. The same survey disclosed that 15 percent of the persons interviewed believed that "The Government bothers you less when the return is signed by an accountant."[19] This is not a very high percentage, but it is more than negligible; and if this many chief executives of manufacturing firms with 20 to 250 employees think an accountant's signature helps to ward off an audit or to ease the way through one, I would guess that the percentage of run-of-the-mine taxpayers with a similar view would be far higher. This surmise in turn suggests to me that we ought not to encourage, even passively; the notion that a tax return will be accepted more easily if it passes through the hands of a practitioner whose professional contribution is limited to transcribing the taxpayer's figures onto the form and applying his mathematical skill to these amounts.

For these reasons, then, I favor the development of a professional practice under which the practitioner would indicate whether or not he has verified the information submitted by his client in the course of preparing the return. It would be most desirable, in my opinion, if the appropriate professional societies could develop, in consultation with the Internal Revenue Service, a standard formula — comparable in its function to the "generally accepted accounting principles" letter now used in opinions on financial statements — to describe the extent of the accountant's labors in preparing an income tax return.[20]

I should like to turn, finally, to another aspect of disclosure in the preparation of tax returns, one that has stimulated a good deal of vigorous but inconclusive debate — the extent to which the practitioner has a professional obligation to call the Internal Revenue Service's attention to the fact that he has resolved a debatable issue

---

[19] Roper, What Manufacturers Think of CPA's, J. Accy., July, 1963, p. 35, and Roper, As Others See You, J. Accy., Jan., 1964, p. 32.

[20] The Committee on Federal Taxation of the American Institute of Accountants has made such a proposal to the Internal Revenue Service. See Carey, Professional Ethics of Certified Public Accountants 119 (1956).

differently from the way in which the Service might, or probably would, decide it. An example is a payment received by a widow from her deceased husband's company. If the practitioner thinks that the payment is properly treated as an excludable gift, but that the Service might disagree, ought he to attach a rider to the return calling the item to the government's attention? Sometimes, of course, the taxpayer or the person who prepares his return will make mention of such items on an attached statement so as to enhance his reputation for candor, possibly in the hope that this will be of tactical advantage vis-a-vis other debatable items in the return, or to avoid the possibility of a penalty for fraud, negligence, or intentional disregard of rules and regulations.[21] Another reason for volunteering such information on the return is to avoid the 6-year extended statute of limitations applicable to omissions of more than 25 percent of gross income by complying with §6501(e)(1)(A)(ii). What I am concerned with here, however, is whether there is any professional obligation to disclose the item, despite the practitioner's belief that it is non-taxable, and even though he thinks that disclosure will generate an unnecessary controversy with the government.

I might say, parenthetically, that I am not at all sure that this is really a question of professional responsibility. If there is a duty of disclosure, I should suppose that it applies to the taxpayer himself, and that the practitioner's duty differs from the taxpayer's only insofar as his professional skill may lead him to see that an item is debatable though the taxpayer thinks it is indisputable, and vice versa. Given the same information and skill, the taxpayer and the practitioner ought not to have varying responsibilities to disclose. Because the full-disclosure theory is usually discussed at professional meetings as an issue of professional responsibility, however, I am dealing with it here.

I should suppose that many persons would argue for full disclosure of debatable items, at least on first thinking about the question, and this view is also espoused by some authorities of eminent

---

[21] On the question whether disclosure will protect the taxpayer against the penalty imposed by §6653(a) for "intentional disregard of rules and regulations," see Hoffman, Intentional Disregard of Rules and Regulations, 28 Taxes 111 (1950), with which compare the discussion in 21 N.Y.U. Inst. on Fed. Taxation 23, at 31-33 (1963).

standing and long experience.[22] They would point out that the practitioner may be wrong in his belief (and, indeed, he may be temperamentally inclined to give his client the benefit of any doubts he may entertain); and disclosure will permit the issue to be resolved in an orderly fashion — in the taxpayer's favor if the item was properly excludable; in the government's favor, if it was not. The taxpayer ought not to get an exclusion to which he was not entitled, it will be argued, merely because the volume of tax returns is too great for all of them to be adequately audited by the government. A policy of full disclosure will enlarge the number of controversies, it may be argued, only if the additional disputes uncover a reasonable number of genuine deficiencies; but even if it were to generate a large volume of baseless claims by the Internal Revenue Service, this is a reasonable price to pay for our self-assessment system.

The opposing argument would begin by noting the absence of any provision in the Internal Revenue Code or the Treasury Regulations imposing a general obligation to list or otherwise identify debatable items that the taxpayer has resolved in his own favor. Indeed, the fact that the Regulations explicitly require disclosure of certain items might be taken to imply that the taxpayer need disclose only those items that are so specified by the Service,[23] and this inference draws additional strength from the fact that the tax return asks for various items of information for the obvious purpose of putting the

---

[22]Darrell, Responsibilities of the Lawyer in Tax Practice, reprinted in Trumbull, Materials on the Lawyer's Professional Responsibility (1957) 291, 296 ("by and large, wherever there is an item in doubt which might be considered taxable by the tax authorities, it should be disclosed somewhere, even though it is not actually reported as involving taxable income"); Hellerstein, Taxes, Loopholes and Morals (1963) 239 (seemingly favoring disclosure on the tax return of "all relevant facts, hurtful as well as helpful, that bear on the correct determination of the taxpayer's liability"); see also Shaw, What is Good Tax Practice: A Panel Discussion, 21 N.Y.U. Inst. on Fed. Taxation (1964) 23, 28 ("an honest return that will disclose all material facts").

Randolph Paul was evidently more doubtful about full disclosure. Referring to two questions posed by Hellerstein in Ethical Problems of Tax Practitioners, 8 Tax L. Rev. 1, 8 (involving possible applications of the *Clifford* and "thin corporation" doctrines), Paul said that the question of disclosure was "not easily answered." Speaking of "information in the possession of the tax attorney which is harmful to, but not dispositive of, a taxpayer's case" before the Appellate Division of the Internal Revenue Service, Paul said that most tax attorneys would "rarely volunteer" such information and that he "would be the last to condemn them for not doing so," vouching Samuel Williston as authority. Paul, The Lawyer as a Tax Adviser, 25 Rocky Mt. L. Rev. 412, 427-429 (1953).

[23]To cite only a few such requirements: the receipt of stock in an allegedly tax-free divisive reorganization, Treas. Regs. §1.355-5(b); recovery of items excluded from gross income under §111, Regs. §1.111-1(b)(1); information respecting formation, directorships, shareholdings, etc. of foreign corporations, Regs. §1.6046.

government on notice as to such sensitive areas as sick pay exclusions, tax-free annuity receipts, expenses charged by an employee to his employer, and certain travel and entertainment expenses.

A duty to disclose debatable items would apply, of course, not only to the commonly-cited widow's allowance, but to a long list of exclusions, non-recognition transactions, and other items that are not routinely reflected on the tax return if honestly believed to be exempt from tax. Among these are:

- tax-free returns of capital
- gifts and bequests
- prizes for notable achievement
- fellowships
- exchanges of "like kind" property
- loans that might be regarded as constructive dividends
- life insurance proceeds
- strike benefits

Although the overwhelming bulk of items for which an exclusion is claimed by the taxpayer no doubt fall well within the confines of the statutory privilege, there are enough controversies in these areas to suggest that a policy of full disclosure if consistently applied would require tens if not hundreds of thousands of riders to the 65 million federal income tax returns filed annually. Frequently the proper treatment of the item hangs on an interpretation of the facts, including such subtle issues as business purpose, bona fides, prearrangement, family relationships, arm's length bargaining, and fair market value — in respect of which there may well be a difference of opinion between the Service and the taxpayer. Still others involve unsettled and debatable questions of law.

Nor can we confine ourselves, if a duty of disclosure is to be imposed, to items that are not otherwise mentioned on the return. Many deductions and other items claimed on the return would take on a different complexion if they were accompanied by a full or even a partial statement of the facts. I do not think I exaggerate in saying that a payment of rent, salary, or purchase price to a person related to the taxpayer almost always contains within it the seeds of controversy, and that if the taxpayer is obligated to disclose every item that the Service could in good faith dispute, it would be necessary to attach an explanatory rider to the return for many if not most payments to related persons, and for innumerable other deductions as well. A lump sum deduction of $500,000 for rent, salaries, or merchandise purchases hardly alerts the Internal Revenue Service to the fact that $10,000 of the total was paid to the taxpayer's son, and thus to the possibility that part or all of this amount might be disallowed. A full-disclosure policy, in other words, would hardly be realistic if it distinguished exclusions from deductions on the feeble ground that deductions necessarily come to the government's attention because they are formally claimed on the return, whereas exclusions are omitted and thus may never come to light.

Many deductions, especially in business transactions, depend in part on the validity of allocations made by the taxpayer (e.g., in arriving at cost of goods sold; in allocating the cost of a business to its component assets; etc.). Here, too, a policy of disclosure would seem to require the use of riders on many more returns than is now the custom.

At bottom, our difficulties in this area may stem from uncertainty about the function of the federal tax return: If we view it as expressing the taxpayer's opinion of his legal liability, he has discharged his obligation to the government by expressing his opinion honestly—by including those receipts that he honestly believes are taxable and excluding those he honestly believes are excludable, and so on with respect to deductions, credits, and exemptions. If the return's function is viewed in this way, it seems to me that the practitioner's obligations when he prepares a return is to insist that it reflect *his* honest belief, based on *his* professional experience and skill, as to the proper treatment of inclusions, exclusions, deductions, and so on, based on the facts as he knows them. On the other hand, if the return is viewed as a statement by the taxpayer of what the government ought to know in order to make the most efficient use of its auditing facilities, then the taxpayer ought to call attention to all debatable items, because these are obviously the ones that would be most productive of revenue if subjected to examination.

For myself, the honest-belief approach to the tax return is more persuasive than the audit-assistance concept.[23a] When they demand too much, legal and ethical systems fall of their own weight in practice, even though they may linger on to be invoked on ceremonial occasions. I fear that the full-disclosure theory of the federal tax re-

---

[23a] In an opinion issued after these lectures were given, the A.B.A. Committee on Professional Ethics came to the same conclusion: "Thus where the lawyer believes there is a reasonable basis for a position that a particular transaction does not result in taxable income, or that certain expenditures are properly deductible as expenses, the lawyer has no duty to advise that riders be attached to the client's tax return explaining the circumstances surrounding the transaction or the expenditures." Op. 314, 51 A.B.A.J. 671 (1965).

turn, asking in effect that the taxpayer identify every item that the government might reasonably seek to treat differently, goes beyond what can be reasonably expected of the taxpayer. The Internal Revenue Service has ample means to specify those items which in its experience are frequently debatable, or difficult to detect without assistance from the taxpayer, and to require the taxpayer to disclose them. This authority has been exercised with respect to many categories of troublesome items and transactions, as I indicated earlier. The Service obviously has ample authority to add questions to the return, to require broad categories of deductions and other items to be broken down, and to require excludable items to be disclosed. It also has the power to require information returns to be filed in many areas, and its electronic data processing equipment now insures the speedy and accurate correlation of these information returns with the relevant tax returns. With these techniques for specifying what it wants of the taxpayer, coupled with the statutory penalties for negligence, fraud, and intentional disregard of rules and regulations, the Internal Revenue Service ought not to depend on a vague concept of taxpayer disclosure for debatable items and transactions.

I freely acknowledge that my view is less lofty than the vision of taxpayer cooperation with the government in a common search for truth that is offered by the full-disclosure theory. In practice, however, I suspect that the full-disclosure theory would be less likely to produce the flood of riders and statements that its conscientious application would require, than to encourage hypocritical claims that the items in question are not "really" debatable. Even the most conscientious practitioner would not be immune to this kind of self-deception. Whatever gain in information would be derived from a full-disclosure theory could be obtained, as I have suggested, more efficiently and with less moral wear and tear by the normal exercise of the Internal Revenue Service's power to prescribe the form of the tax return, and thus to specify in explicit fashion the categories of items that should be disclosed, segregated, or explained by the taxpayer. In addition, as I have suggested, the penalties for negligence, intentional disregard of rules and regulations, and fraud provide an impetus to disclosure; for many taxpayers and their tax advisers, these penalties create a broad penumbra of items to be disclosed in order to avoid even a suspicion of irregularity. The "honest belief" formulation of the tax return's function does not, of course, avoid the need for hard decisions by the taxpayer or his practitioner. As a standard, however, it seems to me easier to apply, less likely to induce hypocrisy, and less susceptible than "full disclosure" to the abuse that is unavoidable in the sporadic enforcement of a rule that is unknown to or customarily disregarded by the public.

II. Professional Responsibility in Representing Taxpayers

I propose in this lecture to discuss professional responsibility in the representation of taxpayers in administrative proceedings before the Internal Revenue Service — at the audit stage, in informal conferences, in the Appellate Division, and in the Tax Rulings Division and other sections of the national office. At the outset, we must take account of Treasury Department Circular No. 230, providing that no person may practice before the Internal Revenue Service unless he is enrolled for practice by the Treasury's Director of Practice, and defining the term "practice" as follows:

> Practice before the Internal Revenue Service comprehends all matters connected with presentations to the Internal Revenue Service or any of its officers or employees relating to a client's rights, privileges or liabilities under laws or regulations administered by the Internal Revenue Service. Such presentations include the preparation and filing of necessary documents, correspondence with and communications to the Internal Revenue Service, and the representation of a client at conferences, hearings, and meetings.

As I pointed out in my first lecture, in discussing professional responsibility in the preparation of tax returns, the term "practice before the Internal Revenue Service" as defined by Department Circular No. 230 does not include the preparation of tax returns, although if a person who is enrolled commits an impropriety in the preparation of a return, he may be disbarred or suspended from practice.

Since my concern is primarily with persons who represent taxpayers before the Internal Revenue Service for compensation and as a part of their profession or occupation, I will exclude from my discussion the representation of taxpayers by their employees, partners, or members of their immediate family; these persons need not be enrolled, but their practice before the Service is usually sporadic and uncompensated. In turning my back on them, however, I do not mean to suggest that their practice does not generate some problems of professional responsibility — it may, for example, in the case of attorneys and accountants who are employed in the tax department of a business corporation or bank and who regularly represent their employers in proceedings before the Service[24] — but their status is rather different from that of persons whose business or profession is not confined to representing a single employer, but consists of representing the public at large. In concerning myself with practitioners in this sense, however, I would include persons who are permitted by §10.7(7) of Department Circular No. 230 to practice to a limited extent before the Internal Revenue Service without enrollment, by virtue of having prepared the tax return under examination.[25] This exemption from the enrollment requirements, first promulgated in 1959, differs from earlier exemptions in the fact that it embraces persons who do not confine their practice to a single employer, but rather serve the public at large on a continuing basis and for compensation. Even though such a practitioner is permitted to appear as a taxpayer's representative only in the Audit Division of the District Director's office, and only with respect to the client's tax liability for the year covered by the return he prepared, he must comply with the standards of conduct prescribed by the Internal Revenue Service; and some of my observations about professional responsibility in representing clients before the Service will be as applicable to these so-called "unenrolled preparers of returns" (if they act for compensation and in the ordinary course of their business activities) as to enrolled practitioners.

Before attempting to examine the problems of professional responsibility that may arise under Department Circular 230, I must comment on two preliminary issues, since my views on these issues are intertwined with much of what I shall have to say on the principal subject of this lecture: Does practice before the Internal Revenue Service constitute the practice of law? It is does, can state courts in the exercise of their jurisdiction over the unlawful practice of law, regulate or forbid such practice by persons who are acceptable to the Internal Revenue Service as practitioners but are not members of the bar of the state in which their activities are conducted?

I shall begin boldly by expressing my conviction that much, perhaps most, of the practice before the Internal Revenue Service that

[24]See Kust, Standards of Conduct For Tax Executives, 14 Tax Exec. 283 (1962), which discusses and reprints a statement of principles ("Standards of Conduct") approved by the Board of Directors of Tax Executives Institute, Inc. in 1962; see also State Bar Ass'n of Conn. v. Connecticut Bank & Trust Co., 145 Conn. 222, 140 A. 2d 863 (1958); Austern, Corporate Counsel Communication: Is Anybody Listening? 17 Bus. Law. 868 (1962).

[25]The conduct of such "unenrolled preparers of returns" is regulated by Rev. Proc. 64-47, 1964-2 C. B. 988.

is governed by Department Circular 230 comes within the ordinary meaning of the "practice of law." The principal exception, in my view, is the representation of taxpayers before the Audit Division of the District Director's office, where the practitioner may be requested by the revenue agent to relate items in the tax return to the taxpayer's books and records, to assemble checks, bills, and invoices in support of deductions or other allowances, to explain the method of classifying accounts, and so on. These activities may be carried on by an unenrolled practitioner if he prepared the tax return under examination, and this exception to the general rule requiring enrollment to practice before the Internal Revenue Service seems to acknowledge that this kind of representation is more of a bookkeeping or clerical function than a professional one. When the proper treatment of an item is disputed, however, and resolution of the dispute requires study and interpretation of the Internal Revenue Code, Treasury Regulations, Service rulings, and judicial decisions, the practitioner must perform functions that are normally characterized as the "practice of law." This kind of research, which may culminate in the submission of a memorandum on legal issues, occurs frequently but not invariably in the representation of clients before the Audit Division, and it is almost always necessary in representing clients before the Appellate Division and in the national office.

Moreover, I do not think that activities of this type are any the less the practice of law if they are confined to the representation of clients for whom the practitioner regularly performs accounting services, or for whom he prepared the tax returns under examination. The character of the work itself is not changed by such a restriction; and while the practitioner who thus limits himself may not hold himself out for the practice of law (or of "tax law") in general, he does hold himself out as ready to perform legal services for his accounting clients.

If I am right in asserting that much of the process of representing clients before the Internal Revenue Service comes within the usual definition of "practice of law," does it necessarily follow that an enrolled practitioner performing such functions is engaged in the *unauthorized* or *unlawful* practice of law if he is not a member of the bar of his state? The answer to this question turns on whether state laws forbidding non-attorneys to engage in the practice of law are superseded by the Treasury's enrollment procedure, so far as practice before the Internal Revenue Service is concerned. Considering the volume of such activities by persons who are not attorneys, and taking into account the zeal of some bar association committees on the unauthorized practice of law, it is surprising to find that there is very little legal authority directly responsive to this issue. (This gap is partly explicable, I suppose, by the relatively low visibility of practice before the Internal Revenue Service. Unlike the incidental legal services rendered by claims adjusters, real estate brokers, and other laymen, whose work for clients usually comes rapidly and routinely to the attention of opposing private parties and hence of the local unauthorized practice committee, the activities of non-lawyer practitioners before the Internal Revenue Service are often known only to their clients and the government.)

The *Bercu* case, the leading New York decision in this area, held that an accountant was engaged in the unauthorized practice of law when he engaged in research and prepared a memorandum advising a client that it would be able to take a federal income tax deduction for an amount to be paid in settlement of a New York City claim for unpaid sales and use taxes. The services which were held to constitute the unlawful practice of law in that case were performed for a client for whom the accountant was not performing any accounting services, however, and no proceeding before the Internal Revenue Service was involved; and the injunction issued by the lower court forbidding him to engage further in the unlawful practice of law expressly exempted "services in the presentation of a client's interest to [the Internal Revenue Service] as authorized by its rules and regulations."[26] This exemption might be taken as a tacit admission that practice before the Internal Revenue Service is not subject to regulation by the state, even if it would otherwise be considered as the unlawful practice of law; but it might be construed more narrowly, as simply leaving that issue to be faced when, as and if it should arise. Outside of New York, we find a decision of the Florida Supreme Court holding that a "Treasury card" does not permit the practitioner to perform services that would constitute the practice of law, even if he confines himself to representing clients before the Internal Revenue Service, a California decision to the same effect, and a Massachusetts decision that reserves judgment on this issue.[27]

These state court decisions were largely superseded by a 1963 decision of the United States Supreme Court, holding that a person

[26] Re New York County Lawyers Ass'n. (Bercu case), 273 App. Div. 524, 78 N.Y.S. 2d 209, 87 N.E. 2d 451 (1948). Bercu was enrolled at the time the injunction was issued, but not when he performed the services in dispute.
[27] In re Kearney, 63 So. 2d 630 (Sup. Ct. of Fla. 1953); Agran v. Shapiro, 127 Cal. App. 2d 807, 273 P. 2d 619 (1954); In re Lyon, 301 Mass. 30, 35-36, 16 N.E. 2d 74, 77 (1938); but see Noble v. Hunt, infra note 29.

who was enrolled to practice before the United States Patent Office could carry on this practice in Florida; he was not a member of the Florida bar and his activities constituted the practice of law, but the Supreme Court ruled that Florida had no right to prevent him from doing what the Patent Office had authorized him to do.[28]

The federal statute under which non-lawyers are admitted to practice before the Patent Office, which the Court in this case held transcended any conflicting state laws, is virtually identical to the statute under which the Treasury established the enrollment procedure set out in Department Circular 230. Despite some differences of detail, the two enrollment procedures are sufficiently alike to lead me to the conclusion that practice before the Internal Revenue Service by an enrolled practitioner is not subject to regulation by the states, and that this practice therefore cannot be treated as the unauthorized practice of law.[29] I say this even though Department Circular 230, after providing that an enrolled agent shall have the "same rights, powers, and privileges and be subject to the same duties as an enrolled attorney," goes on to state that "nothing in the regulations in this part shall be construed as authorizing persons not members of the bar to practice law." In my opinion, this proviso is only a warning against activities, *other than practice before the Internal Revenue Service*, that might constitute the practice of law. This position is confirmed, in my view, by a 1956 interpretation of this proviso by the Treasury, which, among other things, expresses satisfaction with the current practice (which unquestionably has customarily included research into legal issues and the preparation of legal memoranda by non-lawyer practitioners), speaks of the necessity for "uniform inter-

---

[28] Sperry v. Florida, 373 U.S. 379 (1963).
[29] In its brief as amicus curiae in *Sperry v. Florida*, the United States said:
The impact of the decision [of the Florida Supreme Court, holding that the practitioner's activities constituted the unlawful practice of law even though he was enrolled by the Patent Office] on Patent Office practice is reason enough for concern. But the implications of the ruling are more far-reaching. There are a host of federal agencies which admit non-lawyers to their practice. Those most directly affected include the Department of Commerce . . .; the Treasury Department . . .; the United States Tax Court . . . [Br., pp. 3-4.]
The amicus brief (p. 49) of the American Bar Association similarly treated the Treasury Department enrollment procedure as analogous to the Patent Office's, and quoted at length from Agran v. Shapiro, supra note 27, "because of its pertinence to the question."
The argument in the text, to the effect that the federal enrollment procedure has pre-empted the field so as to preclude a state from requiring admission to its bar as a condition to practice before the federal agency, seems to have been accepted in Noble v. Hunt, 95 Ga. App. 804, 99 S.E. 2d 345 (1957), involving an enrolled accountant's right to his fee for representing a client in a fraud case before the Internal Revenue Service, Department of Justice, and Tax Court.

pretation and administration" of Department Circular 230 (which would be destroyed if all 50 states were free to decide for themselves what aspects of practice before the Treasury are reserved for attorneys), and states that in Circular 230 it fully exercised "its responsibility to determine the proper scope of practice by enrolled agents and attorneys before the Department."[30]

Although an enrolled practitioner's performance of services before the Internal Revenue Service cannot be regulated by state law (if I am right in my reading of *Sperry* v. *Florida*), this does not necessarily mean that there are no other limits on his freedom. In its 1956 statement, the Treasury said that it has "placed on its enrolled agents and enrolled attorneys the responsibility of determining when the assistance of a member of the other profession is required," and it referred favorably to the Joint Statement of Principles Relating to Practice in the Field of Federal Income Taxation, approved in 1951 by the American Bar Association and the American Institute of Accountants. With respect to practice before the Internal Revenue Service, this statement provides:

> If, in the course of such proceedings, questions arise involving the application of legal principles, a lawyer should be retained, and if, in the course of such proceedings, accounting questions arise, a certified public accountant should be retained.[31]

Although the Treasury warned in its 1956 statement that it may take formal action if it finds "that enrolled agents and attorneys are not respecting the appropriate fields of each in accordance with [the 1951] Joint Statement," this may suggest only the promulgation of prospective rules attempting to define the fields more precisely, not disciplinary action against a practitioner who oversteps the boundary line. Whether disciplinary action by the Treasury is possible or not,

---

[30] 21 Fed. Reg. 833 (1956), reprinted in 42 A.B.A.J. 349 (1956).

[31] National Conference Adopts Code for Practice in Income Tax Field, 37 A.B.A.J. 517 (1951); see also Carey, Professional Ethics of Certified Public Accountants, p. 129 (1956); Carey, Ethics, "Unauthorized Practice," and Federal Income Taxation—An Accountant's Viewpoint, 25 Rocky Mt. L. Rev. 435 (1953).

For a counterpart to the 1951 Joint Statement, see Principles Applicable to Legal and Accounting Practice in the Field of Taxation, Joint Statement of New York State Bar Association and New York State Society of Certified Public Accountants, 29 McKinney's Consol. Laws of N. Y. (Judiciary) (1964 Appendix), p. 348.

Whatever the function of the 1951 Joint Statement may be, it concerns itself only with lawyers and certified public accountants and says nothing about the proper role of other enrolled practitioners, who hold about 5,000 of the 77,000 outstanding "Treasury cards." The Treasury's 1956 interpretation, however, may have implied that all enrolled practitioners, not merely lawyers and certified public accountants, are bound by the 1951 Joint Statement.

however, the practitioner's professional obligation to his client surely requires him to accept only those engagements that his training and experience fit him to discharge properly.

As a lawyer, for example, I would not want to plunge into a proceeding involving the mysteries of the dollar-value method of pricing LIFO inventories without the aid of an accountant; and I daresay that most accountants would want an attorney's assistance before preparing a memorandum on the use of a joint husband-and-wife tax return by a man and woman who were married in Bulgaria after getting Mexican divorces from their previous mates. Extreme cases like these aside, however, I doubt that the current customs of enrolled practitioners conform to the 1951 Joint Statement. It is common practice, I think we would all agree, for accountants holding "Treasury cards" to engage in research culminating in oral argument and written submissions on such question as these:

—whether a taxpayer selling building lots is an investor entitled to report his profit as capital gain or a dealer whose profit is ordinary income;
—whether a loan by a shareholder to his corporation is a business or a nonbusiness debt;
—whether entertainment expenses incurred by a businessman were "directly related to the active conduct" of his trade or business;
—whether a salary paid by a closely-held corporation to one of its principal shareholders was reasonable compensation for services rendered.

Questions of this type — the list could easily be extended — are the bread and butter of the enrolled practitioner, but all involve "the application of legal principles," and thus require that a lawyer be retained if the language used in the Joint Statement of 1951 is to be given its normal meaning. I do not doubt, however, that accountants and other non-lawyer practitioners regularly undertake to represent clients in such matters, and that they read Treasury rulings, judicial decisions, treaties, and articles to ascertain how the Code has been applied to similar disputes, prepare briefs and other memoranda to fortify their oral arguments, argue with the government's representatives about the probable outcome of litigation should their case not be settled at the administrative level, negotiate compromise settlements, and advise their clients on the legal effects of signing Forms 870, 870-AD, and 872 in connection with their proceedings.

I might add that many issues that might be classified as accounting (or "tax accounting") questions also involve "the application of legal principles" just as inescapably as the issues I have mentioned above, and thus would seem to require that a lawyer be retained to satisfy the Joint Statement of 1951. To cite only a few recent examples of the fact that accounting follows the law in the determination of federal income tax liability (as for many other purposes, also), rather than vice versa, I may mention:

> —the deductibility of depreciation in a year in which the asset is sold for more than its adjusted basis at the beginning of the year
> —the determination of salvage value for assets that are customarily sold before their normal economic life is exhausted
> —the proper treatment of amounts received in advance for services to be rendered in the future
> —whether a tax liability which is being contested may be accrued as a liability by an accrual basis taxpayer
> —whether an accrual basis dealer who sells installment obligations received from his customers must accrue the reserve held back by the finance company that buys the obligations

Are these "accounting questions" that require the use of a certified public accountant to conform to the principles of the 1951 Joint Statement? If so, many lawyers would find themselves in non-compliance, since they would unquestionably feel competent to deal with these issues without an accountant, and other lawyers would use an accountant only as a witness or source of information, which is presumably not what the Joint Statement contemplates. Similarly, I should suppose that attorneys regularly deal with questions arising under the "tax benefit" doctrine (although the Supreme Court has said that at least one important aspect of this doctrine is "purely an accounting problem"),[32] with the concept of constructive receipt, and even with the question of whether an accounting method "clearly reflects income," without the assistance of an accountant.

Thus, one can scarcely avoid the conclusion that enrolled practitioners cross the line between "questions involving the application of legal principles" and "accounting questions" in proceedings before the Internal Revenue Service every hour of the working day, and that they would continue to do so on Saturdays, Sundays, and national holidays if the Service were open on these days. Whether this violates the 1951 Joint Statement, I do not know; only the ambassadors who negotiated and signed that treaty know whether it was intended to alter the practices of the day, or only to symbolize the cessation of

---

[32]Dobson v. Commissioner, 320 U.S. 489, 504 (1943).

open hostilities between the two professional organizations in the hope that their differences could be resolved gradually in the quiet of committee meetings.

Whatever may have been the intended function of the 1951 Joint Statement, however, I am far from convinced that changing current practices in this area would be in the public interest. Of course, if all of the legal work now being performed by the least able of the non-lawyer enrolled practitioners could be transferred to the best tax lawyers, their clients would be better off; but a similar transfer of engagements from inadequately trained lawyers to the best accountants would also elevate the level of practice before the Internal Revenue Service. In general, of course, amateur lawyers are at a disadvantage in coping with legal questions. Familiarity with the legal materials to be found in the loose-leaf tax services easily induces a false security; law is a seamless web from which tax rules and decisions cannot be safely detached. In my experience, non-lawyers underestimate the evolutionary character of the law, and, more Catholic than the Pope, tend to read and cite judicial decisions with more reverence than is appropriate.

While all this leads me to conclude that, in general, legal work is done better by lawyers than by laymen, so many lawyers are so ill-equipped for handling tax controversies that a crusade to oust non-lawyers from this area holds little appeal for me or even, I dare say, for most lawyers who work extensively in this area. Moreover, if I am right in thinking that *Sperry* v. *Florida* has the effect of vesting exclusive control over the practices of enrolled agents and attorneys in the Treasury, I would be surprised if the Treasury would wish to alter a state of affairs that it has characterized as "beneficial to the taxpayers and to the Government."

Since enrolled practitioners are likely to continue to prepare and submit briefs and memoranda on debatable legal questions in representing their clients before the Internal Revenue Service even though they are not members of the bar, I think that more attention must be given to certain issues in the area of professional responsibility.

One basic problem grows out of the fact, which I mentioned earlier, that "tax law"—if such an area can be defined—is not a self-contained system, but rather is part of the larger process of social control that we call law. Let me offer three examples of the way in which tax law draws upon other legal sources that are not to be found in the tax treatises, not even if they are as up-to-date and as bulky as the looseleaf services:

1. If a business corporation is prosecuted for violating the anti-trust laws and is convicted, can the legal expenses incurred in its unsuccessful defense be deducted as "ordinary and necessary" business expenses under §162? For many years, the routine answer was "no"; the expenses were not "necessary," it was asserted, because they could be avoided by complying with the anti-trust laws, and a deduction would "frustrate public policy" by encouraging violations of law. Recently, however, the United States Court of Appeals for the Second Circuit reversed this line of authority, citing (inter alia) the Sixth Amendment (providing for the right of counsel in criminal cases), the recently-enacted Criminal Justice Act, providing that the United States will pay for counsel for indigent defendants, *Powell v. Alabama* (the so-called Scottsboro case, holding that indigent defendants are entitled to have counsel assigned to them in capital cases), and several other cases that are not even indexed, let alone discussed, in the tax services.[33]

2. If a closely-held corporation borrows funds from a bank on notes endorsed by its principal shareholder, and the shareholder is compelled to pay the debt because the corporation becomes bankrupt, does he have an ordinary loss under §165 or a bad debt under §166? (The answer is important because if §166 applies, and the debt is a "nonbusiness debt," §166(d) confines the taxpayer to a short term capital loss.) The choice between §165 and §166 ultimately turned not on "tax law," but on the law of suretyship, which governs the rights of an endorser whose principal fails to meet his obligation on the due date.[34]

3. If a taxpayer buys securities on January 19th and sells them on July 19th of the same year, has he held them for "more than six months" so that his gain is long term capital gain? In deciding this question as recently as 1953, the United States Court of Appeals for the Fifth Circuit found it necessary to consider the implications of a number of non-tax cases, and it followed an 1864 decision of the United States Supreme Court involving an obscure issue of English land law.[35]

The non-lawyer who undertakes to prepare a protest or a brief

---

[33] Tellier v. Commissioner, 342 F. 2d 690, 15 AFTR 2d 416 (2d Cir. 1965). The fees before the court were incurred by a taxpayer who was convicted of fraud under the Securities Act of 1933 and the mail fraud statute, but the rationale of the decision is equally applicable to anti-trust violations.
This decision was affirmed by the Supreme Court, Commissioner v. Tellier, 383 U. S. 687 (1966).
[34] Whipple v. Commissioner, 373 U.S. 193 (1963).
[35] Fogel v. Commissioner, 203 F. 2d 347 (5th Cir. 1953).

for the Appellate Division, then, may be well-versed in the details of the Internal Revenue Code, but he is less well qualified by training and experience to see or sense the link between the tax question before him and the whole body of law; and he and his client may never learn of the damage done by this shortcoming. I do not suggest that all, or even most, lawyers have so broad an angle of vision that they will see what the non-lawyer has overlooked; but their training and experience will ordinarily give them an advantage in this respect. This disparity in professional competence does not run solely in one direction, of course; the accountant has a compensating advantage when an accounting question is in dispute—but it is usually easy to see when an accountant's special training would be helpful or necessary in resolving a disputed tax question. The need for legal training may be equally obvious if the tax dispute is known to involve the validity of a marriage, a will, or a trust; but many legal issues arising under the Internal Revenue Code carry no such signs advising the practitioner that the law of contracts, agency, or suretyship may be relevant or controlling—and thus he has no reason to know, or even to suspect, that his conscientious search through the loose-leaf tax services is inadequate.

Except in extreme cases, however, I see little chance of effectively enforcing the 1951 Joint Statement. If a practitioner plunges ahead to deal with a matter that anyone can see is beyond his professional competence, to be sure, a disciplinary action by his professional organization (if he belongs to one) or by the Treasury might be in order; and if the client is injured by the practitioner's negligence, he might be held liable for the client's financial loss. In most cases, however, the non-lawyer who represents a client in a reasonable salary, constructive dividend, thin capitalization, or real estate subdivision case is not departing from current practice in reading and citing judicial decisions and Treasury rulings, nor will he have any reason to know when a more difficult legal issue is lurking beneath a seemingly normal surface. Some practitioners, of course, may decide not to represent clients simply because they do not want to skate on thin ice, but most, I dare say, will not restrain themselves in this way. If so, and if the appropriate professional organizations and the Treasury are content with the current working rules governing practice before the Internal Revenue Service, it may be that the professional training of the accountant ought to include a larger element of legal education.[36] Conscious of my inability to do justice to this suggestion tonight, I offer it as no more than a tentative outgrowth of my view that much of the practitioner's work in representing clients before the Internal Revenue Service inescapably carries him into "the application of legal principles," to use the language of the 1951 Joint Statement.

I should like to turn now to another aspect of representing clients before the Internal Revenue Service: the extent of the practitioner's duty to disclose facts that may be troublesome to his client's case. The lawyer approaches this question from a background of experience with an adversary system that stresses the lawyer's duty to his client. This duty is described in the Canons of Professional Ethics as follows:

> The lawyer owes "entire devotion to the interest of the client, warm zeal in the maintenance and defense of his rights, and the exertion of his utmost learning and ability," to the end that nothing be taken or be withheld from him, save by the rules of law, legally applied.

Although the lawyer is not to engage in fraud or chicanery to assist his client, and although he must be candid and fair with judges and other lawyers, he is obligated to assert for his client "any and every remedy and defense that is authorized by the law of the land."

It is sometimes argued that this heavy emphasis on the lawyer's obligation to his client is more appropriate for the trial of private lawsuits than for the representation of a client in an administrative proceeding where the other "side" is the government. Quite apart from the fact that the canon of loyalty is at least as applicable to criminal prosecutions (where the government is always on the other "side") as to private lawsuits, I do not find this distinction between "private adversaries" and "the government" very persuasive, at least not in the context under discussion. Nor do I think that that the lawyer's obligation to his client should be diluted by the fact that the Internal Revenue Service is an agency of the Treasury Department, which has admitted the lawyer to practice; if anything, this

---

[36] In Summerfeld and Ritzwoller, Income Taxes on the CPA Exam: What Role Do They Play, 23 J. Taxation 54 (1965), it is said that federal income tax questions have occupied about 21 percent of the time allotted to Accounting Practice on the CPA examinations during the period 1951-64, and that "[t]hese questions have dealt generally with highly esoteric legal provisions requiring the candidate to have a relatively sophisticated comprehension of the current law."

dual role of the government as opposing party on the one hand, and enrollment and disciplinary agency on the other, suggests that great care should be exercised lest the lawyer's independence of the body before which he is practicing be jeopardized. There is a shadow of Big Brother, disturbing even though faint, in these suggestions that the lawyer has special obligations to the Treasury because it regulates his admission to practice or because it represents "all of us" and hence embodies a virtue superior to that of any of us.

It may be, of course, that these competing visions or abstractions of the lawyer's role in administrative proceedings are both straw men. Those who stress the practitioner's duty to act energetically and loyally for his client acknowledge that fraudulent behavior is beyond the pale; and those who argue that the practitioner must be candid with the government agency before which he is practicing do not insist that he open his files to opposing counsel. General propositions do not decide concrete cases in this area, any more than in other branches of the law. Let me, therefore, illustrate my views with a few concrete cases. In exposing my own conclusions on these cases, I am less eager to persuade you of their validity than to stimulate a more extensive exchange of views on a troublesome subject. This forum, I may add, is an especially appropriate place for such public introspection, since the N. Y. U. Institute on Federal Taxation and the Tax Law Review have both notably contributed to this process by sponsoring symposiums on professional responsibility in recent years.

To turn to my cases:

1. In computing his taxable income for a given year, the taxpayer deducted the loss on a sale of a farm to his sister, not knowing that a loss on such a sale to a related person is made non-deductible by §267. On audit of the tax return, the revenue agent fails to discover this error, but he disputes the taxpayer's deductions for travel and entertainment expenses for the same year. If a practitioner engaged to represent the taxpayer on the travel and entertainment issue learns of the non-deductible loss on the sale of the farm, he would be obligated by §10.23 of Department Circular 230 to advise the taxpayer of this error;[37] and I think it would be improper for the practitioner to represent the taxpayer on the travel and entertainment issue if he refuses to permit the non-deductible loss to be called to the revenue

[37] I am assuming here that the original error was innocent; if it was, or might have been, fraudulent, the practitioner's obligation to his client would include, in the case of a lawyer, advice as to the possible criminal or other consequences of admitting the error.

agent's attention. The ultimate question at stake in the proceeding before the Internal Revenue Service is the amount of tax liability for the entire year, not the amount of liability attributable to any separable item; and to claim the travel and entertainment deduction without offering to correct the clear error on the sale of property to the sister seems to me to be comparable to filing the return itself with knowledge of this unjustifiable deduction.

Let me vary the facts by assuming that the revenue agent disallows the loss on the sale itself, but on the ground that the farm was used as a residence so that the loss did not occur in a transaction entered into for profit. I do not think a practitioner could properly undertake to prove that the property was business property, knowing that the revenue agent had overlooked a clear barrier to the deduction either because he did not know that the buyer was the taxpayer's sister or because he had forgotten about the existence of §267.

I reach these conclusions, I should emphasize, not because I think that there is a special obligation of disclosure in tax cases, but because it seems to me that concealment of the improper deduction would be equally improper in a private lawsuit. A private parallel, in my opinion, would be a suit for the price of goods in which the only defense asserted by the defendant was that they had been paid for. If the seller's attorney were to discover during the trial that the goods had never been delivered to the buyer, I should think it would be improper to take advantage of the buyer's ignorance by continuing to press the claim.

2. Let me vary my sale-to-a-related-party illustration by assuming that the farm was sold to a corporation of which the seller was a shareholder. When the practitioner is engaged on the travel and entertainment expense matter, he learns of the loss on the sale of the farm, and he also learns that the taxpayer's stock in the corporation may or may not be worth more than 50 percent of the value of all outstanding shares. If his client's stock was worth more than 50 percent of all shares, the deduction was improper under §267; if his stock was worth 50 percent or less of all shares, the loss was deductible.

On discovering that there is a genuine doubt about the fair market value of the taxpayer's stock in the purchasing corporation, does the practitioner have an obligation to inform the Internal Revenue Service of this fact so that it can make an independent examination of the issue, or to withdraw from the case if his client will not sanction such a disclosure?

I would resolve this issue by applying the standard I suggested in my first lecture when discussing the obligation to disclose facts on the tax return itself: if the practitioner honestly believes the question can be properly resolved in the taxpayer's favor (or has no reason to believe that it cannot be so resolved), I do not think he is obligated to inform the Service that there might be a difference of opinion on this question. I express this view not because I think that we are engaged in a game of catch-me-if-you-can with the government, or because I think that sharp practice could be justified by the fact that revenue agents sometimes seek to take advantage of every slip that the taxpayer may make;[38] but because a policy of full disclosure, if conscientiously applied, would be intolerable. Every tax return of any complexity is a summary of a number of decisions; to ask not only that the taxpayer or his practitioner reach the result that he honestly believes is the right one, but that he also disclose all the facts in respect of every decision that a conscientious revenue agent might wish to review, would be, in my judgment, to impose too heavy a moral load, as well as to clog the process of adjudication. I say this despite my recognition that many practitioners are imbued with formidable powers of self-persuasion, leading them to resolve many doubtful issues in their client's favor.

The adversary system of administering governmental rules and regulations unquestionably has its drawbacks but I think it contributes to the preservation of a democratic society by assuring the citizen that in disputes with the government, he will have the vigorous assistance of independent practitioners; and I would pay a good deal, including an increased budget for the Internal Revenue Service's enforcement activities, rather than deny the public the right to deal at arm's length with public officials.[39]

3. Continuing with my example of a sale of the taxpayer's farm to a corporation in which he is a shareholder, let me now assume that the only issue in dispute in the proceeding before the Internal Revenue Service is whether his stock is worth more than 50 percent of

---

[38]It may be that revenue agents or other Service employees will be less ready to act impartially if they find that practitioners adopt an adversary position in disputed cases, but I am inclined to think that impartiality is best inculcated by the Service's training and personnel policies. There is, after all, no inconsistency in urging that government employees have a public responsibility to act in a judicial manner even while dealing with practitioners whose role is of an adversary character; this is what we regularly ask of district attorneys.

[39]For a brief statement of the function of the adversary system and of its bearing on the lawyer's professional responsibility, see Professional Responsibility: Report of the Joint Conference, by a joint committee of the ABA and the Association of American Law Schools, 44 A.B.A.J. 1159 (1958); see also Fowler v. Wirtz, 236 F. Supp. 22, 35-36 (S.D. Fla. 1964) (re disclosure of attorney-client under Labor-Management Reporting and Disclosure Act).

all outstanding shares.

Is there a duty to disclose fully all evidence bearing on *this* question, or can the practitioner properly put forward the favorable evidence and refrain from offering the rest? Here too, I find that I part company with the full disclosure school. I think, for example, that the practitioner could properly offer evidence of the dividends paid on his client's class of stock over a five-year period as evidence of value without disclosing that a seven or ten year record would put a different face on the matter, and without referring to other items of evidence, such as sales of stock by other shareholders, negotiations by the taxpayer to sell his shares, and so on.

The "full disclosure" school, I suspect, comes out of a background of legal practice in which registration statements under the Securities Act of 1933 and applications for rulings on corporate reorganizations are common. Documents of this character, filed only after painstaking revisions by attorneys of great ability, may be able to attain a standard of full disclosure; but experience in this area is not readily transferred to the day-in-day-out representation of small businesses and other taxpayers in the Audit and Appellate Divisions of the Internal Revenue Service. In view of the revenue agent's undisputed authority to ask questions, to issue subpoenas, and to assert a deficiency if he is not satisfied with what he has learned, I see no ground for insisting upon the kind of disclosure that some commentators seem to demand.

Let me now turn to another aspect of disclosure: when information is not furnished voluntarily by the taxpayer or his representative, must the Service confine its investigative activities to the taxpayer and third parties, or may the practitioner himself be required to disgorge whatever evidence is within his knowledge or under his control? Section 10.22(a) of Department Circular 230 provides that enrolled practitioners must submit any records or information requested by a duly authorized officer or employee of the Internal Revenue Service "unless the information or testimony is privileged or [the practitioner] has reasonable grounds to believe and does believe that the said demand is of doubtful legality." If the privilege against self-incrimination with which the client is clothed by the Fifth Amendment warrants withholding the records or information requested by the Service, it is clear that Department Circular 230 does not require the practitioner to comply with the revenue agent's request. Under a recent Supreme Court decision, the practitioner can properly refuse to comply with the revenue agent's request unless and until he is ordered to comply by a federal court after a hearing at which the taxpayer would be entitled to present his claim of self-incrimination.[40] Not only is the practitioner entitled to refuse to comply with such a request until the client's claim is adjudicated by a court of proper jurisdiction, but I venture the opinion that the practitioner would be derelict in his duty of loyalty to his client if he were to comply voluntarily. The client, it seems to me, is entitled to notice from the practitioner that the demand has been made, so that he can take the appropriate action to protect his Fifth Amendment privilege.

The provision in Department Circular 230 requiring enrolled practitioners to comply with requests for records and information suggests another question of professional responsibility, growing out of the concept of privileged communications between attorney and client. If the taxpayer is represented by an attorney, the long-established attorney-client privilege will entitle the attorney to refuse to disclose his client's confidential communications, and his refusal will not violate Department Circular 230.[41] The protection accorded by this privilege sometimes overlaps the protection arising from the Fifth Amendment, so that a communication between the client and his attorney may be sacrosanct on both grounds; but the attorney-client privilege is often broader, in that it protects communications that would not in any sense incriminate the client. Although sometimes criticized as an obstacle to the administration of justice, the privilege has withstood these assaults, and it has been vigorously defended on the ground that the public interest in the administration of justice is best served by allowing citizens to talk fully and frankly with their attorneys.

Most states, including New York, do not confer confidentiality on communications between an accountant or other non-attorney practitioner and his client; and even when such an accountant-client privilege is created by state law (as in Pennsylvania), it has been held inapplicable to the federal government in a number of litigated cases.[42] These cases make it clear that communications between an

---

[40] Reisman v. Caplin, 375 U.S. 440 (1964).
[41] See Lofts, The Attorney-Client Privilege in Federal Tax Investigations, 19 Tax L. Rev. 405 (1964); Note, The Attorney and His Client's Privileges, 74 Yale L. J. 539 (1965); Report on Attorney-Client Privilege Study, 18 Bulletin of ABA Section of Taxation, No. 3 (April, 1965) p. 83.
[42] United States v. Bowman, 236 F. Supp. 548 (M.D. Pa. 1964); see also FTC v. St. Regis Paper Co., 304 F. 2d 731 (7th Cir. 1962); Falsone v. United States, 205 F. 2d 734 (5th Cir. 1953); Dorfman v. Rombs, 218 F. Supp. 905 (N.D. Ill., 1963); cf. Palmer v. Fisher, 228 F. 2d 603 (7th Cir. 1955) (civil suit in which federal jurisdiction was based on diversity; state-created privilege allowed).

There is some evidence that CPAs, and accountants in general, are not interested in the creation of an accountant-client privilege. Comment, Functional Overlap Between the Lawyer and Other Professionals: Its Implications for the Privileged Communications Doctrine, 71 Yale L. J. 1226, 1248 (1962).

accountant and his client in connection with ordinary accounting services, including the preparation of tax returns, are not privileged as against the federal government even if state law purports to make them so; but they do not, in my opinion, settle a more limited but nevertheless important issue. This is whether a taxpayer's confidential communications to an accountant, or other enrolled practitioner, *made in connection with a pending proceeding in the Internal Revenue Service*, are entitled to a privilege against disclosure.

Much can be said, in my view, for the proposition that the Treasury Department, by admitting accountants and other non-attorneys to practice, implicitly invites taxpayers to avail themselves of the services of all enrolled practitioners without discrimination between attorneys and others. Having failed to warn the taxpayer that the confidentiality of his communications will be respected only if he employs an attorney as his representative, the Treasury would be engaging in dirty business, in my opinion, if it were to require an accountant or other non-attorney practitioner to divulge information that was imparted to him by the client in connection with a proceeding in the Internal Revenue Service. Such an extension of the attorney-client privilege to other enrolled practitioners might be implied from §10.39 of Department Circular 230, providing that agents enrolled before the Internal Revenue Service, "shall have the same rights, powers, and privileges" as enrolled attorneys, and further support for this position might be found in the constitutional guarantee of due process of law.[43]

---

[43]See United States v. O'Connor, 118 F. Supp. 248 (D. Mass. 1953), as interpreted in Application of Myers, 202 F. Supp. 212, 213 (E.D. Pa. 1962):
 It is clear that the purpose underlying the Special Agent's summons is to obtain information from Myers in aid of the Government's criminal trial of the indictment against Sherman . . . We believe the Government's purpose, openly avowed, is contrary to our fundamental and deep seated conceptions of fair play. See United States v. O'Connor . . . It [subpoena] aims to circumvent the policy of the Federal Rules of Criminal Procedure which deny the Government the advantage of pre-trial discovery. Surely the United States should set the example of law observance.

There is a suggestion in Falsone v. United States, 205 F. 2d 734 (5th Cir. 1953), that Department Circular 230 would violate Section 7602 of the Internal Revenue Code if it conferred confidentiality on a client's communications to an enrolled agent, but this theory overlooks the fact that the Circular itself rests on a statutory foundation (supra note 1); thus, the issue is whether the Treasury's statutory authority to regulate practice before the Service permits it to confer confidentiality on communications essential to that practice.

If confidentiality of client-practitioner communications were to be recognized, it would be necessary in some instances to distinguish between communications leading up to the preparation of the tax return and subsequent communications relating to the practitioner's representation of the client before the Service. The same distinction must be made under existing law if a taxpayer is represented before the Service by an attorney who prepared the tax return. See Colton v. United States, 306 F. 2d 633 (2d Cir. 1962).

Having expressed my conviction that a taxpayer's communications to an enrolled practitioner in connection with a proceeding before the Internal Revenue Service ought to enjoy the same immunity from disclosure whether the practitioner is an attorney or not, I hasten to add that I am not recommending that you offer up your clients as guinea pigs to test the validity of my theory. Moreover, unless and until the confidentiality of such communications has been clearly recognized by the courts, the non-attorney practitioner may in some instances owe it to his client to advise him that their conversations may be subject to compulsory disclosure. I should think that such a warning ought to be a routine matter in fraud cases, and that it might be wise in many ordinary civil cases in which testimony concerning the taxpayer's intent or purpose may be crucial (e.g., §531 cases).

I realize that much of what I have said in this lecture about the practitioner's professional responsibility in proceedings before the Internal Revenue Service reflects the standards, experience, and practices of the lawyer. I readily acknowledge that only about half of the enrolled practitioners are lawyers, and it may well be that they handle less than half of the cases before the Service. Yet I do not think that my heavy reliance on the lawyer's standards in discussing this subject is parochial, or that it stems mainly from my own professional training. The simple fact is that the conduct of adversary proceedings of every type is entrusted by our society to lawyers, and that tax practice makes up only a small fraction of this type of activity. Unless tax practice is unique, and I do not think it is, the standards and practices that have developed in the conduct of adversary proceedings elsewhere are bound to influence, and more likely to dominate, the conduct of proceedings before the Service. Moreover, even if we confine our attention to federal tax practice, we find that proceedings before the Service are only a segment of the taxpayer's relations in tax matters with the government; many controversies with the Service are preceded by legal advice given to the taxpayer by his lawyer and will be followed by litigation in the courts.

In thus suggesting that the non-lawyer who represents a taxpayer before the Service is swimming far from shore in a sea of legal customs and standards, I do not mean to assert that he will drown unless he clings tightly to the lawyer's rules and practices. Perhaps there is room for the development of another set of professional standards to govern the non-lawyer in representing taxpayers before the Service. I have seen no signs of such a development as yet, however, and I am inclined to think that all enrolled practitioners, regardless of their professional background, will in the end accept the same basic criteria for answering questions of professional responsibility arising in proceedings before the Service; and that these criteria will be heavily influenced by, and perhaps identical with, those developed by lawyers for administrative proceedings generally.

III. Professional Responsibility in the Planning of Business Transactions

The subject of this, my third and last lecture, is professional responsibility in the planning of business transactions. When Dean Prime first asked me to supply the titles of my three lectures, I thought of discussing tonight's subject first, on the ground that tax planning logically precedes the preparation of the tax return and the representation of clients before the Internal Revenue Service. On reflection, however, I concluded that my views on professional responsibility in the preparation of returns and in the representation of clients in tax controversies ought to be laid before you as a foundation for my discussion of tax planning. My reasons for discussing the subjects in this order will become clear, I think, in the course of tonight's lecture.

When I compare the tax practitioner's function in planning business transactions with his functions in preparing tax returns and in representing clients before the Internal Revenue Service, I am struck by three aspects of the planning process that are not characteristic of the practitioner's work in preparing returns and representing clients. The first difference is the much wider range of choice that confronts the practitioner who is advising his client in the planning of a business transaction; the second difference is that choices made at the planning stage will often have more drastic and irreversible consequences than choices made when the return is prepared or a brief is submitted to the Internal Revenue Service; and the third difference is that a decision to take one route rather than another on entering into a business transaction will affect much more directly the taxpayer's legal rights and duties as against his business associates, customers, and other persons. I should like to discuss each of these points a bit more fully because of their bearing, as I view the subject, on the practitioner's professional responsibility in planning business transactions.

When the practitioner prepares a tax return, he is concerned with the consequences of events that have already occurred; however much he and the taxpayer may wish it, the past cannot be revised. Of course, our knowledge of past events depends on memories that may be, or that may become, unreliable and on documents that are ambiguous; this means that the preparation of a tax return may require the practitioner to spend part of his time, like an archeologist, in digging up the past. Even more important, the practitioner must interpret what he has dug up, and this task calls for the exercise of judgment in applying canons of relevance and reliability to the facts he has before him; and we hope, though perhaps vainly, that his conclusions are more likely than the archeologist's to correspond to reality. The process of finding, selecting, classifying, and interpreting the facts as a foundation for determining their impact on the client's tax liability is of immense importance, obviously, but it requires the practitioner to work within predetermined limits with facts that are no longer malleable. In a few instances, of course, decisions can be made after the close of the taxable year that will govern the tax results of last year's events. Elections to use one accounting method rather than another, the payment of certain accrued liabilities, and a few other choices of this type may still be open when the return is prepared. In general, however, the practitioner is confined when preparing a return by brute facts that he can interpret but not modify.

The practitioner is similarly restricted when he represents a taxpayer before the Internal Revenue Service. The process of finding, selecting, classifying, and interpreting the facts continues to be important, and the practitioner will often find it necessary to engage in this process *de novo*, even if he prepared the tax return, in order to insure that the client's case is properly presented to the Service. Even though this reinvestigation and reappraisal of the facts may lead him to view the transaction very differently from the way it was reflected on the tax return, however, he is still working with events that he cannot control. Nothing, I suppose, is more painful to the practitioner than this iron link to the unalterable past. How often, when a revenue agent points to a troublesome book entry, a sloppily-drafted corporate resolution, or a hasty answer to a question on a tax return, is the practitioner reminded of these lines in Omar Khayyam's *Rubaiyat*:

> The Moving Finger writes; and having writ,
> Moves on; nor all your Piety nor Wit
>   Shall lure it back to cancel half a Line,
> Nor all your Tears wash out a Word of it.

By contrast, the practitioner who is advising his client at the planning stage of a transaction has a good deal of control over the facts. He may recommend that a business be conducted in corporate form rather than as an individual proprietorship, that property be leased rather than sold, or that the taxpayer's compensation be paid in cash rather than in stock; and the client's tax liability will ordinarily be determined by whichever of these routes is taken to achieve his business aim. Of course, the practitioner is often hemmed in even when he is planning a transaction; the client may not come to him until the die is cast, business pressures may narrow his range of choice, or the client's business purpose may predetermine the practitioner's recommendations because it can be achieved by only one route. Often, however, the practitioner can play a creative role at this stage, and even if he can see only one method of accomplishing the client's business aim, the phraseology of contracts, corporate minutes, or other documents that are employed to put this method into effect may avoid, or create, trouble at a later time.

I do not mean to suggest that the practitioner, if he appears on the scene early enough, can always insure that the transaction will look to others the way it looks to him, or the way he wants it to look to them. Granting that revenue agents and judges have their own eyes, microscopes, and telescopes, however, one may still maintain with confidence that the practitioner at the planning stage has a degree of control over the facts that he will never enjoy again.

If I am right in this conclusion, it follows that the practitioner's responsibility to his client at the planning stage is unusually burdensome. When one sees that a given business purpose might be achieved in a particular way, how does one find out whether there are other, possibly better, ways of accomplishing the same purpose? If you have found three possibilities, how can you be sure that there is not a fourth? The answer, of course, is that the practitioner must rely on his own experience and training, and on the advice of his associates and others, in deciding whether he has perceived all of the possible routes to his client's destination; there is no other source of assurance. In preparing tax returns and in representing taxpayers before the Service, the practitioner must similarly rely in the last analysis on his intuition and skill in ferreting out all possible theories and arguments before deciding which ones to pursue; but this task, demanding as it is, calls for less imagination and, ultimately, less self-confidence than the unavoidably open-ended inquiry that is called for at the planning stage.

The second characteristic of the practitioner's function in planning business transactions that I wish to stress is the finality of the decisions that result from his advice. If the taxpayer organizes a corporation instead of operating his business as a proprietorship, he will almost certainly be foreclosed from asserting subsequently that he did not understand the consequences of his decision, or that the corporation may have existed in form, but that in substance the business was a proprietorship and should be so treated for tax purposes. The government can disregard the corporate form in appropriate cases in order to tax the business on another basis, but rarely will the taxpayer be successful in such an argument; and even for the government, the form chosen by the taxpayer will be controlling in the overwhelming bulk of cases. Decisions made in the planning stage of business transactions, then, are usually irreversible. For good or for ill, they establish the boundaries within which the practitioner must work in deciding how the transaction should be reflected on the tax return and how it should be presented to the Internal Revenue Service and the courts in the event of a controversy.

These later decisions, however, are endowed with far less finality. If an item is deducted as a bad debt on the 1965 return, the taxpayer is not ordinarily precluded from later asserting that it should have been deducted in 1964 or 1966, nor is he ordinarily estopped from claiming that the original transaction did not create a debt after all, and that it should properly have been treated as a business expense, loss, or investment. Such a shift in theory may come too late because the statute of limitations has run in the meantime, or it may require adjustments to prevent double deductions or other duplicate benefits; or it may be tactically unwise because it betrays a lack of confidence in the taxpayer's position. These qualifications aside, the fact that the tax return is prepared on one theory is ordinarily not a barrier to the assertion of an inconsistent explanation of the same transaction later on, nor is there any impropriety in suggesting several competing and inconsistent theories at the same time. The practitioner may properly change his theories as the case moves through the Internal Revenue Service from the revenue agent to the Appellate Division, and if a better theory occurs to him — or to his successor — when the case goes to the Tax Court, a shift is perfectly proper at that time.[44] Because the practitioner is not forever wedded to every idea

[44]E.g., Dorminey v. Commissioner, 26 T.C. 940 (1956), Gutterman Strauss Co. v. Commissioner, 1 B.T.A. 243 (1924); Barry v. Commissioner, 1 B.T.A. 156 (1924). By contrast, a taxpayer is not so free to shift his theory in a suit in the District Court or Court of Claims for a refund, once the time to amend the claim for refund has expired. For examples in which a variance between the claim for refund and the issues litigated caused a non-suit, see Ronald

that appeals to him when he prepares a return, argues with a revenue agent, or files a brief in the Appellate Division, there is room for experiment and improvisation in the performance of these functions. Not so when the practitioner is planning a business transaction — here he (more precisely, his client) must usually marry for life.[45] If the practitioner does not have the skill needed for the undertaking, the damage is usually irreparable.

At the risk of offering to illustrate the obvious, let me refer to a recent suit in Louisiana by a taxpayer against his accountant's insurer for a loss caused by the accountant's faulty tax advice. The taxpayer, who was the principal shareholder in two closely-held corporations, asked his accountant about the tax consequences of a sale of his stock in one of the corporations to the other corporation, and the accountant advised him that if his basis for the stock was equal to its fair market value, a sale at that price would produce neither gain nor loss. The accountant was presumably acquainted with the elementary principle that a pro rata redemption by a corporation of its own stock is usually taxable as a dividend to the extent of the corporation's earnings and profits, but he evidently thought that the proposed transaction could be distinguished because the stock in question was not to be sold to the issuing corporation, but to another corporation owned by the same shareholder. In assuming that this distinction would be sufficient to produce a different tax result, he overlooked §304, which had been amended in the previous year to require the proposed transaction to be treated like a redemption by the "sister" corporation of its own stock.[46] When the impact of the amended provision was pointed out by the revenue agent on an audit of the return, the accountant admitted to his client, with commendable candor, that he made a mistake because "I simply, in my re-

Press Co. v. Shea, 114 F. 2d 453 (2d Cir. 1940); Zachary v. United States, 220 F. 2d 749 (2d Cir. 1955); Stewart v. United States, 50 F. Supp. 224 (Ct. Cl. 1943); cf. Scovill Mfg. Co. v. Fitzpatrick, 215 F. 2d 567 (2d Cir. 1954) (substantial compliance even though the claim for refund characterized as a "loan" a transaction which the parties later came to characterize as a purchase of accounts receivable).

[45] For possible escape routes, see Sugarman, Drafting Clauses of Escape in Agreements with Uncertain Tax Consequences, 1960 So. Calif. Tax Inst. 131; Barker, Planning Business Transactions in View of Uncertainties in Tax Law, 1964 ibid. 79.

[46] Section 304 of the 1954 Code is based on §115(g)(2) of the 1939 Code, which required parent-subsidiary redemptions to be treated like redemptions by a corporation of its own stock. In Cramer v. Commissioner, 20 T.C. 679 (1953), this provision of pre-1954 law was held inapplicable to "brother-sister" redemptions; non-acquiescence in this decision was announced in 1954 but withdrawn in 1960, 1960-1 C.B. 4, after the Service lost several other cases in this area, Rev. Rul. 59-97, 1959-1 C.B. 684. In the meantime, §304 of the 1954 Code was enacted, to provide a firm statutory foundation for taxing brother-sister redemptions as dividends in appropriate cases.

search, missed the new law." Because of this mistake, the taxpayer had to report about $60,000 of unexpected dividend income, resulting in an additional tax liability of about $35,000. He then sued the accountant's insurance company. The court held that the loss was covered by the accountant's professional liability insurance, notwithstanding the insurance company's claim that the policy was inapplicable because the accountant was unlawfully practicing law when he gave the advice in question (a defense to which I will return later).[47]

The facts of this case illustrate another aspect of the irreversibility of tax advice, viz., the possibility that the taxpayer will continue to rely on the practitioner's advice in later years. The advice requested by the client was followed by two transactions, one in 1955 (the year of the advice) and a second in 1957. The court held that the taxpayer was justified in relying on the accountant's advice not only in 1955 but also in 1957, since there had been no change in the law, the earlier transaction had not yet been challenged by the Service, and the accountant had not advised him of the error.[48] This possibility that bad advice may render the practitioner liable for a series of losses, for as many years as the client may reasonably rely on the advice, is reminiscent of the court's fear in the *Ultramares* case that if accountants were held liable to third parties for negligently-prepared financial statements, they would be exposed "to a liability in an indeterminate amount for an indeterminate time to an indeterminate class."[49] In the case of tax advice, the liability is to the client rather than to an "indeterminate class," but this limitation will be of little comfort to the practitioner if the client engages in larger, or more, transactions than were anticipated when the advice was given. To guard against this possibility, the practitioner might of

[47]Bancroft v. Indemnity Insurance Co. of North America, 203 F. Supp. 49 (W.D.La. 1962). The insurance company tendered several other defenses, including the claim that the taxpayer's loss was less than the amount of his tax deficiency for the year of the transaction because the basis of the redeemed stock could be added to the basis of the retained stock. The court held that the resulting reduction in capital gain that would be realized on a future sale of the retained stock was too speculative to be taken into account in assessing damages for the year of the transaction.

[48]In *Bancroft,* the 1955 advice was bad when given; the court was not called upon to consider the scope of a practitioner's liability for failing to inform his client that advice that was valid when given became invalid as a result of a later change in the law. The practitioner might contract explicitly to keep his advice up to date, in which event a failure to do so would be a breach of contract. More troublesome, however, is the possibility of an implicit undertaking to this effect, as well as the conflicting possibility that the volunteering of advice in a later year might be construed as an unethical solicitation of business.

[49]Supra, note 14.

course warn his client that his advice is good for one trip only, but the practitioner would ordinarily be reluctant to issue a disclaimer that seems to impugn the validity of his advice for the original transaction as well.

To return for a moment to the luckless Louisiana accountant who overlooked the 1954 amendment to §304: liability for negligence was imposed because of this error, but perhaps his professional shortcoming was more fundamental. If he knew that a corporation's redemption of its own stock on a pro rata basis is ordinarily taxable as a dividend to the extent of the corporation's earnings and profits, should he not have been skeptical about the success of a sale to an affiliated corporation? Although a number of taxpayers who tried this alternative in taxable years before the 1954 change were successful,[50] they had to go to court to win their point; and I doubt that many practitioners would have been confident of this outcome. If the Louisiana practitioner had been temperamentally inclined to doubt the effectiveness of any arrangement that seems too good to be true, he might have carried his research far enough to discover the 1954 statutory change; or, failing that, he might have qualified his advice to the client by pointing out the economic similarity of the proposed transaction to an ordinary dividend.

I cannot improve on Randolph Paul's expression of this point:

> Above all things, a tax attorney must be an indefatigable skeptic; he must discount everything he hears and reads. The market place abounds with unsound avoidance schemes which will not stand the test of objective analysis and litigation. The escaped tax, a favorite topic of conversation at the best clubs and the most sumptuous pleasure resorts, expands with repetition into fantastic legends. But clients want opinions with happy endings, and he smiles best who smiles last. It is wiser to state misgivings at the beginning than to have to acknowledge them ungracefully at the end. The tax adviser has, therefore, to spend a large part of his time advising against schemes of this character. I sometimes think that the most important word in his vocabulary is "No"; certainly he must frequently use this word most emphatically when it will be an unwelcome answer to a valuable client, and even when he knows that the client may shop for a more welcome answer in other offices which are more interested in pleasing clients than they are in rendering sound opinions.[51]

I should like to add to this definitive statement a comment on

[50] Supra, note 46.
[51] Paul, The Lawyer as a Tax Adviser, 25 Rocky Mt. L. Rev. 412, 416 (1953).

another aspect of the practitioner's responsibility in tax planning — the issue of disclosure. In my two earlier lectures, I have explained why I think that the practitioner is not required to reveal all of the weak spots in his client's position to the Internal Revenue Service. When he is concerned with planning a business transaction, however, he ought as a matter of simple prudence to assume that all of the relevant facts will become known to the government; any plan that depends for its success on the withholding of information or embarrassing documents or on a guess that it will not come to the government's attention is likely to be a poor plan. I am talking here not merely of "side" agreements and oral understandings that conflict with the transaction's public face, where it would be fraudulent to withhold the private arrangements. I am speaking also of a much wider circle of facts and plans, including negotiations that have been broken off in order to change the character of a planned transaction, and similar background material. In many circumstances, in my opinion, there is no affirmative obligation to supply information of the latter type to the government; but in advising the client, one surely ought as a general rule to assume that everything will come out into the open sooner or later. Moreover, if the background is so embarrassing that secrecy seems important, there is grave danger that the client and perhaps even the practitioner will step over the line from non-disclosure to misrepresentation.

I should like now to turn to my third major distinction between advising the taxpayer in the planning of business transactions, on the one hand, and preparing his tax return or representing him before the Internal Revenue Service, on the other. This distinction is to be found in the fact that business planning usually affects the taxpayer's rights and duties vis-a-vis third persons, while the preparation of the client's tax return or the settlement of his controversy with the Internal Revenue Service seldom does so. There are exceptions, of course. Sometimes the practitioner may recommend one method of consummating a business transaction rather than another with complete assurance that the taxpayer's partners, customers, and other business associates will be quite unaffected by the choice; conversely, the way the client's tax return reflects a debatable item or the way his case is presented to the Service may have an impact on third persons as well as on him. By and large, however, business planning, even if it is labelled "tax planning," does affect the taxpayer's legal relations with others, while his tax return and his disputes with the Service do not. When the practitioner is engaged in the planning of a business transaction, accordingly, he cannot confine his attention to the client's tax liability, to the exclusion of his non-tax rights and duties.

I am well aware of the platitudinous flavor of the point I have just made, but I would like to suggest, by offering an illustration, that it has ramifications that are not fully understood. Many of you are familiar, I am sure, with bank-financed life insurance, under which the insured pays the annual premiums by borrowing against the increasing cash surrender value of the policy, so that his only cash outlay is the interest due on the debt. For persons in high tax brackets, the tax deduction allowed for the interest paid to the lending institution (assuming it is not disallowed by §264) serves to decrease the cost of carrying such insurance, with the result that the insured may obtain a large face amount of insurance at a low cash outlay. As the years go by, however, the taxpayer's insurance protection diminishes because the loan increases inexorably, while the face amount of the policy remains constant. For some persons, this is not a serious drawback because their need for life insurance declines as the years go by; for others, the reducing feature of the policy is unfortunate.

A recent decision of the Court of Appeals for the Ninth Circuit involved a life insurance agent's sale of such a bank-financed insurance policy, with a face amount of $100,000, to a 36-year old employee whose income was about $10,000. In order to pay the first annual premium, the employee converted and pledged his existing life insurance policies. Within a short time, he found that the new plan was not advantageous to him — although it was generating large commissions for the insurance agent — and he found it necessary to cancel and convert his various policies. He then sued the insurance agent for fraud and misrepresentation, alleging that the plan was represented as suitable to his economic and family status, but that in fact it disregarded his family obligations and produced a tax deduction that was too small, considering his modest income, to outweigh the plan's insurance short-comings. After an extended trial, at which expert witnesses were called by both sides to testify to the suitability of the plan, the court decided for the plaintiff, and awarded compensatory damages of about $13,000 in recognition of the interest and other out-of-pocket costs to him, punitive damages of $10,000 to discourage a repetition of such behavior, and $2500 for his mental anguish. The award was upheld by the appellate court.[52] It is interesting

---

[52] *Anderson* v. *Knox*, 297 F, 2d 702 (9th Cir. 1961), reh. den., 300 F. 2d 296, cert. den., 370 U. S. 915 (1962); see also Gediman v. Anheuser Busch, Inc., supra note 17.

to speculate on the agent's potential liability for even more substantial damages if his customer had been forced by economic pressure to surrender all of his policies, and had died or become uninsurable before the suit was brought.

Another case in this area: A taxpayer was advised by her accountant that she had realized a gain on the sale of certain shares of stock, and that she could reduce her tax liability by selling some other securities which were worth less than their adjusted basis and setting off this loss against the realized gain on the first sale. The taxpayer discovered a year later that the accountant's advice was erroneous in that the first sale had produced not a gain but a loss, so that she had derived no tax advantage from the second sale. She then sued the accountant for the difference between the price at which she had sold the second group of securities and their market value when the error was discovered. The court held that the accountant was liable for negligence, but laid down a different measure of damages. Pointing out that the taxpayer could have revived her investment by repurchasing the securities in question 31 days after the sale (when the "wash sale" period expired), the court held that her loss from the accountant's negligence was the difference between the price at which she sold the securities and the price she would have had to pay if she had repurchased them at the expiration of the "wash sale" period.[53]

These cases, and other recent decisions of similar tenor,[54] amply demonstrate the hazards of recommending tax reduction or avoidance plans to a client who does not fully comprehend the plan's non-tax results. In discussing in my first lecture the practitioner's possible liability for overstating the client's tax liability when preparing a tax return, I pointed out that such an error on the return does not invariably saddle the taxpayer with a loss, since it can be rectified until the statute of limitations has run. In the case of negligent planning, however, the loss is often irretrievable, and its amount, as the cases

[53] *Rassieur v. Charles*, 354 Mo. 117, 188 S.W. 2d 817 (1945). The defendant evidently did not contend that the increase in the taxpayer's capital loss as a result of the second sale was of tax benefit to her, via a capital loss carry-forward, in a later year; conversely, the taxpayer's claim that the ill-advised sale damaged her by destroying a potential "useful" capital loss was held too speculative (because dependent on her realizing capital gains in the future, on a continuation of the depreciation in the securities, and on future tax laws).

[54] Livingstone Securities Corp. v. Martin, 327 F. 2d 937 (1st Cir. 1964); Miles v. Livingstone, 301 F. 2d 99 (1st Cir. 1962) (suit for damages when tax avoidance scheme failed; action dismissed because plaintiff was privy to fictitious character of transactions); see also Nichols v. Commissioner, 43 T.C. 842 (1965) (similar plan; taxpayer held to have suffered loss from "theft").

just described indicate, may greatly exceed the anticipated tax advantage because planning so often affects the client's non-tax legal rights and duties.

This aspect of planning leads almost inevitably to a discussion of the professional qualifications of non-lawyers to engage in so-called tax planning, and their legal right to do so. In my first lecture, I pointed out that the Treasury does not require enrollment as a condition to preparing tax returns, not even if they are prepared for compensation in the regular course of the practitioner's business. As to whether such activities constitute the unauthorized practice of law when the practitioner must resolve legal issues, I reminded you that the *Bercu* case in New York enunciated the proposition that an accountant may "assume jurisdiction of the incidental legal questions that may arise in connection with preparing tax returns," without defining the concept of "incidental legal questions"; as for other states, some have indicated that they would be less tolerant than New York of the resolution of legal questions by laymen, even in preparing a tax return.[55] In my second lecture, I argued that much of the practitioner's work before the Internal Revenue Service, especially at the conference and Appellate Division levels, falls within the usual boundaries of the practice of law; but I also expressed the view that the Treasury Department's enrollment procedure pre-empts this field so as to preclude the assertion of jurisdiction by state and local authorities.

What I have said tonight about the impact of most tax planning on the taxpayer's legal relations with other persons leads me to express the view that such work, *a fortiori*, usually involves the practice of law. Moreover, the irreversible character of decisions made at the planning stage suggests that faulty advice at this stage is often more costly to the client than errors in preparing his return or in representing him before the Internal Revenue Service. In the case described earlier in this lecture of the Louisiana practitioner who overlooked §304 in advising his client on the sale of stock of one corporation to another corporation owned by the same client, the defendant insurance company argued that its policy of professional liability insurance did not cover the client's loss because the accountant was improperly practicing law when he gave the bad advice. This defense had a double aspect: the insurer argued that its policy did not apply because the accountant was not engaged in furnishing "professional

---

[55]Supra, note 4.

services" within the meaning of the policy and also because the rendition of legal advice by non-lawyers was a criminal act under Louisiana law.

The court's answer, in holding the company liable for the loss caused by the accountant's negligence, was that accountants in Louisiana "regularly render opinions and advise their clients on matters of federal and state income tax liability as a routine matter in performance of their professional services"; that the insurance company must have known of this practice — whether it was lawful or not — in writing the policy; and that because of the inability of the legal and accounting professions to delineate clearly the boundaries of their respective callings, the court had an obligation to protect "innocent clients who have been damaged by a C.P.A.'s professional negligence, from the hiatus which the professions themeselves have been unable to resolve." This approach to the problem, it will be noted, does not confer legitimacy on the accountant's activity; it merely holds that the injured client, who no doubt assumed in good faith that his adviser was professionally qualified to render the opinion, should be allowed to recover his loss from the insurance company on a policy that did not clearly exclude coverage in such circumstances. I suspect, however, that the court's description of Louisiana custom — which concerned, it should be noted, the planning of a business transaction rather than the preparation of a tax return after the event — could be accurately applied to many other areas of the nation as well.[56]

Sometimes, of course, advice by an accountant or other non-lawyer on the tax consequences of a transaction is accompanied by an explicit warning that the client's legal rights and duties vis-a-vis third persons may be affected and that he should seek legal counsel on these issues. This is most likely to occur when the tax advice relates to family matters, such as wills, trusts, alimony settlements, and the like, though even here the client is often blithely advised on gifts to minor children and other arrangements as though they can have no substantial effect on his rights and obligations. And it is even more common for the accountant to assume almost complete jurisdiction over the planning process when business transactions are involved. The hazards in doing so are, or should be, clear enough when the con-

---

[56]For examples, see Coastal Club, Inc. v. Commissioner, 43 T.C. 783 (1965) (accounting firm's opinion letters re tax exemption of hunting club, recommending transfer of property to trustee and liquidation of club); O. Falk's Department Store, Inc. v. Commissioner, 20 T.C. 56 (1953) (advice re personal holding company status of corporations on consummation of proposed transaction); Haygood v. Commissioner, 42 T.C. 936 (1964) (advice re transfer of property to children at minimum gift tax cost).

templated transactions will affect the client's legal relations with third persons, but — for the reasons that I advanced in my second lecture — troublesome legal issues may be overlooked by the layman even if the transaction will affect nothing but the client's income tax liability.

It is sometimes suggested that the right of an accountant or other non-lawyer to prepare income tax returns carries with it the right to advise the client on contemplated transactions. I do not think that this position can be successfully maintained, not even if the advice is carefully couched in the form "If you do A, I would report it as a taxable transaction when preparing your return; if you do B, on the other hand, I would report it as non-taxable; etc." This goes far beyond the assumption of "jurisdiction of the incidental legal questions that may arise in connection with preparing tax returns" that was validated for accountants by the *Bercu* case and *a fortiori* it goes beyond what less tolerant states would permit[56a] I would also reject, as ingenious but equally unpersuasive, the alternative theory that an enrolled practitioner can engage in the planning of business transactions as a corollary of his power to represent the taxpayer before the Internal Revenue Service in requesting a ruling on the transaction or in a controversy should one arise at a later time. Section 10.39 of Department Circular 230 provides that "nothing in the regulations in this part shall be construed as authorizing persons not members of the bar to practice law." If this proviso means anything, it is surely inconsistent with the theory that the right to represent clients in disputes with the Service carries with it the right to plan the transactions out of which such a controversy (and need for representation) may arise.

Nor do I think that the accountant in such cases is adequately protected against the charge of unauthorized practice of law by the fact that an attorney will be called in to draft the operative documents — contracts, leases, corporate charters and minutes, etc. By this time, the important decisions may well have been made; the process of considering and discarding alternatives in arriving at the final plan may constitute the practice of law if legal issues have been studied and resolved along the way. Collaboration between the client's counsel and his accountant or other advisers is obviously an altogether different matter, provided it is a genuine joint undertaking,

---

[56a] In Oregon State Bar v. John H. Miller & Co., 385 Pac. 2d 181 (1963), the court held that estimates by an insurance agent of a client's cash requirements for estate tax payments would usually "require an understanding and application of the tax laws to the client's estate" and that this would constitute the unlawful practice of law.

and not merely a cloak in which the accounting firm is engaged to plan the transaction with the understanding that the final result will be retyped on the lawyer's stationery.[57]

I should like, in concluding this final lecture in the series, to turn from the unauthorized practice question to two broader aspects of the problems that I have been discussing. Whatever may be the merits of the lawyer's view that current practices in the tax field are vulnerable to the charge of unauthorized practice of law, lawyers must ask themselves why these practices have developed and whether the public will clearly be benefitted by a change. As I have suggested earlier, many lawyers are not professionally qualified to advise on the tax aspects of business transactions. This in itself would be of little moment if they emulated general practitioners of medicine by referring their clients to specialists when a preliminary diagnosis indicates a need for a consultation. This practice may have gone too far in medicine, but it has barely reached its infancy in the legal profession; and I suspect that the reason is not a valid concern for protecting the "whole man" against the fragmented views of narrow specialists, but the fear of losing the client to a better-qualified competitor. Improvement of the quality of legal service is not the whole answer to the unauthorized practice issue, however, since there is another reason for the role played by the accountant in the tax field. This is his continuing relation to the client, which serves to bring problems and possibilities to the accountant's attention as a routine matter, to give him a factual context out of which realistic proposals can emerge, and to permit suggestions to be made without an aura of soliciting business.[58] Sooner or later, the bar must come to terms with these underlying reasons for the accountant's role in the tax field.

Conversely, it seems to me that the accounting profession has not sufficiently concerned itself with the implications of its growing activ-

[57]See Blumenberg v. Neubecker, 12 N. Y. 2d 456 (1963) (retainer between client and attorney and accountant; each practitioner to work in own field). On the employment of lawyers by accounting firms, see Griswold, Role of Lawyer in Tax Practice, 1958 So. Calif. Tax Inst. 1, 9-13; Queenan, Role of Accountant in Tax Practice, *ibid.* 15, 19-20; Editorial, Employment of Lawyers by Accounting Firms, J. Accy., Sept., 1957, p. 28; Professional Ethics Comm. Op. No. 297, 47 A.B.A.J. 527 (1961); Reports of Special Committee on Professional Relations, 89 A.B.A. Reports 253 and 625. On the problem of "dual practice," see 23 J. Taxation 53 (1965).

[58]In this respect, the accountant's position resembles that of house counsel in large corporations. See Brown, Accountant as Problem-Discoverer, 1958 So. Calif. Tax Inst. 27, and the same author's The Law Office—A Preventive Law Laboratory, 104 U. of Pa. L. Rev. 940 (1956), recommending that lawyers exercise more initiative in calling the attention of regular clients to changes in statutes and regulations.

ities in this area. Much has been said about the independence of the accountant, especially his obligation to prepare financial statements in accord with professional standards, however much this may offend his client, because lenders and other members of the public rely on these statements. This is a noble ambition, but I cannot help but feel that its achievement is jeopardized by the accountant's role as planner and as advocate in tax matters.[59] If the accountant has advised his client on the tax consequences of a contemplated sale of property or a liquidation of a subsidiary, what is he to do when preparing a financial statement if further research or a new administrative ruling or judicial decision casts doubt on the validity of his original views? Put in these terms, the question may answer itself; I presume that he must act on the basis of his opinion as revised by the later developments. The question is more troublesome, however, if the focus is changed. Once we acknowledge how prone we all are to cling to our opinons, even professional ones, if a change will disclose sloppiness, haste, or ignorance, we may conclude that the practitioner should not allow himself to pass judgment on his own earlier recommendations or opinions. Similarly, if an accountant represents his client before the Internal Revenue Service in a tax dispute, can he properly claim to be independent in certifying to the client's financial statements? If in the administrative proceeding the legal validity of the accountant's classification of items in the taxpayer's accounts is disputed, can he properly be both a witness to the facts and a representative of the client urging a partisan position? Viewing these issues as a lawyer, I am doubtful that independence can be maintained under the pressure of a competing role, and even more doubtful that the public appearance of independence, which is also of importance to the profession, can be preserved in such cases.

Postscript: P. L. 89-332

In expressing the view (pp. 259-262) that state restrictions on the unauthorized practice of law do not apply to CPAs and other enrolled practitioners in their representation of clients before the IRS, I relied on the "Federal pre-emption" doctrine of the *Sperry* case. The status of practitioners enrolled to practice before the Service was, as of 1964, substantially the same as that of the patent agent who was before the court in the *Sperry* case.

[59]See comments on this problem in Johnson, Does the Tax Practitioner Owe a Dual Responsibility to his Client and to the Government?—The Theory, 1963 So. Calif. Tax Inst. 25, 33-35.

But this conclusion is subject to an important caveat. Congress, late in 1965, enacted P. L. 89-332 (5 U.S.C. 1012-14). Section 1(b) of this law superseded the Treasury's admissions practice by permitting any qualified CPA to represent others before the IRS "upon filing with that agency a written declaration that he is currently qualified. . . .and is authorized to represent the particular party in whose behalf he acts." (A similar privilege, but broad enough to embrace any Federal agency, is granted to lawyers in good standing at the bar of the highest court of any state.) By withdrawing the authority that was previously vested by Congress in the Service to regulate the admission of CPAs to practice, Section 1(b) of P. L. 89-332 weakens the "Federal pre-emption" argument. It is no longer possible for the Service to impose its own competency restrictions on the scope of a CPA's activities in representing his clients. Therefore, to this extent, the *Sperry* case is no longer controlling.

On the other hand, Congress clearly has the power, so far as practice before federal agencies is concerned, to displace state prohibitions on the practice of law—if if chooses—without substituting an alternative administrative method of regulating the practice of non-attorney practitioners. The status of CPAs *vis-a-vis* state prohibitions on the unauthorized practice of law, therefore, now depends upon the intent of Congress as embodied in Section 1(b) of P. L. 89-332. Unfortunately, the legislative history on this important question is not entirely clear.

The principal function of P. L. 89-332 was to free *attorneys* from all federal agency-imposed admission requirements and thus allow members of the public to be represented before Federal administrative agencies by counsel of their choice. At the same time, however, the right of "automatic admission" to practice before the Internal Revenue Service was conferred on CPAs. This by-product of P. L. 89-332 was designed to eliminate the opposition of the American Institute of Certified Public Accountants to earlier proposals that would have applied only to attorneys. The AICPA had argued that these automatic admission proposals should not apply to the Treasury Department because "each individual agency ought to retain the right to determine the extent to which it will permit non-lawyers to practice before it and the rules under which such practice should be conducted." If the Treasury was not to be exempted from the automatic admission procedure, however, the AICPA asked that CPAs be treated the same as attorneys as to this one agency; and this suggestion prevailed. Thereafter, the Treasury Department amended Department Circular 230 to provide that "[a]ny certified public accountant who is not currently under suspension or disbarment from practice before the Internal Revenue Service may practice before the Service upon filing with the Service a written declaration that he is currently qualified as a certified public accountant and is authorized to represent the particular party on whose behalf he acts." See 1966-2 C.B. 1171, 1173-74.

The House Judiciary Committee's report on P. L. 89-332 states that "Section 1(b), while it would eliminate the special enrollment requirements for certified public accountants in representing others before the Internal Revenue Service, is not intended to change the scope of service performed by certified public accountants in the practice of accountancy before the Internal Revenue Service." This reference to "the practice of accountancy" is puzzling in view of the fact, described above (pp. 261-264), that in representing their clients before the Service, accountants regularly engage in research, preparation of briefs, and oral argument of a kind that constitutes the practice of law when carried on before other governmental agencies. If P. L. 89-332 authorizes a continuation of the status quo, however, such services may be properly performed hereafter by a CPA, whatever may be the appropriate label for them.

On balance, I believe that the "Federal pre-emption" that formerly resulted from the Treasury's right to admit and regulate its enrolled practitioners was preserved by Section 1(b) of P. L. 89-332; and that CPAs—while representing clients before the Service—are now subject neither to state prohibitions on the unauthorized practice of law nor to administrative regulation by the Service. (I am referring here to administrative restrictions based on standards of competency, training, and experience; disciplinary proceedings for dishonesty, etc. are another matter.)

In reaching this conclusion, I am influenced in part by the fact that P. L. 89-332 did not alter the status of enrolled practitioners who are *neither* attorneys *nor* certified public accountants, with the result that these persons (who remain subject to the Service's admissions procedure) continue to be protected by the *Sperry* case against state regulation. Since such persons are free to represent their clients without state interference, I think it unlikely that the Federal courts will permit such state controls to be imposed on CPAs who are entitled to automatic admission under P. L. 89-332. The enactment of P. L. 89-332 muddied the waters, however, so that the right of CPAs to the mantle of "Federal pre-emption" is less clear than formerly.

13. Motivation and Responsibility in Tax Practice: The Need For Definition   *Francis C. Oatway*

ONE of the essential characteristics of a profession is the existence and voluntary acceptance of a standard of conduct governing the relations of the practitioners with their clients, their professional colleagues and with the public. Given this as a fact, it should not be surprising to note that over the past several years much has been written and said about the ethical responsibility and standards of conduct of the professional tax advisor.

Typically, these discussions, most of which have been led or initiated by prominent members of the accounting and legal professions, have concluded that the modern tax practitioner observes a standard of conduct supplementing the general standards applicable to all members of the practitioners' respective professions. In other words, there seems to be fairly general agreement among these spokesmen that the modern tax practitioner has either assumed or had thrust upon him certain responsibilities peculiar to his practice, and not common to all areas of practice within the legal and accounting professions.

In sharp contrast to this general agreement is the general disagreement regarding the exact nature and extent of these responsibilities. It would be a gross misstatement of fact to contend that even among these spokesmen there is unanimous agreement as to just what these special responsibilities are. Certainly, there is general agreement that the CPA and the lawyer tax practitioner are bound to observe the highest standards of technical competence, morality, and integrity. Also, it would be generally, if not unanimously, agreed that the work of these practitioners is endowed with a special public interest. But beyond these areas of agreement, and admittedly there are still other areas in which there is majority agreement, the concepts of special responsibility are many and varied. It is not at all uncommon in every day practice to hear expressed such diverse views as "The tax practitioner does not regard it as his duty to recommend full and fair disclosure of the facts as to items questionable in law"[1] and "[The practitioner] is not bound to support interpretations of the facts which might help the government, but is duty bound not to conceal facts which are material to the issue which is being considered. In the ordinary case, a lawyer is generally free to furnish his adversary facts or refuse them, depending upon the tactics of the case. This is of course one of the striking differences between the ordinary situation and the tax situation."[2] These views and others like them are not from fringe practitioners but from responsible members of the accounting and legal professions.

Should the existence of such diverse views among individuals who believe themselves to be honorably and ethically practicing as members of professions be permitted to continue? The answer to this question should be obvious if we can agree that the simultaneous maintenance of these views and the conduct that must follow them are dangerous and potentially fatal to the maintenance of a professional reputation. It is hoped that subsequent discussion will produce such agreement.

During this continuing discussion of responsibilities, one voice has not been heard from and by its absence has been somewhat conspicuous. The voice is that of the public—that collection of individuals who will call upon the professional tax advisor for service and who expect from the advisor a level of conduct that will do credit to himself, to his profession, and to the public. It is to this collection of individuals and interests that many of these responsibilities are actually owed. Hence, the surprise that in the discussions the public's voice has been the silent one.

At this juncture, two premises appear to have emerged:

1. There is general agreement among tax practitioners that they assume special responsibilities when they take on the mantle of their practice but there is general disagreement on specifics.

2. The public probably has a concept of what these responsibilities are but it is not known whether this concept coincides with that observed individually or collectively by tax practitioners.

Implicit in these two premises is a deficiency. Conceivably, the deficiency lies in a failure on the part of the accounting and legal

---

[1] See *Ethical Problems of Tax Practitioners*, 8 TAX L. REV. 1 (1952), the transcript of an open discussion among tax law practitioners.

[2] *Ibid.*

professions to formulate and to agree upon these responsibilities. After all, are not these responsibilities in the main voluntarily assumed? If this is the deficiency, it is suggested that this should be no more understandable or excusable than would be a failure to agree that a profession owes integrity to the public it serves.

On the other hand, possibly there is a consensus; perhaps the deficiency lies in the failure or inability of public and practitioners alike to seek out this consensus and to become knowledgeable about these responsibilities. If this is so, the fault could lie either in shortcomings in the individuals (largely a cause beyond the control of the professions) or in shortcomings in the means of making such a consensus known (a cause over which the professions can exercise some corrective action).

All of the discussion to this point is, of course, very speculative and largely theoretical. The essence of it is this. Do the tax practitioners of the accounting and legal professions have the means whereby they can readily determine what their special responsibilities are, and does the public have a standard to which it can refer in order to make a measure of the comparability of expected and actual standards of professional responsibility and conduct? Put another way, are the codes of conduct of the legal and accounting professions adequate for the modern tax practitioner in the fulfillment of the purposes they are intended to serve?

The Need for Reevaluation

The Narrow View

To many, the mere utterance of such a question would be viewed as heresy. They would take the position that to question the adequacy of a code of professional conduct or, even worse, to point out a shortcoming is nothing less than a direct affront to the profession itself. If it is assumed that a code of conduct is in and of itself a detailed mirror of what professional conduct is in fact, then perhaps there is some ground for this fear. It would indeed seem to follow that a shortcoming in the code is a shortcoming in the level of professional conduct and, therefore, potentially an adverse reflection upon the profession itself. It is, however, a narrow and confining view that sees a code as a mirror of conduct. A good code of professional conduct should evidence aims and guideposts rather than specifics. Most codes of professional conduct and at least those with which this discussion is concerned contain a specific admonition against the drawing of any inference that the enumeration of rules permits the denial of the existence of others not specifically mentioned.[3] As a matter of fact, experience indicates that members of the accounting and legal professions typically supplement the written rules of conduct with their own unwritten ones which frequently portray a level of conduct higher by far than the level specifically required by the written rules.

For this reason, it should not be assumed that a deficiency in a code is indicative of a deficiency in the level of professional conduct governed by that code. More often than not it would probably be found that any generally suggested additions to a code would have no greater effect than the formalization of existing standards and the public proclamation of the fact that such standards are in practice maintained.

A Good and Necessary Procedure

In contrast to the view of those who would utter "heresy," there is another with which the writer would agree. That is, that rather than look upon a reappraisal of rules of conduct as a fearful thing and something to be avoided in the professions' best interests, it would be better to regard it as good and necessary in these best interests. A reappraisal is necessary because of the status of a code of conduct as an essential element in the definition of a profession. It is good also for somewhat more selfish reasons.

Because of its very nature and by virtue of its special public-service function, a profession cannot survive without the confidence of the public. Without it the profession would indeed be a hollow thing. Confidence can, of course, be engendered in many ways, public relations being an example of a particular stimulant. But even public relations needs a foundation.

No one item would seem to be more capable of fostering public confidence or, alternatively, of providing a foundation for other stimulants than the conduct of the profession itself. And while agreeing that a code of conduct should not be exclusively reflective of actual conduct, a code looms as the best vehicle for informing the public of the high standards observed and to which the public can look with confidence when requesting or observing professional pursuits. From this standpoint, then, a periodic reappraisal is good.

---

[3] The reference is to the Preamble of each of the Canons of Professional Ethics of the American Bar Association and the Code of Professional Ethics of the American Institute of Certified Public Accountants. These will be frequently referred to hereafter merely as "Canons" and "Code."

Standards of Responsibility

Obviously, before we can intelligently consider the adequacy of standards of responsibility or rules of ethical conduct in tax practice we must have at least a general concept of what these standards are. What, then, are the ethical standards applicable generally to members of the legal and accounting professions and, more specifically, how do these standards evidence the ethical responsibility of the CPA and the attorney in tax practice?

From the answer to the first part of this question comes the first hint of the reason for all of the aforementioned difficulty in identifying professional responsibilities. There really is nothing to which one might refer and thereafter conclude that he had examined the code of professional conduct of one or both of these professions. In both professions, these guides to proper professional behavior are a great blend of conceptual materials.

Canons or Codes of Practice

They are, first and foremost, the written standards adopted by and for their members by national organizations of CPAs and attorneys. In this sense then they are at least the Code of Professional Ethics of the American Institute of Certified Public Accountants and the Canons of Professional Ethics of the American Bar Association. Next, they are the written standards adopted by various regional, state, and local CPA societies and bar associations. In addition, they are also the rules adopted or prescribed by state boards of accountancy in those jurisdictions where such rules have been promulgated under authority of law. In sum and substance, they are all of the written standards of conduct, canons of practice and codes of ethics, by whatever name identified. With respect to each profession individually, by and large the rules of all of these bodies are similar. The basic principles are in all cases the same even though the form, arrangement, and extent of coverage may differ.[4]

Customs of Practice

But this is not all that makes up this body of standards. These standards are also the unwritten ethical practices of the two professions, the customs of practice generally observed by reputable

---

[4] The framework for this definition is borrowed from John L. Carey's concept of "the origin of the rules of conduct of the accounting proession" in his book entitled Professional Ethics of Certified Public Accountants.

members of each profession. In many ways these customs are even more comprehensive than the codes; comprehensive enough, at least, so that no really meaningful consideration of the adequacy of standards could be undertaken if these customs were ignored. This is particularly true in a discussion of standards in tax practice since this branch of the practice of law and accounting is, generally speaking, younger than the written standards themselves. Generally, the written standards emphasize the more traditional functions of the two professions, namely litigation for the attorney and the attest function of the CPA.

By their very nature, written standards of conduct must be general. As was mentioned previously, even the codes themselves recognize this. Most of us would agree that when dealing in abstracts such as standards of responsibility, no one body can be expected to be wholly comprehensive. It is doubtful whether those adopting the standards would even want it to be that way since the more specific a body of rules becomes, the more mechanical their observance becomes. At some point, with a high degree of specifics, some element of professionalism is lost. Individuals then act not out of respect for the high principles characteristic of their profession but rather out of a feeling of obligation dictated by one or another specific rule of conduct. Robert T. McCracken, a former chairman of the America Bar Association Committee on Professional Ethics and Grievances, highlights what he believes to be the intended nature of a written code of conduct when he says of the Canons of Professional Ethics:

> Much of the intendment of the Canons has to do with the eternal verities, with the fundamentals of right or wrong conduct of the members of an ancient and honorable profession.... For lawyers of experience and the right instincts, no Canons are required. As a guide to the young, and even, in rare instances, for those of mature years, they are most useful. But they are intended to serve only as signposts at the crossroads, not as a fence along the entire length of the highway.[5]

United States Treasury Department Rules

For the tax practitioner, the standards of conduct include something in addition to these canons and customs of practice. They are the rules of conduct that must be observed by the CPA or the attorney who wishes to practice as an enrolled taxpayer representative before the United States Treasury Department. These rules and standards are embodied in Treasury Department Circular No.

---

[5] *Canons of Ethics: Some Observations on a Reappraisal*, 43 A.B.A.J. 1098 (1957).

230.[6] From the standpoint of standards, the Circular consists of two things. First, in a general way it requires that enrolled agents or attorneys conduct themselves in accordance with recognized ethical standards applicable to members of their respective professions generally.[7] Secondly, it enumerates a series of negative acts, the performance of which will constitute grounds for disbarment.[8]

Clearly, Circular No. 230 is something very different from the other standards just described. Among other things, it is almost entirely negative. As such, it presents a sharp contrast with the positive exhortations to high principles of responsibility that we observe in the various Canons and Codes.

In a way it would be desirable if the rules of Circular No. 230 could be ignored in a discussion of standards of professional responsibility on the grounds that they are otherwise embodied in the voluntarily assumed canons and customs of practice. Until we are satisfied that they are mere duplication, however, they cannot be ignored. In any event, Circular No. 230 is determinative of good and responsible tax practice and, therefore, in this sense, even if in no other, the Circular must be considered part of this elusive body of standards, the adequacy of which is being questioned.

NECESSARY LIMITATIONS AS TO SCOPE

It has probably been noted that up to this point, the preliminary discussion and particularly the definition of standards has been limited to the CPA and the attorney in tax practice. By so doing, there is no intention to imply that any one individual outside these professional groups is not qualified to render competent tax advice. On the contrary, it is recognized that there are such individuals. However, when discussing standards of conduct in the broadest sense and, particularly, standards that have general rather than individual application, it does become somewhat necessary to impose this limitation. On a group basis, only the accounting and legal professions have voluntarily imposed the general standards of conduct with which we are concerned. To be sure, individual practitioners, not properly includible as members of these professions, have imposed upon themselves rigid standards of conduct which, from all appearances, measure up to the best. No matter how admirable, however, these standards have no broader application than the seri-

---

[6] 31 C.F.R. §§ 10.1–10.8. The Circular was most recently published in revised form at 29 Federal Register 9647–9655, dated July 17, 1964.

[7] Treasury Circular No. 230 § 10.21, and § 10.51(a) (by inference).

[8] *Id.* at § 10.51(b)(1) through (30).

ous intention of the individual who assumes them, and for their adequacy the individual is accountable to no one but himself.

Having obtained a general idea of what is comprehended by the phrase "standards of responsibility," let us now consider the purposes for which these standards are designed. Pinning these down is, in many respects, more difficult than identifying the standards themselves. In one sense they can be said to serve whatever purpose the group of individuals assuming them wants them to serve. This would be the easy way out! More realistically, however, it would seem that something much more specific is in fact intended—fundamental purposes like the maintenance of the professions and the protection of the public interests that the professions dedicate themselves to serve, and practical purposes like providing day-to-day guides to right action.

Fundamental Purposes

In the case of the Canons of Professional Ethics of the ABA, the Canons themselves provide the first indication of what these purposes are. The Preamble to the Canons speaks of molding the conduct and motives of the members of the legal profession so as to merit the approval of all just men. The Canons speak in terms of so engendering this public confidence as to maintain pure and unsullied the system of establishing and dispensing Justice. Similarly, the Code of Professional Ethics of the AICPA emphasizes this confidence or reliance of the public, except in this instance the principal emphasis is on sound financial reporting and business advice. Since not much in the way of day-in-and-day-out tax practice affects either the administration of justice or the rendering of independent opinions on financial statements, these aims are, of course, somewhat removed. It seems nevertheless, that the basic purposes are still there. From the narrow standpoint of the professional tax practitioner, it does not seem unreasonable to expect that his code of ethics should similarly operate to instill the confidence of the public in this instance that the administration of the tax system is not being undermined. From an observation of the conduct of the tax practitioner and from a study of the standards set by these practitioners, the public should be able to come away assured that the motives of the professions are such that our self-assessment tax system is in no way in jeopardy. Do the respective Codes accomplish this purpose? Hopefully they do, but frequently there appears to be misunderstanding.

Misunderstandings

In 1961, in a speech on the floor of the Senate of the United States, Senator Paul Douglas expressed what is not an isolated view of the conduct and motives of the accounting and legal professions when he said:

> We all know that our present tax system has so many loopholes or "truck" holes that certain favored groups are able to escape taxation on large parts of their income. These exemptions are steadily widened by legislation and perhaps even more by the rise of two well paid new professions, namely tax lawyers and tax accountants. These gentlemen help citizens avoid and, in some cases, evade the payment of taxes which in all good conscience they should pay. A bewildering variety of tax "gimmicks" and arguments are developed with which the revenue officials and the courts are either unable or unwilling to cope. All this has been sanctioned by sage counsel which I have heard promulgated from this body, and from even more august quarters, that it is a patriotic duty for a citizen to pay as little taxes as possible.[9]

These remarks leave little doubt concerning their meaning. Senator Douglas claims that as a result of the combined efforts of legislators and tax practitioners our self-assessment system is being eroded. If this is true, obviously the conduct of the professions is not evidencing the high motivation to which the Canons and Code should be exhorting it and without which public confidence is not possible. But it is not true. Senator Douglas and others who share his view fail to differentiate between assisting a client in a plan of tax evasion and assisting a client in the determination of his legal tax burden.

Again, from the standpoint of misunderstanding, consider the unsophisticated public who know not what special responsibility the tax practitioner has accepted. As incomprehensible as it may seem to attorneys, CPAs and their clients, all of whom know better, it is an undeniable fact than an alarmingly large segment of the public considers tax advice to be a slightly shady business. Widely publicized congressional inquiries have uncovered tax evasion schemes so ingenious as to imply dishonest tax advice. It takes little imagination on the part of any taxpayer who wrestles with his own conscience to speculate on the integrity of other taxpayers confronted with much larger problems than his own and who are in a position to afford expert advice.[10]

---

[9] 107 CONG. REC. (daily ed. May 25, 1961).

[10] These thoughts are taken from an article by Charles P. Rockwood—*The Changing Image of a Profession*, 110 J. ACCOUNTANCY No. 4, pp. 35–43 (1960).

THE RESPONSIBILITY OF THE PROFESSIONS

Surely the tax practitioner has a responsibility to do his part to make the tax laws work; this is every citizen's duty. It is really a social rather than a professional responsibility. But can it be denied that for the tax practitioner there exists an even greater responsibility—one that emanates from the practitioner's special talents and experiences? Realistically it cannot. The practitioner's duty is real. It is a duty to recommend and to suggest correction and simplification of the statute. Certainly, it needs it if it is complicated enough to cause the eminent jurist Judge Learned Hand to describe it as words that "dance before (our) eyes in a meaningless procession: cross-reference to cross-reference, exception upon exception—couched in abstract terms that offer no handle to seize hold of"—leaving in our minds "only a confused sense of some vitally important, but successful(ly) concealed purport." [11] The duty is also, however, a duty to make existing law work, a duty to advise or otherwise influence his client to avoid plans and actions that tend to undermine the tax system.

Each and every day we see and hear of tax-practitioner groups attempting to improve the system. The AICPA and the ABA regularly testify or otherwise comment on proposed legislation and regulations. Tax-practitioner groups are continually meeting with the Treasury Department and the Internal Revenue Service in an attempt to encourage cooperative tax administration. One need only observe some of these activities to see clearly that self-serving interests are not the motivation for these efforts.

THE DUTY OF THE PRACTITIONER

But what is the individual practitioner called on to do to foster this purpose? Is he anywhere in his standards of conduct exhorted to activities that would tend to improve rather than circumvent our system? Is his motivation and responsibility clear?

In everyday tax practice there often arises the opportunity for the individual practitioner to make his contribution toward the effective and efficient operation of our tax system. Frequently he is in the position of being able to influence his client to follow the noble course of action without in any way abridging his clear responsibility to his client. For example, how often is the tax practitioner asked to advise upon the tax consequences of a plan that apparently has only tax motives as its sole purpose for existence and execution,

---

[11] Swan, *Learned Hand*, 57 YALE L. J. 167, 169 (1947).

but which requires a business purpose in order to have substance under the law? Motives by their very nature are not always obvious and often a client needs help in articulating his true objectives. But there is a fine line between assisting in the development of real purposes and unconsciously providing motives for a tax-conscious client. It is quite probable that most practitioners when faced with such an opportunity to make a contribution to the effective operation of the tax system turn in the right direction. But they probably do so in response to their own citizen's and moral consciences rather than in response to a clearly enunciated professional responsibility. Clearly defined responsibilities would widen considerably this fine line.

Existing Exhortations

The closest that existing canons of practice come to exhorting or requiring constructive activity is at best in terms of vague generalities. Canon 16 of the Canons of Professional Ethics requires the lawyer to use his best efforts to restrain his client from doing those things that the lawyer himself ought not to do. Does this mean that because the lawyer himself would feel that his citizen's duty requires that he observe the intent rather than the letter of the law in a particular situation, that he should restrain his client from an action that stretches or conflicts with this intent? The general language of Canon 16 would not seem to reflect such a responsibility. It is directed toward restraining clients from improprieties. But there is obviously a wide area between improprieties and the average citizen's duty. It is this area that needs to be defined. The Code of Professional Ethics of the AICPA is even more general than Canon 16 in this regard. In this instance, it requires a search for even a general hint as to the accountant's responsibility. Article 1.02 requires that a member or associate not commit an act discreditable to his profession. The Preamble to the Code requires that a member uphold the dignity and honor of his profession and maintain high standards of personal conduct. But, again, neither of these exhortations confers the special responsibility such as some believe exists.

It would be a simple matter to point to the aforementioned customs of practice and to accurately conclude that the practitioner's responsibility is embraced therein. But should such a basic concept be left to general understanding? The written Codes pay a great deal of attention to other specifics, for example, advertising,[12] rec-

---

[12] Canon 27 of the Canons and Article 3.01 of the Code, along with other references to promotional practices and numerous interpretative opinions.

ognizing the adverse effect that such activity would have on the professions' reputations. Certainly, public suspicion and misunderstanding of the tax practitioner's motivation has the potential of being even more destructive of this reputation.

THE DEFICIENCY

When the Canons and Codes were proclaimed, surely the right emphasis was placed. Maintenance of the system of justice and reliance upon sound financial reporting were and still are prime motivations for the highest level of professional conduct. It is suggested, however, that in this era when tax practice comprises such an important part of the practice of law and accounting, no less important is the confidence of the public that the professional tax advisor is doing his part to foster rather than undermine the system of taxation. The very existence of our self-assessment system might depend on this confidence.

If the failure of the Canons and Codes to enunciate this responsibility is a deficiency, and there is by no means unanimous agreement that it is, it is nothing to be ashamed of. It is merely a product of changing times. But this should be no excuse for ignoring it. In this regard, the words of Mr. Justice Stone seem to have a particularly soothing, yet suggestive effect:

> ... we cannot expect the bar to function as it did in other days and under other conditions. Before it can function at all as the guardian of public interests committed to its care, there must be appraisal and comprehension of the new conditions and the changed relationships of the lawyer to his clients, to his professional brethren and to the public. That appraisal must pass beyond the petty details of form and manner which have so largely been our code of ethics, to more fundamental consideration of the way in which our professional activities affect the welfare of the public as a whole.[13]

PRACTICAL PURPOSES

Fostering the confidence of the public by a manifestion of motivation is, of course, not the sole aim of a code of professional conduct. Certainly, this is a very fundamental purpose and, in many respects, it might even be the end of all proximate aims. However, closer to everyday practice there is a more practical purpose, namely, the provision of day-to-day guides to right action. In other words, providing the "signposts at the crossroads" to which Mr.

---

[13] *The Public Influence of the Bar,* 48 HARV. L. REV. 1.

McCracken referred.[14] It is in the fulfillment of this purpose that the adequacy or inadequacy of standards of professional conduct are truly experienced by the modern tax practitioner.

AN APPROPRIATE APPROACH

In attempting to consider the fulfillment of a purpose as broad as this, two approaches have potential merit. The first is to approach the matter in a very general way and to attempt to draw conclusions on the basis of the apparent presence or absence of broad guiding principles, the application of which to specific situations would hopefully provide the proper direction for action. The second approach would be to consider a series of borderline cases in which questions of propriety commonly arise and to attempt to determine in each instance if the standards available provide adequate means of direction. A combination of these two approaches appears most desirable in these circumstances.[15]

Before proceeding, a few limitations should be recognized. First, it is not the function of this discussion to provide authoritative answers to common ethical problems. On the contrary, this is merely an attempt to determine if such answers can be arrived at by the application of existing standards of practice. Secondly, it would be a mistake to speak positively or precisely on the basis of facts necessarily sketchily drawn. Briefly drawn facts must ignore the very human element and do not ordinarily permit the slight variations and shadings that could well permit different conclusions. Finally, a consideration of a series of cases must always be something less than all-inclusive. No matter how much effort might be put into the attempt to provide broad coverage, it would always be possible to point to another specific instance not so covered.

TAX RETURN SITUATIONS

Consider a succession of circumstances surrounding the tax return of a client whom the lawyer or CPA tax practitioner has accepted.

---

[14] *Supra*, note 5.

[15] In following this approach the writer will borrow the nucleus of each factual situation and the suggested answer from more experienced practitioners than himself; notably from, *Ethical Problems of Tax Practitioners*, 8 TAX L. REV. 1 (1952), an open discussion among highly competent tax practitioners; Darrell, *Conscience and Propriety in Tax Practice*, PROCEEDINGS OF NEW YORK UNIVERSITY SEVENTEENTH ANNUAL INSTITUTE ON FEDERAL TAXATION, 1–24 (1959); Graves, *Responsibility of the Tax Advisor*, 114 J. ACCOUNTANCY No. 6, pp. 33–38 (1962); and Lees, *Moral Responsibility in Tax Practice— A CPA's View*, 107 J. OF ACCOUNTANCY No. 4, pp. 30–33 (1959).

Inadvertent Omission of Income. The client asks the practitioner for advice concerning a material item of income that the client believes to be taxable but which was inadvertently omitted from his income tax return. Assume for the moment that the return in question has been filed but was not prepared by the practitioner.

The practitioner's immediate reaction should be to ascertain if in fact the item in question is as clearly taxable as the client suggests that it is. If it is not, there is, of course, no ethical problem. If it is questionable, there may or may not be a problem depending on the basis underlying the nontaxability. This type of problem will be discussed further on. But, assuming that the item is clearly taxable, the practitioner's response should be in the form of advice that an amended return be filed. Alternatively, if the client is one for whom an annual audit is normal, he might advise that steps be taken to ensure that the omission be appropriately brought to the attention of the examining agent.

Most clients will want to correct their errors and, accordingly, will follow this advice. If, however, the client refuses to do so, what does the practitioner then do? How far must he go toward encouraging the disclosure of the item? It is clear that he may not disclose the omission to the Internal Revenue Service without his client's permission. This would be true even if the omissions had been deliberate since to do so would violate the practitioner's confidential relationship with his client.[16] But, may the practitioner continue to serve this client as if the incident had never occurred, merely because he was not directly connected with the return in question? There is respectable authority for the view that the giving of the unheeded advice is enough.[17] But Canon 16 certainly seems to imply that if the practitioner is a lawyer, some consideration should be given to the termination of the relationship. There is also indication that the CPA practitioner should similarly consider withdrawal,[18] but in neither case is there a clear mandate.[19]

---

[16] Aside from the legal concept of privileged communication which would not, of course, extend to all situations of this type, both the Canons and Code require that, as a matter of ethics, the client's confidence be respected. Canon 37 and Article 1.03.

[17] Maguire, *Conscience and Propriety in Lawyer's Tax Practice*, 13 TAX L. REV. 27, 41 n.53 (1957).

[18] Graves, *Responsibility of the Tax Advisor*, 114 J. ACCOUNTANCY No. 6, p. 36 (1962).

[19] It should be noted that even though there is not a clear answer to this type of problem within the framework of existing standards of practice, frequently the practitioner's course of action will be dictated by other considerations. For example, many practitioners would feel compelled to withdraw in circumstances such as these because of a belief that the client's best interests could not be served in the future as a result of the breach of mutual trust and understanding.

Subsequent Revenue Agent's Examination. Assume further in the case of this same client and return that the client does not heed the practitioner's advice but at a later date requests that the practitioner handle the revenue agent's examination of the return. May the practitioner accept this engagement knowing what he does but also knowing that he may not disclose the omission? Circular No. 230 precludes the practitioner from knowingly aiding in any way an attempt to conceal the failure to report an item of income.[20] Similarly, the Circular [21] and the basic ethical concept of integrity would preclude the concealment of the item if information with respect to it was requested. These standards, then, would tend to indicate that the engagement should not be taken. But what if the client authorized disclosure only if asked or, alternatively, only as a tactical offset to some other item that might be questioned?[22]

Involvement of Practitioner's Reputation. Consider now a second situation with respect to a client's return. Assume in this case the same facts as in the former except that the return in question had been prepared or otherwise approved for filing by the practitioner. Again the client refuses to authorize the practitioner to inform the Internal Revenue Service of the omission that has been disclosed to him.

At this point, another interest becomes involved. The practitioner's carefully cultivated professional reputation is now directly concerned since his name has been associated with a return that he now knows to be materially incorrect. Many have suggested that because of this it is not enough to terminate the client-practitioner relationship.[23] The answer, however, is by no means clear. The doctrine of privileged communications comes directly into play and even in those cases where the doctrine has no legal standing, the ethical obligation to maintain the client's confidence is clearly applicable.[24]

Variations. A common variation of all phases of these two tax return situations is encountered when the practitioner and the client

---

[20] Treasury Circular No. 230, § 10.51(b)(27).

[21] *Id.* at § 10.51(b)(9).

[22] The ethical answer to this question might well turn on the exact nature of the conditions that the client imposes and consequently depend on whether compliance with that condition would constitute suppression of information. Treasury Circular No. 230, §§ 10.51(b)(6), (9) and (27). The practical answer, however, might be the same as is indicated in Note 19 *supra*, particularly in a case such as this where the choice is between taking and rejecting a new engagement rather than withdrawing from one.

[23] Maguire, *Conscience and Propriety in Lawyer's Tax Practice*, 13 TAX L. REV. 27, 41, n.55 (1957).

[24] *See* note 16 *supra*.

are faced with an item of income or deduction, the tax consequences of which are debatable. The most troublesome of these is one for which the Treasury Department regulations take a clear position contrary to that which the practitioner and his client believe to be supportable. In some such situations, there may even be many Tax Court and Courts of Appeal decisions favorable to the client but the Internal Revenue Service doggedly refuses to acquiesce.

On the strength of Circular No. 230, the practitioner's obligation is relatively clear. He may not participate in the willful failure to make a return in violation of the internal revenue laws and the regulations thereunder.[25] Accordingly, he must advise his client either to report the item in accordance with the regulations with the idea of claiming refund at a later date or to take a position and adequately disclose the nature of the item in the return.

But in situations such as this few practitioners can truthfully deny that, in the words of John M. Maguire, they have often and rather artfully held "the cards tight against their wishbone and played to the limit the game of 'caveat fiscus'." In public discussion, one fears, there are more words of conscientious subservience to the idea of full disclosure in returns than unpublicized practice justifies in fact.[26]

PLANNING AND ADVISORY PROBLEMS

This situational category overlaps to a large extent the prior discussion of motivation covered under the heading of "Fundamental Purposes." Many problems encountered in tax planning or in rendering tax advice are unduly complicated by the lack of clear guidelines on the practitioner's motivation and his responsibility to the effective functioning of the tax system. It is in this area that the varied interests and responsibilities of the practitioner all too often clash head on. On the one hand, the practitioner will frequently be asked to advise about proposals that are personally distasteful to him. On the other hand, there will be the duty and desire of the practitioner to serve his client and to provide him with all of the tax relief the law permits.

One of the most basic qualifications for the effective resolution of problems encountered in this area is not a set of standards. Rather, this requires first of all a firm and unyielding resolve on the part of the practitioner to follow his own moral and professional judgment with the detachment necessary to be able to firmly

---

[25] Treasury Circular No. 230, § 10.51(b)(4).
[26] Maguire, *Conscience and Propriety in Lawyer's Tax Practice*, 13 TAX L. REV. 27, 42 (1957).

tell his clients the truth. This is not to suggest that in this area there will be constant conflict between practitioner and client. After all, the client is coming to the practitioner for advice, so usually he will follow it. Nevertheless, this is the area in which reasons can very easily be colored or even fabricated. The practitioner will often find himself faced with the choice of assisting or discouraging arrangements that appear to be legally intact but are in fact artificial.

Substance versus Form. For example, consider the practitioner who is consulted about a proposed family partnership between husband and wife, valid in form but to be operated pursuant to an unwritten understanding that may never be discovered. The understanding will be that the husband will continue to control the property and manage the partnership, that the wife will pay family expenses out of her share of the profits, and that the wife will hold her interest subject entirely to the husband's control.

A question of propriety of action and attitude is clearly concerned in a situation such as this. Circular No. 230 provides no guidance and neither for that matter do the Canons or Code. At best, they provide a conflict of interests with no tie breaker in sight.

A Manufactured Situation. Consider now the plight of the practitioner who is informed on the last day of his corporate client's taxable year that the client has just consummated the sale of a capital asset at a substantial gain. The effect of this gain will be to use up completely an operating loss that would otherwise have been available for carry-back. After assuring himself that the sale has in fact been consummated and informing the client of the unfortunate tax results, the client suggests that the papers can be changed so as to put the sale in the following taxable year. The client rationalizes that, from a business standpoint, the timing of the sale was not a significant factor and it could just as well have been consummated on one day as the next.

The practitioner may not prepare or approve the client's return if the client insists on arranging the alteration of the documents and omitting the gain from the return.[27] But what is the practitioner's responsibility beyond this? If he either chooses or is required to terminate his relationship with the client, may he suggest another practitioner who is unaware of all of the facts? Is it possible that no matter what he does, short of informing on his client, that he has advised or aided in the preparation of a false tax return, knowing the same to be false?[28]

---

[27] Treasury Circular No. 230, §§ 10.51(b)(9) and (14) make this quite clear.

[28] Section 10.51(b)(9) of Treasury Circular No. 230 prohibits such action but it must

The Deficiency

It would be possible to go on indefinitely with instances of this type in which clear and unmistakable questions of propriety arise. No real purpose would be served by such expansion. But the list is endless. Consider all of the provisions of the Internal Revenue Code that require a business purpose.[29] Consider the distinction between the words "transaction entered into for profit" and "transaction entered into solely for tax purposes" and it should become obvious that the conflicts which arise will cover the broadest spectrum of tax practice. The need for answers is clear and standards permitting the formulation of such answers should be just as clear.

In all situations and variations just described in which unanswered questions were raised, it must be said in all fairness that existing broad general standards such as morality, integrity, duty to client, and fidelity to profession do permit the formulation of answers. To be sure these will be varying answers if arrived at solely on the basis of those broad standards but to a lesser degree the same would be true even if there were more specific standards to be applied. The shortcoming that does exist, however, and that renders an answer most difficult in all these situations is this: Nowhere, except in the limited "don'ts" of Circular No. 230 is the tax practitioner's duty to the government properly defined. As to the lawyer, he has not been adequately informed if the government is his adversary in the traditional sense. While the CPA clearly does not owe the government the independence he owes the reader of a certified financial statement,[30] the degree of independence he does owe has not been defined.

Concept of Dual Responsibility

Most will agree that some form of dual responsibility to both client and government does exist. For the CPA it stems from the independence that he has gone to great and extreme lengths to maintain. For the lawyer it comes from the integrity, candor, and fairness that he owes to his adversary in any legal proceeding.

---

be conceded that it would be stretching the intent of this section to contend that it applies in a situation such as this.

[29] Generally this "business purpose" requirement is imposed indirectly by statutory provisions which necessitate a demonstration that tax avoidance was not a principal purpose for the particular transaction or activity. See, for example, I.R.C. §§ 269, 367, and 532 (1954). In some instances, however, notably section 357(b) of the Internal Revenue Code of 1954, the requirement is a direct one and in still other instances it has been imposed by court decisions and subsequently reflected in Treasury regulations.

[30] Opinion No. 13 of AICPA Committee on Professional Ethics Numbered Opinions.

For both, it comes ultimately from a sense of professional obligation to the government and society of which both are a part and to the tax system with whose administration they are to some extent charged.

It was pointed out previously that it is not the function of this discussion to provide answers. On this specific point it would be presumptuous to do so since this is one of the larger unresolved questions of responsibility in tax practice. It may well be that a complete and honest examination of the facts will justify the conclusion that no special responsibility is owed. On the other hand, the conclusion might be that a limited and non-conflicting responsibility exists. The fact remains, however, that until responsibility is properly identified, neither profession can be said to have received "adequate marching orders or advice as to its proper attitudes and conduct in a number of commonplace situations produced by tax practice."[31]

ACTIVITIES OF PROFESSIONAL GROUPS

This discussion was introduced with a question—a question regarding the adequacy of the standards of practice available for the guidance of the modern tax practitioner. It is believed that the foregoing commentary has provided one form of answer to that question. On the assumption that it does, it seems only fitting to conclude the discussion with an indication of what is being done by the accounting and legal professions to correct the deficiency that apparently exists. It is gratifying to note that these efforts are indeed comprehensive.

ACTIVITIES OF THE LEGAL PROFESSION

In 1962 the Council of the ABA passed a resolution authorizing the appointment of a Special Committee on Standards of Tax Practice. Subsequently, this Committee was expanded into a Joint Committee comprised of members of the ABA's Section of Taxation and members of the Federal Bar Association. The Joint Committee has functioned as such since that time and has chosen for consideration and study two specific areas:

1. The application of existing Canons of Ethics to facts peculiar to tax practice
2. Whether present Canons devised for county seat practice are

---

[31] Maguire, *Conscience and Propriety in Lawyer's Tax Practice*, 13 TAX L. REV. 45 (1957).

adequate for resolving conflicts of duty arising in the administrative practice, particularly in the tax area.

As the first step in its consideration, the Joint Committee has chosen as an approach, the development of a series of specific fact situations for which possible solutions to ethical problems will be formulated on the basis of existing Canons of Ethics. It is proposed that these problems will be explored, briefed, and argued at membership meetings and that formal opinions thereon will be obtained from the ABA Committee on Professional Ethics.

As the Joint Committee envisions it, the work remaining to be done is as follows:

> The principal problem area in the field of professional legal ethics is not in the distinguishing between right and wrong, or good and bad, but rather in deciding which duties shall prevail under certain circumstances. According to the Canons of Ethics, a lawyer owes a duty to his client, to the court, to the members of his profession and to himself. Many times these duties conflict and the problem is which shall prevail under given circumstances. Members of this committee who have had the opportunity of meeting together frequently have come to feel that a lawyer's first reaction to this type of situation is almost always wrong. This is not because he is good or bad, but because the resolving of these competing duties requires as much study as any other field of law.
>
> The second basic problem is whether our present Canons of Ethics sufficiently cover the competing duties of lawyers practicing before the Internal Revenue Service. An answer to this question requires a complete knowledge of the application of our present Canons of Ethics to existing problems and hence may require further exploration by subsequent committees before embarking upon a recommendation in this area.[32]

ACTIVITIES OF THE ACCOUNTING PROFESSION

In a similar manner, the AICPA has also instituted a program aimed at the development and identification of standards of responsibility in tax practice. This program is being conducted by a special Subcommittee of the Committee on Federal Taxation and contemplates the promulgation and publication of a numbered series of Statements of Responsibility in Tax Practice.[33]

Whereas the ABA program includes ultimately an inquiry into the sufficiency of existing Canons, the AICPA program is based on the premise that adequate bases are available to assist the practi-

---

[32] "Report of Special Committee on Standards of Tax Practice," *Bulletin of Section of Taxation, ABA*, Volume XVII, No. 4, July 1964.

[33] Statement Number 1 of the series was issued by the Committee on Federal Taxation of the AICPA in September, 1964. The first statement considers the responsibility of a CPA to sign as preparer certain Federal tax returns.

tioner in determining his responsibilities. The potential deficiency that the AICPA sees is in the means of identification and communication of these bases. The stated objectives of the AICPA program are as follows:

1. To identify and develop minimum standards of responsibilities in tax practice and to encourage and promote their uniform application by CPAs
2. To protect CPAs against charges of misconduct resulting from misunderstanding regarding the extent of the CPA's responsibility
3. To encourage the development of increased understanding of the responsibilities of the CPA by the Internal Revenue Service
4. To foster increased public integrity and confidence in the tax system through awareness of self-imposed standards of conduct accepted by CPAs

The statements are not intended to establish a separate Code of Conduct in tax practice apart from the general ethical precepts of the Institute's Code of Professional Ethics. They are intended to guide a CPA in his tax practice within the general tenets of the Code of Professional Ethics. This Code imposes upon members and associates obligations to maintain high standards of technical competence and integrity in dealing with clients and the public. These obligations apply in all phases of the professional activities of members and associates, including tax practice.[34]

While the approaches of these two organizations differ, the actions of both tend to support in their own separate ways the conclusion of this entire discussion: that some basic deficiencies do in fact exist and that it is in the best interests of the professions to take steps to resolve them.

---

[34] Excerpts from the prospectus of the AICPA responsibilities program as described by Matthew F. Blake in *Responsibilities in Tax Practice*, 117 J. ACCOUNTANCY No. 4, pp. 37–41 (1964).

14. Ethical Considerations on Discovery of Error in Tax Returns
Marvin K. Collie and Thomas P. Marinis, Jr.

Although the various aspects of the "professional responsibility" of the tax practitioner have been the subject of increasing attention, much of this scrutiny reflects continued uncertainty.[1] An illuminating facet of the current difficulties is reflected in the problems members of the accounting profession are having with a Proposed Statement by the Division of Federal Taxation of the American Institute of Certified Public Accountants on the responsibilities of the accountant upon discovery of an error in a client's tax return.

Obviously these problems also have interesting implications for lawyers considering legal problems arising from the Internal Revenue Code. Hence, here we will consider the relatively narrow ethical problem raised by the accountants as it relates to the legal profession. This is not to intimate that the standards of conduct in the area of tax practice should be the same for both professions,[2] but only reflects a belief that both professions are faced with ethical problems having the same genesis and that each can profit from the other's experience.[3]

THE ACCOUNTANT'S PROPOSED STATEMENT

The Proposed Statement by the accountants is the most recent in a series of Statements prepared by the Division of Federal Taxation of the

---

[1] See generally, Bittker, PROFESSIONAL RESPONSIBILITY AND FEDERAL TAX PRACTICE (1965); Brown, *Responsibilities of the Taxpayer*, U. So. Cal. 1963 Tax Inst. 1; Darrell, *Conscience and Propriety in Tax Practice*, 17 N.Y.U. Inst. on Fed. Tax., 1 (1959); Darrell, *Responsibilities of the Lawyer in Tax Practice*, reprinted in Trumbull, MATERIALS ON THE LAWYER'S PROFESSIONAL RESPONSIBILITY, 291 (1957); Johnson, *Does the Tax Practitioner Owe a Dual Responsibility to His Client and to the Government?—The Theory*, U. So. Cal. 1963 Tax Inst. 25; Maguire, *Conscience and Propriety in Lawyers' Tax Practice*, 13 Tax L. Rev. 27 (1957); Young, *Does The Tax Practitioner Owe a Dual Responsibility to His Client and the Government?—The Practice*, U. So. Cal. 1963 Tax Inst. 39. Other works are cited in the footnotes.

[2] The ABA and AICPA have recognized that accountants and lawyers have different roles in tax practice, which may indicate a different standard of conduct. See ABA and AICPA, JOINT STATEMENT OF PRINCIPLES RELATING TO PRACTICE IN THE FIELD OF FEDERAL INCOME TAXATION (1951). The Joint Statement is reprinted at 53 A.B.A.J. 549 (1967).

[3] The accountant's perspective is discussed in Carey, PROFESSIONAL ETHICS OF CERTIFIED PUBLIC ACCOUNTANTS 110-136 (1956); Graves, *An Accountant's View of the Responsibilities of the Tax Advisor*, 40 Taxes 1040 (1962). See also, Oatway, *Motivation and Responsibility in Tax Practice: The Need For Definition*, 20 Tax. L. Rev. 237 (1965).

AICPA as part of that Institute's tax responsibilities program.[4] The series is intended to constitute a body of opinion on what are good standards of tax practice, outlining the accountant's responsibility to his client, the public, the Government and his profession.

By way of a general summary, Statement No. 1 makes its contribution to this goal by stating that a CPA should sign every return that he prepares. Statement No. 2 reflects the conclusion that there is additional credibility attached to a return signed by a CPA and that this credibility should be substantiated by an investigation on the part of the signer equivalent to that of a preparer. Statement No. 3 deals with the answers to questions asked on tax returns. Statement No. 4 discusses the extent to which consistency is required in the treatment of an item following the conclusion of an administrative proceeding in which that item was at issue.[5] Statement No. 5 concerns the use of estimates on Federal tax returns.[6]

The Proposed Statement, which has been in draft form for over two years, deals with how a CPA should react when a mistake in a tax return or other relevant document comes to his attention.[7] In its present form, the Statement proposes three principal guidelines to this problem. First, the CPA should promptly advise his client upon the discovery of an error in a previously filed return or upon discovery of the client's failure to file a required return. This advice should be accompanied by a recommendation of the appropriate action to be taken, which ordinarily will be to disclose the error promptly, e.g., by filing an amended return. The CPA is under no obligation to inform the Internal Revenue Service of the error, nor will he be permitted to do so without the client's permission.

Secondly, if the CPA is engaged to prepare the current year's return and the client has refused to take appropriate measures to correct an error in a prior return, the CPA should consider whether to continue with preparation of the current return. If the CPA decides to proceed with the current year's return, he should take appropriate steps to assure

---

[4] The AICPA program, as well as the Proposed Statement, is thoroughly discussed in an article by William T. Barnes, entitled *Responsibilities in Tax Practice*, J. Accy., March 1968, p. 27. Mr. Barnes is Chairman of the AICPA Division of Federal Taxation and former Chairman of the subcommittee in charge of the Proposed Statement. The authors are heavily indebted to him for information with regard to the reaction of the accounting profession to circulation of the Proposed Statement.

[5] Barnes, *supra* note 4, at 29.

[6] Statement No. 5 is reported in J. Accy., March, 1969, pp. 61-62. This issue also reports changes made in the introduction to the Statement series. *Id.* at 60-61.

[7] The Proposed Statement is still a draft and is not currently available in printed form. A detailed description of the general principles may be found in Barnes, *supra* note 4.

himself that the error is not repeated and that the error is not allowed to reduce the current year's tax liability either directly or indirectly.

Thirdly, if the CPA is engaged to represent the client in an administrative proceeding with respect to a return in which there is an error that has resulted in a material understatement of tax liability, he should request the client's agreement to disclose the error to the Internal Revenue Service. Lacking such agreement, preferred practice requires that the CPA withdraw from that engagement except where the mere act of withdrawal would constitute a violation of the confidential relationship between himself and the client.

The introduction to the Statement makes it clear that these guidelines would not apply in cases where there is reasonable support for the positions taken by the taxpayer or there was reasonable support at the time the return was filed. The guidelines do not apply unless the error results, or may result, in a material understatement of tax liability. The guidelines were stated to apply whether the CPA prepared the return that contained the error or whether it was prepared by someone else, but they would not govern the conduct of a CPA who has been engaged by legal counsel to provide accounting assistance to him in a matter relating to the counsel's client.

Objections to the Proposed Statement

As is only natural in these matters, the circulation of the Proposed Statement by the accountants generated considerable controversy among members of that profession. Many of the objections apparently were of a purely definitional nature and concerned questions of what would be considered a material error [8] and what was meant by the requirement (omitted from the present draft) that the current year's return should not "conceal the existence of the prior year's error or omission."

There were several more basic objections to what in effect was an unqualified requirement that the client be advised to file an amended return to correct his error or, if he corrected it in the current year's return, to include a rider explaining the correction. These objections were that filing an amended return or including the rider in a subsequent year's return only invited trouble, and that it was proper to correct the error in a subsequent year's return without attaching a rider. Those who supported this view stressed the fact that procedures followed in some Internal Revenue districts were prejudicial to the filing of amended returns and that investigation and settlement of

---

[8] The latest draft of the Statement provides:

"The concept of materiality is not a simple one and generally it has a more restrictive connotation in tax law practice than in the determination of income for financial reporting purposes. Accordingly, the determination of whether an error is material should be left to the judgment of the individual CPA."

See Proposed Statement (Committee Ballot Draft dated 9-18-1968).

tax controversies can be extremely costly to taxpayers, apart from any tax deficiencies that may be involved.

Although admitting that the "wait and see" approach might be acceptable in unusual circumstances, the present draft of the Statement sees the omission of an explanatory rider to the current year's return as presenting a problem of whether that return will be "true, correct and complete" within the meaning of the preparer's declaration and therefore advises against it as a regular procedure.[9]

This position of the Statement logically leads to the more general ground that although any Internal Revenue Service procedure prejudicial to the filing of amended returns is to be abhorred, such a Service practice should be no excuse to shortcut the proper procedures for correcting errors in prior years. This is a matter that should be dealt with through negotiations with the Treasury Department rather than through unilateral "take-a-chance" acts by tax practitioners.

The most difficult problem with the Proposed Statement arose in connection with the situation in which the CPA is engaged to represent

---

[9] The draft of the Proposed Statement dated May 22, 1967 included the following:
"Moreover, the current year's return should not be prepared in such a manner as to conceal the existence of the prior year's error. For example, where the client has refused to file an amended return for an open year (one with respect to which the statute of limitations has not run) in which an error occurred but is willing to correct the effect of such error on his cumulative Federal income tax liability by an adjustment in the current year's return, appropriate disclosure must be made in such return."

That passage was omitted from the draft of September 18, 1968 and the following included in lieu thereof:

"Although taxable income should be determined on the basis of separate taxable years, there are instances in which a client desires to compensate for a prior year's error in his next tax return. This course of action is frequently motivated by the belief that the filing of an amended return will add to the cost and inconvenience of determining the ultimate tax liability, over and above the tax deficiencies which might be determined. While there may be unusual circumstances where this practice may be followed, it is not recommended.

"Moreover, such a course of action raises the question of disclosure. It can be argued that such a return is not 'true, correct and complete' within the meaning of the preparer's declaration, since it overstates the taxpayer's tax liability for the particular year. On the other hand, it can be asserted that the intent of the jurat is not contravened in cases of overpayment. While it is preferred and recommended that disclosure be made, this is not a requirement provided the error appears to have been made in good faith and, that the tax effects of this approach are substantially the same as would follow from the filing of an amended return."

* This proposed ruling is to be compared with the following statement in *Opinion 314* issued by the Committee on Professional Ethics of the American Bar Association, note 11, *infra:*

"Similarly, a lawyer who is asked to advise his client in the course of the preparation of the client's tax returns may freely urge the statement of positions most favorable to the client just as long as there is reasonable basis for those positions. Thus where the lawyer believes there is a reasonable basis for a position that a particular transaction does not result in taxable income, or that certain expenditures are properly deductible as expenses, the lawyer has no duty to advise that riders be attached to the client's tax return explaining the circumstances surrounding the transaction or the expenditures."

a client in an administrative proceeding with respect to a return known by the CPA to contain an error that resulted in a material understatement of tax liability. No one could quarrel with the Statement position that a CPA should not be false or devious in dealing with any issue that is raised by the Internal Revenue Service, but there was general disagreement about what should be done about the known and patent error if it is not discovered by the Service. This lack of agreement centered on differences among the accountants as to the true nature of practice before the Internal Revenue Service.

The controversy centered on the view that administrative practice before the Internal Revenue Service cannot be viewed as a true adversary proceeding. The critics take the position that practice before the Internal Revenue Service is always adversary and the CPA, subject to his obligation to be truthful and candid, should do only those things which are calculated to produce the least amount of tax liability for the client. It the revenue agents operate under the philosophy of "protecting the revenue," this argument goes, let them protect it. Other accountants have objected that the recommendation for withdrawal of CPAs from engagements of this variety would place a more onerous burden on them than that placed upon lawyers and other non-CPA enrolled agents and that such disparity is unwarranted.[10] This argument with respect to the lawyers is based on *Opinion 314* issued by the Committee on Professional Ethics of the American Bar Association in 1965, discussed below.[11]

It should be noted that in an earlier draft, the discussion of the Proposed Statement contained the following language:

"We have concluded that it is not in the public interest—or even in the long term interest of a particular taxpayer—to view practice before the Internal Revenue Service as an adversary proceeding. Ours is a self-assessment tax system and that system is not suddenly transformed when a return is filed. An error which would cause a CPA to refuse to sign the preparer's declaration on a tax return, if its existence were known at such time, cannot be countenanced by a CPA when he is representing the client in an administrative proceeding before the IRS." [12]

Thus the Statement took the position that when the CPA was engaged to represent a client in an administrative proceeding with respect to a return known to contain a material and patent error, he should request the client's permisssion to disclose the error, and if he refused, the CPA should decline to represent him.[13] As indicated before, the Statement has since retracted this strong language and now only states that it is arguable

---

[10] Barnes, *supra* note 4, at 30-31.
[11] ABA Reports, Vol. 90, Appendix p. 5 (1965); ABA COMM. ON PROFESSIONAL ETHICS, OPINIONS, No. 314 (1967); 51 A.B.A.J. 671 (1965).
[12] Proposed Statement (Exposure Draft dated 11-17-67 as revised 4-10-68).
[13] *Id.*

that administrative practice before the Internal Revenue Service is adversary, and, instead of stating flatly that if the client refuses to disclose, the CPA should decline to represent him, it now states:

> "Preferred practice in most instances requires that, if the client refuses [to disclose the error], the CPA should decline to represent him, lest his continuing representation of the client have the effect of misleading the IRS." [14]

The last clause in the above-quoted sentence, which gives the reason for the rule, was added in the most recent draft of the Proposed Statement. This reference to the possibility of misleading the Service by continued representation of the client is similar to the reason given in *Opinion 314,* discussed below, for the holding that a lawyer should disassociate himself from a client if, under all the circumstances, he believes that the Service "relies on him as corroborating statements of his client which he knows to be false."

Some may take the position that the changes made by the present draft are not ones of substance, but merely ones of form to soothe the more vocal objections to the original wording of the Statement. The current draft, however, does appear to reflect a change in the basic philosophy of the prior draft of the Statement that administrative practice before the Internal Revenue Service is not an adversary proceeding. Rather, the Statement now appears to recognize a limited adversary role for the accountant, which would only require disclosure in the case of patent and uncontroverted errors.[15]

The Legal Profession's Approach

The remainder of this article will compare the accountant's view of practice before the Internal Revenue Service as explained in the Proposed Statement to the lawyer's view as expressed in *Opinion 314,* and attempt to discover any differences that may exist between the two.

The legal profession has never felt the need to designate a separate body of rules to govern the lawyer's conduct in the area of tax practice. This decision, which has been discussed from time to time,[16] is based

---

[14] Proposed Statement (Committee Ballot Draft dated 9-18-68).

[15] In this connection the Proposed Statement includes the following:

> "A CPA has both the right and responsibility to be an advocate for his client with respect to any position for which he has reasonable support, and he has no obligation to disclose any weakness which may be inherent in such a position. He is in a different position, however, with respect to an error which, if its existence had been known at the time the return was prepared, would have caused him to refuse to sign the preparer's declaration on the tax return."

[16] At the beginning of the work of the ABA Special Committee on Evaluation of Ethical Standards, the Chairman of the ABA Tax Section's Committee on Standards of Practice, inquired of the Tax Section Committee whether the revision of the Canons of Ethics should provide special rules for tax lawyers. Such survey found the Committee overwhelmingly opposed to such an approach.

on a belief among most "tax lawyers" that the ethical problems faced in the tax area are not significantly different from those faced by lawyers generally. Thus, there are no statements of standards of conduct for members of the legal profession practicing primarily in the tax area other than the general principles of the American Bar Association Canons of Ethics [17] and the various written standards of state and local bar associations, as well as the writings on ethical practices by reputable members of the profession.

An expansion of this general approach to the ethical problems of tax practice is *Opinion 314* of the Committee on Professional Ethics, which is a comprehensive attempt to define, within the standards of the Canons, the ethical relationship between the Internal Revenue Service and lawyers practicing before it.

The crux of this problem for the legal profession, and as a result, the point of departure for *Opinion 314,* is the basic conflict between the lawyer's duty of warm zeal for his client as expressed in Canon 15 [18] and the lawyer's duty of loyalty to the courts as expressed in Canons 1,[19] 16 [20] and 22.[21] This conflict is always present and is not an easy one to resolve. The problem is perhaps at its peak in the area of tax practice because of the unique aspects of the Internal Revenue Service. Although it has been argued that the Service is an administrative arm of the Federal government with regulation of its practitioners and thus should be treated in the same manner as courts and perhaps other administrative agencies, the Service has never provided at the outset for independent hearing officers or trial examiners of the kind that are familiar in other administrative proceedings. Rather the Internal Revenue Service provides initially individuals to deal with the taxpayer both in the role of adversary and judge of fact, two obviously inconsistent roles. Hence most lawyers would agree with *Opinion 314,* which characterizes the Internal Revenue Service as follows:

> "The Internal Revenue Service is neither a true tribunal, nor even a quasi-judicial institution. It has no machinery or procedure for adversary proceedings before impartial judges or arbiters, involving the weighing of conflicting testimony of witnesses examined and cross-examined by opposing counsel and the consideration of arguments of counsel for both sides of a dispute. While its procedure provides for 'fresh looks' through departmental reviews and informal and formal conference procedures, few will contend that the service provides any truly dispassionate and unbiased consideration to the taxpayer. Although willing to listen to taxpayers

---

[17] The preliminary draft of the proposed Code of Professional Responsibility does not depart from this policy. See note 16 *supra.*
[18] ABA CANONS OF PROFESSIONAL ETHICS No. 15.
[19] ABA CANONS OF PROFESSIONAL ETHICS No. 1.
[20] ABA CANONS OF PROFESSIONAL ETHICS No. 16.
[21] ABA CANONS OF PROFESSIONAL ETHICS No. 22.

and their representatives and obviously intending to be fair, the service is not designed and does not purport to be unprejudiced and unbiased in the judicial sense."

This view is not meant to be a harsh criticism of the Internal Revenue Service. On the contrary, this is merely a practical and realistic view of the Service based on the basic nature of its organization. The problem is especially critical in the lower echelons of the Service where agents and conferees are faced with the normal responsibility of loyalty to their employer, and the career pressures to perform their functions efficiently.

Once the Internal Revenue Service is characterized as *Opinion 314* has done, the ethical problem of the lawyer becomes less difficult. Because the lawyer is an advocate before a service which represents the adversary point of view, where his client's case is reasonably arguable, a lawyer is under no duty to disclose its weaknesses, anymore than he would be to a brother lawyer. The lawyer is free to resolve factual questions in favor of his client and make statements of positions most favorable to the client, so long as there is reasonable basis for these positions.

This is not to suggest that the lawyer may deal less than fairly with the Internal Revenue Service. *Opinion 314* adopts the logical position that the attorney is under a duty both in the preparation of returns and negotiating administrative settlements not to mislead the Internal Revenue Service deliberately and affirmatively, either by misstatements or by silence or by permitting the client to mislead. This duty is clear from the mandate of Canon 22 which requires that the conduct of the lawyer be characterized by candor and fairness. Thus when a Service representative requests data and information pertaining to a case of a particular taxpayer, they are entitled to such information if it is relevant to the issue under consideration, and the lawyer assumes the responsibility for the accuracy of the information furnished.[22] Similarly, a problem may arise if, in the course of representation of a taxpayer on a particular issue, the lawyer discovers that the taxpayer has made an unrelated but uncontrovertible error in the same return, but this patent error has been overlooked by the Service. In this case, *Opinion 314* indicates that the lawyer must advise the client to disclose the existence of an unrelated error.[23]

But should the lawyer advise his client to inform the Service voluntarily of all of the material facts of the client's situation as to an issue already in controversy, or of collateral facts that *may* lead to another issue, the outcome of which would be in doubt?[24] And is the lawyer under a duty to withdraw from the matter if the client refuses

---
[22] See Tarleau, *Ethical Problems in Dealing with Treasury Representatives* 8 Tax. L. Rev. 10 (1952).
[23] See Bittker, *supra* note 1, at 42-43; Tarleau, *supra* note 22, at 12-13.
[24] See Tarleau, *supra* note 22, at 12.

to make such disclosure? Most lawyers instinctively would have a negative answer to both of these questions. The obligation of candor and fairness should not require the lawyer to go this far in helping the Service establish its case.

The possibility of withdrawal question is likely to arise in a situation where the client has misled the Internal Revenue Service without the knowledge or participation of the lawyer. If the client refuses to correct the statement, *Opinion 314* states that the lawyer's obligation "depends on all the circumstances," and that "fundamentally" the lawyer, subject to the restrictions of the attorney-client privilege,[25] may be under a duty to withdraw from the matter. *Opinion 314* closely resembles the Proposed Statement when it goes on to specify that, if the lawyer believes that the Service relies on him as corroborating or agreeing with false statements of his client, then he is under a duty to disassociate himself from such reliance unless such disassociation would have the effect of violating the attorney-client privilege. Here the lawyer must advise the Service that he is not in a position to answer if questions regarding the false statement are raised.[26]

Some lawyers apparently would argue that when a client refuses to correct a material misrepresentation to the Service the lawyer should withdraw from representation in all circumstances.[27] Proponents of this view take the position that if a client owes someone money he ought to pay it, and that the lawyer should not be a party to a refusal to pay it. The rationale for this position may be that a lawyer works with a client on the basis of mutual confidence and trust, and if this error and refusal to correct undermines a lawyer's trust in his client, he has no business representing him in any way. The lawyer may feel that through continued representation he might in the future be placed in the embarrassing position of having built upon an uncorrected error. There is also a possibility that this kind of client, having refused to correct one error, may refuse to do it again. These are not clear cases, however, and it is unrealistic to state a general rule of withdrawal on the basis of such circumstances.

This raises a practical point that may be an overriding consideration to tax lawyers. In the area of practice before the Internal Revenue

---

[25] ABA CANONS OF PROFESSIONAL ETHICS No. 37. See Lofts, *The Attorney-Client Privilege in Federal Tax Investigations*, 19 Tax. L. Rev. 405 (1964).

[26] The Proposed Statement includes a similar rule:

> "While a CPA should generally conform to the principles of this Statement, there may be cases where the effect of the withdrawal itself would clearly be to reveal information which had been imparted to the CPA in confidence. In such cases, the CPA need not withdraw but should advise the client, who has refused permission to make the disclosure, of the resultant possibility of the CPA being unable to answer other questions asked of him and of the prejudicial effect on his client's case which might follow from his inability to do so."

[27] See *What is Good Tax Practice: A Panel Discussion*, 21 N.Y.U. Inst. on Fed. Tax., 23, 50-53 (1963). See also Tarleau, *supra* note 22.

Service the lawyer faces the same group of adversaries on a regular basis. If the lawyer is well-known and of good repute he may be placed in a position of trust by his Government opponents, which usually results in heavy reliance by the Service representatives on the truth and completeness of the lawyer's statements. Although this situation, of course, may be advantageous to such lawyer, it places a high, and sometimes unappreciated, responsibility on him to deal fairly with those that trust him. Counsel not only must utilize great care in the accurate presentation of material to the Service, he must be equally careful not to allow others to trade on his good reputation by furnishing him with inaccurate material they know will be accepted without question. If the lawyer does not take steps to guard against this problem, he may find that he has jeopardized his most valuable professional asset—his good reputation.[28]

A discussion of this type runs the risk of over-simplifying in order to extract abstract principles. Any attorney representing those subject to the Internal Revenue Code will face, sooner or later, the desire (perhaps it would be more accurate to say the pressure) to present only the favorable facts and not the unfavorable ones, the desire to comply only with the minimum necessary to satisfy the Internal Revenue Service and not to furnish the complete story. In following the traditional legal approach one must never forget that there is often a thin line between mere nondisclosure of evidentiary facts and misrepresentation.

A Concluding Comparison of the Differences

The discussion to this point has suggested that the legal profession sees the problem of the ethical relationship of the tax lawyer and the Internal Revenue Service differently from the accountants. Basically this difference lies in the fact that many accountants do not see their role as an advocate to the full meaning of that word as it is used in the legal profession. Such accountants tend to think that there is a point in which they must assume a judicial role between the Government and the taxpayer. Admittedly this theory has been received in the tax area with favor by some members of the legal profession—especially in light of the fact that the Internal Revenue Service is an arm of the Federal government and ours is a self-assessment tax system [29]—but the great majority of the legal profession has tended to discount the idea as having at best only a limited theoretical appeal.[30] This is based on the consideration that it is the lawyer's professional tradition and primary obligation to give undivided loyalty to the client, and any obligation to the Government must come second to the interests of the client.

---

[28] See Tarleau, *supra* note 22, at 13.
[29] See note 27 *supra*.
[30] See Johnson, *supra* note 1; Young, *supra* note 1.

At first this difference may be surprising to some in light of the prestige of the two professions and the fact that they perform similar roles in the area of tax practice.[31] However, the variance may be explained by the basic differences between lawyers and accountants that are not necessarily related to the particular problems of tax practice.

While the professional tradition of the lawyer always has been that of an advocate, the accountant on the other hand has an opposite tradition. The primary role of the accountant initially has been (and may still be) that of a certifier of financial statements. In this status he necessarily and ethically must act independently of, and sometimes adversely to, his client. His liability to creditors and the public gives him a responsibility to third parties whose interests may be adverse to his client. It is only recently with the expansion of the tax practice and other counseling roles that the accountant has taken on the additional roles of advisor and advocate which tend to bring a schizophrenic effect.

In this light, it would be surprising that the accountants did not feel a greater responsibility to the Government than the legal profession in the area of tax practice.[32] In our tax system the Government is in reality a creditor, and by showing a concern for the Government in the preparation of tax returns and negotiations with the Internal Revenue Service, the accountant is acting in a similar role to his certification functions.

The Proposed Statement apparently recognizes this problem and attempts to solve it with the following language:

> "Opinion No. 13 of the Committee on Professional Ethics holds that neither the technical standards (Article 2) of the Code of Professional Ethics nor any other sections of the Code which relate only to examinations of financial statements have any application to tax practice. Thus, the independence rules of Section 1.01 are inapplicable. Opinion No. 13 also holds that a member or associate must observe in tax practice the same standards of truthfulness and integrity as he is required to observe in any other professional work, but that he may resolve doubts in favor of his client if there is reasonable support for his position. Therefore, it is appropriate for the CPA to serve as an advocate for his client." [33]

However, this dichotomy borders on sophistry in trying to paper over the dilemma. The accountant's difficulty is demonstrated in the preparing and signing of a tax return by an accountant if he adopts a position in the return that he believes proper under law but is contrary to a ruling by the Service. Can the accountant then certify

---

[31] See Bittker, *supra* note 1, at 33-41. Mr. Bittker does not believe that the line drawn between accounting questions and legal questions by the 1951 Joint Statement has worked in practice. See note 2 *supra*.

[32] The accountants' view may be influenced by the fact that they are not entitled to the protection of the attorney-client privilege in tax cases.

[33] Proposed Statement (Committee Ballot Draft dated 9-18-68).

the financial statements, including the tax liability shown by the return without a footnote showing the contingent liability? Such a footnote could be hard on the client. Can the accountant proceed without such a footnote if supporting opinion by an attorney is secured? [34]

Although it apparently is not possible for the accountant to reconcile in a logical manner these basically contradictory functions of certification, counseling and advocacy, the very confidence of a taxpayer in his representative must come first to preserve and protect our self-assessment system.[35] The Proposed Statement on discovery of error as presently drafted is a significant step in the right direction in accomplishing this goal.

---

[34] One solution for the accountants might be adoption of a system of certified tax returns. See Johnson, *supra* note 1, at 33-35.

[35] See Johnson, *supra* note 1, at 35.

15. Ethical Restraints on Tax Practice in Great Britain
F. S. A. Wheatcroft

When one discusses ethics in relation to an area of professional practice, he is postulating a code of conduct which is different from, and, in his opinion, higher than, the minimum code required by law. We assume an obligation on the part of every citizen, and particularly a professional man, to conform strictly to the law, although we may have to consider situations in which a professional man has to deal with other persons who do not have that minimum standard. In addition to the code prescribed by law, a professional man is also subject to a code of conduct prescribed by his own professional body and as a member of that body he can take a part in framing and applying that code. This, again, is a minimum standard with which all members of his professional body are expected to comply and any member who falls below that standard is subject to the sanctions of that body. In addition a professional man may endeavor to base his own actions on some still higher standard of conduct which is dictated to him by the society in which he lives or by his own conscience.

I have been asked to deal with some of the ethical problems in which accountants in tax practice in Great Britain may currently find themselves involved. As I am dealing with a field which is similar to, but in some respects different from, that in the U.S.A., I must start by outlining certain basic factors relating to tax practice in Great Britain which affect the situations in which ethical problems arise.

There are a number of professional bodies of accountants, but the bulk of the important work is concentrated in the hands of the members of the Institute of Chartered Accountants in England and Wales, who have recently absorbed another smaller but important body known as the Society of Incorporated Accountants. The Institute now has over 33,000 members and membership in the Institute is generally regarded as a hallmark of professional integrity and competence. Scottish chartered accountants frequently emigrate south of the border and have the same professional standing in England as have members of the English Institute. The next largest body in England is called the Association of Certified and Corporate Accountants, and there are a number of others. Each body has its own professional standards of conduct, but in this article I propose to refer to the code of the Institute of Chartered Accountants in England and Wales — known for short as "The Institute."

Auditors, solicitors and barristers

While a number of professional accountants are directly employed by large business organizations, company law requires that company accounts be audited by an independent accountant or firm of accountants. Many unincorporated traders and private individuals employ accountants to prepare and submit accounts and tax returns to the Inland Revenue, so that the majority of accounts submitted as a basis for tax computations are audited or prepared by accountants who practice independently and are not salaried servants of the taxpayer.

The legal profession is also divided, but here there are only two bodies, barristers and solicitors. Barristers are, in general, specialists and most of them specialize in advocacy within particular fields. The general body of barristers know little about taxation and neither tax nor accounting are subjects in the Bar qualification examination. A small number of barristers, however, specialize in tax work and act as advisers and advocates in tax cases. They have a high degree of expert knowledge. The professional etiquette of a barrister requires that he can only receive instructions through a solicitor, who is a general legal adviser dealing directly with the public. His position is like a general medical practitioner who deals with the day-to-day problems of his patient but refers him to a specialist in case of difficulty. Until comparatively recently solicitors took little interest in tax work, apart from death duties, but this is rapidly changing. Taxation law has now been for some years a compulsory subject for the solicitors' qualification examination and most large firms of solicitors in London, and other big towns, now tend to have at least one partner with a fair knowledge of taxation. A barrister may not receive instructions directly from an accountant, so that a client who is advised by an accountant and who desires expert legal advice on some particular tax problem will have to instruct a solicitor, who will in turn obtain the opinion of one of the tax specialists at the Bar.

Owing to the neglect of tax by the legal profession, there has been a similar neglect in the legal faculties of the universities. Until I was appointed as a Professor of London University last year, there was no Professor of Law at any British university who had specialized in taxation law, and at present the only legal degree in which taxation law can be offered as a subject is the LL.M. (post-graduate) degree of London University. I believe this situation is about to change rapidly and that taxation law will shortly become much more extensively taught in universities. There is, however, a striking contrast at present between British and American universities; many of the outstanding Deans of American Law Schools and Professors of Law are well-known figures in the tax field. On the other hand, those British universities which offer degrees involving specialization in accountancy have paid considerable attention to tax from the accountancy aspect. This reflects the general attitude in Great Britain that tax is normally a matter for accountants and that lawyers should only be called in when the client stands in need of special advice or legal representation.

Features of the British tax system

I must now say something about the British income tax system in order to explain the roles accountants and lawyers play in it.

1. *Withholding procedure.* One of the main features of the British system is that income tax is collected by withholding at source as far as possible. There is an elaborate pay-as-you-earn (P.A.Y.E.) system which requires employers to deduct and account to the Revenue for tax on their employees' earnings. The system is so arranged that the amount of the tax withheld is adjusted to meet the particular tax circumstances of each employee as reported by him (i.e., his tax allowances for marriage, children, housekeeper, earned income, life insurance, etc., are taken into account) and is computed at four successive different progressive rates (at present 8¾% on the first £60 of taxable income, 21¼% on the next £150, 31¼% on the next £150 and 38¾% — what we call standard rate — on the remainder). The system can also cope with small amounts of unearned income reported by the taxpayer which are not subject to withholding at source — e.g., bank interest on deposits. For the great majority of employees the tax deducted under P.A.Y.E. is sufficiently near to the taxpayer's total liability to require no further adjustment at the end of the year.

Withholding at standard rate also applies in relation to company dividends, interest on government stocks and mortgage interest. The paying agent for foreign dividends and interest has to withhold tax at source and pay it to the Revenue. In addition, the tax we call Schedule A, which is based on the imputed income of the value of land and buildings, is collected from the occupier on a geographical basis, who in turn, if he is a tenant, may reimburse himself by deduction from his rent so that the landlord thus suffers the tax.

Although we have pushed the withholding system practically as far as it will go, there is still a substantial area in which it cannot be applied. Tax on the profits of a trade or profession clearly cannot be collected by withholding. It is not until the accounts have been prepared that the profits, and consequently the amount of tax, can be ascertained. Our highly progressive surtax, which is additional to income tax, applies to individuals with an income over £2,000 per annum, and in the highest range takes a further 50% of income in that range (i.e., the top rate of income tax and surtax is 88¾%). This tax requires a computation of total income with various permitted deductions which are different from those allowed for income tax; hence it is also inappropriate for tax deduction at source. There are also certain other items of income which have to be assessed directly on the taxpayer.

2. *Assessment procedure.* We have no system of direct assessment by the taxpayer himself. His obligation is to make a return to the Inland Revenue showing his total sources of income and the respective amounts under each head. Unless the amounts are trivial, he is also expected to supply accounts showing how the amounts of profits, etc., have been arrived at. He also supplies the Revenue with the necessary information as to any deductions or allowances he may be entitled to. On this information the officials of the Revenue fix his code number for P.A.Y.E. (if he is an employee) and assess to him any tax due from him which is not collected by withholding, for which he receives a demand note from the Collector in due course. In most cases of any substance or difficulty the taxpayer is assisted in the preparation of his return by an accountant or, in some cases, by a solicitor, and in these cases the computation of tax is normally agreed upon between the professional adviser and the Revenue official concerned. The person, however, who is primarily responsible for the correctness of the return is the taxpayer himself and if he makes an inaccurate return through fraud or negligence, he is liable to substantial monetary penalties. A professional advisor who assists in prepar-

ing an incorrect return is also liable to a penalty if he knows that the return is incorrect. Financial penalties are the main Revenue sanction; in extreme cases, however, they will initiate a criminal prosecution for fraud or forgery.

When accounts are submitted to the Revenue by an accountant the inspector will scrutinize carefully the accountant's report on those accounts. If there is a clear audit certificate then the Revenue will normally accept the basic facts as true and will only raise questions on tax problems arising from those facts. If, however, the report shows that the accountant takes little responsibility for the accuracy of the figures and has only prepared accounts from figures supplied to him by the taxpayer, then the Revenue's questions will be more searching. The Revenue, while expecting full answers to their questions, rarely audit a taxpayer's books. If they are not satisfied with the answers they get, their remedy is to assess the taxpayer in a higher figure than that shown by his return and accounts and leave him to appeal. On an appeal, the Commissioners hearing the appeal have power to order the taxpayer's books to be produced to the Revenue, but the onus is on the taxpayer to show the Revenue assessment is wrong so that he will normally have to produce his books in order to succeed in his appeal.

Hence the normal practice is for the independent accountant acting for the taxpayer to submit accounts to the Revenue, then deal with their queries, and finally negotiate the computation of tax. The Revenue will normally accept as accurate, statements made to them by an accountant which he states he has verified. Members of the accountancy profession in England are very proud that this trust placed in them by the Revenue has become an integral part of our tax system. Even in what we call "back duty" cases, i.e., where the Revenue have discovered that income has been understated in past returns, they normally arrange for an independent accountant to make a general investigation on behalf of both the Revenue and the client and submit full details to the Revenue. In back duty cases it is made clear to the client that the accountant owes this double duty; but even in the ordinary case the accountant regards himself as under a duty to the Revenue not to put forward any facts which he knows to be inaccurate, and to investigate, as far as he can, the truth of facts put to him by his client if he has reasonable grounds for being suspicious of their accuracy. The fact that the Revenue normally rely on the figures put forward by the client's accountant is a substantial benefit both to the client and to the accountant and in those rare cases where the Revenue are not prepared to accept a particular accountant's figures, the queries and investigations that follow from the Revenue tend to make both client's and accountant's position so intolerable that such an accountant may have to abandon tax business.

The fact that the Revenue rely on the taxpayer's accountant for the basic facts does not mean that they do not enquire into the basis upon which accounts have been prepared, or valuations made, so as to satisfy themselves that the accounts have been prepared in accordance with income tax law and practice, the criteria of which vary in some degree from the criteria required in a profit and loss account prepared in accordance with the Companies Acts. An accountant is fully entitled to argue as strongly as he can on his client's behalf on all matters where two views can reasonably be taken as to the way in which tax accounts should be prepared. What he is not entitled to do is to misrepresent or conceal the basic facts which are relevant to his client's tax position.

3. *Appeal procedure.* When a taxpayer has been assessed to tax by the Revenue he has a right of appeal if he disputes the assessment; such an appeal is heard by the General Commissioners for his district (unpaid local men of business experience who are similar to our Justices of the Peace) or by the Special Commissioners (who are fulltime judicial officers). In either case he may appear himself or be represented by a barrister, solicitor or accountant and most of the simpler cases are conducted by accountants. From the Commissioners an appeal lies, on law only, to the ordinary High Court and here only a barrister (instructed by a solicitor), has a right of audience.

4. *Attitude of legal and accountancy professions to each other.* There has not been the same conflict in England between accountants and lawyers over the division between them of tax work as has occurred in the United States. Although occasionally one hears complaints by a member of one profession against a member of the other, in general they work in collaboration. It is becoming generally recognized that a client is best served by joint advice from both professions in any sizeable tax problem and the most common complaint from accountants is that there are not enough solicitors who have specialized in tax so that they frequently find themselves in collaboration with a client's solicitor who does not appreciate the technicalities and merely acts as a post office between the accountant and the specialist barrister. With the growing appreciation by solicitors of the importance of tax, this complaint is now less often heard.

5. *The attitude of the Courts to tax cases.* If we turn to the at-

titude of the Courts to tax problems, the first point to notice is that we have no written constitution, and no law duly passed by Parliament can be attacked in the courts on grounds of unconstitutionality. Whatever Parliament says is the law; it can legislate retrospectively and does so occasionally in Revenue matters. The Courts construe tax laws as literally as possible. It is only when there is ambiguity in the wording of some taxing provision that the Courts will look behind the wording of the relevant clause to see which of two or more possible constructions is the one likely to have been intended by Parliament. Where the words are unambiguous the approach of the Courts is that laid down by Lord Cairns in the House of Lords (our final Appeal Court) in 1869:

> If the person sought to be taxed comes within the letter of the law he must be taxed however great the hardship may appear to the judicial mind to be. On the other hand if the Crown, seeking to recover the tax, cannot bring the subject within the letter of the law, the subject is free, however apparently within the spirit of the law the case might otherwise appear to be. In other words, if there be admissible, in any statute, what is called an equitable construction, certainly such a construction is not admissible in a taxing statute, where you simply adhere to the words of the statute.[1]

Similarly, in dealing with the tax effect of transactions by the taxpayer with third parties, the Courts do not go behind the strict legal effect of the contractual engagements entered into by the taxpayer. If on the true construction of the documents and acts of the taxpayer, certain legal results follow as between himself and third parties, the Courts will apply those results in considering the consequences of the tax to the taxpayer. In particular, unless authorized by a specific tax provision to do otherwise, the Courts will treat a corporation as a different legal entity from its shareholders, even though it is substantially a one man company controlled by the taxpayer. A number of special tax provisions do require the "veil of incorporation" to be lifted for closely-held corporations but our Courts do not go as far as your Supreme Court appears to have gone in *Gregory v. Helvering* and similar cases. Our Courts will only discard "form" in favour of substance when they are satisfied that the documents presented to them are a sham and are not intended to be acted upon, a state of affairs which is generally extremely difficult for

---

[1] Partington v. A.-G. (1869), L.R. 4 H.L. 100 at p. 122. The statement has been since approved in A.-G. v. Selbourne [1902] 1 K.B. 388 at p. 396, in IRC v. Barclays Bank, [1951] A.C. 421 at p. 439 and in Potts' Executors v. IRC [1951] A.C. 443 at p. 456.

the Revenue to prove. This attitude of the Courts has led to much legislation being passed which disregards "form" in special cases by "deeming" certain transactions or situations to be quite different transactions or situations for tax purposes. This has reduced the number of situations in which the Courts might be asked to look at "substance" and has tended to confirm the Judges in their strictly legal approach.

Prior to the last war there was a steady flow of judicial dicta which made it clear that the Courts would not be astute to prevent tax avoidance so long as it was carried out by lawful means. Here are a few quotations:

> No man in this country is under the smallest obligation, moral or other, so to arrange his legal relations to his business or to his property as to enable the Inland Revenue to put the largest possible shovel into his stores. The Inland Revenue is not slow—and quite rightly—to take every advantage which is open to it under the taxing statutes for the purpose of depleting the taxpayer's pocket. And the taxpayer is, in like manner, entitled to be astute to prevent, so far as he honestly can, the depletion of his means by the Inland Revenue. (Lord Clyde)[2]

> My Lords, the highest authorities have always recognized that the subject is entitled so to arrange his affairs as not to attract taxes imposed by the Crown, so far as he can do so within the law, and that he may legitimately claim the advantage of any express term or of any omissions that he can find in his favour in the taxing Acts. In so doing he neither comes under liability nor incurs blame. (Lord Summer)[3]

> It is trite law that His Majesty's subjects are free, if they can, to make their own arrangements so that their cases may fall outside the scope of the taxing Acts. They incur no legal penalties, and, strictly speaking, no moral censure if having considered the lines drawn by the legislature for the imposition of taxes, they make it their business to walk outside them. (Lord Summer)[4]

> Every man is entitled if he can to order his affairs so as that the tax attracted under the appropriate Act is less than it otherwise would be. If he succeeds in ordering them so as to secure this result, then, however unappreciative the Commissioners of Inland Revenue or his fellow taxpayers may be of his ingenuity, he cannot be compelled to pay an increased tax. (Lord Tomlin)[5]

[2]Ayrshire Pullman Motor Services v. IRC (1920) 14 T.C. 754 at p. 763.
[3]IRC v. Fisher's Executors [1926] A.C. 395 at p. 412.
[4]Levene v. IRC [1928] A.C. 217 at p. 227.
[5]Westminster (Duke) v. IRC [1936] A.C. 1 at pp. 19, 20.

You will notice that Lord Sumner not only stressed the legality of a tax avoidance transaction, but indicated that in his view it was perfectly ethical. During the war the climate of judicial opinion changed somewhat, as is shown by two more quotations:

> My Lords, of recent years much ingenuity has been expended in certain quarters to devise methods of disposition of income by which those who were prepared to adopt them might enjoy the benefits of residence in this country while receiving the equivalent of such income without sharing in the appropriate burden of British taxation. Judicial dicta may be cited which point out that however elaborate and artificial such methods may be, those who adopt them are "entitled" to do so. There is, of course, no doubt that they are within their legal rights, but that is no reason why their efforts, or those of the professional gentlemen who assist them in the matter, should be regarded as a commendable exercise of ingenuity or as a discharge of the duties of good citizenship. On the contrary, one result of such methods, if they succeed, is, of course to increase *pro tanto* the load of tax on the shoulders of the great body of good citizens who do not desire, or do not know how, to adopt these manoeuvres. (Lord Simon)[6]

> The section is a penal one, and, whatever its consequences may be, they are intended to be an effective deterrent to practices which the legislature considers to be against the public interest. For years a battle of manoeuvres has been waged between the legislature and those who are minded to throw the burden of taxation off their own shoulders on to those of their fellow-subjects. In the battle the legislature has often been worsted by the skill, determination and resourcefulness of its opponents, of whom the present appellant has not been the least successful. It would not shock us in the least to find that the legislature has determined to put an end to the struggle by imposing the severest of penalties. It scarcely lies in the mouth of the taxpayer who plays with fire to complain of burnt fingers. (Lord Greene)[7]

It will be observed, however, that neither of these two latter eminent judges dissented from the legal proposition that tax avoidance was perfectly lawful and should be sharply distinguished from tax evasion which involves some illegal act or concealment. Since the war, judges have unhesitatingly adopted the legalistic approach and have never, so far as I am aware, again indicated any ethical doubts.

---

[6] Latilla v. IRC [1943] A.C. 377 at p. 381; [1943] 1 All E.R. 265.
[7] Lord Howard de Walden v. IRC [1942] 1 K.B. 389 at p. 397; [1942] 1 All E.R. 287.

An important consequence of this judicial attitude is that, except in a few special cases where legislation has designated a tax avoidance motive as being an element in the taxability of a transaction, there is no advantage in pretending that a tax avoidance transaction has any other motive or in dressing it up with some "good business purpose."

6. *The British concept of capital gains.* Another important feature underlying British income tax is that many of its main principles took shape in the last century. The tax was then a proportional tax and was not progressive except that there was a minimum exemption for small incomes. With tax at a flat rate and an emphasis on withholding, it is natural that the system was based on taxing "income" rather than on taxing the taxpayer. The basic structure of our income tax, which still reflects the principles established in 1801, thus looks primarily for a "source" of income and only taxes that which is derived from the source. This led to a clear judicial distinction being drawn between the tree, which was regarded as capital, and the fruit, which was regarded as income; from which followed the British doctrine that capital appreciation is not income. On the other hand, a realized profit on the stock in trade of a trader is taxable as part of his trading profit, and over the last 40 years the Courts have steadily extended the concept of trading. Even one purchase and resale may be deemed to constitute trading if the subject matter of the transaction is something which is not normally regarded as a medium for investment and is not acquired for personal use of enjoyment.

There is thus a fairly wide field in which the profit of a transaction may be either capital or income according to the form which that transaction takes, and in sizeable business and family transactions close attention to "form" may result in considerable tax savings, while lack of it may bring an otherwise untaxable transaction into charge to tax. Some lawyers and accountants have specialized in devising elaborate tax avoidance methods which have usually led to anti-avoidance legislation. In turn these experts have found new loopholes and more legislation has followed in still more sweeping terms. Many of our tax provisions are now highly complicated and difficult to construe. Hence the general body of taxpayers are often forced to study the tax aspects of perfectly innocent transactions to make sure there are no unexpected tax repercussions and many lawyers and accountants are kept busy on tax advising as few sizeable business or family transactions can be carried through without a check on the tax effects.

The areas in which ethical problems arise

With this general background, may I now pass on to consider the main areas in which ethical problems arise in tax practice. A professional man, like any other man, may often find himself faced with a problem in which his self-interest clashes with his conscience; in addition he has problems which arise from a conflict of professional duties and loyalties, and it is these last which I propose to consider.

The professional adviser's first duty is to do his best for his client, but he also owes duties and loyalties (1) to his profession and the other members of it, (2) to the community, its laws and its social and political institutions, and (3) to his own personal ethical standards which may well be different from those of his client. The two main occasions when conflicts between these duties and loyalties may occur in relation to tax practice are (1) when acting for a client in connection with some proposed transaction which is designed to minimize that client's tax and there are certain features in that transaction which the adviser may consider unethical or of doubtful legality, but which the client desires him to carry through, and (2) when acting for a client in relation to some transaction in the past which the adviser has now discovered to have been wrongful.

Problems regarding a future transaction

In the case of a future transaction which is only in contemplation, the main principles are clear. The adviser must not advise or assist in the commission of a crime, but problems do arise as to what he should do if he suspects that his client intends some wrongful act despite his advice to the contrary. Except in the case of a limited number of serious crimes, classified as "felonies," the law imposes no duty to inform on one's neighbor to the police, and except in the case of these crimes a professional adviser must respect his client's confidence although he must clearly disassociate himself from all participation in any criminal act.

When the proposed transaction is lawful but of a highly artificial nature designed solely for tax avoidance purposes, a professional man may well hold ethical views which would prevent him from using it for himself. Should he apply a similar standard to his client's affairs? Clearly a man who holds strong ethical views on tax avoidance will devote his energies to other fields and not undertake tax practice, but those with similar, but less strong views, may well draw a distinction between advising a client as to possible methods of tax avoidance when asked or generally retained to do so, and encouraging clients, unasked, to adopt highly artificial tax avoidance schemes.

In view of the judicial dicta I have quoted, the majority of professional men practicing in this field are prepared to devise and implement schemes for minimizing their clients' tax so long as the schemes comply with the law. In cases where the law is uncertain there is one good general rule for the adviser to follow which will usually prevent him from coming into difficulties. He must be satisfied that, when the scheme has been carried out, all the relevant facts can be disclosed to the Revenue and the scheme will still work. If, however, the scheme depends in essence on the Revenue not ascertaining some material fact, even though it may not be a fact which would normally be expected to be put before the Revenue in the first instance, the scheme is undesirable and should not be pursued. If the professional adviser can foresee that he may not be able to give a frank answer to some query of the Revenue without destroying the tax advantage proposed by the scheme, then this must be taken as a clear warning signal not to go on with it. He must be prepared to put all his cards on the table.

There are, of course, border line cases where a lot must be left to individual judgment. The law on any point may not be clear and different opinions may be held by different experts. If a particular transaction is clearly a capital one and nontaxable it may well require no disclosure to the Revenue. Suppose there is doubt about its taxability but an adviser, on the whole, believes that it is not taxable. Should he go ahead and not report it? Clearly the safe course is to report the facts and submit that they do not involve liability to tax, but a client may object to this.

Here the independent professional man, who is not whole time employed by some business firm, is in a much stronger position than the full time employee, although the small independent accountant with only a few large clients may equally find himself in practical difficulties. One cannot dogmatize about such situations; each has to be dealt with on its own merits; but the climate of professional opinion in Great Britain is such that in most cases a professional man can take a fairly strong line with his client, or even his employer, if he feels that he should do so.

Problems in relation to past transactions

We must now consider the second occasion when difficulties arise. This is when the professional adviser discovers that his client has already committed some tax irregularity or fraud. Is he under any duty of disclosure to the Revenue and, if not, to what extent may he assist the client in avoiding or minimizing the consequences of the fraud?

1. *Felonies and misdemeanors.* Before dealing with the main issue, one or two preliminary points should be mentioned. I mentioned before that certain crimes in England are classified as felonies. A person, whether a professional man or not, who intentionally helps a man who has committed a felony to escape conviction, commits the criminal offence of being an accessory after the fact; similarly a person who knowingly fails to report a felony to the police commits the offence of misprision of felony if the concealment of the crime is for that person's own advantage and possibly even if it is not. It is extremely rare for a prosecution to take place for misprision of felony, but the existence of this possibility makes it obvious that an accountant who discovers that his client has committed a felony should, both in his own and his client's interest, arrange for legal advice to be taken and for the client in future to act on that advice. Most tax frauds, however, are not felonies but are only "misdemeanors" so that this problem is only likely to occur in relation to tax matters when the client has committed forgery, which is a felony.

2. *No legal privilege for accountants.* Another point to bear in mind, which I believe to be the same in the United States, is that while a client can claim legal professional privilege in criminal or civil proceedings for statements made to his lawyer, he cannot do the same for statements made to an accountant or other person who is not a lawyer. Hence statements made to an accountant and documents supplied to him may subsequently have to be given in evidence, whereas they would be protected from disclosure if made to the lawyer. This applies to all classes of crime and not only to felonies, so that there are other cases in which, acting in the interests of the client, the accountant should hand the client over to the lawyer at an early stage.

3. *General duty to advise disclosure.* In every case it is clearly the duty of the accountant to advise his client to confess the crime and make full disclosure. If this is done, no professional problem arises. Owing to the practice of the Revenue to be more lenient in penalties and much less likely to prosecute in cases where the offender confesses before he is found out, an adviser can nearly always advise his client that to confess his wrongdoing is not only ethically right but also good business. If, however, the client is not prepared to

make disclosure, then a conflict may easily develop between the accountant's professional duty and the client's instructions.

4. *Duty if client refuses to make disclosure.* The Institute has published a long and detailed statement as to the action to be taken by their members in these circumstances. Its recommendations may be summarized as follows: If the accountant has been a party, although an innocent party, to the fraud by the submission of returns on his client's behalf which he now knows are inaccurate and the client is not prepared to make disclosure, then the accountant may no longer act for that client and, in addition, it is his professional duty to inform the Inland Revenue that the accounts he had previously submitted cannot be relied upon and that he has ceased to act for the client. He is under no duty to specify the respects in which the accounts are inaccurate and it would be unprofessional for him to do so without first obtaining the client's consent.

If the accountant discovers that past accounts submitted on behalf of that client to the Inland Revenue were defective, but he was in no way responsible for transmitting them to the Inland Revenue, then he is under no duty to make any communication to the Inland Revenue, but equally he cannot continue to act in submitting subsequent accounts unless those accounts contain all adjustments that are necessary in view of the previous defects. Since such adjustments often disclose the previous inaccuracies to the Revenue, this means that in those cases the accountant cannot continue to act for the client unless disclosure is permitted.

In the rare case when the previous fraud does not involve any adjustments to current accounts and the accountant had no part in it, there is no strict obligation on him to refuse to act in future. The Institute, however, in their Memorandum give a fairly broad hint that in general it would be unwise for one of their members to do so.

Substantially these rules of professional conduct mean that if an accountant discovers that his client has committed a fraud which the client will not disclose to the Revenue, he will in most cases be unable to continue to act for the client, and in those rare cases where he can, he probably will not do so.

5. *Duty on change of accountants.* The obvious alternative for a client in these circumstances, who does not wish to make disclosure, is to consult another accountant. Here again strict rules have been prescribed by the Institute which ensure that no member may accept nomination as auditor or professional accountant to a company, partnership or private individual without first communicating with

the previous auditor or professional accountant in order to ascertain the circumstances in which the change takes place. If a former accountant of a client receives such a communication, he is now under a professional duty to inform the prospective successor of the general nature of the reason for the change in order to put that successor adequately on his guard. There is thus some extremely effective machinery in operation to prevent another accountant taking over, in ignorance of the tax fraud, in a case where the previous accountant, with knowledge of the tax fraud, has declined to act, and this machinery puts strong pressure on clients to make disclosure, because they will in practice be unable to get any reputable accountant to act for them in future unless they do so. Even if the client does find some less reputable accountant, who is not a member of the Institute and not bound by its rules, who is prepared to act in these circumstances, the sudden change will almost certainly put the Revenue on their guard and they will naturally subject such a client's accounts to as thorough an enquiry as they can.

By the adoption of these rules, accountancy in England has gone a long way toward eliminating tax frauds, except in those cases where the fraud is such that the client can successfully keep the accountant in ignorance, or the fraud is of a type which does not involve an accountant's participation.

6. *Borderline cases*. While there still remains a considerable area in which individual judgment is required, particularly in cases where the accountant has suspicions and cannot obtain proof, the rules applied by the profession as a whole enable most problems to be resolved without too great difficulty. If the problem is one of fact, then it is clearly the duty of the adviser to ascertain the relevant facts and to ensure that no material fact is concealed from the Revenue. If the problem is clearly one of law, so long as the facts are disclosed an accountant, just as a lawyer, may put forward his client's contentions, whatever his own view of the law may be. There is, of course, an area where facts and law intermingle. If, in preparing some accounts, an accountant sees some item of expenditure, the lawful deductibility of which he is uncertain about, how far should he separate that item from others of a similar nature which are clearly allowable so that the Revenue's attention is drawn to it? This is clearly a question of degree, and I think most accountants take the view that where the item is at all substantial any accounts prepared for submission to the Revenue should contain sufficient information to distinguish such an item. Problems also arise where the accountant has

not audited accounts but is merely submitting them for tax purposes, e.g., for an individual in business or a partnership where there is not the same statutory obligation to audit as there is in the case of a company. It will, of course, be made clear to the Revenue in such a case that the accounts have not been audited by the accountant and he will not be expected to vouch for their accuracy to the extent that he would if he had conducted an audit. Equally clearly, however, he will not satisfy his professional duty if he merely passes on accounts prepared by the client containing items which he has reasonable grounds for suspecting are inaccurate, without further investigation of those items. Here again, individual judgment and the size of the item in question will play a part.

Conclusions

In all walks of professional life ethical problems arise. Speaking as a lawyer who has had many contacts with accountants, I do not believe that such problems arise in the tax practice of accountants in Great Britain as much as one might expect at first sight. This I believe to be due to the high standard of personal integrity which the public expects to find—and generally does find—in members of the accountancy profession, and the resulting attitude of the Revenue in relying on and trusting the accountancy profession. This in turn results in the members of the profession rarely abusing that trust, and loyally abiding by the detailed and practical rules which the profession has laid down.

Postcript

This article was written 8 years ago and a number of statements in it are now out of date. There has been a big change in the attitude of university law schools and tax law is now taught at most of them. Schedule A (the tax on the imputed value of land and buildings owned by the taxpayer) has been abolished and capital gains are now taxed in much the same way as they are taxed in U.S.A. The main rules about ethics, however, remain much the same and our Internal Revenue still basically rely on the accountancy profession for the accuracy of the accounts and returns they submit.

G.S.A.W., 1969

Documentary Appendix

Treasury Department Circular 230

1959-1 C.B. 745*

SUBPART A.—RULES GOVERNING AUTHORITY TO PRACTICE

§ 10.1 DIRECTOR OF PRACTICE.—(a) *Establishment of office.*—There is established in the Internal Revenue Service the office of Director of Practice. The Director of Practice shall be appointed by the Secretary of the Treasury and shall be under the direction and supervision of the Secretary of the Treasury.

(b) *Duties.*—The Director of Practice shall receive and act upon applications for enrollment to practice as attorneys or agents before the Internal Revenue Service; institute and provide for the conduct of disciplinary proceedings relating to enrolled attorneys and agents; make inquiries with respect to matters under his jurisdiction; and perform such other duties as are necessary or appropriate to carry out the provisions of this part or as are prescribed by the Secretary of the Treasury. Decisions of the Director of Practice in individual cases relating to enrollment, disbarment, or disciplinary measures shall not be subject to change by the Commissioner of Internal Revenue.

(c) *Acting Director.*—The Secretary of the Treasury will designate an officer or employee of the Treasury Department to act as Director of Practice in the event of the absence of the Director or of a vacancy in that office.

§ 10.2 REGULATION OF PRACTICE.—(a) *In general.*—Except as provided by § 10.7 or other sections of this part no person shall be recognized or permitted to practice before the Internal Revenue Service unless he is enrolled as an attorney or agent pursuant to this part. An enrollment card issued pursuant to the regulations superseded by this part will be recognized to evidence enrollment to practice pursuant to the regulations in this part and subject to the limitations specified by that card.

(b) *Definition of Practice.*—Practice before the Internal Revenue Service comprehends all matters connected with presentations to the Internal Revenue Service or any of its officers or employees relating to a client's rights, privileges or liabilities under laws or regulations administered by the Internal Revenue Service. Such presentations include the preparation and filing of necessary documents, correspondence with and communications to the Internal Revenue Service, and the representation of a client at conferences, hearings, and meetings. Neither the preparation of tax returns nor the furnishing of information at the request of the Internal Revenue Service or any of its officers

---

*For this document as later amended, see infra p.359.

or employees is considered practice before the Service, and enrollment is not necessary for either of such activities.

§ 10.3 ELIGIBILITY FOR ENROLLMENT.—(a) *In general.*—Persons applying for enrollment to practice before the Internal Revenue Service must show to the satisfaction of the Director of Practice that they are of good character and in good repute, possessed of the necessary qualifications to enable them to render valuable service to clients, and otherwise competent to advise and assist clients in the presentation of their interests to the Internal Revenue Service. Applicants for enrollment have the burden of establishing that they possess a good character and reputation, an adequate education, knowledge and understanding of the laws and regulations relating to tax matters and other subjects administered by the Internal Revenue Service, and a knowledge of the rules governing practice before the Internal Revenue Service.

(b) *Character and reputation.*—Good character and good reputation are not identical requirements. The former is determined by the applicant's actual qualities; the latter depends upon the opinion entertained of the applicant by those who have had the opportunity of knowing him in the community in which he resides or in which he practices his profession. It follows that evidence of any act or omission which tends to establish lack of integrity or untrustworthiness or other qualities reprehensible in a professional man, is material as bearing upon the character of the applicant, notwithstanding there is clear proof that his reputation is good.

(c) *Citizens; natural persons.*—Enrollment to practice may be granted only to natural persons who are citizens of the United States and who are over the age of 21 years.

(d) *Attorneys and certified public accountants.*—If found to possess the qualifications provided for in this part, the Director of Practice may grant enrollment to practice before the Internal Revenue Service to persons of the following classes:

(1) Any attorney at law who is a member in good standing of the bar of the highest court of a State, Territory, or possession of the United States, or of the courts of the District of Columbia, and who is lawfully engaged in the active practice of his profession;

(2) Any certified public accountant who has duly qualified to practice as a certified public accountant in a State, Territory, possession of the United States, or in the District of Columbia, and who is lawfully engaged in the active practice of his profession.*

(e) *Persons not attorneys or certified public accountants.*—With respect to applicants other than attorneys or certified public accountants, the Director of Practice, in his discretion, may grant special enrollment to practice if the applicant demonstrates special competence by written examination or as provided in paragraph (f). Persons interested in obtaining special enrollment pursuant to paragraph (e) should apply to the Director of Practice for information as to requirements.

---

*Secs. 10.3(d)(1) and (2) were amended in 1962 to eliminate the qualifying phrase "and who is lawfully engaged in the active practice of his profession." See 1962-2 C.B. 394.

(f) *Special enrollment for former Internal Revenue Service employees.*—Former employees of the Internal Revenue Service may be granted special enrollment by the Director of Practice under paragraph (e), in cases where their service and technical experience in the Internal Revenue Service has qualified them for such enrollment, as follows:

(1) Application for special enrollment on account of former employment in the Internal Revenue Service shall be made to the Director of Practice. Each applicant will be supplied a form by the Director, which shall indicate the information required respecting the applicant's qualifications. In addition to the applicant's name, address, citizenship, age, educational experience, etc., such information shall specifically include a detailed account of the applicant's employment in the Internal Revenue Service, which account shall show (1) positions held, (2) date of each appointment and termination thereof, (3) nature of services rendered in each position, with particular reference to the degree of technical experience involved, and (4) name of supervisor in such positions, together with such other information regarding the experience and training of the applicant as may be relevant.

(2) Upon receipt of each such application, it shall be transmitted to the appropriate officer of the Internal Revenue Service with the request that a detailed report of the nature and rating of the applicant's services in the Internal Revenue Service, accompanied by the recommendation of the superior officer in the particular unit or division of the Internal Revenue Service that such employment does or does not qualify the applicant technically and otherwise for the desired authorization, be furnished to the Director of Practice. (Such report shall be requested in addition to the usual reports requested in cases of application for enrollment.)

(3) In examining the qualifications of an applicant for special enrollment on account of employment in the Internal Revenue Service, the Director of Practice will be governed by the following policies:

(*i*) Special enrollment on account of such employment may be of the same scope as enrollment granted pursuant to paragraph (d)(2) or the scope may be limited to permit the presentation of matters only of the particular class or only before the particular unit or division of the Internal Revenue Service for which his former employment in the Internal Revenue Service has qualified the applicant.

(*ii*) In the case of employees separated from employment in the Internal Revenue Service, application for special enrollment on account of such employment must be made within 3 years after the termination thereof.

(*iii*) It shall be requisite for special enrollment on account of such employment for practice before the Internal Revenue Service that the applicant shall have had a minimum of 7 years continuous employment in the Internal Revenue Service during at least 5 years of which service he shall have been regularly engaged in applying and interpreting the provisions of the Internal Revenue Code and the regulations thereunder relating to income, estate, gift, employment, or excise taxes.

(*iv*) For the purposes of subdivision (*iii*), an aggregate of 10 or more years of employment, at least three of which occurred within the 5 years preceding the date of application, shall be deemed the equivalent of 7 years continuous employment.

§ 10.4 INELIGIBILITY FOR ENROLLMENT.—(a) *In general.*—No person shall be eligible for enrollment to practice before the Internal Revenue Service if he fails in any particular to show to the satisfaction of the Director of Practice that he is possessed of the qualities contemplated by section 3 of the Act of July 7, 1884, 23 Stat. 258 (5 U.S.C. 261) and the regulations contained in this part, or if such practice by him would be inconsistent with any of the laws of the United States.

(b) *Particular grounds.*—Among the causes sufficient to justify denial of an application for enrollment are failure to show good character or reputation; any conduct or practices which would constitute a violation of any of the provisions of this part if the applicant were enrolled; any conduct which would be a ground for disbarment or suspension from practice pursuant to this part; and any conduct which would be deemed grossly improper in commercial transactions by accepted standards.

(c) *Government officers and employees; judges.*—Officers and employees of the United States or of the District of Columbia, Members of Congress or a Delegate or Resident Commissioner thereto, and judges of the Tax Court or any courts of record, unless such judges are permitted by law to practice their profession, shall be ineligible for enrollment. Officers and employees of any State, or subdivision thereof, whose duties require them to pass upon, investigate, or deal with tax matters of such State or subdivision, shall be ineligible for enrollment, provided such employment may disclose facts or information applicable to Federal tax matters.

(d) *Full-time employees of corporations and others.*—Except for employees of individuals or partnerships engaged in the practice of law or accounting, persons employed by individuals, partnerships, corporations or other organizations on a full-time basis, and who do not maintain offices apart from their employment, with services available to the general public, shall not be eligible for enrollment.

(e) *Violation by Internal Revenue Service employee of tenure agreement.*—Application for enrollment may be denied in any case in which it appears that the applicant without reasonable cause has terminated his employment with the Internal Revenue Service in violation of an obligation assumed as a condition of employment to remain in the service of the Internal Revenue Service for a specified period or for a reasonable time.

(f) *Oath of allegiance.*—No person shall be enrolled to practice if he is unable for any reason to take the oath of allegiance, and to support the Constitution of the United States, as required of persons prosecuting claims against the United States by section 3478 of the Revised Statutes (31 U.S.C. 204).

§ 10.5 APPLICATION FOR ENROLLMENT.—(a) *Form; fee.*—An applicant for enrollment shall file with the Director of Practice an application on Form 23, properly executed under oath or affirmation. Such application shall be accompanied by a check or money order in the amount of $25.00, payable to the Treasurer of the United States, which amount shall constitute a fee which shall be charged to each applicant for enrollment. The fee shall be retained by the United States whether or not the applicant is granted enrollment. Attorneys at law shall apply for enrollment as attorneys, and all other applicants shall apply for enrollment as agents, except that an applicant who is qualified to enroll either as an attorney at law or as an agent may elect whether to apply as attorney or agent.

(b) *Additional information; examination.*—The Director of Practice, as a condition to consideration of an application for enrollment, may require the applicant to file additional information and to submit to any written or oral examination under oath or otherwise. Upon request of the Director of Practice an applicant shall endeavor to stipulate with an officer or employee of the Internal Revenue Service facts pertaining to the application to the fullest extent to which either complete or qualified agreement can be reached. The Director shall grant a hearing on an application at the applicant's written request.

(c) *Temporary recognition.*—Upon receipt of a properly executed application, the Director of Practice may grant the applicant temporary recognition to practice pending investigation of the applicant and a determination as to whether enrollment to practice should be granted. Such temporary recognition shall not be granted if the application is not regular on its face; if the information stated therein, if true, is not sufficient to warrant enrollment to practice; or if there is any information before the Director of Practice which indicates that the statements in the application are untrue or that the applicant is not of good character or reputation. Issuance of temporary recognition shall not constitute enrollment to practice or a finding of eligibility for enrollment, and the temporary recognition may be withdrawn at any time by the Director of Practice.

(d) *Appeal from denial of application.*—Decisions of the Director of Practice denying enrollment to practice before the Internal Revenue Service may be appealed to the Secretary of the Treasury. (Sec. 501, 65 Stat. 290; 5 U.S.C. 140.)

§ 10.6 ENROLLMENT.—(a) *Roster.*—The Director of Practice shall maintain rosters of all attorneys and agents who are enrolled to practice, of all attorneys and agents who have been disbarred or suspended from practice before the Internal Revenue Service, and of persons whose applications for enrollment have been denied.

(b) *Enrollment cards.*—The Director of Practice shall issue an enrollment card to each attorney or agent who is enrolled to practice before the Internal Revenue Service. Unless advised to the contrary by the Director of Practice, any officer or employee of the Internal Revenue Service may consider the holder of an unexpired enrollment card to be duly authorized to practice before the Internal Revenue Service.

(c) *Period of enrollment card.*—Every enrollment card shall by its terms become void five years after the date of its issuance. A holder of a void card is not entitled to practice before the Internal Revenue Service.

(d) *Application for renewal.*—Application for renewal of enrollment card may be made at any time during a twenty-four month period commencing twelve months before and ending twelve months after the expiration of an enrollment card. Such application shall be filed on Form 23A at such place or places as may be designated by the Director of Practice and there shall be annexed thereto the enrollment card last outstanding. Copies of Form 23A may be obtained from the Director of Practice and at the offices of District Directors of Internal Revenue. Each application shall be accompanied by a check or money order in the amount of $5.00, payable to the Treasurer of the United States, which amount shall constitute a fee which shall be charged each person who applies for issuance of a new enrollment card pursuant to the provisions of this paragraph.

(e) *Expiration of enrollment.*—Unless application for a new enrollment card is filed with the Director of Practice within twelve months after the expiration date of an enrollment card, the enrollment of the holder of the card shall automatically terminate, his name shall be stricken from the roster of enrollees, and he shall not be authorized to practice before the Internal Revenue Service except by filing a new application for enrollment, as provided by § 10.5, and obtaining authority to practice from the Director of Practice. (Sec. 501, 65 Stat. 290; 5 U.S.C. 140.)

§ 10.7 PRACTICE WITHOUT ENROLLMENT.—(a) *In general.*—Individuals may appear on their own behalf, and individuals who are qualified, of good character and reputation, and are not under disbarment or suspension from practice before the Internal Revenue Service or from practice of their profession by any other authority, may be permitted to appear without enrollment, provided they present satisfactory identification, in the following classes of cases:

(1) An individual may represent another individual who is his regular full-time employer, may represent a partnership of which he is a member or a regular full-time employee, or may represent without compensation a member of his immediate family.

(2) Corporations (including a parent, subsidiary or affiliated corporation), trusts, estates, associations, or organized groups may be represented by a bona fide officer or regular full-time employee.

(3) Trusts, receiverships, guardianships, or estates may be represented by their trustees, receivers, guardians, administrators or executors or their regular full-time employees.

(4) Any governmental unit, agency, or authority may be represented by an officer or regular employee in the course of his official duties.

(5) Unenrolled persons may participate in rule making as provided by section 4 of the Administrative Procedure Act, 60 Stat. 238 (5 U.S.C. 1003).

(6) Enrollment is not required for representation outside of the

United States before personnel of the International Operations Division of the Internal Revenue Service.

(7) [2] Any person who signs a return, other than an estate or gift tax return or an income tax or excess profits tax return of a corporation, as having prepared it for the taxpayer may appear, without enrollment, as the taxpayer's representative, with or without the taxpayer, before revenue agents and examining officers of the Audit Division in the offices of District Directors (but not at the Informal Conference in a District Director's office) with respect to the tax liability of the taxpayer for the taxable year or period covered by that return; provided that any person who prepared the income tax return of a corporation and the individual returns of any of the corporate officers for the same taxable year or period, or any part thereof, covered by such corporate return, may also so appear as the corporation's representative. Proper authorization from the taxpayer will be required. Any person who prepared a return with respect to which the instructions or regulations do not require that it be signed by the person who prepared the return for the taxpayer may likewise appear as the taxpayer's representative when properly authorized. Unless the taxpayer is present, such persons must present satisfactory identification. All such persons will be subject to such rules regarding standards of conduct, the extent of their authority, and other matters as the Director of Practice, with approval of the Commissioner of Internal Revenue, shall prescribe. Such persons will be permitted to represent taxpayers within those limits without enrollment.

(b) *Special appearance.*—The Director of Practice, subject to such conditions as he deems appropriate, may authorize any person to represent another without enrollment for the purpose of a particular matter.

§ 10.8 CUSTOMHOUSE BROKERS.—Nothing contained in the regulations in this part shall be deemed to affect or limit the right of a customhouse broker, licensed as such by the Commissioner of Customs in accordance with the regulations prescribed therefor, in any customs district in which he is so licensed, at the office of the District Director of Internal Revenue or before the National Office of the Internal Revenue Service, to act as a representative in respect to any matters relating specifically to the importation or exportation of merchandise under the customs or internal revenue laws, for any person for whom he has acted as a customhouse broker.

SUBPART B.—DUTIES AND RESTRICTIONS RELATING TO ENROLLED ATTORNEYS AND AGENTS

§ 10.20 LOSS OF STATUS.—Loss of status to practice as an attorney, as a certified public accountant, or as a public accountant shall constitute good cause for disbarment.

---

[2] Subparagraph (7) of section 10.7(a), approved by Acting Secretary Fred C. Scribner, Jr., on January 29, 1959, will become effective on March 15, 1959. For standards of conduct governing practice under this subparagraph, see Rev. Proc. 59-3, page 801, this Bulletin.

§ 10.21 ETHICS. — (a) *Professional ethics.* — Enrolled attorneys shall conduct themselves and their practice before the Internal Revenue Service in accordance with recognized ethical standards applicable to attorneys generally. Enrolled agents who are certified public accountants or public accountants shall conduct themselves and their practice before the Internal Revenue Service in accordance with recognized ethical standards applicable to certified public accountants or public accountants generally.

(b) *Observance of regulations.*—Enrolled attorneys and agents shall conduct themselves and their practice before the Internal Revenue Service in such manner as not to commit any act of disreputable conduct referred to in § 10.51 or to violate any other provisions of this part.

§ 10.22 INFORMATION TO BE FURNISHED.—(a) *To the Internal Revenue Service generally.*—No enrolled attorney or agent shall neglect or refuse to submit records or information in any matter before the Internal Revenue Service, upon proper and lawful request by a duly authorized officer or employee of the Internal Revenue Service, unless the information or testimony is privileged or such attorney or agent has reasonable grounds to believe and does believe that the said demand is of doubtful legality; and no such attorney or agent shall interfere, or attempt to interfere, with any proper and lawful efforts by the Internal Revenue Service or its officers or employees to obtain information relative to any matter before the Internal Revenue Service.

(b) *To Director of Practice.*—It shall be the duty of an enrolled attorney or agent, when requested by the Director of Practice, to provide the Director with any information he may have concerning violation of the regulations in this part by any person, and to testify thereto in any proceeding instituted under this part for the disbarment or suspension of an enrolled attorney or agent, unless such information is privileged.

§ 10.23 KNOWLEDGE OF CLIENT'S OMISSION.—Each enrolled attorney or agent who knows that a client has not complied with the law, or has made an error in or omission from any return, document, affidavit, or other paper which the client is required by law to execute in connection with any matter administered by the Internal Revenue Service, shall advise the client promptly of the fact of such noncompliance, error, or omission.

§ 10.24 DILIGENCE AS TO ACCURACY.—(a) *In general.*—Each enrolled attorney or agent shall exercise due diligence in preparing or assisting in the preparation of, approving, and filing returns, documents, affidavits, and other papers relating to Internal Revenue Service matters.

(b) *Representations to service.*—Each enrolled attorney or agent shall exercise due diligence to determine the correctness of representations made by him to the Internal Revenue Service.

(c) *Representations to clients.*—Each enrolled attorney or agent shall exercise due diligence to determine the correctness of representations made by him to clients with reference to any matter administered by the Internal Revenue Service.

§ 10.25 MONEYS RECEIVED FROM OR FOR A CLIENT.—Each enrolled attorney or agent shall promptly pay over to the United States when due all sums received for the payment of any tax, duty, or other debt or obligation owing to the United States, and shall promptly account to a client for funds received for him from the United States, or received from a client in excess of the charges properly payable in respect of the client's business.

§ 10.26 ENDORSEMENT OF CLIENT'S CHECKS.—No enrolled attorney or agent shall, without authority of his client, accept or endorse any Government draft, check, or warrant drawn to the order of such client.

§ 10.27 PROMPT DISPOSITION OF PENDING MATTERS.—No enrolled attorney or agent shall unreasonably delay the prompt disposition of any matter before the Internal Revenue Service.

§ 10.28 ASSISTANCE FROM UNENROLLED PERSONS.—No enrolled attorney or agent shall in any Internal Revenue Service matter knowingly and directly or indirectly:

(a) Employ or accept assistance from any unenrolled person who is disbarred from practice before the Internal Revenue Service or any other department or agency of the Federal Government or before any court of record; who is under suspension from practice before any such department, agency, or court; who has been deprived of his certificate as a certified public accountant or public accountant; or who to the knowledge of the enrolled attorney or agent solicits business, obtains clients, or otherwise conducts his practice in a manner forbidden under the regulations in this part to enrolled persons; or

(b) Accept employment as associate, correspondent, or sub-agent from, or share fees with, any such person, or any person who is not an attorney, a certified public accountant, or a public accountant. Nothing in this section shall be construed to authorize the acceptance of employment or the sharing of fees contrary to recognized ethical standards which are to be followed pursuant to § 10.21.

§ 10.29 EMPLOYEES OF ACCOUNTING CORPORATIONS.—No enrolled attorney or agent shall be connected with an accounting corporation either as an officer, employee, or stockholder.

§ 10.30 CERTAIN PARTNERSHIPS PROHIBITED.—No enrolled attorney or agent shall maintain a partnership for the practice of law, accountancy, or other related professional service with a person who is under disbarment from practice before the Internal Revenue Service or any other department or agency of the Federal Government, or with an unenrolled person who is neither an attorney legally practicing law nor a certified public accountant or a public accountant legally practicing accounting. Nothing in this section shall be construed to authorize the maintenance of a partnership contrary to recognized ethical standards which are to be followed pursuant to § 10.21.

§ 10.31 EMPLOYEES OF AGRICULTURAL COOPERATIVE ASSOCIATIONS.—Nothing contained in the regulations in this part shall prevent an enrolled person from being employed by agricultural cooperative associations (which are on a nonprofit basis and not subject to Federal income taxes) to represent before the Service the groups or units constituting membership of such associations: *Provided*, That individuals may not be so represented.

§ 10.32 PRACTICE BY FORMER GOVERNMENT EMPLOYEES.—(a) *In general.*—No former officer or employee of the United States, whether or not enrolled to practice before the Internal Revenue Service, shall represent anyone in any matter administered by the Internal Revenue Service if the representation would violate any of the laws of the United States, including the laws which under certain circumstances prohibit former officers and employees of the United States from acting as representatives of others in matters to which the United States is a party or in which it is interested. See section 190 of the Revised Satutes (5 U.S.C. 99) and 18 U.S.C., Chapter 15.

(b) *Personal consideration.*—No former officer or employee of the United States, whether or not enrolled to practice before the Internal Revenue Service, shall represent anyone in any matter administered by the Internal Revenue Service to which he gave personal consideration or as to the facts of which he gained knowledge during and by reason of his Government service.

§ 10.33 PRACTICE BY FORMER INTERNAL REVENUE SERVICE EMPLOYEES.—(a) *Matters pending while employed.*—No former officer or employee of the Internal Revenue Service shall, within two years after the termination of his Internal Revenue Service employment, practice or in any manner act as attorney or agent or as the employee of an attorney or agent in any matter which was pending in the Internal Revenue Service during the period of his employment therein, unless he shall first obtain the written consent of the Director of Practice. This consent will not be granted unless it appears that the applicant, as an officer or employee of the Internal Revenue Service, did not give personal consideration to the matter or gain knowledge of the facts of it during and by reason of his employment in the Internal Revenue Service.

(b) *Application for consent.*—An applicant for the consent provided for in paragraph (a) shall file a declaration to the effect that he gave no personal consideration to the matter and that he obtained no knowledge of the facts involved in the matter during and by reason of his employment by the Internal Revenue Service, that he is not and will not knowingly be associated with any former officer or employee who gained knowledge of the matter during and by reason of employment by the Internal Revenue Service, and that his employment is not prohibited by law or by the regulations of the Internal Revenue Service. The application shall be denied by the Director of Practice if the statements contained therein are disproved by an examination of files, records or circumstances pertaining to the matter. Applications for consent should be transmitted to the Director of Practice on Form 901 and should state the applicant's former connection with the Internal Revenue Service and identify the matter in which he desires to act. The applicant shall be advised as to his privilege to appear in the matter, and he shall

APPENDIX

file the notice of advice in the Internal Revenue Service's record of the matter concerning which he has applied for permission to appear or act as attorney or agent.

(c) *Pending matter.*—For the purpose of this section, a matter shall not be deemed pending in the Internal Revenue Service merely by virtue of the filing of a tax return, but it shall be considered as pending from the time an examination was commenced by interviewing, corresponding with, or examining the books and records of, a taxpayer, or from the time a taxpayer made a representation or inquiry to the Internal Revenue Service which is related to the matter. Pursuant to section 190 of the Revised Statutes (5 U.S.C. 99), a pending matter includes any claim against the United States pending in any department of the Government.

§ 10.34 ASSISTANCE FROM OR TO FORMER EMPLOYEES.—In connection with any matter involving practice before the Internal Revenue Service, no enrolled attorney or agent shall knowingly assist, accept assistance from, or share fees with, any person who gave personal consideration to the matter or gained knowledge of facts involved in it during and by reason of his Government service.

§ 10.35 ENROLLEES AS NOTARIES.—No enrolled attorney or agent as notary public shall take acknowledgments, administer oaths, certify papers, or perform any official act in connection with matters in which he is employed as counsel, attorney, or agent, or in which he may be in any way interested before the Internal Revenue Service. Under the provisions of this section an enrolled person who is a notary public is prohibited from taking any acknowledgment, oath, or certification as a notary public in connection with any tax return, protest, or other document which he has prepared or in the preparation of which he has assisted. (26 Op. Atty. Gen. 236.)

§ 10.36 ATTEMPTING TO OBTAIN INFORMATION.—No enrolled person shall procure, or attempt to procure, directly or indirectly, from Government records or other Government sources information of any kind which is not made available by proper authority.

§ 10.37 FEES.—(a) *In general.*—An enrolled attorney or agent shall not charge a manifestly unreasonable fee for representation of a client in any matter before the Internal Revenue Service. The reasonableness of a fee is within limits a matter of judgment and depends upon all the facts and circumstances of the case, including its complexity and difficulty, the time and effort required, the amount involved, and the professional standing and experience of the enrolled attorney or agent.

(b) *Contingent fees.*—An enrolled attorney or agent shall not enter into a wholly contingent fee agreement with a client for representation in any matter before the Internal Revenue Service unless the client is financially unable to pay a reasonable fee on any other terms. Partially contingent fee agreements are permissible where provision is made for the payment of a minimum, substantial in relation to the possible maximum fee, which minimum fee is to be paid and retained irrespective of the outcome of the proceeding.

§ 10.38 SOLICITATION AND ADVERTISING.—(a) *Solicitation.*—No enrolled attorney or agent shall, in any manner whatsoever not warranted by personal relations, directly or indirectly solicit employment in matters related to the Internal Revenue Service.

(b) *Advertising special relationships.*—No enrolled attorney or agent shall use, directly or indirectly, signs, printing or other written matter indicating some past or present connection with, or relationship to, the Internal Revenue Service, nor shall he represent in any manner that he possesses influence or a special relationship with officers or employees of the Internal Revenue Service.

(c) *Letterheads and announcements.*—The following shall not be presumed to constitute a violation of this paragraph:

(1) Letterheads, professional cards, and the customary professional insertions in telephone, and city directories, or in newspapers, trade or professional journals, or other publications admitted to second-class mailing privileges, provided they set forth only the name and address of the attorney or agent, or the name of the firm of which he is a member or with which he is associated, and a notation of the nature of his practice, to wit, whether he practices as an attorney, certified public accountant, or public accountant (there is no objection to the use of the words "Enrolled to practice before the Internal Revenue Service"); and the customary professional insertions in professional directories provided they set forth only the above information and customary biographical and professional data;

(2) The distribution by former officers or employees of the Government of cards briefly stating the fact of their former official status and announcing their new status or association, provided the cards are addressed only to personal or business acquaintances and provided such cards are distributed only once, within a reasonable time after severance of official connection with the Government, and within 30 days after the creation of the new status or the formation of the new association.

§ 10.39 RIGHTS AND DUTIES OF AGENTS.—An agent enrolled before the Internal Revenue Service shall have the same rights, powers, and privileges and be subject to the same duties as an enrolled attorney: *Provided,* That an enrolled agent shall not have the privilege of drafting or preparing any written instrument by which title to real or personal property may be conveyed or transferred for the purpose of affecting Federal taxes, nor shall such enrolled agent advise a client as to the legal sufficiency of such an instrument or its legal effect upon the Federal taxes of such client: *And provided further,* That nothing in the regulations in this part shall be construed as authorizing persons not members of the bar to practice law.

NOTE: An interpretation by the Secretary of the Treasury of § 10.39 (31 CFR, 1949 ed., 10.2(f)), among other sections, appeared at 21 F.R. 833, Feb. 7, 1956.

SUBPART C.—RULES APPLICABLE TO DISCIPLINARY PROCEEDINGS

§ 10.50 AUTHORITY TO DISBAR OR SUSPEND.—Pursuant to section 3 of the Act of July 7, 1884, 23 Stat. 258 (5 U.S.C. 261), the Secretary of the Treasury, after due notice and opportunity for hearing, may suspend or disbar from further practice before the Internal Revenue Service any enrolled attorney or agent shown to be incompetent, disreputable or who refuses to comply with the rules and regulations in this part, or who shall, with intent to defraud, in any manner willfully and knowingly deceive, mislead, or threaten any claimant or prospective claimant, by word, circular, letter, or by advertisement.

§ 10.51 DISREPUTABLE CONDUCT.—(a) *Nature.*—Disreputable conduct, for which any enrolled attorney or agent may be disbarred or suspended from practice before the Internal Revenue Service, includes any conduct violative of the ordinary standards of professional obligation and honor.

(b) *Forms.*—Among other forms of disreputable conduct, the following are deemed to constitute such conduct:

(1) Conviction of any criminal offense prescribed by the internal revenue laws or conviction of any crime involving moral turpitude;

(2) Making false answers in an application for enrollment or for renewal of an enrollment card with knowledge that such answers are false;

(3) Preparing or filing for himself or another a false Federal tax return or other statement on which Federal taxes may be based, knowing the same to be false;

(4) Willful failure to make a Federal tax return in violation of provisions of the internal revenue laws and the regulations issued thereunder;

(5) Suggesting to a client or a prospective client an illegal plan for evading Federal taxes or the payment thereof, knowing the same to be illegal;

(6) Giving false testimony in any proceeding before the Internal Revenue Service or before any tribunal authorized to pass upon Federal tax matters, knowing the same to be false;

(7) Filing any false or fraudulently altered document or affidavit in any case or other proceeding before the Internal Revenue Service, or procuring the filing thereof, knowing the same to be false or fraudulently altered;

(8) Using, with intent to deceive, false or misleading representations to procure employment in any case or proceeding before the Internal Revenue Service;

(9) Knowingly giving false or misleading information relative to a matter pending before the Internal Revenue Service to any officer or employee of the Internal Revenue Service;

(10) Preparing a false financial statement for a corporation, partnership, association, or individual, or certifying the correctness of such false statement, knowing the same to be false;

(11) Imparting to a client false information relative to the progress of a case or other proceeding before the Internal Revenue Service, knowing the same to be false;

(12) False representations by an enrolled agent that he is an attorney or a certified public accountant;

(13) Preparing or assisting in the preparation of, or filing, a false claim against the United States, knowing the same to be false;

(14) Approving, for filing, a false Federal tax return prepared by some other person, or advising or aiding in the preparation of such a false tax return, knowing the same to be false;

(15) Misappropriation of, or failure properly and promptly to remit, funds received from a client for the purpose of payment of taxes or other obligations due the United States, or misappropriation of funds or other property belonging to a client;

(16) Improper retention of a fee for which no services have been rendered;

(17) Obtaining or attempting to obtain money or other thing of value from a client or other person by false representations, knowing the same to be false;

(18) Obtaining or attempting to obtain money or other thing of value from a client or other person by duress or undue influence;

(19) Concealing or attempting to conceal assets of himself or another in order to evade or assist in evading Federal taxes or the payment thereof;

(20) Representing to a client or prospective client that the attorney or agent can improperly obtain special consideration or action from the Internal Revenue Service or an officer or employee thereof, or that he has access to unusual sources of information within the Internal Revenue Service;

(21) Soliciting or procuring the false testimony of any person in any proceeding before the Internal Revenue Service;

(22) Directly or indirectly attempting to influence, or offering or agreeing to attempt to influence, the official action of any officer or employee of the Internal Revenue Service by the use of threats, false accusations, duress, or coercion, by the offer of any special inducement or promise of advantage, or by the bestowing of any gift, favor or thing of value;

(23) Failure of an enrolled attorney to conduct himself and his practice before the Internal Revenue Service in accordance with recognized ethical standards applicable to attorneys generally;

(24) Failure of an enrolled agent to conduct himself and his practice before the Internal Revenue Service in accordance with recognized ethical standards:

(25) Disbarment or suspension from practice as an attorney, certified public accountant, or public accountant by any duly constituted authority of any State, Territory, possession of the United States, the District of Columbia, or by any department or agency of the Federal Government;

(26) In connection with practice before the Internal Revenue Service, using intemperate and abusive language, making false accusations or statements knowing them to be false, or circulating or publishing malicious and libelous matter;

(27) Knowingly aiding or abetting another by any means to defraud or attempt to defraud the United States, as by affirmatively assisting or participating in any way in the concealment of or failure to report income, receipts, or other property subject to taxation by the United States;

APPENDIX

(28) Solicitation of practice in any unethical or unprofessional manner;*

(29) Representing, as an agent or associate, an attorney, accountant, or other person known by the enrollee to solicit practice in any unethical or unprofessional manner;

(30) Knowingly aiding and abetting another person to practice his profession during a period of disbarment of such other person.

[Sections 10.52-10.75, concerning disciplinary proceedings, and 10.90-10.94, relating to records, effective date, and other general matters are omitted.]

Treasury Interpretation of Treas. Dept. Circular 230, §10.2

1956-1 C.B. 1007

For some months the Treasury Department has had under consideration the revision of Treasury Department Circular 230 relating to practice before the Department.

Congress has given the Treasury Department the responsibility of regulating practice before the Department. It is in the exercise of this responsibility that the Department has issued the rules and regulations set forth in Circular 230, taking into consideration, among other things, the need of taxpayers for tax advice and assistance, the number of tax returns filed each year, the volume and complexity of problems relating thereto, the skills and training required for proper representation of taxpayers' interests and the availability of people who can provide such service.

The Department believes the standards prescribed in Circular 230 have generally operated in a highly satisfactory manner, have made available to taxpayers representatives to assist them in presenting their interests to the Department, and have facilitated fair and orderly administration of the tax laws.

It is the intention of the Department that all persons enrolled

---

* Sec. 10.51(b)(28) was amended in 1962 to read:
  Solicitation of practice in any unethical or unprofessional manner, including, but not limited to, employment unethically arranged directly or indirectly by or through any individual, partnership, association, corporation or employee thereof.
See 1962-2 C.B. 394.

to practice before it be permitted to fully represent their clients before the Department, in the manner hereinafter indicated. This is apparent from section 10.2(b), which states that the scope of practice (of agents as well as attorneys) before the Department comprehends "all matters connected with the presentation of a client's interest to the Treasury Department". Enrollees, whether agents or attorneys, have been satisfactorily fully representing clients before the Department for many years. The Department believes this has been beneficial to the taxpayers and to the Government and that there presently appears no reason why the present scope and type of practice should not continue as it has in the past.

The Department's attention has been called to the decisions of certain State courts and to statements which suggest varying interpretations of section 10.2(f) of the Circular. This subsection makes it clear that an enrolled agent shall have the same rights, powers, and privileges and be subject to the same duties as an enrolled attorney, except that an enrolled agent may not prepare and interpret certain written instruments. The second proviso of the subsection states that nothing in the regulations is to be construed as authorizing persons not members of the bar to practice law. The uniform interpretation and administration of this and other sections of Circular 230 by the Department are essential to the proper discharge of the above responsibility imposed on it by the Congress.

It is not the intention of the Department that this second proviso should be interpreted as an election by the Department not to exercise fully its responsibility to determine the proper scope of practice by enrolled agents and attorneys before the Department. It should be equally clear that the Department does not have the responsibility nor the authority to regulate the professional activities of lawyers and accountants beyond the scope of their practice before the Department as defined in section 10.2(b) and nothing in Circular 230 is so intended.

The Department has properly placed on its enrolled agents and enrolled attorneys the responsibility of determining when the assistance of a member of the other profession is required. This follows from the provisions in section 10.2(z) that enrolled attorneys must observe the canons of ethics of the American Bar Association and enrolled agents must observe the ethical standards of the accounting profession. The Department has been gratified to note the extent to which the two professions over the years have made progress toward mutual understanding of the proper sphere of each, as for example in the Joint Statement of Principles Relating to Practice in the Field of Federal Income Taxation.

The question of Treasury practice will be kept under surveillance so that if at any time the Department finds that the professional responsibilities of its enrolled agents and enrolled attorneys are not being properly carried out or understood, or that enrolled agents and attorneys are not respecting the appropriate fields of each in accordance with the Joint Statement, it can review the matter to determine whether it is necessary to amend these provisions of the Circular or take other appropriate action.

Treasury Department Circular 230

1966-2 C.B. 1171*

SUBPART A—RULES GOVERNING AUTHORITY TO PRACTICE

§ 10.1 DIRECTOR OF PRACTICE.

(a) *Establishment of office.*—There is established in the Office of the Secretary of the Treasury the office of Director of Practice. The Director of Practice shall be appointed by the Secretary of the Treasury.

(b) *Duties.*— The Director of Practice shall act upon appeals from decisions of the Commissioner of Internal Revenue denying applications for enrollment to practice before the Internal Revenue Service; institute and provide for the conduct of disciplinary proceedings relating to attorneys, certified public accountants, and enrolled agents; make inquiries with respect to matters under his jurisdiction; and perform such other duties as are necessary or appropriate to carry out his functions under this part or as are prescribed by the Secretary of the Treasury.

(c) *Acting Director.*—The Secretary of the Treasury will designate an officer or employee of the Treasury Department to act as Director of Practice in the event of the absence of the Director or of a vacancy in that office.

§ 10.2 DEFINITIONS.

As used in this part, except where the context clearly indicates otherwise, the term:

(a) "Practice before the Internal Revenue Service" comprehends all matters connected with presentation to the Internal Revenue Service or any of its officers or employees relating to a client's rights, privileges, or liabilities under laws or regulations administered by the Internal Revenue Service. Such presentations include the preparation and filing of necessary documents, correspondence with and communications to the Internal Revenue Service, and the representation

---

*For an earlier version of this document, see supra p. 343; see also discussion, supra pp. 289-291.

of a client at conferences, hearings, and meetings. Neither the preparation of a tax return, nor the appearance of an individual as a witness for the taxpayer, nor the furnishing of information at the request of the Internal Revenue Service or any of its officers or employees is considered practice before the Service.

(b) "Attorney" means any person who is a member in good standing of the bar of the highest court of any State, possession, territory, Commonwealth, or the District of Columbia.

(c) "Certified public accountant" means any person who is duly qualified to practice as a certified public accountant in any State, possession, territory, Commonwealth, or the District of Columbia.

(d) "Commissioner" refers to the Commissioner of Internal Revenue.

§ 10.3 WHO MAY PRACTICE.

(a) *Attorneys.*—Any attorney who is not currently under suspension or disbarment from practice before the Internal Revenue Service may practice before the Service upon filing with the Service a written declaration that he is currently qualified as an attorney and is authorized to represent the particular party on whose behalf he acts. An enrollment card issued to such person before the effective date of this regulation shall be invalid and may not be used in lieu of such written declaration.[2]

(b) *Certified public accountants.*—Any certified public accountant who is not currently under suspension or disbarment from practice before the Internal Revenue Service may practice before the Service upon filing with the Service a written declaration that he is currently qualified as a certified public accountant and is authorized to represent the particular party on whose behalf he acts. An enrollment card issued to such person before the effective date of this regulation shall be invalid and may not be used in lieu of such written declaration.[2]

(c) *Enrolled agents.*—Any person enrolled as an agent pursuant to this part may practice before the Internal Revenue Service.

(d) *Others.*—Any person qualifying under section 10.7 or section 10.5(c) may practice before Internal Revenue Service.

(e) *Government officers and employees; others.*—No officer or employee of the United States in the executive, legislative, or judicial branch of the Government, or in any agency of the United States, including the District of Columbia, may practice before the Service, except that such officer or employee may, subject to the conditions and requirements of these regulations and of 18 U.S.C. 205, represent a member of his immediate family or any other person or estate for which he serves as guardian, executor, administrator, trustee, or other personal fiduciary. No Member of Congress or Resident Commissioner (elect or serving) may practice before the Service in connection with any matter for which he directly or indirectly receives, agrees to receive, or seeks any compensation. 18 U.S.C. 203, 205.

[2] This supersedes the provision contained in a notice of interim course of action published in the Federal Register, Nov. 16, 1965 (30 F.R. 14331), which permitted attorneys and certified public accountants, who were enrolled as of Nov. 8, 1965, to continue to use their enrollment cards as evidence of authority to practice before the Service. [C.B. 1965-2, 954]

APPENDIX 361

(f) *State officers and employees.*—No officer or employee of any State, or subdivision thereof, whose duties require him to pass upon, investigate, or deal with tax matters of such State or subdivision, may practice before the Service, if such State employment may disclose facts or information applicable to Federal tax matters.

§ 10.4 ELIGIBILITY FOR ENROLLMENT.

(a) *Enrollment upon examination.*—The Commissioner may grant enrollment to an applicant who demonstrates special competence in tax matters by written examination administered by the Internal Revenue Service and who has not engaged in any conduct which would justify the suspension or disbarment of any attorney, certified public accountant, or enrolled agent under the provisions of this part.

(b) *Enrollment of former Internal Revenue Service employees.*— The Commissioner may grant enrollment to an applicant who has not engaged in any conduct which would justify the suspension or disbarment of any attorney, certified public accountant, or enrolled agent under the provisions of this part and who, by virtue of his past service and technical experience in the Internal Revenue Service has qualified for such enrollment, as follows:

(1) Application for enrollment on account of former employment in the Internal Revenue Service shall be made to the Commissioner. Each applicant will be supplied a form by the Commissioner, which shall indicate the information required respecting the applicant's qualifications. In addition to the applicant's name, address, citizenship, age, educational experience, etc., such information shall specifically include a detailed account of the applicant's employment in the Internal Revenue Service, which account shall show (i) positions held, (ii) date of each appointment and termination thereof, (iii) nature of services rendered in each position, with particular reference to the degree of technical experience involved, and (iv) name of supervisor in such positions, together with such other information, regarding the experience and training of the applicant as may be relevant.

(2) Upon receipt of each such application, it shall be transmitted to the appropriate officer of the Internal Revenue Service with the request that a detailed report of the nature and rating of the applicant's services in the Internal Revenue Service, accompanied by the recommendation of the superior officer in the particular unit or division of the Internal Revenue Service that such employment does or does not qualify the applicant technically or otherwise for the desired authorization, be furnished to the Commissioner.

(3) In examining the qualification of an applicant for enrollment on account of employment in the Internal Revenue Service, the Commissioner will be governed by the following policies:

(i) Enrollment on account of such employment may be of unlimited scope or may be limited to permit the presentation of matters only of the particular class or only before the particular unit or division of the Internal Revenue Service for which his former employment in the Internal Revenue Service has qualified the applicant.

(ii) In the case of employees separated from employment in the Internal Revenue Service, application for enrollment on account of such employment must be made within 3 years after the termination thereof.

(iii) It shall be requisite for enrollment on account of such employment that the applicant shall have had a minimum of 5 years' continuous employment in the Service during which he shall have been regularly engaged in applying and interpreting the provisions of the Internal Revenue Code and the regulations thereunder relating to income, estate, gift, employment, or excise taxes.

(iv) For the purposes of subdivision (iii) of this subparagraph, an aggregate of 10 or more years of employment, at least 3 of which occurred within the 5 years preceding the date of application, shall be deemed the equivalent of 5 years' continuous employment.

(c) *Citizens; natural persons.*—Enrollment to practice may be granted only to natural persons who are citizens of the United States and who are over the age of 21 years.

(d) *Oath of allegiance.*—No person shall be enrolled to practice if he is unable for any reason to take the oath of allegiance, and to support the Constitution of the United States, as required of persons prosecuting claims against the United States by section 3478 of the Revised Statutes (31 U.S.C. 204).

(e) *Attorneys; certified public accountants.*—Enrollment is not available to persons who qualify to practice under section 10.3 (a) or (b).

§ 10.5 APPLICATION FOR ENROLLMENT.

(a) *Form; fee.*—An applicant for enrollment shall file with the Commissioner of Internal Revenue an application on form 23, properly executed under oath or affirmation. Such application shall be accompanied by a check or money order in the amount of $25, payable to the Internal Revenue Service, which amount shall constitute a fee which shall be charged to each applicant for enrollment. The fee shall be retained by the United States whether or not the applicant is granted enrollment.

(b) *Additional information; examination.*—The Commissioner, as a condition to consideration of an application for enrollment, may require the applicant to file additional information and to submit to any written or oral examination under oath or otherwise. The Commissioner shall, upon written request, afford an applicant the opportunity to be heard with respect to his application for enrollment.

(c) *Temporary recognition.*—Upon receipt of a properly executed application, the Commissioner may grant the applicant temporary recognition to practice pending a determination as to whether enrollment to practice should be granted. Such temporary recognition shall not be granted if the application is not regular on its face; if the information stated therein, if true, is not sufficient to warrant enrollment to practice; if there is any information before the Commissioner which indicates that the statements in the application are untrue; or which indicates that the applicant would not otherwise qualify for enrollment. Issuance of temporary recognition shall not constitute enrollment to practice or a finding of eligibility for enrollment, and the temporary recognition may be withdrawn at any time by the Commissioner.

(d) *Appeal from denial of application.*—(1) The Commissioner, in denying an application for enrollment, shall inform the applicant as to the reason(s) therefor. The applicant may, within 30 days after receipt of the notice of denial, file a written appeal therefrom, together with his reasons in support thereof, to the Director of Practice. A decision on the appeal will be rendered by the Director of Practice as soon as practicable.

(2) A decision of the Director of Practice in sustaining a denial of enrollment may be appealed to the Secretary of the Treasury within 30 days after receipt of the decision of the Director.

§10.6 ENROLLMENT.

(a) *Roster.*—The Commissioner shall maintain rosters of all agents who are enrolled to practice, of all persons who have been disbarred or suspended from practice before the Internal Revenue Service, and of persons whose applications for enrollment have been denied.

(b) *Enrollment card.*—(1) The Commissioner shall issue an enrollment card to each agent who is enrolled to practice before the Internal Revenue Service after the effective date of this regulation. Each such enrollment card shall be valid so long as the holder shall remain enrolled and in good standing before the Service. Unless advised to the contrary by the Commissioner, any officer or employee of the Internal Revenue Service may consider the holder of a valid enrollment card to be duly authorized to practice before the Service.

(2) An enrollment card issued prior to the effective date of this regulation to a person who continues to qualify for enrollment under the provisions of this part shall by its terms remain valid for a period of 5 years after the date of issuance.

(c) *Application for permanent enrollment card.*—Application for a permanent enrollment card may be made at any time during a 24-month period commencing 12 months before and ending 12 months after the expiration of an enrollment card. Such application shall be filed on form 23A at such place or places as may be designated by the Commissioner and there shall be annexed thereto the outstanding enrollment card. Copies of form 23A may be obtained from the Commissioner of Internal Revenue and at the offices of District Directors of Internal Revenue. Each application shall be accompanied by a check or money order in the amount of $5, payable to the Internal Revenue Service, which amount shall constitute a fee which shall be charged each person who applies for issuance of a permanent enrollment card pursuant to the provisions of this paragraph.

(Sec. 501, 65 Stat. 290; 5 U.S.C. 140)

(d) *Termination of enrollment.*—(1) Unless application for a permanent enrollment card is filed with the Commissioner of Internal Revenue within 12 months after the expiration date of an enrollment card, the enrollment of the holder of the card shall automatically terminate, his name shall be stricken from the roster of enrollees, and he shall not be authorized to practice before the Internal Revenue Service except by filing a new application for enrollment, as provided by section 10.5 and obtaining authority to practice from the Commissioner.

(2) The enrollment of any agent to whom an enrollment card is

issued after the effective date of this regulation shall terminate at such time as such agent may become eligible to practice without enrollment under section 10.3 (a) or (b), and such agent shall forthwith return his enrollment card to the Commissioner of Internal Revenue for cancellation.

§ 10.7 LIMITED PRACTICE WITHOUT ENROLLMENT.

(a) *In general.*—Individuals may appear on their own behalf, and may otherwise appear without enrollment, provided they present satisfactory identification, in the following classes of cases:

(1) An individual may represent another individual who is his regular full-time employer, may represent a partnership of which he is a member or a regular full-time employee, or may represent without compensation a member of his immediate family.

(2) Corporations (including parents, subsidiaries, or affiliated corporations), trusts, estates, associations, or organized groups may be represented by bona fide officers or regular full-time employees.

(3) Trusts, receiverships, guardianships, or estates may be represented by their trustees, receivers, guardians, administrators, or executors or their regular full-time employees.

(4) Any governmental unit, agency, or authority may be represented by an officer or regular employee in the course of his official duties.

(5) Unenrolled persons may participate in rulemaking as provided by section 4 of the Administrative Procedure Act, 60 Stat. 238 (5 U.S.C. 1003).

(6) Enrollment is not required for representation outside of the United States before personnel of the Internal Revenue Service.

(7) Any person, who is not under disbarment or suspension from practice before the Internal Revenue Service or from practice of his profession by any other authority (in the case of attorneys, certified public accountants, and public accountants) and who signs a return as having prepared it for the taxpayer, or who prepared a return with respect to which the instructions or regulations do not require that it be signed by the person who prepared the return for the taxpayer, may appear without enrollment as the taxpayer's representative, with or without the taxpayer, before revenue agents and examining officers of the Audit Division in the offices of District Directors (but not at the district conference in a District Director's office) with respect to the tax liability of the taxpayer for the taxable year or period covered by that return. Proper authorization from the taxpayer will be required. All such persons will be subject to such rules regarding standards of conduct, the extent of their authority, and other matters as the Commissioner of Internal Revenue shall prescribe. Such persons will be permitted to represent taxpayers within those limits without enrollment, except that the Commissioner may deny permission to engage in such limited practice to any person who has engaged in conduct which would justify suspension or disbarment of any attorney, certified public accountant, or enrolled agent under the provisions of this part.

(b) *Special appearance.*—The Commissioner, subject to such conditions as he deems appropriate, may authorize any person to represent another without enrollment for the purpose of a particular matter.

§ 10.8 CUSTOMHOUSE BROKERS.

Nothing contained in the regulations in this part shall be deemed to affect or limit the right of a customhouse broker, licensed as such by the Commissioner of Customs in accordance with the regulations prescribed therefor, in any customs district in which he is so licensed, at the office of the District Director of Internal Revenue or before the national office of the Internal Revenue Service, to act as a representative in respect to any matters relating specifically to the importation or exportation of merchandise under the customs or internal revenue laws, for any person for whom he has acted as a customhouse broker.

SUBPART B—DUTIES AND RESTRICTIONS RELATING TO PRACTICE BEFORE THE INTERNAL REVENUE SERVICE

§ 10.20 INFORMATION TO BE FURNISHED.

(a) *To the Internal Revenue Service.*—No attorney, certified public accountant, or enrolled agent shall neglect or refuse promptly to submit records or information in any matter before the Internal Revenue Service, upon proper and lawful request by a duly authorized officer or employee of the Internal Revenue Service, or shall interfere, or attempt to interfere, with any proper and lawful effort by the Internal Revenue Service or its officers or employees to obtain any such record or information, unless he believes in good faith and on reasonable grounds that such record or information is privileged or that the request for, or effort to obtain, such record or information is of doubtful legality.

(b) *To the Director of Practice.*—It shall be the duty of an attorney or certified public accountant, who practices before the Internal Revenue Service, or enrolled agent, when requested by the Director of Practice, to provide the Director with any information he may have concerning violation of the regulations in this part by any person, and to testify thereto, in any proceeding instituted under this part for the disbarment or suspension of an attorney, certified public accountant, or enrolled agent, unless he believes in good faith and on reasonable grounds that such information is privileged or that the request therefor is of doubtful legality.

§ 10.21 KNOWLEDGE OF CLIENT'S OMISSION.

Each attorney, certified public accountant, or enrolled agent who knows that a client has not complied with the revenue laws of the United States, or has made an error in or omission from any return, document, affidavit, or other paper which the client is required by law to execute in connection with any matter administered by the Internal Revenue Service, shall advise the client promptly of the fact of such noncompliance, error, or omission.

§ 10.22 DILIGENCE AS TO ACCURACY.

Each attorney, certified public accountant, or enrolled agent shall exercise due diligence in preparing or assisting in the preparation of, approving, and filing returns, documents, affidavits, and other papers relating to Internal Revenue Service matters, in determining the correctness of representations made by him to the Internal Revenue Service, and in determining the correctness of representations made by him to clients with reference to any matter administered by the Internal Revenue Service.

§ 10.23 PROMPT DISPOSITION OF PENDING MATTERS.

No attorney, certified public accountant, or enrolled agent shall unreasonably delay the prompt disposition of any matter before the Internal Revenue Service.

§ 10.24 ASSISTANCE FROM DISBARRED OR SUSPENDED PERSONS.

No attorney, certified public accountant, or enrolled agent shall in any Internal Revenue Service matter knowingly and directly or indirectly:

(a) Employ or accept assistance from any person who is under disbarment or suspension from practice before the Internal Revenue Service, or who to the knowledge of the attorney, certified public accountant, or enrolled agent solicits business, obtains clients, or otherwise conducts his practice in a manner forbidden under the regulations of this part; or

(b) Accept employment as associate, correspondent, or subagent from, or share fees with, any such person.

§ 10.25 PRACTICE BY PARTNERS OF GOVERNMENT EMPLOYEES.

No partner of an officer or employee of the executive branch of the U.S. Government, of any independent agency of the United States, or of the District of Columbia, shall represent anyone in any matter administered by the Internal Revenue Service in which such officer or employee of the Government participates or has participated personally and substantially as a Government employee or which is the subject of his official responsibility (18 U.S.C. 207(c)).

§ 10.26 PRACTICE BY FORMER GOVERNMENT EMPLOYEES.

(a) *In general.*—No former officer or employee of the U.S. Government, of any independent agency of the United States, or of the District of Columbia, shall represent anyone in any matter administered by the Internal Revenue Service if the representation would violate any of the laws of the United States.

(b) *Personal and substantial participation.*—No former officer or employee of the executive branch of the U.S. Government, of any independent agency of the United States, or of the District of Columbia, shall represent anyone in any matter administered by the Internal Revenue Service, involving a specific party or parties, in which he participated personally and substantially as an officer or employee. See 18 U.S.C. 207(a).

(c) *Official responsibility.*—No former officer or employee of the executive branch of the U.S. Government, of any independent agency of the United States, or of the District of Columbia, shall, within 1 year after his employment has ceased, appear personally as agent or attorney for anyone before the Internal Revenue Service in any matter administered by the Internal Revenue Service, involving a specific party or parties, which was under his official responsibility as an officer or employee of the Government at any time within a period of 1 year prior to the termination of such responsibility. See 18 U.S.C. 207(b).

§ 10.27 NOTARIES.

No attorney, certified public accountant, or enrolled agent as notary public shall with respect to any matter administered by the Internal Revenue Service take acknowledgments, administer oaths, certify papers, or perform any official act in connection with matters in which he is employed as counsel, attorney, or agent, or in which he may be in any way interested before the Internal Revenue Service (26 Op. Atty. Gen. 236).

§ 10.28 FEES.

No attorney, certified public accountant, or enrolled agent shall charge an unconscionable fee for representation of a client in any matter before the Internal Revenue Service.

§ 10.29 CONFLICTING INTERESTS.

No attorney, certified public accountant, or enrolled agent shall represent conflicting interests in his practice before the Internal Revenue Service, except by express consent of all directly interested parties after full disclosure has been made.

§ 10.30 SOLICITATION.

No attorney, certified public accountant, or enrolled agent shall solicit employment, directly or indirectly, in matters related to the Internal Revenue Service. Solicitation includes the advertising of professional attainments or services. In the case of an enrolled agent, the phrase "enrolled to practice before the Internal Revenue Service," when appearing on the stationery, letterhead or professional card of such enrolled agent, is not considered to violate this prohibition.

§ 10.31 PRACTICE OF LAW.

Nothing in the regulations in this part shall be construed as authorizing persons not members of the bar to practice law.

SUBPART C—RULES APPLICABLE TO DISCIPLINARY PROCEEDINGS

§ 10.50 AUTHORITY TO DISBAR OR SUSPEND.

Pursuant to section 3 of the Act of July 7, 1884, 23 Stat. 258 (5 U.S.C. 261), the Secretary of the Treasury, after due notice and opportunity for hearing, may suspend or disbar from practice before the Internal Revenue Service any attorney, certified public accountant, or enrolled agent shown to be incompetent, disreputable or who refuses to comply with the rules and regulations in this part or who shall, with intent to defraud, in any manner willfully and knowingly deceive, mislead, or threaten any claimant or prospective claimant, by word, circular, letter, or by advertisement.

§ 10.51 DISREPUTABLE CONDUCT.

Disreputable conduct for which an attorney, certified public accountant, or enrolled agent may be disbarred or suspended from practice before the Internal Revenue Service includes, but is not limited to:

(a) Conviction of any criminal offense under the revenue laws of the United States, or of any offense involving dishonesty, or breach of trust.

(b) Giving false or misleading information, or participating in any way in the giving of false or misleading information, to the Internal Revenue Service or any officer or employee thereof, or to any tribunal authorized to pass upon Federal tax matters, in connection with any matter pending or likely to be pending before them, knowing such information to be false or misleading. Facts or other matters contained in testimony, Federal tax returns, financial statements, applications for enrollment, affidavits, declarations, or any other document or statement, written or oral, are included in the term "information."

(c) Solicitation of employment as prohibited under section 10.30 of this part, the use of false or misleading representations with intent to deceive a client or a prospective client in order to procure employment, or the use of signs, printing, or other written matter indicating some past or present connection with, or relationship to, the Internal Revenue Service or otherwise intimating that the practitioner is able improperly to obtain special consideration or action from the Internal Revenue Service or officer or employee thereof.

(d) Willfully failing to make a Federal tax return in violation of the revenue laws of the United States, or evading, attempting to evade, or participating in any way in evading or attempting to evade any Federal tax or payment thereof, knowingly counseling or suggesting to a client or prospective client an illegal plan to evade Federal taxes or payment thereof, or concealing assets of himself or another to evade Federal taxes or payment thereof.

(e) Misappropriation of, or failure properly and promptly to remit funds received from a client for the purpose of payment of taxes or other obligations due the United States.

(f) Directly or indirectly attempting to influence, or offering or agreeing to attempt to influence, the official action of any officer or employee of the Internal Revenue Service by the use of threats, false accusations, duress or coercion, by the offer of any special inducement or promise of advantage or by the bestowing of any gift, favor or thing of value.

(g) Disbarment or suspension from practice as an attorney, certified public accountant, or public accountant by any duly constituted authority of any State, possession, territory, Commonwealth, or the District of Columbia.

(h) Knowingly aiding and abetting another person to practice before the Internal Revenue Service during a period of suspension, disbarment, or ineligibility of such other person. Maintaining a partnership for the practice of law, accountancy, or other related professional service with a person who is under disbarment from practice before the Service shall be presumed to be a violation of this provision.

(i) Contemptuous conduct in connection with practice before the Internal Revenue Service, including the use of abusive language, making false accusations and statements knowing them to be false, or circulating or publishing malicious or libelous matter.

> [Sections 10.52-10.75, concerning disciplinary proceedings, and 10.90-10.94, relating to records, effective date, and other general matters are omitted.]

Practice by Unenrolled Preparers of Tax Returns

Rev. Proc. 68-20, 1968-1 C.B. 812

SECTION 1. PURPOSE.

The purpose of this Revenue Procedure is to prescribe, pursuant to Section 10.7(a)(7) of Treasury Department Circular No. 230 revised effective after September 12, 1966, and with amendments dated September 27, 1966, C.B. 1966–2, 1171, and October 28, 1966 (31 CFR Part 10) C.B. 1967–1, 433, the standards of conduct, the extent of authority, and the circumstances and conditions under which an individual preparer of tax returns may exercise, without enrollment, the privilege of limited practice as a taxpayer's representative before the Internal Revenue Service.

SEC. 2. APPLICABILITY.

.01 This Revenue Procedure, issued pursuant to section 10.7(a)(7) of Circular 230, applies to all unenrolled individual preparers of returns who seek to represent taxpayers, within the United States, before revenue agents or examining officers in the Audit Division of an Office of a District Director of Internal Revenue or in the Office of International Operations. Any reference herein to the District Director will be construed, where appropriate, to include the Office of International Operations or the Director of International Operations.

.02 This Revenue Procedure does not apply to attorneys, certified public accountants, or agents who are enrolled to practice before the Internal Revenue Service. The rules governing the practice of such persons before the Service are contained in the provisions of Circular 230.

SEC. 3. SCOPE OF AUTHORITY.

.01 An unenrolled individual who signs a return as its preparer may act as the taxpayer's representative if accompanied by the taxpayer, or by filing a written authorization from the taxpayer as provided herein in section 5. Such representation is limited to practice before a revenue agent or an examining officer in the Field Audit or Office Audit Branch in the Audit Division of an Office of the District Director of Internal Revenue, and may only encompass matters concerning the tax liability of the taxpayer for the taxable year covered by that return, subject to the limitations herein prescribed.

.02 Privilege of limited practice before the Internal Revenue Service is limited to any person who is not under disbarment or suspension from practice before the Internal Revenue Service or from practice of his profession by any other authority (in the case of attorneys, certified public accountants, and public accountants).

.03 An unenrolled individual who prepared a return which provides no space on the prescribed form for signature of the preparer, or who prepared a return with respect to which the instructions or regulations do not require that it be signed by the preparer, may appear as the taxpayer's representative, if properly authorized, as set forth in 3.01.

.04 If the unenrolled preparer appears before the revenue agent or examining officer without the taxpayer, written authorization from the taxpayer for such representation must be filed with the revenue agent or examining officer. The unenrolled preparer may also be required to furnish satisfactory identification.

.05 The unenrolled preparer will be expected to remain alert to questions, issues and factual situations of such difficulty as to require the assistance of an attorney, a certified public accountant, or an enrolled agent and, when such assistance is required, to suggest to the taxpayer that he seek the advice or services of an attorney, certified public accountant, or an enrolled agent.

.06 Where a carryback or carryforward, or both, are involved in a tax return, the unenrolled preparer will not be recognized as the taxpayer's representative with respect to the taxable year in which the carryback or carryforward arose unless he prepared and signed a return for such year or years.

.07 The privilege to practice as a taxpayer's representative in accordance with this Revenue Procedure shall not constitute enrollment nor a finding of eligibility for enrollment.

SEC. 4. LIMITATIONS OF THE PRIVILEGE OF LIMITED PRACTICE.

.01 Privilege of limited practice without enrollment afforded an individual preparer of returns is restricted to representation before the examining officer stated in section 3. No unenrolled preparer shall represent or correspond as the taxpayer's representative at a district conference in the Audit Division, District Director's Office; nor as a taxpayer's representative before the Appellate Division, nor before officials in the National Office.

.02 In addition, the following acts on behalf of the taxpayer are beyond the scope of authority permitted an unenrolled preparer:

(a) Executing claims for refund.

(b) Receiving checks in payment of any refund of Internal Revenue taxes, penalties, or interest.

(c) Executing consents to extend the statutory period for assessment or collection of a tax.

(d) Executing closing agreements with respect to a tax liability or specific matter.

(e) Executing waivers of restriction on assessment or collection of a deficiency in tax.

APPENDIX 371

Sec. 5. Form of Authorization From the Taxpayer.

.01 Internal Revenue Service Form 2848–D, Tax Information Authorization (or any other properly executed written authorization), will be accepted as the unenrolled preparer's authorization to appear without the taxpayer under this Revenue Procedure.

.02 Tax Information Authorization forms may be obtained from local Internal Revenue Service offices.

.03 The authorization must be signed by the taxpayer. It may be revoked by the taxpayer at anytime, but such revocation shall not be effective so far as the Service is concerned prior to the receipt of written notification.

Sec. 6. Ethics and Conduct.

.01 An unenrolled preparer shall conduct himself in such manner as not to commit any act of disreputable conduct. Disreputable conduct includes, but is not limited to, the items contained in section 10.51 of Circular 230.

.02 An unenrolled preparer shall not charge an unconscionable fee for representation of a client in any matter before the Internal Revenue Service.

.03 An unenrolled preparer shall not neglect or refuse to submit records or information in any matter before the Internal Revenue Service upon proper and lawful request by a duly authorized officer or employee of the Service; and the unenrolled preparer shall not interfere, or attempt to interfere, with any proper and lawful efforts by the officers or employees of the Service to obtain information, unless he believes in good faith and on reasonable grounds that the request for, or effort to obtain, such record or information is of doubtful legality.

.04 Any unenrolled preparer who knows that the client has not complied with the law, or that he has made an error in or omission from any return, document, affidavit, or other paper which the client is required by law to execute in connection with any matter administered by the Service, shall advise the client promptly of the fact of such noncompliance, error, or omission.

.05 An unenrolled preparer shall exercise due diligence in preparing or assisting in the preparation, approving, and filing of returns, documents, affidavits, or other papers relating to Internal Revenue Service matters. He shall also exercise due diligence in determining: (1) The correctness of representation made by him to the Service, and (2) the correctness of representation made by him to his client with reference to any matter administered by the Service.

.06 An unenrolled preparer shall not unreasonably delay the prompt disposition of any matter before the Internal Revenue Service.

.07 An unenrolled preparer, as a Notary Public, shall not take acknowledgements, administer oaths, certify papers, or perform any official act in connection with matters relating to his client's tax liabilities, or in connection with any other matter in which he may in any way have given assistance or been employed. In addition, he may not take any acknowledgements, oaths, or certification as a Notary Public relating to any tax return, protest, or other document which he has prepared or which he has assisted in preparing. (26 OP. Atty. Gen. 236.)

.08 An unenrolled preparer shall not procure, or attempt to procure, directly or indirectly, from Government records or Government sources, information of any kind which is not made available by proper authority.

.09 An unenrolled preparer shall not represent conflicting interests in his limited practice before the Service, except by express consent of all directly interested parties after full disclosure has been made.

SEC. 7. SOLICITATION AND ADVERTISING.

.01 An unenrolled preparer shall not, in any manner whatsoever that is not warranted by personal relations, directly or indirectly, solicit employment in matters relating to the Internal Revenue Service; nor shall he advertise that he is authorized to represent taxpayers before the Service.

.02 An unenrolled preparer shall not use false or misleading representations with intent to deceive a client or prospective client in order to procure employment, or use signs, printing, or other written matter indicating some past or present connection with, or relationship to the Internal Revenue Service or otherwise intimating that the unenrolled preparer is able improperly to obtain special consideration or action from the Service or officer or employee thereof.

SEC. 8. PERSONS INELIGIBLE TO PRACTICE UNDER THIS REVENUE PROCEDURE

.01 The following persons shall be ineligible to exercise the privilege of limited practice before the Internal Revenue Service:

(a) Any individual who has been convicted of any criminal offense under the Revenue Laws of the United States or of any offense involving dishonesty or breach of trust;

(b) Any individual who is under disbarment or suspension from the practice of his profession as an attorney, certified public accountant, or public accountant by a state authority or the District of Columbia;

(c) Any individual who has been disbarred or suspended from practice before the Internal Revenue Service;

(d) Any individual whose application for enrollment to practice before the Internal Revenue Service has been denied;

(e) Any individual who refuses to comply with this Revenue Procedure;

(f) Any individual whose conduct or practices have been or are such as to constitute a violation of Sec. 6 or 7 of this Revenue Procedure;

(g) Any individual who is an officer or employee of the United States or of the District of Columbia; and

(h) Any individual who is an officer or employee of any state or any subdivision thereof, whose duties authorize him to investigate, pass upon, or act with respect to tax matters of such state or subdivision, if such employment may make available to him facts or information applicable to Federal tax matters.

.02 In addition corporations, associations, partnerships, or other business entities are ineligible to practice before the Internal Revenue Service.

[*Sections 9-13, relating to certain administrative matters are omitted.*]

National Conference of Lawyers and Certified Public Accountants

1944 Resolution (76 ABA Reports 699)

WHEREAS, Lawyers and certified public accountants are trained professional men, licensed by the several states, and required to bring to their public service qualifications both as to competency and character; and

WHEREAS, The American Bar Association and the American Institute of Accountants have adopted codes of ethics to assure high standards of practice in both professions;

Be It Resolved, In the opinion of the National Conference of Lawyers and Certified Public Accountants,

(1) That the public will be best served if income-tax returns are prepared either by certified public accountants or lawyers;

(2) That it is in the public interest for lawyers to recommend the employment of certified public accountants, and for certified public accountants to recommend the employment of lawyers, in any matter where the services of either would be helpful to the client; and that neither should assume to perform the functions of the other;

(3) That certified public accountants should not prepare legal documents, such as articles of incorporation, corporate by-laws, contracts, deeds, trust agreements, wills, and similar documents, where in connection with such documents questions of accountancy are involved or may result, it is advisable that certified accountants be consulted.

1951 Statement of Principles (76 ABA Reports 699)

Preamble

In our present complex society, the average citizen conducting a business is confronted with a myriad of governmental laws and regulations which cover every phase of human endeavor and raise intricate and perplexing problems. These are further complicated by the tax incidents attendant upon all business transactions. As a result, citizens in increasing numbers have sought the professional services of lawyers and certified public accountants. Each of these groups is well qualified to serve the public in its respective field. The primary function of the lawyer is to advise the public with respect to the legal implications involved in such problems, whereas the certified public accountant has to do with the accounting aspects thereof. Frequently the legal and accounting phases are so inter-related and interdependent and overlapping that they are difficult to distinguish. Particularly is this true in the field of income taxation where questions of law and accounting have sometimes been inextricably intermingled. As a result, there has been some doubt as to where the functions of one profession end and those of the other begin.

For the guidance of members of each profession the National Conference of Lawyers and Certified Public Accountants recommends the following statement of principles relating to practice in the field of federal income taxation:

1. *Collaboration of lawyers and certified public accountants desirable*

It is in the best public interest that services and assistance in federal income tax matters be rendered by lawyers and certified public accountants, who are trained in their fields by education and experience, and for whose admission to professional standing there are requirements as to education, citizenship and high moral character. They are required to pass written examinations and are subject to rules of professional ethics, such as those of the American Bar Association and American Institute of Accountants, which set a high standard of professional practice and conduct, including prohibition of advertising and solicitation. Many problems connected with business require the skills of both lawyers and certified public accountants and there is every reason for a close and friendly cooperation between the two professions. Lawyers should encourage their clients to seek

APPENDIX

the advice of certified public accountants whenever accounting problems arise and certified public accountants should encourage clients to seek the advice of lawyers whenever legal questions are presented.

2. *Preparation of federal income tax returns*

It is a proper function of a lawyer or a certified public accountant to prepare federal income tax returns.

When a lawyer prepares a return in which questions of accounting arise, he should advise the taxpayer to enlist the assistance of a certified public accountant.

When a certified public accountant prepares a return in which questions of law arise, he should advise the taxpayer to enlist the assistance of a lawyer.

3. *Ascertainment of probable tax effects of transactions*

In the course of the practice of law and in the course of the practice of accounting, lawyers and certified public accountants are often asked about the probable tax effects of transactions.

The ascertainment of probable tax effects of transactions frequently is within the function of either a certified public accountant or a lawyer. However, in many instances, problems arise which require the attention of a member of one or the other profession, or members of both. When such ascertainment raises uncertainties as to the interpretation of law (both tax law and general law), or uncertainties as to the application of law to the transaction involved, the certified public accountant should advise the taxpayer to enlist the services of a lawyer. When such ascertainment involves difficult questions of classifying and summarizing the transaction in a significant manner and in terms of money, or interpreting the financial results thereof, the lawyer should advise the taxpayer to enlist the services of a certified public accountant.

In many cases, therefore, the public will be best served by utilizing the joint skills of both professions.

4. *Preparation of legal and accounting documents*

Only a lawyer may prepare legal documents such as agreements, conveyances, trust instruments, wills, or corporate minutes, or give advice as to the legal sufficiency or effect thereof, or take the necessary steps to create, amend or dissolve a partnership, corporation, trust, or other legal entity.

Only an accountant may properly advise as to the preparation of financial statements included in reports or submitted with tax returns, or as to accounting methods and procedures.

5. *Prohibited self-designations*

An accountant should not describe himself as a "tax consultant" or "tax expert" or use any similar phrase. Lawyers, similarly, are prohibited by the canons of ethics of the American Bar Association and the opinions relating thereto, from advertising a special branch of law practice.

6. *Representation of taxpayers before Treasury Department*

Under Treasury Department regulations lawyers and certified public accountants are authorized, upon a showing of their professional status, and subject to certain limitations as defined in the Treasury rules, to represent taxpayers in proceedings before that Department. If, in the course of such proceedings, questions arise involving the application of legal principles, a lawyer should be retained, and if, in the course of such proceedings accounting questions arise, a certified public accountant should be retained.

7. *Practice before the Tax Court of the United States*

Under the Tax Court rules non-lawyers may be admitted to practice.

However, since upon issuance of a formal notice of deficiency by the Commissioner of Internal Revenue a choice of legal remedies is afforded the taxpayer under existing law (either before the Tax Court of the United States, a United States District Court, or the Court of Claims), it is in the best interests of the taxpayer that the advice of a lawyer be sought if further proceedings are contemplated. It is not intended hereby to foreclose the right of non-lawyers to practice before the Tax Court of the United States pursuant to its rules.

Here also, as in proceedings before the Treasury Department, the taxpayer, in many cases, is best served by the combined skills of both lawyers and certified public accountants, and the taxpayers, in such cases, should be advised accordingly.

8. *Claims for refund*

Claims for refund may be prepared by lawyers or certified public accountants, provided, however, that where a controversial legal issue is involved or where the claim is to be made the basis of litigation, the services of a lawyer should be obtained.

9. *Criminal tax investigations*

When a certified public accountant learns that his client is being specially investigated for possible criminal violation of the Income Tax Law, he should advise his client to seek the advice of a lawyer as to his legal and constitutional rights.

Conclusion

This statement of principles should be regarded as tentative and subject to revision and amplification in the light of future experience. The principal purpose is to indicate the importance of voluntary cooperation between our professions, whose members should use their knowledge and skills to the best advantage of the public. It is recommended that joint committees representing the local societies of both professions be established. Such committees might well take permanent form as local conferences of lawyers and certified public accountants patterned after this conference, or could take the form of special committees to handle a specific situation.

ABA Committee on Professional Ethics

Opinion 314 (51 ABAJ 671, 1965)

The Committee has received a number of specific inquiries regarding the ethical relationship between the Internal Revenue Service and lawyers practicing before it. Rather than answer each of these separately, the Committee, believing this to be a matter of general interest, has formulated the following general principles governing this relationship.

Canon 1 says: "It is the duty of the lawyer to maintain towards the Courts a respectful attitude." Canon 15 says that the lawyer owes "warm zeal" to his client and that "The office of attorney does not permit, much less does it demand of him for any client, violation of law or any manner of fraud or chicane." Canon 16 says: "A lawyer should use his best efforts to prevent his clients from doing those things which the lawyer himself ought not to do, particularly with reference to their conduct towards Courts . . .". Canon 22 says: "The conduct of the lawyer before the court and with other lawyers should be characterized by candor and fairness."

All of these canons are pertinent to the subject here under consideration, for Canon 26 provides: "A lawyer openly, and in his true character, may render professional services . . . in advocacy of claims before departments of government, upon the same principles of ethics which justify his appearance before the Courts . . .".

Certainly a lawyer's advocacy before the Internal Revenue Service must be governed by "the same principles of ethics which justify his appearance before the Courts". But since the service, however fair and impartial it may try to be, is the representative of one of the parties, does the lawyer owe it the same duty of disclosure which is owed to the courts? Or is his duty to it more nearly analogous to that which he owes his brother attorneys in the conduct of cases which should be conducted in an atmosphere of candor and fairness but are admittedly adversary in nature? An analysis of the nature of the Internal Revenue Service will serve to throw some light upon the answer to these questions.

The Internal Revenue Service is neither a true tribunal, nor even a quasi-judicial institution. It has no machinery or procedure for adversary proceedings before impartial judges or arbiters, involving the weighing of conflicting testimony of witnesses examined and cross-examined by opposing counsel and the consideration of arguments of counsel for both sides of a dispute. While its procedures provide for "fresh looks" through departmental reviews and informal and formal conference procedures, few will contend that the service provides any truly dispassionate and unbiased consideration to the taxpayer. Although willing to listen to taxpayers and their representatives and obviously intending to be fair, the service is not designed and does not purport to be unprejudiced and unbiased in the judicial sense.

It by no means follows that a lawyer is relieved of all ethical responsibility when he practices before this agency. There are certain things which he clearly cannot do, and they are set forth explicitly in the canons of ethics.

Canon 15 scorns the false claim that it is the duty of the lawyer to do whatever may enable him to succeed in winning his client's cause no matter how unscrupulous, and after making it clear that the lawyer owes entire devotion to the interest of his client, Canon 15 concludes as follows:

> ... But it is steadfastly to be borne in mind that the great trust of the lawyer is to be performed within and not without the bounds of the law. The office of attorney *does not permit*, much less does it *demand* of him for any client, violation of law or any manner of fraud or chicane. He must obey his own conscience and not that of his client [emphasis supplied].

Canon 22, relating to candor and fairness, states that

> It is unprofessional and dishonorable to deal other than candidly with the facts ... in the presentation of causes.
>
> These and all kindred practices are unprofessional and unworthy of an officer of the law charged, as is the lawyer, with the duty of aiding in the administration of justice.

Canon 29 provides in part that a lawyer

> should strive at all times to uphold the honor and to maintain the dignity of the profession and to improve not only the law but the administration of justice.

Canon 32 states that

> No client ... is entitled to receive nor should any lawyer render ... any advice involving disloyalty to the law whose ministers we are. ... [He] advances the honor of his profession and the best interests of his client when he ... gives advice tending to impress upon the client and his undertaking exact compliance with the strictest principles of moral law. ... [A] lawyer will find his highest honor in a deserved reputation for fidelity to private trust and to public duty, as an honest man and as a patriotic and loyal citizen.

In addition, the preamble to the canons concludes as follows:

> No code or set of rules can be framed, which will particularize all the duties of the lawyer ... in all the relations of professional life. The following canons of ethics are adopted by the American Bar Association as a general guide, yet the enumeration of particular duties should not be construed as a denial of the existence of others equally imperative, though not specifically mentioned.

The problem arises when, in the course of his professional employment, the attorney acquires information bearing upon the strength of his client's claim. Although a number of canons have general bearing on the problem (Canons 15, 16, 22 and 26), Canon 37 regarding client confidences and Canons 29, 41 and 44 regarding perjury, fraud and deception and the withdrawal of an attorney are most relevant.

For example, what is the duty of a lawyer in regard to disclosure of the weaknesses in his client's case in the course of negotiations for the settlement of a tax case?

Negotiation and settlement procedures of the tax system do not carry with them the guarantee that a correct tax result necessarily occurs. The latter happens, if at all, solely by reason of chance in settlement of tax controversies just as it might happen with regard to other civil disputes. In the absence of either judicial determination or of a hypothetical exchange of files by adversaries, counsel will always urge in aid of settlement of a controversy the strong points of his case and minimize the weak; this is in keeping with Canon 15, which does require "warm zeal" on behalf of the client. Nor does the absolute duty not to make false assertions of fact require the disclosure of weaknesses in the client's case and in no event does it require the disclosure of his confidences, unless the facts in the attorney's possession indicate beyond reasonable doubt that a crime will be committed. A wrong, or indeed sometimes an unjust, tax result in the settlement of a controversy is not a crime.

Similarly, a lawyer who is asked to advise his client in the course of the preparation of the client's tax returns may freely urge the statement of positions most favorable to the client just as long as there is reasonable basis for those positions. Thus where the lawyer believes there is a reasonable basis for a position that a particular transaction does not result in taxable income, or that certain expenditures are properly deductible as expenses, the lawyer has no duty to advise that riders be attached to the client's tax return explaining the circumstances surrounding the transaction or the expenditures.

The foregoing principle necessarily relates to the lawyer's ethical obligations — what he is *required* to do. Prudence may recommend procedures not required by ethical considerations. Thus, even where the lawyer believes that there is no obligation to reflect a transaction in or with his client's return, nevertheless he *may*, as a tactical matter, advise his client to disclose the transaction in reasonable detail by way of a rider to the return. This occurs when it is to the client's advantage to be free from either a *claim* of fraud (albeit unfounded) or to have the protection of a shorter statute of limitations (which might be available by the full disclosure of such a transaction in detail by way of a rider to the return).

In all cases, with regard both to the preparation of returns and negotiating administrative settlements, the lawyer is under a duty not

APPENDIX 381

to mislead the Internal Revenue Service deliberately and affirmatively, either by misstatements or by silence or by permitting his client to mislead. The difficult problem arises where the client has in fact misled but without the lawyer's knowledge or participation. In that situation, upon discovery of the misrepresentation, the lawyer must advise the client to correct the statement; if the client refuses, the lawyer's obligation depends on all the circumstances.

Fundamentally, subject to the restrictions of the attorney-client privilege imposed by Canon 37, the lawyer may have the duty to withdraw from the matter. If for example, under all the circumstances, the lawyer believes that the service relies on him as corroborating statements of his client which he knows to be false, then he is under a duty to disassociate himself from any such reliance unless it is obvious that the very act of disassociation would have the effect of violating Canon 37. Even then, however, if a direct question is put to the lawyer, he must at least advise the service that he is not in a position to answer.

But as an advocate before a service which itself represents the adversary point of view, where his client's case is fairly arguable, a lawyer is under no duty to disclose its weaknesses, any more than he would be to make such a disclosure to a brother lawyer. The limitations within which he must operate are best expressed in Canon 22:

> It is not candid or fair for the lawyer knowingly to misquote the contents of a paper, the testimony of a witness, the language or the argument of opposing counsel, or the language of a decision or a textbook; or with knowledge of its invalidity, to cite as authority a decision that has been overruled, or a statute that has been repealed; or in argument to assert as a fact that which has not been proved, or in those jurisdictions where a side has the opening and closing arguments to mislead his opponent by concealing or withholding positions in his opening argument upon which his side then intends to rely.

It is unprofessional and dishonorable to deal other than candidly with the facts in taking the statements of witnesses, in drawing affidavits and other documents, and in the presentation of causes.

So long as a lawyer remains within these limitations, and so long as his duty is "performed within and not without the bounds of the law", he "owes 'entire devotion to the interest of the client, warm zeal in the maintenance and defense of his rights and the exertion of his utmost learning and ability', to the end that nothing be taken or be withheld from him, save by the rules of law, legally applied" in his practice before the Internal Revenue Service, as elsewhere (Canon 15).

Statements on Responsibilities in Tax Practice

AICPA Committee on Federal Taxation

1. Signature of Preparer

I. *Introduction*

Is it proper for a certified public accountant to prepare a Federal tax return and deliver it to the taxpayer without having signed the preparer's declaration?

II. *Statement*

A CPA should sign as preparer any Federal tax return which requires the signature of a preparer if he prepares it for and transmits it to the taxpayer or another, whether or not the return was prepared for compensation.

III. *Explanation*

Section 1.6065-1(b)(1) of the Income Tax Regulations requires that a preparer must sign the preparer's declaration on a return providing for such verification where the return is prepared for a taxpayer for compensation or as an incident to the performance of other services for which compensation is received. It is clear that if the CPA is the "preparer" of a return (in the sense of the Regulation) he should sign the preparer's declaration and may not avoid doing so willfully. A CPA also should sign a return prepared by him whether or not it is prepared for compensation. Although this latter requirement goes beyond the scope of the Regulation, it represents a step in the establishment of uniform standards of responsibility in tax return preparation by CPAs.

A typical example of a preparer's declaration (taken from the 1963 Form 1040) follows:

> Under penalties of perjury, I declare that I have examined this return, including accompanying schedules and statements, and to the best of my knowledge and belief it is true, correct and complete. If prepared by a person other than taxpayer, his declaration is based on all information of which he has any knowledge.

APPENDIX 383

The following examples reflect the committee's understanding of when the CPA is a "preparer." The examples are intended to be illustrative and are offered to provide a basis for resolving doubts which may arise in the course of a CPA's practice:

A. Situations considered to constitute the preparation of a return, and in which the CPA's signature as preparer is required.

1. The CPA assembles information pertinent to the taxpayer's return, and completes the return and transmits it to the taxpayer. The CPA is required to sign the return as preparer whether the CPA prepares the return from information supplied by the taxpayer, or from information obtained by the CPA directly or indirectly from the taxpayer's books and records. This requirement is unchanged whether the CPA conducted an examination of the financial statements in accordance with generally accepted auditing standards, or whether he expressed or disclaimed an opinion on them.

2. The CPA assembles information as in Situation A-1 above and completes a draft of the return but does not perform certain mechanical functions, such as typing or reproducing (e.g., the draft of the return is prepared in pencil), and forwards it to the taxpayer. The CPA's arrangement with the taxpayer should provide that before the return is filed, the taxpayer will make the draft and the return to be filed available to the CPA for proofing and signature.

3. The CPA prepares a return as in Situation A-1 above and transmits it to the taxpayer ready for filing, except for certain *minor* items or supplemental information which will not affect the taxable income or loss and which are to be inserted in the return by the taxpayer. The CPA should sign the return before it is transmitted to the taxpayer. An example of a minor item is a taxpayer's identification number; pension plan data is an example of supplemental information.

4. The CPA reviews a return originally prepared by the taxpayer or another and, under authority conferred by the taxpayer, either makes substantial changes in the return or

substantial changes are made by the taxpayer or another at the CPA's direction. In this situation the CPA is considered to be a preparer, should sign the return and, accordingly, should satisfy himself as to the content of the entire return. On the other hand, if the CPA's engagement is limited to submitting recommendations, he is not considered to be a preparer. The term "substantial changes" means the revisions are significant in relation to the taxpayer's taxable income or loss, or the tax liability for the year. (Review situations in which the CPA is not the preparer will be discussed in a subsequent statement.)

B. Situations not considered to constitute the preparation of a return, and in which the CPA's signature as preparer is not required.

1. A taxpayer transmits to a CPA an otherwise completed return with the request that the CPA perform certain mechanical service, such as typing or reproducing.

2. In the course of an examination of financial statements the CPA assembles some, but not a preponderant part, of the information which is used for the preparation of a return by the client or another.

3. The CPA prepares a schedule (e.g., capital gains, foreign tax credit, etc.) and transmits it to the taxpayer for inclusion in a return. The remainder of the return is completed by the taxpayer or another.

4. In the course of an examination of financial statements: (a) The CPA makes a determination of taxable income or loss in considering the client's tax liability, but not in connection with the preparation of a return. (b) The CPA reviews a return prepared by the client or another, before it is filed, for the sole purpose of considering the client's tax liability. The CPA neither makes substantial changes (as described in Situation A-4) in the return nor are substantial changes made by the taxpayer or another at the CPA's direction.

5. During or after the close of the taxable year the CPA advises a taxpayer as to the taxability, deductibility or presentation of certain items in a return.

(In each of the above situations it is assumed that the CPA did not perform additional services which, when taken together with the situation discussed, would constitute preparation of a return.)

C. Other situations.

1. The CPA assembles information pertinent to the taxpayer's return, but discontinues work on it due to a disagreement with the taxpayer as to the presentation of an item. At the taxpayer's request the CPA transmits to him the incomplete return. The CPA is not required to sign the incomplete return, and in his letter of transmittal should disavow responsibility as preparer.

2. The CPA prepared a return, signed and transmitted it to the taxpayer. The taxpayer requests that the CPA make certain changes. If the changes sought by the taxpayer meet with the approval of the CPA, the CPA should sign the return as revised. If the changes sought by the taxpayer are unacceptable to the CPA and an impasse develops, the CPA should refuse to revise the return or to sign a return as revised by the taxpayer.

In connection with an engagement to prepare a return, it should be recognized that the return, upon transmission to the taxpayer, belongs to the taxpayer. Before filing a return prepared by a CPA, a taxpayer could make changes in it without the CPA's knowledge or permission. It is recommended that the CPA preserve a copy of each return in the form in which it was transmitted to the taxpayer.

IV. *Applicability*

This statement is confined to Federal tax practice. It applies to the preparation of Federal tax returns by CPAs in public practice, and by CPAs in private employment to the extent that they prepare returns outside of their regular employment. The Regulations except employees from the requirement of verification of certain tax returns prepared by them, if prepared in the scope of their employment, for their employers or fellow employees. Therefore, they are excepted to that extent from the application of this statement.

Although, for convenience, this statement is written in terms of an individual CPA, it applies equally to the CPA's staff, members of a CPA partnership, and the staff of a CPA partnership.

NOTE

This statement has been approved by at least two-thirds of the members of the committee on Federal taxation, reached on a formal vote after examination of the subject matter. It has not been considered and acted upon by the Council of the Institute. Its authority rests upon the statutes and regulations of the taxing authority and the general acceptability of the committee's interpretations. The statement is not intended to be retroactive.

2. Signature of Preparer: Assumption of Preparer's Responsibility

I. Introduction

Frequently, a certified public accountant is engaged to review a Federal tax return by a taxpayer who seeks added assurance that it has been prepared properly. In many such instances, the taxpayer requests that the CPA sign or cosign the preparer's declaration on the return.

This statement considers whether a CPA who is not the preparer of a return, and therefore is not required to sign the preparer's declaration, nevertheless in his discretion may sign and thus assume the preparer's responsibility.

Statement No. 1 issued in September 1964, discusses the signature requirement for a CPA who is the preparer of a Federal tax return.

II. Statement

If the CPA is not the preparer of a Federal tax return, he is not required to sign the preparer's declaration. However, in his discretion, the CPA may sign the declaration on a return prepared by the taxpayer or another if he reviews the return and, in the course of the review, acquires knowledge with respect to the return substantially equivalent to that which he would have acquired had he prepared the return. Unless such review is made, the CPA should not sign the preparer's declaration.

III. Explanation

A. *General.* This statement is concerned with situations in which the CPA's role is that of a reviewer with no obligation to sign as preparer. Statement No. 1 provides examples and discussion relating to whether in certain situations the CPA is the preparer of a Federal tax return. It also covers one type of situation in which a review becomes tantamount to preparation and the CPA should sign as preparer (Statement No. 1, Part III A-4).

The Internal Revenue Code, the Income Tax Regulations (including Section 1.6065-1(b)(1)) and tax return forms make no reference to the signing by a reviewer of the preparer's declaration. Thus, it appears that the CPA who signs the preparer's declaration assumes the same responsibility whether he is a preparer or a reviewer. Accordingly, unless the CPA-reviewer intends to assume the same responsibility as a preparer for the entire return, he should not sign the preparer's declaration.

A CPA who has reviewed a return (prepared by the taxpayer or another) to the extent set forth in the following paragraph may sign the preparer's declaration. However, he is not required to sign unless he is considered to have become the preparer in circumstances such as those described in Statement No. 1.

Before a CPA-reviewer signs the preparer's declaration on a return prepared by a taxpayer or another, he should acquire knowledge with respect to the return substantially equivalent to that which he would have acquired had he prepared the return. It is contemplated that review procedures will vary from return to return and that the CPA will apply his professional judgment in each engagement to determine the extent of the review needed to acquire such knowledge.

B. *Cosigning.* Where a return has been prepared for a taxpayer by a person who signed as preparer and a CPA is asked to review and cosign the return, the CPA may add his signature to the preparer's declaration provided that his review meets the standard set forth in the preceding paragraph.

IV. *Applicability*

This statement is confined to Federal tax practice. It applies to the review of Federal tax returns by CPAs in public practice and by CPAs in private employment to the extent that they practice outside of their regular employment.

Although, for convenience, this statement is written in terms of an individual CPA, it applies equally to the CPA's staff, members of a CPA partnership, and the staff of a CPA partnership.

NOTE

This statement has been approved by at least two-thirds of the members of the committee on Federal taxation, reached on a formal vote after examination of the subject matter. It has not been considered and acted upon by the Council of the Institute. Its authority rests upon the statutes and regulations of the taxing authority and the general acceptability of the committee's interpretations. The statement is not intended to be retroactive.

3. Answers to Questions on Returns

I. *Introduction*

May a certified public accountant sign the preparer's declaration on a Federal tax return where one or more questions on the return have not been answered? The term "questions" is considered to include requests for information on the return which are not stated in the interrogatory form.

II. *Statement*

A CPA should sign the preparer's declaration on a Federal tax return only if he is satisfied that reasonable effort has been

APPENDIX

made to provide appropriate answers to the questions on the return which are applicable to the taxpayer. Where such a question is left unanswered the reason for such omission should be stated. The possibility that an answer to a question might prove disadvantageous to the taxpayer does not justify omitting an answer or a statement of the reason for such omission.

III. *Explanation*

It is recognized that the questions on tax returns are not of uniform importance, that often they are not applicable to the particular taxpayer, and that the frequency of change of the questions on tax return forms from year to year tends to minimize their significance to the preparer as well as to the taxpayer. Nevertheless, aside from administrative convenience to the Internal Revenue Service, there are at least two considerations which dictate that a CPA-preparer should satisfy himself that reasonable effort has been made to provide appropriate answers to the questions on the return which are applicable to the taxpayer:

1. A question may be of importance in determining taxable income or loss, or the tax liability shown on the return, in which circumstance the omission tends to detract from the quality of the return;
2. It is not consistent with the professional stature of the CPA to sign the preparer's declaration on a return which is incomplete.

While an effort should be made to provide an answer to each question on the return which is applicable to the taxpayer, reasonable grounds may exist for omitting an answer. For example, reasonable grounds include the following:

1. The information is not readily available and the answer is not significant in terms of taxable income or loss, or the tax liability shown on the return; or
2. The answer might prove to be significant as to the particular return, but, either:
    (a) genuine uncertainty exists regarding the meaning of

the question in relation to the particular return; or,

(b) the information which is obtainable is not sufficiently reliable to warrant reporting on the return.

3. The answer to the question is voluminous; however, assurance should be given on the return that the data will be supplied to the revenue agent in the course of his examination.

Where reasonable grounds exist for omission of an answer to an applicable question, a brief explanation of the reason for the omission should be provided on the return.

The purpose of this statement is to discuss the professional responsibility of the CPA concerning answers to questions on tax returns. It should not be construed to have any bearing on other matters such as whether a return which contains one or more unanswered questions is sufficiently complete to start the running of the statute of limitations.

The final sentence of Opinion 13 of the Institute's Committee on Professional Ethics, in effect, states that a CPA may resolve doubt in favor of his client as long as there is reasonable support for his position. The concept of reasonable support does not justify the omission of an answer merely because it may prove disadvantageous to the taxpayer.

This statement is based upon the general nature and scope of the questions currently on Federal tax returns.

NOTE

This statement has been approved by at least two-thirds of the members of the committee on Federal taxation, reached on a formal vote after examination of the subject matter. It has not been considered and acted upon by the Council of the Institute. Its authority rests upon the statutes and regulations of the taxing authority and the general acceptability of the committee's interpretations. The statement is not intended to be retroactive. Its applicability is the same as that stated in Part IV of Statements 1 and 2.

APPENDIX 391

4. Recognition of Administrative Proceeding of a Prior Year

I. Introduction

This statement considers whether a certified public accountant may sign the preparer's declaration on a Federal tax return in which the treatment of an item differs from that consented to by the taxpayer for a similar item as a result of an administrative proceeding concerning a prior year's return. This statement refers to an administrative proceeding which was concluded by the execution of a waiver by the taxpayer.

An "administrative proceeding" includes an examination by a revenue agent, a district conference or an appellate conference relating to a return or a claim for refund.

The term "waiver" includes a waiver of restrictions on the assessment of a deficiency in tax, the acceptance of the Internal Revenue Service's findings by a partnership, fiduciary or Subchapter S corporation, and the acceptance of an overassessment.

Any reference to "item" or "year" is intended to cover the plural of those terms.

II. Statement

The selection of the treatment of an item in the course of the preparation of a tax return should be based upon the facts and the rules as they are evaluated at the time the return is prepared. Unless the taxpayer is bound as to treatment in the later year, such as by a closing agreement, the disposition of an item as a part of concluding an administrative proceeding by the execution of a waiver for a prior year does not govern the taxpayer in selecting the treatment of a similar item in a later year's return. Therefore, if justified by the facts and rules then applicable, a CPA may sign the preparer's declaration on a return containing a departure from the treatment of an item arrived at as a part of concluding an administrative proceeding regarding a prior year's return. Such departure need not be disclosed.

III. Explanation

A taxpayer as a matter of course usually will treat an item in the same manner as was arrived at in concluding an administrative proceeding for a prior year when a similar item arises in a subsequent year. The question is whether the taxpayer is required to do so. The considerations in deriving an answer include:

1. The Internal Revenue Service tends to act consistently with the manner in which a similar item was disposed of in a prior administrative proceeding, but maintains that it must look upon the examination of each return as a new matter. Broadly speaking, it has no alternative to this policy because of its responsibility as an administrative agency.

2. The taxpayer's position may be influenced by facts or circumstances such as the following:

    (a) his assent in the administrative proceeding may have been caused by a lack of substantiation while supporting data for the later year is adequate,

    (b) he may have yielded in the administrative proceeding for settlement purposes even though there was and is reasonable support for his position, or

    (c) taking into account the applicable court decisions, rulings, etc., the climate now may be more favorable to the taxpayer's position than it was when the administrative proceeding was concluded.

When valid reasons exist such as those cited above, there is no requirement that a disclosure of the dissimilarity be made in a later year's return.

NOTE

This statement has been approved by at least two-thirds of the members of the committee on Federal taxation, reached on a formal vote after examination of the subject matter. It has not been considered and acted upon by the Council of the Institute. Its authority rests upon the statutes and regulations of the taxing authority and the general acceptability of the committee's interpretations. The statement is not intended to be retroactive. Its applicability is the same as that stated in Part IV of Statements 1 and 2.

5. Use of Estimates

I. Introduction

This Statement considers the responsibility of a certified public accountant in connection with the use of estimates in the preparation of a Federal tax return which he signs as preparer.

II. Statement

A certified public accountant may prepare tax returns involving the use of estimates if such use is generally acceptable or, under the circumstances, it is impracticable to obtain exact data. When estimates are used, they should be presented in such a manner as to avoid the implication of greater accuracy than exists. The CPA should be satisfied that estimated amounts are not unreasonable under the circumstances.

III. Explanation

A. *Accounting Judgments*—Accounting requires the exercise of judgment and in many instances the use of approximations based on judgment. For example, in computing depreciation charged against the income of a given time period, judgment enters into the determination of useful life, salvage value, obsolescence, and other factors determining the amount of cost. Similarly, judgment enters into the valuation of inventory, the addition to a reserve for bad debts, the allocation of acquisition costs to individual units of property bought in bulk for a lump sum, the determination of an overhead rate and similar matters. The application of such accounting judgments is accepted and expected and these judgments are not estimates within the purview of this Statement.

B. *Accruals*—The income tax regulations provide, in effect, that if all other conditions for accrual are met, the exact amount of income or expense need not be known or ascertainable at year end and it is permissible to make a reasonable estimate of the amount.

C. *Small Expenditures*—In the case of transactions involving small expenditures, accuracy in recording some data is difficult to achieve. It is not practicable, for example, to require accurate recording of frequently recurring minor expenditures, such as sales and gasoline taxes. Use of estimates in determining the amount to be deducted for such items is an accepted practice.

D. *Unavailable Data*—In other cases where all of the facts relating to a transaction are not accurately known, either because records are missing or because precise information is not available at the time the return must be filed, estimates of the missing data may be made.

E. *Manner of Presentation*—It is not acceptable practice to present estimates in such a way as to imply greater accuracy than exists. Estimated amounts should be presented in any manner which will avoid deception or a misleading impression of the facts. Under some circumstances it may be necessary to state expressly that an amount has been estimated. In other instances use of a round amount, or an amount suggested in a Treasury Department guideline, may constitute a sufficient designation as an estimate. If a tax return entry is an aggregation of items which includes a significant estimated amount, such estimated amount should be disclosed.

F. *Record keeping*—The CPA should encourage the use of appropriate records to support, where practical, all entries on a client's tax return. The fact that some estimates may be used as set forth in this Statement should not serve to condone poor record-keeping practices.

NOTE

The Division of Federal Taxation through its committee on responsibilities in tax practice and executive group has been granted authority by the Institute to issue pronouncements on matters of tax practice. This Statement has been approved by at least two-thirds of the members of the committee and of the executive group. This Statement is not intended to be retroactive.

Statements on Responsibilities in Tax Practice containing standards of responsibility which are more restrictive than those established by the Treasury Department or by the Institute's Code of Professional Ethics depend for their authority on the general acceptability of the opinions expressed.

Lowell Bar Ass'n v. Loeb
Supreme Judicial Court of Massachusetts, Middlesex
52 N.E. 2d 27 (1943)

LUMMUS, Justice.

This is a petition in equity . . . , brought by an incorporated association of members of the bar, to restrain the respondents, who are not members of the bar, from holding themselves out as authorized, entitled, competent, qualified and able to practice law, from engaging in the practice of law, and from giving legal advice in respect to liability to pay income taxes and the preparation and execution of income tax returns. . . . By the final decree, entered on March 15, 1943, those respondents were "permanently enjoined and restrained from advertising a tax service in any form whatsoever, whether in newspapers, placards or signs displayed in their various offices, and from engaging in the making out of income tax returns as a regular occupation and other than the occasional drafting thereof and from engaging in the practice of the law in any of its aspects," and were ordered to pay costs. From each decree these respondents appealed. . . .

The facts may be summarized as follows: One Louis G. Loeb, an attorney at law practising in Boston, the husband of the respondent Birdie T. Loeb, had an interest in a business of making out income tax returns for wage earners which was carried on in Quincy in 1941, and was then discontinued. In the summer of 1942 he planned to establish a similar business in a number of manufacturing cities. Recent statutes had required income tax returns from many wage earners previously exempt, and the trend was toward a further extension of tax liability. . . .

To carry out his plan, he organized the unincorporated American Tax Service, with headquarters in Boston which soon after establishment were moved to his law office, and with branch offices in Lowell, Lawrence and other manufacturing cities. He is the real owner of the business, although he devotes little time to it. The respondent Birdie T. Loeb devotes all her time to the business, and ostensibly is the proprietor. The respondent Friedman is general manager, and has his office at the Boston headquarters. The respondent Koch was manager of the Lowell branch until succeeded by one Shea. The business has about one hundred employees during the season for income tax returns. None of them is a member of the bar. None of them appears to be an accountant, with the exception of the respondent Friedman.

The American Tax Service does not attempt to make out income tax returns for corporations, partnerships, estates, fiduciaries or business men conducting a business. Its patrons are exclusively persons whose income consists wholly, or almost wholly, of salary or wages. It advertises extensively in newspapers and by signs in its windows. There is little modesty or restraint about its advertising, which is designed to arrest attention and to bring in a large volume of business. Its uniform prices are $2 for a State or Federal return, and $3.75 for both returns. Its "maximum charge for all returns to any one person" is advertised to be the latter sum.

The legal principles underlying this case are now well established. The judicial department of government, and no other, has power to license persons to practise law. Statutes may aid by providing machinery and criminal penalties, but may not extend the privilege of practising law to persons not admitted to practice by the judicial department. . . . As constituted at present, the Massachusetts bar is a unit. Each member may practise in any State court and in any branch of legal work, without regard to his special qualifications in one branch or his comparative lack of them in another. In England, the legal profession is divided, and lawyers may practise only in the branch of work for which they have been admitted. Formerly a similar division existed in this Commonwealth. . . . The justification for excluding from the practice of law persons not admitted to the bar is to be found, not in the protection of the bar from competition, but in the protection of the public from being advised and represented in legal matters by incompetent and unreliable persons, over whom the judicial department could exercise little control. . . .

A member of the bar is held to a high standard of honor and of ethical conduct. He may not advertise for business or solicit employment. . . . But "a member of the bar is free to engage in commercial pursuits of an honorable character and to advertise and to extend his purely mercantile business honestly and fairly by ordinary commercial methods." . . .

The judicial department is necessarily the sole arbiter of what constitutes the practice of law. Opinion of the Justices, 289 Mass. 607, 614, 194 N.E. 313. . . . It is not easy to define the practice of law. Since it undertakes to determine all controversies as to rights that may arise among men, the law pervades all human affairs. This has become increasingly evident in recent years. Statutes familiar to everyone have made almost every citizen feel the heavy hand of the law, helping him or hampering him, often adding to his financial burdens, and markedly increasing his dependence upon experts, especially in law and in accounting.

The proposition cannot be maintained, that whenever, for compensation, one person gives to another advice that involves some element of law, or performs for another some service that requires some knowledge of law, or drafts for another some document that has legal effect, he is practising law. All these things are done in the usual course of the work of occupations that are universally recognized as distinct from the practice of law. There is authority for the proposition that the drafting of documents, when merely incidental to the work of a distinct occupation, is not the practice of law, although the documents have legal consequences. . . .

For example, an architect cannot advise a landowner properly, or plan for him intelligently, without an adequate knowledge of the building laws and regulations. In practice, an architect prepares the building contract, and drafts the specifications that accompany it and determine to a great extent the rights and liabilities of the land-owner. An insurance agent or broker, in order to be of service, must know the legal effect of different forms of policies and of various provisions in them. Often he is the agent of the insured . . . , and as such drafts riders, to be attached to a policy, which have important legal effect. An appraiser or valuer of property, real or personal, must be acquainted with the principles of value that find acceptance in the courts. Bonbright, Valuation of Property (1937). An auctioneer or broker often drafts sale notes, receipts and memoranda for his employer which may affect his legal rights. . . . A so called customhouse broker (U.S.C.A. Title 19, § 1641) commonly prepares for the importer documents that have important legal effect, and to do so requires considerable knowledge of the law of customs duties. . . .

The work of an accountant necessarily brings him into touch with rules of law which he must understand if his computations and conclusions are to stand the test of possible litigation. He must know the nature and general legal effect of negotiable instruments, patent rights, corporate stock and bonds of different kinds, insurance policies, and other contracts. He must appreciate the distinction between buying goods, and taking them as bailee, agent, broker or factor. He could hardly prepare a correct account for a partnership without a working knowledge of the main principles of the law of partnership. In preparing an account for a trust estate, he must understand the difference between principal and income, and the rules of law governing the allocation of receipts and expenses to the one or the other. Income taxes have produced a flood of judicial decisions and departmental rulings with which he must have adequate acquaintance, even though he merely works with figures and does not draft tax returns. A sharp line cannot be drawn between the field of the lawyer and that of the accountant. Some matters lie in a penumbra. But any service that lies wholly within the practice of law cannot lawfully be performed by an accountant or any other person not a member of the bar.

Plainly the commencement and prosecution for another of legal proceedings in court and the advocacy for another of a cause before a court, in cases relating to taxes as in other cases, are reserved exclusively for members of the bar. Doubtless the examination of statutes, judicial decisions, and departmental rulings, for the purpose of advising upon a question of law relative to taxation, and the rendering to a client of an opinion thereon, are likewise part of the practice of law in which only members of the bar may engage. . . .

When we pass beyond these propositions we enter debatable ground. The present case does not require us to delimit either the practice of law in tax matters or the right of persons not admitted to the bar to engage for compensation in the business of assisting others in such matters. It would be unwise and perhaps unfair to future litigants, to enunciate at this time broad principles not necessary to the decision of the case before us.

Specifically, we do not deal at this time with the validity of Rule 1 of the Massachusetts Appellate Tax Board which purports to give to a certified public accountant the right to practise before that tribunal, or with the question whether a person not a member of the bar may be allowed to practise before any administrative tribunal in this Commonwealth. If such practice by one not a member of the bar is the practice of law, no rule of such a tribunal can legalize it. The statutes of this Commonwealth give to a certified public accountant no right not possessed by other accountants and other persons generally, except the right to style himself "certified public accountant." G.L. (Ter. Ed.) c. 112, §§ 87D, 87E. Whether practice before an administrative tribunal in tax matters is the practice of law has been the subject of decisions elsewhere that appear to be in some conflict.

Neither do we consider at this time whether the permission granted to certified public accountants and other persons not members of the bar to practise in tax matters by the rules of the United States Treasury Department and of the administrative tribunal . . . now called the Tax Court of the United States, can have the effect of granting by implication to holders of "Treasury enrollment cards" a right to perform in this Commonwealth services in connection with Federal taxes which in their nature are comprised in the practice of law. It may deserve consideration whether the rules of a Federal administrative tribunal can legalize acts done in the States in matters not actually before the tribunal, though of a class that might eventually come before it. . . .

Moreover, we do not decide at this time whether considering, or advising upon, questions of law only so far as they are incidental to the preparation for another of an income tax return may constitute the practice of law where the return is more complicated than were those in the case before us, and the questions of law as well as of accounting are correspondingly more difficult and important.

Confining our decision to the case at bar, we find the respondents engaged in the business of making out income tax returns of the least difficult kind. The blank forms furnished by the tax officials for that class of returns are made simple, and are accompanied by plain printed instructions. The forms may appear formidable to persons unused to mental concentration and to clerical exactness, but they can readily be filled out by any intelligent taxpayer whose income is derived wholly or almost wholly from salary or wages and who has the patience to study the instructions.

We are aware that there has been said to be no difference in principle between the drafting of simple instruments and the drafting of complex ones. . . . But though the difference is one of degree, it may nevertheless be real. . . . There are instruments that no one but a well trained lawyer should ever undertake to draw. But there are others, common in the commercial world, and fraught with substantial legal consequences, that lawyers seldom are employed to draw, and that in the course of recognized occupations other than the practice of law are often drawn by laymen for other laymen, as has already been shown. The actual practices of the community have an important bearing on the scope of the practice of law. . . .

We think that the preparation of the income tax returns in question, though it had to be done with some consideration of the law, did not lie wholly within the field of the practice of law. . . . The final decree should not have enjoined the respondents from preparing such returns.

But though the permanent injunction which was granted was too broad, a final decree for the petitioner was required by facts that remain to be stated. For the small fee charged, which was advertised at "the most any one taxpayer pays us," patrons were promised "counsel in handling income tax matters should any develop after the official audit by the U.S. Tax Department during the year." The "legal counsel" was advertised to be Louis G. Loeb. Patrons were promised that "we stay with your taxes." Signs in the windows stated, "We take care of all correspondence and all interviews with the tax department. ATS stays with your taxes. Its services are available to you throughout the year."

We think that what was promised patrons was not the recommendation or the payment of a lawyer who would serve them in the direct and usual relation of attorney and client, as in Matter of Thibodeau, 295 Mass. 374, 378, 3 N.E.2d 749. What the respondents advertised and undertook to do was to sell the legal services of a lawyer who was to act for the American Tax Service. That was unlawful under Matter of Maclub of America, Inc., 295 Mass. 45, 3 N.E.2d 272, and Matter of Shoe Manufacturers Protective Association, Inc., 295 Mass. 369, 3 N.E.2d 746, whether done by an attorney or by a layman. Although Louis G. Loeb was the undisclosed principal, the respondent Birdie T. Loeb as the ostensible proprietor bound herself by contract to sell legal services.

[Discussion of procedural issues is omitted.]

The interlocutory decree permitting the Attorney General to intervene is affirmed. The final decree is modified so that it will enjoin and restrain the respondents permanently only from furnishing, or advertising or undertaking to furnish, for a consideration, legal services, and will give costs to the plaintiffs. As so modified it is affirmed.

Ordered accordingly.

Application of N. Y. County Lawyers Ass'n
(In re Bercu)
Supreme Court, Appellate Division, First Department
78 N. Y. S. 2d 209 (1948)

PECK, Presiding Justice.
The New York County Lawyers Association brought this pro-

ceeding to punish respondent for contempt and to enjoin him from pursuing certain activities which petitioner claims constitute the practice of law. The substantive question is whether the professional practice in which respondent is admittedly engaged constitutes the practice of law. A preliminary procedural question is whether the substantive question may be entertained and determined by the court in this summary proceeding.

Petitioner contends that respondent, an accountant, has engaged in the unlawful practice of law in giving tax advice to clients, and that as the facts are not disputed respondent may summarily be punished for contempt of court and enjoined.* Respondent contends that the advice given was in the nature of an accounting service, rather than a legal service, and that in any event his activity outside of court may not be regarded or treated as a contempt of court and may not be made the subject matter of an injunction except through an action brought under Article 75-A of the Civil Practice Act, which would require petitioner to make written request of the Attorney General to bring the action. Such request was not made. Respondent therefore contends the proceeding may not be maintained.

[Discussion of procedural question, which was decided against respondent, is omitted.]

We come, therefore, to the substantive question. Respondent is an accountant. He gave certain advice to the Croft Company on a tax question. He was not the auditor for the company, nor did he do any work of any kind on the books of the company. He did not prepare the tax return. The question on which he gave advice arose as follows: The City of New York had claims against the Croft Company for retail sales taxes and compensating use taxes attributable to business done in the years 1935, 1936 and 1937. The claims had not been paid in those years, in which the company had no taxable profits. In 1943 the company made large profits which would require it to pay a minimum of 80% federal tax on its net profits. It seemed advantageous to the company, therefore, to settle the City tax claims for the prior years in the year 1943, if a deduction for the payment could be taken on the federal income tax return for 1943. The company was thus considering compromising the City's claims if it was legal for the company to deduct the payment as an expense in 1943, rather than attribute the expense to the years in which the claims accrued.

---

*This proceeding arose out of an action brought in the Municipal Court by respondent against the Croft Company for professional services. Judgment was rendered in favor of the company on the ground that respondent's services were legal services. All the facts stated in this opinion are taken from respondent's testimony in the Municipal Court action. There is thus no dispute as to the facts.

The Croft Company kept its books on an accrual basis. The company's regular accountant, who was also a lawyer, had given his opinion, based on a decision of the United States Supreme Court, that any such payment would have to be charged back to the year in which the tax obligations were incurred. The president of the company consulted respondent, wanting to know why payment was not properly deductible in the year in which made. Respondent testified: "As an accountant, I said, 'No,' and he said he could not understand as a business man why it was not deductible, and he wanted my advice based on what I know of the tax law."

Respondent had several conferences with the president of the company and/or the company's accountant-lawyer. He first stated that he was confident that there was a case similar to the Croft case and in its favor, and that he would make his own research on the subject. Thereafter he made a study of the reported decisions on the subject, examining a score or more of the hundreds of cases on the question, and found a Treasury decision which in his view supported the position the Croft Company wished to take. Respondent then addressed the following letter to the Croft Company:

August 21, 1943

Mr. Joseph C. Bancroft
Croft Steel Products, Inc.
370 Lexington Avenue
New York, N. Y.

Dear Sir:

You will recall our conference of Friday last, when we discussed the question as to the year in which a New York City sales tax, assessed upon your company and payable in 1943, is properly deductible by your company on its Federal tax returns.

At that conference, Mr. Jacques Levy contended that under the general rule laid down by the U. S. Supreme Court, a sales tax which accrued in prior years is properly deductible only in those years, since the books of your company have been kept on an accrual basis. You will recall my contention that despite this general rule, your case could be shown to be an exception, in that there was no definite ruling as to the taxability of your products in those years, and you did not bill any sales tax to your customers in those years.

At your request, I have examined the available sources of information on this question, and find that, in 1941, the Internal Revenue Department had ruled on precisely this question, in favor of the business man's viewpoint, that a disputed tax liability is properly due and accruable in the year in which the dispute is settled.

This decision (I.T. 3441) (C.B.1941—1 p. 208) cites facts which are apparently exactly comparable to your situation and which may be summarized as follows:

> The M. Company had not added sales tax on material installed under lump-sum contracts in the years 1935, 1936 and 1937. It considered these installations as being affixed to realty, and the sales not subject to tax because made for the improvement of real property. The tax authorities ruled otherwise, and in 1939 the company was assessed. Also, a small portion of the additional assessment covered taxes on sales of material shipped from without the state into New York City, which the company considered interstate commerce, and not subject to the tax. The tax authorities also ruled such sales taxable, and the ruling was upheld by the U. S. Supreme Court.
>
> It is held that taxes assessed in 1939, paid out of the company's own funds which the company should have collected from its vendees in earlier years are deductible not as a tax, but as a business expense under [§ 23(a), 1939 Code, § 162, 1954 Code.]

In view of this specific favorable ruling, I have gone no further in marshalling precedents to sustain your position.

I shall be pleased to discuss this matter with you at your convenience, and help you to conclude the City case in a manner which will be squarely within the scope of the Federal Revenue Department ruling.

Very truly yours,
BB:rl
cc to:
Mr. Jacques M. Levy

For his services respondent submitted a bill for $500, describing the services as follows:

"Consultations in re deductibility in current taxable year of N. Y. City excise taxes for prior years" and "Memorandum in re above."

The charge was at the rate of about $50 an hour for his time. Respondent admitted that this work was not an isolated instance of its kind and that he often gave advice of the character which he gave to the Croft Company, without examining books or preparing tax returns. For auditing he charged $15 an hour, but for services as a tax consultant he received as high as $50 an hour.

As the tax problem confronting the Croft Company was a dual problem involving both a sales tax and compensating use tax, which could not be assimilated in legal treatment, there is force in petitioner's argument that respondent oversimplified the problem and inadequately covered it in his research and advice, which were confined to considering a sales tax problem. Petitioner's point is that respondent was dealing with complex questions of law, on which the numerous decisions were far from clear, and the questions were not susceptible to the cavalier answer which respondent gave. Thus, petitioner contends, respondent was entering into a field of law and fine legal distinctions far removed from the practice of accountancy. Respondent contends, on the other hand, that he was dealing with a subject which was primarily a matter of accounting and though touching upon the law within the field of accounting practice, and that the advice he gave met and correctly answered the question put to him.

We shall not dwell on the adequacy or accuracy of the advice given, or discuss the applicable law, for the decision in a case of this kind should not turn on the quality of the advice given. The decision must rest on the nature of the services rendered and on whether they were inherently legal or accounting services.

Petitioner acknowledges that law enters into accounting and accounting into tax law and that it is a proper function of an accountant to prepare tax returns, which work requires a knowledge and application of the law, but contends that giving advice with respect to the tax law, unconnected with work on the books or tax returns, is giving legal advice and practicing law. As much is implicit in respondent's testimony.

> Q. Answer me: did you say you knew what the legal point was involved in this question? A. I knew the point.
> Q. Did you say "Legal" point, just then? A. I did, and I withdraw it just now.
> Q. Why? A. Because it is not a question of legal point but it is a question of applicability of the tax law as understood by accountants.
> Q. Isn't that a legal point, applicability of the tax law? A. Well, accountants have to determine questions.
> Q. You mean accountants practice law? A. No, accountants have to understand the tax law in order to be able to keep books and prepare tax returns.

Respondent then went on to say that he did no work on the books or tax return of the Croft Company.

The case is not an easy one because of the overlapping of law and accounting. An accountant must be familiar to a considerable extent with tax law and must employ his knowledge of the law in his accounting practice. By the same token, a tax lawyer must have an understanding of accounting. It is difficult, therefore, to draw a precise line in the tax area between the field of the accountant and the field of the lawyer. Unless we are to say, however, that because common ground exists between the lawyer and accountant in the tax area no bounds may be recognized between them, some line of demarcation must be observed. We believe that the line has not been altogether obliterated, and with due regard to the latitude which should be given to the accountant, a majority of this Court is quite clear in its mind that respondent's services in this matter were well into the field of the law and outside of the field of accounting. To hold otherwise would be tantamount to saying that an accountant may practice tax law.

The accountant serves in setting up or auditing books, or advising with respect to the keeping of books and records, the making of entries therein and the handling of transactions for tax purposes and the preparation of tax returns. Naturally his work and advice must take cognizance of the law and conform with the law, particularly the tax law. The application of legal knowledge in such work, however, is only incidental to the accounting functions. It is not expected or permitted of the accountant, despite his knowledge or use of the law, to give legal advice which is unconnected with accounting work. That is exactly what this respondent did. He was doing no accounting work for the Croft Company within the ordinary or proper conception of an accountant's work. He had nothing to do with the Croft Company's books or its tax return. He was not giving any advice as to how the books should be kept or how entries should be made or transactions or figures recorded. There was no question of the book or record handling of the facts and figures involved in the City's tax claims. The facts were all fixed and the only question was what view the tax authorities and ultimately the courts would take as to the years in which the payment of the City's tax claims would be deductible for federal tax purposes. In short, legal advice was sought and given on a question of law.

That question was put to respondent not even in connection with the preparation of a tax return but for the purpose of determining whether the City's tax claims should be compromised. What the Croft Company proposed to do in reference to the disposition of those claims depended upon the advice it received as to law applicable to the proposed settlement if made. The question respondent undertook to answer was in nature a question of law, as is made all the more evident when one considers the research respondent undertook in the matter and the legal labyrinth into which any thorough research in the matter would lead.

We are told in behalf of respondent that the basis of the tax law is accounting and that the tax subject upon which respondent gave his advice is a matter of proper accounting practice. We are also told that the administration of the tax law in the Treasury Department and other agencies of government is mainly in the hands of accountants, and that taxation is a particular specialty of accountants in which they are more expert than lawyers.

Fortunately the tax law conforms largely with accepted principles of accounting, as most law conforms with business customs and practices. One need only thumb through the Internal Revenue Code relating to income taxes, however, or listen to the criticism leveled at the tax laws and decisions by some writers on accountancy, to note the many respects in which tax law is at variance with usual accounting principles. And it is certainly contrary to fact to view the advice which respondent gave in this case as following accounting principles. The Croft Company kept its books on an accrual basis and as an accounting matter would be expected to charge the City's tax claims against the years in which they accrued. Undoubtedly that is why the company's accountant advised that the income tax deductions for those claims would have to be taken in the years in which they accrued and could not be taken in 1943. Undoubtedly, also, that is why respondent, "as an accountant," said "No" to the question of the Croft Company's president as to whether the deduction could be taken in 1943. He undertook, nevertheless, and in his opinion successfully, to find a different answer in the "tax law."

An accountant may know more about the tax law than some law practitioners, just as a labor relations adviser, trust officer or customs broker may know more about the law relating to their businesses than many lawyers not specialists in the law relating to such business. A layman may know a lot of law about a particular subject, upon the knowledge of which he may rely at his own risk in his own business. He may not, however, set himself up as a public consultant on the law of his specialty. If the services of a specialist in some particular branch of the law are required, the public must still turn to the bar, for all the reasons of public protection for which the bar and bar standards are maintained. The law specialist offers more and much more is required of him for admission to practice than knowledge of his specialty. He must have a grounding in the law and a legal education and training, must pass examinations in the law and attain and maintain standards which are imposed by the bench and bar for the protection of the public.

The law includes many specialties, perhaps as diverse as specialties in medicine, but they are all related and integrated in the common body of the law, much the same as specialties in medicine are linked in the whole body of medicine. One might become informed, and even expert, in some narrow specialty of medicine without the general training, preparation and experience required for admission to practice medicine. Yet we know that only the generally trained doctor, grounded in medicine as a whole, has the understanding requisite to practice medicine in any of its branches, albeit the laboratories, so intimately and vitally connected with medical service, are staffed by technicians who are not medical doctors.

Similarly, the law specialist should be trained and grounded in the law. A thorough knowledge and understanding of basic legal concepts, legal processes and the interrelation of the law in its parts are quite essential to the practice of law in any of its branches. Technicians are needed to serve in bureaus and agencies and in numerous non-legal capacities, but the counsellor licensed and trusted to advise the public with respect to the law must be a duly qualified and admitted lawyer. We are unable, therefore, to regard the admission of accountants, subject to certain qualifications and regulations of the Treasury Department and the Tax Court, to practice before those agencies, as an authorization to accountants to practice tax law at large or as an eradication of the distinction between the lawyer's and the accountant's function in the tax field.

It is much too narrow a view, and one revealing inadequate perception, to regard the tax law as mainly a matter of accounting. More than most specialties in the law, tax law is drawn from and involved with many branches of law. It bridges and is intimately connected, for example, with corporation law, partnership law, property law, the law of sales, trusts and frequently constitutional law. Quite obviously, one trained only in accounting, regardless of specific tax knowledge, does not have the orientation even in tax law to qualify as a tax lawyer. Equally obviously, as a matter of administration, he may not practice any phase of tax law, regardless of what might be his subjective qualifications for the particular undertaking. Inquiry cannot be made in each case as to whether the particular accountant or accountants generally are sufficiently familiar with the law on a particular tax question to be qualified to answer it. An objective line must be drawn, and the point at which it must be drawn, at very least, is where the accountant or non-lawyer undertakes to pass upon a legal question apart from the regular pursuit of his calling.

Respondent concedes that an accountant may not practice law. He is obliged, therefore, in support of his claimed freedom of action in the tax field, to resort to nomenclature which eliminates the word and concept of "law" from the tax area. The excellent brief in behalf of respondent, always employing the word "taxation" instead of "tax law," presents "taxation" as something sui generis and apart from law. The negation of taxation as law is made complete by presenting the question upon which respondent passed in this case, after studying a score or more of the hundreds of cases on the subject, as a question of "tax accounting" and as such a question of fact and not a question of law.

May the accountant then handle any tax problem and as a "tax consultant" entertain any tax question? Respondent appreciates his involvement and though denying taxation as law recognizes that frequently taxation is involved with law. Seeking to square his position with that fact and to allow for it, respondent states that not included in "income tax advice" by accountants is advice as to collateral questions of general law upon which tax liability may on occasions depend, such as domicile or the validity of a marriage, which questions may be conceded to lie within the exclusive competence of the lawyer. The concession is only a nod at reality, not a full facing of the fact. Taxation, which permeates almost every phase of modern life, is so inextricably interwoven with nearly every branch of law that one could hardly pick any tax *problem* and say this is a question of pure taxation or pure tax law wholly unconnected with other legal principles, incidents or ramifications.

This does not mean, of course, that many or most questions which may arise in preparing a tax return may not be answered by an accountant handling such work. But if the question is such a problem that an outside consultant, besides the regular accountant preparing the tax return, must be called in to do legal research of the kind which was necessary in this case and to advise as to the none too clear, if not obscure, law, that consultant must be a lawyer.

When such problems arise who is to say how much "general" law is involved? Essential to the solution of any problem is recognizing

APPENDIX 409

all the elements of the problem. It is a fair question whether respondent recognized all the elements in this case. Will anyone but the generally trained lawyer be competent to analyze difficult tax problems, which are beyond the regular accountant's ken, and be able to say what other law besides tax law is involved? And when confronted with any question of whether an accountant, acting as a tax consultant, is practicing law, are we to decide it upon the basis of determining whether any law besides tax law is involved in the matter upon which he was consulted?

Any attempt at such delineation and control would be wholly impractical. We must either admit frankly that taxation is a hybrid of law and accounting and, as a matter of practical administration, permit accountants to practice tax law, or, also as a matter of practical administration, while allowing the accountant jurisdiction of incidental questions of law which may arise in connection with auditing books or preparing tax returns, deny him the right as a consultant to give legal advice. We are of the opinion that the latter alternative accords to the accountant all necessary and desirable latitude and that nothing less would accord to the public the protection that is necessary when it seeks legal advice.

Respondent is most persuasive when he challenges the consistency of recognizing an accountant's right to prepare income tax returns while denying him the right to give income tax advice. As respondent says, precisely the same question may at one time arise during the preparation of an income tax return and at another time serve as the subject of a request for advice by a client. The difference is that in the one case the accountant is dealing with a question of law which is only incidental to preparing a tax return and in the other case he is addressing himself to a question of law alone.

The preparation of an income tax return is not primarily a matter of law and generally and mainly is not a matter of law. It may usually be prepared by one having no legal knowledge, from instructions prepared for lay consumption, or by one having only incidental legal knowledge. A taxpayer should not be required, therefore, and is not required, to go to a lawyer to have a tax return prepared. It is a practical, reasonable and proper accommodation to business men and the accounting profession not only to permit accountants to prepare tax returns but to permit them, despite the risks involved, to assume jurisdiction of the incidental legal questions that may arise in connection with preparing tax returns. It is quite another thing to say that apart from preparing a tax return and from doing the accounting work in connection with the return, an accountant should be permitted as an independent consultant to pass upon specific questions which are questions of law, especially when the occasion for such consultation is apt to be, as it was in this case, a particularly knotty question of law. The distinction is altogether valid and desirable. The law here, as elsewhere, is a rational and practical adjustment of conflicting interests, objectively calculated to be of the greatest public benefit.

Respondent, therefore properly, makes an appeal of public interest, under the heading: "The public would be materially inconvenienced if accountants were ousted from the income tax field." His brief states that a decision adverse to respondent would prevent accountants from continuing to act as advisers in the income tax field and would give the legal profession a monopoly in this field. The consequent inconvenience to the public is illustrated with the observation that larger corporate taxpayers can afford to retain both lawyers and accountants on a regular basis, but that it would be unreasonable to expect the average small taxpayer to do so or to bear the expense of a lawyer's education in tax accounting and administration. The argument bears analysis.

We have heard no proposal that accountants be ousted from the income tax field. It is precisely out of consideration of the interests which respondent emphasizes, that a taxpayer may, if he wishes, leave the entire preparation of the tax return to his accountant, legal incidents included, without the necessity of engaging a lawyer. It may and probably will remain true, as respondent quotes the American Bar Association as noting, that the bulk of income tax work is not handled by lawyers. When, however, a taxpayer is confronted with a tax question so involved and difficult that it must go beyond its regular accountant and seek outside tax law advice, the considerations of convenience and economy in favor of letting its accountant handle the matter no longer apply, and considerations of public protection require that such advice be sought from a qualified lawyer. At that point, at least, the line must be drawn. The line does not impinge upon any of the business or public interests which respondent cites or oust the accountant from the tax field or prejudice him in any way in the pursuit of his profession or create any monopoly in the tax field in favor of the legal profession. It allows the accountant maximum freedom of action within the field which might be called "tax accounting" and is the minimum of control necessary to give the public protection when it seeks advice as to tax law.

The order appealed from should be reversed, respondent adjudged in contempt and fined $50 and an injunction as prayed for issued.

Order reversed, respondent adjudged in contempt and fined $50, and an injunction as prayed for issued. Settle order on notice.

DORE, COHN, and CALLAHAN, JJ., concur.

GLENNON, J., dissents and votes to affirm.

Gardner v. Conway
Supreme Court of Minnesota
48 N.W. 2d 788 (1951)

MATSON, Justice.

Defendant appeals from an order denying his motion for a new trial.

This action, to have the defendant perpetually *enjoined* from further engaging in the unauthorized practice of law and to have him *adjudged in contempt* of court therefor, was brought by the plaintiffs[1] in their own behalf as licensed lawyers and in a representative capacity in behalf of every other licensed lawyer in Minnesota, as well as in behalf of the courts and the public.[2]

Defendant, who is possessed of only a grade-school education, has never been admitted to the practice of law in Minnesota or elsewhere. During a two-year period immediately prior to the time of trial, he followed the occupation of a public accountant. Prior thereto, he served for three years as a United States deputy collector of internal revenue. Before that, he had worked for six years as the credit manager of a hardware company, about five years as the operator of a collection agency, and for four years as an insurance solicitor and risk inspector.

At and prior to the time with which we are concerned, defendant held himself out to the public by newspaper advertisements and by other advertising media as an "Income Tax Expert," duly qualified to give advice, aid, and assistance to the public generally in the discharge

---

1. Plaintiffs are the members of a committee on the unauthorized and illegal practice of law, which is a subcommittee of the Committee on Practice of Law of the Ramsey County Bar Association.

2. As *amici curiae* the following organizations have filed briefs with the court: Minnesota Association of Public Accountants, National Society of Public Accountants, Minnesota Society of Certified Public Accountants, American Institute of Accountants, Minnesota State Bar Association, and the American Bar Association.

of a taxpayer's duty to make accurate returns of income to the federal government. Defendant alleges that he is thoroughly familiar with income tax rules and regulations. He has used a business card on which he describes himself as a "Tax Consultant" and prominently calls attention thereon to the fact that he was a former deputy collector of internal revenue.

On or about March 4, 1948, Cecil G. Germain, a private investigator employed by plaintiffs to obtain information as to whether defendant was engaged in the practice of law, went to the office of defendant under the assumed name and identity of an alleged taxpayer, George Heinl. Germain, as George Heinl, informed defendant that he operated a truck farm, that he had come to have his income tax return prepared, and that he needed help with certain questions. For a cash consideration, defendant prepared the income tax return and gave Germain professional advice for the determination of the following questions:

(a) Whether the taxpayer, who himself had exclusive control of the operation of the truck farm, was in partnership with his wife, who had contributed one-half of the purchase price, who helped with the work, and who received one-half the profits.

(b) Whether the taxpayer was entitled to claim his wife as an exemption,. since he had never been ceremonially married, though maintaining a common-law marriage status.

(c) Whether the taxpayer should file his separate return and advise his so-called common-law wife to file a separate return.

(d) Whether certain money expended on improvements of buildings on the truck farm was deductible from his earnings.

(e) Whether a certain produce loss sustained by frost and subsequent flood was a deductible item.

Aside from the fundamental issue of whether defendant's activities constituted the unauthorized practice of law, we are concerned with these procedural issues:

1. Does the *district court* have the power to adjudge defendant in contempt of court and to punish him for the unauthorized practice of law?

2. Does the district court have jurisdiction to enjoin the unauthorized practice of law where defendant's acts of purported law practice did not involve any act or appearance before said court?

3. Is a justiciable issue presented when the evidentiary base of an action to enjoin the unauthorized practice of law consists primarily of professional acts of advice and service which were furnished for a

consideration to a person who was not a bona fide taxpayer, upon a fabricated and hypothetical state of facts, and in connection with the preparation of an income tax return which was never intended to be filed? . . .

4. Does a justiciable issue arise when the purported acts of unauthorized practice of law were intentionally performed by defendant upon the mistaken assumption that he was then advising a bona fide taxpayer and was preparing for him a tax return for use in reporting an actual taxpayer's income?

[Discussion of procedural issues, which were decided against the defendant, omitted.]

5. Was defendant, however, practicing law when, as a preliminary to and as part of his preparation of an income tax return he advised the purported taxpayer as to whether he had acquired a partnership status, a valid marriage for exemption purposes, whether he should file a joint return with a woman to whom he had never been ceremonially married, and whether certain building and truck farm improvements, as well as certain losses sustained by frost and subsequent flood, were deductible items?

Much of what is law practice is conducted outside the courtroom, and as to that field of activity we have said: "* * * The line between what is and what is not the practice of law cannot be drawn with precision. Lawyers should be the first to recognize that between the two there is a region wherein much of what lawyers do every day in their practice may also be done by others without wrongful invasion of the lawyers' field." Cowern v. Nelson, 207 Minn. 642, 646, 290 N.W. 795, 797.

Although it is difficult to draw any precise dividing line, the task is ours to find some criterion for distinguishing that which is from that which is not law practice. The development of any practical criterion, as well as its subsequent application, must be closely related to the purpose for which lawyers are licensed as the exclusive occupants of their field. That purpose is to protect the public from the intolerable evils which are brought upon people by those who assume to practice law without having the proper qualifications. See, 29 Mich.L.Rev. 989. The need for public protection is not of new origin. As early as 1292, the problem was recognized when Edward I, by royal ordinance, limited the number of attorneys and directed his justices "to provide for every county a sufficient number of attornies and apprentices from among the best, the most lawful and the most teachable, so *that king and people might be well served.*" (Italics supplied.) 1 Pollock and Maitland, History of English Law, p. 194. See Herbert, Antiquities of the Inns of Court and Chancery, pp. 166, 167. The limitation and selection of lawyers, without strict regulation, proved inadequate.

"* * * The evil finally became so great that in the year 1402 Parliament this time took cognizance of it and enacted the now famous statute, 4 Henry IV, Ch. 18, which provided that all attorneys should be examined by the justices, and in their discretion, only those found to be good and virtuous, and of good fame, learned and sworn to do their duty, be allowed to be put upon the roll and all others put out." Rhode Island Bar Ass'n v. Automobile Service Ass'n, 55 R.I. 122, 133, 179 A. 139, 144, 100 A.L.R. 226. These early English statutes illustrate that a licensed bar subject to the supervision of the courts originated with a public demand for the exclusion of those who assumed to practice without being qualified therefor.

6. The protection of the public, as the purpose of confining law practice to a licensed bar, ancient as it is in its origin, is of vital importance today. . . . Any criterion for distinguishing law practice from that which belongs to other fields can be properly geared to the public welfare only if we keep in mind the manner in which the licensing of lawyers serves its purpose. The law practice franchise or privilege is based upon the threefold requirements of *ability, character*, and *responsible supervision*. The public welfare is safeguarded not merely by limiting law practice to individuals who are possessed of the requisite ability and character, but also by the further requirement that such practitioners shall thenceforth be officers of the court and subject to its supervision. See, 40 Dickinson L.Rev. 225, 229. In consequence, lawyers are not merely bound by a high code of professional ethics, but as officers of the court they are subject to its inherent supervisory jurisdiction, which embraces the power to remove from the profession those practitioners who are unfaithful or incompetent in the discharge of their trust. . . . This is in itself an important reason why law practice should be confined to members of the bar. Protection of the public is set at naught if laymen who are not subject to court supervision are permitted to practice law. Although professional standards for safeguarding the public interest must be sufficiently flexible to allow for adaptation to changes in conditions, they must in any event be of such stability and permanence as to protect the individual practitioner in the enjoyment of his professional franchise; otherwise men of ability and character will find no inducement to undergo the years of training necessary to qualify them as lawyers. This principle, as a

part of the public weal, is applicable to any profession which demands of its members high skill and proficiency based upon years of intensive preparatory training. . . .

7. If we bear in mind that any choice of criterion must find its ultimate justification in the interest of the public and not in that of advantage for either lawyer or nonlawyer, we soon cease to look for an answer in any rule of thumb such as that based upon a distinction between the incidental and the primary. . . . Any rule which holds that a layman who prepares legal papers or furnishes other services of a legal nature is not practicing law when such services are incidental to another business or profession completely ignores the public welfare. A service performed by one individual for another, even though it be incidental to some other occupation, may entail a difficult question of law which requires a determination by a trained legal mind. See, 33 Minn.L.Rev. 445. Are we to say that a real estate broker who examines an abstract of title and furnishes an opinion thereon may not be held to practice law merely because the examination of a title is ancillary to a sale and purchase of real estate? Can we say that a lawyer employed to bring a suit for damages for personal injuries is competent to diagnose the nature of his client's injuries and that he is not practicing medicine merely because such diagnosis is incidental to a proper presentation of his client's case? The drawing of a simple instrument or the application of an elementary legal principle is one thing in the incidental classification, but it is wholly another when such incidental act or service requires professional skill. The incidental test has no value except in the negative sense that if the furnishing of the legal service is the primary business of the actor such activity is the practice of law, even though such service is of an elementary nature. In other words, a layman's legal service activities are the practice of law unless they are incidental to his regular calling; but the mere fact that they are incidental is by no means decisive. In a positive sense, the incidental test ignores the interest of the public as the controlling determinant.

8-9. In rejecting the incidental test, it follows that the distinction between law practice and that which is not may be determined only from a consideration of the nature of the acts of service performed in each case. No difficulty arises where such service is the primary business of the actor. We then have law practice. Difficulty comes, however, when the service furnished is incidental to the performance of other service of a nonlegal character in the pursuit of another calling such as that of accounting. In the field of income taxation, as in the instant case, we have an overlapping of both law and accounting. An accountant must adapt his accounting skill to the requirements of tax law, and therefore he must have a workable knowledge of law as applied to his field. By the same token, a lawyer must have some understanding of accounting. In the income tax area, they occupy much common ground where the skills of both professions may be required and where it is difficult to draw a precise line to separate their respective functions. The public interest does not permit an obliteration of all lines of demarcation. We cannot escape reality by hiding behind a facade of nomenclature and assume that "taxation," though composed of both law and accounting is something *sui generis* and apart from the law. See, Matter of New York County Lawyers Ass'n (Bercu) 273 App.Div. 524, 78 N.Y.S.2d 209, affirmed, 299 N.Y. 728, 87 N.E.2d 451. If taxation is a hybrid of law and accounting, it does not follow that it is so wholly without the law that its legal activities may be pursued without proper qualifications and without court supervision. The interest of the public is not protected by the narrow specialization of an individual who lacks the perspective and the orientation which comes only from a thorough knowledge and understanding of basic legal concepts, of legal processes, and of the interrelation of the law in all its branches. Generally speaking, whenever, as incidental to another transaction or calling, a layman, as part of his regular course of conduct, resolves legal questions for another—at the latter's request and for a consideration—by giving him advice or by taking action for and in his behalf, he is practicing law if difficult or doubtful legal questions are involved which, to safeguard the public, reasonably demand the application of a trained legal mind. What is a difficult or doubtful question of law is not to be measured by the comprehension of a trained legal mind, but by the understanding thereof which is possessed by a reasonably intelligent layman who is reasonably familiar with similar transactions. A criterion which designates the determination of a difficult or complex question of law as law practice, and the application of an elementary or simple legal principle as not, may indeed be criticized for uncertainty if a rule of thumb is sought which can be applied with mechanical precision to all cases. Any rule of law which purports to reflect the needs of the public welfare in a changing society, by reason of its essential and inherent flexibility, will, however, be as variable in operation as the particular facts to which it is applied.

10-11-12. In restraining laymen from improper activity, *the difficult question of law criterion* is to be applied in a common-sense way which will protect primarily the interest of the public and not hamper or burden that interest with impractical and technical restrictions which have no reasonable justification. . . . We are therefore not concerned with a technical application which would ban the giving of any and all legal advice or the taking of any and all action for another.[3] Whether a difficult or doubtful question of law is resolved by the giving of advice to, or the doing of an act for, another must in each case depend upon the nature of the problem involved. As ancillary to the closing of a real estate transaction, a real estate broker may draw the ordinary instruments of conveyance. . . . No layman, however, except when dire emergency prevents the calling of a lawyer, may draw another's will. . . . As applied to the preparation of income tax returns, it has been well said: "* * * Federal income taxation is founded on statute, elaborated and interpreted by administrative regulations and rulings, and construed by court decisions. Matters in this field, as in other statutory subjects, will at times involve difficult questions of interpretation of statute or court decision, and the validity of regulations or statute; they will also involve doubtful questions of nontax law on which the tax issues may depend, and questions of liability for criminal or civil penalties or of statutes of limitation or of liability as transferee for the taxes of another. Such questions, in general, are the kind for which lawyers are equipped by training and practice." [4]

When an accountant or other layman who is employed to prepare an income tax return is faced with difficult or doubtful questions of the interpretation or application of statutes, administrative regulations and rulings, court decisions, or general law, it is his duty to leave the determination of such questions to a lawyer. In so holding that the determination of difficult or doubtful questions is the practice of law, it does not follow that the entire income tax field has been preempted by lawyers to the exclusion of accountants. The work of an accountant disassociated from the resolving of difficult or doubtful questions of law is not law practice. See, Opinion of the Justices, 289 Mass. 607, 615, 194 N.E. 313, 318. In the determination of income—

---

3. " 'Giving any legal advice' would include telling a man whether it is lawful to write 'Please do not open until Christmas' on a parcel post package. 'Any action taken for others in any matter connected with the law' would include parking a man's automobile for him parallel to the curb not over six inches from it." 19 American Bar Assn. Journal 652.

4. Maurice Austin, Relations Between Lawyers and Certified Public Accountants in Income Tax Practice (1951), 36 Iowa L.Rev. 227, 228.

the subject of taxation—difficult accounting problems may arise by presenting "such aspects as inventory pricing methods (last-in-first-out, first-in-first-out, retail method, cost determination, actual costs, standard costs, cost of in-process merchandise, market price valuation, etc.), accrual and installment accounting, carryover and carryback of net operating losses, depreciation, depletion and corporate distributions. The taxation of such income may involve such concepts as consolidated returns, taxable years of less than twelve months, invested capital, etc. All of these are concepts of accounting, * * *." 36 Iowa L.Rev. 227, 229.

Where difficult accounting questions arise, the careful lawyer will naturally advise his client to enlist the aid of an accountant. In the income tax field, the lawyer and the accountant each has a function to perform in the interest of the public.

13. In the instant case, the evidence sustains the trial court's findings and conclusions that defendant was engaged in the practice of law. For a consideration, and as part of his regular income tax work, defendant advised and determined for the taxpayer whether the latter had attained the status of a lawful marriage with a woman with whom he had been living but to whom he had never been ceremonially married. He further gave advice as to whether such taxpayer and his consort should file separate or joint returns. The purported taxpayer was likewise uncertain as to whether he occupied the status of a partner with his so-called common-law wife in the operation of a truck farm, over which he himself exercised exclusive control but in which the latter shared equally in the labor, investment, and profit. This question, the answer to which obviously required legal training, he also resolved. We do not here have the case of a taxpayer whose legal status was established or known beforehand. In addition, defendant gave advice as to the deductions which the taxpayer might claim for certain farm improvements and for certain produce loss by frost and subsequent flood. Although the preparation of the income tax return was not of itself the practice of law, defendant, incidental to such preparation, resolved certain difficult legal questions which, taken as a whole, constituted the practice of law.

14. In further confirmation of the conclusion that defendant was practicing law, the evidence establishes that he advertised and held himself out as a "Tax Consultant," which by reasonable implication advised the public that he was competent to give legal advice on the law of taxation. A layman, whether he is or is not an accountant, may not hold himself out to the public as a tax consultant or a tax expert,

or describe himself by any similar phrase which implies that he has a knowledge of tax law. It should be noted that lawyers, by the canons of ethics of the American Bar Association and the opinions thereto pertaining, are likewise prohibited from advertising any special branch of law practice. Canons of Professional and Judicial Ethics, American Bar Association, Canons 27 and 45, and see Opinion 260.

The order of the trial court is affirmed.

Affirmed.

Agran v. Shapiro
Appellate Department, Superior Court, California
273 Pac. 2d 619 (1954)

PATROSSO, Judge.

Plaintiff instituted this action to recover the sum of $2,000 for what his complaint denominates as "accounting services" rendered to the defendants, and from a resulting judgment in favor of the plaintiff for the amount sued for, defendants appeal.

Plaintiff is a certified public accountant practicing his profession in the city of Los Angeles, and admitted to practice as an agent before the Treasury Department of the United States. He is not, however, a member of the bar, and the question presented is whether the services in question or some portion thereof constitute the practice of law and for which he is not entitled to recover. The evidence discloses that in 1948 plaintiff was retained by the defendants as an accountant and auditor for a corporation, Motor Sales of California, Inc., which was owned or controlled by them, and also for the preparation of defendants' individual income tax returns. We are not concerned with the services rendered by plaintiff to the corporation, but only with those performed for the defendants as individuals. These consisted of the preparation of their Federal income tax returns for each of the years 1947 to 1950, inclusive, as well as their estimated return for 1951 and other services related thereto as hereinafter set forth.

In the preparation of the joint return of the defendants for the calendar year 1948 plaintiff claimed as a deduction a loss in the sum of $43,260.56, which was incurred in this manner: defendants were the owners of a building in the city of Los Angeles which, under date of July 19, 1946, they had leased to one Pritchard, a dealer in used automobiles, for a fixed rental of $1,500 per month, plus 5 per cent of the net profits from lessee's operations in the demised premises. This lease, on November 5, 1947, was amended or superseded by a new agreement under which the rental to be paid was $1,500 per month, plus 5 per cent of the profits from lessee's operations upon the demised premises, as well as of the profits derived from four other used-car lots operated by the lessee at other locations, in consideration of which defendants agreed with the lessee that they would, and did, guarantee the Bank of America against loss upon all "used cars financed by and contracts discounted with the" bank by the lessee. As part of this agreement the defendants agreed to, and did, deposit with the bank the sum of $115,000 in cash to secure their guaranty. The lessee thereafter became financially embarrassed, with the result that on December 14, 1947 the bank foreclosed against the lessee, and defendants' deposit was retained by it to cover any losses which it might sustain as the result of the bank's transactions with the lessee, and as of December 31, 1948 the bank had charged defendants' deposit with losses totalling the sum of $43,260.56, the amount claimed as a deduction in the 1948 return, as previously stated.

Following the preparation by plaintiff of the defendants' 1948 return, the exact date not appearing, plaintiff prepared and filed on behalf of each defendant a separate "application for a tentative carry-back adjustment" [§ 3780, 1939 Code; § 6411, 1954 Code] of the excess loss shown by the 1948 return ($29,074.83) to the two preceding years, 1946 and 1947. The allowance of the adjustment requested in this application, if granted by the Commissioner of Internal Revenue, would have the effect of extinguishing defendants' tax liability for the years 1946 and 1947 and as a result each of the defendants would be entitled to a refund (which they therein claimed) of the taxes paid for said preceding two years, in the total sum of $1,804.65. While the record is somewhat obscure on this point, it appears inferentially at least that such applications were granted and each of the defendants received a refund in the amount stated.

For the preparation of the 1947 return plaintiff charged and was paid the sum of $30. Plaintiff, however, submitted no statement to the defendants for the preparation of the returns for the years subsequent to 1947 except insofar as a charge for such services may be included in the bill which he submitted to the defendants under date of March 31, 1952, to which reference will hereinafter be made. In explanation of this plaintiff testified that early in 1949 he advised the defendants "that he could not state what his fee at that time would be because as a matter of ordinary practice in the Bureau of Internal

Revenue all tentative tax refund claims and income tax returns related thereto would be audited and investigated within three years from the date thereof by a revenue agent from said bureau, and therefore plaintiff would not be able to fix his accounting fee now but would charge defendants at a latter date for the time and work involved in preparing said tax returns, refund claim, subsequent returns related thereto and in conferring and discussing said problem regarding this net operating business loss with revenue agent, and also would base said fee on any tax savings accomplished thereby." It does not appear that plaintiff performed any services in connection with income tax matters for the defendants other than as stated, and seemingly no "problem" arose in connection with any of the previous returns until August, 1951, at which time he received a call from Mr. Manson, a treasury agent, in regard to the 1949 return, in which there had been claimed as a deduction the unused portion ($7,776.01) of the Pritchard loss sustained, as hereinbefore stated, in 1948. Several meetings were held between plaintiff and Mr. Manson, in the course of which the latter stated that the so-called Pritchard loss did not qualify as a "net operating loss" and that as a result in re-computing the returns for 1946 to 1949, inclusive, the defendants were subject to an additional assessment in the sum of $15,000. Plantiff disputed this contention of Mr. Manson, countering with the claim that the loss was a "net operating loss," which could be "carried back" and "that tax benefits and refunds could be secured for the years 1946 through 1950." Plaintiff further testified that in his several conferences with Mr. Manson he "cited him numerous cases" and "spent five days in the county law library and in his office reading tax services, cases, reports and decisions." Again he testified that "he spent approximately four days in reading and reviewing over one hundred cases on the proposition of law involved." As a final result of the conferences between himself and plaintiff, Mr. Manson stated that he would submit a report recommending an additional assessment of $6,280, and such report was thereafter filed by him. At a later date another treasury agent, Mr. Stewart, was assigned to the case, with whom plaintiff met upon at least one occasion and had at least two telephone conferences. Following these conferences plaintiff was advised by Mr. Stewart that he was in agreement with plaintiff's contention but that he "wanted to talk to the defendant once more"; Mr. Stewart further stating that the assessment would be reduced from $6,280 as recommended by Mr. Manson to $200, which latter amount would be assessed because of certain errors in the return unrelated to the matter of the loss in question. Some time later, in January or February, 1952, plaintiff was advised by Mr. Shapiro that he no longer needed plaintiff's services, and at the same time was advised that Mr. Shapiro had signed an agreement with Mr. Stewart closing the matter. Following this, and under date of March 31, 1952, plaintiff submitted a bill to the defendants in the sum of $2,000 which reads as follows:

> To Professional Services Rendered:—Conferences with revenue agent Edgar Manson re his examination of the income tax returns of Morris and Helen Shapiro for the years 1946, 1947, 1948 and 1949.
>
> Research of the problems involved and preparation of arguments to overcome the following proposed assessments of income tax:
>
> | 1946 and 1947 | Morris | $1,804.65 |
> | | Helen | 1,804.65 |
> | 1949 | | 2,671.29 |
> | Total Proposed Assessment | | $6,280.59 |
>
> Conference with conferee James A. Stewart and subsequent discussion of the questions involved by telephone, resulting in a reversal of all disputed items contained in revenue agent Manson's report.
>
> Report submitted by conferee James A. Stewart resulted in a tax saving in excess of $6,000.00 and was cleared to the Collector of Internal Revenue on February 5, 1952.
>
> Total due for services to date $2,000.00.

While courts have experienced difficulty in formulating a precise and all-embracing definition as to what constitutes the practice of law, the one generally accepted is that announced in Eley v. Miller, 7 Ind. App. 529, 535, 34 N.E. 836, 837, and adopted by our Supreme Court in People v. Merchants' Protective Corp., 1922, 189 Cal. 531, 535, 209 P. 363, 365, as follows:

> As the term is generally understood, the practice of the law is the doing and performing services in a court of justice, in any matter depending therein, throughout its various stages, and in conformity to the adopted rules of procedure. But *in a larger sense it includes legal advice and counsel, and the preparation of legal instruments and contracts by which legal rights are secured although such matter may or may not be depending in court.* (Emphasis added.)

... However, whether a particular activity falls within this general definition is frequently a question of considerable difficulty, and particularly is this true in the field of taxation where questions of law and accounting are frequently inextricably intermingled as a result of which doubt arises as to where the functions of one profession end and those of the other begin. Specifically, whether practice before an administrative tribunal in tax matters constitutes the practice of law has been the subject of decisions elsewhere which appear to be in some conflict. See cases collected in note 111 A.L.R. 32, 36, and authorities cited in Lowell Bar Ass'n v. Loeb, 1943, 315 Mass. 176, 183, 52 N.E.2d 27, 33. The question, under the circumstances here, is a particularly perplexing one, and we acknowledge the aid and assistance which has been afforded us in our efforts to resolve it by the excellent briefs filed by counsel as *amici curiae* on behalf on the State Bar of California and the California Society of Certified Public Accountants, respectively.

It appears to be generally conceded that it is within the proper function of a public accountant, although not a member of the bar, to prepare federal income tax returns, except perhaps in those instances where substantial questions of law arise which may competently be determined only by a lawyer. In the case at hand we find no real difficulty in concluding that in the preparation of the income tax returns in question plaintiff did not engage in the practice of law. They are of such a simple character that an ordinary layman without legal or accounting training might have prepared them in the first instance. An inspection thereof discloses that the defendants had but three sources of taxable income: Mr. Shapiro's salary, the rental received from the building leased to Mr. Pritchard, and the rental from a two-flat building, one-half of which was occupied by the defendants as their residence, with the exception of the year 1950 in which the defendants in addition received interest from savings and loan associations in the total sum of $612.68. Likewise the deductions claimed therein, other than the portion of the Pritchard loss carried forward into the 1949 return were usual and ordinary expenses incident to the ownership and operation of income producing real property, the determination of the propriety of which required no particular legal knowledge.

A different and more serious question arises, however, with respect to the services rendered by the plaintiff in preparing the applications for a carry back adjustment and refund of taxes paid for the previous two years, and the preparation of the 1949 return wherein a deduction was claimed for a portion of the Pritchard loss, as well as his subsequent services in resisting the additional assessment proposed by the Treasury Department upon the ground that the Pritchard loss did not constitute a "net operating loss" within the meaning of the "carry back" provisions of the statute. At this stage no question of accounting was involved. Neither the fact that the loss had been sustained nor the manner in which it arose was questioned. The only question was whether, under the admitted facts, the loss was one which could be "carried back," the answer to which depended upon whether or not it was a loss "attributable to the operation of a trade or business regularly carried on by the taxpayer" within the meaning of that phrase as used in [§ 122(d) (5), 1939 Code; § 172 (d), 1954 Code]. We see no escape from the conclusion that under the circumstances this question was purely one of law. A substantially similar question was presented in Wilson v. Eisner, 2 Cir., 1922, 282 F. 38, and the court, at page 41, says: "The question presented was whether the plaintiff was engaged in this enterprise as a business for profit or for pleasure. We think that on this proof, no question of fact was presented for submission to the jury. The undisputed proof made it a question of law for the court. Was the plaintiff carrying on a business within the meaning of the taxing act?" and continuing, 282 F. on page 42, the court said: "Since the facts and circumstances are admitted or undisputed, the question of whether the plaintiff was engaged in business for profit or pleasure became one for the court to decide, and it was error to leave the question of law to the determination of a jury * * *." . . . And in Commissioner of Internal Revenue v. Smith, 2 Cir., 1953, 203 F.2d 310, 311, . . . the court said: "Whether a particular loss or expense is incurred in a taxpayer's trade or business is a question of fact in each particular case. . . . But insofar as this determination involves interpretation of the statutory language, it raises an issue of law on which the Tax Court's decision is subject to review here. Washburn v. C. I. R., 8 Cir., 51 F.2d 949, 951."

Not only was the question which arose here one of law but a difficult and doubtful one as well, as evidenced by the many occasions upon which the courts and the Treasury Department have had occasion to consider it. . . . Moreover, it is evident that the plaintiff himself fully appreciated this. He not only testified that "in his opinion it was a tough case because it was an isolated one" but he detailed at length the extensive research of the legal authorities which he was required to make in order to support his position that the loss was one which qualified as a "net operating loss" under a proper interpretation of the statutory definition.

Both parties place reliance upon the decision in the Matter of New York County Lawyers Ass'n, 1948, 273 App.Div. 524, 78

N.Y.S.2d 209, 9 A.L.R.2d 787, commonly referred to as the Bercu case, which was affirmed without opinion in 299 N.Y. 728, 87 N.E.2d 451. There one Bercu, an accountant, not a member of the bar, was consulted by a corporation [which kept its books upon an accrual basis] as to whether or not certain sales taxes accrued but not paid in a preceding year could be deducted in the income tax return for a subsequent year. Thereafter he rendered an opinion to the effect that such taxes might be deducted in the year of their payment, for which services he submitted a bill for $500. This not being paid, he instituted suit in the municipal court and was denied recovery upon the ground that the services for which he sought payment constituted the practice of law. Thereafter the reported proceeding was instituted by the Lawyers' Association to have him adjudged guilty of contempt of court and to enjoin him from similar activities in the future. The court held that in undertaking to render an opinion upon the point in question Mr. Bercu was unlawfully undertaking to practice law. However, the court seems to have been influenced in reaching the conclusion which it did largely by reason of the fact that Mr. Bercu had not previously performed any accounting work for the corporation, nor was the advice given in connection with the preparation by him of an income tax return for the corporation. It must be admitted that, as contended by plaintiff here, the language of the opinion suggests that if Bercu had been the accountant of the corporation or engaged to prepare its income tax return, he might have advised it as he did in his opinion without subjecting himself to the charge of practicing law in so doing. In the course of the opinion it said, 78 N.Y.S. 2d 220, 9 A.L.R.2d 796:

> Respondent is most persuasive when he challenges the consistency of recognizing an accountant's right to prepare income tax returns while denying him the right to give income tax advice. As respondent says, precisely the same question may at one time arise during the preparation of an income tax return and at another time serve as the subject of a request for advice by a client. The difference is that in the one case the accountant is dealing with a question of law which is only incidental to preparing a tax return and in the other case he is addressing himself to a question of law alone.

Thus it would appear that the New York court adopts, as the criterion for determining whether advice relative to tax matters constitutes the practice of law, whether or not it is given as an incident to accounting work or in the preparation of tax returns. While for reasons hereinafter stated we are not prepared to accept the view to its fullest extent, we do not believe that the court necessarily entertained the view that, as plaintiff here contends, having prepared the return, an accountant who is not a member of the bar may thereafter undertake to advise his client with respect to difficult or doubtful legal questions arising therefrom or undertake to seek a refund, the right to which depends wholly upon the interpretation of the taxing statutes. No such question was there presented, and we are not prepared to accept the decision as holding that a non-lawyer may properly perform services such as those last enumerated.

We believe, however, that the criterion formulated by the New York court for determining whether a particular activity does or does not constitute the practice of law is unsatisfactory for the reasons well stated by the Supreme Court of Minnesota in Gardner v. Conway, 1951, 234 Minn. 468, 48 N.W.2d 788.

[Extensive quotation from Gardner v. Conway, reprinted at p. 411, omitted.]

We are confirmed in our conclusion that the activities of the plaintiff which we have detailed fall within the domain of the lawyer by a consideration of The Statement of Principles Relating to Practice in the Field of Federal Income Taxation, which was recommended by the National Conference of Lawyers and Certified Public Accountants and approved by The Council of the American Institute of Accountants May 8, 1951, wherein it is stated (par. 3, 6, 8):

[Quotation from 1951 Statement of National Conference of Lawyers and Certified Public Accountants, reprinted at p. 373, omitted.]

From what has been said, it appears that plaintiff undertook to determine the "tax effect" of defendant's transaction with Pritchard, the ascertainment of which involved uncertainties both as to the interpretation of the taxing statute as well as the application thereof to the transaction in question. It is likewise evident from the plaintiff's testimony that at the time of preparing the application for carry back adjustment and refund he realized that a "controversial legal issue" was involved with respect to which the Treasury Department might take a contrary view, for he assigned this as a reason why he could not then advise defendants as to what his fee in the matter would be. And when he finally submits his bill we find that, in detailing therein the services covered thereby, no mention is made of accounting work or that involved in the preparation of the returns, but rather he describes the same as consisting of "conferences with revenue agent(s)" and *"research of the problems involved and preparation of arguments to overcome"* the proposed additional assessments, the only basis for which could be the Treasury Department's claim that the Pritchard loss did not constitute a "net operating loss" under [§122, 1939 Code; § 172, 1954 Code]. Surely the solution of this "problem" did not involve or depend upon the application of accounting principles or procedure, but of legal principles and precedents. These were the subject of plaintiff's "research" and these alone could serve as the foundation for his "arguments" addressed to the representatives of the Treasury Department in resisting the "proposed assessments."

From what has been said, we would have but little hesitancy in concluding that the services rendered by plaintiff other than those involved in the preparation of the income tax returns and possibly others of an accounting character constitute the practice of law as that term has been judicially defined in this State. Kountz v. Rowlands, 1943, 46 Pa.Dist. & Co. 461, 463. The more serious questions which present themselves, however, are (1) whether the controlling test of what constitutes the practice of law in the field of federal income taxation is dictated by federal legislation, congressional or administrative, and (2) the effect of the federal regulations which have been adopted in this field. Upon behalf of the plaintiff, it is urged by *amicus curiae* that an affirmative answer is required to the first inquiry and that, inasmuch as plaintiff was enrolled as an agent in the Treasury Department, and by virtue thereof licensed to practice before that Department, all of his activities in the instant case were within the scope of such license, and any action by a state court which would interfere with or curtail the right so granted is not only unwarranted but unconstitutional.

By the Act of July 7, 1884, sec. 3, 23 Stats. 258, 5 U.S.C.A. § 261, the Secretary of the Treasury is authorized to prescribe "regulations governing the recognition of agents * * * representing claimants before his departments * * *." Pursuant to this statutory authority, the Secretary issued Circular 230, which insofar as material here reads as follows:

[Quotations from what is now § 10.39 and § 10.2(b) of Treasury Circular, reprinted supra at p. 354 and p. 343, omitted.]

In this connection also, reference should be made to Rule 2 of the ... Tax Court of the United States, for the admission to practice, after examination, of citizens without restriction to members of the bar or certified public accountants, and the validity of such rule has been recognized. Goldsmith v. U.S. Board of Tax Appeals, 1926, 270 U.S. 117; Crane-Johnson Co. v. Commissioner of Internal Revenue,

8 Cir., 1939, 105 F.2d 740, 744. In the latter case, however, the court expressly stated that it did not undertake "to determine the question as to whether the appearance before the Board [of Tax Appeals] by a certified public accountant constituted the unlawful practice of law in the District of Columbia." With this particular question, however, we are not here concerned.

No case which we have been able to discover has undertaken to directly decide the precise question with which we are confronted, namely, whether the Treasury Regulations referred to have the effect of declaring that services performed by an enrolled agent in connection with federal income tax matters do not constitute the practice of law in the sense that such practice is prohibited, by state law, when engaged in by other than members of the bar. We direct our attention, however, to such as have been cited as having a more or less bearing upon the question.

The first is Brooks v. Mandel-Witte Co., 2 Cir., 1932, 54 F.2d 992, 993. There the defendant, an importing concern, entered into a contract with one Stern, a customs house broker—not a member of the bar—to make, file and prosecute protests and appeals, and "to retain counsel" at his (Stern's) expense, to secure the allowance of refunds of custom duties, upon a contingent fee of one-third of all amounts refunded. Pursuant to this contract, Stern engaged plaintiff, an attorney at law, to institute and prosecute the necessary proceedings in the United States Customs Court, upon an agreement to pay plaintiff a portion of his contingent fee. The proceedings resulted in the recovery of a substantial sum for the defendant, and the plaintiff, not having received payment of his fee, instituted suit to enforce an attorney's lien, as provided by the New York statute, against the fund. The defense interposed was two-fold: (1) that, inasmuch as, under the rules of the Customs Court, admission to the bar was not required as a prerequisite to practice therein, the services rendered by plaintiff were not legal, and hence no lien existed; and (2) that if the services rendered by plaintiff constituted the practice of law, he was barred from recovery by virtue of a statute of the state which made it unlawful for one " 'to make it a business to solicit employment for a lawyer, or to furnish attorneys or counsel or an attorney and counsel to render legal services, * * * without having first been duly and regularly licensed and admitted to practice law in the courts of record of this state.' " The majority held (1) that although the services rendered by plaintiff were such as, under the rules of the Customs Court, might lawfully be performed by a layman, the plaintiff nonetheless was entitled to an "attorney's lien," and (2) that the statute referred to, which prohibited laymen from soliciting employment for a lawyer or furnish an attorney to render legal services, was inapplicable because the Customs Court permitted custom house brokers to practice and appear before it. It was in connection with this last holding that the majority used the language relied upon by plaintiff, that "The state statute could not prohibit this" (practice by laymen before that court). Not only does Byrne v. Kansas City, etc., Ry. Co., C.C., 55 F. 44, cited in support of this statement, fail to sustain it, but the incongruity of the reasoning employed and the result reached by the majority is evident and is tersely pointed out in one sentence by Judge Learned Hand in his dissent. He says, 54 F.2d at page 996: "Either the services were not those of an attorney at law, and there was no lien; or the agreement was unlawful, and there was no pay." Under the circumstances, we attach little weight to this case.

More closely in point and supporting plaintiff's position is De Pass v. B. Harris Wool Co., 1940, 346 Mo. 1038, 144 S.W.2d 146, wherein plaintiff, a non-lawyer licensed to practice before the Interstate Commerce Commission, sought to recover for services rendered before that body in certain rate reduction cases on behalf of the defendant. Defendant demurred upon the ground that the alleged contract called for services which, under the law of Missouri, constituted the practice of law, and hence plaintiff was barred from recovery. The Supreme Court of Missouri, though apparently of the view that, judged by Missouri law, the services in question constituted the practice of law, held that the question was foreclosed by the Rules of Practice of the Interstate Commerce Commission, 49 U.S.C.A. Appendix following sec. 1185, which permitted laymen licensed by it to practice before it. Says the court, 144 S.W.2d at page 148: "Defendant seems to argue that the right to define the practice of law and to regulate persons engaging in such practice falls within the police power of the state. So it does, except in so far as that right does not run contra to an Act 'made in pursuance' to the Federal constitution."

It does not appear, however, that the rule of the Interstate Commission there involved contained any limitation with respect to the practice of law as does the Treasury Regulation under consideration.

In re Lyon, 1938, 301 Mass. 30, 16 N.E.2d 74, cited on behalf of plaintiff, and relied upon in De Pass v. B. Harris Wool Co., just considered by us, is, we believe, factually distinguishable. Moreover, it must be viewed in the light of the discussion in the more recent decision of the same court—Lowell Bar Ass'n v. Loeb, 1943, 315 Mass.

176, 52 N.E.2d 27, wherein the court adverted to but did not undertake to determine the effect of the Treasury Regulations previously referred to. The court there said, 52 N.E.2d at page 33:

> Neither do we consider at this time whether the permission granted to certified public accountants and other persons not members of the bar to practise in tax matters by the rules of the United States Treasury Department and of the administrative tribunal . . . now called the Tax Court of the United States, can have the effect of granting by implication to holders of "Treasury enrollment cards" a right to perform in this Commonwealth services in connection with Federal taxes which in their nature are comprised in the practice of law. It may deserve consideration whether the rules of a Federal administrative tribunal can legalize acts done in the States in matters not actually before the tribunal, though of a class that might eventually come before it. . . .

Were we convinced that the effect of the Treasury Regulations is to declare that acts constituting the practice of law in the accepted sense could lawfully be performed by non-members of the bar, we would entertain the same doubts as those suggested by the Supreme Judicial Court of Massachusetts in the portion of the opinion quoted above. Cf. Chicago Bar Ass'n v. United Taxpayers of America, 1941, 312 Ill.App. 243, 38 N.E.2d 349, holding the rule of Department of Finance permitting non-lawyers to appear before it in behalf of taxpayers void insofar as it purported to authorize such to perform acts constituting practice of law. We do not, however, believe that the regulations in question were intended to or have the effect contended for on behalf of plaintiff. We regard as highly significant the concluding clause in [Treasury Circular 230, § 10.39] "that nothing in the regulations in this part shall be construed as authorizing persons not members of the Bar to practice law." This statment must be read in context with the opening sentence of the section providing that "An agent enrolled before the Treasury Department shall have the same rights, powers and privileges * * * as an enrolled attorney" and as qualifying the same. As admittedly the Treasury Department is without authority to prescribe the rights and privileges to be exercised by persons except those appearing before it upon behalf of others, this provision could only have been intended as a disavowal of any intent upon the part of the Secretary of the Treasury to confer authority upon enrolled agents, not members of the bar, to perform acts upon behalf of others in connection with matters before the department which would otherwise constitute the practice of law. We cannot subscribe to the argument advanced upon behalf of the plaintiff that this provision was merely "a catch-all clause designed to prevent enrolled agents from holding themselves out as general attorneys" and "to limit the authority granted an enrolled agent to the precise field of Federal income taxation." Rather it suggests a recognition that "practice before the Treasury Department," while it may include acts which do not constitute the practice of law, and hence within the authority of enrolled agents, though not lawyers, to perform, also comprehends others of such character as to bring them within this classification. See Petition of Kearney, Fla. 1953, 63 So.2d 630.

In essence plaintiff's contention is that the effect of the Treasury Regulations is to declare that an enrolled agent, though not a lawyer, may, in the representation of others in tax matters before the Treasury Department, lawfully perform all of the services which a member of the bar is authorized to perform except "the privilege of drafting or preparing any written instrument by which title to real or personal property may be conveyed or transferred for the purpose of affecting Federal taxes" or advising "a client as to the legal sufficiency of such an instrument or its legal effect upon the Federal taxes of such client." If this be true, we see no reason for the concluding proviso in [§ 10.39], disavowing any intent to thereby authorize non-lawyers to perform acts in connection with tax matters before the Department which would constitute the practice of law.

Yet another consideration confirms us in the conclusion we have reached. We refer to the Statement of Principles previously adverted to which were approved by the American Institute of Accountants, wherein it is recognized that representation before the Treasury Department may involve the "application of legal principles" necessitating the retention of a lawyer. We can hardly believe that, if the conferees representing the certified public accountants who joined in recommending the adoption of the Statement and the Members of the Council of the American Institute of Accountants who approved it, were of the view that the effect of the Treasury Regulations authorized an enrolled agent who was not a lawyer to perform any and all services on behalf of others before the Treasury Department that might be performed by a lawyer, they would have given their adherence thereto.

Thus we conclude that, as indicated, the judgment in favor of plaintiff includes an award for services which constituted the practice of law, for which, not being a member of the bar he was not entitled to recover. . . .

The judgment is reversed, and the cause remanded for a new trial in accordance with the views herein expressed.

SHAW, P. J., concurs.

BISHOP, Judge.

I concur, not only in the judgment, but with most all that is said in the opinion. I do not agree with the criticism of the Bercu case . . . in Gardner v. Conway, 1951, 234 Minn. 468, 48 N.W.2d 788. Neither case furnishes a standard that fits all situations. I am agreed, however, that some of the services for which the plaintiff made his charge must be characterized as legal services, and the consequence is that the judgment was for too large a sum.

Oregon State Bar v. John H. Miller & Co.
Supreme Court of Oregon
385 Pac. 2d 181 (1963)

O'CONNELL, Justice.

Plaintiff seeks to enjoin defendants from the unauthorized practice of law. ORS 9.160. The trial court entered a decree enjoining defendants from carrying on certain activities related to the business of preparing estate plans. The decree also specified that certain conduct in carrying on the business of defendants did not constitute the practice of law. Plaintiff appeals, praying for a modification of the decree on the grounds that it is vague and inconsistent and that it permits defendants to practice law in connection with the conduct of some of its business.

Defendant Miller is the principal stockholder and president of defendant, Executive Estate Planners, Inc. Mr. Miller is not a lawyer. The nature of defendants' business is described by Mr. Miller as follows:

> A service organization offering a service to aid in financial and estate planning of individuals. That primarily. They have ventured into the field of pension and profit-sharing plans for businesses, individuals—businesses, I think. We have sold life insurance, received commission on it. That is what we do.
>
> * * * The planning of a person's affairs in order to maximize the benefits to their family while living and in the event of

death, and to attempt to conserve as much of the estate as possible consistent with the client or the estate owner's desires.

Mr. Miller also engages in the business of selling insurance. He argues that the estate planning business is merely incidental to the business of selling insurance. However, it was clearly established that the estate planning business was carried on as a distinct enterprise offering service to clients irrespective of their insurance needs.

The defendant company solicits business through salesmen who are paid a percentage of the fee charged for an analysis of the client's estate. A variety of factors reflecting upon tax liability are considered in preparing the analysis. For example, a report to the client might contain suggestions relating to the transfer of assets, the making of gifts, the use of the marital deduction, the use of inter vivos and testamentary trusts, and other devices designed to minimize taxes. The client's will is examined for the purpose of determining the need for change with regard to reducing taxes. These and other suggestions are a standard part of the service performed by defendants.

Much of the advice contained in the report to the client could not be given without an understanding of various aspects of the law, principally the law of taxation. Most of the advice is in terms of "suggestions." In each instance the client is urged to consult his own attorney. But whether the report takes the form of suggestions for further study or as a recommendation that the suggestions be subjected to further scrutiny by a lawyer, the fact remains that the client receives advice from defendants and the advice involves the application of legal principles. This constitutes the practice of law.

Defendants contend that they employ the law in essentially the same manner as many types of businesses which require the understanding and application of legal principles by those who are not admitted to the bar, as for example, the architect who advises a prospective builder that a proposed structure does not conform to the applicable building code, or the travel agent who advises his customer of passport requirements. It must be conceded that frequently advice given in the course of carrying on a business is shaped by a knowledge of the applicable law. But the giving of such advice is not in every instance regarded as the practice of law. The legal ingredient in the advice may be so insubstantial as to call for the application of the principle of de minimis non curat lex. This is not to say that we adopt the view permitting the practice of law where the legal element is merely incidental to the business activity being carried on. To fall outside the proscription of the statute the legal element must not only be incidental, it must be insubstantial. It cannot be said that one who plans another person's estate employs the law only in an insubstantial way.

There remains only the question of the adequacy of the lower court's decree. The decree was as follows:

> 1. Defendants are declared not to be engaged in the unauthorized practice of law when they perform the following activities:
>   a. Collecting information on customer or potential customer's financial affairs, including kind and value of assets.
>   b. Questioning customers as to the customer's desires as to the amount of estate to be left in the case of death.
>   c. Advising the customer as to his life insurance requirements, amount, kind, etc., including approximate estate cash requirements brought about by taxes.
>   d. Advising customers on the tax consequences of life insurance and on methods of premium payments and settlement options and other matters affecting the tax consequences of the insurance.
>   e. Preparing the policies of insurance.
> 2. Defendants are declared to be engaged in the unauthorized practice of law when they perform the following activities:
>   a. Suggesting, recommending, or advising on the form or contents, in whole or in part, of legal documents, and particularly wills and trusts;
>   b. Directly or indirectly preparing, construing, or drafting legal documents, including wills and trusts;
>   c. Rendering any legal opinion or advice, particularly as to the tax consequences of any activity or asset except life insurance or annuity plans;
>   d. Preparing any estate plan, except that part of the plan which directly concerns life insurance or annuities;
>   e. Holding themselves out as persons who prepare legal documents, give legal advice, or prepare estate plans, whether by use of business names or otherwise; and
>   f. Employing any person, firm or corporation, to give legal advice to customers of defendants.
> 3. Defendants are hereby perpetually enjoined from performing any of the activities set forth in paragraph 2 of this decree.

Plaintiff objects to the decree on the ground that it permits defendants to practice law as an incident to the business of selling life insurance. Part 1(c) of the decree permits defendants to estimate the cash requirements for estate tax purposes. In many, if not in most cases, to make such an estimate would require an understanding and application of the tax laws to the client's estate. This would constitute the practice of law. Part 1(d) permits defendants to advise customers on the tax consequence of life insurance.

The life insurance needs of the client can be determined only in relation to the client's estate as a whole. Whether life insurance is preferable to some other method of distributing the assets of the estate calls for an appraisal requiring an understanding of relevant legal principles. An insurance salesman can explain to his prospective customer alternative methods of disposing of assets, including life insurance, which are available to taxpayers *generally*. He may inform his prospect in general terms that life insurance may be an effective means of minimizing his taxes. He cannot properly advise a prospective purchaser with respect to his *specific* need for life insurance as against some other form of disposition of his estate, unless the advice can be given without drawing upon the law to explain the basis for making the choice of alternatives.

The decree of the lower court can be construed to permit this type of advice. To eliminate the ambiguity the following decree is substituted for that entered by the lower court. Defendants are enjoined from preparing estate plans embodying legal analysis either as a separate service or as an incident to carrying on the business of selling insurance.

Blumenberg v. Neubecker
New York Court of Appeals
12 N.Y. 2d 456 (1963)

FOSTER, J. This controversy involves an agreement whereby an attorney and accountant agreed to represent the defendant in a Federal income tax matter. The Internal Revenue Service had filed a deficiency tax claim against defendant in the sum of $918,220.96. Through the efforts of the plaintiff, an attorney, and the accountant, a settlement was made with the Government in the sum of $293,157.08. The plaintiff and the accountant, one Glickman, through the intervention of another attorney, were retained by the defendant under a written agreement providing for a contingent fee of one third of the difference between the amount of the deficiency claim and that of the ultimate determination by the Internal Revenue Service. After the final settlement, the defendant refused to honor the retainer agreement, and thereafter the plaintiff, suing in his own right and as assignee on the claim of Glickman, brought this action, alleging two causes of action, one upon the retainer agreement and the other upon *quantum meruit*.

After a trial in the Supreme Court, a jury awarded the plaintiff a verdict in the sum of $208,354.69 upon the retainer agreement. By a divided court, the Appellate Division, Second Department, reversed the judgment and dismissed the cause of action on the retainer agreement on the ground that the agreement contemplated legal services by a layman, and that the arrangement between the parties involved illegal fee splitting between a layman and a lawyer (Penal Law, § 276). The order of reversal, however, permitted the plaintiff to pursue his claim based on *quantum meruit* for services which he alone rendered.

A contract for the rendition of legal services, or the performance of such services, by one not a lawyer, is invalid and the fact that the nonlawyer is to act jointly or alone with an attorney will not alter this result. However, we agree with the conclusion reached by the two Justices who dissented in the Appellate Division that the contract here under consideration did not on its face contemplate the rendition of legal services by the accountant. Furthermore, there is proof in this record from which a jury could find not only that Glickman confined his activities to accountancy procedures and accounting problems, but also that the understanding among the parties when the agreement was made was that Glickman's responsibility was in the area of accountancy and that plaintiff's responsibility, in the field of law, was to represent the defendant in the Tax Court and to deal with the legal problems involved.

An arrangement such as was here arrived at assures the sort of co-operative effort whereby the expertise of both lawyer and accountant in their respective fields may be availed of and is designed to achieve for the client who retained them the best possible result. Indeed, such an arrangement comes close to the ideal setup contemplated by the New York State Bar Association and the New York State Society of Certified Public Accountants acting jointly in 1962. (See Principles Applicable to Legal and Accounting Practice in the Field of Taxation, McKinney's Cons. Laws of N. Y., Book 29, Judiciary Law, Appendix [1962 Supp.], pp. 300-302.) Thus, in their joint statement, the two associations declared (Principles, *loc. cit.*, p. 300): "In the large areas in the tax field where the legal and accounting aspects are interrelated and overlap, it is often in the public interest that the services of both professions be utilized. Indeed, experience has shown that a lawyer and a certified public accountant working together on behalf of a common client in the tax field constitute a very effective team. When the lawyer and accountant have joined hands in the preparation and presentation of a case before the Internal Revenue Service, the taxpayer is most effectively represented." *

*Joint Statement of New York State Bar Association and New York State Society of Certified Public Accountants (in part):

The intricacies of both our federal and state tax systems more and more demand the professional services of lawyers and certified public accountants. While the primary function of the lawyer is to advise the public with respect to legal implications involved in tax matters and the certified public accountant has to do with accounting aspects of them, frequently the legal and accounting phases are so interrelated, interdependent or overlapping that they are difficult to distinguish. In 1951, the National Conference of Lawyers and Certified Public Accountants considered these problems and adopted a Statement of Principles as a guide for both professions in dealing with them. The New York State Bar Association and the New York State Society of Certified Public Accountants concur in and ratify that Statement.

As pointed out in the Statement of Principles, in some areas clear lines of demarcation are possible between the professional services which should be undertaken only by a lawyer and those which should be undertaken only by a certified public accountant. For instance, only a lawyer may prepare legal documents such as agreements, conveyances, trust instruments, wills, corporate minutes or give advice as to legal sufficiency or effect of any such instrument or take the necessary steps to create, amend or dissolve a partnership, corporation, trust or other legal entity. It is equally clear that only an accountant may properly advise as to the preparation of financial statements included in reports or submitted with tax returns or as to accounting methods and procedures.

In other areas it is settled that certain matters are within the competency of both professions. This is true for instance in the preparation of federal income tax returns, although it is recognized by both professions that if a substantial question of law or accountancy arises in the preparation of a return, it should be referred to a member of the appropriate profession.

In the large areas in the tax field where the legal and accounting aspects are interrelated and overlap, it is often in the public interest that the services of both professions be utilized. Indeed, experience has shown that a lawyer and a certified public accountant working together on behalf of a common client in the tax field constitute a very effective team. When the lawyer and accountant have joined hands in the preparation and presentation of a case before the Internal Revenue Service, the taxpayer is most effectively represented. It is not intended, of course, that the services of both a lawyer and a certified public accountant need to be utilized in matters which do not involve uncertainties as to legal or accounting questions or in matters of minor significance, particularly where litigation is not indicated.

The services of a lawyer should be obtained in connection with the organization of corporations, effecting corporate reorganizations, the creation of partnerships and trusts, the setting up of pension and profit-sharing trusts and the like, since in these matters there are involved not only very complex tax statutes but also substantial non-tax legal problems under State law. On the other hand, the services of a certified public accountant should be obtained in connection with the accounting problems and effects of the organization and reorganization and development of corporations, partnerships, and trusts, including pension and profit-sharing trusts; with the accounting problems involved in income determination, such as questions relating to operating losses, earnings and profits, surplus accumulations and the like; and in those matters requriing the experience and training of the certified public accountant in the fields of financial and operational planning.

In those cases, where it is important to the client's cause that a client's communications remain privileged, it may well be imperative that the lawyer bear a rather larger share of the total responsibility for a matter than would otherwise occur in deference to the rule that certain communications by a client to a lawyer are privileged while those to an accountant are not. In criminal tax investigations, the services of a lawyer should be obtained to protect the legal and constitutional rights of the client.

As already indicated, a jury could find from the proof in this record that defendant personally retained both the plaintiff and Glickman to render services in their respective fields. It is of no consequence that their retainer was effected by a single agreement or that their compensation was to be equal or that it was specified in a lump sum contingency percentage, as long as the fee provided for the accountant was to be for accounting services rendered by him, and the fee for the lawyer for legal services which he was to perform. It is only necessary to add, as the dissenters below observed, that the defendant has received a benefit which was "remarkable, unusual and eminently satisfactory", and, since a jury could find that there was no fraud or overreaching on the part of the plaintiff or Glickman, either in the making of the retainer agreement or in the rendition of services, the judgment and order of the Appellate Division should be reversed and a new trial granted.

The judgment and order appealed from should be reversed and a new trial granted, with costs to abide the event.

BURKE, J. (dissenting). I dissent and vote to affirm.

The contract, a single joint retainer, typewritten on one sheet of paper, did provide for one indivisible fee for services which were at least partly legal and for the payment of all expenses and disbursements by the lawyer, a former employee of the Internal Revenue Bureau, and accountant. Plaintiff, a lawyer-accountant admitted to practice in the Tax Court, and the accountant, Glickman, who was not so admitted, were clearly partners in the strictest sense, sharing jointly profits and losses (expenses) with respect to a legal matter. It requires no extended discussion to demonstrate that this violates the canons of ethics governing the independence required of a lawyer in his dealings with his client. (See Rules of Practice of U. S. Tax Court, rule 2; Canons of Professional Ethics of American Bar Assn., Nos. 12, 33, 34, 35, 47; Opinion 614 of Association of Bar of City of New York; Opinion 343 of New York County Lawyers Assn.; Opinion 297 of American Bar Assn. Committee on Professional Ethics.) These canons are declarative of the policy of this State respecting the conduct of attorneys and I think the general rule applicable to contracts against public policy should control. No cause of action should be held good where the complaint states on its face an illegal agreement. The agreement also violates the Treasury Department Regulations prohibiting wholly contingent fees for services in matters before the Internal Revenue Service. (Code of Fed. Reg., § 10.37, subd. [b]; 1963 Fed. Tax Regs., vol. 2, p. 1672.) (*Stone v. Freeman*, 298 N. Y.

268; *McConnell* v. *Commonwealth Pictures Corp.*, 7 N. Y. 2d 465; *Van Bergh* v. *Simons*, 286 F. 2d 325.) The fact that the illegality lies in the violation of an attorney's canons of ethics rather than a statute should in no way diminish a court's disapprobation. (*Matter of Annunziato*, 201 Misc. 971; *Matter of Rothman*, 12 N. J. 528, 535.)

Chief Judge DESMOND and Judges DYE, FULD, VAN VOORHIS and SCILEPPI concur with Judge FOSTER; Judge BURKE dissents and votes to affirm in an opinion.

Rassieur v. Charles
Supreme Court of Missouri
188 S. W. 2d 817 (1945)

HYDE, Presiding Judge.

This is an action for $15,000 damages for alleged negligence of public accountants in preparing and auditing books and statements made in connection with plaintiff's income tax return. Demurrers were sustained to plaintiff's third petition and plaintiff has appealed from the judgment of dismissal entered.

The facts stated in the petition are summarized as follows:

(1) That defendants were public accountants engaged in the business of preparing and auditing books and records, preparing financial statements, and preparing income tax returns; (2) that plaintiff hired defendants to prepare for her a set of books which would reflect clearly the cost or value of plaintiff's securities for the purpose of determining gains or losses under the income tax laws and regulations upon a sale or sales of such securities and to prepare her income tax return and compute the taxes owed by plaintiff for the year 1940; (3) that for a valuable consideration, defendants undertook this employment and in fact did set up such a set of books and did prepare her income tax returns for the year 1940; (4) that in November, 1940, defendants falsely represented to her that she had realized a taxable profit resulting from the sale of shares of North American Company stock, and then defendants undertook to advise her that under the income tax laws she had the right to sell other securities at a loss during 1940 for the purpose of off-setting such loss against the profit which defendants represented plaintiff had made on the sale of North American Company stock; (5) that defendants represented to plaintiff that making the sales of other securities at a loss would reduce her income tax liability for the year

1940 and that defendants advised plaintiff to make such sales; (6) that plaintiff relied on the representations made by defendants and the books and records prepared by them and did make sales of other securities which were selected by defendants with aid of plaintiff's broker; (7) that as a result of making the sales of other stocks, plaintiff received for such stocks an amount less than they had cost her and actually suffered a pecuniary loss; (8) that defendants, instead of correctly recording the proper cost to plaintiff of the North American stock, recorded the cost of such stock to her at a value which was less than its proper cost to her with the result that it appeared from the books and records prepared by defendants that plaintiff had realized a taxable gain on the sale of the North American Company stock when in fact she had sustained a capital loss on said sale; (9) that if defendants had used due care they could have ascertained the true cost to plaintiff of the North American Company stock, and that plaintiff was misled and misinformed by defendants as to the true result of her investment transaction during the year 1940.

The petition also stated that, by selling such securities in 1940, she was deprived of her right under income tax laws "to off-set, in any subsequent year, any losses which might be sustained by her in the sale of the same." The petition further stated that plaintiff first learned the true facts (that the North American stock was sold at a loss instead of a gain) on November 1, 1941, and "that on November 1, 1941, the market value of the securities she sold during the months of November and December, 1940, as a result of the representations and advice of defendants, was greatly in excess of the amount she had realized from the sale of the same on broker's board." Plaintiff contends that she is entitled to recover this difference between the 1940 sale price and the November 1, 1941, market value.

Defendants do not seriously contend that this petition failed to show negligence in preparing the statement upon which plaintiff acted in selling her stocks; nor do defendants contend that they would not be liable for damages caused by their negligence. For liability of accountants, see 10 Am.Jur. 520, Sec. 7; 8 A.L.R. 462; 74 A.L.R. 1153. Defendants, however, claim the petition failed to state a cause of action because they say that plaintiff was not damaged by sale of her securities if they were sold for their full value at the time she sold them; that their value a year later is immaterial; that nominal damages cannot be recovered in a case of this kind; and that the sale of the securities in 1940 was not the proximate cause of plaintiff's situation in November 1941. In contending that plaintiff was not damaged, defendants rely on cases fixing the measure of damages as the value of property at the time of loss, conversion, or sale. . . . We do not understand plaintiff to claim that she was entitled to recover the difference between the sale price of her stocks and their original cost; and of course that would not be a loss caused by defendants' negligence but was due instead to depreciation in value before they were employed.

Plaintiff, however, contends that a rule of damages analogous to that established in Baker v. Drake, 53 N.Y. 211, 13 Am.Rep. 507, should be applied. This rule, known as the New York rule, "is that the measure of damages when a broker wrongfully sells his customer's stock is the highest market price of the stock between the time the customer has notice of a sale and a reasonable time thereafter within which he could go into the market and purchase the stock." 8 Am.Jur. 1114, Sec. 217. . . . The basis of this rule as stated in the Gallagher case [129 U.S. 193] is:

> The real injury sustained by the principal consists not merely in the assumption of control over the stock, but in the sale of it at an unfavorable time, and for an unfavorable price. Other goods wrongfully converted are generally supposed to have a fixed market value at which they can be replaced at any time; and hence, with regard to them, the ordinary measure of damages is their value at the time of conversion, or, in case of sale and purchase, at the time fixed for their delivery. But the application of this rule to stocks would, as before said, be very inadequate and unjust.

The principle applied is, as stated in Baker v. Drake, that "the customer is entitled to recover such damages as would naturally be sustained in restoring himself to the position of which he has been deprived."

We think it is obvious that for the same reason a sale at an unfavorable time and for an unfavorable price (absent the benefit of the expected off-set against a taxable gain) as the result of defendants' negligence could likewise result in injury and damage; and that the measure of damages should be the difference between the sale price and the cost of restoring plaintiff to her original position. We see no reason why this rule should not apply to such a sale caused by negligence as well as to a sale made in violation of or without instructions. We, therefore, hold that the petition does state facts from which actual damage to plaintiff could be found.

Plaintiff considers that this rule would allow her as damages the cost of replacing her stocks within a reasonable time after discovery of the negligence of defendants, namely, at November 1941 value. However, this does not take into consideration the actual situation herein involved. Plaintiff here knew when the stocks were sold. She sold them herself to get a benefit (on her 1940 tax return) permitted by federal income tax law. Under the same law authorizing off-set of losses on stock sales against gains on such transactions, plaintiff was permitted to repurchase the same stocks after 30 days (from the date of sales made at a loss for such purpose) without affecting her right of off-set. [§ 118, 1939 Code; § 1091, 1954 Code.] Therefore, after the end of this 30 day period, plaintiff was free to repurchase the stocks sold at defendants' direction, without in any way affecting the benefit she expected to obtain by selling them. So if she desired to own them, either as investments which she thought would produce income or increase in price or for the purpose of offsetting future capital gains if they depreciated, she was not prevented from doing so for more than 30 days by reason of the erroneous information furnished by defendants. Thus plaintiff's negligence could not have been the proximate cause of her failure to do so thereafter, because the sales which she made as a result of defendants' alleged negligence in no way affected the replacement of her holdings after 30 days. In other words, while defendants' negligence caused plaintiff to sell the stocks (to take losses for the purpose of off-setting the supposed capital gain) and likewise caused her to refrain from repurchasing the stocks in less than 30 days thereafter (because she would have lost the supposed benefit, for which she sold the stocks, by repurchase within that period), nevertheless after this 30 day period had elapsed she had no reason based on defendants' negligence, or anything resulting therefrom, for failing to repurchase these stocks, if she had any desire to own them. Thus her failure to repurchase them after that time was the result of her own choice and not of defendants' negligence.

Plaintiff also claims damage by reason of loss of future rights (on selling these stocks at a loss) to take off-sets against prospective capital gains of some later year. However, that is far too speculative (much more speculative than loss of future profits disallowed in Walker v. Borland, supra, and cases disallowing contingent speculative damages) . . . , because it depends on plaintiff having a future capital gain (and selling when she had it), on the stocks sold remaining at the same market value (which according to the petition was not true even for one year), and on income tax laws and all interpretations thereof remaining exactly the same (no comment necessary) on the matter of rates, exemptions and capital gains and losses. We, therefore, hold that, on the allegations of her petition, plaintiff is entitled to recover the difference between the sales price of her stocks and the cost of replacing them within a reasonable time after the expiration of the 30 day period.

The judgment is reversed and the cause remanded.

All concur.

Anderson v. Knox
U. S. Court of Appeals, Ninth Circuit
297 F.2d 702 (1961)

Before CHAMBERS, POPE and HAMLIN, Circuit Judges.
POPE, Circuit Judge.

The appellee Knox, who was plaintiff below, brought this action to recover damages alleged to have been incurred by him in consequence of alleged fraud and misrepresentation on the part of Anderson, the appellant, in inducing Knox to purchase a certain life insurance contract of the New York Life Insurance Co. Anderson was the company's agent. Knox had judgment in the court below from which this appeal is taken. . . .

The negotiations which led to the purchase of the insurance began in August, 1952. Knox, then 36 years of age, lived with his wife and three children on the Island of Maui where he was employed as a field superintendent on a sugar plantation. Anderson, a resident of Los Angeles, had been for many years an insurance representative and salesman, and in 1952 he established an office in Honolulu in association with one Kreidler, also an insurance agent, with a view to selling insurance in the Hawaiian Islands. Anderson had specialized in the sale of what is referred to throughout the record as bank financed insurance or insurance under the bank loan plan. The features of this type of insurance as it was sold to Knox may be illustrated by describing the method of financing the policy which he purchased covering his own life. This was a $100,000 ten payment life policy. As the annual premiums on this policy were $7,265 and Knox's total annual cash income was only in the neighborhood of $10,000, the insurance was offered to him under this bank financed plan which involved among other things these features:

1. Knox turned over to Anderson his existing life policies with various life insurance companies. These had been issued in sundry face amounts aggregating something in excess of $35,000. In doing so he authorized Anderson to convert them in the manner which will hereafter be described, and to borrow thereon sufficient cash to pay the first premium of $7,265, and to pledge the remaining cash values of those policies as collateral for the bank loans hereafter mentioned.

2. The plan was that subsequent premiums would be provided by borrowing the amounts thereof from a bank and securing the bank by assignment of the old and new policies. It was calculated that by the time the first such loan was procured the assignable cash value for security purposes would be such that the necessary loan would not exceed 95 per cent of the assigned values.

3. Knox, the insured, would pay each year only the interest on the bank loans, but since his interest payments would be tax deductible the annual net out-of-pocket payment required to be made by Knox in order to carry the plan would be only the interest on the loan less the amount of taxes he would be able to save by deducting this interest in his income tax return. (Obviously the net cost to Knox calculated in this manner would depend in a substantial degree upon the tax bracket in which his income tax was calculated. This saving through deduction of interest paid was deemed to be the main attractive feature of the bank financed plan of paying life insurance.)

4. The purported advantages of obtaining this extra $100,000 of life insurance was that it would at once provide for Knox a large coverage at an early age when the premiums would be low and for a minimal outlay, that outlay being as above indicated merely the interest on bank loans for successive premiums reduced by his tax savings. (As against this, as we shall later have occasion to note, as each year's premium came due, the insured must increase his loan at the bank by the amount of the annual premium and in ten years he finds himself with a very substantial amount owing to the bank, and each year his interest payments increase accordingly.)

5. An aspect of this plan primarily attractive to the selling agent was the size of the agent's commission, computed on the basis of an annual premium far in excess of what would ordinarily be procurable through selling a person in Knox's financial situation the type of policy which an insurance agent might be likely to be able to sell.

For a man whose income and financial condition is such that his income tax puts him in high brackets and who has the means to liquidate the steadily increasing debt out of other sources, the bank finance plan can well be useful. Much use has been made of the plan under these conditions. Thus X paying taxes in a high income bracket, with resources which he currently wishes to use for other purposes, as for instance in the stock market, may find the bank finance plan of insurance an attractive arrangement. Such a man gets an immediate large coverage of insurance with premiums based on his early age at a time when he is sure of his own insurability.

It is clear from the record that what brought about this controversy, wholly apart from its merits, was that Knox was not that kind of man. Knox had an annual salary of $8100 per year; he had investment income which was not in excess of $1600 per year. This came from securities which he testified had a value of about $12,000. In addition, in his position as superintendent of the sugar plantation, Knox had the free use of an ample dwelling house and the free use of a company automobile. The court found that Knox's income was such that he was placed in the 26 per cent tax bracket. It also found that Knox had expectations of being raised at some time in the future to be assistant manager of the sugar plantation at a salary of $12,000 per year.

The court found that Knox was induced to buy the life insurance policies above mentioned by certain representations made to him by Anderson which were false and fraudulent. These representations upon which plaintiff relied are listed at length and in some detail under paragraph 8 of the findings beginning on page 340 of 162 F.Supp.

In a subsequent paragraph 9, the court found that Anderson failed to disclose to plaintiff certain material information and facts which he knew with respect to the proposed insurance plan; that Anderson was under a duty to make disclosure because of a relationship of trust and confidence, and because of Anderson's superior knowledge; and the court concluded that liability on the part of Anderson accrued not only from the alleged false and fraudulent representations, but also from these failures to disclose.

We think that for the purpose of disposing of this appeal we need go no further than to consider the facts relating to what the court found to be the central and primary representation made by Anderson with respect to the policies purchased, namely, that Anderson represented to Knox, under circumstances permitting him to rely thereon, that the proposed plan for bank financed insurance which Knox agreed to purchase "was a suitable program for plaintiff and his family and fitted their needs."

We shall note as we proceed that the trial court treated this representation as one of fact and not as a mere expression of opinion. Our discussion of that question will await our primary inquiry: did the evidence here warrant the judge in finding that there was such a representation and that the representation as made was false.

It is our opinion that the evidence before the trial court warranted its findings that there was such a representation of suitability and that such representation was not true in that the insurance program sold to Knox was in fact not a suitable one in view of all the facts then existing with respect to him—his income, his financial condition, his prospects, his family, and their prospective needs.

The question whether the representations made by Anderson to Knox were actually false or made with such recklessness as to make them substantially fraudulent, is a more difficult one; it turns in part upon a decision as to whether the representation of suitability was in truth a representation of fact and not a mere expression of opinion. In approaching these matters it is not the function of this court to find the facts initially but merely to ascertain whether the facts as found by the trial court were, in view of the record, clearly erroneous. . . .

Whether the Representation Was Made

At the time Knox was approached for the purpose of inducing him to buy the insurance which Anderson was undertaking to sell, Anderson was using the Honolulu agent Kreidler above mentioned. Kreidler had made advance arrangements with Knox for Anderson's visit to the latter's home, and Kreidler was present at the time the sales efforts were being made by Anderson. Kreidler testified that Anderson then expressed his opinion as to the suitability of his plan for Knox and his family. He said: "Mr. Anderson explained that it was advantageous to Roger Knox and his family, that it would benefit him at all times and that it was cheaper too, as long as he could afford it under a credit of tax deductibility, that he might as well have it and not need it than to need it and not have it, that it was an excellent plan throughout the entire period of this man's life."

The opinion of the district court sets out at length (159 F.Supp. p. 803), a letter written later by Anderson to Knox which it found "exemplifies [Anderson's] method of presentation." Among other things to the same effect, the letter stated: "I am sure you can readily see the advantages of this outstanding program", and "There are four fundamental essentials to a good investment, namely, 1st, Security, 2nd, Guaranteed Increase in Value, 3rd, Quick Marketability, 4th, Flexibility of Contract. This Plan embraces all four of these fundamental essentials."

In substance the testimony of the witness Kreidler as well as that of Knox and his wife was to the effect that many similar statements were made by Anderson to Knox at the time that Anderson first presented the insurance deal to him.

Anderson testified that he made no such representation as to the suitability of the program he was selling. Plainly the trial judge did not believe him. Indeed, as we note hereafter, Anderson testified that the question of the suitability of the bank loan for Knox and his needs did not concern him.

That Anderson did in fact inform Knox that the program was a suitable one and strongly urged him to purchase the insurance as meeting his needs and consistent with his capabilities is supported by evidence which the trial court had the right to believe.

Knox's Right To Rely

We are also of the opinion that under the circumstances of this case the court was fully warranted in finding that Knox had the right to rely upon these representations of suitability. The court's opinion and its findings reflect the view that Anderson went to considerable pains to lay the ground work for a maximum impact of his salesmanship upon Knox.

As there noted Knox first received a letter of introduction from E. E. Bodge, president of a Honolulu business corporation, describing Anderson as an insurance and annuity counsellor who was temporarily in the Islands and who had the latest information about a bank financed loan plan. Bodge indicated that at first he was skeptical about the plan but he had made inquiries and found the plan entirely legal; that some insurance companies were not enthusiastic about it because they could not write this plan. It was suggested that Knox might care to give Mr. Anderson some time for presentation of this matter. The plain inference was that Anderson had superior knowledge on the subject. Anderson had suggested the writing of the letter and examined its form before it was sent.

Anderson gave Kreidler instructions to approach his prospects keeping them in "anticipation of meeting me" and explaining that "I will be able to give them all the information they desire." Kreidler testified: "I, naturally, as a part of my work gave Mr. Anderson a big buildup as to his ability and capability and qualifications."

The finding of the trial court (162 F.Supp. 343), that when Knox purchased this program of bank financed insurance "defendant knew that he did not understand said program and did not intend that he understand same and Plaintiff did not make an independent decision thereon but relied completely upon Defendent" cannot be said to be clearly erroneous, not merely because of the assurance which Kreidler gave Knox that he was about to meet a man who was especially qualified to give information in this field, indeed "the only one that was qualified to do this tremendous job", but also because there were circumstances from which the court could infer that Knox was obliged to take the program on faith and in many important respects to act in the dark. . . .

We are of the opinion that there was sufficient evidence in the record to warrant the trial judge in believing and finding that Anderson, either in person or through Kreidler, represented to Knox that here in Anderson he found the man who was not only an expert in the field but practically the only man alive who understood the plan fully and that here was a man upon whom Knox could rely for information as to what he was buying. In short, Anderson, the court found, in substance said: You can take my word for what I am now telling you; later I will give you a schedule showing just what you have bought and how it works.

It is clear that in fact Knox did rely upon Anderson's statements and we think that it would be idle to argue here that Knox should have found out for himself because of some principle of caveat emptor that the program was not at all what it was represented to be. Knox testified: "I had my faith in him because he was recommended by a leading business man in the Territory. I figured he knew what he was talking about. He had all the facts in my case. I figured he was giving me something that was designed for me." . . .

The facts here related, and thus credited by the trial court, sufficiently establish Knox's right, as a matter of law, to rely on these representations as to suitability, if, as the court found, the representations were false, and were made with intent to deceive. Appellant argues, quoting from Kerr, Fraud & Mistake, 254: "A man who abstains from inquiry where inquiry ought to have been made cannot be heard to say so and to rely on his ignorance. * * * In the absence of inquiry where inquiry ought to have been made, the Court is bound to assume that the person from whom inquiry should have been made would have done what it is his duty to do." Such a rule is not apposite to the fact situation present here. As Prosser has noted (Law of Torts, 2nd Ed. p. 552): "The last half-century has seen a marked change in the attitude of the courts toward the question of justifiable reliance," and quotes from Chamberlin v. Fuller, 59 Vt. 247, 256, 9 A. 832, 836, the now classic statement that "no rogue should enjoy his illgotten plunder for the simple reason that his victim is by chance a fool." . . .

Was The Program Suitable, As Represented?

This brings us to the next inquiry which is: does the record support the court's finding that the program sold to Knox was in fact not suitable?

Here again we must say that the court's finding on this point was not clearly erroneous. There was considerable evidence to support it. Some of it came from qualified experts in the insurance field who undertook to demonstrate through analysis of the Anderson proposals and with the aid of charts, diagrams and mathematical calculations that the program sold to Anderson was not a suitable one. While the schedules (Exhibits 4, 8 and 10A) furnished by Anderson were not self-explanatory, and required extensive mathematical calculations to disclose just what the program contemplated, yet once those calculations were made, it was not difficult for the court to draw its factual inference of unsuitability from these figures.

The expert witnesses, both those for the plaintiff and for the defendant, were in substantial agreement as to what would constitute a suitable insurance plan for Knox and his family and as to what factors would have to be considered in order to determine such suitability. We think that appellee has correctly summarized the views of these witnesses in saying that they agreed "it was necessary to know (i) the details of the existing insurance program; (ii) its values and benefits, (iii) the cost of continuing the old program, (iv) the additional cash outlay for the new program, (v) loss of values and benefits, if any, under the old program, and (vi) the additional values and benefits of the new program."

Van Cleve, a thoroughly qualified expert in the insurance field, with 37 years of experience, demonstrated with a great degree of clarity and reference to specific details, the reasons why the Anderson program was not suitable for Knox. With the use of figures and amounts he demonstrated that the program failed to provide the protection Knox was led to think he was getting; that it in fact destroyed some protections he already had; that the program was not worth the money it would cost; that Knox could not afford it; and that he did not understand it.

A rather striking thing about the pattern of the new program was that under it Knox's insurance protection sharply decreased for the first ten years during which premiums had to be paid so that at the end of that time the amounts receivable in the event of death were hardly more than he would have collected had he left his insurance policies as they were under his old program. The reason for this was that Knox himself would start out with a new $100,000 New York Life Insurance policy added to his old policies, but in initiating the new policy, as previously indicated, he had to borrow substantial sums from the cash reserves of his old policies thus reducing their protection and in each year thereafter he had to borrow from a bank the annual premiums of $7265 payable each year for the ten year period. Although the plan contemplated that he would only pay the interest on that $7265, yet each year during the ten years his bank indebtedness would increase by another $7265. In like manner he had to borrow on account of the premiums on Ellen's policy $3758 each year and thus enhance the total bank loan by that additional amount.

The net result of this was that at the end of ten years he would owe the bank $125,000. If he could have died in the first two or three years, under this program his beneficiaries would reap some substantial benefits from the Anderson plan; but these benefits taper off very rapidly because all of his policies, old and new, were required to be pledged with the bank as collateral for the loan; therefore the amount collectible on death would be only the balance remaining after payment to the bank. . . .

The various charts furnished by Anderson to Knox recited in their caption: "Interest rates and dividends are not guaranteed." It is apparent, however, that if the calculations made on those charts are based upon unrealistic assumptions of interest rates and tax brackets, that fact alone has an important bearing upon the suitability of the program and whether Knox was entered upon a safe or a hazardous undertaking.

None of the schedules stated the interest rates used in the calculations but Van Cleve was able to calculate them from the figures shown. Exhibit 10A started with 4.25 percent in 1953, reduced to 4% in 1954, to 3.75% in 1956, and to 3.5% in 1960, continuing at that rate until 1973. As counsel for Knox pointed out, in judging as to the suitability of the proposed program, fair allowance must be made for contingencies. Van Cleve testified that any one selling this program should take into consideration certain contingencies and variables which would alter its usefulness in important particulars. One variable was the tax bracket which for Knox might remain at about 25%. Another variable was the interest. Van Cleve said that the interest rate instead of going down to 3.5% might well go to 5%, which would be the probable rate at which a loan would be made by the insurance companies themselves.

If the necessary outlay which Knox would have to make to carry this new program were based on an interest rate of 5% (which later experience showed would have been the case) and upon the stipulated tax bracket of 24.6%, then Knox's gross interest for 1960 would have been $5446.15, and his net interest $4106.40, 40% of his gross annual income. This would be a preposterous burden for a man in Knox's situation. Obviously the court could properly hold that a program which involved such contingencies, so possible and so real, was not suitable for a man of Knox's earning capacity.

In this same connection Van Cleve testified that the bank financed insurance plan could not be justified for any person whose taxes were under the 50% bracket. As previously stated, Knox's gross income was far below the $24,000, which it was stipulated would be the lowest gross income which would provide a tax as high as 40%. With his actual income tax bracket at the stipulated 24.6%, we have to note here a further reason why this bank financed insurance program was unsuitable for Knox....

The Question Of Fraud

This brings us to the consideration of two questions which we think must be answered together. The first question is: was the representation made by Anderson as to the suitability of this program a representation of fact and not a mere expression of opinion? The second question is: assuming that we find here a statement or representation of fact, was it made falsely and fraudulently with intent to deceive, or was the representation made with reckless disregard whether it was true or false?

With respect to the first question, dealing with the opinion problem, we think that a fair statement of the applicable rule is to be found in the case of Ed. Barron Estate Co. v. Woodruff Co., supra, 163 Cal. 561, 126 P. 351, p. 356. There the court said:

> It is, of course, generally speaking, true that an action for deceit cannot be founded upon the mere expression of an opinion. But the qualifications and modifications of this general rule are as important as the rule itself. Those qualifications and modifications are numerous. It is unnecessary to attempt to illustrate them all. But, bearing in mind that an expression of an opinion, if honestly made, is an expression of what the speaker believes to be a fact, it becomes apparent that, by the expression of a dishonest opinion to one entitled to rely upon it, deceit is practiced,

injury may be worked, and an action will lie. Thus the opinion of an expert employed to report upon a mine would be but the expression of his judgment, and if honestly, though mistakenly, made, of course, no injury cognizable in law, equity, or good morals could result. But instantly that the expert expresses a dishonest opinion, though it still be but an opinion, he has made himself liable in an action for deceit.

This is a rule generally recognized. It has been restated in the Restatement of the Law of Torts, § 542(a), and has received general approval from the text writers.

The question which the trial court had to consider was whether Anderson's statement of opinion was an honest one. If therefore when Anderson spoke he knew or believed his statement to be false or unwarranted, he would be liable, for obviously he expected that Knox would rely upon his statements. In like manner, if he gave this assurance of suitability when he knew that he had no basis for such an assertion, he would be liable for this would be a case of a representation with reckless disregard whether it was true or false.

The trial court found, as noted: "That this representation of suitability was known or ought to have been known to defendant to be false and fraudulent and was made by defendant to plaintiff with intent that he rely upon it in buying said integrated program." [162 F.Supp. 340.] Our inquiry is therefore whether that finding is supported by evidence or whether it is clearly erroneous.

In his brief here the appellee takes pains to state that he is not attacking the bank plan as such; that that plan is not on trial; and he concedes that under some circumstances this type of plan may be satisfactorily useful and suitable.

That it has usefulness in some cases we noted at the outset of this opinion. However, it is apparent that a mere look at the characteristic features of the plan is sufficient to make it apparent to any one, and particularly to the trial judge, that it contains within it features which make it inherently a system readily adaptable to sharp practices. In short, any insurance agent using this system and familiar with it must be aware of the fact that in employing it he must resist any temptation to overreach a purchaser. The court could well find that Anderson must have known that an indiscriminate use of the bank loan plan was fraught with hazards. . . .

But from Anderson's own testimony the trial court could conclude that Anderson was unconcerned about these matters. The cross-examination of Anderson by counsel for Knox endeavored to find out his thoughts and mental attitude with respect to the suitability of this program at the time of sale. For a considerable period of his testimony Anderson evaded the question. The court intervened telling him that "counsel is trying to find out how you felt at the time of this transaction, specifically whether or not you felt that you owed a duty to protect the Knoxes against what in your opinion might be poor judgment in deciding how much insurance to take under this proposed loan financed plan." The witness evaded this question by stating that he went to the time and expense to prepare the schedules so that the Knoxes themselves could decide. Finally, however, the testimony was as follows: "The Court: Let's go over it again. From the answers you have given me, I take it that you are saying, no, that you felt you owed them no duty to protect them against any bad judgment that in your opinion they might be exercising in relation to the insurance that they had decided to purchase? The witness. I guess that's right with this qualification, that it was their responsibility to determine what they should buy and could buy. I was selling life insurance. But at the time I felt I was using the judgment of the insuring company in the amount that would be issued. As to what they decide, what they should buy, is their responsibility."

We believe that this answer alone would be sufficient to warrant the trial judge in finding that Anderson, in making his representations respecting the suitability of the program did so with reckless disregard as to whether his representation was true or false. . . .

The court could fairly infer from the circumstances here that Anderson's sole interest was in collecting his immense commission; that he felt no responsibility whatever, as he himself indicated, with respect to the truth or falsity of his representation of suitability. Indeed, the court might well regard seriously the argument that any insurance agent who would sell a man with Knox's limited income and prospects an insurance program that involved saddling him with a bank indebtedness of $125,000, an essentially term insurance type of protection, and dissipation of the accumulated cash values of his old insurance, must have known that he was not acting honestly in making the sale.

We hold therefore that the record sustains the court's findings, first, as to the representation alleged; second, that the representation was false, and third, that Anderson either knew and intended it to be false, or made the representation with reckless disregard of the facts.

Damages.

This brings us to the question of damages.

The trial court awarded Knox compensatory damages in the sum of $13,309.98 plus interest, exemplary and punitive damages in the sum of $10,000, and damages for "grievous mental anguish and great distress of body and mind" in the sum of $2500. . . .

[Discussion of damages omitted.]

The judgment is affirmed.

CHAMBERS, Circuit Judge (concurring).

The foregoing exhaustive opinion gives me no trouble as to liability. In short, I regard it as a reasonable inference that the multiplicity of figures given to Knox were not intended to enlighten but were intended to put a film of sweet lusciousness over the shell of a bitter coconut.

As to the element of damage for mental suffering, I cannot yet say I am satisfied with the American Law Institute's work in the field. Some day I may be. Fraser v. Blue Cross Animal Hospital, 39 Haw. 370, convinces me, in a diversity case, I should concur in the allowance for that item. In another case from another state, the question will have to be reexamined.

If history repeats itself, many good insurance men will be encouraged to be alarmed that this decision puts their livelihood in jeopardy. There is no reason to think so. The answer is: "Read the facts—if you have a full hour to do so."

Lindner v. Barlow, Davis & Wood
District Court of Appeal, California
210 Calif. App. 2d 660, 27 Calif. Rptr. 101 (1962)

BRAY, P. J.—Plaintiff appeals from an adverse judgment in a nonjury trial, in an action for alleged malpractice by defendants.

QUESTIONS PRESENTED

1. Sufficiency of findings and evidence to support them.

2. Was plaintiff's examination of defendant Wood improperly restricted?

EVIDENCE

Plaintiff is the widow of Clarence Lindner who died in January, 1952. Defendants are certified public accountants, engaged in the practice of accounting, including tax phases thereof. From time to time, since before 1948, defendants were employed by Clarence Lindner and plaintiff to prepare federal and California income tax returns, income tax estimates, and to do related accounting work as requested.

For many years Lindner had been and at the time of death was publisher of the San Francisco Examiner; director and vice president of Hearst Publishing Company, Inc., the owner of the Examiner; and director and vice president of Hearst Consolidated Publications, Inc., the owner of all the stock of Hearst Publishing Company, Inc.

For a period of approximately five years commencing in about March 1952, Hearst Publishing Company, Inc. (hereinafter called Hearst) paid plaintiff certain monies in weekly installments pursuant to and in accordance with a resolution of its board of directors. These payments were made after deducting United States income tax withheld by Hearst, and by it remitted to the government.

The payments were made pursuant to and as part of a plan, practice, custom and policy of Hearst to make payments to widows of deceased publishers and certain lesser executives who had rendered long and faithful service. This practice was known to Lindner during his lifetime. He and Hearst contemplated that if he remained faithfully in Hearst's employment and service, his widow would receive such payments.

In March, 1952, Garrett McEnerney, of the law firm of McEnerney & Jacobs, Hearst's attorney, who was also attorney for plaintiff as executrix of her husband's will and for her individually in all matters arising out of his death, informed plaintiff that Hearst would make such payments, subject to Hearst's obligation to withhold federal income taxes thereon on the grounds that they constituted taxable income to plaintiff; at about that time plaintiff received a copy of the above mentioned resolution.

In April 1952, plaintiff told defendant Wood that she was to receive payments from Hearst, that McEnerney had advised her that Hearst would withhold taxes thereon, and that Wood should speak to Attorney Haile, an employee of McEnerney & Jacobs. Wood was informed by Haile that Hearst would withhold the taxes. Wood so informed plaintiff.

There is a conflict in the testimony of plaintiff and Wood as to whether plaintiff protested to Wood that the payments should not constitute taxable income.

In February 1953, Hearst issued a withholding statement (W-2 form) and McEnerney & Jacobs forwarded it to plaintiff. This showed the belief of plaintiff's counsel that said weekly payments made in 1952 were taxable, and showed the withholding and payment by Hearst of plaintiff's federal income taxes thereon. In April 1952, defendants prepared an amended estimate of plaintiff's 1952 income tax and in April 1953, defendants prepared plaintiff's 1952 income tax return with the withholding statement attached. The latter was accompanied by defendants' written statement to plaintiff that said return was based upon records and information not independently verified by them. Both statements showed the Hearst payments as taxable income and were signed and filed by plaintiff without comment. In the years 1954 through 1957, Hearst sent plaintiff similar withholding statements. She in turn sent them to defendants, who prepared each year's returns showing the payments as taxable income. Each return was accompanied by a written statement to the effect that such return was based upon information not independently verified by defendants. Each was signed and filed by plaintiff without comment.

In April 1957, plaintiff read of a tax court decision holding that corporation payments to the widow of a deceased executive were not taxable. She then consulted with lawyers who filed for her claims for refund of the federal income taxes paid on account of the Hearst payments for the years 1954, 1955 and 1956. The claims were denied. Suit was then filed thereon and in November 1958, the suit was settled by the refund to plaintiff of all of said taxes plus interest. Thereafter, plaintiff obtained administrative refund of the California income taxes paid for the years 1953 to 1956, inclusive.

March 13, 1959, this action was commenced. The action is essentially one for alleged malpractice of defendants as certified public accountants. It is based partly on contract and partly on negligence. Count I is for the recovery of the 1952 federal taxes plus interest, alleged to have been lost through defendant's negligence, because any claim therefor was barred by the statute of limitations. Count II for the 1953 federal taxes, and count III for the 1952 California taxes are likewise based upon negligence. Counts IV, V, and VI are respectively for the same recovery, but based on alleged breach of contract.

1. *Findings and Evidence.*

Plaintiff conceded that defendants acted properly and without negligence in the preparation of each year's tax returns. She claims, however, that defendants breached an alleged duty to file protective claims for refund or to advise plaintiff to do so through an attorney. Plaintiff contends that such a duty arises where a doubtful question exists with respect to whether or not payments are taxable income and that defendants knew, or should have known, that such doubtful question existed.

The court's findings on certain key questions of fact in the case,

APPENDIX 457

if supported, make consideration of most of the questions of law and of other findings raised by plaintiff immaterial. The findings on the key questions of fact are: (1) That defendants were employed to do the work on the basis of data, records, and information supplied by plaintiff, by her attorneys, and by others designated by her, without independent verification by defendants. (2) That plaintiff never disclosed the existence of the Hearst resolution to defendants and they did not learn of its existence until the bringing of this action. (3) That defendants understood that the McEnerney law firm was plaintiff's counsel in regard to the payments here involved. (4) That the care, skill and learning ordinarily possessed by certified public accountants in San Francisco did not require defendants to file or advise plaintiff to file claims for refund or require the accountants to make independent investigations; that it is the accepted standard of practice in San Francisco of certified public accountants engaged in income tax work in such a case as this to rely upon withholding statements (W-2 forms) issued by corporate payors as to taxable status of moneys so reported. (5) That plaintiff at no time protested to defendants that the Hearst payments were not taxable income.

As to (1) the evidence clearly shows that the agreement between plaintiff and defendants did not contemplate independent verification of the data received by defendants from plaintiff. As to (2) plaintiff concedes that at no time did she inform defendants of the Hearst resolution. As to (3) defendant Wood testified that it was his understanding that plaintiff was being advised by the McEnerney firm. The McEnerney firm was the attorney for Mrs. Lindner as executrix of her husband's estate and in all matters arising out of her husband's death including "these Hearst payments." The fact that plaintiff had Wood contact an employee of that firm justified such an assumption. There was no evidence that Wood was ever informed to the contrary. As to (4) there was expert evidence to the effect that certified public accountants in San Francisco rely upon the withholding forms unless the client indicates that he is not satisfied that the payments indicated thereon are taxable.

[A]ccountants have been recognized as 'a skilled professional class . . . subject generally to the same rules of liability for negligence in the practice of their profession as are members of other skilled professions.' " (Hawkins, *Professional Negligence Liability of Public Accountants*, (1959) 12 Vanderbilt L. Rev. 797; see also Prosser on Torts, p. 132; Rest., Torts, § 299, com. d, p. 805.)

As members of a skilled profession they are experts. The duty of experts is well expressed in *Gagne v. Bertran* (1954) 43 Cal.2d 481, 489 [275 P.2d 15]: "The services of experts are sought because of their special skill. They have a duty to exercise the ordinary skill and competence of members of their profession, and a failure to discharge that duty will subject them to liability for negligence. Those who hire such persons are not justified in expecting infallibility, but can expect only reasonable care and competence. They purchase service, not insurance. [Citations.]"

It is conceded that the standards of care of accountants in this area ("the ordinary skill and competence" referred to in *Gagne, supra*) does not require in the absence of complaint by the client that the payment is not taxable, an independent investigation by the accountant, in a situation where, as here, the employer determines withholding to be necessary.

This brings us to (5): Did plaintiff so protest? As to this, plaintiff testified that on three occasions in the spring and summer of 1952 she protested that the payments did not constitute taxable income. Defendant Wood denied that she had so protested. He admitted that she had mentioned a certain case to him and asked whether it affected the taxability of the payments she was receiving. He looked up the case and found it dealt with a distinction between capital gain and ordinary income, and had nothing to do with the taxability or non-taxability of payments, and he so told her. It is contended that on cross-examination he appears to have hedged somewhat on his denial. However, it needs no citation of authority for the well known rule that in a conflict in the testimony of two witnesses this court is bound by the finding of the trial court.

Plaintiff contends that the court indirectly found that plaintiff did so protest. This contention is based upon the following: Defendants proposed a finding of fact to the effect that plaintiff never asserted to defendants that the Hearst payments were not taxable and never complained of McEnerney's advice, or the withholding of the tax or of defendants' treatment of the payments as taxable. Plaintiff objected to this proposed finding and requested a specific finding "Whether or not plaintiff protested to defendant Wood in 1952 that the Hearst payments did not constitute taxable income to her." The court found: "At no time from February, 1953, when the first W-2 form herein was issued by Hearst, until the date of suit did the plaintiff ever protest to the defendant that the payments which were the subject of such withholdings were not subject to income tax." Additionally the court found: " At all times between April 1952 and April

1957, the plaintiff acquiesced in defendants' action and conduct as set forth above, and plaintiff never during said period nor prior to the filing of this suit in March 1959, objected to defendants of said actions and conduct. Defendants at all times prior to the filing of this suit relied upon the said acquiescence and said failure to object."

At first blush there appears to be some ambiguity or uncertainty between these two findings. It is the duty of this court to attempt to reconcile the ambiguities and uncertainties and to resolve them in favor of sustaining the judgment.... The finding first above was set forth in the final sentence of a finding dealing with the right of defendants to rely on the W-2 forms, and the corresponding absence of duty to undertake individual investigations. Taken in that context it is understandable why the sentence begins "At no time from February, 1953, when the first W-2 form herein was issued...." It therefore cannot be considered an indirect finding that plaintiff did protest prior to that date. The second finding above set forth to the effect that "At all times between April 1952 and April 1957," plaintiff acquiesced in defendants' action and "never during said period . . . objected" is a definite finding adverse to plaintiff's testimony. The lack of objection to defendants' conduct found encompasses the lack of any protest regarding the tax status. Findings should be liberally construed so as to uphold the judgment. Thus, even if the duty of care included the duty to investigate after protest, the findings are that no protest was made.

Plaintiff concedes that if no protest was made to defendants, they were entitled to rely on Hearst's action in withholding and on the W-2 forms. As stated, the findings are supported. There was the above mentioned testimony of Wood; plaintiff's testimony that she never showed a copy of the resolution to Wood; plaintiff's admitted failure to protest the taxability when the first W-2 form was received and in subsequent years; plaintiff's signing under oath the tax returns for the various years, which were accompanied by defendant's statements of no independent verification, and her failure to pursue the question of taxability with McEnerney.

OTHER FINDINGS

The court found that had defendants known that payments were being made pursuant to the Hearst resolution, they would have had no more reason to believe that a doubtful question of law existed than without this information; that the solution of the question as to the taxability of the payments involved difficult and doubtful legal questions as opposed to simple or routine legal questions; that on the basis of decisions prior to 1952 and information furnished defendants by plaintiff, defendants did not know, nor should they have known, as certified public accountants, that there was any question of law as to the taxability of the payments. "Subsequent decisions indicating a more liberal attitude with respect to the taxability of such payments culminating in the promulgation of a more liberal policy announced by the Commissioner on August 25, 1958 did not impose any duty on defendants to recommend the filing of protective refund claims or the employment of an attorney prior to that date."

In view of the fact that the court found that defendants did not see the Hearst resolution and that defendants were entitled to rely on the W-2 forms, we deem it unnecessary to consider the evidence upon which the court made the above findings. They are immaterial and not necessary to the judgment. In view of the fact that defendants had no duty under the circumstances to inquire into the effect of the resolution or to act otherwise than they did, it is futile to inquire into what might have been the situation had the facts in the case been otherwise.

In view of the court's findings on failure of plaintiff to object to the withholding, we deem it unnecessary to consider the other questions raised by plaintiff, all of which are based upon the assumption that plaintiff did so object. Nor do we deem it necessary to discuss defendants' contention that the action is barred by the statute of limitations, a matter which the court, although asked to make a direct finding, did not include in its conclusions of law.

2. *Examination of Defendant Wood.*

Plaintiff examined defendant Wood under section 2055 of the Code of Civil Procedure. Wood was asked, "Now, a CPA who prepared a return and computed the tax without familiarizing himself concerning the facts and the law to the end that the client's tax would be held to the amount legally due and no more would not be exercising the amount of learning and skill ordinarily exercised, would he?" The court sustained its own objection that the question called for the opinion and conclusion of the witness on the ultimate issue. Obviously this was a "loaded" question and did not take into consideration the real issue in the case, namely, whether or not defendants under the circumstances were entitled to rely on the W-2 forms.

Plaintiff asked several similar questions to which the court sustained objections. Finally, plaintiff asked the question, including in it the element of protest by the client. The question should have been permitted. However, the ruling sustaining an objection to it could not have been prejudicial for two reasons: one, the court then asked Wood what he conceived was the function of a certified public accountant employed to prepare a tax return, and Wood's answer covered the matter asked for in plaintiff's question; and secondly, the standard of care required of an accountant in this area was never in dispute.

The judgment is affirmed.

Bancroft v. Indemnity Insurance Co. of North America
U. S. District Court, Western District of Louisiana
203 F. Supp. 49 (1962)

BEN C. DAWKINS, Jr., Chief Judge.

Presented here is an action for damages arising from an alleged breach of contract involving professional accounting services. It is brought by T. O. Bancroft, president of Bancroft Bag Factory, Inc., and his wife, of Monroe, Louisiana, against the professional liability insurer of a firm of Certified Public Accountants practicing in Monroe.

The facts forming the basis of the suit occurred during an accountant-client relationship which had existed between plaintiffs and defendant's insured since approximately 1938, the insured having been employed originally by plaintiffs while Bancroft was operating as an individual, then as a partnership, and later as principal stockholder of Bancroft Bag Factory, Inc., and Bancroft Paper Company, Inc.

May 23, 1955, Bancroft directed a letter to a member of the insured firm in which he explained that several stockholders in the bag factory, who were children of the Bancroft family, owed money to the bag factory and that a plan had occurred to him which possibly would effect a means of payment with minimum tax consequences. The following question was asked.

> T. O. Bancroft, Sr. owns a certain amount of stock in the Bancroft Paper Company, Inc. This stock was acquired during the married life of T. O. Bancroft, Sr., and Vada Speed Bancroft, and is community property. Would it be possible, and not in violation of any law, for a sufficient amount of this stock to be sold to the Bancroft Bag Factory, Inc., and one-half of the sale price to be credited to Vada Speed Bancroft account on Bancroft Bag Factory, Inc. books, and one half sale price credited to T. O. Bancroft, Sr. on Bancroft Bag Factory, Inc. books, and these

credits could set-off the debit charges by gifts from Vada and myself to the three children at the rate of legal gift limits per year until the accounts are balanced.

The Bancroft Paper Company stock is Par $100.00 per share, and is maintained at that value by the distribution of dividends and bonuses each year.

Please let me have your opinion in writing concerning this proposal.

The insured C.P.A. replied May 25, 1955, in a letter addressed to Bancroft, in the following language:

Reply to your letter of May 23, 1955, is made as follows:
You and Mrs. Bancroft propose to sell a certain amount of Bancroft Paper Company, Inc. stock at $100.00 per share to Bancroft Bag Factory, Inc. We understand that Bancroft Paper Company, Inc. stock has been kept at a book value of about $100.00 per share by the payment of dividends and that its selling price is $100.00 per share and your cost is the same amount per share. In our opinion, there would be no Federal or Louisiana income tax on the sale of the stock.

We further understand that you are not to receive cash for the stock but that a credit will be set up for you and Mrs. Bancroft on the books of the Bancroft Bag Factory, Inc. Each calendar year you propose to make a gift of $3,000.00 to each of your three children by crediting their account due the Bancroft Bag Factory, Inc. and charging your account. Mrs. Bancroft will do likewise. The total gifts to the three children will be $18,000.00 annually. Such a transaction would not involve any Federal Gift Tax as a person may give $3,000.00 (the maximum annual exclusion) per year to as many individuals as he may choose without gift tax.

Relying on this advice, September 15, 1955, plaintiffs sold 410 shares of their stock in the paper company to the bag factory for $41,000.00; and October 18, 1957, they sold an additional 187 shares of paper company stock to the bag factory for $18,700.00. These two transactions were accomplished by bookkeeping entries on the accounts of the two corporations, the two sums being credited to plaintiffs' accounts on the books of the bag factory, thereby satisfying their children's indebtedness and leaving a credit balance. Following the 1955 transaction, plaintiffs' accounts in the bag factory were debited for $8,149.17 and the accounts of their children were credited with an equal amount to reflect gifts from the parents to the children.

In 1959, the Internal Revenue Service audited plaintiffs' income tax returns, including those for 1955 and 1957, and subsequently notified them that the two stock transactions were subject to the provisions of Section 304 of the 1954 Internal Revenue Code (26 U.S.C. § 304); that the sums received by plaintiffs from the sales of stock in 1955 and 1957 would be treated, for tax purposes, as dividends and taxed accordingly. The government's position was summarized in a letter dated December 1, 1959, from the office of the District Director, Internal Revenue Service, addressed to plaintiffs. After listing net adjustments (increases) to taxable income in the sum of $41,000.00 and describing them as "Dividends from Bancroft Bag Factory, Inc.," the letter explained:

(1) The sale of 410 shares of stock of Bancroft Paper Co., Inc., in year 1955 to Bancroft Bag Factory, Inc., and the sale of 187 shares of stock of Bancroft Paper Co., Inc., to Bancroft Bag Factory, Inc., in year 1957, by the taxpayers, constitutes a distribution in redemption of the stock of Bancroft Bag Factory, Inc., in the amount of the sales proceeds. The proposed adjustment is to include in income the dividends resulting from the redemption. See Sec. 304 of the Internal Revenue Code of 1954. The assessment of additional tax in year 1955 is not barred by the statute of limitations because of the omission of over 25% of the amount of gross income stated in the return. See Sec. 6501(e) of the Internal Revenue Code of 1954.

In an effort to reach an accord with the Internal Revenue Service and for purposes of securing a review of the adjustments, an informal conference was held among Bancroft, representatives of the Internal Revenue Service, the insured C.P.A., and D. C. Bernhardt, an attorney and certified public accountant then representing plaintiffs. The insured C.P.A. testified that all parties agreed that the assessment was owed for the stock sales in 1955 and 1957:

Q. You agreed to the assessment by the Federal Government and, in substance, told Mr. Bancroft he would have to pay it; isn't that right?
A. Yes, sir.
Q. When did you tell him he would have to pay it? Would that be before this conference or after it?
A. No, sir. In this conference we all agreed the tax was owed. I don't believe the computation was made that day, but we discussed the items to be included in the settlement and he later submitted a computation to me of the tax.
Q. That result, * * * was very different from the advice set forth in your letter of May 25, 1955, that there would be no tax?
A. It sure was.
Q. How do you account for the results you got—let us say, bad result?
A. I simply, in my research, missed the new law.
THE COURT: What section was it you missed?

A. 304.
THE COURT: Of the 1954 Code?
A. Yes, sir.
BY MR. KING:
Q. Didn't you just, frankly, admit to Mr. Bancroft that you made a mistake?
A. Yes, sir.
Q. When you say you missed this Section 304, you were not aware of it, or what do you mean by that, * * *?
A. I think when he posed the question, or rather outlining there was no profit or loss in the question, I simply didn't carry my research far enough.
Q. It was there.
A. The Section was there, yes, sir.
Q. Didn't the section fit this pretty much like a glove?
A. I would say so.
Q. Has there been any change in that law since then?
A. Not that I know of.

The insured further testified that he considered himself employed by Bancroft and his wife at the time the advice was given and when the 1955 stock transaction occurred. He also testified, as did Bancroft, that the latter paid the assessment on the strength of his opinion that the additional tax was due, Bancroft thus relying further, at least partially, at the date of the extra assessment, on the professional advice of the insured.

Following the conference, adjustments were made by I. R. S., including an allowance for the tax-exempt gifts from the parents to the children, and a total additional assessment for the years 1955 and 1957 was fixed at $35,419.74. This amount was paid to the government April 5, 1960, and is the sum sued for here.

Defendant denies liability to plaintiffs for the amount of the additional income tax paid on the grounds that, notwithstanding payment of the extra assessment, the taxes were not legally owed under Section 304 and related sections of the Internal Revenue Code of 1954; that its insured did not fall below the standard of reasonable care required of professional accountants in advising his clients as to their tax problems; that, assuming the advice given plaintiffs was erroneous and the result of professional negligence, plaintiffs were not "justified" in relying thereon in the transactions which occurred, in the first instance, approximately four months and, in the second, two years and five months after rendition of the written opinion; that the insured C.P.A. committed a criminal act within the meaning of LSA— R.S. 37:213 (1950) by engaging in the unauthorized practice of law and, therefore, the terms of the professional liability policy did not extend coverage to include this.

We must, accordingly, determine the duty owed to plaintiffs by the insured. Accountants, "a skilled professional class * * * subject generally to the same rules of liability for negligence in the practice of their profession as are members of other skilled professions," have been held liable for damage to clients resulting from malpractice in actions founded both on contract and tort. . . .

This standard, which requires that an accountant exercise that degree of skill and competence reasonably expected of persons in his profession in the community, is implied in the contract for professional services and is brought about by the accountant-client relationship. The contract, therefore, creates the relationship out of which arises the duty to exercise reasonable care to render skillful performance according to local professional standards. Hawkins, Professional Negligence Liability of Public Accountants, 12 Vand.L.Rev. 797 (1959), and 54 A.L.R.2d 324, et seq. . . .

As noted, defendant argues that plaintiffs were not "justified" in either instance in relying on the written opinion which was rendered some four months prior to the first stock sale and approximately two years and five months prior to the second. We find that plaintiffs were reasonable in their belief that the advice given four months earlier was correct and still reliable when the first sale occurred.

Not having been challenged about the first transaction by I.R.S., plaintiffs understandably followed the identical procedure in selling the stock in 1957. The insured having been retained as plaintiffs' C.P.A. and tax consultant for approximately seventeen years, surely plaintiffs were entitled to believe that, should a change in the Code have occurred within the four-months period, the insured would have notified them of it. Bancroft testified that in selling the stock in both 1955 and 1957 he relied on the advice of the insured. But for the insured's advice and the failure of the I.R.S. to question that transaction, presumably the 1957 stock transfer would not have been effected and that loss would not have occurred. It is reasonable to conclude, we think, that as time passed without objection from I.R.S. or notice from the insured Bancroft was justified in having confidence in the plan and in following the same procedure for sale of the additional stock in 1957.

Defendant contends that the advice given plaintiffs by the insured C.P.A. was not within the proper area of accounting; that his opinion actually was a legal view which lawfully could be rendered only by a licensed attorney-at-law; that, therefore, the insured committed a crime within the purview of LSA-R.S. 37:213 (1950), and that neither he nor his insurer can be held liable for his negligently rendering legal advice because plaintiffs knew that he was not licensed to practice law. Defendant urges, *ergo*, that its professional liability policy does not extend coverage to the risk of liability for its insured's performance of a criminal act.

Without judging the merits of the accounting profession's *de facto* rendition of quasi-legal services, we must take judicial notice of the fact that, in Monroe, Louisiana, as elsewhere, C.P.A.'s regularly render opinions and advise their clients on matters of federal and state income tax liability as a routine matter in performance of their professional services. As a matter of fact, attorneys-at-law frequently refer clients to C.P.A.'s for such advice, which is in a specialized field; and attorneys also seek such advice directly from C.P.A.'s. In writing the policy here sued upon, defendant is bound to have known of this almost universal practice.

This is further borne out by the testimony of the insured, who stated that he has rendered opinions and given advice as to tax consequences of various transactions during the whole of his professional career; and by the testimony of Lambert, who said that the problem was one both of accounting and taxation and it therefore was within the proper province of a C.P.A. to render an opinion on the probable tax results of the proposed stock transfer. We hold, therefore, that, had the action been brought against the insured, the mixed legal and accounting nature of the opinion would not have been a valid defense on the grounds urged by defendant, i. e., that plaintiffs knew the insured could not practice law.

Defendant further maintains that the policy itself does not extend coverage to include the risk of liability for professional negligence in rendering what defendant insists was a purely legal opinion. The insuring agreement provides, in part:

1. Accountant's Professional Liability
To pay on behalf of the insured all sums which the insured shall become legally obligated to pay for damages caused or alleged to have been caused by the insured, any predecessor in business, any accounting organization acting under contract with the insured or any partner or employee of any of the foregoing, in the performance of professional services for others, including but not limited to breach of contract,

(a) through *neglect, error or omission;* [Emphasis supplied.]
(b) through dishonesty, misrepresentation or fraud, except if made or committed by the insured or any partner with affirmative dishonesty or actual intent to deceive or defraud;
(c) through civil libel or slander or defamation of character, except if committed by an insured in bad faith and except loss and expense due to criminal libel or criminal slander by the insured or by any partner or employee of the insured.

As we read the insurance contract, the form of liability for professional negligence incurred in this instance is reasonably included within the broad coverage of the policy, that is, liability for professional negligence occurring in a mixed area of accounting and law, a twilight zone where both professions find common ground and, in some instances at least, are equally competent to render expert advice. Authorities cited by defendant point up the deep significance of the professional disagreement between the American, State and local Bar Associations on the one hand, and the American, State and local Institutes of Accountants on the other.

We ask this pertinent question: Had defendant not undertaken to insure against the risk of professional liability for negligence in rendering an opinion as to tax consequences, knowing full well that C.P.A.'s give such opinions every day, why was this not made a specific exception or exclusion in the insurance contract here in view of continuing disagreement between the two professional groups as to appropriate spheres of services for each?

Because this policy was written without the insured having been consulted as to its form or content, under the rule of liberal construction, every reasonable effort should be invoked to secure coverage to the insured and in favor of the damaged parties. Collard v. Globe Indemnity Co., 50 So.2d 838 (1st Cir., La.App., 1951). Jones v. Standard Life & Acc. Ins. Co., 115 So.2d 630 (2d Cir., La.App., 1959), and authorities cited therein.

Moreover, we do not think that these plaintiffs, the damaged clients, should be left without a remedy because of the frustrated attempts of the two professions to delineate the outer limits of their respective activities and competence. Admittedly, there is a valid difference of opinion on this subject but we are not, in this ruling, attempting to further the cause of either side. *We are, however, protecting innocent clients who have been damaged by a C.P.A.'s professional negligence, from the hiatus which the professions themselves have been unable to resolve.*

Defendant submits that, if it is liable, its liability is considerably less than the $35,419.74 assessment paid by the Bancrofts to I.R.S.; that in the 1955 transaction plaintiffs did not lose their cost or basis in the Bancroft Paper Company stock because under Section 304 plaintiffs are treated as having made a contribution to capital of the bag factory in the sum of $32,850.83. Therefore, argues defendant, plaintiffs may sell their stock in the bag factory and recover not only their initial cost but $32,850.83 in addition without paying any income tax. Defendant concludes, therefore, that plaintiffs will be left in a superior position to that existing before the transactions occurred because besides receiving $32,850.83 "tax free," plaintiffs will have an investment in that amount which they may recover without taxes at any time in the future.

We are not impressed with this argument, first, because plaintiffs, through the sale, have lost direct ownership of the 597 shares of stock in the paper company, and those shares now belong to the bag factory. . . . Moreover, an increased basis, or cost, in the capital of the bag factory may be a tax benefit in some years but not in others, depending on the then status of the I.R.C. The future possibilities are too speculative to calculate with any degree of exactness and would depend upon many variables, e. g., the current market value of the stock, other income received in the same year by plaintiffs, and whether the stock is subject to estate taxes.

Finding the defenses asserted to be invalid, and for the reasons given, there will be judgment for plaintiffs as prayed.

Present decree.

Miles v. Livingstone
U. S. Court of Appeals, First Circuit
301 F. 2d 99 (1962)

Before WOODBURY, Chief Judge, and HARTIGAN and ALDRICH, Circuit Judges.

HARTIGAN, Circuit Judge.

This is an appeal from a judgment of the United States District Court for the District of Massachusetts directing a verdict for the defendant in a civil action to recover prepaid interest on three loans arranged by the defendant, a dealer in government securities, the proceeds of which were to be used by the plaintiff to buy certain government securities from the defendant for the dual purpose of obtaining an advantageous deduction on his federal income tax return for the interest paid, and insuring that any profit realized on the transaction would be taxed at capital gains rates.

Plaintiff-appellant's complaint is in three counts: the first count alleging a scheme or artifice to defraud under federal securities regulations; the second count alleging an action in common-law deceit and the third count alleging a breach of the three contracts. In his answer the defendant admitted that he contracted with the plaintiff on three occasions relative to arranging loans and selling bonds, but denied that the loans and sales did not in fact take place. As affirmative defenses he alleged the statute of limitations and knowledge on the part of the plaintiff of all facts and circumstances concerning the transactions.

The type of transaction which forms the basis of the present action has been a source of a great deal of litigation. The facts underlying two of the three transactions involved here are virtually identical with those before us and recounted at length in Goodstein v. Commissioner, 267 F.2d 127 (1 Cir. 1959).[1] We do not believe it essential to repeat them here in detail. In general, however, the record indicates that the transactions as envisioned by the parties were to unfold as follows: defendant would enter into a contract to sell certain government bonds to the plaintiff on a given date at a stipulated price. At or about the same time defendant would arrange a loan for the plaintiff with a finance company to finance the purchase price of the bonds. The finance company would forward the proceeds of the loan to the defendant in payment of the bonds. Plaintiff would execute a nonrecourse note for the loan in favor of the finance company and pledge the bonds as security. Defendant would send to the finance company the bonds which the plaintiff had purchased. The excess of the proceeds of the loan over the purchase price of the bonds would be forwarded to the plaintiff. The plaintiff would then send a check to the finance company prepaying the total interest due on the loan. When plaintiff's note became due, the finance company would be instructed to sell the bonds and use the proceeds to pay the note. The finance company would do this and then render the plaintiff a final statement.

In the course of the three transactions plaintiff contracted to purchase $1,375,000 of United States Treasury notes and bonds. The only money which he paid out was an aggregate of some $18,000 in

[1] The third transaction differed only in the time interval which elapsed during certain steps of the transaction.

interest payments to the finance companies. All of the foregoing constituent stages in each transaction were duly reflected in elaborate bookkeeping entries and in the drawing of notes and checks. However, the transactions were essentially "paper" ones and the finance companies which were utilized to finance the transactions were in fact alter egos of the defendant.

Unlike the instant case, the type of transactions usually involved here have been analyzed in the context of a dispute involving the deductibility of interest payments under the federal income tax laws. In such a context, courts have unvaryingly held that the purported interest payments could not be deducted as their underlying events lacked substance. One court in noting the lack of economic reality to the transactions, stated "[The] Decision here can be placed on the more fundamental ground that all the elaborate drawing of checks, execution of notes and bookkeeping entries performed by taxpayers, Livingstone and Gail, did not in fact produce the legal transactions which they simulated." Lynch v. Commissioner, 273 F.2d 867, 871 (2 Cir. 1959). Another court, in disallowing a similar attempted interest deduction, stated that "In reality, this financial round robin was only a paper transaction that did not involve any real Treasury notes or any real money. * * * " Broome v. United States, 170 F.Supp. 613, 614, 145 Ct.Cl. 298 (1959). This court reached the same conclusion in Goodstein v. Commissioner, supra.

After plaintiff's attempt to deduct the interest which he had prepaid on the "loans" was disallowed, he initiated the instant action. His central position is that until the attempted deductions were disallowed, he was unaware that these transactions lacked substance. Relying on the line of cases of which Goodstein, supra, is an example, he argues that neither a sale of the bonds nor a loan of money ever took place and that the paper shuffling of the defendant was a fraudulent device or artifice as to him.

Despite the arguments advanced in the brief of defendant's counsel, we believe that the district court was correct in directing a verdict for the defendant.

First of all, so far as the sale aspects of the transactions went, viz., the sale of bonds from Livingstone to Miles, this phase of the transactions was sufficiently viable that Miles could and did claim a capital gain on each of these transactions and duly recorded the gain on his income tax returns. If the sales were valid to this extent it is extremely difficult for us to see how plaintiff can now claim that there was in fact no sale.

Secondly, concerning the loans, it is true that several courts, including our own, have held that facts similar to those involved here did not give rise to a "loan" in the sense that interest paid incident thereto could be deducted under the tax laws. However, none of those cases had been decided at the time that the present transactions were negotiated. The question of how these arrangements would pass judicial scrutiny was then an open one. It is true that subsequently, in keeping with the well settled principle that substance and not form governs the administration of the revenue laws, the transactions were held incapable of effectuating their desired result. However, because a court might later hold that a particular transaction did not achieve a desired tax result in that it lacked economic reality, it does not necessarily follow that such a transaction must be branded as a fraudulent device or artifice. Plaintiff makes such an argument here.

In this case plaintiff, a college graduate, was an extremely successful and obviously astute business man. He earned a salary that ranged between $50,000 and $75,000 a year during the period that these transactions were negotiated. His motives in entering the instant transactions were not to physically acquire bonds but, obviously, to generate a structure of documentation which would present advantageous tax benefits to him. To be sure, as he contends, he wanted the transactions to be *bona fide*, but it does not appear that the specific physical form in which the transactions were to be cast was of particular moment to him. This he admitted at the trial.

The record indicates that throughout the proceedings he was guided by a tax advisor who was also a lawyer to whom he granted complete authority to handle all the pertinent details—short of actually consummating the transactions. In addition he was advised by another counsel who apparently watched over the activities of the "tax advisor."

Our reading of the entire record leads us to agree with the conclusion of the district judge that:

> * * * It is quite plain that the three transactions were spurious and without substance and that both the plaintiff and the defendant knew it.
>
> No reasonable person could accept as true the plaintiff's story that he really believed he could buy $1,375,000 in United States Treasury notes and bonds by paying out a little more than $18,000 without incurring further liability and at the same time acquire the right to claim on his income tax returns deductions for alleged interest payments totaling more than $77,000, resulting in a tax savings amounting to several times his original outlay of $18,000.

Judgment will be entered affirming the judgment of the district court.

United States v. Bowman
U. S. District Court, Middle District of Pennsylvania
236 F. Supp. 548 (1964)

NEALON, District Judge.

This action has been brought pursuant to Section 7402(b) of the Internal Revenue Code of 1954, for the purpose of judicially enforcing an Internal Revenue summons issued to Melvyn R. Bowman, as resident partner of the accounting firm of Main, LaFrentz and Comany.

The summons herein involved was issued by the petitioner, John P. Wright, Special Agent of the Internal Revenue Service, on May 20, 1964, in connection with an investigation by the Internal Revenue Service of the tax liabilities of New Enterprise Stone & Lime Company for the years 1956 through 1962, and directed respondent to produce for examination certain work papers, schedules, memoranda, correspondence and accounting reports prepared by his firm for said company. On June 2, 1964, the respondent, Melvyn R. Bowman, appeared in response to the summons, but refused to comply, relying on the provisions of Title 63 of Purdon's Pennsylvania Statutes Annotated, Section 9.11a, which makes communications between an accountant and his client privileged.

A hearing was held before this Court on October 2, 1964, and at that time C. Galen Detwiler, Dale W. Detwiler, Emmert I. Detwiler, Paul I. Detwiler, all brothers, and New Enterprise Stone & Lime Company, Inc., New Enterprise Equipment & Supply Company, Inc., and Somerset Limestone Company, Inc., of which corporations the Detwiler brothers are the sole stockholders, were allowed to intervene. The documents requested in the summons pertain to the abovementioned corporations. The respondent, Melvyn R. Bowman, argued that his refusal to comply with the summons was justified in light of the Accountant-Client Privilege in Pennsylvania and, in the alternative, that the summons issued is too broad and too vague and, therefore, should be set aside. The intervening respondents contend that the Accountant-Client Privilege applies and, also, that their rights under the Fourth and Fifth Amendments of the United States Constitution and under the provisions of § 7605 of the Internal Revenue

APPENDIX 473

Code of 1954 would be violated if obedience to the summons was ordered.

The first question raised by both the respondent and respondent-intervenors is whether or not the State-created privilege of confidential communications between a Certified Public Accountant and his client is applicable in an investigation before a Special Agent of the Internal Revenue Service. The Pennsylvania Statute relating to the privilege reads as follows:

§ 9.11a   Privileged communication

Except for permission of the client or person or firm or corporation engaging him or the heirs, successors or personal representatives of such client or person or firm or corporation, a certified public accountant or a person employed by a certified public accountant shall not be required to, and shall not voluntarily, disclose or divulge information of which he may have become possessed relative to and in connection with any professional services as a certified public accountant other than the examination of audit of or report on any financial statements, books, records or accounts, which he may be engaged to make or requested by a prospective client to discuss. The information derived from or as the result of such professional services shall be deemed confidential and privileged: Provided, however, That nothing herein shall be taken or construed as modifying, changing or affecting the criminal or bankruptcy laws of this Commonwealth or of the United States. 1947, May 26, P.L. 318, § 11.1, added 1961, Sept. 2, P.L. 1165, § 8.

The respondent and respondent-intervenors contend that just as the confidential relationship between attorney and client is recognized in both State and Federal proceedings, so, too, should the accountant-client relationship be equally recognized. In support of his argument, the respondent relies on Baird v. Koerner, Special Agent, Internal Revenue Service, 279 F.2d 623, 95 A.L.R.2d 303 (9th Cir. 1960). The petitioner, on the other hand, asserts that a State evidentiary statute is not applicable to a Federal administrative proceeding which is being conducted pursuant to the provisions of Section 7602 of the Internal Revenue Code of 1954. In support of this argument the petitioner cites Falsone v. United States, 205 F.2d 734 (5th Cir. 1953), certiorari denied 346 U.S. 864; In Re Albert Lindley Lee Memorial Hospital, 209 F.2d 122 (2d Cir. 1953); F. T. C. v. St. Regis Paper Co., 304 F.2d 731 (7th Cir. 1962).

The law is clear that investigations by Federal administrative agencies are not judicial proceedings and are not, therefore, restricted by rules of evidence applicable in courts of law. In Re Albert Lindley

Lee Memorial Hospital (supra); In Re Colton v. United States, 306 F.2d 633 (2d Cir. 1962). Furthermore, "(i)nvestigators for federal purposes may not be prevented by matters depending upon state law." United States v. Murdock, 284 U.S. 141, 149 (1931). In the case at bar the respondent's papers are being summoned by an administrative agency of the Federal government. Such an investigation is not a judicial proceeding to which a State evidentiary statute should apply. Moreover, it is well established that there is no accountant-client privilege recognizable in the Federal system. Petition of Borden Co., 75 F.Supp. 857 (E.D.Ill.1948); United States v. Culver, 224 F.Supp. 419 (D.C. Md.1963); In Re Kearney, 227 F.Supp. 174 (S.D.N.Y.1964). In recent years legislation has been enacted in several States extending the privilege to accountants, journalists and psychologists, but in none of these instances have the Federal Courts given recognition to the State-created privilege.

In Falsone v. United States (supra), the Court refused to apply the accountant-client privilege, provided by the Florida statute, to a proceeding before an Internal Revenue Agent. The Court noted that "the system of rules of evidence in force for trials by jury or even in courts of equity is not applicable, either by historical precedent, or by sound practical policy, to inquiries of fact determinable by administrative tribunals or officers." The Federal Courts of Illinois have refused to recognize the accountant statute for the reason that "to do so would result in a frustration of the Federal Government's performance of a necessary investigatory function." See F.T.C. v. St. Regis Paper Co. (supra) and also, Petition of Borden Co. (supra).

The Court of Appeals for the Third Circuit has not had an opportunity to pass on the question of the applicability of Pennsylvania's statute involved herein, but in the recent case of Lustman v. C. I. R., 322 F.2d 253 (3d Cir. 1963), Falsone v. United States (supra) was cited with approval. The Court noted as follows:

> Confidential communications between a client and an accountant are not generally recognized as privileged. There is no sanction for the privilege in common law. See Wigmore, Evidence, § 2286 (McNaughton rev. 1961). And there is no state or federal statute applicable here which would confer such privilege. Moreover, where records relating to tax liability are the subject matter of inquiry, the Internal Revenue Code, Section 7602 (26 U.S.C.A. § 7602), negates any privilege which might otherwise exist. . . .

In my opinion, the decision in the Falsone case (supra) is based on sound and logical reasoning. The great weight of authority appears to be in agreement with it. Indeed, Professor Wigmore has cautioned against the expansion of privileges, stating:

> For more than three centuries it has now been recognized as a fundamental maxim that the public (in the words sanctioned by Lord Hardwicke) has a right to every man's evidence. When we come to examine the various claims of exemption, we start with the primary assumption that there is a general duty to give what testimony one is capable of giving, and that any exemptions which may exist are distinctly exceptional, being so many derogations from a positive general rule.... The investigation of truth and the enforcement of testimonial duty demand the restriction, not the expansion, of these privileges. They should be recognized only within the narrowest limits required by principle. Every step beyond these limits helps to provide, without any real necessity, an obstacle to the administration of justice. (8 Wigmore on Evidence (3d ed.), Sec. 2192, pp. 64, 67.)

Therefore, it is the conclusion of this Court that the Pennsylvania accountant-client privilege does not extend to an accountant summoned by a Special Agent of the Internal Revenue pursuant to the authority of Section 7402(b) of the Internal Revenue Code of 1954.

[Discussion of other issues omitted.]

United States Code, Title 5, Appendix
5 U.S.C. (Appendix) §1012

§ *1012. Representation of parties.*

(a) Federal agencies in general; membership of the bar of the highest court; declaration of qualification and authorization.

Any person who is a member in good standing of the bar of the highest court of any State, possession, territory, Commonwealth, or the District of Columbia may represent others before any agency upon filing with the agency a written declaration that he is currently qualified as provided by this subsection and is authorized to represent the particular party in whose behalf he acts.

(b) Internal Revenue Service; certified public accountants; declaration of qualification and authorization.

Any person who is duly qualified to practice as a certified public accountant in any State, possession, territory, Commonwealth, or the District of Columbia may represent others before the Internal Revenue Service of the Treasury Department upon filing with that agency a written declaration that he is currently qualified as provided by this subsection and is authorized to represent the particular party in whose behalf he acts.

(c) Appearance or representation by other persons; discipline; former officers or employees; power of attorney.

Nothing herein shall be construed (i) to grant or deny to any person who is not qualified as provided by subsection (a) or (b) of this section the right to appear for or represent others before any agency or in any agency proceeding; (ii) to authorize or limit the discipline, including disbarment, of persons who appear in a representative capacity before any agency; (iii) to authorize any person who is a former officer or employee of an agency to represent others before an agency where such representation is prohibited by statute or regulation; or (iv) to prevent an agency from requiring a power of attorney as a condition to the settlement of any controversy involving the payment of money.

Editor's Notes

18 § 102 (1939 Code) is now § 351 (accumulated earnings tax). The citations of the *Court Holding Co.* and *Cumberland Public Service Co.* cases are 324 U.S. 331 (1945) and 338 U.S. 451 (1950). For the effect of § 337, enacted in 1954, on these cases, see Bittker & Eustice, Federal Income Taxation of Corporations and Shareholders (3d ed., 1966), pp. 386ff.

20 The *Clifford* doctrine was laid down by Helvering v. Clifford, 309 U.S. 331 (1940). It was the basis of the so-called "Clifford Regulations," Treas. Regs. 118, § 39.22(a)-21, promulgated in 1945. In 1954, this area was covered by statutory provisions, §§ 673-675. Canons of Professional Ethics: For the new Code of Professional Responsibility, to supersede the 1908 Canons, see ABA Special Committee on Evaluation of Ethical Standards, Code of Professional Responsibility (1969), adopted by the ABA House of Delegates, Aug., 1969. See 55 A.B.A.J. 970 (1969).

25 Treasury Circular 230: See Appendix, this volume, p. 359.

26 *Mitchell:* The reference is evidently to Helvering v. Mitchell, 303 U.S. 391 (1938), involving an assessment of fraud penalties against Charles E. Mitchell, former president of the National City Bank.

29 On the accountant-client privilege, see United States v. Bowman, Appendix, this volume, p. 472.

32 Canons of Professional Ethics: See note to p. 20, supra.

33 Participation in bar association activities: A report to the Council of the ABA Section of Taxation by its Rules Committee states that "members of the Tax Section should always be mindful of their dual capacity." See 22 The Tax Lawyer, No. 4 (1968) (inside back cover).

37 King Committee: See Hearings before Subcommittee of House Committee on Ways and Means, 82d Cong., 1st sess., on Administration of the Internal Revenue Laws (4 vols., 1951); ibid., 82d Cong., 2d sess. (1952).

38 *Court Holding Co.* case: See note to p. 18, supra.

39 Sale to brother: See § 267(a)(1), disallowing a deduction for a loss on such a sale.

40 See Gregory v. Helvering, 293 U.S. 465 (1935); Helvering v. Horst, 311 U.S. 112 (1940); Helvering v. Clifford, 309 U.S. 331 (1940); Commissioner v. Tower, 327 U.S. 280 (1946).

42	"Recent scandals": See note to p. 37, supra.
44	Mr. Miller's paper is reprinted as Chapter 3 of this volume, p. 47.
50	§ 129 of the 1939 Code is now, with amendments, § 269 of the 1954 Code.
53	For subsequent statutory change, see note to p. 18, supra.
57	The "premiums paid" test of § 811(g) (1939 Code) has been repealed; see § 2042.
59	§ 102 (1939 Code) is now § 531 (accumulated earnings tax).
60	§ 112(k) (1939 Code) is now § 357.
62	King Committee: See note to p. 37, supra.
64	Note 2: The Tax Law Review symposium is reprinted as Chapter 2 of this volume; the Paul article is reprinted as Chapter 1.
66	"Double taxation" on corporate liquidation: see note to p. 18, supra.
72	§ 129 (1939 Code) is now § 269.
76	Treasury control over practice by attorneys: For a change in the law, see Bittker, Postscript, this volume, p. 289. Treasury Circular 230; See Appendix, this volume, p. 359.
77	Tax Law Review symposium: Reprinted as Chapter 1 of this volume.
79	*Clifford* doctrine: See note to p. 20, supra.
80	Lobbying: This area was changed in 1962 by the enactment of § 162(e).
85	Mr. Paul suffered a heart attack while testifying at a hearing of the Joint Committee on the Economic Report on national tax policy, and died shortly thereafter. New York Times, Feb. 7, 1956, p. 19.
89	Tax scandals: See note to p. 37, supra.
91	Preferred stock dividend: This area was altered by the enactment in 1954 of § 306. See Bittker & Eustice, Federal Income Taxation of Corporations and Shareholders (2d ed., 1966), pp. 326-328.
96	Lawyer-client privilege: See discussion of this matter by Maguire, this volume, at pp. 110-111 and 119-121.
101	Life insurance trusts: See § 677(a) (3).
106	Statute of limitations: § 6501(c)(1)-(3) (no limitation on assessment of tax in case of fraud, willful attempt to evade, or failure to file return); § 6501(e) (six years, formerly five, in case of omission in excess of 25% of income).
110	Note 6: The Tax Law Review symposium is reprinted as Chapter 2 of this volume; the Miller article as Chapter 3; the Paul article as Chapter 4; and the Harvard Law School pamphlet (a speech by Darrell) as Chapter 5.
111	Canons of Professional Ethics: See note to p. 20, supra. Treasury Circular 230: See Appendix, this volume, p. 359.
116	Tax practice as a field of specialization: See 21 The Tax Lawyer 728 (1968) and 22 ibid. 759 (1969), raising doubts about a certification procedure.
133	Dividends received deduction: § 243.
136	Treasury Circular 230: See Appendix, this volume, p. 359.
140	See Lykes v. United States, 343 U.S. 118 (1952); and its statutory aftermath, § 212(3).

EDITOR'S NOTES

142   Voluntary disclosure policy: See ABA Tax Section Bulletin, Oct. 1961, p. 32; Shotwell Mfg. Co. v. United States, 371 U.S. 341 (1963).
152   Treasury Circular 230: See Appendix, this volume, p. 359.
159   The AICPA's Committee on Federal Taxation has issued five "Statements on Responsibilities in Tax Practice," reprinted in Appendix, this volume, p. 382.
170   British practice: See Wheatcroft, this volume, p. 331.
176   See Eisenstein, A Critical View of the Treasury, 15 N.Y.U. Inst. on Fed. Taxation 21 (1957).
183   *Gregory* case: See note to p. 40, supra.
184   See Henry v. Commissioner, 36 T.C. 879 (1961) (yacht owned by tax lawyer and accountant, with red, white and blue flag bearing numerals "1040," allegedly to generate inquiries leading to business).
188   Treasury Circular 230: See Appendix, this volume, p. 359. Canons of Professional Ethics: See note to p. 20, supra.
195   Negligence penalty: See § 6653(a) (5% penalty for underpayment due to "negligence or intentional disregard of rules and regulations"); Hoffman, Intentional Disregard of Rules and Regulations, 28 Taxes 111 (1950).
201   *Livingstone* case: See Nichols v. Commissioner, 43 T.C. 842 (1965); Miles v. Livingstone, reprinted in Appendix, this volume, p. 468.
205   Traveling and entertainment expenses: See § 274, enacted in 1962.
206   Footnote: Treas. Regs. 1.274-5(c)(iii).
213   Business gifts: See § 274(b).
214   Allocation of purchase price to good will or contract not to compete on sale of business: See Danielson v. Commissioner, 378 F.2d 771 (3d Cir. 1967), cert. denied, 389 U.S. 858 (1968).
216   Treasury Circular 230: See Appendix, this volume, p. 359.
217   Voluntary disclosure: See note to p. 142, supra. King Committee: See note to p. 37, supra.
219   Canons of Professional Ethics: See note to p. 20, supra.
222   Rulings: Rev. Proc. 62-28, 1962-2 C.B. 496, superseded by Rev. Proc. 67-1, 1967-1 C.B. 544.
234   National Conference's Statement of Principles: See Appendix, this volume, p. 374.
237   Treasury Circular 230: See Appendix, this volume, p. 359.
238   For the *Bercu* and *Lowell Bar Ass'n* cases, see Appendix, p. 400 and p. 395.
239   Gardner v. Conway and Agran v. Shapiro are reprinted in Appendix, p. 411 and p. 419. The National Conference Statement is reprinted at p. 374.
240   The *Lindner, Bancroft,* and *Rassieur* cases are reprinted in Appendix, p. 454, p. 461, and p. 439.
241   AICPA Statement: See Appendix, this volume, p. 382.
249   Wheatcroft article: Reprinted as Chapter 15 of this volume, p. 327.
251   The discussion cited in note 21 appears in this volume, at pp. 195-198.

252 The Darrell article cited in note 22 appears in this volume as Chapter 5, p. 87; the Shaw discussion is at pp. 191-192; the Paul-Hellerstein discussion is at pp. 20-21 and 79-81; and the Paul article is reprinted as Chapter 4 of this volume, p. 64.

254 ABA Op. 314, cited in note 23a, appears in this volume, Appendix, p. 377.

257 Treasury Circular 230: See Appendix, this volume, p. 343. Rev. Proc. 64-47, cited in note 25, was superseded in 1968 by Rev. Proc. 68-20, reprinted in Appendix, p. 369.

259 The *Bercu* case and Agran v. Shapiro are reprinted in Appendix, this volume, p. 400 and p. 419.

260 For subsequent changes in this area, see Postscript, p. 289.

261 The Treasury interpretation cited in note 30 is reprinted in the Appendix, p. 357. The ABA-AICPA National Conference statement is reprinted at p. 374. The New York statement cited in note 31 is quoted in Blumenberg v. Neubecker, Appendix, p. 435.

267 For the new Code of Professional Responsibility, see note to p. 20, supra.

272 United States v. Bowman, cited in note 42, is reprinted in Appendix, p. 472.

273 With the change in Treasury Circular 230 resulting from the enactment of P. L. 89-332 (see text at p. 289, and revised version of the Circular at p. 359), this argument is no longer available, but the due process point remains applicable.

280 The *Bancroft* case is reprinted in Appendix, p. 461.

281 The Paul article cited in note 51 is reprinted as Chapter 4, p. 64.

283 Anderson v. Knox is reprinted in Appendix, p. 433.

284 Rassieur v. Charles and Miles v. Livingstone are reprinted in Appendix, p. 439 and p. 468.

287 The *Oregon State Bar* case is reprinted in Appendix, p. 432.

288 Blumenberg v. Neubecker is reprinted in Appendix, p. 435.

289 The Johnson article cited in note 59 is reprinted as Chapter 9 of this volume, p. 161.

290 P.L. 89-332 is reprinted in Appendix, p. 475.

291 Amendment to Treasury Circular 230: See Appendix, p. 343.

294 Note 1: The Tax Law Review symposium is reprinted as Chapter 2, this volume, p. 13.

298 Canons of Professional Ethics: See note to p. 20, supra.

299 Treasury Circular 230: See Appendix, this volume, p. 343.

305 Note 15: The Tax Law Review symposium is reprinted as Chapter 2, this volume, p. 13; the Graves article as Chapter 8, p. 149.

306 Notes 17 and 18: The Maguire and Graves articles are reprinted as Chapters 6 and 8 of this volume, p. 109 and p. 149.

307 Treasury Circular 230: See Appendix, this volume, p. 343.

312 AICPA statements: See Appendix, this volume, p. 382.

315 Notes 1 and 3: Of the cited articles, the following are reprinted in this volume: Bittker, Chapter 12, p. 233; Darrell, Chapter 5, p. 87; Johnson, Chapter 9, p. 161; Maguire, Chapter 6, p. 109; Young, Chapter 10,

p. 175; Graves, Chapter 8, p. 149; and Oatway, Chapter 13, p. 293. Note 2: For the ABA-AICPA Joint Statement, see Appendix, p. 374.
316 AICPA Statements: See Appendix, this volume, p. 382.
318 Note 9: ABA Opinion 314 is reprinted in Appendix, this volume, p. 377.
322 Note 22: The Tarleau comments are part of Chapter 2, this volume, p. 22.
323 Note 27: This symposium is reprinted as Chapter 11, this volume, p. 187.
333 Gregory v. Helvering, 293 U.S. 465 (1935).

Index

Accountants
   Cooperation with lawyers, 234-235, 261-264, 288-289, 374-375
   Dual responsibility of, 191-193
   In criminal cases, 29-30
   In Great Britain, 337-342
   Responsibilities compared with lawyers, 169-171, 324-326
Advertising, 115-117
Agran v. Shapiro, 419
American Bar Association
   Opinion 314, 320-324, 377-381
   Special Committee on Standards of Tax Practice, 311-312
American Institute of Certified Public Accountants
   Program to develop standards, 312-313
   Statements on Responsibilities in Tax Practice, 315-320, 381-393
Anderson v. Knox, 433
Application of N. Y. County Lawyers Ass'n (In re Bercu), 400
Audits, 226-228

Bancroft v. Indemnity Insurance Co. of North America, 461
Belief in arguments, 83-85
Blumenberg v. Neubecker, 435
Bribes, 26, 31, 36-37, 145
Canons of Professional Ethics of A.B.A.
   Advertising, 115-117
   Application to tax practice, 130, 302-304
   Fundamental principles, 112-113, 200

Inciting litigation, 113-115
Lawyer's duties, 378-379
Lobbying, 32-33
Clients
   Advising as to non-tax considerations, 99, 282-285
   Educating, 101-102, 198-199
   Inconsistent taxpayers' positions, 212-214
   Loyalty to, 73-74, 167-169
Code of Professional Ethics of A.I.C.P.A.
   Adequacy, 152-153
   Purpose, 300
Codes of conduct (See also specific names)
   Customs, 297-298
   Need for, 109-112, 127-130
   Purposes, 304-305
   Re-evaluation of, 293-296
Congressional intervention, 221-222
Courts
   Attitude to tax cases, in Great Britain, 332-336
   Moral sensibility of, 50-54, 101
Criminal litigation, 27-31, 83
Disclosure
   Accountants' duty, in Great Britain, 339-340
   Adverse authorities, 103-104, 140-141
   Doubtful items, 307-308, 341-342
   Effect of statute of limitations on, 94-95, 106
   Officer use of corporate facilities, 210-212

INDEX

Past fraud, 90-91, 105, 142-143, 214-216
Risk of negligence penalty, 195-198
Unfavorable facts, 23-24, 78-79, 141, 180-181, 268-269
Unrelated errors, 93-94, 137, 322
Voluntary, 217-219
Weak points, 379-381
Dual responsibility, 74-76, 146-148, 149, 188-190, 267-268
  Effect on duty to disclose, 322-324
  Explaining to client, 191
  Imposing double ethical standard, 77-85
  Source of, 310-311, 321-322
Fees, 60-61, 144-145
Gardner v. Conway, 411
Inciting litigation, 113-115
Independence of clients, 102-103
  Expressing personal views, 9-10, 69-70, 83-85
  Urging reform, 85-86, 107, 146, 172-173
Interstate duties, 97, 119, 138-139
Jurat
  Proposed changes in, 158
Legal ethics
  Decline of standards, 13-15, 22, 26-27, 39-40
  Defined, 16-17
  Establishing, 15-16, 39-40
  In tax practice, 64-65
Lindner v. Barlow, Davis & Wood, 454
Lobbying, 31-34, 106, 127, 143-144
  Disclosure of attorneyship, 32-33
  Special legislation, 33-34, 38
Lowell Bar Ass'n v. Loeb, 395
Manufactured situations, 17-19, 57-60, 72-73, 122, 134-135, 178-179, 202-205, 308-309
Miles v. Livingstone, 468
Minimizing taxes
  Considerations in, 190-191
  Killing poor tax schemes, 55-57
  Legitimacy of, 38-41, 70-72, 99-100, 133-134
  Philosophy of tax avoidance, 65-68
  Public attitude to tax schemes, 49-50
  Technical advantages, 223-224
  Under unjust law, 38-39, 44-45

National Conference of Lawyers and Certified Public Accountants
  Joint Statement of Principles, 234, 261-264, 266, 373-377
  1944 Resolution, 373
Oregon State Bar v. John H. Miller & Co., 432
Planning
  Continuing impact, 281-282
  Danger of overcleverness, 100-101
  Distinguished from lawyer's other functions, 275-277
  Finality of decisions, 278-280
  Involving practice of law, 285-288
  Morality in, 55-57, 134, 202
  Tax adviser's role in, 69-73, 337-338, 199-202
Practice before the Internal Revenue Service
  By non-lawyers, 261-267
  By unenrolled preparers of tax returns, 369-373
  Constituting practice of law, 257-258
  Danger of deception, 24
  Disciplinary proceedings, 354-359
  Distinguished from Tax Court proceedings, 82
  Due diligence requirement, 156, 247-248, 350
  Duties and restrictions, 349-354, 365-369
  Enrollment, 343-349, 359-365
  Federal regulation of, 258-261, 289-291
  Nature of, 319-320, 321-322, 378
  No duty to volunteer information, 80-82, 271-272
  Relations with the government, 8, 25, 75-76, 125-127, 324
  Rules of, 76-77, 156-158, 298-299, 343-357
Privileged communications, 272-274
  Disclosure of, 110-111, 120
  Effect on duty to disclose, 96, 106-107, 141-142
  In preparing tax return, 25-26, 92-93, 136-137
Public service obligations, 146-148
  Educating public, 21, 61-63
  Improving tax system, 10-12, 171-173, 184-185, 302
  Of accountants, 152-154

Rassieur v. Charles, 439
Reliance on client's information, 6-7, 91, 206-210, 246-249
Representing guilty client, 27-28, 84
Reputation, 29, 121, 193, 307, 324
Revenue Agents
   Attitude to taxpayers, 193-194
   Role of, 222-223
   Social relations with, 219-221
Tax Court proceedings, 82-83, 376
Tax law
   Relation to other areas of law, 3-6, 264-267
Tax returns (See also Disclosure)
   Accountants' disclosure of error, 316-320
   Amended returns, 317-318
   Change in treatment of items, 390-392
   Definition of "preparation," 241-242
   Doubtful items, 92, 95, 251-254
   Estimates, 392-395
   Extended time for filing, 229-231
   False returns, 157
   Full-disclosure theory, 254-256
   Function of, 254
   Liability for fraudulent return, 243
   Liability for negligent preparation, 239-241, 244-246
   Omissions, 92, 105, 122-124, 135-137, 158, 306-307
   Overassessments, 228-229
   Qualifications for preparing, 237-239
   Refusal to sign, 105-157
   Signature of preparer, 381-388
   Unanswered questions, 224-226, 388-390
   Unauthorized deductions, 19-20, 138, 179-180, 268-269
   Verification, 154-155, 205-210, 241-243, 248-250
Tax system
   In Great Britain, 329-336
   Need for confidence in, 161-167, 194
   Public attitude towards, 150-151, 301
Treasury Department Circular 230, 343-357
   Changes in, 359-369
   Treasury interpretation of, 357-358
Uncertain tax consequences
   Disclosure in case of, 20-21, 79-80, 195-198
   Resolving in client's favor, 124-125, 250-253, 269-271, 322-323
United States v. Bowman, 472
United States Code, Title 5 (App.), § 1012, 475
Withdrawal of representation, 104-105, 215-216, 322-323
   In Great Britain, 340